Financing

the PUBLIC SCHOOLS

ROE L. JOHNS
Head, Department of Educational
Administration, University of Florida

EDGAR L. MORPHET
Professor of Education,
University of California, Berkeley

PRENTICE-HALL, INC.

Englewood Cliffs, N. J.

42505

PRENTICE-HALL EDUCATION SERIES

Dan H. Cooper, Editor

LIBRARY OF CONGRESS
CATALOG CARD NO.: 60-8327

First printing ...... *February, 1960*
Second printing .... *March, 1962*
Third printing .... *May, 1964*
Fourth printing .... *June, 1965*

PRINTED IN THE UNITED STATES OF AMERICA

31631—C

TO OUR WIVES—

Gladys and Camilla

Preface

The kinds of decisions made by a nation with respect to the quantity and quality of the educational services provided for children, youth, and adults vitally affect the future of that nation. The basic decisions on educational policy in the United States are made by the people or their duly elected representatives at the Federal, state, and local levels. The consent of the governed must be obtained before such decisions are made. Not only the educational and lay leadership, but also the mass of the people must understand educational policies before intelligent decisions can be made. The arrangements for making educational decisions in America place greater responsibilities on its educational administrators than in any other nation.

One of the major responsibilities of American school administrators is to provide leadership in determining fiscal policies for public education. In a popular government particularly, the wisdom of the decisions that are made is determined largely by the quality and quantity of the leadership provided. Therefore, school administrators must not only provide leadership themselves, but they must facilitate the development of other intelligent leadership both in the profession and in the lay public.

This book is concerned primarily with the financing of the public schools and with the business administration policies and procedures essential to the conservation and wise utilization of funds, facilities,

v

and people. To furnish adequate leadership in school finance, not only must one know the processes by which decisions are made in a democratic society, but he must also possess much specific knowledge needed by the group when it makes decisions. Therefore, the processes of decision-making as well as specific information concerning school finance and business administration are presented in this book.

The financing of education is a very broad field of knowledge. It encompasses educational planning based on the goals and purposes of education in a democratic society. It is directly concerned with the organizational structures and the fiscal arrangements provided for implementing educational plans. It is closely involved with the national economy and the financing of other governmental services.

Teachers of school finance have long known that students need an understanding of the basic concepts of economics and public finance in order to study school finance. It has not always been practicable to require students to take courses in these areas as a prerequisite to the study of school finance. Therefore, the authors have included in this book the concepts of economics and public finance that are considered basic to an understanding of school finance.

Ideally, the materials of school finance should be presented as an organic whole, but it seems impossible to do so. Therefore, the first seven chapters of this book deal with the over-all problems of school financing that affect the entire nation, including all levels of government—Federal, state, and local. Chapter 8 deals specifically with the role of the local school district in public school financing. Chapters 9 to 12 deal with the role of the states, Chapter 13 with the role of the Federal government, and Chapters 14 to 19 with the operational aspects of business administration having particular significance for school financing.

One of the features of this book is the emphasis given to the problems and issues of school financing on which decisions are being made. A section of each chapter is devoted to pointing up the significant problems and issues which have not been fully resolved. It is believed that this dynamic approach will be stimulating to practicing school administrators as well as to the teachers and the students of the subject.

Roe L. Johns
Edgar L. Morphet

Table of Contents

CHAPTER ONE

Finance

and the Educational Program

Education may represent the difference between catastrophe and a rapidly improving civilization. Illiteracy and ignorance lay the predicate for injustice, turmoil, and eventual waste or destruction of both natural and human resources. Education is essential for survival and progress.

The leaders, and gradually the common citizens, of every nation are coming to realize the truth and implications of these statements. The time is approaching when no nation will dare to permit any substantial proportion of its citizens to continue in ignorance. Modern civilization demands knowledge, understanding, and technological skills. Development of these through education provides the opportunity for progress. Neglect invites misery, exploitation, and eventual disaster.

Among the problems faced by various nations in attempting to develop an adequate program of education are the following:

1. The group in power may not want the masses to be educated. These leaders may seek to control the people and use them for their own selfish purposes. Limited education may be permitted—even encouraged—but opportunities for most are likely to be narrowly restricted. Potential leaders will probably be educated—or indoctrinated —to help in directing and controlling the masses.

2. The traditions and beliefs of the people may tend to perpetuate existing conditions. Learning and thinking beyond or contrary to these traditions may be discouraged for women, for certain minority groups,

1

or for all except the upper classes, who may or may not want to perpetuate the existing mores. Under such conditions, the development of a satisfactory program is likely to come slowly.

3. The people and their leaders may earnestly desire a good program of education, but the resources may be so limited that little progress can be made. Low subsistence levels tend to be associated with ignorance and lack of educational opportunity. At best, progress is likely to be slow and halting until more adequate resources are available.

4. The people may believe in a good program of education and may have the resources to make it possible but may not be willing to make the effort to assure that it is adequate to meet the needs. They may become complacent because their material needs are easily satisfied and consequently may handicap themselves by failing to prepare their children properly to meet the needs and deal with the problems of the future.

A substantial proportion of the resources of each nation must be devoted to education if the lot of mankind is to be improved. As pointed out by the Education Committee of the United States Chamber of Commerce a few years ago: "Education [is] an investment in people." [1] The investment may be good or bad, depending on the purposes, objectives, and procedures. It may be adequate or totally inadequate to meet the needs, depending on the resources and purposes of the people and their willingness to make the necessary effort. It may and should help mankind to avoid catastrophe and to develop an ever-improving civilization. But if that is to be accomplished, schools and other educational institutions must be adequately supported and financed in every part of the world.

SOME BASIC ISSUES

The people and their leaders in every nation are confronted with several basic issues relating to education and its financial support. In some countries, these issues are clearly recognized and faced. In others, at least some of them seem to be largely unrecognized or ignored.

Among the most important issues which must be resolved satisfactorily if an adequate program of education is to be provided in any nation are the following:

1. *What purposes should be accomplished through education?* The accepted purposes of education differ greatly. They range from ex-

---

[1] Chamber of Commerce of the United States, Committee on Education, *Education—An Investment in People* (Washington, D.C.: The Chamber, 1954).

treme emphasis on conformity with the mores or religious beliefs of the leaders to a bona fide desire to help everyone develop the ability to recognize and work out satisfactory solutions for the major problems facing civilization; from an attempt to dominate and control the masses to an effort to free them and help them contribute to the betterment of humanity; from an interest in increasing material comforts for the privileged to a genuine desire to improve the level and quality of living for all. The purposes of education that are accepted in any country influence greatly the development, and consequently the destiny, of the people. Divergent purposes tend to contribute to national and international tension and conflict. Greater agreement on defensible purposes could and should result in a rapidly improving civilization.

2. *What quantity and quality of education are needed?* Many factors influence the quantity and quality of education provided in any community, state, or nation. Among these are the stated or accepted purposes, the insights, the stage of development, the form of government, and the resources available. Low quantity and quality of organized education have tended to be associated with primitive or underdeveloped peoples; high quantity and quality, with peoples who are contributing most to the progress of the world.

3. *How much should education cost?* A characteristic of every normal human being is his natural tendency to learn. This learning may be unorganized and haphazard or organized and relatively scientific. Any learning necessitates an investment of time, effort, and financial resources. But how much of an investment is necessary for the quantity and quality of education needed to achieve the accepted purposes? The search for a reasonably satisfactory answer to this question will undoubtedly continue. It is apparent that, in many parts of the world and for substantial numbers in every nation, the investment is still far too limited. It has increased greatly during the present century and undoubtedly will continue to increase. In fact, there is no evidence that the limit has been attained in any nation thus far.

4. *What percentage of a nation's resources should be devoted to education?* In the past, a substantial proportion of the world's human and natural resources has either been wasted or utilized inefficiently. Resources may be utilized destructively, as for wars of conquest or exploitation, or constructively, as for improved health. The developed resources of some nations are much greater than those of others. How much of these resources should be used for education of the people? If the resources are too limited or too small a proportion is used, the people make little progress; they remain "backward," cannot develop their own potential effectively, and are subject to exploitation. Increas-

ing the percentage somewhat seems to result generally in increasing progress. Will a greater increase result in greater progress? There seems to be good reason for believing that most nations have been too timid or conservative thus far and that a larger percentage of their resources could profitably be devoted to education in the future than has been the practice in the past.

SOME IMPORTANT CONCEPTS

Concepts regarding education and its financial support vary considerably among the local school systems found in each state and likewise among the different states comprising the United States of America. However, in many respects, the similarities are more striking and more significant than the differences. These similarities grow out of the principles underlying the democratic form of government established in this country and out of the beliefs of the citizens regarding policies and procedures that are essential to the perpetuation and improvement of the democratic way of life.

Among the pertinent concepts and beliefs generally held by citizens throughout this nation are the following:

1. *Education should be provided for all through the elementary grades, for virtually all through the high school grades, for a large proportion through the junior college grades, and for the most competent through the colleges and universities.* This belief has evolved slowly but persistently. At present, few people in any state would question the necessity of an elementary education for all. Kindergartens are accepted as desirable by a large proportion of leading citizens, but, largely because of financial and other complicating factors, they have not been established in many communities. Some doubt whether everyone can benefit from a high school education. Others believe it is desirable for all under present conditions. There is a growing tendency in many states to believe that a large proportion of the young people should expect to continue through the junior or community college grades and that the most able should continue through the university—a practice that is still far from universal.

2. *Throughout each state, provision should be made for an adequate program of education designed, insofar as possible, to meet the needs of each person.* Although much progress has been made toward implementing this objective, the practice in some states and in many communities falls far short of the goal. Studies have shown that there are many children who do not have access to an adequate program of

education [2] and that many schools have not yet satisfactorily solved the problem of providing optimum opportunities, especially for those children who are considerably below and for those who are decidedly above the average in aptitudes and ability.[3]

3. *Everyone should have equality of opportunity for the kind and quality of educational program which will best meet his needs and those of the society in which he lives.* Apparently almost every American citizen accepts this concept in theory. However, it has not been fully implemented in many communities, because of handicaps arising from ineffective district organization, limiting provisions in state laws, inadequate financial plans and programs, ineffective local policies, inept leadership and teaching, and many similar factors. The fact that it has been accepted as an objective in most states and communities should mean, however, that further improvements will be made during coming years.

4. *Adequate educational opportunities should be provided in the public schools and at public institutions of higher learning for all who desire education in those institutions and can benefit from the program; adequate opportunities should similarly be provided in non-public schools and institutions of higher learning for all others.* Everyone has access to and has an opportunity to be educated in the public schools. However, no one may be required or compelled to attend public schools. Citizens have a right to determine the kind of elementary and secondary schools their children will attend. The citizens of each state determine the minimum quality and quantity of education to be provided. No one is required to attend any institution of higher learning. Most states have attempted to provide public higher institutions for all who desire to attend and can benefit from the program at such institutions. Non-public higher institutions of one kind or another are available in all states for those who do not wish to attend public institutions.

5. *Public elementary and secondary schools should be entirely supported by funds provided, directly or indirectly, through public taxation; public institutions of higher learning should be largely, if not entirely, supported by such funds; non-public schools and institutions of higher learning should be supported on a voluntary basis and not from public tax funds.* This objective has been reasonably well attained in

---

[2] For example, see: Clayton D. Hutchins and Albert R. Munse, *Expenditures for Education at the Midcentury*, U. S. Office of Education (Washington, D.C.: U. S. Government Printing Office, 1953); and National Education Association, Research Division, *Rankings of the States* (Washington, D.C.: The Association, April, 1959).

[3] Malcolm S. MacLean and Edwin A. Lee, *Change and Process in Education* (New York: Dryden Press, Inc., 1956), Chapters IX to XIII.

most states except that the support provided in many instances is far from adequate. In no states are fees required for elementary schools and in few are they permitted. Voluntary contributions are often encouraged and sometimes found necessary. Public high schools are likewise generally supported from public tax funds but in some cases limited fees are permitted. Varying charges are permitted, and often required, to cover part of the cost for those attending public institutions of higher learning. Non-public schools and institutions of higher learning are supported from endowments, fees, tuition charges, and from voluntary contributions encouraged through provisions in the income tax laws. On the basis of provisions in the Federal Constitution and in most state constitutions, it is generally accepted that public tax funds may not be used for the support of non-public educational institutions.

6. *Each state should provide, through its constitution or laws, for adequate financial support of public schools and institutions of higher learning, wherever they should be located in the state.* All states authorize local financial support for public schools and provide some state funds for support of both public schools and public institutions of higher learning. However, few states give sufficient consideration to the significance of local variations in ability to provide financial support for public schools. Some make limited state funds available for schools with the hope and expectation that local school systems will meet most of the cost, ignoring the fact that some do not have the ability to do so. Other states provide substantial funds but ignore local variations in ability and thus perpetuate inequities. During the past few years, an increasing proportion of the states have taken steps to assure that reasonably adequate financial support will be available for schools in all districts, regardless of local wealth and other related factors beyond the control of local boards of education.

7. *Each citizen in the state should contribute in accordance with his ability to the support of public schools and public institutions of higher learning in the state.* In the early days, public schools and institutions were supported largely by the parents of children attending those schools. The inequity and inconsistency with democratic theory of this practice were soon recognized. Now everyone who has taxpaying ability is expected to help meet the costs of providing public schools and institutions of higher learning. However, there are some inequities in the tax systems of all states. The citizens in some of the less wealthy school systems, because of inequities in the plan for apportioning state school funds, frequently have to pay much more for the support of their schools than do citizens in many of the more wealthy communities.

8. *The resources of the nation should be used to assist in providing educational opportunities in public schools and institutions of higher learning for the citizens of the nation, regardless of the state or community in which they live.* This concept is still controversial as far as many citizens are concerned. Even the idea that the resources of the state should be used to assure adequate educational opportunities for children throughout the state, regardless of the wealth of the area in which they live, has not been fully implemented. As each new state has been admitted to the Union, Congress has recognized the principle of Federal concern by providing generous land grants for public school purposes. Land grants have also been made for the support of public institutions of higher learning providing education in agriculture and the mechanic arts. Various special grants have been provided for certain aspects of public education ranging from vocational education through school lunches. Thus some of the resources of the nation have been used to help to implement this principle but, for one reason or another, Congress has not provided for more than token implementation, except in instances similar to those discussed here.

DIFFERENCES BETWEEN CONCEPTS AND PRACTICES

As has been noted above, there are certain respects in which practices are not entirely consistent with the generally accepted concepts relating to provision of educational opportunities and financial support for schools. It is relatively easy for many people to subscribe to a desirable objective or to give verbal support to sound concepts, but developing and implementing a program of action that is consistent with the ideal becomes a different matter. Americans, like most other peoples, tend to be more idealistic in verbal expression than in things they actually do. This tendency creates a problem but at the same time provides a challenge.

Some Important Differences

Three of the major differences between generally accepted objectives and common practices relating to the educational program and its financial support may be summarized as follows:

1. While a large proportion of the youth of the nation now complete high school and substantial numbers attend college, there are many who drop out for one reason or another before completing the high school grades. Studies have shown that a large proportion of the most able students either do not enter, or do not continue through, institu-

tions of higher learning. Thus the human resources of the nation are not being developed or utilized as effectively as is desirable.

2. The educational program in many communities is not adequate. Appropriate educational opportunities are lacking due to insufficient funds, ineffective leadership, or a program that is not designed to meet the needs of many of the students. One or more of these conditions is found in many communities, with consequences that are sometimes tragic. There are wide differences in financial support for schools and, consequently, wide variations in educational opportunities. The place of residence of a student has considerable significance for his educational program. Discrimination presumably is illegal or at least is indefensible. Yet discrimination based on place of residence is practiced and condoned in many parts of the country.

3. Many citizens do not contribute to the support of public schools and institutions of higher learning in accordance with their abilities. This situation exists in many cases not because these individuals attempt to avoid their proper responsibility, but because the laws provide for or permit inequities. Neither the resources of many states nor of the nation are utilized as effectively as they should be to assist in providing adequate educational opportunities for all.

Reasons for Differences

There are many reasons for such differences in what we believe and in what we do. Some of the reasons are understood by a large proportion of the people. Others are more subtle and may not yet be fully understood by anyone. A few of the more important, considered in greater detail in subsequent chapters, are discussed briefly below.

Different Concepts of Purpose. There are many differences in philosophy or point of view regarding the place and role of public education among the citizens of each state and community. Some differences, of course, are to be expected. However, sharp differences among any substantial proportion of the citizens mean that the schools will inevitably be handicapped in one way or another. In the final analysis they may be denied some of the financial support that is essential if satisfactory educational opportunities are to be provided. In some communities, for example, there are people who do not believe in public education. If this belief is held by only a few, the educational program may not be appreciably affected. However, if it is held by a majority the consequences are likely to be disastrous.

A few years ago, Scott and Hill assembled and classified many of the criticisms of the public schools current at that time, attempted to evaluate them, and presented a number of constructive suggestions for dealing with criticisms.[4] Since that time there have been even greater waves of criticism. It seems either that there are sharper differences of opinion or that the critics are more vociferous than some years ago. Some of these criticisms have been well founded, and as a result adjustments and improvements have been made in the educational program. Other criticisms have come from individuals or groups who have made no study of education, do not seem to be interested in making any study, but want changes to conform to their own purposes and objectives.

In the meantime, however, earnest and conscientious lay citizens and educators in many communities have cooperated in careful studies that resulted in constructive suggestions for improvements. The constructive approach offers the most promise; it provides an opportunity for studies and discussions which should help to bring about improvements.

Reliance on Property Taxes. Property taxes have been the chief, and until recent years, almost the sole source of school support. In several states, more than two-thirds of all revenues for support of schools still come from property tax sources. Yet property is only a relatively minor source of income for the citizens of the nation and, in many cases, is not a good measure of ability to support the schools. Variations in local wealth based on property have resulted in marked differences in local funds available for school support and consequently in serious inequities in educational opportunity.

Inequities in Local Ability. The people in most states assumed for many years that schools should be supported chiefly from local funds which, in practice, meant chiefly from property taxes. With the spread of industrialization, local differences in wealth and ability were greatly accentuated. States gradually began to face up to the realities of this situation and sought some equitable means of providing funds from state sources, which in most cases meant sources other than property tax. However, some people in all districts thought they were entitled to state funds because they paid state taxes. As a result, the wealthy districts often received, in proportion, as much money as the less wealthy. Thus existing differences were sometimes either perpetuated or exaggerated. More recently, states have become increasingly impressed with the need for assuring equitable educational opportunities. Progress has been slow, because it has often been resisted and sometimes even thwarted by vested interest groups. The struggle for equity is far from resolved in many of the states.

---

[4] Winfield Scott and Clyde M. Hill, *Public Education Under Criticism* (Englewood Cliffs, N.J.: Prentice-Hall, Inc., 1954).

Continuation of Inadequate Districts. The local school district structure established during Colonial days has tended to be continued in many of the states. Studies show that small districts tend to be inadequate and cannot economically provide a satisfactory program of education. Yet changes in district organization have come slowly in most states. Small districts perpetuate extreme differences in wealth which would be considerably decreased under any logical plan of district organization. Furthermore, when states began to provide funds in an effort to help to assure adequate educational opportunities in all communities, the amounts made available to small and inefficient districts were frequently sufficient to perpetuate them but not to improve them. The prevailing district structure, therefore, is one of the reasons for inequalities in educational opportunity in many states.

Limitations on Local Responsibility. Although the American people seem to believe in the desirability of local initiative and responsibility, they have, in some states, permitted restrictive or handicapping features to be incorporated in their laws or constitutions. Some states have legally made it either difficult or impossible for the people in many local school systems to provide the kind of educational program they would like to have for their children. Some have limited taxes that may be levied locally for the current school program or for all purposes including schools. Several of these states have given some assistance through state funds but have not provided enough funds to offset the handicaps which have been imposed by local limitations.

Continuation of Outmoded Finance Practices. There has been an unwillingness in many states and communities to abandon outmoded financial practices that have been sanctioned by law and to which the people have become accustomed. Some of these have been shown by studies to be extremely inequitable and indefensible. Yet they have been difficult to change. It is now possible, as a result of studies made over a period of years, to devise (in terms of commonly accepted principles) an equitable and defensible program of financial support for schools in every state. Yet there are usually school districts or groups of taxpayers that resist change because they do not want to give up their privileged position. Inequities are thus perpetuated partly by inertia and partly because of the resistance of groups that place their own interests above the interests of the entire program.

Differences in Leadership and Management. Some states and local school systems, for one reason or another, have had more capable and forward-looking leadership than others. Good leadership tends to result in progress in solving problems and in developing practices that are consistent with sound theory. Inept leadership often means perpetuation of undesirable and inequitable practices, inefficiency in development and management of resources and, consequently, unsatisfactory educational opportunities. Adequate financial support alone does not solve the problems facing the schools; it facilitates their solution. Good leadership and management must be combined with adequate and soundly conceived financial support in order to produce a good educational program.

Summary of Developments and Problems

Much progress has been made in improving education and the financial support of education in nearly every state. Our concepts of what constitutes adequate educational opportunities and adequate financial support have been broadened and improved. There is substantial agreement in many states and communities on the characteristics of a good program of education. However, there are differences of opinion in many parts of the nation that have not been resolved. These differences tend to result in criticisms that make progress difficult and handicap the schools. Constructive studies are being made in a number of places in an effort to determine facts, promote better understanding, and reach greater agreement on desirable objectives and procedures. However, schools continue to be handicapped in many communities because of unresolved differences of opinion, reliance on property taxes as the chief source of revenue, the expectation that each local school system should provide most of the funds for the support of schools regardless of its ability, differences in local ability, obsolete and antiquated district structure, handicapping restrictions in the constitution or law, the tendency to continue existing practices regardless of their justification or desirability, and ineffective leadership or inefficient management.

EDUCATIONAL QUALITY AND FINANCIAL SUPPORT

The two basic questions that have been directly or indirectly involved in most of the discussions and controversy about public education in the various states from the beginning are:

(1) What should be accomplished through the public schools, and

(2) How much should the public school program cost, and how should it be financed?

These two questions are obviously interrelated. Any agreements and policies relating to the first have implications for the second, and any solutions agreed upon for the second question are likely to have implications for the first. When the quantity or quality of education is increased, financial support generally needs to be increased. When the financial support is restricted, the quantity or quality of education is likely to be limited.

Some people begin their consideration of these problems with the assumption that any reasonable quantity and quality of education that is found desirable can and should be financed. Others begin with the assumption that taxes are high and financial support must be limited and conclude that the educational program provided must be limited accordingly.

Cost-Quantity Relationships Apparent

It is much easier for most people to see relationships between *quantity* and educational expenditures than between *quality* and expenditures or costs. In fact, there are only a limited number of situations where increased quantity does not require increased expenditures if quality is to be maintained. In some schools a few students could be added to certain classes without increasing costs appreciably. However, if the enrollment in a local or state school system increases by 10 per cent, the costs probably would be increased in nearly the same proportion provided the same quality is maintained. Likewise, it can be seen that if a larger proportion of the student population attends high school or college, if vocational or business education is added to an academic program, if special classes are organized for exceptional children, if transportation is provided for children who previously have been transported by their parents, or if any other similar changes are made which increase the quantity of education or educational services, the cost is likely to be increased.

The quantity of education provided in most state and local school systems has increased considerably over a period of years. That is one of the reasons school costs and expenditures have increased. Still further increases may be expected in the future. For example, on the basis of recent and projected birth rates, it is apparent that there will be approximately a 20 per cent increase in the number of school age children in the United States during the next ten years. Thus the quantity of education provided must be increased to meet this need, and the expenditures for education will increase somewhat accordingly if there are no significant changes in quality or in the purchasing power of the dollar.

Cost-Quality Relationships

When it comes to *quality* of education, as related to cost, there are usually greater differences of opinion. Many people would agree that increasing the quality is likely to add somewhat to the cost, but fewer would agree that increasing the cost would add to the quality.

Cost Not Always Related to Quality. Before undertaking to analyze cost-quality relationships it is desirable to call attention to certain conditions under which there are no necessary relationships between cost and quality:

1. Small schools tend to cost more per pupil than average or larger sized schools, even though the quality of education provided in the smaller schools is frequently found to be lower than in the larger schools. Thus increasing the number of small schools could add to the cost without increasing, or perhaps even while decreasing, the quality. On the other hand, in certain areas it might be possible to decrease the cost or improve the quality by eliminating small schools and organizing larger schools. However, where small schools have to be maintained there is some evidence to indicate that the quality could in many cases be improved by increasing the expenditures for such schools.

2. In some school systems the quality of education may be adversely affected by inept leadership and administration. For example, teachers and other employees may not be carefully selected, with the result that a large number have limited competence. In other systems, employment policies may be unusually good, with the result that only the most competent persons are selected for service in the system. Although the cost may not be any greater in the second system than in the first, the quality of education provided may be higher. Similarly, factors that contribute to low morale may result in relatively low quality of service in one district whereas in other districts high morale may result in higher quality. In individual school systems, therefore, quality may be affected to some extent by a number of factors that are not directly related to finance.

3. In some instances, state laws or local board policies may require the continuation of outmoded practices that limit or do not add to the quality of education provided. A change in law or board policy in such instances could result in improvement of quality without any material change in financial support.

Quality Difficult to Measure. Aside from situations such as these, however, is there any relationship between the cost or expenditures and the quality of education provided? Some contend that in spite of greatly increased expenditures for the schools, the quality or standards of education have generally been lowered in this country. Others hold that the quality of education has improved, partly because there are more well-prepared teachers, better facilities and services and, in general, better learning conditions and opportunities.

One problem arises from the fact that it is difficult to define or t(

measure quality of education. The measurement of quantity is relatively easy. Different people define the term "quality" in different ways. Some think of quality only in terms of academic achievement of pupils in schools, whereas others insist that quality be judged by the all-round development and progress as well as by the knowledge of pupils. Where different bases are used for judging, the judgments are bound to differ.

Tests of Quality. Paul R. Mort, who has sponsored and conducted a number of studies in this area over a period of years, has proposed the following tests for analyzing data in cost-quality studies:

1. The basic skills should include speech and learning how to think, both considered matters of continuous constructive concern for all children.
2. The basic skills should be taught in such real or realistic situations that there is enhancement of the probabilities that children of all levels of ability not only will master these skills and retain them but will also make intelligent use of them in solving problems met in later life.
3. The range of knowledge should be extended in the scientific and social fields.
4. The knowledge taught should be selected for its probable usefulness in solving life problems rather than solely for its "cultural" values.
5. The knowledges taught should be learned in real or realistic situations in order to enhance the probabilities that children not only will learn them and remember them but will also make intelligent use of them in solving problems in later life.
6. The schooling years should be used to discover the aptitudes of individuals for the arts we live by in our complex society, both useful arts and fine arts.
7. The schooling years should be used to develop individual aptitudes into knowledge and skills that will enhance life for the individual and for our people, both culturally and economically.
8. Children and young people should be under continuous positive guidance in the development of good life behavior habits in such areas as personality, citizenship, character, and home life.
9. Children and young people should be under continuous positive guidance in the development of knowledge and behavior habits that will promote mental and physical stamina.
10. The school should be so operated as to use the personal resources of the citizens not only to help the school but also to give citizens experience in self-government.[5]

Probably most people would agree that many of these tests are reasonable and realistic. Few would insist that quality in the educa-

---

[5] Paul R. Mort, "Cost-Quality Relationship in Education," Chapter 2 of *Problems and Issues in Public School Finance*, R. L. Johns and E. L. Morphet, editors (New York: Bureau of Publications, Teachers College, Columbia University, 1952), pp. 13–14.

tional program be judged solely on the basis of achievement tests in the academic subjects.

Tentative Conclusions. On the basis of numerous studies made thus far, it seems that the following conclusions are justified:

1. The quality of education provided by the schools of today is generally superior to that provided a generation or two ago.[6] This does not mean that the quality is as good as it should be, or that there are no weaknesses to be corrected. In fact, there are many communities throughout the nation where the quality is undoubtedly much lower than it should be. There unquestionably have been weaknesses in the program provided for some of the more able students, as well as failures to meet adequately the individual needs of many others. Although there seems to be no sound basis for the conclusion that educational standards generally have declined, there is much reason for concluding that they are not as high as they should be.

2. In spite of numerous reports to the contrary, the evidence seems to indicate that the products of the public schools generally compare favorably with those of private and parochial schools. In fact, there are many indications that public school graduates generally do at least as well and perhaps even better in college than graduates of other schools and that the quality of education in public schools is at least equal to that in other schools.[7]

3. The quality of education provided in the school systems where expenditures are low is far less satisfactory than that in systems where expenditures are above the national average.[8] Low expenditures tend to mean inadequate leadership, large classes, poor teachers and teaching, and many other features that contribute to low quality.

4. Even in the higher expenditure level school systems, there seems to be a strong relationship between expenditures and quality of education. The districts which spend more "appear generally to contribute more per dollar to individuals and to our national life than those who spend less." As expenditure levels increase, expenditures seem to have "more of the characteristics of a productive investment for the nation."[9]

The case, however, is not closed. Some laymen and educators still

---

[6] See, for example, Archibald W. Anderson, "The Charges against American Education: What Is the Evidence?" *Progressive Education* (January, 1952), pp. 91–105.

[7] David Iwamoto, "Don't Sneer at Public Education," *National Education Association Journal* (February, 1958), pp. 118–19.

[8] William P. McLure, *Let Us Pay for the Kind of Education We Need: Report of a Study of State and Local Support of Mississippi Schools* (University: Bureau of Educational Research, University of Mississippi, 1948); also Mort, *op. cit.,* Chapter II.

[9] Mort, *op. cit.,* pp. 9–10.

contend that schools should be rated by the progress of pupils in acquiring skills and knowledge and not by criteria which attempt to list desirable features of an educational program. Many additional studies will undoubtedly be needed before final statements can be made as to conditions under which increased expenditures result in increased quality.

SOME PROBLEMS AND ISSUES

Many of the specific problems and issues relating to the various aspects of educational finance are considered in subsequent chapters of this book. Some of those especially pertinent to this chapter are discussed briefly on the following pages.

How Significant Is a Well-planned and Properly Financed Program of Education?

Every group, society, or nation has had to develop some plan and certain standards for educating its children. Most primitive societies accepted the idea that there was little to learn except how to survive, to conform to tribal mores, and to propitiate the spirits and unknown forces. But those conditions have changed or are changing rapidly even in the more remote parts of the world.

In modern civilization the need for learning and understanding is more impelling than ever before. This need is generally recognized and accepted. An illiterate might survive, but he would encounter innumerable difficulties. Even a literate person who knew little about history, geography, economics, psychology, or the physical sciences would be seriously handicapped. There seems to be a demand and a necessity for more and more education by a larger proportion of the people with each passing generation. The better educated people become, the more clearly they seem to recognize the need for increased education. Thus education becomes more necessary, more complex, and more costly. There is a growing belief that the nations with the largest proportion of citizens educated to think and to help solve the problems facing humanity will inevitably become the leading nations of the world. In fact, many hold that the hope of saving civilization from catastrophe lies in the citizens of such nations.

Some time ago, H. G. Wells expressed the thought that civilization is a race between education and catastrophe. Is this statement justified? Does a better program of education provide the best hope for civilization?

Studies of expenditures for education, of educational attainments, and of other related developments in selected states in this nation and in certain other countries have led to the conclusion that "education steps up living standards." [10] It seems to be generally true that nations with the least adequate programs of education are among the most backward in many respects and tend to have the lowest standards of living. Whereas some of these countries have limited resources and do not seem to be able at present to afford high expenditures for education, others have an abundance of resources which could be developed and utilized for the benefit of their citizens. Some nations with limited resources but a good program of education have made remarkable progress.

How do differences in the kind and quality of education provided affect communities, states, or nations? Can a state or nation ever afford low or decreasing expenditures for education? Under what conditions should a state or nation devote an unusually high percentage of its resources to education?

How Much Education Should Be Provided at Public Expense?

In most communities, during the early history of this country, even elementary schools were financed largely by rates or fees paid chiefly by the patrons of the schools. Gradually the idea was accepted that all public schools should be supported by public tax funds.

However, the issue of public support has not yet been fully resolved. Some people—chiefly supporters of non-public schools—still object to the idea of paying taxes for support of public schools. Many others, particularly rural residents in certain states, resist the idea of tax-supported or "free" kindergartens. On the other hand, some urban residents oppose the idea of "free" or tax-financed transportation from which rural or village children have been the chief beneficiaries.

There are many who seriously question the desirability of publicly supported high schools for any except the most able students. The matter of how special classes for slow learners or physically handicapped children, courses such as driver training, and other similar programs should be financed is quite controversial in many communities. Even more controversial is the question as to how much tax support should be provided for public junior colleges and institutions of higher learning.

Some people believe that unless students or their parents pay directly

---

[10] Harold F. Clark, *Education Steps Up Living Standards* (Washington, D.C.: Chamber of Commerce of the United States, 1945).

at least part of the cost of education they do not fully appreciate it. They contend that if too much is "given" to people they tend to become complacent and expect even more services from their government. In short, the people who hold this point of view may honestly think that "free" schools and educational institutions tend to encourage socialistic tendencies in the population.

On the other hand, it must be recognized that many people could not afford to pay for special classes when needed for their children, to meet the expenses of sending them through high school, or to pay all the costs of a college education. With a system of private schools or of substantial fees for public schools, many of the nation's citizens would undoubtedly be less well educated than they are at present. If a democracy depends for its successful functioning on a relatively high level of education for all citizens, the nation would be seriously handicapped by those who have limited education. Much of the nation's talent is not now being adequately developed. Much more might remain undeveloped if high fees were required for secondary schools and colleges.

What aspects of the public school program should be financed at public expense? Should any courses or other aspects of the program be financed by fees? What should be the plan of financial support for public kindergartens? For driver training? For public junior colleges? For other public institutions of higher learning?

To What Extent Do Differences of Opinion Concerning the Objectives and Scope of Public Education Affect Financial Support?

In Community "A," representative lay citizens and educators for several years have been studying and discussing many aspects of their program of education, including desirable purposes and objectives. There now seems to be substantial, although not unanimous, agreement on many phases of the program. As a result of their consideration of the problem, some of the lay citizens have changed certain of their ideas about what the schools should be doing, and the board of education has made some changes in its policies. Several public meetings have been held at which proposed policy statements have been presented and rather fully discussed. Most people seem to be in general agreement regarding the basic proposals, but a few still have serious reservations.

In Community "B," the superintendent and his staff have been trying to do a good job with their schools. They have seldom discussed objectives but have assumed that there is general agreement with the objectives they have in mind. Some teachers, however, have been critical of certain policies. There has been some comment that certain teachers seem to be moving in one direction, and that others apparently have different purposes in mind. As far as the superintendent and board are concerned, there never has been a serious attempt to involve lay citizens in discussions of purposes, scope, or aspects of the program other than buildings, bond issues, and tax levies. During the past few years there have been several letters to the newspaper, and quite a number of citizens have openly objected to some of the things the schools are doing. Recently a committee of lay citizens has been organized by an outspoken critic to "study the school program."

In which of these communities would you expect to find more adequate financial support for the schools? Does general agreement on purposes and scope of the educational program tend to mean good financial support? Do wide differences of opinion decrease the probability of adequate financial support?

Many citizens during the past few years have become increasingly tax conscious. They have become concerned about the prospect of higher local and state taxes in addition to what they consider already high Federal taxes. In many states, citizens have an opportunity to vote directly for or against local bond issues and tax levies for schools. In a number of cases proposed increases have been voted down. A few school systems, as a result, have had to curtail certain aspects of their program.

Which is likely to have a more adverse effect on financial support for schools: disagreement as to the purposes and objectives of the educational program, or fear that taxes for school purposes may be increased? What have been the chief factors in the failure of some proposed tax levies or bond issues for schools?

When Do Increased Expenditures Mean Better Educational Opportunities?

The board of a medium-sized school system has decided that additional local funds are needed to improve the educational program. Salaries have not kept pace with the cost-of-living increases during the past few years, but additional state funds authorized for the ensuing year will help to remedy this situation.

The board has decided to ask the voters to approve an increase in the local tax levy for schools to provide about $10 per pupil additional. It is understood that these additional funds are to be used primarily to improve the *quality* of the educational program provided. Some of the leading citizens in the community have reached the conclusion that considerable emphasis in the past has been placed on attempting to achieve national norms and that excellence may not have been sufficiently emphasized. The board and superintendent have tentatively accepted this point of view and believe that greater attention should be given to quality.

There seems to be considerable difference of opinion in the community, however, as to how quality improvement could best be effected. Several teachers have proposed that most of the new funds should be devoted to increasing salaries. They contend that considerably higher salaries would enable the school system to attract and retain more competent teachers; also, that higher morale would result, and would in turn assure higher quality work. A few believe that the average class size of 33 should be reduced as much as possible; that with smaller classes much better work could be done. A number of parents seem to concur in this point of view.

The lay citizens of the community seem to have a variety of ideas. Some contend that salary increases should be given only to the most capable teachers; that some merit plan of compensation should be used. A few think the term, which is now 172 days, should be extended to 180 days. Several believe that major attention should be centered on improving programs for the more gifted students; that special classes taught by particularly competent teachers should be organized for the more able. Others believe part of the new funds should be used for improving the appearance of many classrooms that are now rather dull and unattractive, thus improving the learning environment. Some do not think any increases in local funds are necessary or can be justified. They contend that quality can be improved without additional funds if the administration will provide proper leadership and give sufficient attention to the problem.

How could additional funds best be used to improve the quality of education in such a school system? Will quality be increased because additional state funds are used to improve salaries? Under the conditions explained above, are the voters likely to approve the proposal for increasing the local tax levy? What should be done to effect a satisfactory solution in this situation?

SELECTED REFERENCES

Burke, Arvid J., *Financing Public Schools in the United States*, rev. ed. New York: Harper and Brothers, 1957. Chapters 3, 4, and 5.

Counts, George S., *Education and American Civilization*. New York: Bureau of Publications, Teachers College, Columbia University, 1952. Chapters 1, 2, 19 and 27.

Harris, Seymour E., *How Shall We Pay for Education?* New York: Harper and Brothers, 1948. Chapters 1 to 4.

Johns, R. L., and E. L. Morphet, editors, *Problems and Issues in Public School Finance.* New York: Bureau of Publications, Teachers College, Columbia University, 1952. Chapters I and II.

MacLean, Malcolm S., and Edwin A. Lee, *Change and Process in Education.* New York: The Dryden Press, 1956. Chapters 5 and 6.

Melby, Ernest O., *Administering Community Education.* Englewood Cliffs, N.J.: Prentice-Hall, Inc., 1955. Chapters 2 and 4.

Miller, Van, and Willard B. Spalding, *The Public Administration of American Schools,* 2nd ed. Yonkers-on-Hudson, N.Y.: World Book Company, 1958. Chapters 1 to 3.

Morphet, Edgar L., chairman, "Some Effects of Finance Policies and Practices on the Public School Program," Phi Delta Kappa Commission on Support of Public Education, *The Phi Delta Kappan,* Vol. XXXIII, No. 1 (September, 1951), pp. 5–45.

————, R. L. Johns, and Theodore L. Reller, *Educational Administration.* Englewood Cliffs, N.J.: Prentice-Hall, Inc., 1959. Chapter I.

National Education Association, Committee on Tax Education and School Finance, *Does Better Education Cost More?* Washington, D.C.: The Association, 1959.

Ross, Donald H. (ed.), *Administration for Adaptability,* rev. ed. New York: Metropolitan School Study Council, Teachers College, Columbia University, 1958. Chapters 3 and 14.

CHAPTER TWO

The Problem
of Support

Those who are especially concerned about an adequate program of education believe that *the best possibilities for good schools exist when sufficient funds are available each year to assure that adequate and well-rounded educational opportunities can be provided for all who should be educated.* This does not mean they believe that money alone will assure a satisfactory program of education. In fact they know it will not. They recognize that resources must be used wisely and effectively if satisfactory progress is to be made. However, unless adequate financial and other resources are available and are wisely used, it is not possible to have good schools or to provide satisfactory educational opportunities in any country. There are many people in this country who would agree with a statement in the report of a recent study of the costs of education in the United Kingdom: "Every teacher, every councillor, every parent must be aware that the grave inadequacies, past and present, of our educational provision can be ascribed in large part to inadequate expenditure." [1]

On the other hand, there are always substantial numbers of people who are so concerned with the impact and implications of high taxes, the high cost of living, and the struggle for personal or corporate financial security that they believe neither the schools nor other agencies of government should be entitled to or receive all of the financial support

[1] John Vazey, *Costs of Education* (London: Ruskin House, George Allen and Unwin, Ltd., 1958), p. 17.

their leaders and representatives believe to be desirable. Those who hold this point of view frequently criticize the public schools and other educational institutions for being extravagant and for jeopardizing the economy through excessive demands.

These sharp differences in points of view regarding financial support are not unique to this country. In the foreword to Vazey's book, Richard M. Titmuss calls attention to this conflict in the United Kingdom:

> In the past, two opposing views have competed for influence. One has asked whether the concept of cheapness and efficiency can satisfy the needs of an industrial society. . . . But what is also noticeable is the extent to which the educational service is simultaneously criticized in a social role for being excessively costly and a burden on industry. The dilemma of cheapness against adequacy is a real one. . . .[2]

Because of the varying points of view regarding the support of education held by substantial numbers of people, there is continuing conflict, actual or incipient, in practically every community, in every state, and at the national level. Many citizens are confused and troubled by this conflict. Most of them want good schools and an adequate program of education, but are not willing to encourage extravagance or inefficiency.

What are the needs? How can the facts be determined? How can lay citizens know whether their schools are underfinanced, overfinanced, or are properly supported? How can teachers or others judge whether too large a proportion of the budget is devoted to operation, to maintenance, or to other aspects not directly related to the instructional program? How can a sound program of finance be developed for all schools and educational institutions in a state?

These and many similar questions are considered in subsequent chapters of this book. In this chapter, primary attention is given to the problem of studying and evaluating financial support as it relates to the entire educational program and of developing insights and understandings that are necessary if progress is to be made in resolving some of the basic conflicts and differences in points of view such as those discussed above.

UNDERSTANDING EDUCATIONAL FINANCE

There are certain things every citizen needs to know and understand about educational finance as well as about the educational program. In the final analysis, misunderstanding or lack of understanding could

---

[2] *Ibid.*, p. 7.

lead to serious difficulties not only for the schools and educational institutions but for the nation as well.

In this country educators cannot determine the amount of financial support to be provided for the schools, the sources of support, or even the purposes for which available funds are to be used. They can make recommendations to the board of education, to the citizens of their community, to the legislature, to the citizens of the state, to Congress, or to the citizens of the nation. However, the basic decisions are made directly or indirectly by the citizens themselves. They elect the members of the board of education, of the state legislature, and of Congress. They determine by their votes the people who are to serve as their representatives—liberal or conservative, wise or short-sighted—and thus whether the basic policies are to be sound or unsound. In short they determine, directly or indirectly, whether schools and educational institutions are to be adequately financed or are to be so seriously handicapped in terms of financial support that the educational program will be inadequate.

While many aspects of educational finance are somewhat technical and difficult for anyone except persons who have made a thorough study of the area to understand, the basic issues and policies can be reduced to relatively simple terms. In our society every citizen has the obligation to understand these essentials sufficiently to participate intelligently in making sound and wise decisions. Any administrator or leader in education who assumes that only experts in finance should have sufficient understanding to make decisions in this area is accepting a point of view which is contrary to realities as they exist in this country. Voters will make the ultimate decisions, but if the issues are not shared with them, their decisions are liable to be hasty and unwise.

Some Background Considerations

In the first place, every citizen should recognize that if children are to be satisfactorily educated in our modern complex civilization it is necessary to provide schools and other appropriate educational institutions. There must be a plan for providing a sound program of education. This plan should be designed to meet the needs. All types and kinds of schools and other educational institutions require financial support if they are to operate satisfactorily. There is no way to avoid this fact. If the support provided is too limited, the schools will be unsatisfactory and the children will be handicapped. In the long run, not only the national economy but even our democratic way of life would be jeopardized if the educational opportunities provided are not adequate to meet the needs. If, on the other hand, too much money is provided, uneconomical practices and inefficient organization may be encouraged. The basic problem, therefore, is: (1) *to provide sufficient funds to assure a good educational program for all who should be educated and* (2) *to develop a plan of organization and administration which will assure optimum returns for all expenditures.*

The problem is complicated in many states and communities because a large proportion of the school districts and consequently many of the schools are too small to be efficient and economical. Inefficient practices are more commonly found in small schools and districts than in those which are properly organized. Limiting the funds provided for school support would not be a satisfactory way to solve this problem because children would then be handicapped. They would be punished because of the failure of their parents and other adults to recognize problems and needs and to develop a satisfactory solution. This means that the problem of financial support cannot be solved merely by centering attention on finance but that it must be considered in relationship to problems of organization and administration.

Another basic concept grows out of the fact that finance is not an end in itself. The objective should never be to obtain more money or to provide less money for financing schools. The purpose of the schools should be to provide an adequate program of education designed to meet the needs of those who should be educated. The purpose of school finance should be to provide whatever funds are necessary to assure a program of education that is designed to meet these needs. Studies of finance should, therefore, begin with studies of the educational program. What program is needed? What services and facilities are required if the needs are to be met? What will these services and facilities cost and how can that cost best be met?

A major difficulty for many people arises from the fact that there is no way to prove conclusively what kind and quality of educational program is required to meet the needs of modern society. The question as to what education is of most worth has been debated from the beginning of civilization and should be debated seriously in the future. However, there should be general recognition of and agreement on a number of points of view which must be considered and utilized in determining the kind and quality of educational program needed in any community or state. This is vitally important in a democracy. These include:

1. Insofar as possible the people in each community, in each state, and even the citizens of the nation, should constantly endeavor to reach greater agreement on the aims and purposes of education. Greater

agreement will provide a better basis than now exists for developing a program and determining the extent of financial support needed for the program designed to meet these purposes and objectives.

2. Each citizen should be seeking constantly to reassess and reappraise his values and to bring sound values to bear in forming his judgments regarding what constitutes a satisfactory program of education and what is needed in the way of adequate financial support. The values people hold and the assumptions they make tend to determine their points of view regarding the educational program and its financial support.

3. All available information should be utilized in arriving at conclusions and decisions. Studies which have been made thus far contribute much information which should be used by everyone who is considering the problem of financial support. These studies show that certain needs are common to all communities, that certain programs and procedures are much more effective than others, and that some provisions for organization and administration are much more likely to result in effective schools than others.

Provisions for Financing Schools

While specific provisions for financing schools vary considerably from state to state and from community to community, some basic patterns are found throughout the country. Some of the most important, discussed in detail in later chapters, are:

Local Finance. Some provision has been made for the local financing of schools in every state. While local school systems range from one-teacher districts found in many parts of some states to county and city districts in others, there is invariably a board of education that is basically responsible, within limits prescribed by state law, for policies relating to finance as well as to other aspects of the educational program. In a few states, and in certain types of districts in other states, some agency other than the school board has been assigned responsibility for making the final determination as to the extent of financial support to be provided from local resources. When finance policies for schools are determined by the board of education or directly by the people, the district is said to be *fiscally independent.* When finance policies are determined by some other agency of local government, the district is *fiscally dependent.*

The superintendent and his staff are usually expected to recommend finance policies for consideration of the board but these recommendations do not have to be followed. The board may authorize the superintendent and his staff to make limited expenditures but even these must be approved by the board which makes the decisions regarding all major expenditures. Provision is made in many states for the citizens of each district to decide by vote on proposals for tax levies which exceed some maximum prescribed by law, as well as on proposals for bond issues for schools. The finance plan for the district in most cases is set forth in a budget which is adopted by the board and has to be followed or amended. Generally local funds for schools are derived from property taxes but in some states other local sources of revenue may be used. Most local school districts receive some funds from state sources and many receive Federal funds.

State Finance. Every state provides some funds for the support of public schools and educational institutions. These funds, however, are provided on various bases and in varying amounts. In some states, they are reasonably adequate and in others they are obviously inadequate. State funds that are made available to the local school systems, as provided by the legislature, must be used by those local systems in accordance with the purposes for which the funds are provided and the limitations placed on the use of those funds. Sometimes state funds have to be kept in separate accounts. Sometimes they may be added to local revenues and used for general school purposes. The practice that must be followed in every case is determined by the legislature.

Federal Finance. The Federal government, by Congressional action, has provided land grants and direct appropriations for schools and educational institutions since the nation was established. Most of the Federal grants of funds thus far have been for specific educational purposes. These are made available, in accordance with the various Acts of Congress, to the states or to the districts which are eligible to participate and must be used in accordance with the purposes set forth in the Federal law authorizing the appropriation.

School Finance Terms

There are many technical terms used in finance which must be understood by all who work extensively in finance. Most of these are defined or discussed in appropriate chapters of this book. There are, however, a few basic terms discussed below which everyone should understand if confusion is to be avoided because they are so commonly used: [3]

---

[3] See Paul L. Reason and Alpheus L. White, *Financial Accounting for the Local and State School Systems: Standard Receipt and Expenditure Accounts,* State Educational Records and Reports Series, Handbook II; Bulletin 1957, No. 4, Office of Education, U. S. Department of Health, Education, and Welfare (Washington, D.C.: United States Government Printing Office, 1957), Chapters 2 and 6.

Receipts. This general term applies to all funds made available for school purposes regardless of source. The term *revenue receipts* includes all monies which add to the assets of a school system and do not involve an obligation to be met at some future date (such as loans). On the other hand, *nonrevenue receipts* do not add to the assets of a school system and include money received from loans and bond sales, sale of property, and other similar sources. It is always important to distinguish between revenue and nonrevenue receipts.

There is another important way of classifying money received for school purposes—that is, on the basis of the level of government from which the funds are derived. Thus funds derived from sources within the school system are commonly classified as *local revenues* or *local school funds.* Those from state sources are listed as *state aid* or *state support* and those from Federal sources as *Federal aid* or *Federal support.*

Expenditures. This is another general term that may be confusing. It is generally more meaningful to use the following: *current expense* means the expenditure for the current on-going program, that is all expenditures except for capital outlay and debt service; *gross expenditure* includes current expense plus capital outlay and debt service. Where summer schools, adult education, or similar programs are provided, it is important to determine whether current expense applies only to the expense of the regular term for the grades commonly included in the regular school program or includes expenses beyond that. The two chief items not included in current expense are *capital outlay* which includes expenditures for sites, buildings, and equipment (either from current or from bond funds) and *debt service* which usually includes payments (principal and interest) made on indebtedness previously contracted to extend beyond the year during which it was incurred.

Current Expense per Pupil in Average Daily Attendance. This term is commonly used for cost analyses and comparisons and, when properly used, is much more satisfactory than gross expenditure per pupil because the latter includes items which may vary considerably from year to year. The current expense per pupil in average daily attendance is found by dividing the current expense of the school system by the number of pupils in average daily attendance.

Budget. The budget is the statement of the plan for financing the various aspects of the educational program to be provided during the year or other stated period of time. It comprises a detailed and carefully prepared estimate of the anticipated receipts, expenditures, and balances for the period for which the budget is prepared.

Foundation Program. This term has come into common usage during the past few years, and refers to what is sometimes called the "minimum program" or even the "minimum foundation program." The foundation program is the program of services and facilities, the financing of which is guaranteed by the state. It may be financed entirely from state funds, as it is in a few states, or, more commonly, through a combination of state and local funds, and may even include some Federal funds.

THE PUBLIC AND SCHOOL FINANCE

As indicated above, every citizen is or should be interested in school finance since the citizens of this country are responsible for the schools. If the citizens of any community, state, or of the nation understand the basic facts and issues relating to the educational program and the provisions for financing the schools, they should be in a good position to make intelligent decisions regarding school support. If, however, they do not understand much about the schools and their needs, the decisions cannot be expected to be either intelligent or wise.

People who do not believe in public schools or who, for some reason, may be prejudiced against the schools, may not make very intelligent decisions even though they have access to the facts. Everyone recognizes that open-mindedness and ability to study and analyze the situation may be just as important, or even more important, than familiarity with facts. Facts may be used either to support a preconceived notion or conclusion or as an aid in thinking through problems and arriving at sound conclusions.

Since so many important decisions regarding the schools have to be made by the public or by representatives elected by the public, one important conclusion should be evident to everyone: *Each and every citizen in this country has a responsibility to attempt to keep informed regarding the public schools and their needs and to participate intelligently and fairly in decisions which relate to the financial support of the schools in his community, in the state, and in the nation.* If each citizen is to be well informed and in a position to act intelligently, he needs not only to know how the schools operate and to have access to facts relating to their operation and financing, but he also needs to understand the respective roles of educators, of the board of education, of the legislature, and of state officials.

Both the lay citizens and the educators of every community should, therefore, be interested in and concerned about ways of improving understanding of the problems and needs of the schools as a basis for improving the climate of support for the schools. Thus educators, board members, and others who have direct responsibilities for the educational program and its support should at all times be concerned with the public and its attitude toward schools and school finance. This does not mean that they should merely attempt to ascertain the attitude of the public and to conform to that attitude; rather that *their chief concern and obligation should be to help the public and all members of the public to develop basic attitudes and understandings which are essential for intelligent decisions and action.* Lay citizens should similarly be concerned because they have such an important obligation to the schools and cannot meet that obligation unless they have, and can help others to have, the basic understandings and attitudes necessary for intelligent participation.

Public understanding of finance and financial problems does not come easily. Seldom do the citizens of a community or state attain the level of understanding which is desirable and in fact necessary for intelligent support at all times. Kindred has pointed out that:

> The failure of school boards and administrators to supply them [the people] with accurate and understandable information, to establish communication, or to give them a part in the educational and financial planning, has been responsible for the inadequate support of public education.[4]

Many ways of increasing public understanding of the problems of school finance have been attempted. Some of these have been reasonably successful. Others have not. Among the points of view which seem to have been adopted or at least generally followed in various districts are the following:

1. The public should have unquestioning confidence in the board they have elected, in the administrator and staff selected by the board, and in the program they have developed. If carried to its logical conclusion, this point of view would mean that the board and staff would concentrate on doing the best job possible and would not be particularly concerned about informing the public about the problems and needs of the schools. However, in this country people have seldom been willing merely to select a board and assume that the board will do a good job. The people have learned that their representatives can and often do make mistakes; that they sometimes may not make a serious effort to meet the responsibilities the people have imposed on them. The public likes to have an opportunity, at least, to become informed. Neither the board nor school personnel can afford to ignore

---

[4] Leslie W. Kindred, *School Public Relations* (Englewood Cliffs, N.J.: Prentice-Hall, Inc., 1957), p. 30.

the public nor to proceed on the assumption that if they do a good job all will be well.

2. The board and the staff should be in a position to decide what information the public needs and should conscientiously make that information available. In some cases they have done a very satisfactory job. However, there is a basic weakness in this assumption also. The public usually is not satisfied to have its officials decide what information should be made available. People like to know they have access to any and all information. The officials of any state or local school system should, of course, seek opportunities to assemble and analyze information and make it available in readily understandable form to newspapers, over radio and television, for public meetings, and through reports of various types. This should be a definite part of the plan and program for every school system but many would hold that such a plan does not go far enough.

3. The best understanding and support usually come through participation. Many school boards and educational leaders believe that if representatives from the public have an opportunity to participate in studying and analyzing various aspects of the educational program, they will become informed regarding the program, will develop an understanding of the problems and needs, will have an opportunity to help plan needed improvements, and thus will have a sound basis for supporting the program. *Studies have shown that people tend to support what they have helped to plan and develop.* Public participation is therefore essential for adequate public understanding and support.

The search for ways of improving understanding and increasing the support for plans to improve the educational program and its financing continues and will undoubtedly continue for many years to come. Much has been learned about what is desirable and what is undesirable. Methods of reporting to the public have been greatly improved. Boards and administrators have learned that classroom teachers and pupils as well as lay citizens have contributions to make and that their contributions must be based on understanding and ability to interpret. More and more state and local school systems have been placing increasing emphasis on public understanding through public participation.

EDUCATORS AND SCHOOL FINANCE

A basic obligation of all educators and of all boards is to recognize the fact that they are responsible to the public for the educational program. The schools do not belong to the educators or to the board. Board members and educators serve as agents of the local citizens, on the one hand, and of the people of the state, on the other, to administer and operate the schools. In fact they may be considered as trustees for the children, for the buildings, and for the funds that are used in financing the schools.

The first concern of educators as well as of board members, therefore, should be to do the best possible job in their capacity as trustees. If they are careless or indifferent in any respect, the public will sooner or later become aware of that carelessness and, because of lack of confidence, may either insist that the board make some changes, may even change the board itself, or finally may reduce the financial support for the schools even though this may handicap the children. As far as the public is concerned, there can be no substitute for capable, honest, and conscientious operation of the schools and of all aspects of the educational program. To the extent that the public is convinced that the staff is doing a good job, is helping the board to establish and implement policies that will assure wise and prudent expenditure of funds, and is accounting periodically for the stewardship to which they have been entrusted, the staff is likely to have and maintain the confidence of the public. This is one of the first necessities in school-public relations and constitutes an important step in assuring adequate financial support insofar as this can be provided by the community.

As far as finance and financial support are concerned, the following should be considered essentials for all school personnel:

1. To seek not only to understand the local problems and needs of education, but also to understand state and national problems and their inter-relationships with local problems.

2. To be able to see clearly the implications of the educational program for finance and of financial support for the educational program, and to interpret these inter-relationships.

3. To recognize finance as merely a means to the end of providing an adequate program of education and seek to understand all phases and aspects of educational finance.

4. To recognize that all laws and board requirements should be scrupulously observed and at all times seek to operate in accordance with those requirements or, if the requirements are not realistic, seek to have them changed.

5. To maintain conscientiously all records including attendance and personnel as well as financial records and render honest and intelligible accounting based on those records.

6. To recognize that continuing studies constitute the basis for evaluating the educational and financial program and for planning needed improvements; to plan and conduct such studies as are necessary and as are within their province to undertake.

7. To recognize that teamwork and cooperation are essential, and that all members of the team should be fully informed, and thus be in a position to help to inform others at all times.

8. To recognize that public participation tends to improve public understanding and support and seek opportunities to provide for such participation in appropriate aspects of the program.

9. To recognize that educators frequently have difficulty communicating with lay citizens concerning educational problems and that lay citizens also have difficulty communicating with educators. They should, therefore, constantly be interested in and seeking ways of improving lay-professional communication.

RESEARCH, LEADERSHIP, AND FINANCE

Satisfactory provisions for financing schools cannot be developed on the basis of expediency. Just as there should be sound reasons for deciding what is to be included in the educational program, there should be sound bases for determining the amount and kind of financial support to be provided. Schools that are under-financed cannot provide satisfactory plant facilities, maintain the quantity and quality of teachers needed or attempt to assure an adequate program of education for the children. Over-financed schools (if there are any) might become careless and not provide the quality of educational program that should be available on the basis of expenditures.

Research studies of various kinds are needed to provide a sound basis for financing schools in each state and in each local school system. Some of these studies will involve immediate and practical problems such as: How many children may be expected to enroll in each grade in each school, school system, or in the state during the next five to ten years? What building facilities will be needed to house these children satisfactorily? How many teachers will be required? What will be the cost of building facilities? Of teachers' salaries? What supplies will be needed? Many questions along this line will need to be asked and answered in each local school system and in each state.

Many other needed studies will have greater value in connection with the solution of long-range rather than immediate problems. Under what conditions do improvements in quality result from increased financial support? What inequities have developed in the educational program? How can these best be corrected? Is there any way of determining the social and economic returns from the investment in education? What percentage of the income of the people should be used for the support of public education?

Research must be carefully planned if it is to be both profitable and meaningful but so must all other phases of the educational program. Good planning requires good leadership as well as able staff members and technicians. Leadership is undoubtedly related to quality. Wise direction and leadership on the part of the local board and superintendent are necessary to assure that there is a sound program of education, that it is properly financed, and is operated economically and efficiently.

Good leadership implies good planning. Failure to plan properly can result, and often has resulted, in inefficiency and long-range extravagance. Anticipating the need for and obtaining adequate sites before property is subdivided, planning and constructing buildings before half-day sessions become necessary, employing additional teachers before enrollment results in overcrowded classes, anticipating and planning for additional funds before the schools face a financial crisis, and taking many other similar steps based on careful studies should help to make possible an adequate, yet economical and efficient program that is properly financed.

State leadership and planning in the field of finance are also of great importance. Failure to plan effectively at the state level may result in handicapping even a far larger number of children than failure in a district. The state program of finance needs to be studied constantly and evaluated in light of defensible principles. Inequities in the program should be ascertained before they become serious. The need for additional state funds should be determined before there is an acute shortage of revenue. In fact, good state leadership and planning based on sound and continuing studies could mean the difference between a continuously improving program that is properly financed and one which lags hopelessly behind the needs.

STUDYING SCHOOL FINANCE

No state or local school system can expect to continue for a number of years without important changes in its program of financial support. The educational program itself is constantly changing in one respect or another. Some of the changes are of major importance, others of relatively minor importance. Some may represent improvements, others may, from a long-range point of view, be considered backward steps. The financial situation of the schools is also constantly changing.

Every state and local school system should have some plan for making both continuing and periodic studies of various aspects of educational finance as it relates to the educational program. Details of these plans will differ from one community to another and from one state to another, but there are certain basic considerations which should be kept in mind in every state and community as studies are planned. A few of the problems to be considered are discussed briefly below.

Scope of Studies

National studies of some aspects of education and of financial support are constantly undertaken by one group or another. These may be concerned with problems in and among the states, with the need for Federal support and the possibility of providing Federal support without Federal control, with revenues and costs, or with some combination of these or other aspects of the problem of finance.

State studies may be concerned with equitable provisions for apportioning funds, with adequacy of support, with equity for taxpayers, with trends in receipts and expenditures, or with any one or more of various other aspects of finance. Such studies are periodically being made in many of the states.

In local school systems there is likely to be concern with population trends and their implications for finance, with building needs and costs, with personnel and salary needs, or with other problems. Some local school systems may make such studies periodically; others almost never. There is undoubtedly need for more and better studies in the financing of schools than have been made in many local school systems during recent years.

Thus national, state, or local studies may be concerned with one aspect of finance, with practically all aspects and their inter-relationships, or with the educational program and its relationship to and implications for finance. Before any study is undertaken by any national, state, or local group or agency, the group needs to determine whether the study should be comprehensive or of some one aspect of finance, and for what purpose and how it should be made.

Timing of Study

There are certain studies that need to be carried on almost continuously in every state and local school system. In a state, for example, continuing information needs to be assembled regarding enrollment trends, changes in value of the dollar and in adequacy of legal provisions which relate to financial support, as a means of making projections and determining what further improvements should be made. Periodic studies, that is studies planned and carried out every few years, for each of the various aspects of the program should be considered essential. From time to time a comprehensive study is desirable. Many authorities would hold that a state-wide comprehensive study should be planned and carried out every five to ten years; others believe that in some states, at least, adjustments made from time to time should suffice to meet the needs and that a comprehensive study should probably be made only about once every ten to twenty years.

Local school systems likewise have continuing studies to make involving such matters as relation of receipts and expenditures to amounts which should be included in the budget, population projections and their implications for finance, and so on. In all districts a comprehensive study is probably desirable every few years. It should not be postponed until there is serious difficulty between the board and the community, until proposals for bond issues have failed, or until there is some other dramatic illustration of difficulties that have arisen. A comprehensive study should not be considered as a device to be used when there are difficulties but as a basis for planning which should assure needed adjustments and avoid serious difficulties.

Kind of Study

Many studies can and should be made by the staff members of local and state school systems, of the U. S. Office of Education, or of various groups interested in education. These include studies which involve assembling, analyzing, and interpreting technical information essential for satisfactory planning. It is important in every case to determine which studies should be carried out by regular members of the staff and which ones should be made in some other manner.

For many years studies involving technical problems as well as comprehensive studies were conducted largely by outside experts. The state or local school system contracted with some group, usually an educational group, to carry on the study and make the report. Many excellent studies were made by such groups and the reports were usually well prepared. Sometimes, particularly in the case of state studies, groups composed primarily of governmental and financial experts made the study either with or without the assistance of educators. Generally such studies have not been as helpful as studies by educational experts who understand all aspects of education and likewise are well grounded in finance. Fewer outside expert-type studies have been made in the past few years than during the earlier stages of the survey movement which first became widespread forty or fifty years ago.

During the past decade or two, more and more local school systems have begun to operate on a different assumption regarding the plan and procedure to be used in making comprehensive surveys or studies. One of the early movements in this direction was to involve members of the staff of the school system. This had considerable value because it provided a basis for better understanding of the educational and finance programs on the part of members of the staff who participated. It also had some limitations. The study was still made by educators, and lay citizens were usually not involved. Moreover the school staffs sometimes had "blind spots" or traditional concepts which were projected into the study and limited the improvements which could be made.

The most recent tendency has been to plan cooperative studies which involve not only members of the local school staff but also lay citizens, and "experts" from without the community or state who serve as consultants. Many of these studies have been quite successful from the standpoint of providing for more widespread participation and understanding as well as of establishing the basis for implementation of recommendations for improvements in the program.

Among the states which have carried out cooperative studies during the past few years are: Alabama, Florida, Indiana, Kentucky, Missouri, Mississippi, North Carolina, Ohio, Texas, Utah, and Wyoming. Some of these have been much more successful than others but most of them have resulted in marked improvements in public support as well as in the educational and finance programs.

More and more local school systems have also been planning cooperative studies which follow essentially the same procedures. The studies are made primarily by educators and lay citizens in the community, usually under the direction of a policy committee which reports to the board. Often consultants from without the community are obtained to assist in planning and carrying out the study.

Some Problems

There are always problems in planning and carrying out studies of any phase of the educational program. One of the most important of these seems to be finding time and the resources to conduct the study. In too many cases, months and even years pass without anyone finding time to do the planning or carry it out. The resources must, of course, include personnel who can devote adequate time to the study and sufficient financial support to pay the expenses of collecting, interpreting, and distributing pertinent materials.

Another important problem involves the development of plans. Some boards and administrators are still hesitant about releasing members of their staffs part-time to help with such studies (this involves the need for additional funds to pay for the services of people who can take over some of the regular responsibilities) and may even be more hesitant about involving lay people. There are, of course, many other problems which involve the collection, analysis and interpretation of information, the establishment of bases for evaluating the information that is obtained, and the development of conclusions and recommendations. Some important safeguards and cautions are listed below:

1. The board of education (or in case of the state, perhaps the governor or the legislature) should authorize the study and propose the general plan. The details should be left to the sponsoring committee or the study group.

2. The problems inherent in the cooperative procedures should be carefully explored and understood insofar as possible by everyone involved. Unless there is definite and nearly universal understanding regarding the cooperative process from the beginning, there are likely to be misunderstandings and difficulties.[5]

3. If any consultants are to be used, they should be selected because they believe in the cooperative process and know how to work with groups which are engaged in the process, as well as because they are recognized authorities and have contributions to make.

4. Sufficient financial resources should be provided by the board or by the state to assure that a satisfactory study can be carried out and completed without serious limitations due to inadequate resources.

5. Ample time should be allowed for the study. Whereas an "expert-type" study might be carried out and completed within a few weeks, a cooperative study requires enough time for everyone to develop the basic understandings and ways of working on the problems that are essential for success. Thus more time should be allowed for a cooperative study than for other kinds of studies.

6. Everyone should understand that the study is concerned with the educational and financial program and not with personalities. Attention should be centered on problems, issues, and needs and the ways of meeting those satisfactorily.

7. It should be clearly understood that the major objective of the study is not to prepare a report but to develop better understanding and insight as well as sound recommendations which can be satisfactorily implemented; the report should be considered a means to an end rather than an end in itself.

---

[5] See Dorwin Cartwright and Alvin Zander, *Group Dynamics: Research and Theory* (Evanston, Illinois: Row, Peterson and Company, 1958), Chapter 22.

COOPERATIVE STUDIES [6]

There probably should be many more cooperative comprehensive studies in state and local school systems during the next few years than have been made in the past. Finance and other special phase studies will still be important but will not meet all needs in many situations. Many people will be seeking an opportunity to reconsider the entire program of education and its support and to study each aspect in relationship to other aspects. Such studies can represent one of the most important single developments in helping to bring order out of potential chaos and in assuring that changes in the educational program will represent progress.

Some Guidelines

Some guidelines which should be followed generally in planning and carrying out either comprehensive *state* or *local* studies or studies of finance are discussed briefly below:

1. *Competent representative citizens from the state or local school system should assume the basic responsibility for planning and conducting the study.* When people participate in a study, they are likely to grow in insight and understanding and to see more clearly than would otherwise be the case the strengths and weaknesses in the educational or financial program. If improvements are found to be needed, those who have assisted with the study should be in excellent position to help assure that the proposals are implemented.

2. *The committee responsible for planning the scope of the study and for determining the general policies, that is for sponsoring the study, should generally be comprised of lay citizens.* Many educators might hesitate to entrust the responsibility for planning a major study of education to a group of lay citizens. However, superintendents of schools constantly work with lay boards of education who are responsible for the policies of the school system.

The sponsoring committee, with the assistance of the coordinator and consultants, should adopt policies and procedures designed to facilitate the planning and conducting of a superior and bona fide study. For example, the committee should agree to: (1) make every reasonable effort to obtain and verify all pertinent information, get agreement on objectives, and arrive at conclusions designed to assist in attaining

[6] Adapted in part from Edgar L. Morphet, "Who Should Solve School Problems?" *The Nation's Schools*, Vol. 63, No. 4 (April, 1959), pp. 67–68. By permission.

the purposes and objectives; (2) arrive at decisions only after careful study of the evidence involved and preferably on the basis of a bona fide consensus rather than simply by a majority vote; and (3) emphasize and use procedures which encourage widespread understanding of state or community educational and financial problems and needs.

3. *The sponsoring or policy committee should be selected on a basis that will justify the confidence and support of both educators and laymen.* It should include people from throughout the state or community and, while it should be representative of the people, should not generally include representatives selected by organizations as such. Any one who has the following characteristics should be eligible for selection: (a) a genuine interest in and concern about public education; (b) honesty and sincerity of purpose; (c) the ability to recognize problems, interpret information fairly, and reach sound conclusions; (d) relative freedom from strong biases that might interfere with impartial interpretations or judgments.[7]

The method of selection should be such as to convince the people that plans are being developed for a thorough and unbiased study of education and of finance. The members of such a committtee should generally not be selected by educators or even by the state or local board of education. In a number of communities, each community-wide organization not sectarian or political in nature is asked to designate a representative for a nominating committee which in turn is authorized to select the sponsoring committee for the study.

4. *Consultants who know how to work constructively with people, both educators and laymen, and who have special competence in their areas of work should be selected to help in planning and conducting the study.* Such consultants can bring insights, understandings, and interpretations which otherwise might be overlooked. While they should be specialists in their respective areas, they must by all means be able to see and appreciate the significance of relationships between their own area of specialization and other areas concerned.

5. *The sponsoring committee should select a competent person to serve as coordinator or executive director.* The sponsoring committee cannot plan and carry out all phases of the study on its own initiative. Members probably will not have time to collect some of the information needed and may not have the competence to deal with details. The coordinator should usually be an educator who can work with lay citizens as well as with educators and who has a broad knowledge and

[7] National Society for the Study of Education, *Citizen Cooperation for Better Public Schools*, Fifty-Third Yearbook, Part I (Chicago: University of Chicago Press, 1954), Chapter X, especially p. 254.

understanding of all major aspects of the educational program. His relationship to the sponsoring committee should be similar to that between the superintendent, as secretary and executive officer of the board, and the board of education. He will, of course, also help to direct and coordinate the work of the various study groups.

6. *When a comprehensive study is planned, study committees comprising six to fourteen competent educators and laymen should be appointed to assume responsibility for planning and conducting the study of each major aspect of the program.* These committees should be carefully selected to assure that they are composed of persons who have the characteristics previously suggested for members of the sponsoring committee. The number of study committees should usually not exceed five or six. Study committees might be designated, for example, for areas such as the following: (a) the educational or instructional program, (b) personnel, (c) organization and administration, (d) pupils and pupil welfare, (e) school plant and transportation, (f) finance. If the study is concerned primarily with finance, study committees might be developed for phases such as (1) salaries and salary schedules, (2) the budget, (3) the capital outlay program, and (4) ability and effort. Each study committee should be responsible to the policy committee for determining the scope of its study, the procedures to be used in collecting and interpreting information, and for tentative conclusions and recommendations.

7. *The objective of the policy or sponsoring committee, the consultants, the coordinator, and the study committee should be to develop the best possible proposals for improving the program of education.* Everyone should recognize that a cooperative study involving major aspects of education cannot be rushed. However, there should be a definite time schedule and the study should move along as expeditiously as possible. Major insights and understandings should develop as the study progresses and some of these are likely to be missed if there is too much haste. Insofar as practicable all conclusions and recommendations should be reached by consensus rather than by majority vote. Some of the greatest values from such a study arise from the insights and understandings gained while the study is in progress.

8. *Close bona fide cooperation between the educational staff and the committee is essential from the beginning.* Neither educators nor lay citizens should attempt to work in isolation nor to conceal or control information.

9. *The committee, after considering suggestions from the board, members of the staff, and consultants, should carefully define the scope of the study, agree upon procedures, and proceed as scientifically and systematically as possible.* The scope should be sufficiently compre-

hensive to cover all important aspects of the program and the plan should provide for assembling, evaluating, and interpreting pertinent data and for completing the study within a reasonable time limit.

10. *One of the important objectives of the committee should be to study and attempt to reach agreement on the characteristics of a satisfactory and well-balanced program of education and finance.* This statement of characteristics should be carefully prepared in written form and used as the basis for evaluating various aspects of the existing program.

11. *The present status of the program should be determined as fully and accurately as possible.* In the course of this determination the committee should attempt to ascertain strong and weak points, and to agree upon problems which need particularly careful study as a basis for prompt solution.

12. *After the committee has agreed upon the characteristics of a satisfactory program, and has determined the present status, it should consider and propose steps which should be taken to solve major problems.* The committee should then prepare recommendations as to priority of these steps and perhaps as to means of taking each major step.

13. *When the committee has completed its studies, it should prepare and submit a report for the interested public and for the board or for the legislature.* Such a committee will be serving in an advisory capacity and of course will not have authority to require the adoption of the findings and recommendations, or to implement them. That responsibility, by law, belongs to the board of education or to the legislature.

Some Cautions

The suggestions above are not designed as a blue print for making a study but as criteria which must be generally observed if real progress is to be made in improving the program and its support. The detailed procedures used in planning and conducting studies will necessarily vary from state to state and from community to community. Special phase or limited studies will require a number of adaptations, but the basic criteria should apply except in the case of certain technical studies. At all times the organization should be kept as simple as possible consistent with the requirements based on the problems to be studied.

Following the procedures suggested here will not necessarily result in a successful study. Much depends on the sponsoring committee, the consultants, the coordinator, the study committees, and the climate of opinion in the community or state. There are certain conditions under which no study is likely to be very successful until the climate improves. Yet a carefully planned, bona fide study may result in sufficient improvement of the climate to enable more meaningful studies to be made at a later time.

Other things being equal, studies developed along these lines are likely to be good studies, and to result in significant improvements, provided all those associated with such studies want to do the best possible job and are willing to make the effort.

Since nearly every state and local school system has some weaknesses and problems, and since many improvements both in education and in finance are obviously needed in most parts of the country, procedures such as those suggested in this section should help to assure that changes are beneficial and that better programs of education will be provided for a larger proportion of the population of the nation.

SOME PROBLEMS AND ISSUES

Some of the problems and issues which should be considered in developing better understanding of school support and in planning and conducting studies of school finance are discussed briefly on the following pages.

When Should Studies of School Finance Be Undertaken?

It should be obvious that factual information regarding various aspects of school finance should be tabulated continuously in accordance with a plan which is designed to make available specific types of information whenever it is needed. Such tabulations supplemented by official pertinent information can be used as a basis for estimates and projections. Studies of special aspects of the entire problem of finance should be made from time to time during the year or from year to year as needed.

Theoretically if a local or state finance program has been developed through careful study and is based on sound principles, a comprehensive re-study should be needed only after a lapse of several years. However, few finance programs have been implemented as fully as would be considered desirable. Sometimes traditional practices have been continued even though they are not consistent with sound principles. Conditions within a community or state are constantly changing and sometimes change quite rapidly. Therefore each program should be re-appraised more frequently than has been the customary practice.

The situation in a local school system is affected by many factors. State laws, requirements, and appropriations are likely to be changed from time to time. In the meantime the local assessed valuation probably is changing but so is the enrollment and the number of teachers. The assessed valuation may increase more rapidly proportionately than enrollment, or less rapidly. Tax levies that sufficed during previous years may no longer be adequate. Some of the policies relating to the educational program may have been modified and these, of course, have implications for financial needs. The buildings may be becoming obsolete and an extensive renovation or construction program may be in order. Some of the needs can be met by special studies but the time will come in almost every local school system when a comprehensive study of all phases of finance and of the educational program may be urgently needed to solve or to avoid serious problems. There is always a danger of failing to plan and carry out a comprehensive study when such a study is needed.

What criteria should be used as a basis for determining when a comprehensive study of finance in a local school system will be needed? How often should such a study generally be undertaken?

Conditions throughout a state are also changing continually. Some local school systems grow much more rapidly than others. Some are increasing in wealth and ability while others are decreasing. New laws result in new demands. The pattern of district organization is likely to change in certain respects. New insights and understandings may open up promising possibilities that cannot be realized without careful study of all aspects of the situation. Outmoded practices may result in much more serious handicaps with changing conditions than had previously been apparent.

Almost every state at one time or another has had a more or less comprehensive study of the educational program including finance. Sometimes attention has been centered chiefly on finance but usually finance has been studied in relationship to the entire program and needs. Several states have undertaken systematic and comprehensive studies about once every ten years. Others have had only special phase studies and may never have undertaken a comprehensive study.

Under what conditions should a comprehensive state study be considered desirable? How frequently should such studies be made in the typical state?

National studies of finance or finance in relationship to various aspects of the educational program have been conducted from time to time. Some of these have been carried out by government agencies; others by various groups and organizations. In 1940 and again in 1950, for example, the Office of Education with the help of a national advisory committee conducted a special study of the ranges in financial support of the schools among the various states and within each of the states.[8] The Office of Education conducts other special studies periodically. For example, every four years a study is made of the provisions for financing schools in each of the states.[9] The Office has also conducted studies of provisions for financing capital outlay and plans to conduct other studies in this area once every four or five years.

The Commission on Intergovernmental Relations in 1955 conducted a study of provisions for financing schools as well as other aspects of government.[10] The White House Conference on Education included studies of finance as one aspect of the national conference sponsored by that organization in 1955.[11]

Why are national studies of school finance important? Are other studies of this type needed? How often and by whom should the studies of various aspects of finance among the states be conducted?

What Should Laymen Contribute?

Many educators have believed in the past that they are the only ones in position to make defensible studies of school finance. Sometimes the local superintendent of schools has assumed that he and the business manager, perhaps with the help of experts from some college or university or the state department of education, should assume full responsibility for all finance studies that are made in the local school system.

During the past few years, however, there has been a tendency for laymen and lay organizations to insist that they should participate in such studies. Sometimes they have plainly stated that they believe educators are sufficiently biased that they are not likely to make a fair or impartial study. In some local school systems lay groups have been organized to obtain "the facts" and work out conclusions and recommendations without consulting or involving anyone from education.

On several occasions groups that have excluded educators have sought to determine the facts and work out solutions for the state prob-

---

[8] See Clayton D. Hutchins and Albert R. Munse, *Expenditures for Education at the Midcentury*, U. S. Office of Education (Washington, D.C.: U. S. Government Printing Office, 1953).

[9] Albert R. Munse and Eugene P. McLoone, *Public School Finance Programs in the United States, 1957–58*, U. S. Office of Education (Washington, D.C.: U. S. Government Printing Office, 1959).

[10] See The Commission on Intergovernmental Relations, *A Report to the President for Transmittal to the Congress* (Washington, D.C.: The Commission, 1955), Chapter 9.

[11] The Committee for the White House Conference on Education, *A Report to the President* (Washington, D.C.: U. S. Government Printing Office, 1956).

lems of financing schools. In one state, for example, an organization which was dissatisfied with provisions for financing schools employed an economist to make an analysis and work out a proposal. The proposal which was developed ignored many of the commonly accepted principles and criteria customarily used in developing state programs of school finance and included recommendations which, if adopted, would have "saved" the state money but would have thrown much of the financial burden back on local school systems. The citizens of the state were not satisfied with the proposal and consequently it was not adopted.

Several organizations interested in studying the management and financing of governmental agencies and of industrial concerns have "offered their services" for proper compensation to conduct state or local studies involving school finance. Sometimes these organizations have employed one or more educators to work with them in such studies, whereas in other cases they have felt it was not necessary to involve educators.

Since the schools in this country belong to the people, the citizens of a community or state must have some understanding of the financial problems and needs of the schools if they are to support a plan which will assure adequate financing. This seems to imply that laymen should be involved in many studies of school finance. In fact laymen have demonstrated again and again that they have many valuable contributions to make to such studies. Since educators generally have at hand much information which would not be readily available to laymen, it seems evident that they should also be involved.

Laymen can assist in assembling or, at any rate, can help to verify much of the information needed for finance studies. They can and should help to think through and decide upon policies which are sound. However, in making such decisions they should have an opportunity to consider the implications of every such policy for the educational program. It seems apparent, therefore, that both laymen and educators should be involved in finance studies and that each has an important contribution to make.

To what extent should laymen be expected to help to assemble pertinent information? What are some examples of policies that might be financially sound but educationally unwise? How can educators point out the fallacies in such policies without controlling or dominating the study?

How Can the Average Teacher or Lay Citizen Know What Can Be Accepted as Facts?

Teachers as well as lay citizens sometimes are suspicious of finance "facts" compiled and reported by administrators or boards of education. In fact, many times lay groups or individual laymen are not willing to accept data compiled by teachers' associations or other educational groups or even by educational administrators. Facts, of course, can always be verified by adequate records. The official reports, then, constitute the basis for much of the information which will need to be assembled in finance studies. Facts can be verified by those who are willing to take the time and make the necessary effort. However, the problem does not end with verification of isolated facts.

Everyone knows that facts can be assembled, organized, and interpreted in such a way as to give the wrong impression. Some important information may be overlooked or deliberately omitted. The data used may show only the favorable or unfavorable aspects of a situation and other equally important information may be left out. Charts may be developed in such a way as to center attention on certain things and to ignore or minimize other developments which are equally significant.

When teachers and lay citizens are involved in studies of finance, the first and most important step is to establish mutual confidence. If there are any suspicions, reservations, or doubts, they should diplomatically be brought into the open. The members of the group should agree on the source or sources for all information, on what constitutes facts, on procedures to be used in tracing trends and making comparisons. When the group works together on a bona fide basis, mutual trust and confidence should be improved. Anyone who betrays that trust in one way or another is likely to be discredited.

For any bona fide study group, the first few meetings are usually the most difficult. Each member of the group needs to become well acquainted with other members, learn to respect them and their competencies, and in turn earn the respect of the other members. The principles of good cooperative procedure should be carefully observed at all times. No "smart" moves to gain a point or to attempt to discredit valid information or anyone's judgment should be permitted. A bona fide cooperative study can result in better understanding on the part of everyone concerned and provide the basis for confidence and increased public support of the entire program of school finance.

How can an administrator proceed to gain the confidence of teachers when some of them have had previous experience with administrators who have attempted to withhold some of the facts? What assumptions

48   THE PROBLEM OF SUPPORT

are teachers likely to make which may handicap the cooperative process? What assumptions made by laymen are likely to arouse the suspicion of educators?

What Should Be the Role of the "'Expert" or Consultant?

While there will continue to be special studies which can best be carried out by experts, their role in connection with most studies of finance has changed considerably during the past few years. In the future, experts will usually be expected to serve as consultants for committees involving teachers and lay citizens and perhaps for committees which are composed largely of laymen.

The role of an expert who is serving as consultant is quite different from the role of one who makes the study. The consultant will need to gain the confidence of all members of the committee with whom he works; he cannot assume that he will have that confidence. He should not expect to have all of the "good" ideas. In fact he will find that every member of a good committee will have some worthy ideas.

The consultant should be interested in the development of the group and its members. This should be as important to him as the report. In fact the process and procedure may be even more important than a highly polished report.

The consultant should at all times seek to encourage and promote understanding. There are some things perhaps he can explain better than other members of the group. On the other hand, as the study moves along, there should be members of the group who can explain some things just as well or nearly as well as the consultant. He should therefore encourage such explanation and not become impatient with those who do not attain perfection.

The consultant should try to avoid being the first one to make a suggestion unless it becomes evident that the suggestion is needed for the progress of the study. Sometimes he can propose an idea which will be recognized by the group as valid but which the group will then put in somewhat different form than originally proposed by the consultant. The objective should be a good study and everyone should be expected to contribute to the development of the study. Suggestions made by the consultant should be accepted on their merit, not because he, as consultant, has made the contribution. If his proposals are rejected, he cannot afford to be offended. Rejection may come because the idea has not been properly explained. Later the same idea may be picked up by someone else and accepted by the group. Such a procedure is not unusual. The consultant who has good ideas to suggest and knows when to make the suggestion will soon be accepted by the group as the expert he is.

Are all experts in finance equally suited to serve as consultants? What should be the chief characteristics of a person who is to serve as consultant for a study of school finance?

SELECTED REFERENCES

American Association of School Administrators, *Public Relations for America's Schools*, Twenty-Eighth Yearbook. Washington, D.C.: The Association, 1950. Chapters I, IV, and X.

Campbell, Roald F., and John A. Ramseyer, *School-Community Relations*. Boston: Allyn and Bacon, Inc., 1955. Chapters 3, 5, and 6.

Johns, R. L., and Edgar L. Morphet, editors, *Problems and Issues in Public School Finance*, National Conference of Professors of Educational Administration. New York: Bureau of Publications, Teachers College, Columbia University, 1951. Chapters I, II, and III.

Kindred, Leslie W., *School Public Relations*. Englewood Cliffs, N.J.: Prentice-Hall, Inc., 1957. Chapters 1, 9, 11, and 12.

Miller, Van, and Willard B. Spalding, *Public Administration of American Schools*, 2nd ed. Yonkers-on-Hudson, New York: World Book Company, 1958. Chapters 1 and 18.

Moehlman, Arthur B., and James A. van Zwoll, *School Public Relations*. New York: Appleton-Century-Crofts, Inc., 1957. Chapters 9, 11, and 24.

Morphet, Edgar L., Roe L. Johns, and Theodore L. Reller, *Educational Administration*. Englewood Cliffs, N.J.: Prentice-Hall, Inc., 1959. Chapters 1, 4, and 5.

National Society for the Study of Education, *Citizen Cooperation for Better Public Schools*, Fifty-Third Yearbook, Part I. Chicago: University of Chicago Press, 1954. Chapters I, II, IV, VII, VIII, X, and XI.

Report of the Ohio School Survey Committee. Columbus, Ohio: The Ohio School Survey Committee, 1955. Chapters 1 and 8.

Still, Rae, *The Gilmer-Aiken Bills: A Study in the Legislative Process*. Austin, Texas: Steck Publishing Company, 1950.

Sumption, Merle R., *How to Conduct a Citizens School Survey*. Englewood Cliffs, N.J.: Prentice-Hall, Inc., 1952.

CHAPTER THREE

The Economics
of School Finance

The financing of education cannot be adequately studied without giving full consideration to its effect on the national economy. The American people have many aspirations. One of the more important of those aspirations is that the economy shall produce a rising standard of living for all the people. Therefore a major purpose of the economy is to maximize the production and consumption of goods and services which satisfy human wants. The goods and services produced and consumed in the economy are both private and public.

Education is vital to the economy of any modern nation. Some of the more fundamental concepts of economics are treated briefly in the following section of this chapter in order to demonstrate the relationship of education to the economy.

SOME FUNDAMENTAL CONCEPTS IN ECONOMICS

Economics has been defined in many ways. One of the simplest and most satisfactory definitions is that economics is the study of human wants and their satisfaction. The economic system provides an arrangement for the production, exchange, and consumption of whatever is needed to satisfy human wants. Some concepts essential to an understanding of the economy are presented, with necessary brevity, in the following paragraphs.

Goods

Anything that satisfies or is capable of satisfying a human want is a good. Goods can be classified as free goods or economic goods. If a good is so abundant, such as air, that it need not be economized, it is called a free good. If a good is scarce and capable of being apportioned or economized, it is called an economic good. Economics is concerned only with economic goods. Education is an economic good.

Material and Nonmaterial Goods. Economic goods are either material or nonmaterial. A material good is physical and tangible. A nonmaterial good is a service rendered by a free person which satisfies a want. Economists generally consider slaves themselves as goods so therefore their services cannot be counted as goods. Education is one of the most important of the nonmaterial goods produced by the economy.

Single Use, Multiple Use, Durable and Nondurable Goods. Economists classify material goods such as food, which can be used only once for their original purpose, as single-use goods. Those goods such as typewriters which can be used many times are classified as multiple-use goods. A closely related classification of material goods is durable and nondurable. A durable good is one which can be kept or stored for an extended period of time before use.

Economists do not usually classify education under these categories because it is a nonmaterial good. However the educated person has acquired a nonmaterial, multiple use, durable good of great importance, both to himself and to society. Education has the peculiar characteristic that, unlike material goods, it appreciates rather than depreciates with use. On the other hand, education loses its durability with storage or non-use. For example, if one acquires a knowledge of the German language and does not speak, read or write that language for ten years, most of the knowledge of the language is forgotten and the "good" is found to have a limited durability. Furthermore many kinds of education, like machinery, rapidly become obsolete. For example, teachers, physicians, engineers, farmers—in fact, practically all educated persons—find that certain aspects of an education acquired at any one time soon becomes obsolete because of the continuous discovery of new knowledge. This is particularly true in a rapidly advancing culture.

The phenomenon of the accelerated rate of obsolescence of education in a dynamic culture with a growing economy has great significance for the financing of education. If education satisfies the wants of society and the individuals in that society, it is necessary to extend the time spent in schooling the young and also to continue throughout life the inservice and adult education facilities provided for adults.

Progressive nations will undoubtedly find it necessary in future years to spend increasing amounts of their income in order to satisfy urgent wants for education.

Consumers' and Producers' Goods. The distinction between consumers' goods and producers' goods is of fundamental importance to an understanding of the economy. Economists commonly classify both material and nonmaterial goods under these categories. A good used by a consumer to satisfy his wants is a consumer's good and a good used in the process of producing other goods is a producer's good. Education is both a producer's good and a consumer's good. When knowledge [1] is acquired to become an engineer, a teacher, a physician, a mechanic or for any vocational objective which has as its major purpose the production of material or nonmaterial goods that satisfy human wants, education is a producer's good. When knowledge is acquired to use, enjoy, or appreciate any material or nonmaterial good, education is a consumer's good. Education can be used to enjoy both free goods, such as the beauties and mysteries of nature, and economic goods. It would be futile to produce such economic goods as art, music, and literature if individuals in the society did not possess the consumer knowledge necessary to enjoy them. It would be equally futile to produce such economic goods as bathrooms and healing medicines if the population were too ignorant or superstitious to utilize them.

For these reasons, the arguments between those who insist that education should be for economic and vocational efficiency and those who insist that knowledge should be acquired for its own sake are futile. It seems that both functions are important. There is every reason to believe that in future years, human wants for education both as a producer's good and a consumer's good will greatly increase.

Public and Private Goods. Economic goods can be classified as public and private. When the use of a good such as a public school or a highway is free to an individual but obtained at a cost to the community, it is a public good. When an individual or a corporation acquires a good for private use, it is a private good. A tax-supported school is a public good and is commonly called a public school. Goods which cannot be produced at all or as efficiently by the private economy as by the public economy are usually produced as public goods.

Value and Price

The usefulness of a good for satisfying human wants is called its use value. As pointed out above education is a nonmaterial, multiple use,

---
[1] Knowledge in the broad sense including all things learned.

durable, consumer's and producer's economic good produced in both the public and private economy. It is also one of the most useful goods produced by human society.

The exchange value of a good is the purchasing power over other goods which is possessed by the owner of a good when he exchanges it for other goods. A person may not directly sell or exchange his education for another economic good. However education can be used to produce both material and nonmaterial goods which have an exchange value, therefore education might be considered as having an exchange value.

The price of a good is its exchange value expressed in money. Therefore whether education is considered to have a price depends upon whether one accepts the concept that education has an exchange value.

Wealth

Wealth is usually defined by economists as the accumulated stock of material goods which satisfy our wants. Since services are consumed as they are produced, they are not considered by economists as wealth. This seems to be an unnecessarily limited concept of wealth. For example, the services rendered by a teacher at a particular moment are consumed at that time and cannot be accumulated.[2] But the learning possessed by the teacher represents an accumulated stock of knowledge. Therefore it might well be considered as wealth. Certainly a nation with a highly educated population with a vast store of technological knowledge and skill has a type of wealth not possessed in the same amount by such a country as Indonesia.

Wealth can be both public and private. Therefore the total wealth of a country is the sum of public and private wealth.

Capital

Most economists generally use the term capital to mean the aggregate of man-made goods used in production. Sometimes unconsumed goods in the hands of consumers are called consumers' capital but it is less confusing to consider such goods as consumers' goods.

Capital is generally considered by economists as man-made material wealth used in production. "The process of adding to productive capacity is capital formation; the thing created is real capital."[3] How-

---

[2] It might be argued that the services of the teacher are accumulated by pupils.

[3] C. Lowell Harriss, *The American Economy*, rev. ed. (New York: Rinehart and Company, Inc., 1946), p. 40.

ever non-material wealth such as education may be the most important capital used in many kinds of production.

Traditionally, economists have directed most of their efforts to the study of the production, exchange, and consumption of material economic goods. Adam Smith gave major attention to that aspect of the economy in his monumental work, "The Wealth of Nations" written in 1776. His work has had a powerful influence on the thinking of economists. However many modern economists are giving much more emphasis than their predecessors to the production, exchange, and consumption of non-material economic goods such as education.

Income

Concepts of income are very important to students of school finance. Income can be defined as ". . . the sum of economic goods that becomes available to an individual, firm, or community during a given period, e.g., a year. Whereas wealth and capital are stocks of goods or accumulations, income is a flow of goods." [4] Although it is relatively easy to define income, it is much more difficult for the statistician to assign a dollar value to income because everyone receives considerable non-monetary income. For example, the services rendered within one's own family; the rent income equivalent of one's own house; the income value of government services received such as public schools, highways, protection, and parks are difficult to estimate in dollars but they represent real income. This is particularly important for low income families because the proportion of the income of a low income family that is non-monetary is probably greater than for high income families. Since much non-monetary income is not included in published data on income, the actual inequalities in income are probably not quite as great as reported. [5] However, the United States Department of Commerce in recent years has made a greater effort than previously to report non-monetary income.

All taxes for schools and other purposes are paid from income received at one time or another. The ability to pay taxes, the effect of taxes on income, the effect of education on income, and the financial effort made to support schools are all important to the study of school finance.

Measures of Income. Different measures of the productivity of the national economy are frequently confused. It is important that these measures be carefully defined in order to avoid confusion. The 1955

[4] Anatol Murad, *Economic Principles and Problems,* rev. ed. (Ames, Iowa: Littlefield, Adams and Company, 1954), p. 13.
[5] Harriss, *op. cit.,* p. 385.

Statistical Supplement to the Survey of Current Business, United States Department of Commerce, presents and defines the following five measures of the productivity of the nation:

1. Gross national product is the market value of the output of goods and services produced by the nation's economy before deduction of depreciation charges and other allowances for business and institutional consumption of durable capital goods.
2. National income is the aggregate earnings of labor and property which arise from the current production of goods and services by the nation's economy.
3. Personal income or income payments to individuals is the current income received by persons from all sources, inclusive of transfers from government and business but exclusive of transfers among persons.
4. Net national product is the market value of the net output of goods and services produced by the nation's economy. All business products used up by business in the accounting period are excluded.
5. Disposable income is the income remaining to persons after deduction of personal tax and non-tax payments to general government.

The first three measures—gross national product, national income and personal income—are most useful in studying the ability of the nation to finance education. Only one of these measures, personal income, is available regularly for individual states.

Investment and Saving

The economic concepts of investment and saving are very important to the study of educational financing. Investment is defined as the incurring of costs for the purpose of adding to capital. Therefore expenditures for education are an investment for the purpose of adding to the educational capital of the people.

When people save, they refrain from consuming that part of current income which is added to capital. When consumers save, they reduce proportionately the income stream from the circular flow of production and consumption. If much of the amount saved is not invested, the economy stagnates because both production and consumption will decline. Investments increase the income stream and add to both production and consumption. Investments must approximately equal saving in order to keep the economy in equilibrium. Uninvested saving results in a decline in the economy. Unused goods and services [6] do not add to the level of living. They must be consumed or invested be-

---

[6] Although economists use the word *goods* to include both material and non-material goods, common usage usually reserves the word to mean material goods and *services* to mean non-material goods.

cause the amount saved by the community cannot be more than the amount invested no matter how much collectively the people intend to save.

Those charged with the responsibility of securing funds for financing the schools have frequently encountered the old New England theory of "do without and make it do." The refusal to invest funds in education has frequently been justified on the grounds of thrift and economy. Murad's comment on thrift is interesting at this point:

> When people want to save more, they consume less. A decline in consumption discourages investment. And since the volume of investment determines the amounts actually saved by the community as a whole, saving declines as investment declines. Therefore, the net result of the people's efforts to save *more* is that they save *less*. This is known as the *paradox of thrift*.[7]

Investment and Exchange Media

The relationship of the quantity of exchange media (money) to investment is frequently misunderstood. It is a popular notion that there can be no investment unless someone first saves some money and the money saved is invested by the "saver" or by someone who borrows it from the "saver." This idea is based on the assumption that there is a fixed volume of money available and therefore it must be spent sparingly because if more money is spent for one purpose, there will be a smaller quantity available for other purposes.

The Relationship of Money to Investment. This concept is erroneous for a number of reasons. Recently the authors were serving as consultants for a state school survey in which school building needs were being studied along with other matters. A careful analysis revealed that the aggregate of the building needs of the state was approximately $300,000,000. The ability of the state to finance a program of this size became an issue. It was argued by some that "the money" simply was not available. It was also argued that it would hurt business to spend that much money for school buildings because it would reduce the purchasing power of consumers by the amount spent. Still another argument advanced was that it would reduce seriously the amount of "investment capital" available for private enterprise.

But money actually cannot be invested. Money will not build a school house. School plants are built by architects, contractors, skilled workers and laborers using lumber, brick, concrete, steel and many other materials. These economic goods are the real capital invested. At the time the school building program was being debated there was

---

[7] Murad, *Economic Principles and Problems*, p. 180.

considerable unemployment of all the professional and labor groups named and also large unsold inventories of all the materials used in constructing school buildings. These unconsumed goods and services represented a potential saving but they could not become a real saving unless and until they were invested in the productive mechanism. Real capital would be in short supply only if there were not enough services and goods available to build school houses and at the same time satisfy other urgent human wants such as residential housing.

But where is the money coming from?[8] Obviously workers and suppliers of building materials must be paid in currency of some kind.[9] To answer this question fully would require an extensive treatment of exchange media and banking which is beyond the scope of this book. In simple terms however the state (and boards of education) can obtain the money needed: (1) from cash balances on hand, (2) by borrowing from individuals who have exchange media, or (3) by borrowing from commercial banks which can create exchange media.[10]

The Creation of Exchange Media. Let us now see how commercial banks can create exchange media. Eighty-five per cent of the commercial bank deposits in this country are in member banks of the Federal Reserve System. Therefore this discussion of how commercial banks can increase the media of exchange is confined to banks that are members of that System. Those banks are required to deposit a legal cash reserve in a Federal Reserve Bank. The amount of the reserve is calculated in terms of a percentage of deposits. The Federal Reserve System may vary this percentage within the maximum and minimum limits prescribed by law. The legal limits vary for different classes of commercial banks and higher reserves are required for demand deposits than for time deposits. An example will show how a commercial bank can expand the media of exchange.

Let us assume that the bank is a central reserve city bank for which the legal minimum cash reserve is 13 per cent of deposits and the legal maximum 26 per cent but that the reserve requirement has been set at 20 per cent. Now let us study the effect of a $1,000 primary deposit in that bank. The bank, of course, wants to loan money at interest in order to make a profit. The bank can loan $800 or 80 per cent of the deposit to some competent borrower and it does so. The borrower deposits $800 in the lending bank or in some other bank, creating another

---

[8] The terms *money* and *currency* are defined differently by economists. In order to avoid confusion to the reader of this book, *money* is used to mean the total of all media of exchange including coins, notes, and bank deposits. *Currency* is used to mean coins and paper media of exchange such as bank notes.

[9] Corporations sometimes pay the persons building a factory in ownership shares.

[10] Murad, *Economic Principles and Problems,* p. 181.

deposit. Then $640 or 80 per cent of the $800 deposit can also be loaned creating still another deposit. This process can be continued until theoretically $4,000 of secondary deposits are created which added to the primary deposit of $1,000 makes a total of $5,000 in bank deposits. Ninety per cent of all cash transactions in the United States are by checks and they serve as important media of exchange.

It will also be observed that the Federal Reserve System can create bank deposits and exchange media by lowering the legal reserve requirement for member banks. In the example just cited, the deposits could total much more than $5,000 if the required reserve were 15 per cent instead of 20.

Thus it is seen that the scarcity of money is not a real problem in our economy. "The existence of money depends upon debt. We have money only if someone—individual, business or government—is willing to assume an obligation. The growth or contraction of money depends upon changes in debt." [11]

The Source of Currency. But, as was pointed out above, workers and suppliers of materials for school buildings must be paid in currency. Where is the currency coming from? The supply of currency can readily be regulated by the Federal Reserve System. Ninety per cent of the currency in circulation is in the form of Federal Reserve notes. The notes are printed and guaranteed by the United States Treasury but are issued by the twelve Federal Reserve Banks. These banks can issue such notes, but at least twenty-five per cent must be backed by gold certificates and the remainder by notes or other eligible debts of business firms, U. S. Government obligations or gold certificates.

Money, Banking, and Investment. This is a very inadequate discussion of money, banking and investment. [12] But it is sufficient to demonstrate that our economy does not depend on the supply of money or the currency saved by individuals. Real capital consists of economic goods and services invested in the productive mechanism. In the example given of a state which was considering the construction of needed school buildings costing $300,000,000, the issue is not whether this investment is possible but rather whether these buildings are necessary to the production of the educational enterprise or whether education itself is a good investment.

Too often our economic thinking has been based upon the "economics of scarcity." Economics has frequently been defined as the administration or use of scarce resources. To a certain extent this is

---

[11] Harriss, *The American Economy*, p. 163.
[12] For further information the serious student of school finance should read some standard work on money and banking.

true but how scarce are resources in a given country at a given time? The level of scarcity is quite different in America from that in Pakistan.

Microeconomics and Macroeconomics. Furthermore, classical economics [13] has emphasized the study of individuals and corporations and largely ignored a study of the total economy. This type of economics is sometimes called microeconomics, that is the study of the small or particle. Within recent years the emphasis has shifted to a study of aggregates or macroeconomics.[14] It is now apparent that one cannot obtain an adequate concept of the total economy by summing the economic activities of all the individuals and corporations in the economy. The vital, growing, productive, free enterprise, capitalist economy of the United States was not built upon the "do without and make it do" sayings of the New England sages.

For example, when the automobile came along many said that people would not have any money to build houses or buy other things because they would spend so much on automobiles. The same things were said as each new invention such as central heating, radios, refrigerators, and television sets came along. Incidentally the same thing has been said many places in the United States as new educational activities have been added to the program. Needless to say these fears have not been realized. The productive capacity per man hour of the nation has increased from 2½ to 3 per cent per year since the beginning of the century. Ours has been an economy of plenty and not one of scarcity. We have not been compelled to eat less food, live in poorer houses or go poorly clothed in order to enjoy such want satisfying goods as automobiles, television, refrigeration, and education. Indeed, we have more of everything. We can continue to do so unless we accept the defeatist theory that in order to have more of any one thing we must have less of something else. That outworn belief seems to have been based on the assumption that there is a fixed stock of economic goods available which must be parceled out parsimoniously. That assumption ignores our increasing wants and our increasing capacity to satisfy those wants.

It should not be assumed from this discussion that the spending of money, personal and public, is a sure road to progress. Neither should it be concluded that the less we save and the more we spend the greater our wealth. The purposes for which we save and the purposes for which we invest are all important in this process. For example, our

---

[13] Perhaps starting with Adam Smith's *Wealth of Nations* (1776).

[14] See John Maynard Keynes, *General Theory of Employment, Interest and Money* (New York: Harcourt, Brace and Company, 1936). Perhaps the classic initial statement, although by no means the last word in macroeconomics, was set forth by Keynes in this work.

productive capacity has increased steadily as a result of progressive mechanization, which is based upon technological knowledge, which in turn is based on education. Therefore, the key to progress is not spending but wise investment. Later in this chapter, attention is given to the necessity for investment in education as a part of the productive mechanism.

The next section of this chapter deals with the effect of governmental expenditures on the national economy.

GOVERNMENT EXPENDITURES AND THE NATIONAL ECONOMY [15]

No economic system is purely private enterprise, socialist, or communist. The governments of all civilized nations supply certain human wants because private enterprise cannot meet them or can provide for them only inadequately.[16] Furthermore the private enterprise system cannot function successfully unless government performs certain services. Every civilized nation needs a system of laws, methods of enforcing those laws, a police force for protecting life and property, a plan for educating the young, health protection, highways, national defense, and many other services and facilities.

Wagner's Law

The more advanced the civilization, the greater the number and proportion of human wants which must be supplied by government. Adolph Wagner, a famous German economist of the 19th century, stated the law of increased state functions as follows:

> Comprehensive comparisons of different countries and different times show that, among progressive peoples, with which alone we are concerned, an increase regularly takes place in the activity of both the central and the local governments. This increase is both extensive and intensive: the central and local governments constantly undertake new functions, while they perform both old and new functions more efficiently and completely. In this way the economic needs of the people, to an increasing extent and in a more satisfactory fashion, are satisfied by the central and local governments.[17]

---

[15] A considerable part of the material of this section has been adapted from R. L. Johns, "Education and the National Economy," National Education Association, Legislative Commission (Washington, D.C.: The Association, 1958).

[16] See William H. Anderson, *Taxation and the American Economy* (Englewood Cliffs, N.J.: Prentice-Hall, Inc., 1951), p. 13.

[17] Adolph Wagner, *Grundlegung der politischen Oekonomie* ("Principles of Political Economy"), 3rd ed. (1893), Book VI, Chapter 3. Translated and quoted

Wagner derived his law from a study of the economics of a number of progressive countries of western Europe over a long period of time. It will be noted that it is not implied by Wagner's law that the government economy in progressive nations will ever supplant the private economy. That is, the private economy will continue to satisfy human wants which can best be supplied by private enterprise. However, as civilization advances the proportion of human wants which are non-material in nature increases. Many of these nonmaterial wants cannot be supplied at all or as well by private enterprise as by government.

The Economy of Prehistoric Man. In order to understand the operation of Wagner's law, let us first consider the wants of a prehistoric human being. He had no culture, so his wants at that stage of development were biological or primary wants. Such wants had to be satisfied in order for man to survive in the struggle for existence. He had to have air, water, food, and shelter in order to survive and he had to reproduce the species. Air and water were free economic goods. However, he had to contrive somehow to secure his food and shelter by his own individual efforts.

His economic system was a purely private enterprise system. He paid no taxes and government supplied him no services. His standard of living was low and his span of life was short. He found it difficult indeed to compete with other animals for survival.

Anthropologists have observed that the human animal was probably the poorest equipped physically of any of the animals that avoided extinction in the struggle for survival. He couldn't swim instinctively, he couldn't fly, he couldn't run as fast as many other animals, he was not very strong and his physical equipment in tooth and claw for either offense or defense was very poor.

The Development of Culture. The only thing that saved man from extinction was a brain that enabled him to think and reason and predict the consequences of his acts and the acts of other persons and animals. However, the purely private enterprise system under which he lived produced such a low standard of living that man existed precariously on earth hundreds of thousands of years before he started to develop a culture. When he discovered that his chances of survival would be better if he cooperated with other human beings instead of relying exclusively on a purely individualistic private enterprise system, the tribe was created. By banding themselves together human beings found that they could defend themselves better from predatory animals and could also obtain better food and shelter.

---

in C. J. Bullock, *Selected Readings in Public Finance,* 3rd ed. (Boston: Ginn and Company, 1924), p. 32.

As the standard of living of the primitive man improved he began to develop a culture. Wants other than the primary wants of food and shelter developed. Anthropologists have found that even in prehistoric times man attempted to satisfy such nonmaterial wants as art and music, the beginnings of a literature, the education of the young, and healing.

We have no authentic record of the economics of prehistoric man but we have learned a great deal from artifacts. We know that after the development of oral and especially written languages civilization developed rapidly. Communication made it possible to exchange the goods and cultures of different human societies. This greatly accelerated human progress.

The Development of Government. Man soon found that he could not live in a civilized society without government. Systems of laws were developed and government began to assume a variety of functions that were not recognized as necessary in a primitive society. Therefore when man discovered the art of government he really unlocked the potentialities of free enterprise. It is true that when one studies the history of mankind, he finds many examples in which government has not supplied the human wants it should have supplied. Furthermore government at times, as Adam Smith pointed out, has handicapped the free enterprise of human beings. Nevertheless government which satisfies human wants is necessary to the survival of the culture of any nation. Despite this fact which is well known to all students of anthropology, there are some people who believe that the smaller the role played by government, the better the society.

Wagner's Law and the American Economy

Let us now consider the application of Wagner's law to the economy of the United States. Table 3-1 presents certain pertinent information for selected years beginning with 1923. In studying economic trends over a period of time it is usually desirable to avoid peak war expenditure years and very low depression years. The year 1923 was selected because it was the first fairly normal year after World War I. The years 1930, 1940 and 1950 are good intermediate years because they were neither low depression years nor peak war expenditure years. The year 1957 was selected because it was the latest for which all needed data were available from reasonably reliable sources.

It appears from Table 3-1 that the national income for 1957 was five and one-half times greater than for 1923 but expenditures for all government (Federal, state, and local) in 1957 were 12 times the expenditures in 1923. The various costs of government rose from 13.7 per cent of the national income in 1923 to 30.3 per cent in 1957. Many people have viewed this trend with great alarm.

TABLE 3–1

TOTAL NATIONAL INCOME AND TOTAL EXPENDITURES FOR GOVERNMENT IN
CURRENT DOLLARS FOR SELECTED YEARS 1923–1957

Year	Total National Income (in millions)	Total Expenditures for All Government (in millions)	Per Cent of National Income Spent for Government
(1)	(2)	(3)	(4)
1923	$ 64,600	$ 8,850	13.7
1930	75,729	11,022	14.6
1940	81,634	18,467	22.6
1950	239,956	61,247	25.5
1957	358,200	108,674	30.3

Sources:
Column 2: Data from the *Survey of Current Business*, U. S. Department of Commerce, except for the year 1923 which is from *Tax Facts and Figures, 1941*. New York: The Tax Foundation.
Column 3: Data for 1957, 1950, 1940 and 1930 from *Facts and Figures on Government Finance*, 10th ed., 1957–58, New York: The Tax Foundation; and for 1923 from *Tax Facts and Figures, 1941*, New York: The Tax Foundation.
Column 4: Column 2 divided by Column 1 × 100.

Effect on National Income of Increased Governmental Expenditures

What is the real effect on the private economy of this trend toward increasing the proportion of the national income spent on government? In order to answer this question it is necessary to convert current dollars for the different years into dollars of the same purchasing power and also the total income into per capita income. Table 3-2 sets forth the data necessary to make these conversions. It will be noted from Table 3-2 that the price index for the years shown ranges from a low of 59.9 in 1940 to 120.2 in 1957, based on 1947–49 prices as 100. The population also increased from 111,950,000 in 1923 to 171,229,000 in 1957.

Table 3-3 shows national income in terms of the purchasing power of the 1947–49 dollar.[18] Therefore each year is comparable to every other year. It will be noted that the real national income for 1957 was slightly more than 3.4 times the income of 1923 in terms of the same purchasing power. The real expenditure for government in 1957 was 7.5 times the expenditure for 1923.

---

[18] In order to convert current dollars for any year into dollars with the purchasing power of 1947–49 dollars, divide current dollars for the year being converted by the 1947–49 Consumer Price Index and multiply by 100. For example, in order to convert national income of 1957 into 1947 dollars proceed as follows: $358,200 million divided by 120.2 equals 2980.03 million times 100 equals $298,003 million.

TABLE 3-2

CHANGES IN PRICE INDEX AND POPULATION

Year	Consumer Price Index (1947-49 = 100)	Total Population (in thousands)
(1)	(2)	(3)
1923	72.9	111,950
1930	71.4	122,775
1940	59.9	131,669
1950	102.8	150,697
1957	120.2	171,229

Sources:
Column 2: *Monthly Labor Review*, U. S. Department of Labor, Bureau of Labor Statistics.
Column 3: U. S. Bureau of the Census.

However, trends become more meaningful when expressed in per capita amounts rather than in total amounts because the population increased 53 per cent during this 34-year period. Table 3-3 shows that the per capita national income increased from $792 in 1923 to $1,740 in 1957, an increase of 120 per cent. It will also be observed that the per capita expenditures for government during this same period of time increased from $108 to $529, an increase of 391 per cent.

TABLE 3-3

NATIONAL INCOME AND EXPENDITURES FOR GOVERNMENT IN TERMS OF 1947-49 PURCHASING POWER

Year	National Income (in millions)	Total Expenditures for all Governments (in millions)	Per Capita National Income	Per Capita Expenditures for Government	(6) Per Capita Expenditure and Capital Accumulation in the Private Economy
(1)	(2)	(3	(4)	(5)	(6)
1923 ...	$ 88,615	$12,140	$ 792	$108	$ 684
1930 ...	106,063	15,437	864	126	738
1940 ...	136,284	30,829	1,035	234	801
1950 ...	233,420	59,581	1,549	395	1,154
1957 ...	298,003	90,562	1,740	529	1,211

Sources:
Columns 2 and 3: Data from Table 3-1 converted into 1947-49 dollars.
Columns 4 and 5: Data from Columns 2 and 3 divided by the total population.
Column 6: Column 4 less Column 5.

This radical change in policy in a relatively short period of time has caused many people to feel that the public economy is destroying the private economy. However, the facts do not support this theory. It will be observed that the private economy (exclusive of the expenditures for government) increased from $684 per capita in 1923 to $1,211 in

1957. This increase amounted to 2.3 per cent per year or 77 per cent over this 34 year period.

Thus the application of Wagner's law to the American economy shows that the government economy is increasing rapidly but that it is not destroying the private economy. On the other hand the private economy has undoubtedly increased as a result of the increase in the government economy. This can be seen clearly from the following analysis. The proportion of the total national income expended for government increased only from 13.7 per cent in 1923 to 14.6 per cent in 1930. During this same period of time the per capita private economy increased from $684 to $738 or an increase of only 7.9 per cent or 1.1 per cent per year over this 7 year period. But expenditures for government increased from 14.6 per cent in 1930 to 30.3 per cent in 1957.

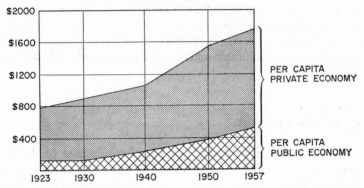

CHART I. Per Capita Private and Public Economy, 1923–57 (1947–49 dollars).

The private economy increased from $738 to $1,211 during this 27-year period. This represents an increase of 64.1 per cent or 2.4 per cent per year. Therefore it might be argued that the increase in the proportion of the national income spent for government during the past 34 years did not hinder the private economy but greatly aided it. In Chart I the relationship between the government economy and the private economy is presented graphically. There are some who believe that our traditional attitude toward government spending has been so conservative that it took a major depression and a world war to bludgeon the United States into sufficient government spending to save the private economy.

The conservative point of view is that the great expansion of the private economy made possible the great expansion of the public economy. There is no doubt that this has been true to some extent; however, the evidence available for the years following 1939 seems to indicate that the increase in the government economy caused an increase in the production of the private economy because the increase in the government economy preceded the increase in the private economy. Actually, the government economy and the private economy are as closely related to each other as different sectors of the private economy are inter-related. Over a long period of time, the government economy and the private economy affect each other in much the same way as the production of steel and the production of automobiles affect each other.

The authors do not intend to imply that government spending *per se* will cause a rise in the level of living. Some unproductive government spending is no doubt due in part to the tendency of government bureaus to proliferate and expand more than the service requires. This tendency is made explicit in what is now known as Parkinson's Law.[19] But the tendency of officials to expand their own departments operates in business and industry as well as in government. The purpose of government service is to satisfy the wants of the people served, not to create meaningless jobs. Inefficiency in either the public or the private economy has an unfavorable effect on the standard of living of the people.

The Effect of Governmental Expenditures on the Standard of Living

It is not the function of students of school finance to defend all governmental expenditures but rather to examine the effect of governmental expenditures on the economy and to relate the general effect of all governmental expenditures to the effect of educational expenditures. Between 1923 and 1957 the American nation passed through a major depression, World War II, the Korean War and was still in the cold war at the end of that period. Many expenditures of the national government especially during these national emergencies were not made to contribute maximally to the national economy. Despite this fact the standard of living of the American people has risen rapidly during these 34 years. Some would credit all of this gain to private enterprise and some would credit all of it to government. The evidence seems to indicate that each part of our economy has complemented the other.

Human wants are satisfied by government as well as by the private economy. Generally speaking there is a close relationship between rising expenditures and a rising standard of living when each is measured

---

[19] C. Northcote Parkinson, *Parkinson's Law* (Boston: Houghton Mifflin Company, 1957), pp. 2–13.

in terms of dollars of the same purchasing power. But expenditures for national security however necessary for national survival do not satisfy basic human wants to the same degree as other types of expenditures. In order to make an estimate of the actual increase in the standard of living of the people it is advisable to deduct national security expenditures from the national income. Table 3-4 shows the expenditures for national security of the Federal government.

TABLE 3–4

MAJOR NATIONAL SECURITY EXPENDITURES OF THE FEDERAL GOVERNMENT

Year	Amount in Current Dollars (in millions)	Amount in 1947–49 Dollars (in millions)	Per Capita Amount in 1947–49 Dollars
1923	$ 664	$ 911	$ 8
1930	734	1,028	8
1940	1,657	2,766	21
1950	13,009	12,654	84
1957	44,414	36,950	216

Source: Data for Column 1 for the years 1923, 1930, and 1940 include only expenditures for the armed forces and are from *Facts and Figures on Government Finance*, 9th ed., 1956–57, The Tax Foundation, Inc., p. 73; the data for 1950 and 1957 are from the 10th ed., 1958–59, p. 83.

In Table 3-5 the expenditures for national security are deducted from the national income and an estimate is made of the total per capita want-satisfying economy. It will be observed from Table 3-5 that the per capita want-satisfying expenditures by government increased from $100 in 1923 to $313 in 1957. This excludes government expenditures for national security. When the per capita want-satisfying expenditures of government are added to the per capita private economy, it is found that the total per capita want-satisfying economy increased from $784 to $1524 in 1957. This can be considered as a measure of the standard of living of the people. It has increased 94.4 per cent over this 34 year period or approximately 2.8 per cent per year using 1923 as the base.

It is doubtful that any other nation in any period of history has ever had as great an increase in the level of living of the people over an equal period of time. The vigor and productivity of the American private enterprise system and the vital role of the government economy have been fully demonstrated during this period of time.

Our economy is basically a private enterprise economy. Actually the percentage of the total national income spent by government to satisfy human wants has not increased nearly so much between 1923 and 1957 as is generally assumed. After excluding government expenditures for national defense, the want-satisfying government expenditures increased only from 12.6 per cent of the total national income in 1923

TABLE 3-5

TRENDS IN THE STANDARD OF LIVING (1947–49 DOLLARS)

Year	Per Capita National Income	Per Capita Expenditures for All Governments	Per Capita Expenditures for National Security	Per Capita Want-Satisfying Expenditures by Government Economy	Per Capita Private Economy	Total Per Capita Want-Satisfying Economy
(1)	(2)	(3)	(4)	(5)	(6)	(7)
1923	$ 792	$108	$ 8	$100	$ 684	$ 784
1930	864	126	8	118	738	856
1940	1,035	234	21	213	801	1,014
1950	1,549	395	84	311	1,154	1,465
1957	1,740	529	216	313	1,211	1,524

Sources:
Columns 2, 3, and 6: From Table 3–1.
Column 4: From Table 3–4.
Column 5: Column 3 less Column 4.
Column 7: The sum of Columns 5 and 6.

to 18.0 per cent in 1957. If the interest on the national debt (incurred largely for national defense) is also excluded from government expenditures, want-satisfying government expenditures increased only from 11.5 per cent of the total national income in 1923 to 15.9 in 1957. It would seem that there is little danger that the want-satisfying government economy will ever supplant the private economy.

Two of the most important functions of government in the United States are to provide an environment in which private enterprise can function with maximum efficiency and to provide those services which cannot be supplied by private enterprise or which can better be supplied by government. Government which performs these functions not only assures a high standard of living but it also gives the greatest possible chance for enjoying individual liberties.

EDUCATIONAL EXPENDITURES AND
THE NATIONAL ECONOMY

The effect of government expenditures generally on the national economy has been examined in some detail in the previous section. Educational expenditures have been included in the total expenditures of government. It is difficult if not impossible to isolate all of the effects of educational expenditures on the national economy. It is pertinent however to ask the following questions: Do educational expenditures satisfy human wants? Can educational wants best be satisfied by the government economy or by the private economy? Do expenditures for education represent a subtraction from the private economy or do expenditures for education add to the private economy?

It is easy to answer the first of these questions. Organized educational opportunities are provided by every civilized nation. Education is necessary to the survival of civilization. Therefore education is universally recognized as a human want that must be satisfied.

Can education, especially elementary and secondary education, with which we are primarily concerned in this book, be better provided by the private economy than the public economy? Most public elementary and secondary education in all advanced countries is provided in tax supported schools. As pointed out in Chapter 1, it seems to be the universal experience of all civilized nations that most elementary and secondary education can best be provided by the public economy. This does not imply that private schools should not be permitted to operate. Private schools serve important purposes but they cannot meet the needs that are satisfied by the public schools.

Expenditures for Public Education in the United States

The total expenditures for elementary and secondary education for selected years between 1923 and 1957 are set forth in Table 3-6.

TABLE 3-6

EXPENDITURES FOR THE PUBLIC ELEMENTARY AND SECONDARY SCHOOLS
FOR SELECTED YEARS 1923–1957

Year	Total Expenditures in Current Dollars (in millions)	Total Expenditures in 1947–49 Dollars (in millions)	Per Capita Expenditures in 1947–49 Dollars	Per Cent of National Income Expended for Public Schools
(1)	(2)	(3)	(4)	(5)
1923	$ 1,701	$ 2,333	$21	2.63
1930	2,317	3,245	26	3.06
1940	2,344	3,913	30	2.87
1950	5,838	5,679	38	2.43
1957	12,884	10,719	63	3.60

Sources:
Column 2: *Statistical Abstract of the U. S.*, U. S. Department of Commerce, except for the year 1957 which was estimated by the National Education Association. Expenditures include current expenses, capital outlay, and interest.
Column 3: Current dollars converted into 1947–49 dollars.
Column 4: Derived by dividing Column 3 by the total population for the respective years.
Column 5: Derived by dividing Column 3 by the national income expressed in 1947–49 dollars.

In terms of the purchasing power of 1947–49 dollars the total per capita expenditures for the public schools increased from $21 in 1923 to $63 in 1957. This is an increase of 200 per cent compared to an increase of 390 per cent for all government purposes. The proportion of the national income allocated to public school expenditures increased only from 2.63 per cent in 1923 to 3.60 per cent in 1957.

In 1923 expenditures for the public schools made up 19 per cent of the expenditures for all government, but only 12 per cent of all government expenditures were allocated to the public schools in 1957. It is true that much of the increase in total governmental expenditures has been due to the requirements of national defense. But after excluding these national defense expenditures the public school expenditures accounted for 21 per cent of all governmental expenditures in 1923 and 20 per cent in 1957. Therefore the expenditures for the public schools have not quite kept pace with other government want-satisfying expenditures since 1923.

The effect of total governmental expenditures on the private economy has been pointed out. But what governmental expenditures have had the most favorable effect on the national economy? Education has made up only 20 to 21 per cent of want-satisfying government expenditures from 1923 to 1957. As explained in the following paragraphs there is considerable evidence to indicate that if the nation had followed the policy of allocating a higher proportion of its income to education the standard of living would have been greater than at present. Furthermore our ability to defend ourselves from external aggression would also be greater. Let us examine the broad effects of education.

Effect of Educational Expenditures on Production

Education increases the productive capacity of the individual and and of the nation. It is essential to the development of the technological processes and the machines necessary for the extension of human power. The productive capacity of all uneducated populations is much lower than the productive capacity of an educated nation.

Production requires the collaboration of five factors: labor, land, capital, management, and government. Early writers on economics considered only land, labor, and capital as factors in production. After the industrial revolution, management was recognized as a factor. Only comparatively recently have economists begun to recognize government as a factor. Education has a favorable effect on the development or utilization of all of the five factors of production.

Effect of Educational Expenditures on Consumption

The products of an expanding economy must be consumed or they cannot be produced. Education enlarges the area of human wants which are necessary to consume the goods and services produced by an expanding economy. It also develops the purchasing power necessary for the exchange of economic goods.

Effect of Educational Expenditures on Investment

Education produces investment capital because it enables individuals to earn a surplus of income above that necessary to provide for basic needs. This surplus or saving is then available for investment and more production. Education from an economic standpoint is therefore an important part of the production mechanism.

It is difficult to find any expenditure in either the public economy or the private economy that contributes more to the standard of living of the people than expenditures for education. The Chamber of Commerce of the United States in its booklet "Education, an Investment in People" (1954), published some interesting information concerning the effect of education on production and consumption. This information was derived largely from data provided by the 1950 census. Following are some significant facts abstracted from that publication:

1. Eighty-two per cent of the men who had incomes of $10,000 or more had a college or high school education, but 61 per cent of those having had an eighth-grade education or less had incomes of $1,500 to $2,000.

2. Fifty-seven per cent of the farms producing $10,000 or more were operated by men having had a college or high school education, but 84 per cent of the farms producing less than $1,200 annually were operated by persons with an eighth-grade education or less.

3. In metropolitan areas with the highest level of education (11 to 12 years of school completed), retail sales per person averaged 20 per cent higher than in the metropolitan areas with the lowest education levels (8 to 9 years).

4. Magazine subscriptions, in states with the highest education levels, were three times as high per 1,000 population as in states having the lowest education levels.

These facts furnish further evidence concerning the favorable effect of education on the national economy.

SOME PROBLEMS AND ISSUES

The effect education should have on the economy and on society as a whole are quite controversial matters. Some of the more important issues are presented in the following section of this chapter.

Should Education Remove Barriers to Class and Caste?

From the standpoint of economics, one of the major functions of education is to break down the barriers between caste and class and to provide for social mobility. It is not necessary to justify this viewpoint in terms of social justice or Judeo-Christian ethics although it could be so justified. Removing the barriers between caste and class and providing for social mobility are conditions necessary for maximizing production and consumption and thereby raising the standard of living of the people. Therefore, according to this theory, the education system should develop all the talents of all the people without regard to class, caste, race, religion, or national origin. It is necessary to do this in order to maximize the production and consumption of each individual and thereby to raise the standard of living of the total society.

No nation has fully accomplished this goal. But the nations of the world which have most nearly reached this goal are the nations which have attained the highest standards of living or which are increasing their standards of living most rapidly. The United States of America is an example of a nation which is moving in the direction of using its public school system to remove the barriers between caste and class, largely justifying this policy by concepts of social justice and Judeo-Christian ethics. Our standard of living is high and continuously increasing. The U.S.S.R. has been moving in this same direction for the past forty years in order to raise the standard of living of the people and to make the nation strong. Despite the inherent defects of the communist economic system, that nation has made remarkable economic progress during the past forty years and its economy is continuing to grow at a very rapid rate.

It is interesting to note that the U.S.S.R., using an economic justification, has been allocating approximately six per cent of its national income to the public schools, while the United States, using the justifications of social and Judeo-Christian ethical norms, has been allocating approximately three per cent of its national income to the public schools. It would seem that if there were a better general public understanding of the economic implications of education in the United States, a higher proportion of the national income would be allocated to education.

The development of a universal system of public education in the United States has met with considerable opposition. Much of this opposition has been based on resistance to the removal of barriers of caste and class. There have been some who have argued that education is an individual family responsibility and should be provided exclusively at the expense of the parents of the children who receive an education. This policy would restrict education largely to those who have the money to pay for it. It would give special privileges to those with money and tend to strengthen class barriers based on wealth lines.

There are others who have opposed universal education beyond the elementary school because they feared that no one would be left to do common labor. That point of view prevailed in many sections of the South thirty years ago. It was common to operate Negro schools in many Southern counties for shorter terms and with poorer facilities because it was believed that if a Negro were given an education, he would no longer be willing to pick cotton for the white land owners. Fortunately the practice of providing poorer schools for Negroes has now almost entirely disappeared in the Southern states. The issue in the South is no longer "equal facilities" but desegregated schools. Mechanical cotton pickers largely solved the cotton picking problem.

There are many other instances which could be given of the fallacy of restricting education to the few in order to assure a supply of common labor. In fact it was common practice thirty years ago in most states to operate rural schools for shorter terms than urban schools. The justification was that the labor of children was needed on the farms. Our rapid technological advances in all fields have actually created a surplus of unskilled common laborers.

Do private schools, the entrance to which is largely governed by social class and wealth, strengthen or weaken the barriers of class and caste?

Do parochial schools strengthen or weaken the barriers of class and caste?

What impact have the public schools had on class barriers?

What further barriers to class or caste should be removed?

Do Taxes for Education Cause a Reduction in the Private Economy?

There are some people who believe that taxes of any kind for any function of government levied by any level of government result in a subtraction from the private economy. Let us first examine the effect on the economic activity or the standard of living of the people of a governmental expenditure that does not satisfy a human want. A good example would be the expenditure by the Federal government of $1,000,000 for a ballistic missile which is launched at Cape Canaveral and lands in the Atlantic Ocean seven minutes after its launching. The missile satisfies no human want.[20] The Federal government must collect $1,000,000 in taxes to pay for the missile. These taxes might be collected before the missile is purchased, while it is being constructed or even after it is used. In any event the taxes collected would reduce private spending by an equal amount. But the missile was constructed in the private economy and the government paid $1,000,000 to a private enterprise for the missile. This money was used to pay for labor and materials used in the construction of the missile and to provide profits for the owners of the enterprise. The government returned to the private economy all that it had subtracted from it by taxes. Therefore the net effect of this government expenditure on the economy should be zero because no human want was satisfied by the missile.

But what effect does this kind of activity have on the standard of

---

[20] Unless the want is to possess the capability of destroying other human beings on the assumption that this would prevent aggression against the possessor of the missile. Also some information might be obtained which would be useful for other purposes.

living of the people? If the construction of the missile required the use of labor and materials which were necessary to supply human wants such as food, clothing, shelter, and other valid wants, then it would reduce the standard of living of the people. This might be the result in an undeveloped country such as Pakistan. But in a highly industrialized country such as the United States, it would probably have no measurable effect on the standard of living. Such missiles were being constructed by the United States at a time when more than 5,000,000 people were unemployed and when there was a surplus of practically all kinds of consumers' goods.

Let us now consider the effect on the economy of constructing a high school building costing $1,000,000. The board of education constructing the building would have to take $1,000,000 in taxes from the private economy. But the board would return a like amount to the private economy when it paid the contractor, the architect, the suppliers of equipment, and others involved in constructing and equipping the building. However, assuming that a plant of this size is needed to house the student population, it satisfies a human want and it will last for fifty years instead of seven minutes. This building if wisely planned will contribute to the improvement of the educational program for half a century. Therefore during its life it will increase the producing and consuming capacity of thousands of persons, and thus will have a favorable effect on the standard of living of the people.

Next let us consider the effect on the economy of current expenditures for education. Let us assume that it costs $400,000 annually to pay the current expenses of operating this school. This would include the salaries of teachers and other employees and all other expenses of maintaining and operating the school. The board would have to take $400,000 annually from the private economy by taxes. But the employees of the board would provide purchasing power for the private economy and spend this income in the private economy in the same proportion as the employees in the private enterprise system. Furthermore, the board purchases many supplies, materials, and equipment replacements from the private economy. For example, the board's purchase of a typewriter has exactly the same effect on the private economy as the purchase of a typewriter by a merchant. Finally, the education of the pupils will increase their capacity to produce and to consume.

Under what conditions would a capital expenditure for a public school have a neutral or negative effect on the economy?

Under what conditions would a current expenditure have a neutral or negative effect on the economy?

Do Non-Tax-Supported Schools Have a More Favorable
Effect on the Economy Than Public Schools?

In the private enterprise system of the United States, votes are cast by dollars. This has proved to be an extraordinarily efficient system for producing and distributing material economic goods such as automobiles, washing machines, food, and clothing. Mankind has not yet discovered a better system for supplying material economic goods. Even the material economic goods used by the government economy are almost all produced by the private economy. No other system is as sensitive to material human wants. The competitive, profit incentive elements of the free enterprise system continually force private enterprise to supply those wants efficiently. Furthermore, numerous nonmaterial human wants are also well satisfied by the private economy.

A small minority of persons in the United States believe that the nonmaterial economic good called education can best be supplied by the private economy. It has been charged that the public schools constitute a monopoly and that if the public school system were broken up, private schools could then be established which would compete with one another and dollars would vote in the same manner as in the private enterprise system. This argument is readily answered by directing attention to the fact that it has been found necessary to establish government approved monopolies in the private economy in order to satisfy certain kinds of human wants. Examples are telephone, telegraph, and electric power services. An atomized school system directed by numerous independent groups and individuals would create the same type of chaos as a public utility system similarly administered. A monopoly would have to be granted to some private group to administer the schools. Just what church or corporation should be trusted with the monopoly for supplying education? The overwhelming majority of the people of the United States apparently want to trust only themselves to control their schools. They do this when they cast their votes.

It has been argued by certain parochial school leaders, especially in those schools that pay their teachers no salary, that their schools help the economy because they cost less than tax supported schools. But as has been pointed out above, the employees of a public school spend their salaries in the private economy and provide an important market for the private enterprise system. A school that pays its teachers nothing but board, room, and clothing has no more favorable effect on the economy of a community than a factory in that community which would pay its employees only in board, room, and clothing.

Let us next consider the effect on the economy of a private high school operating on the same budget as the public high school described above. Let us assume that the educational programs of both schools are of comparable quality. Both schools would provide equivalent markets for the private economy. Both schools would make equivalent contributions to the producing and consuming capacities of pupils. The only real difference would be the impact on the economy and on individuals of the methods used to procure the funds necessary to operate the school. In the case of the public school, the funds would be obtained by taxation and the school would be open to all. The private school would have to obtain its funds by levying fees on the parents of pupils or by donations or a combination of the two methods. If fees are the chief basis of financial support, either some parents must pay out of proportion to their ability or the school is patronized only by people of wealth. If people pay beyond their financial ability, their standard of living is lowered. If the school is patronized only by the wealthy, it strengthens the barriers of caste and class and injures the economy. Therefore an equitable taxing system is a more efficient method of financing a school than by fees and donations because it has a more favorable effect on the economy.

What would be the effect on the economy if all the public schools were closed?

What would be the effect on the economy if all the private and parochial schools were closed?

What Effect Do Public School Expenditures Have on Deflation and Inflation?

Economists and the people generally have been concerned for many years about business cycles. Periodically throughout our history the nation has passed through "booms" and "depressions" which have caused much suffering and economic dislocation. Some have thought that these cycles are an inevitable part of a free enterprise economy. Others have thought that it is possible even in a free economy to minimize the severity of business cycles. The Federal government has made many attempts to regulate these cycles by both long-range and emergency measures. Some of the long-range measures have been the establishment of the Federal Reserve System, Federal insurance of bank deposits, various types of social security measures, the regulation of the securities exchanges, and similar measures. Emergency measures have included increasing or decreasing government expenditure for public works, devaluation of the currency, extension or contraction of credit, emergency relief expenditures, increase or decrease in taxes, and many other devices.

It is beyond the scope of this book to describe and analyze all of the activities of government to regulate the economy. But it is evident that the policy of the Federal government through many different administrations has been to reduce the severity of business cycles and at the same time facilitate an expanding economy. It is in this context that the effect of school expenditures on business cycles is discussed.

The public school enterprise is one of the most stable factors in our economy. The demand for education is affected very little by business cycles. Pupils report to the public schools regardless of booms or depressions.[21] Therefore there is little or no unemployment in the schools during periods of economic depression and general unemployment. On the other hand there is little or no increase in employment in the public schools in business booms. The number of persons employed by the schools is governed much more by the number of pupils to be served than by business cycles. School budgets rise slowly in inflationary periods and decline slowly in periods of depression. Changes that are made in school budgets during business cycles are due much more to changes in the wage and price structure than to changes in the number of persons employed or material goods consumed.[22] Therefore public school expenditures generally constitute an important stabilizing influence in the economy.

Should public school expenditures be reduced or increased in deflationary times and should public school expenditures be reduced or increased during times of inflation? There are those who argue that school expenditures should be reduced in depression times in order to provide more money for the private economy and there are others who argue that expenditures should be reduced during inflationary times in order to reduce inflationary pressures. A number of state legislators with a considerable number of years of service have used these same arguments at different points in business cycles. Obviously such legislators could not be correct in their reasoning at both points.

It seems that it would be unwise as a general policy to increase or decrease school expenditures as an emergency measure to regulate inflation or deflation. An exception might be a stepping up of school building construction during periods of unemployment as a part of a general public works program. Certainly if the Federal government inaugurated such a program during depression times, the public schools should be included. But such a program would be of little benefit to the people unless the buildings constructed were actually needed.

---

[21] School enrollment of high school age pupils actually increases slightly in times of mass unemployment.

[22] Unless there is a rapid increase or decrease in school enrollment.

Educational expenditures affect the economy most favorably when they are determined by human wants for education. Such a policy makes educational expenditures a stabilizing factor in the economy and also satisfies human wants. Increases in educational expenditures can be justified in either deflationary or inflationary times if such expenditures are necessary to maintain or increase the quantity and quality of educational services desired by the people.

Public education is a part of the public economy but it must do business with a competitive private economy when it employs teachers, buys material goods, or spends money for anything. Therefore as long as the schools exist in a dynamic expanding economy with an increasing population, educational expenditures will increase. Educational expenditures must keep pace with the rest of the economy or the effect on the total economy will be unfavorable.

What would be the effect on the purchasing power of the dollar if wages generally were increased more than the increase in productivity of workers?

Have teachers increased their productivity during the past twenty-five years as much as the increases they have received in salary after making due allowances for differences in the purchasing power of the dollar?

Would a Major Increase in the Investment in Education Be of Assistance in Preventing a Stagnation of the Economy?

As a civilization advances, the proportion of the total economy allocated to the satisfaction of nonmaterial human wants increases at the expense of the proportion allocated to material human wants. It is true that the total number and variety of material wants continue to increase as civilization advances and the economy expands, but nonmaterial wants increase even at a faster rate. This phenomenon is related to Wagner's Law describing the increasing services of government in a developing civilization.

An economy stagnates when human wants both material and nonmaterial cease to increase or when the productive system fails to satisfy those wants. An economy can get out of equilibrium when it produces more material goods than can be consumed and less nonmaterial goods than are wanted. In such a situation an increasing rate of investment in education is one of the surest ways to revitalize a stagnated economy and to keep that economy expanding in an advancing civilization.

On the other hand, if an economy produces more nonmaterial goods than are wanted and leaves unsatisfied a substantial part of the material wants of the people, the economy would get out of balance and the standard of living of the people would decline.

The American economy is noted for its production of material goods. We are capable of and have produced a surplus of many types of material goods. The American economy has not produced a surplus of any important nonmaterial good. For instance education, medical and hospital care, wholesome recreation, good art and music, and worth-while literature have always been in short supply. Our civilization has been called a materialistic civilization. Would a greater production of nonmaterial goods promote the growth of our economy and a continued increase in the standard of living of the people?

Galbraith has shown that our private economy is affluent but that our public economy is poverty stricken.[23] Are the human wants satisfied by the private economy more or less urgent than those satisfied by the government economy?

SELECTED REFERENCES

Blodgett, Ralph H., *Principles of Economics,* rev. ed. New York: Holt, Rinehart & Winston, Inc., 1946. Chapters 2 and 13.

Galbraith, John Kenneth, *The Affluent Society.* Boston: Houghton Mifflin Company, 1958.

Harriss, C. Lowell, *The American Economy,* rev. ed. Homewood, Illinois: Richard D. Irvin Inc., 1956. Chapters 1, 2, 3, 4, 10, and 11.

Johns, R. L., and E. L. Morphet, editors, *Problems and Issues in Public School Finance.* New York: Bureau of Publications, Teachers College, Columbia University, 1952. Chapter 4.

Kurihara, Kenneth K., *Introduction to Keynesian Dynamics.* New York: Columbia University, 1956. Chapters 1, 3, 5.

Murad, Anatol, *Economics Principles and Problems,* rev. ed. Ames, Iowa: Littlefield, Adams and Company, 1954. Chapters 1, 2, 3, 4, 11, 13, and 25.

Poole, Kenyon E., *Public Finance and Economic Welfare.* New York: Holt, Rinehart & Winston, Inc., 1956. Chapters 1, 3.

Samuelson, Paul A., *Economics,* rev. ed. New York: McGraw-Hill Book Company, Inc., 1958. Chapters 2, 3, 6, 10, 11, 14, 16, and 18.

[23] John Kenneth Galbraith, *The Affluent Society* (Boston: Houghton Mifflin Co., 1958), Chapter XVIII.

CHAPTER FOUR

Trends
in Demand and Expenditures
for Public Education

In the private economy of a free enterprise nation, the individual votes with his dollars for the economic goods he chooses to purchase. This economic system forces the private economy to produce quickly the goods needed to satisfy consumer wants. But, as has been pointed out in the previous chapter, some consumer wants cannot be supplied by the private economy as well as by the public economy. Public education is one of the principal goods provided by the public economy.

The machinery for determining what economic goods should be produced and the quantity and quality of those goods differs considerably in the two economies. The machinery of the private economy moves very quickly to supply a human want very soon after it emerges, provided the enterprise can earn a profit. For example, the private economy is so responsive to public demand that it has the power to supply within a few months great quantities of such trivial economic goods as the latest children's toy fads. On the other hand, after the launching of Sputnik I, a great demand was created for increasing the quantity and quality of science and mathematics taught in public schools. But the public economy moved slowly to supply this want because political consensus had to be obtained before the decision to supply the want could be made. Those political decisions had to be made by some 45,000 local school administrative units, fifty states, and the Federal government.[1]

There is another important difference in the two economies. In the private economy, the individual purchases only the economic goods he wants. He may buy a washing machine and his neighbor may buy a television set. But in the public economy, once a political decision has been made to provide an economic good, all individuals subject to the taxes levied must purchase the good whether they want it or not. For example, if the decision has been made to provide public kindergartens, each eligible taxpayer must participate in the financing of kindergartens regardless of whether he wants them. The political decision may be made by popular vote of the electorate concerned or by representatives of the electorate in legislative bodies such as boards of education and legislatures. Usually these decisions are made by a majority vote but in some cases more than a majority is required. The process of obtaining a political decision frequently involves much controversy. For these reasons the time required to supply a human want is usually much greater in the public economy than in the private economy.

Expenditures for different economic goods in the private economy represent fairly accurately current consumer choices, assuming that the supply of goods is equal to the demand. But the same thing is not true in the public economy because consumer wants may go unsatisfied for a long period of time. Also demands for goods produced in the private economy are stimulated by clever advertising and high pressure selling. Public funds cannot be expended directly for these purposes by most governments. Therefore it is not entirely accurate to assume that expenditures for public education for a given year represent consumer demand for public education during that year.

The purpose of this chapter is to explore trends in expenditures for the public schools during the past third of a century and to appraise the social and economic forces that will affect demand and expenditures for public education in future years.

TRENDS IN EXPENDITURES FOR
THE PUBLIC SCHOOLS

It is not a simple matter to appraise trends in school expenditures. Comparisons of total current dollar expenditures for one year with those of another reveal nothing but that more total current dollars were

---

[1] Decisions also had to be made by many thousands of individual school faculties.

expended during one than another year. When only the current dollar expenditures for one year are being compared with those for another year, the comparison becomes more misleading as the time span increases. This is especially true during times of rapid social and economic change.

Trends in educational expenditures between 1923 and 1957 and certain factors affecting those expenditures are presented in this chapter. Certain years were selected as representative of this period. The year 1923–24 was selected as the starting point because it was the first fairly normal year following World War I. The year 1929–30 was selected because it was a pre-depression year, 1939–40 because it was a late depression year, 1949–50 because it was a fairly representative post World War II year, and 1957–58 because it was the latest year for which data were available when the studies were made.[2] The years selected also have the advantage of separating ten-year periods except for the beginning and ending years.

Conclusions regarding the amount of change are vitally affected by the base year or years selected for making comparisons. For example, a biased person attacking an increase in school expenditures may select a low depression year with which to compare expenditures for the current year in order to maximize the percentage increase in expenditures. Also a biased person advocating an increase in educational expenditures may select the base year for comparison which will minimize the percentage increase. The objective student of school finance will avoid insofar as possible either extremely high or low years when appraising long-range trends.

Educational expenditures are affected by many factors. Some of these factors are as follows: Number of pupils educated, the purchasing power of the dollar, the national income, the quantity and quality of educational services provided, and the demand for education. Therefore trends in educational expenditures are appraised in this chapter in terms of these factors.

Trends in Population, Public School Enrollment, and Average Daily Attendance

The data presented in Table 4–1 show that total population, public school enrollment, and average daily attendance in the public schools have all been increasing rapidly in recent years.

The total population increased 52.2 per cent between 1923–24 and

---

[2] The student of school finance may wish to substitute, for the 1957–58 data in these tables, the most recent year available to him and compare the most recent trends with the trends reported here.

1957–58, public school enrollment 38.0 per cent and average daily attendance 55.9 per cent. But most of the growth in enrollment and average daily attendance has occurred since 1949–50. School enrollment actually declined slightly between 1929–30 and 1949–50 and average daily attendance increased only 4.8 per cent during that twenty-year period. On the other hand, the total population has increased during each period since 1923 but the rate of growth has been much greater since 1949 than in the preceding years. The total population increased only 33.3 per cent or 1.3 per cent per year in the twenty-six years preceding 1949 and 14.2 per cent or 1.8 per cent per year in the eight years succeeding 1949.

TABLE 4–1

TRENDS IN PUBLIC SCHOOL ENROLLMENT,
AVERAGE DAILY ATTENDANCE AND POPULATION

Year	Enrollment in Public Schools	Average Daily Attendance in Public Schools	Total Population Residing in the United States
1923–24	24,288,808	19,132,451	111,950,000
1929–30	25,678,015	21,164,886	121,770,000
1939–40	25,433,542	22,042,151	130,880,000
1949–50	25,111,427	22,284,000	149,188,000
1957–58	33,508,814	29,835,000	170,333,000
Per Cent Increase 1923–24 to 1957–58	38.0	55.9	52.2

Sources: Enrollment and attendance from *Biennial Surveys*—U. S. Office of Education except for 1957–58 which was estimated by the National Education Association. Population from Department of Commerce, Bureau of the Census.

School enrollment and attendance changed very little between 1929 and 1949 and increased rapidly after 1949 because of changes in the birth rate. For example, the birth rate was 18.7 per thousand total population in 1935, and 24.1 per thousand in 1950. The birth rate has continued high since 1950; therefore, enrollment increases will continue.

The fertility rate of the female population of child-bearing age has a fundamental effect on population projections. For example, there were 79.9 births per thousand female population 15 to 44 years of age in 1940 and 120.8 in 1956. This upward change in fertility caused the population to increase much more rapidly than was anticipated at the time low fertility rates prevailed.

The total population continued to increase between 1923 and 1949 despite the fact that school enrollment increased very little. This was due largely to the fact that the death rate declined. The rising standard of living and improved medical care were primarily responsible for increased longevity. It is anticipated that the total population will continue to increase due both to high fertility and a further increase in longevity.

All available evidence indicates that the total population will continue to increase at a rapid rate and that the school age population will also continue to increase rapidly. The anticipated increase in total population and in school enrollment will have a powerful influence in future years not only on school expenditures but also the total economy.

It is interesting to note from Table 4–1 that average daily attendance has increased much more rapidly since 1923 than has school enrollment. This proves that pupils attended school better in 1957 than in 1923. This is evidence that the consumer demand for education is increasing because parents are insisting that their children attend school more regularly. Undoubtedly the improved health of children and improved transportation have contributed to better school attendance. But the greater value placed on education by the parents of 1957 as compared with the parents of 1923 has probably accounted for most of the improvement in school attendance. This growth in demand for education will have a major effect on school expenditures in future years.

Trends in Total Public School Expenditures

The term "total school expenditures" as used in this book includes expenditures for current expenses, capital outlay, and interest on school indebtedness but excludes payments to retire the principal of indebtedness. This is the definition used by the United States Office of Education in its biennial surveys.[3] Payments on the principal of indebtedness should be excluded from total expenditures in order to eliminate a meaningless inflation of expenditures. For example, assume that the expenditures of a school system for a twenty-year period are being studied and a five million dollar bond issue maturing over a twenty-year period was floated for buildings during the first year of the period being studied. To include principal payments in total expenditures for each year for twenty years would be double reporting, once for capital

---

[3] Probably a better measure of total expenditures for a given year would be the sum of current expenditures, capital outlay from non-borrowed funds, interest on all types of indebtedness, and payments on the principal of indebtedness incurred for capital outlay. Such a total would approximate the total annual tax effort for schools. It would also equal revenue receipts plus expenditures from non-borrowed revenue receipts assuming the same balance at the beginning and close of the fiscal year. However, the accounting systems commonly used by boards of education do not provide the information necessary for this type of analysis.

outlay and once for payments on principal of indebtedness. The inflation would total five millions of dollars over a twenty-year period.

Many studies of school finance use the term "total expenditures" to include all items of current expense plus capital outlay and debt service even though it includes an unexplained inflation. It would be better to define this type of total as "gross expenditures." Therefore in this book the term gross expenditures will include all expenditures of boards of education for day schools and total expenditures will include all expenditures except payments on the principal of indebtedness. Due to the current lack of uniformity in the use of terms, the student of school finance should examine carefully the composition of any total of school expenditures before it is compared with a total reported from another source.

TABLE 4–2

TRENDS IN TOTAL EXPENDITURES FOR THE PUBLIC SCHOOLS

(includes all items for current expense, capital outlay and payments of interest on school indebtedness)

Year	Expenditures in Current Dollars *	Consumer Price Index 1947–49=100†	Expenditures in 1947–49 Dollars	Total Expenditures Per Pupil in ADA in 1947–49 Dollars	Per Capita Income of Resident Population in 1947–49 Dollars
1923–24 ..	$1,820,743,936	72.9	$2,497,591,000	$131	$791
1929–30 ..	2,306,965,557	73.3	3,147,292,000	148	984
1939–40 ..	2,330,681,788	59.4	3,923,706,000	178	937
1949–50 ..	5,768,218,000	101.8	5,666,226,000	254	1424
1957–58* .	12,883,700,000	120.2	10,718,552,000	359	1750
Per Cent Increase 1923–24 to 1957–58	607.6		329.2	174.0	121.2

Sources:
* All data from *Biennial Surveys*, U. S. Office of Education with the exception of 1957–58 which were estimated by the Research Division of the National Education Association.
† *Monthly Labor Review*, Bureau of Labor Statistics.

The data presented in Table 4–2 show that total expenditures in current dollars increased 607.6 per cent between 1923–24 and 1957–58. This type of comparison is the one most frequently used by those attempting to present an exaggerated picture of school costs. But the consumer price index was 72.9 in 1923 and 120.2 in 1957 when the average of prices between 1947 and 1949 is considered as equaling 100. When expenditures for all the years studied are converted into the purchasing power of 1947–49 dollars, it is seen that school expenditures increased only 329.2 per cent instead of 607.6 per cent.

Other Factors Affecting School Costs. This is still an incomplete picture. Average daily attendance increased 55.9 per cent between 1923 and 1957. The expenditures per pupil in average daily attendance in terms of 1947–49 dollars increased only 174.0 per cent between 1923–24 and 1957–58. Thus we see that the apparent increase in expenditure of 607.6 per cent with which we started is a very misleading figure.

But let us take a closer look at this increase of 174 per cent in per pupil expenditures. Approximately two-thirds of all school expenditures are for the purpose of paying the salaries of teachers and other school employees. The per capita national income increased 121.2 per cent in terms of dollars of the same purchasing power between 1923 and 1957. This is one measure of the economic growth of the nation and the rise in the standard of living. If teachers and other school employees had not been permitted to share in this increase in standard of living, boards of education would not have been able to employ the personnel to operate the schools. Actually boards of education experienced great difficulty in recruiting the qualified personnel needed in the years following World War II even with the increase in expenditures provided.

All of the 174 per cent increase in per pupil expenditures since 1923 has not been used by boards of education to increase the salaries of its employees. The average school term has been increased from 168 days in 1923–24 to 179 days in 1957–58. Only 14 per cent of the total number of pupils was enrolled in the upper four high school grades in 1923–24 and approximately 22 per cent in 1957–58. By 1965, from 28 per cent to 30 per cent of all pupils will be enrolled in senior high school because the senior high school grades will then be composed entirely of pupils born in the high birth rate years. Senior high school education is more expensive than elementary education and therefore the increased proportion of pupils in the high school grades required increased expenditures.

There is also much evidence that the quality of education provided in the public schools has greatly improved. For example, teachers have greatly improved their training; the curricula of both elementary and high schools have been considerably enriched; and school plants including school libraries, laboratories, instructional materials and aids have been improved in quality and increased in quantity.

School expenditures have increased since 1923–24 but there is no evidence whatsoever that the increase has resulted from the extravagance of boards of education. The evidence is overwhelming that the increase has been necessary and unavoidable. Actually school expenditures were not increased sufficiently during this thirty-four-year period to provide the quantity and quality of education needed. The evidence indicates that school expenditures will continue to increase for many years because all of the major factors causing increases in school expenditures between 1923–24 and 1957–58 are still operating.

Trends in Current Expense

Current expense includes all items for which school funds are expended except expenditures for capital outlay and debt service.[4] It is important that this item be considered separately from total expenditures because it represents the amount spent each year for the current operation of schools as contrasted with the amount spent for capital investment and debt service. It will be noted from Table 4–3 that total

TABLE 4–3

TRENDS IN CURRENT EXPENSE FOR THE PUBLIC SCHOOLS

Year	Current Expense in Current Dollars	Current Expense in 1947–49 Dollars	Current Expense Per Pupil in Average Daily Attendance in 1947–49 Dollars
1923–24	$1,432,274,793	$1,964,711,000	$102
1929–30	1,843,551,708	2,515,077,000	118
1939–40	1,941,799,118	3,269,022,000	148
1949–50	4,687,274,000	4,604,395,000	207
1957–58	9,547,320,000	7,942,862,000	266
Per Cent Increase 1923–24 to 1957–58	566.6	304.3	158.3

current expense increased 566.6 per cent between 1923–24 and 1957–58 in current dollars and 304.3 per cent in 1947–49 dollars. Current expense per pupil in average daily attendance increased 158.3 per cent as compared with a per pupil increase of 174 per cent in total expenditures. The per pupil increase has been greater in total expenditures than in current expense because a greater proportion of the budget had to be allocated to capital outlay in 1957 than in 1923 as a result of a rapidly increasing enrollment and inability to increase facilities in keeping with need during the depression and war years.

Trends in current expense could be analyzed further by the same methods used in examining total expenditures but the conclusions would be approximately the same as those drawn from an analysis of total expenditures.

---

[4] For a more complete definition of current expense, see Chapter 16.

Trends in Revenue Receipts

Expenditure trends cannot be adequately appraised without also studying trends in revenue receipts. Revenue receipts include all funds received by a board of education during a fiscal year except borrowed funds or funds obtained by reducing the assets of the board through property sales or insurance adjustments for property loss. It is estimated that more than 95 per cent of the total revenue receipts of boards of education in the United States are derived from local, state, or Federal taxes. Therefore, the amount of revenue receipts available to boards of education is a good measure of tax effort in relation to tax paying ability. Receipts increased 588.5 per cent in current dollars between 1923–24 and 1957–58, 317.6 per cent in 1947–49 dollars and 168.1 per cent per pupil in average daily attendance in 1947–49 dollars. Revenue receipts have not increased as rapidly as total expenditures. This would indicate that boards of education financed more of their expenditures from borrowed funds in 1957–58 than in previous years. Since almost all borrowed funds were invested in school plants needed for the increasing school enrollment, this trend was inevitable.

Per Cent of National Income Allocated to Revenue Receipts. The proportion of the national income allocated to the revenue receipts for the public schools has fluctuated considerably during the 34-year period between 1923 and 1957. Two and fifty-one hundredths per cent of the national income was allocated to public school revenues in the fairly normal post World War I year of 1923, 2.38 per cent in the prosperous year of 1929, 3.11 per cent in the late depression year of 1939, 2.51 per cent in the prosperous post World War II year of 1949, and 3.11 per cent in the prosperous year of 1957. Therefore there is no evidence that there was a marked trend to increase the proportion of the national income allotted to the public schools during this thirty-four-year period. However, the proportion of the national income allocated to public school revenue in 1957 was higher than in any other prosperous year. This might be considered as evidence of an increased consumer demand for education which will be reflected in an increasing proportion of the national income likely to be allocated to public school revenue in the years following 1957.

The data available for 1900 and earlier are not quite comparable with those used in Tables 3–4 and 3–5. But it appears that approximately one per cent of the national income was spent for the public schools during the last years of the nineteenth century. Therefore, the longer the period included in the study the more evident is the long range trend to spend a higher per cent of the national income for the public schools.

Trends in revenue receipts are presented in Table 4–4.

TABLE 4–4

TRENDS IN REVENUE RECEIPTS

Year	Revenue Receipts in Current Dollars	Revenue Receipts in 1947–49 Dollars	Revenue Receipts Per Pupil in ADA in 1947–49 Dollars	Per Cent of National Income Allocated to Revenue for the Public Schools
1923–24 ..	$1,618,437,825	$2,220,079,000	$116	2.51
1929–30 ..	2,088,556,837	2,849,327,000	134	2.38
1939–40 ..	2,260,527,045	3,805,601,000	173	3.11
1949–50 ..	5,437,044,000	5,340,908,000	240	2.51
1957–58 * .	11,143,044,000	9,270,419,000	311	3.11
Per Cent Increase 1923–24 to 1957–58	588.5	317.6	168.1	

Sources: *Biennial Surveys*, U. S. Office of Education and estimates by the National Education Association.
* Estimated by Research Division of National Education Association.

Effect of National Income on School Revenue. Trends in the national income are closely associated with trends in total educational expenditures. Increasing the investment in education undoubtedly increases the national income. On the other hand, the amount of revenue provided for the public schools is vitally affected by general economic conditions. In times of low economic activity, tax levying and appropriating bodies are inclined to hold constant or reduce educational revenues, but in times of high economic activity educational revenues are usually increased. Therefore, the condition of the economy probably has as great or greater effect on educational revenues than the educational needs of the times. The national income increased 121.2 per cent between 1923 and 1957 in terms of the purchasing power of 1947–49 dollars.

Value Placed on Education. The per capita income has rapidly increased since 1923 except for the depression years. Has public school support increased in proportion to the increased economic productivity of the nation? The long-range trend has been for the people to place an increasing value on public education. Chart II shows that total expenditures per pupil in average daily attendance expressed in 1947–49 dollars increased 174 per cent between 1923–24 and 1957–58, current expense 158.3 per cent and revenue receipts 168.1 per cent. Each of these figures is greater than the increase of 121.2 per cent in the per capita income. Therefore, despite the fact that financial provision for the public schools is always behind the demand for public education because of inevitable delays in the decision-making processes of governmental bodies, the public is making progress in seeing that its demands for public education are satisfied.

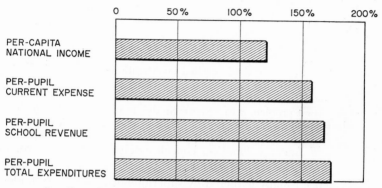

CHART II. *Per Cent Increases 1923–57 in School Revenue, Expenditures, and National Income (1947–49 dollars).*

SOME PROBLEMS AND ISSUES

Sound fiscal planning cannot be done on a year-to-year basis. It is true that boards of education must prepare budgets for each fiscal year. But annual school budgets can best be developed if due consideration is given to social and economic changes, to changes in consumer demand for education and to the quantity and quality of education needed to meet the requirements of the future as well as the present. Every nation attempts to survive in its environment. The nation acts on its environment and the environment acts on the nation. The nation seeks to change its environment in ways favorable to its survival, but the environment may act on the nation either favorably or unfavorably.

In truth, the people of modern nations want more than mere survival. They want growth beyond survival that will result in the better life. What has been said of nations, can also be said of individuals. The nation, the society, the individual all seek survival and growth beyond survival. There is indisputable evidence that education will in the future be increasingly more vital to the survival and growth beyond survival of nations and individuals.

Some of the problems and issues associated with the increasing demand for education are discussed in the remainder of this chapter.

What Criteria Can Be Used To Determine How Much Money Should Be Spent for Public Education?

Taxpayers sometimes complain that schools cost too much. Educational leaders insist that not enough financial support is provided for the public schools. But how much is enough? This is a difficult question. Educational research does not provide an adequate answer. Thomson characterized educational research as follows:

> In the educational field, applied investigation characteristically takes the form of action research or status studies. "Action research" is a label which signifies the miscellaneous generation of energy in the vicinity of an important problem area. "Status Study" is a label which signifies the evaluation of existing practices in terms of existing practices.[5]

The Use of Average Practice. Unfortunately Thomson is probably correct in his caricature of educational research insofar as it applies to the evidence usually gathered by superintendents to justify budgets. Perhaps the most common method is to make comparisons with other systems, thus using average practice as the criterion of what should be expended.

Absurd as it may sound from the standpoint of research, the use of average practice as a criterion of what should be expended for education has resulted in some progress in school support. As those school systems below the average move upward toward the average, the average is increased. This results in a "moving average" which moves upward continuously. Fortunately the demand for education is so great that no school system strives to move downward toward the average. If that were not true, then theoretically the school systems above the average would drop their expenditures to average practice and those below would increase expenditures to the average. All systems would then end on the average without any system's inquiring into what kind of education was being purchased by the average practice. This hypothetical situation reveals the absurdity of using average practice as the criterion of how much money to spend for education.

The Marginal Dollar. Economists sometimes use a concept of the marginal dollar in order to arrive at a criterion of how much should be spent for government. Under this concept

> ... the appropriate level of taxes is given by the point at which the values, advantages and satisfactions secured by the final (marginal) dollar expended by government are equal to the satisfactions which that

---

[5] Procter Thomson, "The Nation's Wealth and the School's Share," *The Elementary School Journal* (October, 1955).

dollar would have secured if left in private hands. The government budget is too large and should be reduced if the sacrifices entailed by the marginal dollar of taxes exceed the benefits secured by the marginal dollar of expenditures.[6]

Let us apply this criterion to a state in which the educational expenditures for a given year were $200,000,000. Exactly the right amount was expended if the final dollar expended secured as many values, advantages, and satisfactions as that dollar would have secured if it had been spent in the private economy. Any additional expenditure would have been too much and any less too little. It is of course impossible to arrive at so fine a point of division by statistical methods, because it is impossible to place an exact money value on values, advantages, and satisfactions. However, it is possible to place a money value on the personal income of the people which is certainly associated with advantages and satisfactions and may be associated with values.

Let us take another example of a state in which the personal income of the people is $5,000,000,000 and educational expenditures $150,000,-000. Educational expenditures therefore consume three per cent of the income of the people. Let us assume that the legislature is contemplating increasing educational expenditures $25,000,000. If this increase in expenditures for education would increase the income of the people by $100,000,000 and if this money left in private hands would increase the economy by $75,000,000 the increase would be justified. It is difficult of course to make an accurate appraisal of how much the economy can be increased by an educational expenditure as compared with an expenditure in the private economy. Nevertheless people must make decisions not only as to what to invest in the government economy as contrasted with the private economy but also as to how much to invest within various sectors of both economies.

Effect of Advertising on Consumer Choices. This concept may seem nebulous but it explains fairly well how people decide to spend their money. In the private economy, producers of goods and services (with the exception of some professions) sell their economic goods by advertising which has been developed to both a science and art. A governmental service such as public education has no vehicle similar to commercial advertising by which it can adroitly present the "values, advantages, and satisfactions" of education. Therefore the consumer does not always have an opportunity to weigh objectively the relative

    6 Eugene S. Lawler and Procter Thomson, "Taxation and Educational Finance," Chapter 4 of *Problems and Issues of Public School Finance*, R. L. Johns and E. L. Morphet, editors (New York: Bureau of Publications, Teachers College, Columbia University, 1952), p. 112.

benefits he will receive from different types of goods and services (both public and private) before he makes decisions. Furthermore some sectors of the private economy carry on a continuous campaign by advertising and other methods against governmental services of all types. Attacks of this kind usually use such epithets as "big government," "the welfare state," and "socialism" as deadly ammunition to hurl at any and all governmental services. When the educational leadership dares to reply it is charged with being opposed to the free enterprise system. Fortunately there are many enlightened sectors of the business community that are staunch advocates of a policy of liberal investment in education.[7]

There should of course be no conflict between the government economy and the private economy because, as was pointed out in Chapter 3, each is essential to the other. This is particularly true of public education and the private economy. What can the schools do to help the leaders of the private economy to understand better the relationship between education and the private economy?

Giving the Consumer a Quality Alternative. There is another criterion which might be used to determine how much to spend for education. The private economy is always trying to build "a better mouse trap." It is continually improving automobiles, airplanes, washing machines, textiles—in fact every economic good it produces. The private economy is never satisfied with what it produces. Research and experimentation are continuously striving for the "best." That is a basic factor in the success of the private economy in satisfying the human wants it is capable of supplying. The cost of the good produced is not as vital as how well the good satisfies the want. For example, the automobile costs much more than a horse and buggy, but it forced the horse and buggy into oblivion.

Many boards of education have traditionally been forced to provide the most expedient types of programs possible with the funds available. Therefore average practice has in effect been an average of expedient practices. Educational programs have seldom been projected in terms of the quantity and quality of educational services actually needed. Should not research and experimentation be utilized in education as well as in the private economy to produce the best types of education we can conceptualize? What would be the characteristics of an excellent public school program? What would an excellent elementary and high school program cost? Is it not as rational to spend what

---

[7] For example, The National Citizens Commission for the Public Schools and its successor, The National Citizens Council for Better Schools.

it takes to buy an excellent educational program as it is to spend what it takes to buy an excellent automobile? Should not the consumer be given the opportunity to purchase a high quality program?

Will Money Alone Solve the School Problem?

This question is frequently asked by both friends and critics of education. It was propounded by a critic of educational expenditures to Dr. Paul R. Mort, a nationally known expert in public school financing. His reply was, "We will never know because no one would ever be fool enough to try it." Money alone will not produce any economic good. But economic goods cannot be produced efficiently without the necessary investment. Elsewhere in this book attention is directed to many factors other than money which must be taken into account before a good educational program can be assured. Among these factors are district organization, parental cooperation, methods of financing, the quality of boards of education, management, and state and local leadership. Perhaps the most important of these factors is leadership, because proper leadership can modify favorably all other factors affecting the quality of the educational program.

Elimination of Inefficiency. Sometimes it is argued that educational expenditures should not be increased until all waste and inefficiency are eliminated. The authors recently served as consultants to a citizens' committee that was making a statewide study of public education. The advisory committee on finance comprised approximately thirty members, most of whom were connected with the most important and successful industries in the state. A task force was assembled to analyze data and study the possibilities of economies which might be made. The needs of education were projected by other study committees. The state was one of the low income states. The finance committee after receiving the reports of other committees and after making its own studies concluded that the additional needs of education totalled more than $100,000,000 and that the possible economies which could be made totalled only a few hundred thousand dollars. The committee stated further that similar studies had shown that every private industry had some waste and inefficiency and that it was possible to minimize but not to eliminate waste and inefficiency from any enterprise either private or public. Therefore if the policy of not investing funds in an enterprise until all waste and inefficiency are entirely eliminated were adopted, no funds would ever be invested in any enterprise either public or private. How can one determine when waste and inefficiency in a public school system have been minimized?

What Are Some of the Social and Economic Factors That Affect Future Demands for Education?

It would require an entire book to give an adequate presentation of this topic. Only a brief discussion of a few of the more important factors can be given here. Some of those factors are growth in national income and productivity, change in pattern of skills and abilities, the changing role of government, changes in the class and caste structure, and social mobility.

Effect of a Rising National Income. Both the total and the per capita income are rising rapidly. The productivity per man hour of labor is increasing at the rate of approximately two per cent per year. This makes a rise in the level of living possible. The rise in the standard of living creates a consumer demand for more and better goods and services of all kinds, both public and private. Therefore consumers will inevitably demand a greater quantity and better quality of education than is now available.

This does not mean that the components of the educational system will remain the same in the future as at present. The consumption of education is similar to the consumption of food with respect to change in components. For example during the past forty years, the percentages of the total diet allocated to potatoes and bread have declined and the percentages allocated to meat and eggs have increased. This has resulted in a better diet. The consumption of food is unlike the consumption of education in that the total intake of food by the human being has a definite limit but there seems to be no limit to the intake of education. There is a limit to the per capita consumption of many physical types of economic goods but the limits of demand for many service types of goods such as education have not been established. Therefore as the standard of living rises the consumption of education will increase more rapidly than the consumption of many other types of economic goods because of increased demand for both quantity and quality.

Effect of Changes in Patterns of Skills and Abilities. The pattern of skills and abilities of the working population is changing rapidly. The proportion of the total national income derived from primary production (farming, fishing, and forestry) is decreasing and the proportion derived from manufacturing and services is increasing. For example the proportion of the total national income derived from agriculture in 1957 was just half the proportion in 1929. There has been a long range trend of migration from the farms to cities. We have changed from a predominantly agrarian economy in 1800 to a predominantly urban industrial economy in 1958. The early waves of migration from the farm to the city and from Europe to our cities were largely absorbed at first by the needs of the nation for a large supply of common labor. But as machines began to replace hand labor in the nineteenth century and as automation developed in the twentieth century, the needs for untrained common labor decreased and the needs for highly skilled and semi-skilled workers increased. The nation no longer has a need for a large supply of unskilled workers. Furthermore with the development of machines, child labor was no longer needed for production and this increased the demand for education. The change in the pattern of skills from emphasis on common labor to emphasis on types of skills and abilities requiring more education added to this demand for more education.

The available evidence indicates that these trends will continue in the future. Increased automation of industry will increase production and decrease the need for the labor of youth. The school term will probably be extended and the number of years of schooling increased. It is quite probable that within twenty years most young people will remain in school through the junior college years. Early marriage has not seemed to slow this trend much since, in 1957, twenty-two per cent of all college students were married. The knowledge, skills, and abilities required to earn a living will require more education in future years than in the past. The increased leisure provided by the shorter work week and the changing pattern of skills will increase the demands for adult education.

Effect of the Changing Role of Government. The changing role of government in our lives requires a constantly rising level of education of the citizenry. Many decisions that were formerly made in the market place are now made by political action. Governmental services consumed 13.7 per cent of the national income in 1923 and 30.3 per cent in 1957. It makes little difference to an individual whether his neighbor buys a washing machine or a desk. In the free market, each individual may purchase or not purchase a good or service. But in the government economy, all must purchase a service or none because decisions to buy or not to buy services must be made collectively by the ballot either directly or indirectly. The wisdom of decisions made by government is determined largely by the level of education of the people in a democratic form of government. Therefore, as government assumes greater importance in our lives, the welfare of the nation is vitally involved in the education of its people. Thomson has summarized the problem as follows:

> Changes in the relative importance of the political-decision making process present a challenge of the first magnitude for the future of American public education. Widening of the sphere of group action,

through the legislative machinery, demands an alert and informed consensus on problems which are both technically complex and of fundamental importance to the preservation of American freedoms.[8]

Effect of the Struggle to Remove Class and Caste Barriers. The twentieth century has been called the age of the common man. Underprivileged nations throughout the world and underprivileged groups within all nations have been struggling for growth beyond mere survival. Caste and class have always been present in all societies, but today as never before the validity of caste and class is being challenged. The denial of equal educational opportunities has always been one of the principal means for perpetuating the barriers between caste and class. Therefore underprivileged groups in the United States as well as throughout the world are demanding equality in educational opportunity. The barriers between caste and class have always hindered social mobility and prevented society from attaining its maximum production potential. Increased investment in education may well be the most productive investment the nation can make. This would be especially true for the underprivileged sectors of our population.

All of these factors will probably produce a greater increase in the demand for education in the latter half of the twentieth century than during the first half. What other factors will increase the demands for education? Are there any factors which are likely to reduce the demands for education?

What Will the Public School Revenues and the National Income Probably Be in 1970?

Long range estimates of this type are subject to rather wide margins of error because they must be based on assumptions which may or may not be valid. Nevertheless, sound fiscal planning requires that long range projections be made. After long range projections are made, the assumptions back of the estimates should be re-examined periodically and new estimates projected. In the following paragraphs projections are presented of public school revenues and total national income in 1970. These estimates give consideration to the trends that have been discussed in this chapter.

Predicted Increase in School Enrollment. The United States Bureau of the Census estimated that the total population of the United States in 1970 (including service men overseas) would be 213,800,000 and

---

[8] Procter Thomson, "Economic Problems and School Finance," unpublished paper presented to the National Education Association Committee on Tax Education and School Finance (March, 1952).

that the population 5–17 years of age would be 54,804,000.[9] In 1956, 80.8 per cent of the population 5–17 years of age was enrolled in the public schools. The per cent of that age group that will be enrolled in the public schools in 1970–71 is of course unknown. However, the demands for education are increasing, the holding power of high schools is increasing, and the public schools are being extended downward to include kindergartens and upward to include the junior college years. Therefore it seems reasonable to assume that 83 per cent of the population 5–17 years of age will be enrolled in the public schools in 1970–71. Based on that assumption, the enrollment in the public schools should be approximately 45,487,000 in 1970–71.[10]

Predicted Increase in School Revenue. The revenue receipts of the public schools totalled approximately $333 per pupil enrolled in 1957–58 in terms of the purchasing power of 1957 dollars. Revenue receipts increased approximately 4.7 per cent per year in constant dollars between 1949 and 1957. Assuming that this rate of increase will continue for thirteen years after 1957, the revenue per pupil will increase 61.1 per cent in constant dollars between 1957 and 1970. Based on this assumption, the revenue per pupil in 1970–71 would be $536 in terms of the purchasing power of 1957 dollars. This amount multiplied by the estimated enrollment of 45,487,000 in 1970 gives a product of $24,381,000,000 which would be the estimated revenue receipts of the public schools in 1970–71 in terms of the purchasing power of 1957 dollars.

But available evidence indicates that there will be continued inflation after 1957 and that the dollar will continue to decline in purchasing power. The consumer price index was 120.2 in 1957 if the average price level from 1947–49 is considered as being 100. Assuming that the price index will rise two points per year between 1957 and 1970 (which seems to be a reasonable assumption at this writing), the consumer price index would be 146.1 in 1970. This would represent a price increase of 21.63 per cent between 1957 and 1970. Therefore in order to estimate school revenues in 1970–71 in terms of the purchasing power of 1970 dollars $24,381,000,000 should be multiplied by 1.21633. This gives a product of $29,655,000,000 which would be the estimated public school revenues in 1970–71 in terms of 1970 dollars.

Predicted Increase in National Income. Let us now attempt to estimate the total national income in 1970 in terms of the probable purchasing power of 1970 dollars. The per capita national income was

[9] U. S. Department of Commerce, Bureau of the Census, "Current Population Reports—Population Estimates," No. 187, Nov. 19, 1958, Series II Estimates, p. 25.
[10] Any substantial change in the proportion of pupils of school age enrolled in private schools would affect this estimate.

approximately $2091 in 1957.[11] But the production per man hour has been increasing at a rate of from 2 to 3 per cent per year. Let us assume that the per capita income in constant dollars will increase 2.25 per cent per year or 29.25 per cent between 1957 and 1970. The 1957 per capita income of $2091 multiplied by 1.2925 gives $2703, the estimated per capita income in 1970 in 1957 dollars. This amount multiplied by 213,800,000 (the estimated population of 1970) gives $577,-901,000,000 as the estimated total national income in 1970 in 1957 dollars. This amount multiplied by 1.21633 gives $702,918,000,000 as the national income in 1970 in terms of 1970 dollars.

Relationship of Predicted School Revenue to Predicted National Income. If the total revenue of the public schools reaches $29,655,000,000 in 1970–71 and the total national income $702,918,000,000, the revenue receipts for the public schools would be 4.2 per cent of the national income in 1970. This compares with 3.11 per cent of the national income allocated to public school revenue in 1957–58. If these estimates are sound, it is apparent that major increases can be made in school revenue between 1957 and 1970 without any serious effect on the total economy because the increase in the percentage of the total national income allocated to the public schools would be small.

The above estimates of school revenue and national income might both be considered as maximums by others making similar estimates. The population estimates by the Bureau of the Census assume a continued high fertility rate. The estimates in enrollment assume a continued increase in consumer demand for education. The estimates of income assume a continuation of the high rate of increase in the efficiency of production. The 1970 dollar value is based on the assumption that the present rate of increase of inflation will continue. But trends at this writing indicate that all of these assumptions are realistic.

What are some other rational assumptions which could be made concerning the increase in school revenue and national income in future years? What would be the estimated school revenue and national income in 1970 using those assumptions?

Should the Productivity of the Educational Enterprise Be Increased?

Much of the knowledge which must be taught in the public schools was not known in 1900. Therefore, the task of the public schools is much greater than at the beginning of the century.

---

[11] Calculated by dividing the national income for 1957 by the total population including armed forces overseas.

Private enterprise has greatly increased the productivity per worker and per organizational unit in the private economy. Should a similar increase in productivity be expected of the educational enterprise? Following are some of the means which have been used to increase the productivity of public education:

1. The reorganization of school districts and the consolidation of schools. This has increased the pupil teacher ratio, broadened the school offering, and enhanced the efficiency of administrative and supervisory services.

2. The improvement of teacher productivity through improvements in knowledge of subject matter and of teaching methods.

3. Increasing the length of the school term. The average length of the school term in the United States is 178 days. In many European countries the schools operate for 220 days. Can the productivity of the educational enterprise of the United States be increased by operating schools for 220 days instead of 178 days?

4. The improvement of the functional planning of school buildings and equipment.

5. The improvement in the quality of books and other instructional materials.

6. The use of audio-visual aids including television.

7. The provision for special pupil personnel services of many types.

8. Extending the age groups served upward and downward.

9. Operating summer and night programs.

10. Extending the length of the school day. Some high schools have increased the capacity of the school plant by approximately 30 per cent by increasing the school day from five to seven periods. It is claimed that this device also makes it possible to provide more enrichment courses.

11. Operating schools for twelve months with three-fourths of the pupils in attendance and one-fourth on vacation at all times. It is claimed that this device increases the capacity of the school plant by 25 per cent.

Which of these plans are desirable and which are not? What other means are used or could be used for increasing the productivity of the educational enterprise?

SELECTED REFERENCES

Burke, Arvid J., *Financing Public Schools in the United States,* rev. ed. New York: Harper and Brothers, 1957. Chapters III, IV, and V.

Hutchins, Clayton D., and Albert R. Munse, *Expenditures for Education at Mid-century.* New York: U.S. Office of Education, U.S. Government Printing Office, 1953.

Hutchins, Clayton D., Albert R. Munse, and Edna D. Booker, *Trends in Significant Facts on School Finance.* Washington, D.C. U.S. Office of Education: U.S. Government Printing Office, 1957.

Johns, R. L., and E. L. Morphet, *Problems and Issues in Public School Finance.* New York: Bureau of Publications, Teachers College, Columbia University, 1952. Chapter IV.

Mort, Paul R., and Walter C. Reusser, *Public School Finance,* 2nd ed. New York: McGraw-Hill Book Company, Inc., 1951. Chapters I and VI.

National Citizens Commission for the Public Schools, *Financing Public Education in the Decade Ahead.* New York: The Commission, 1954.

National Education Association of the U.S., Research Division, *Advanced Estimates of Public Elementary and Secondary Schools for the School Year 1957–58,* and succeeding issues. Washington, D.C.: The Association, 1957, *et seq.*

Rosenstengel, William Everett, and Jefferson N. Eastmond, *School Finance.* New York: The Ronald Press Company, 1957. Chapter VI.

U. S. Office of Education, *Biennial Survey of Education in the United States— Statistics of State School Systems: Organization, Staff, Pupils, and Finances,* and succeeding issues. Washington, D.C.: U.S. Government Printing Office, 1921, *et seq.*

CHAPTER FIVE

Taxation

and Sources of School Revenue

In the previous chapter, attention was called to the fact that the demands for education are rapidly increasing and that school revenues will probably more than double between 1957–58 and 1970– 71. The demand for practically all types of governmental services will increase during that period. The expenditures for many types of governmental services will no doubt be increased proportionally as much as the expenditures for education. The optimistic view is that expenditures for national defense might be reduced. The pessimistic view is that they might be further increased.

Since governmental expenditures of all types in 1957 required approximately thirty per cent of the national income and it is probable that this percentage will continue to rise, the problem of providing tax revenues for all levels of government is a major one. The national income will probably continue to rise and provide more revenue with the same tax rates. But the increased revenue that will be provided from this source will probably not be equal to the increased demands for governmental services.

The provision of needed school revenue is not likely to be accomplished without giving due consideration to the revenue needs of all types of government. The problems and issues of school finance are a part of the whole public finance picture. Therefore in this chapter attention will be given to such factors as expenditures by different levels of government, amounts and types of taxes collected by different levels of government, the relative dependence of different levels of government on various types of taxes, trends in change of dependence on different types of taxes, principles of taxation, shifting of the incidence of taxes, the effect of taxes on production and the distribution of income, sources of school revenue by level of government and by types of taxes, and appraisal of school revenues in terms of certain principles of taxation.

EXPENDITURES BY DIFFERENT LEVELS
OF GOVERNMENT

The different levels of government are broadly classified as Federal, state, and local. Trends in expenditures for different levels of government have significant effects on school financing. Therefore trends in Federal, state, and local governmental expenditures are set forth in Table 5–1 for selected years beginning with 1890. The years were selected so as to represent war years, depression years, prosperous years and fairly normal years in order to consider the relative effects on the different levels of government. If long range trends only were being considered, the most unusual years should not have been included. The expenditures reported in Table 5–1 are in current dollars [1] and they include all expenditures except payments for principal of debts and intergovernmental transfers.

TABLE 5–1

GOVERNMENT EXPENDITURE FOR SELECTED YEARS
(in millions, in current dollars)

Year	Federal	State	Local	Total
1890	$ 318	$ 88	$ 487	$ 893
1903	517	207	912	1,636
1913	697	359	1,607	2,663
1918	12,648	553	1,966	15,167
1923	3,054	1,195	4,056	8,305
1929	2,957	1,928	6,051	10,936
1936	8,611	2,419	5,320	16,350
1940	8,824	3,612	5,640	18,076
1945	98,360	3,750	5,015	107,125
1952	65,999	8,653	17,444	92,096
1954	68,797	10,108	20,593	99,498
1957	68,236	13,774	26,664	108,674

Sources: National Industrial Conference Board, *The Economic Almanac.* Data for 1890–1936 from 1942 volume, p. 408; data for 1940–1954 from 1958 volume, p. 428; data for 1957 from Bureau of the Census, *Summary of Governmental Finances in 1957.*

---

[1] The term *current dollars* means that dollars for different years are unadjusted for differences in the purchasing power of the dollar. The term *constant dollars* means that the current dollars have been adjusted so that the dollars for different years have the same purchasing power.

Expenditures by All Governments

Let us first examine trends in total expenditures for all levels of government. Total expenditures for all governments increased from $893 millions in 1890 to $108,674 millions in 1957 in current dollars. Thus it would appear that governmental expenditures increased approximately 122 fold over this period. But the population increased in number and the dollar decreased in purchasing power during this period. In Table 5–2 total expenditures are converted into per capita expenditures in dollars of constant purchasing power. The per capita expenditure for all government increased from $42 in 1890 to $529 in 1957 in terms of the purchasing power of the 1947–49 dollar. Therefore in constant dollars, the per capita expenditure for government increased approximately 13 fold during this period. This is much less than 122 fold, but it is still quite significant. It is evident that government services will be far more important in the lives of people during the latter half of the twentieth century than at the beginning of the century.

TABLE 5–2

PER CAPITA GOVERNMENT EXPENDITURES IN 1947–49 DOLLARS

Year	Consumer Price Index (1947–49 = 100)	Federal	State	Local	Total
1890	34.1	$ 15	$ 4	$ 23	$ 42
1903	36.1	18	7	31	56
1913	42.3	17	9	39	65
1918	64.3	191	8	30	229
1923	72.9	37	15	50	102
1929	73.3	33	22	68	123
1936	59.3	113	32	70	215
1940	59.9	111	46	71	228
1945	76.9	914	35	47	996
1952	113.5	370	49	98	517
1954	114.8	369	54	111	534
1957	120.2	332	67	130	529

Sources: (1) Consumer price index—Department of Commerce, Bureau of Labor Statistics, except for the years 1890 and 1903 which were estimated by the authors. (2) The per capita data were calculated by converting the expenditure data in Table 1 into 1947–49 dollars and dividing by the total population including armed forces overseas.

It is interesting to note that the per capita government expenditures increased very gradually between 1890 and 1913 but they did increase 50 per cent in constant dollars. This 23-year period was a time of peace except for the short period of the Spanish-American War. Therefore government services were increasing in importance during the last decade of the nineteenth century and the first years of the twentieth century.

Government expenditures increased dramatically during the World War I and World War II years due to the great increases in Federal expenditures. But it is interesting to observe that the per capita expenditures for government did not return to pre-war levels after World War I or II. On the contrary, in the years following each war, government expenditures continued at about half the per capita expenditure of the peak war year, whereas prior to World War I per capita expenditures were about 30 per cent of the peak war year and prior to World War II about 23 per cent. This seems to indicate that wars tend to increase the demand for government services and expenditures in the post-war years. Some of these expenditures resulted from obligations incurred by the Federal government during the wars but state and local expenditures both increased rapidly after each war.

Expenditures by the Federal Government

Per capita Federal expenditures in dollars of the same purchasing power remained almost constant between 1890 and 1913, rose sharply in 1918, declined sharply in the post-war years but remained about double those for the pre-war years, rose rapidly during the depression years, increased to an all time high in the World War II years, and declined rapidly in the years following the war but remained about three times those of the pre-war years. Thus it appears that wars and the Great Depression have caused the greatest fluctuations in Federal expenditures but there has been a long range trend toward increased Federal spending for services other than national defense and relief.

Expenditures by State Governments

The per capita state expenditures were very low in 1890 but they doubled between 1890–1913. Per capita state expenditures dropped slightly in 1918, rose sharply after World War I and by 1929 were 2½ times the pre-war level, continued to rise during the depression years, dropped some during World War II years, and increased in the post-war years to the extent that by 1957 per capita state expenditures were 50 per cent greater than in the pre-war years. Thus it appears that state expenditures declined or remained constant in war years and increased in depression years. The decline in war years was probably due principally to restrictions on construction.

Expenditures by Local Governments

Per capita expenditures of local government increased about 70 per cent between 1890 and 1913, declined during 1918, increased in the post-war years so that by 1929 expenditures were 70 per cent greater than during the pre-war years, remained about constant during the depression, dropped sharply during World War II, and increased in the post-war years so that by 1957 expenditures were 81 per cent greater than in the pre-war years.

Expenditures by Different Types of Local Governments. There are many types of local government in the United States. The principal types are counties, cities, townships, school districts, and special districts such as drainage or irrigation districts. With few exceptions all people living in rural territory are served by a county government and a school government. Likewise with a few exceptions, all people living in cities are served by a county government, a city government, and a school government. Townships and special districts are not universal but they usually have some important functions where they exist. Some people in the United States pay taxes to finance services provided by all of these five types of governments. These local governments are overlapping and sometimes duplicate certain services and facilities. This is one of the major problems of political science because all of these governments spend tax monies.

TABLE 5–3

DIRECT GENERAL EXPENDITURE BY LEVEL OF GOVERNMENT 1957
(*in millions*)

Level of Government	Amount *	Per Cent of Total
Federal	$ 68,236 †	62.8
State	13,774	12.7
Local:		
County	4,785	4.4
City	7,920	7.3
Township	830	.8
School District	12,213	11.2
Special District	916	.8
TOTAL	$108,674	100.0

* Includes all expenditures except payments of debt principal.
† Includes $45,803 millions for national defense and international relations.
Note: The Bureau of the Census data were adjusted by deducting $613 millions from county, $1,360 millions from city and $370,000 millions from township governments and adding to school districts because those units of government spent those amounts for elementary and high schools.
Source: Data adopted from Bureau of the Census, *Summary of Governmental Finances in 1957.*

The direct expenditures in 1957 for each of the five principal types of local government are shown in Table 5–3. The expenditures of the Federal and state governments are also shown for comparative purposes. All expenditures are included except payments on debt principal. Intergovernmental transfers are eliminated and direct expenditures of the state and other units of local government for schools are deducted from those units and added to school districts in order to show total expenditures for the public schools.

In 1957 expenditures of school districts comprised 11.2 per cent of all governmental expenditures, cities 7.3 per cent, counties 4.4 per cent, townships 0.8 per cent, special districts 0.8 per cent, state governments 12.7 per cent, and the Federal government 62.8 per cent. In terms of expenditures, school districts were the most important of all local governments. Expenditures by school districts were exceeded only slightly by those of state governments but the Federal government expended 5.6 times as much as school districts.

Expenditures of All Governments Excluding Expenditures for National Security

Most Federal expenditures during and since World War II have been for national defense and international relations. For example, the direct expenditures of the Federal government totalled $68,236 millions in 1957. Of this amount $45,803 millions were expended for national defense. If the amount expended by the Federal government for national defense and international relations is deducted from Federal expenditures and from total government expenditures, then Federal expenditures would have been 35.7 per cent of the total, state governments 21.9 per cent, county governments 7.6 per cent, city governments 12.6 per cent, township governments 1.3 per cent, school districts 19.4 per cent, and special districts 1.5 per cent. These are purely hypothetical calculations because national defense and international relations are inescapable functions of the Federal government. However they do show roughly the relative expenditures of the different levels of government for functions "internal" to the nation.

Effect of Spending by One Government on the Spending of Other Governments

These patterns of expenditure trends reveal (except in peak war expenditure years), that an increase in the per capita spending of one level of government does not prevent an increase in spending of other levels of government. Actually increases in spending of one level of government seem to be accompanied by increases in the spending of the other levels. It is commonly believed that the different levels of government compete with each other for the taxpayer's dollar. That may be true, but no level of government has as yet gone into a decline as a result of the competition.[2] However the per capita Federal expenditures in 1957 were 18 times the 1903 expenditures, 1957 state expenditures 10 times 1903 expenditures, and 1957 local expenditures 4 times 1903 expenditures.

TAX COLLECTIONS BY DIFFERENT LEVELS
OF GOVERNMENT

Taxes are collected by or for [3] various levels of government. The amount and types of taxes collected are determined by both law and political consensus. The levels of government considered in this section are Federal, state, local governments excluding schools, and school districts.

Amount of Taxes Collected

A study of the taxes collected by the different levels of government reveals to some extent the tax levying capability of each level. The tax levying capability of each level of government is determined by the types of taxes that are legal or practicable for it to levy as well as by its ability to pay. It has been argued that the Federal government has no financial ability other than that possessed by the states and that a state has no financial ability other than that possessed by its units of local government. This reasoning is based on the assumption that the financial ability of the nation is the summation of the ability of the states and the financial ability of a state is the summation of the ability of its subdivisions. This assumption may be theoretically true but it does not follow that the states in total have the same capability to levy and collect taxes as the Federal government nor does it follow that the subdivisions of a state have the same capability to levy and collect taxes as the state.

The amounts of taxes collected by the various levels of goverment in 1957 are shown in Table 5–4. The Federal government collected 70.6 per cent of all taxes collected, state governments 14.7 per cent, local governments excluding schools 9.9 per cent, and school districts 4.8 per cent. The total amount of taxes collected by all local governments including schools was almost identical with the total amount collected

---

[2] This is probably due in part to the fact that some types of government spending increase production. The exchange value of the increased production provides more real dollars with which to pay taxes.

[3] For example, school district taxes are usually collected by county or city tax collectors.

by all state governments. This table excludes payroll taxes for social security and retirement.

TABLE 5–4

TAX COLLECTIONS OF DIFFERENT LEVELS OF GOVERNMENT 1957

(*in millions*)

Type of Tax	*Total of All Governments* *	*Federal Government*	*State Governments*	*Local Governments Excluding Schools*	*School Districts*
Property	$13,097	$ —	$ 479	$7,976	$4,642
Personal Income	37,388	35,620	1,563	205	—
Corporation Income	22,151	21,167	984	**	—
General Sales and Gross Receipts	4,027	—	3,373	654	—
Motor Fuel Sales	4,349	1,498	2,828	23	—
Alcoholic Beverage Sales	3,484	2,893	569	22	—
Tobacco Sales	2,273	1,669	556	48	—
Other Sales and Gross Receipts	5,721	4,333	1,109	279	—
Custom Duties	735	735	—	—	—
Death and Gift	1,711	1,365	338	8	—
Motor Vehicle and Operators Licenses ...	1,462	—	1,368	94	—
All Other Taxes †	2,461	537	1,363	497	64
TOTAL	$98,859	$69,817	$14,530	$9,806	$4,706
PER CENT OF TOTAL	100.0	70.6	14.7	9.9	4.8

     * Excludes payroll taxes for social security and retirement.
     ** Amount included in personal income tax.
     † Principally licenses and permits of various types.
Source: adapted from *Summary of Governmental Finances in 1957,* Department of Commerce, Bureau of the Census.

Grants-in-Aid

The various levels of government collecting taxes do not always directly spend all the taxes they collect. Ignoring deficit financing, the central governments (the Federal and state governments) spend less than they collect and the local governments more. This is due to the various systems of grants-in-aid of central governments to smaller governmental divisions. Intergovernmental transfers in 1957 were, in millions: Federal to state $3,523; Federal to local $350; state to local $7,310; local to state $304; and, local to local $464.

These grants-in-aid are of tremendous importance to government financing in the United States. The various government services needed by the people cannot be neatly allocated to the various levels of government. The direct administration and supervision of many services may be allocated but the central governments still retain an interest in the services. Therefore many governmental services are provided by various types of partnerships between and among different levels of government. These partnerships have necessitated the development of arrangements by which different levels of government could participate in the financing of a service and at the same time provide for an efficient administration of the service.

Types of Taxes Collected

The per cent of the total tax collections of each level of government derived from each tax source in 1957 is shown in Table 5–5. Of the total taxes collected in 1957 by all governments, 37.8 per cent was derived from personal income taxes, 22.4 per cent from corporation income taxes, 20.1 per cent from various types of sales and gross receipts taxes, 13.3 per cent from property taxes and 6.4 per cent from miscellaneous taxes.

TABLE 5–5

PER CENT OF TAX COLLECTIONS DERIVED FROM DIFFERENT TYPES OF TAXES
BY LEVEL OF GOVERNMENT IN 1957

Type of Tax	Total of All Governments	Federal Government	State Governments	Local Governments Excluding Schools	School Districts
Property	13.3	—	3.3	81.3	98.6
Personal Income	37.8	51.0	10.8	2.1	—
Corporation Income	22.4	30.3	6.8	—	—
General Sales and Gross Receipts	4.1	—	23.2	6.7	—
Motor Fuel Sales	4.4	2.1	19.5	.2	—
Alcoholic Beverage Sales	3.5	4.1	3.9	.2	—
Tobacco Sales	2.3	2.4	3.8	.5	—
Other Sales and Gross Receipts	5.8	6.2	7.6	2.8	—
Custom Duties	.7	1.1	—	—	—
Death and Gift	1.7	2.0	2.3	.1	—
Motor Vehicle and Operators' Licenses	1.5	—	9.4	1.0	—
All Other Taxes	2.5	.8	9.4	5.1	1.4
TOTAL	100.0	100.0	100.0	100.0	100.0

Source: Derived from data given in Table 5–4.

But the different levels of government differed very widely in the percentage of taxes derived from different types of taxes. The Federal government derived 51.0 per cent of its tax revenue from the personal income tax, 30.3 per cent from the corporation income tax, 14.8 from sales and gross receipts taxes, 3.9 per cent from miscellaneous taxes, and none from property taxes.

The state governments derived 58.0 per cent of their taxes from sales and gross receipts taxes, 21.1 per cent from miscellaneous sources (mostly licenses and permits), 10.8 per cent from personal income taxes, 6.8 per cent from corporation income taxes, and 3.3 per cent from property taxes.

Local governments other than schools derived 81.3 per cent of their tax revenue from property taxes, 10.4 per cent from sales and gross receipts taxes, 6.2 per cent from miscellaneous sources and 2.1 per cent from personal and corporation income taxes.

School districts derived 98.6 per cent of their tax revenue from property taxes and 1.4 per cent from miscellaneous sources. It is evident that school districts rely almost exclusively on the property tax for local taxes and that local governments other than schools also rely largely on the property tax. The Federal government and the state governments have access to many more types of taxes than local governments. School districts have the least possibility of any important division of government of levying and collecting a wide diversity of local taxes.

TABLE 5-6

PER CENT OF EACH TYPE OF TAX COLLECTED BY DIFFERENT LEVELS
OF GOVERNMENT IN 1957

Type of Tax	Federal Government	State Governments	Local Governments Excluding Schools	School Districts	Total
Property	—	3.7	60.9	35.4	100.0
Personal Income	95.3	4.2	.5	—	100.0
Corporation Income	95.6	4.4	—	—	100.0
General Sales and Gross Receipts	—	83.8	16.2	—	100.0
Motor Fuel Sales	34.5	65.0	.5	—	100.0
Alcoholic Beverage Sales	83.1	16.3	.6	—	100.0
Tobacco Sales	73.4	24.5	2.1	—	100.0
Other Sales and Gross Receipts	75.7	19.4	4.9	—	100.0
Custom Duties	100.0	—	—	—	100.0
Death and Gift	79.8	19.8	.4	—	100.0
Motor Vehicle and Operators' Licenses	—	93.6	6.4	—	100.0
All Other Taxes	21.8	55.4	20.2	2.6	100.0

Source: Derived from data given in Table 5-4.

It is also of importance to consider the per cent of each type of tax collected by different levels of government. This is shown for the year 1957 in Table 5-6. Local governments other than schools collected 60.9 per cent of all property taxes, school districts 35.4 per cent, state governments 3.7 per cent, and the Federal government none. However the Federal government collected more than 95 per cent of all personal and corporation income taxes levied. As will be shown later in this chapter, most authorities on government finance consider income taxes the most equitable of all taxes. Furthermore, the Federal government collected more sales and gross receipts taxes than any other level of government except general sales and gross receipts taxes and taxes on motor fuel sales.

State governments collected most of the taxes on general sales and gross receipts, taxes on motor fuel sales, motor vehicle and operators' licenses, and miscellaneous taxes. Table 5–6 further reveals the limited tax collecting capability of school districts.

Trends in Types of Taxes Collected

Table 5–7 shows the per cent of tax revenue derived from different types of taxes by different levels of government in 1942 and 1957. Tax sources are grouped into six broad categories and school districts are included with local governments in order to simplify the data. The proportion of Federal revenues derived from the personal income tax increased from 26.5 per cent in 1942 to 51.0 per cent in 1957, but the proportionate amounts derived from all other sources declined.

TABLE 5–7

TRENDS IN THE PER CENT OF REVENUE DERIVED FROM DIFFERENT TYPES OF TAXES BY LEVEL OF GOVERNMENT

Types of Taxes	1 9 4 2			1 9 5 7		
	Federal	State	Local	Federal	State	Local
Property	—	6.8	92.4	—	3.3	86.9
Personal Income	26.5	6.4	.6	51.0	10.7	1.4
Corporation Income ...	38.5	6.9	*	30.3	6.8	*
Sales, Gross Receipts, and Customs	27.2	56.8	2.9	15.9	58.1	7.1
Death and Gift	3.4	2.8	—	2.0	2.3	.1
Licenses, Permits, and Other	4.4	20.3	4.1	.8	18.8	4.5
TOTAL	100.0	100.0	100.0	100.0	100.0	100.0

* Included in *Personal Income.*
Source: Derived from U. S. Bureau of the Census, *Statistical Abstracts of the United States 1958* and *Summary of Governmental Finances in 1957.*

The proportionate amounts of revenue derived from different types of taxes by state governments were quite similar for the years 1942 and 1957. However the portion derived from property taxes declined from 6.8 per cent in 1942 to 3.3 per cent in 1957 and the portion derived from personal income taxes increased from 6.4 per cent to 10.7 per cent. The per cent derived from sales and gross receipts taxes increased slightly as compared with a slight decrease in the per cent derived from miscellaneous sources.

The pattern of tax sources of local governments in 1957 was similar to that in 1942. The portion derived by local governments from property taxes declined from 92.4 per cent to 86.9. This was accompanied by an increase in the portion derived from sales and gross receipts taxes from 2.9 per cent in 1942 to 7.1 per cent in 1957 and in personal income taxes from six-tenths of one per cent in 1942 to 1.4 per cent in 1957. Other tax sources contributed proportionately about the same in 1957 as in 1942.

It is also interesting to consider changes in the per cent of the total tax collections of all governments derived from different types of taxes. Table 5–8 shows that the portion of the total taxes of all governments derived from the personal income tax increased from 17.0 per cent in 1942 to 37.8 per cent in 1957. The percentages derived from all other major types of taxes declined during this fifteen-year period. The property tax particularly declined in relative importance. It was the third most important type of revenue in 1942 and fourth in importance in 1957. A comparison with personal income tax collections is particularly significant. The property tax yielded more than the personal income tax in 1942 but in 1957 the personal income tax yielded almost three times the yield of the property tax.

TABLE 5–8

TRENDS IN AMOUNT AND PER CENT OF EACH TYPE OF TAX COLLECTED
BY ALL GOVERNMENTS
(in millions)

	1942		1957	
Types of Taxes	Amount	Per Cent of Total	Amount	Per Cent of Total
Property	$ 4,536	21.8	$13,097	13.3
Personal Income	3,530	17.0	37,388	37.8
Corporation Income	4,995	24.0	22,151	22.4
Sales, Gross Receipts and Customs	5,685	27.3	20,589	20.8
Death and Gift	530	2.6	1,711	1.7
Licenses, Permits and Other	1,521	7.3	3,923	4.0
TOTAL	$20,797	100.0	$98,859	100.0

Source: Derived from Statistical Abstract of the United States 1958, and Summary of Governmental Finance in 1957.

Trends in Total Tax Collections by Level of Government

It is difficult to assess trends in tax collections by level of government because of wide fluctuations in Federal tax collections. The total tax collections of the three major levels of government for 1942 and 1957 are shown in Table 5–9. The taxes collected by the Federal government increased from 59.0 per cent of the total in 1942 to 70.6 per cent in 1957. The taxes collected by both state and local governments

TABLE 5–9

TRENDS IN AMOUNT AND TOTAL TAX COLLECTIONS BY LEVEL OF GOVERNMENT
(*in millions of current dollars*)

Level of Government	1942		1957	
	Amount	Per Cent	Amount	Per Cent
Federal *	$12,270	59.0	$69,817	70.6
State *	3,903	18.8	14,530	14.7
Local	4,624	22.2	14,512	14.7
TOTAL	$20,797	100.0	$98,859	100.0

* Excludes social security tax receipts.
Source: Bureau of the Census, *Statistical Abstract of the United States 1958*, and *Summary of Governmental Finance in 1957*.

declined as percentages of the total between 1942 and 1957. However the taxes collected by all levels of government increased between 1942 and 1957, after making due allowance for increases in population and differences in the purchasing power of the dollar. In terms of the purchasing power of the 1947–49 dollar the per capita tax collections of the Federal government increased from $130 in 1942 to $339 in 1957, of state governments from $41 to $71, and of local governments from $49 to $71. Therefore Federal tax collections increased at a much more rapid rate than either state or local tax collections between 1942 and 1957.

TRENDS IN SOURCES OF REVENUE FOR THE PUBLIC SCHOOLS

The revenue receipts for the public schools for selected years beginning with 1929–30 are presented in Table 5–10. We are interested

TABLE 5–10

TRENDS IN SOURCES OF SCHOOL REVENUE RECEIPTS BY LEVEL OF GOVERNMENT
(*in millions of current dollars*)

Source	1929–30		1939–40		1949–50		1957–58	
	Amount	Per Cent	Amount	Per Cent	Amount	Per Cent	Amount	Per Cent
Federal ..	$ 7	.3	$ 40	1.8	$ 156	2.9	$ 396	3.6
State	354	17.0	685	30.3	2,166	39.8	4,527	40.6
Local ...	1,728	82.7	1,536	67.9	3,115	57.3	6,220	55.8
TOTAL ...	$2,089	100.0	$2,261	100.0	$5,437	100.0	$11.143	100.0

Sources: Data for 1929–30, 1939–40, and 1949–50 from *Biennial Surveys* and *Statistical Circulars*, Office of Education and for 1957–58 from *Advanced Estimates of the Public Elementary and Secondary Schools for the Year 1957–58*, National Education Association.

here in sources of revenue rather than trends in real income expressed in constant dollars. Therefore the data in this table are presented in current dollars. The per cent of public school revenue provided by the

Federal government increased from .3 in 1929–30 to 3.6 in 1957–58; the per cent provided by state governments increased from 17.0 in 1929–30 to 40.6 in 1957–58 and the per cent provided locally decreased from 82.7 in 1929–30 to 55.8 in 1957–58. Although the percentage of total school revenue from local sources declined during this period, the amount increased 260 per cent in current dollars and 120 per cent in constant dollars. The relative percentage decline in local revenues was due principally to the larger increase in state funds because the amount of state funds increased 1,179 per cent in current dollars and 680 per cent in constant dollars between 1929–30 and 1957–58.

There has been some increase in Federal funds but most of this increase has been due to the provision of Federal aid for school lunch programs and special Federal assistance for areas unusually affected by Federal activities.

The trend toward increased dependence on grants-in-aid from the state governments was very marked between 1929–30 and 1949–50. However the proportion of revenue provided by the state, which rose sharply between 1929 and 1949, increased only slightly between 1949–50 and 1957–58.

It is impossible to analyze accurately the particular types of taxes from which all the revenue receipts of the public schools are derived. Funds received from Federal sources are derived from the general tax sources of the Federal government. Funds derived from state sources are almost all provided from general state revenues or earmarked taxes although in a few states income from permanent funds and endowment is significant.

About 94 per cent of the local revenue receipts for the public schools was derived from tax sources in 1954. About 98.6 per cent of local tax collections for schools was derived from property taxes. In 1954 approximately 53 per cent of the total revenue receipts of the public schools from all sources was derived from property taxes. That percentage probably continued through 1957–58 because there was but little change in the percentage of revenue derived from state sources. Therefore the property tax is still the most important single type of tax levied for the support of the public schools.

The over-all picture of revenue receipts for the public schools in 1957–58 was somewhat as follows: approximately 53 per cent was derived from property taxes (including both state and local), 42 per cent from non-property taxes and 5 per cent from miscellaneous sources such as income from permanent funds, endowments, gifts, fees, and interest earned. However school revenue patterns vary widely among the states. For example, in 1957–58, six states provided less than 20 per cent of the revenue receipts for schools from state sources and six states more than 67 per cent.[4] This is significant because the states providing a low percentage of total revenue from state sources support schools primarily from property taxes whereas those providing a high percentage of state funds support schools primarily from non-property taxes.

PRINCIPLES OR CRITERIA OF TAXATION

Practically everyone agrees that taxes should be just to individuals and that their economic effect should be to maximize the production and consumption of legitimate want satisfying goods and services.[5] The concept of justice has been popularly expressed in such words as equity, fairness, non-discriminatory, equal treatment of equals and so on. The concept of economic effect has been frequently expressed by the phrase "don't kill the goose that laid the golden egg." The concepts of justice and economic effect are both somewhat abstract and therefore cannot be readily stated in objective terms. Authorities on public finance and economics have advanced many different principles and theories of taxation. There is far from universal agreement on what are valid principles of taxation. Some authors refer to them as doctrines, rather than principles. Whether principles or doctrines, they are useful for analyzing and describing taxes.

However principles of taxation are not very useful for appraising whether a particular tax is good or bad. The taxing system must be appraised as a whole in order to arrive at broadly useful judgments. Our whole taxing system comprises the taxes levied by the Federal, state, and local governments. There has been almost no planned coordination between the taxing systems of the Federal government and of the state governments except that the states are prohibited from levying customs duties and taxes on interstate commerce. There has been some coordination between the taxing systems of states and local governments but even there the coordination is far from evident in some states. Coordination among the taxing systems of the various types of local governments is also fraught with many difficulties.

But political consensus must be reached on the taxes and the rates of taxes to levy at the Federal level, the state levels, and the various local government levels. Thus taxpayers are faced with very perplexing problems because different persons in our representative democracy are making decisions on taxation at different governmental levels.

---

[4] See Chapter 9.
[5] Or should injure as little as possible the production and consumption of legitimate want satisfying goods and services.

Furthermore any type of tax can be either praised or condemned on the basis of one or more principles of taxation. Sometimes taxation is called a "class struggle" in which each economic group (for example labor and capital and various sub-groups of each) strives to minimize the taxes levied on itself and thereby indirectly to maximize the proportion of taxes paid by other groups. Self-interested economic groups have no difficulty in finding one or more principles of taxation by which they can imply that practically any tax suggested is bad. On the other hand, those advocating the extension or continuation of government services can find support in one or more principles of taxation for practically any type of tax proposed.

The principles or doctrines of taxation are somewhat like missiles which the proponents and opponents of taxes toss at each other. But no missile annihilates opposition. The same missile which has hit one side can be picked up and launched at the other side. Since those responsible for financing the public schools inevitably become involved directly or indirectly in tax struggles, it is advisable that they know something about the properties of the missiles being tossed. Therefore the most commonly accepted principles of taxation are discussed briefly in this section.[6] Some of these principles deal primarily with apportioning the tax burden and others with administrative considerations governing the selection of tax sources. Since the two purposes are not mutually exclusive, no attempt is made to classify the principles.

Ability To Pay

Ability to pay is perhaps the most commonly accepted principle of taxation but acceptance of the principle promotes little consensus in the body politic. The principle simply stated is that each should contribute to the support of government according to his ability. But what is ability? Some would accept the possession of property and wealth as the best test of ability, others consider volume of spending and still others income as the most valid test of ability. If one accepts the first test as best, he considers the property tax to be the best tax. If he accepts the second test, he assumes the sales tax to be the best tax. If he accepts the third test, he advocates the income tax as the best tax. Therefore one can justify any one of the three principal taxes used in the United States by the ability-to-pay principle despite the fact that these taxes are quite different in nature.

---

[6] For a more complete discussion of the principles of taxation see: William H. Anderson, *Taxation and the American Economy* (Englewood Cliffs, N.J.: Prentice-Hall, Inc., 1951), pp. 50–95; and William J. Shultz and C. Lowell Harriss, *American Public Finance*, 6th ed. (Englewood Cliffs, N.J.: Prentice-Hall, Inc., 1954), pp. 137–245; or any standard work on Public Finance.

Despite these differences in definitions of ability, there is widespread agreement that the taxing system should bear some relationship to ability to pay. It would be obviously impossible to support government entirely by poll taxes in the same amount per person regardless of variation in the financial circumstances of individuals.

The progressive income tax is usually considered by experts in public finance as the best expression of the ability-to-pay principle although there are those who insist that the proportional income tax is more equitable. Various theories have been advanced to justify the ability-to-pay principle. Some of them are discussed in the following paragraphs.

Distributing Purchasing Power. It is argued by some that the application of the ability-to-pay principle increases consumption and demand and therefore makes possible an increase in production. Progressive income taxes leave proportionately more of the income earned in the hands of the lower income groups. The lower income groups have a need for consuming and they will spend their income. This will produce full employment and high production; conditions necessary for a high standard of living. This policy, it is argued, will also result in a more equitable distribution of wealth and income as well as preventing oversaving and underconsumption. A progressive income tax will make possible some saving by all income levels thereby resulting in some wealth accumulation at all levels. Income is in effect redistributed because the person of low income receives more benefits than he pays for in taxes, whereas the reverse is true of the person of high income.

Privileges Enjoyed. Ability to pay is justified under this theory by the assumption that persons of higher income have received more priviliges from the government or their environment than those of lower income. This is very close to the benefit and unearned increment principles which are discussed later.

Sacrifices Made. The theories concerning sacrifice are highly controversial as are nearly all other theories of taxation. Most theories of sacrifice are built on assumptions concerning the diminishing marginal utility of income. It is assumed that the marginal dollar of a higher income has less utility to the owner than the marginal dollar of lower incomes. For example, it is assumed that the twenty-thousandth dollar of the possessor of a twenty-thousand dollar income is of less utility to the owner than the three-thousandth dollar to the possessor of a three-thousand dollar income. Thus taxes derived from higher incomes result in less personal sacrifice per dollar of taxes taken than the taxes on lower incomes. This line of reasoning strongly supports progressive income taxes.

There are those however who argue that utility to the owner cannot be closely defined. Higher incomes are used both for consumption and investment and these factors are both necessary for production. Persons with higher incomes consume certain products such as furs, yachts, and jewels not consumed in quantity by those with low incomes. To deprive them of their income would destroy the market for such products and create unemployment. Furthermore, high incomes are used more for investment than low incomes and investment is necessary for production and full employment.

Potential Earning Power. This theory concerns the faculty or power to earn money and support government. It is assumed that "money makes money" and the more a person's income, the greater his power to make more. Sometimes this theory is expressed as "tax the money where you find it."

Benefits Received

According to this principle persons, property, and taxable institutions should pay for government according to the benefits received. This is the order of things in the private enterprise system unless one is the object of charity. One pays for what he receives in the private economy so therefore he should do so in the public economy—so assert the supporters of this doctrine.

This principle seems logical at first consideration but careful analysis reveals some serious weaknesses. It is quite easy to apportion the benefits received in the private economy. For example if one wants an automobile he goes to the market place and buys it. It makes no difference to his neighbor whether he buys it.[7] But it is not practicable to apportion most of the benefits received from the public economy. For example, how could the benefits received from $45,000,000,000 expended by the Federal government in 1957 for national defense and international relations have been apportioned among 171,000,000 people and all the property and taxable institutions existing at that time? How could the benefits of the $12,000,000,000 expended for the public schools in 1957 have been apportioned? Education is a necessity for national defense, for the existence of democratic forms of government, and for developing the abilities and talents of individuals. What is the relative importance of each of these purposes? To argue that one is

---

[7] Except as the consumption of the good minutely affects employment, and supply and demand in the industry producing the good. Presumably the purchaser might have purchased some other good which would have had an equally favorable effect on the total economy.

more important than the other is senseless because each is vital for survival.

Application of the Benefits Principle. Despite its limitations, the benefits principle has some application in our taxing systems. Motor fuel taxes and motor vehicle license taxes have been levied in accordance with the theory that highways should be paid for by the users. But highways benefit far more people than the actual operators of motor vehicles. Highways are essential for national defense and the transportation of civilian goods and persons. Our entire economy would collapse if all highways were closed. Therefore it is impossible to apportion accurately even the benefits of motor vehicle fuel and license taxes.

It would seem that "special assessments" for paving and sewer installations on some kind of a front footage basis would be a valid application of the benefits principle. But all persons on the street must purchase paving and sewer installations if those who do purchase receive full benefits. Local governments frequently pay part of the cost of paving and sewer systems from general revenue on the theory that all citizens benefit to some extent. Therefore, the benefits principle has a very limited application in our taxing systems.

Costs-Incurred

Those supporting this principle assert that persons, property, and taxable institutions should be taxed according to the costs incurred by government in providing the good or service. It is not the same as the benefits principle but it is closely allied to it. But the difficulty of apportioning costs is as great as in applying the benefits principle. Therefore the costs-incurred principle has a very limited application in the design of our total tax structure.

Undeserved Income

According to this theory a tax difference should be made not only in relation to the quantity of income received or wealth accumulated but also in relation to how it was acquired. This type of income or wealth is sometimes called "unearned." It would include such items as excessive profits, excessive inheritances, windfall income acquired by luck, excessive capital gains, and similar items. This theory is also limited in its application because most income is not of this character. Furthermore it would seem that most unearned income and wealth could be adequately taxed under the ability-to-pay principle—except possibly excessive inheritances.

Justice and Equity

This is a very nebulous principle. What justice or equity may be depends largely upon the relative emphasis given to the various principles of taxation stated above or to some combination of these principles or other principles. But "The various principles of taxation are of widely different origin; some are based upon ethical postulates intimately linked with the basic assumptions of a democratic social order; others are derived from economic analysis; still others are administrative rules-of-thumb." [8] Therefore concepts of justice and equity in taxation are largely subjective. Despite this fact, the United States Supreme Court has provided some definition of justice or equity with respect to classification for taxation purposes. In an opinion rendered in 1890 the court declared that "clear and hostile discriminations against particular persons or classes" is a violation of the Fourteenth Amendment to the Constitution of the United States.[9] The court in later opinions has held that any classification which has a reasonable relation to the permitted ends of government is constitutional.[10] While these opinions of the Supreme Court have provided some guidance in formulating tax policy, they must of necessity leave to subjective determination most of the major decisions which must be made in constructing tax systems.

Progressive versus Regressive Taxes. An important lay concept of justice in taxation is based on whether a tax is progressive, proportional, or regressive in its effect. Technically, a tax is progressive when the tax rate increases as the income or property base increases, proportional when the tax rate remains constant whether the base increases or decreases, and regressive when the tax rate decreases as the base increases. These concepts are closely related to the ability-to-pay principle.

The Federal personal income tax is an excellent illustration of a progressive tax. The property tax is a proportional tax. There is probably no tax levied in the United States which is technically a regressive tax. Nevertheless, there is frequent public complaint that certain taxes are regressive. The property tax is a good example. A person with an income of $5,000 may own and live in a $15,000 house and pay property taxes totalling $300. Another person living in the same community

---

[8] Eugene S. Lawler and Proctor Thomson, "Taxation and Educational Finance," Chapter 4 of *Problems and Issues in Public School Finance,* R. L. Johns and E. L. Morphet, editors (New York: Bureau of Publications, Teachers College, Columbia University, 1952), p. 113.

[9] Bell's Gap Railroad Company v. Pennsylvania, 134 U.S. 232 (1890).

[10] Heisler v. Thomas Callienz Company, 260 U.S. 245 (1922).

may own a house of the same value and pay the same taxes but his income is $10,000 per year. In this illustration property taxes amount to six per cent of the income of the person earning $5,000 per year and three per cent of the income of the person earning $10,000 per year. Therefore it is asserted that the property tax is regressive in final effect despite the fact that the rates are the same for both persons. This is true to some extent of practically all taxes except income taxes with progressive rates. Furthermore an income tax is more or less progressive depending upon the steepness of rate graduations.

Judging the Justice of Taxes. If it is argued that no tax is just unless it is a progressive tax both in rate structure and ultimate effect, then the tax systems of all levels of government in order to be just would have to consist almost entirely of income taxes with progressive rate structures. This would hardly be feasible as long as we retain our structure of Federal, state, and local governments. Therefore in order to appraise the justice and equity of taxes it is necessary to appraise the tax structure as a whole including all levels of government. If the Federal government continues to collect more than 70 per cent of all taxes collected and it obtains more than 80 per cent of its tax revenues from steeply graduated income taxes, then the state and local governments might levy some taxes which are less progressive in effect without destroying the over-all equity of our total taxing system.

Using the lay concept of progressive and regressive taxes rather than the technical one, the Federal taxing system is the most progressive, state systems next, and the taxing systems of local governments the least progressive. This is important because it affects the tax collecting capabilities of different levels of government. The public generally associates progressive taxes with just taxation and regressive taxes with unjust taxation. Since political consensus must be secured in order to levy a tax, it is easier to secure that consensus at the levels of government which the public thinks levies the most just taxes.

Neutrality

The supporters of this principle argue that a tax should be as neutral in its effects as possible. That is, as far as possible it should leave persons, firms, and corporations in the same relative economic position after the tax is collected as before. Neither should taxes reallocate resources nor should they affect choices or actions made by the taxpayer. This point of view places major emphasis on "tax consequences." This principle has many supporters, especially in the business community, and like all other principles of taxation has some validity. But the determination of the consequences of a tax is as difficult as of the benefits received. Actually tax consequences cannot be determined without at the same time determining benefits.[11]

Adequacy of Yield

Governments must be financially supported or the nation and the economy must fall. The necessary government services cannot be provided without the necessary financing. Deficit financing may be used as a temporary, emergency measure but the costs of government must be paid for eventually or inflation will wreck the monetary system and the economy. State and local governments particularly must "balance their budgets" because of statutory and constitutional provisions. Continued deficits of the Federal government which cause inflation actually utilize inflation as a hidden tax. No reputable authority on taxation advocates inflation as a tax measure because it cannot be defended by any valid principle of taxation or economics. Therefore taxes for any level of government including grants-in-aid should be adequate to provide for essential services.

Stability of Yield

Tax yields should be sufficiently stable and adequate to provide for needed services without the use of deficit financing. The stability principle is the opposite of the flexibility principle discussed below because it implies that there should be an element of stability in the tax yield regardless of fluctuations in the economy. For example, when bonds are issued, the yield of the taxes pledged should be sufficiently stable to pay the necessary debt service on the bonds or they cannot be sold. Stability of revenues is particularly important to local governments which have limited flexibility in obtaining revenues. The property tax has been justified because of its stability in yield. But during a major depression extending over a period of years, even the property tax will lose its stability. Stability in revenues of local governments can be appraised only after giving consideration to the policies of the states with respect to providing grants-in-aid to local governments in periods of declining revenue.

Flexibility of Yield

The needs for government services change and the dollar amounts needed are modified as the purchasing power of the dollar changes.

---

[11] The principles listed above might be described as principles for the allocation of the tax burden, and those which follow might be listed as principles or criteria for the selection and administration of taxes.

Therefore the revenue system should be sufficiently flexible to provide for the government services needed during prosperous times and in times of population increases. In other words when the costs of government rise rapidly, the revenues should rise rapidly. Income taxes and also sales taxes have considerable flexibility because they increase or decrease with the economy and population growth. Flexibility can be provided either by taxes whose yield automatically increases proportionately to a rise in the economy, or by rates which can be changed in times of need. Even property taxes can be given a degree of flexibility by providing for flexible rates. But income taxes and sales taxes are inherently more flexible than the property tax because the yield of these taxes with no increase in rate automatically rises in prosperous times, and still the rates of these taxes can be changed if additional flexibility is needed.

Non-rigidity

This is usually called the adaptability principle. It is similar to flexibility but not the same. A tax system is rigid if constitutional or other restrictions on the rates or types of taxes levied prevent local governments from adapting their revenue systems to local government needs. State governments, by constitutional provisions, have sometimes prevented legislatures from developing appropriate revenue systems. Rigidity is usually built into a constitution to protect special interests. Constitutional and statutory restrictions have greatly handicapped many boards of education in their efforts to provide local school revenues. State imposed exemptions from the property tax also greatly handicap local governments in some states as explained later in this chapter.

Economy of Administration

The cost of collecting the tax should not be excessive. It may cost two per cent of the yield to collect one type of tax and ten per cent to collect another tax. Other things being equal, the tax which can be collected at a low cost is better than one which is expensive to collect.

When different levels of government are using the same tax, economy of administration can be improved by providing for a coordinated administration of the tax. For example county, city, and school governments within the same county can reduce the cost of administering the property tax by using the same assessing and collecting authorities.

Directness and Certainty

Hidden taxes should be avoided in so far as possible and the possibility of tax evasion should be minimized. Hidden taxes may cause irresponsible decisions to be made on the government services provided. Persons and corporations should know that they are subject to the tax and what the amount will be. This is necessary for planning both on the part of individuals and corporations. Tax evasion is unfair to persons who pay their just obligations because it gives an unfair advantage to their competitors who avoid payment of taxes. From an ethical standpoint, government can be justified in spending a rather high percentage of delinquent or evaded taxes in order to require compliance with the tax laws because of the protection given to those who comply.

Ease of Payment

The payment of taxes should be made as convenient to the taxpayer as possible. For example, the retail sales tax is very convenient for the taxpayer to pay. The ease of payment of the income tax was greatly improved when payroll deductions were instituted. The property tax seems inconvenient to pay because in most states the entire year's tax is due at one time. However since the property tax cannot be collected by payroll deductions, its ease of payment cannot be greatly improved by providing for monthly or quarterly payments. The ease of payment of a tax greatly affects public acceptance or resistance to a tax. This is important for public school financing since so high a percentage of the cost of the public schools is provided from the property tax.

The Eclectic Principle

This is sometimes called the "social expediency" theory of taxation. It combines all principles, theories, and criteria of taxation. There is no one satisfactory "field theory" of taxation. It is the eclectic theory which is usually used by tax levying bodies. The eclectic principle is applied by tax levying bodies with varying degrees of equity. Some tax levying bodies interpret this principle as "pluck the goose which squawks the least." Others levy taxes after giving due consideration to recognized principles and criteria of just and equitable taxation. Most tax levying bodies probably operate somewhere between these two extremes.

Economic efficiency is sometimes referred to as a principle or criterion of taxation. It is related to the eclectic principle.

Other things being the same, a high rate of economic progress is more advantageous and desirable than a low rate; in a materialistic society economic welfare is directly proportional to the size of the national income which the community produces and consumes. The relation between taxation and economic progress is shrouded in conjecture; nevertheless there exists an optimum tax structure under given social and economic conditions which offers maximum assistance or minimum handicaps to the attainment of a high level of national product. The major policy problem in designing such a structure is the choice between generous exemptions and low rates on small incomes in order not to discourage the incentive to work, and low rates on the higher brackets in order not to discourage the incentive to invest. . . . Unfortunately the optimum amount of tax and the optimum rate structure from the point of view of economic efficiency may not correspond to the social consensus on tax equity.[12]

SOME PROBLEMS AND ISSUES

The provision of school revenues inevitably involves educational officials in many of the problems and issues of public finance. Some of those problems and issues of particular significance to public school financing are presented in the remainder of this chapter.

To What Extent Do School and Other Revenues Conform to Acceptable Criteria of Taxation?

As stated above, the principles and criteria of taxation can be used best to appraise the taxing system as a whole rather than a particular tax. However local school revenues are derived principally from the property tax, state revenues principally from sales and gross receipts taxes, and Federal revenues principally from income taxes. Therefore a rough appraisal of these three major types of taxes will be presented.

The Property Tax. The property tax does not conform very well to the ability-to-pay principle. At best it is a proportional tax and at worst a regressive tax. It has but little relationship to the benefit and cost-incurred principles. There is little or no application of the undeserved-income theory to the property tax. Legally it is a just tax but it is not considered to be as equitable as progressive types of taxes. The property tax is not a neutral tax. For example, if property taxes are lowered substantially, property values increase and if raised substan-

---

[12] Eugene S. Lawler and Proctor Thomson, "Taxation and Educational Finance, Chapter 4 of *Problems and Issues In Public School Finance*, eds., R. L. Johns and E. L. Morphet (New York, Bureau of Publications, Teachers College, 1952), p. 117.

tially property values decrease. When property changes hands however the effect is neutral as long as the rates remain constant.

The property tax produces a substantial amount of revenue, it is a relatively stable tax, the yield is relatively inflexible, it is rigid because of constitutional and statutory restrictions, it is expensive to administer, it is direct and certain, and it is relatively inconvenient to pay.

Sales and Gross Receipts Taxes. Sales taxes have only a limited relationship to ability to pay. At best they are proportional and at worst regressive in their effect. Sales taxes are probably less regressive than the property tax, especially when levied on luxury articles. Sales taxes generally have but little relationship to benefits received or costs incurred except for motor vehicle fuel taxes. They do not directly tax undeserved income. Legally sales taxes are just, but progressive types of taxes are usually considered to be more equitable. The sales tax is a relatively neutral tax if the rates are uniform and if it is levied over an entire trading area.

Sales taxes yield large sums of money. The yield is not stable because it varies directly with changes in spending but it is flexible because the yield fluctuates with spending. Sales taxes are non-rigid at the state level because of few or no constitutional restrictions. They are relatively economical to administer, they are direct and certain (especially retail sales taxes as contrasted with gross receipts taxes), and they are easy to pay.

Income Taxes. Income taxes are closely related to the ability-to-pay principle. Graduated income taxes are progressive in effect and flat rate income taxes, proportional. They probably have more relationship to benefits received and costs incurred than most other types of taxes. Undeserved income can be taxed by income taxes more readily than by any other type of tax. Income taxes are legally just and are generally considered to be the most equitable of all taxes. Progressive income taxes are not neutral in effect especially if the rates are high.

Income taxes yield large sums of money, but yields are not stable because they fluctuate with the economy. On the other hand, income taxes are flexible because they do fluctuate with the economy. Federal income taxes are non-rigid because of the absence of constitutional restrictions on rates. Income taxes are economical to administer, direct and certain, and convenient to pay.

Voter Evaluation of Different Taxes. The average voter does not have a comprehensive understanding of the canons of taxation. His evaluation of taxes is probably based largely on intuitive judgment tempered by practical experience in paying taxes. But it is only by the acceptance of voters that taxes can be levied. Therefore the feelings of voters toward different types of taxes are important for school financing and for public financing in general. Judging from the evidence presented in Table 5–8, the general public prefers personal income taxes, corporation income taxes, sales and gross receipts taxes, and property taxes in that order when large sums of tax revenue must be raised. Therefore it appears that the principal tax used to support the public schools is the least popular of the major types of taxes. Does this explain in part some of the difficulties that have been experienced in public school financing?

Do the Types of Taxes Levied Bear a Rational Relationship to the Sources of the National Income?

It would seem that the types of taxes levied for school support should bear some relationship to the sources of income. All taxes are paid from income which is currently received, already received, or will be received. Therefore the sources or methods of acquiring income are of significance. Trends in the sources of the national income are presented in Table 5–11. It is significant that income derived from compensation of employees increased from 58.2 per cent of the total national income in 1929 to 71.0 per cent in 1957. Corporate profits composed about the same percentage of the total national income in 1957 as in 1929 although there was a slight decline. All other sources declined substantially in terms of per cent of total income. The per cent of income derived from farms, rental income of persons, and net interest was just about half as much in 1957 as in 1929.

TABLE 5–11

SOURCES OF THE NATIONAL INCOME 1929 AND 1957

(in millions)

	1929		1957	
Source	Amount	Per Cent	Amount	Per Cent
Compensation of Employees	$51,085	58.2	$254,400	71.0
Corporate Profits	10,100	11.5	39,600	11.1
Unincorporated Business and				
Professional Income	8,791	10.0	28,700	8.0
Farm Income	5,968	6.8	12,100	3.4
Rental Income of Persons	5,425	6.2	10,400	2.9
Net Interest	6,445	7.3	12,800	3.6
TOTAL	$87,414	100.0	$358,000	100.0

Source: U. S. Department of Commerce, *Survey of Current Business.*

Table 5–11 shows for 1957 that 90.1 per cent of the national income was derived from compensation of employees, corporate profits, and unincorporated business and professional income. These types of income can be taxed more readily by income and sales taxes than by any other type of tax. Income from farms, rental income from persons, and net interest composed the other 9.9 per cent of the total national income in 1957. It is practicable to tax these types of income by property taxes but there are those who argue that even income from these sources can be more equitably taxed by the use of other types of taxes.

The data presented in Table 5–8 show that 81.0 per cent of the tax revenue of all governments is obtained from income and sales and gross receipts taxes, 13.3 per cent from property taxes, and 5.7 per cent from other sources. Therefore the taxing system as a whole bears a fairly logical relationship to the sources of the income of the people.

But 53 per cent of all public school revenues was obtained from the property tax in 1957. It is evident from Table 5–11 that the property tax did not bear a rational relationship to the sources of national income in 1957, and the trend is for it to be even less rational. Is it possible that the intuitive resistance of the general public to the property tax is in part due to its lack of correspondence to the sources of income of the people? Would an increase in the proportion of school revenues received from state and Federal sources tend to make the public school revenue system more rational?

How Does Shifting the Incidence of Taxes Affect Public School Financing?

The incidence of a tax is its final resting place. The person or firm paying a tax may pass it on through pricing a product or service. The amount of tax shifting that goes on and the extent to which different taxes are shifted are matters of conjecture and controversy. But there is a type of tax shifting of major importance to school financing that can be readily identified. For want of a better term, it will be called the "geographical incidence" of a tax.

Shifting the Geographical Incidence of a Tax. Certain states collect from 20 to 30 per cent of all of their state taxes from severance taxes on mineral products such as petroleum, and taxes on tourists. These types of taxes are practically all paid by non-residents of the states receiving the benefits from those taxes. Therefore, such states are able to shift a substantial portion of their tax burden to the people of other states. These states in effect are levying "Federal taxes" for their own benefit.

In 1955, six states having 30 per cent of the children five to seventeen years of age paid 61 per cent of the corporation taxes. Twenty-one other states containing 29 per cent of the children paid 8 per cent of the corporation taxes. Of course the amount of corporation taxes paid is not a perfect measure of the concentration of manufacturing and business enterprises but it does give some indication of it. Manufacturing states can pass on much of the incidence of both their state and local taxes by pricing their products. This is especially true where substantial monopolies exist such as in the automobile industry, petroleum products, and tourist areas. States that are predominantly agricultural can shift to other states but little of their taxes because of absence of monopoly.

The ability to shift taxes to other states varies widely among the states. In general, the states of greatest wealth shift more of their taxes to other states than the states of least wealth. It is the opposite of equalization because the wealthy states through their taxing systems are actually receiving more tax benefits from the states of least wealth than the reverse. Would general Federal aid to the public schools tend to correct this inequity?

Effect of Tax Shifting on Local Effort. Much has been said about local effort to support schools. The people are quite properly encouraged to make great local effort. Relative local effort to support schools is usually determined by dividing the amount of local school taxes collected by the equalized assessed valuation of the district. But in many school districts, half or more of the assessed valuation is composed of railroad assessments and other public utilities. In such cases, half or more than half of local school taxes is paid by non-residents of the district. The residents of such districts have effectively shifted to the people of other districts the incidence of most of their school taxes. The same thing is true in districts that contain concentrations of business and manufacturing corporations. Does state aid to school districts tend to correct this inequitable advantage?

How Can the Effects of Taxes on Different Segments of the Economy Be Minimized?

This issue might be phrased, "should the effects of taxes on different segments of the economy be minimized?" There are some who argue that the taxing system should be used to stimulate or to retard the production and consumption of different types of economic goods, and others who argue that taxes should be for revenue only. This is one of the oldest controversies in American history. For example, differences over the tariff constituted an important factor in the formation of political parties.

Effect of Taxes on Consumer Choices. Of more significance in recent history is the effect of a particular tax on the production and consumption of a particular good. For example, some states have levied high taxes on oleomargarine in order to give butter a more favorable competitive position in the market. Special taxes have been levied on furs and jewelry on the assumption that these products were not necessities and therefore the persons consuming them could at least afford to pay the special taxes. Still other special taxes have been levied on such products as alcoholic beverages and tobacco perhaps in part to reduce the consumption of these products. It has also been alleged that the Federal government has favored certain industries by granting them unusually generous depletion allowances for the computation of income tax liability.

It is difficult to assess the effects of these different types of taxes. If a heavy tax is levied on a product for which the consumer has a ready substitute, he will increase his consumption of the substitute and reduce his consumption of the heavily taxed product. For example, butter can be substituted for oleomargarine and coal for natural gas. This type of taxation seems to interfere with the normal operation of competition in the free enterprise, private economy. There are many who believe that this is an improper use of taxation.

Special taxes levied on such products as alcoholic beverages and tobacco seem to have but little effect on their consumption and production because there are no ready substitutes for them. The special tax merely becomes a part of the price of the product. However, if the tax is extremely heavy, the temptation to avoid the tax becomes great. The illicit production and sale of alcoholic beverages is a good example of this effect.

Ways of Minimizing Tax Effects. It would seem to be the best policy for those who seek school revenue to avoid becoming involved in the issue of using the taxing system to favor or to discriminate against different segments of the economy. Certainly public school relations are improved if school officials follow the policy of neutrality in taxation when seeking school revenues. Income taxes, general sales taxes, and property taxes are more neutral in their effects on different segments of the economy than many types of special taxes.

The unfavorable effects of income taxes on the economy of the various political subdivisions of the United States would be minimized if the Federal government levied all income taxes (especially corporation income taxes) and shared a part of those taxes with the states. This would also reduce "tax competition" among the states to secure industry which is discussed under the following topic. The unfavorable effects of sales taxes on business would be minimized if within a state all sales taxes other than Federal were levied by the state and shared in part with local governments. These desired ends must be weighed of course against the undesired end of increasing the dependency of each level of government on a higher level. The property tax is discussed more fully in Chapter 8.

How Do Tax Exemptions Affect School Financing?

Tax exemptions substantially affect the amount of both state and local revenue available for the support of the public schools as well as of other governmental services. The four principal types of tax exemptions are: (1) exemptions granted for the purpose of adjusting tax liability to taxpaying ability, (2) exemptions granted in order to attract business and industry, (3) exemptions granted to give preference to certain groups in the population, (4) exemptions granted to governmental, religious, charitable, educational, and other non-profit institutions.

Income Tax Exemptions. The exemption for dependents allowed by the Federal income tax law is a good example of exemptions granted for the purpose of adjusting tax liability to taxpaying ability. This type of exemption is actually a part of the progressive rate structure, therefore it is fully justified if one accepts the progressive income tax as an equitable tax.

Sales Tax Exemptions. The general sales tax laws enacted by the states vary considerably in the number of items exempted. Some states exempt a great many items, usually on the theory that those items are the "necessities." However what may be necessities for one person may not be for another. The purpose back of this type of exemption may be laudible if it is to adjust tax liability to ability to pay. However it is an awkward method of accomplishing this purpose. It could be accomplished much more readily in states having state income tax laws by modifying the exemption granted for dependents or the amount of income which must be earned before tax liability begins. Exemptions from the sales tax also contribute to tax avoidance. It is much easier for a retail establishment to conceal its tax liability when it sells both exempted and non-exempted articles than if all of its sales are subject to the tax. The more items exempted from a sales tax, the higher must be the tax in order to yield a given amount of revenue. The preference is for low rates and a minimum of exemptions rather than high rates and generous exemptions.

Exemptions to Attract Industry. Exemptions granted to attract industry have been particularly troublesome. Conditions for maximizing the economic progress of the nation are unfavorably affected when artificial barriers or subsidies cause industry to locate at points other than those most favorable for efficient production and distribution.

Despite this fact, states and political subdivisions within states frequently give industry (especially new industry) favored tax treatment. States can do this simply by not having a state corporation income tax or by having very low rates. States have also exempted new industries from property taxes for a given number of years.

The competition for new industries is particularly keen among the political subdivisions of a state. Tax favors are granted to such industries usually by exemption from property taxes entirely for a given number of years or by assessing the properties of industries at a very low rate. Some units of local government have given permanent property tax exemption to certain industries by actually constructing industrial plants and leasing them to private corporations. Ownership of the property is retained by the local government and it is completely tax exempt. These types of property tax exemption seriously affect school financing in many school districts. The new industries often bring many additional pupils, but the tax base remains the same. Thus the school district has less taxable wealth per pupil for school support after the new industry is brought to the district than before. Experts on public finance and economics are generally agreed that if an industry cannot operate in a particular locality without a tax subsidy, the community is better off without it. Furthermore it is also believed that the influence of tax exemptions or low tax rates on the location of industries is greatly exaggerated in public thinking. Such factors as access to necessary raw materials; access to markets; and availability of labor, water, power and community services are far more powerful factors affecting the location of industry than tax exemptions or low tax rates.

Exemptions for Favored Groups. Sometimes tax exemptions are given to certain groups, such as veterans and homeowners. Exemptions given to veterans seem to have little or no justification. Certainly this practice cannot be defended by any generally accepted principle or theory of taxation. Its purpose seems to be to establish a group with special privileges, but that practice finds no defense in the principles of American democracy.

The practice of granting exemptions to homeowners emerged in the depression 'thirties. It had great emotional appeal during those times because many financially distressed persons were in danger of losing their homes. While homestead exemption has a laudible purpose, it is difficult to defend from the standpoint of fiscal policy. One state provided an exemption from all property taxes of $5,000 of the assessed valuation of homesteads. Many districts in that state assessed property at only twenty-five per cent of true value or less. Therefore a home had to have a true value of more than $20,000 in order for the owner to pay any property taxes. This resulted in a major reduction in the assessed valuation of many districts and seriously handicapped local school financing. This exemption might have been considered similar to the exemption for dependents provided for in income tax laws but it did not apply to rented houses and apartments. Therefore its ultimate effect was to increase the rents paid by many people who were unable financially to buy homes. If property were assessed uniformly at the same per cent of true value throughout a state, if the exemption applied to rented domiciles as well as owner occupied premises, and if the exemptions were not so great as to exempt entirely large numbers of people from the property tax, homestead exemption might be defended as having some relation to the ability to pay principle. But these conditions do not obtain in any state. In any event, if levying taxes in accordance with ability to pay is the end sought in planning the tax structure, the income tax is by far the best means by which to attain it.

Exemption of Non-Profit Institutions. It is practically universal practice in the United States to exempt from property taxes all property used for governmental, religious, charitable, educational, and philanthropic purposes. Some have questioned the wisdom of this policy but it has become so firmly established that it is not likely to be changed. However, a prominent Protestant leader has recently attracted attention by stating flatly that, if present exemption policies continue, property will be so concentrated in the hands of religious and other nonprofit institutions by the end of the century that for the economic good of all it will have to be taken from them by "revolutionary" means. Since schools receive almost all of their local taxes from the property tax, any policy that exempts property substantially affects school financing.

Property taxes are levied principally on the enterprises at which people work and on the homes in which they live. If the principal enterprises at which people work in a school district are exempted from taxes then the tax base is greatly reduced. Tax-exempt enterprises bring pupils to a community the same as other enterprises and this adds not only to school costs but the costs of other local governments. The Federal government has ameliorated this situation in communities receiving a heavy impact from Federal activities by providing special grants-in-aid for local governments in such communities. The Federal government also provides payments in lieu of taxes where large areas of national forests are located.

But there are many tax exempt institutions other than Federal properties. For example, state institutions and private colleges may be concentrated at certain locations. States which use the equalization method of apportioning state school funds have taken a step toward solving this problem in so far as school financing is concerned.

What criteria can be used to determine which tax exemptions should be abolished, and which, if any, can be justified?

Can State and Local Taxes Be Exported to the Federal Government?

Theoretically, all state and local taxes can be deducted from income before determining Federal income tax liability. Therefore, personal Federal income tax liability may be reduced by approximately 25 per cent of the state and local taxes paid by persons, and Federal corporation income tax liability by approximately 50 per cent of the state and local taxes paid by corporations. Therefore, the greater the amount of state and local taxes paid by the taxpayers of a state, the greater the reduction in Federal income taxes.

It is not practicable, however, for the residents of a state to deduct all state and local taxes before computing Federal income tax liability. Only those taxes can be deducted for which records are kept. It is very difficult to keep records of state and local sales and excise taxes paid. But records of state income taxes paid are readily available. Therefore, it is much easier to deduct state income taxes from income before computing Federal income tax liability than it is to deduct sales and excise taxes paid. Consequently, it is easier to export a part of a state income tax to the Federal government than a part of sales or excise taxes. Should this fact have any bearing on the decisions of a state with respect to the types of taxes it levies?

Some states levying state income taxes permit taxpayers to deduct Federal income taxes paid before computing state income tax liability. This greatly reduces the yield of the state income tax. Other states do not permit the deduction of Federal income taxes. Which is the better practice?

SELECTED REFERENCES

Anderson, William H., *Taxation and the American Economy.* Englewood Cliffs, N.J.: Prentice-Hall, Inc., 1951. Chapters 1, 2, 3, and 4.

Bureau of the Census, *Statistical Abstract of the United States.* Washington, D.C.: U.S. Government Printing Office. Annual volumes.

———, *Summary of Governmental Finances.* Washington, D.C.: U.S. Government Printing Office. Annual volumes.

Burke, Arvid J., *Financing Public Schools in the United States,* rev. ed. New York: Harper and Brothers, Publishers, 1957. Chapters 4, 5, and 9.

Galbraith, John Kenneth, *The Affluent Society.* Boston: Houghton Mifflin Co., 1958.

Johns, R. L., and E. L. Morphet, editors, *Problems and Issues in Public School Finance.* New York: Bureau of Publications, Teachers College, Columbia University, 1952. Chapter 4.

Maxwell, James A., *Fiscal Policy.* New York: Henry Holt and Company, 1955. Chapter 8.

National Education Association, *Advanced Estimates of Public Elementary and Secondary Schools.* Washington, D.C.: The Association. Annual publications.

National Industrial Conference Board, *The Economic Almanac.* New York: The Board. Annual volumes.

Shultz, William J., and C. Lowell Harriss, *American Public Finance,* 6th ed. Englewood Cliffs, N.J.: Prentice-Hall, Inc., 1954. Chapters 1, 2, 3, 7, 8, 9, and 10.

U.S. Department of Commerce, "Survey of Current Business." Washington, D.C.: U.S. Government Printing Office. Monthly issues and annual summaries.

U.S. Office of Education, *Biennial Survey of Education in the United States —Statistics of State School Systems.* Washington, D.C.: U.S. Government Printing Office. Biennial volumes.

CHAPTER SIX

Inequalities in Opportunity, Ability, and Effort

Equality of educational opportunity is an objective to which practically every citizen has subscribed in theory for many years. But practical application is a different matter. Vigorous and emotionally charged arguments occur periodically in every community, in every state legislature, and in Congress concerning the desirability of taking additional steps to help implement the theory.

Equality of educational opportunity for all does not mean that every person should have the same program of education. Instead it means that every person should have the *opportunity* for the kind and quality of education that will best meet his needs as an individual and as a member of the society in which he lives. There should be no controversy about implementing an idea such as this in a democracy, yet there frequently is. Why?

Undoubtedly this problem needs to be faced more realistically in the future by every American citizen than has been the case in the past. Many studies have shown, and numerous authorities have commented on, the tragedy inherent in wasted human and natural resources. There can be no doubt that the nation has been handicapped by this neglect, or that it can be afforded any longer. The maximum development of the human resources of the nation should therefore be the primary concern of every citizen. Of almost equal concern, however, should be the development of human resources throughout the world, because potential leaders and contributors exist in every nation and among all types and kinds of people. Adequacy of opportunity is as important as equality, and the two must go hand in hand if civilization is to flourish.

INEQUALITIES IN OPPORTUNITY

As pointed out in Chapter 1, the idea of equality of educational opportunity has not even been accepted in theory in certain parts of the world. The idea of adequacy seems utterly impossible of attainment under present conditions in many of the underdeveloped areas. However, considerable progress has been made. It is evident that a larger proportion of the people of the world now realize the importance of at least some education for all than was the case even a generation ago. More and more people want more from life than mere survival. Many have begun to learn that human beings need not be handicapped by diseases that can be prevented or cured, by malnutrition, by poverty, or by exploitation. They have begun to recognize that education constitutes the key that may make available to them, their children, and their neighbors, some of the better things life has to offer. However, the task of educating people so that each may make a constructive contribution to society is becoming vastly bigger and much more complex than it was just a few years ago. There is more to learn, greater need for learning, and greater cost as well.

In a recent publication, the Commission on School District Reorganization, after summarizing some of the encouraging developments in the educational program in this country, called attention to a number of conditions that call for sober thought, careful planning, and determined action:

1. The schools are not well manned. Good teachers and good administrators are hard to get and even harder to keep.
2. Many classrooms are out of date, unsafe, unsightly, grossly overcrowded, and improperly equipped.
3. Two out of three secondary schools are too small to do a good job. About one-third of them enroll fewer than 100 children.
4. Too many secondary school programs are meager and barren rather than rich and comprehensive.
5. About 4 out of every 10 young people who enroll in high school drop out before graduation.
6. The talents of mentally superior children are not being fully developed.
7. The tax base for school support is outmoded and in serious need of revision.
8. There is not enough money available to the schools to do what needs to be done.
9. Many school districts are too small to use financial resources effectively or to provide high-quality educational programs.[1]

---

[1] American Association of School Administrators, Commission on School District Reorganization, *School District Organization* (Washington, D.C.: The Association, 1958), pp. 12–13.

Inequalities Among States

Some of the differences in equality of educational opportunity among the states in the United States are difficult to demonstrate convincingly. Perhaps that is one reason many people do not seem to be seriously disturbed about the existing situation.

One difficulty comes from the fact that state averages do not show the extremes. The educational opportunities in the best school systems in some of the handicapped states may compare reasonably well with those in the best systems in other states. In some of the poorest, however, the deficiencies are striking but are not obvious to those who note only the averages. State statistics do not create a visual and dramatic impression of the hundreds or thousands of people who are and will continue to be seriously handicapped during their lifetime because of inadequate educational opportunities provided in the communities in which they happen to be born.

Another difficulty arises from the fact that most of the objective evidence available deals with factors that, while important, provide only indirect evidence of variations in educational opportunity. For example, the percentage of the adults who have completed four or more years of college work does not give any indication of the number who might have completed college had better educational opportunities been provided in the public schools.

The income of the citizens of a state is related to their potential expenditure for education and other governmental services. The expenditures for education on a statewide basis seem to have a rather direct bearing on the quality of education provided.[2]

Table 6–1 lists, in the first column, the five states ranking highest in personal income payments per pupil enrolled in the public schools and the five states ranking lowest on this basis, in 1956–57.[3] The range in personal income payments per pupil enrolled was from $3,754 in Mississippi to $17,432 in Delaware. Each of the five states ranking highest on this measure showed personal income payments per pupil in excess of $14,000, and each of the five ranking lowest showed personal income payments below $5,500. The measurement and extent of variations in ability are considered later in this chapter.

The second column in the table gives the median school years completed in each of these states by persons 25 years of age or older in

---

[2] See discussion of "Educational Quality and Financial Support" in Chapter I.

[3] Data from *Rankings of the States* (Washington, D.C.: National Education Association, Research Division, December, 1957), Table 20, p. 12. Subsequent reports should be consulted for current data on these and other states.

1950. The number of years completed in each of the five top states in income was from a year to more than two years greater than in any of the five lowest states. While these differences may not seem to be very great, even a difference of one year out of twelve possible years of schooling, as an average for all citizens in the state, may constitute a significant difference in educational opportunity. It is interesting to note that the top states in income were not the top states in median years of school completed. The medians for Wyoming, Washington, Nevada, California, and Utah ranged from 11.1 to 12.0 years of schooling.

TABLE 6–1

SOME INDICATIONS OF DIFFERENCES IN EDUCATIONAL OPPORTUNITY
AMONG STATES

Based on Persons 25 Years of Age and Older in 1950

States (based on personal income payments per pupil) *	Median School Years Completed	% with Less than 5 Years Schooling	% with 4 or More Years of High School	% with 4 or More Years of College	% of Selective Service Registrants Disqualified 1956
FIVE HIGHEST:					
Delaware	9.8	9.7	33.8	7.3	10.1
New York	9.6	9.5	34.7	7.4	15.9
New Jersey	9.3	9.2	33.9	6.8	13.4
Connecticut	9.8	8.9	36.2	7.0	10.7
Illinois	9.3	7.8	34.0	5.9	16.2
FIVE LOWEST:					
North Carolina	7.9	21.1	20.5	5.0	39.5
Alabama	7.9	22.6	21.0	3.6	40.7
Arkansas	8.3	19.8	21.2	3.1	32.8
South Carolina	7.6	27.4	18.6	5.0	41.2
Mississippi	8.1	25.2	21.5	3.8	44.9

* Enrolled in public schools in 1956–57.
Source: Rankings of the States, National Education Association, Research Division (Washington, D.C.: The Association, December, 1957), col. 1, from Table 20; col. 2, from Table 1; col. 3, from Table 2; col. 4, from Table 3; col. 5, from Table 4; and col. 6, from Table 5.

Complicating factors in any such analysis involving older people arise from (1) the mobility of the population within the United States, (2) the immigration and the places where large proportions of immigrants have settled, and (3) the composition of the population in each of the states as between rural and urban, white and Negro, and so on. These data, therefore, cannot show the educational situation in the state at present, nor do they give an exact picture of the situation a few years ago. However, even without further refinement, they indicate some important differences among states.

The percentage of the population 25 years or older which had completed less than five years of schooling was at least twice as great in the poorest group of states as in the most wealthy group. However, again not all the extremes are found in these states. The lowest percentage with less than five years of schooling was found in Iowa, Oregon, Utah, Idaho, Washington, and Nebraska, in each of which it was under 5 per cent. The highest percentage was in Louisiana, only slightly higher than in South Carolina.

The per cent of the older population which has completed high school provides a fairly good indication of the extent to which people were being prepared to meet some of the modern demands in the way of education. Many industries today expect most of their new employees to be at least high school graduates. The percentage of high school graduates in the five top states, based on income, ranged from 33.8 in Delaware to 36.2 in Connecticut. In the five lowest states the percentage ranged from 18.6 in South Carolina to 21.5 in Mississippi. In every case the proportion of the population completing high school in the five top states was twelve or more per cent greater than in any of the lowest states. However, again in this instance the states with the highest percentage of the population having completed high school were Utah, California, and Nevada, in each of which the percentage was over 44.

The percentage of the population that had four or more years of college should provide some indication of the number with sufficient education to have considerable leadership potential according to modern standards. In every instance the top states had a higher percentage who had completed college than the others. Again there were other states, not in this group, having a higher percentage. For example in California and Colorado more than eight per cent had completed four or more years of college.

The per cent of Selective Service registrants disqualified by the mental test, including those who also failed the physical test, in 1956, should be of concern. In every case the percentage in the poorer states was at least twice and in some cases three times as great as in the five top states. The lowest percentages, however, were in Montana, Idaho, Iowa, Minnesota, Washington, North Dakota, and Oregon, in each of which the average was below four per cent.

Considerable additional information indicating differences in educational opportunity could readily be presented. While no single set of figures based on one factor should be considered significant, the fact remains that all data tend to show that there have been significant differences in educational opportunity among many of the states in the past and that these differences are still sufficient to warrant considerable concern.

With the great mobility of population at the present time it is evident that inadequate educational opportunities in a state not only handicap the people in that state but may constitute a problem for other states to which some of these people migrate.[4] It seems evident that under modern conditions the nation cannot long afford the losses resulting from the substantial numbers in the total population who have inadequate educational opportunity.

Inequalities within States

As would be expected, the evidence indicates that the range in educational opportunities available within most states is considerably greater than the differences in the averages for the various states. There are a few states in which apparently most children have fairly adequate educational opportunities. State standards have been established and additional funds provided in an attempt to assure that certain minimum requirements will be met. Generally speaking, the states with the greatest extremes seem to be small-district states in which only limited state support is provided to supplement local funds. In some of the small, poverty-stricken districts in such states the evidence indicates clearly that educational opportunities are hopelessly inadequate.

The fact that children attending Negro schools in many of the Southern states have had limited educational opportunities has been widely publicized. However, the opportunities for many other children, regardless of race, in certain districts in many states, have been nearly as inadequate.

To illustrate the extremes found in some states, the educational program in two types of communities will briefly be described.

Schools in District A. This district has ample resources. The people believe in education and are willing to make whatever effort is necessary to provide a good program. The school board consists of leading citizens who are anxious to develop a program that will meet the needs of the community. A competent man has been selected as superintendent and educational leader. He realizes the importance of good planning; of working with the board, the staff, and the community; of studying problems and proceeding promptly to work out solutions before the problems become serious. On his recommendation, the board has adopted an excellent statement of policies. Diligent effort is made to find the most competent teachers available, from within or

---

[4] See *Rankings of the States*, Table 17, for information on net total migration by states from April 1, 1950, to July 1, 1957.

without the state. In-service programs are provided to assist all staff members in improving their work.

Modern school buildings have been provided, and so planned that the work of teachers and pupils is facilitated. Adequate instructional materials and supplies are made available. There is an extensive audio-visual program. The guidance program is designed to diagnose difficulties and determine problems. Special programs are provided for physically handicapped, mentally retarded, and for gifted students. Kindergartens have been in operation for a number of years. There is an extensive program of adult education for those who have completed high school grades and are interested in keeping in touch with developments or improving their learning in certain areas.

A comprehensive high school is maintained. In this school, students who have the ability and interest can get thorough preparation for continuing in college. Other students, with less ability or motivation, can have basic preparation in English, science, mathematics, and social sciences designed to meet their needs but may also take commercial work, a variety of vocational courses, or considerable work in art and music. The community is recognized as having one of the best educational programs in the state. A large percentage of the students go to college (many attend the community college in the area) and do well in college work. Those who go into industry are well prepared and most of them are obviously on their way to becoming good citizens.

Schools in District B. This is a small district that has limited resources and in which the people have done little thinking about education. The people seem to pay little attention to the caliber of members selected for the board, and the board has given little evidence that it is especially interested in education. The district does not have sufficient resources from state and local sources to provide a satisfactory program of education. However, it has the ability to provide funds beyond those customarily made available. The state has made only limited flat grant funds available to this and other communities.

The district is small and has three elementary schools, two of which have only two teachers each. The buildings are in deplorable condition. The superintendent is also principal of the high school but seems to have been selected because he made a good impression on some of the board members, rather than because he had been well prepared or had demonstrated competence in leadership. The high school program is largely college preparatory, with a little vocational agriculture. Many of the elementary teachers have had only two years of college training, and most of the high school teachers have had no graduate work. Many remain in the community for only two or three years because salaries are low and morale at times has seemed to be even lower. There is no counselling program, there are no kindergartens, there are no special provisions for physically handicapped or for exceptional children of other types, and there is no program of adult education except the limited provisions made in connection with vocational agriculture. In fact, there is not much of an educational program, judged by any defensible standard. Very few students go to college; many drop out for one reason or another before completing high school. The schools seem to be as dull and uninspiring as the community itself.

Need for Improvement. It would be fortunate if the situation described in District B did not exist in any state. Unfortunately, it does. In fact, school systems nearly as divergent as these two can be found in at least half the states. The question might well be raised as to who is responsible. Does the blame for obviously inadequate educational opportunities attach to the people in the communities in which they are found, or to the people in the entire state? However, mere criticism and fault-finding will not solve problems such as these. The most encouraging developments are found in those states where people in the state and in the various communities have cooperated in a serious attempt to develop more adequate and more equitable opportunities for all children.

Inequalities within Local School Systems

There is greater equality of educational opportunity within most local school systems than within states. In each local school system a uniform tax base is available for support of the educational program and all schools are operated under the general policies established by the board. As indicated above, the educational opportunities provided may be reasonably adequate or quite inadequate, but inequities generally are not particularly obvious.

However, there are variations in most school systems. Some of these are due to home factors; that is, children from homes in certain areas are much more handicapped than those from other types of homes. Others are due to school factors; that is, some children may have to attend in antiquated buildings or in schools where, for one reason or another, the less competent principals, teachers, and noncertificated personnel have been assigned. In too many systems, many of these are schools in underprivileged areas. However, some school systems have developed policies that result in reasonably good working conditions for all personnel in every part of the community and in a competent staff for every school.

It seems apparent that school systems have an obligation to provide greater equality of educational opportunity than is now available in many districts. Some have made remarkable progress, while others seem content to continue with traditional procedures, regardless of whether they are equitable or meet the need.

REASONS FOR INEQUALITIES IN OPPORTUNITY

Why are serious inequalities in educational opportunity permitted to exist year after year in a country in which a majority of the people seem dedicated to the idea of equality? Some of the background factors involved are: (1) Many people do not realize the extent or implications of inequalities; (2) most people have become accustomed to and are relatively complacent about the existing situation; (3) substantial numbers of people seem to be more concerned about their own personal problems and the rising costs of living and of government than about variations in educational opportunity that do not seem to affect them immediately; and (4) until comparatively recent years the procedures to solve certain aspects of the problem had not been satisfactorily developed or understood.

Some of the important reasons for differences in educational opportunity, in addition to the general background factors listed above, are briefly discussed on the following pages.

Inadequate School Districts

Many studies have shown that both small schools and small school districts usually provide a less satisfactory educational program, are less efficient, and are more expensive to operate than larger schools and districts.

In spite of the fact that the number of school districts in the United States is less than one-half of the number found a quarter of a century ago, there were still more than 45,000 in the nation in 1958–59. Most districts were organized about early settlements. Although roads and means of transportation have been greatly improved, many of these districts have continued without change. Nine states have more than 2,000 districts each. On the other hand, many or practically all districts have been reorganized in a number of states in the past few years.

Studies have shown that it is not possible to operate an effective and economical school system in a district having fewer than 1,200 to 1,500 pupils in grades one through twelve. Where districts below this size are maintained, costs tend to be high and some of the services needed cannot be provided except, perhaps, through an intermediate district. A district having 5,000 to 10,000 pupils has some potential advantages over one with a smaller number.

However, there are nearly 37,000 districts that have fewer than 10 teachers or 300 pupils. Nearly 40,000 have fewer than 1,500 pupils. Thus approximately 90 per cent of the operating local school districts in the United States are still inadequate in size to meet the needs of a modern program of education. School costs are unnecessarily high in areas where these districts are located, or many children are deprived of satisfactory educational opportunities, or both may occur. This situation tends to result in unjustifiable inequalities in educational opportunity and in undesirable complexities in programs designed by the state for financing schools.

Any state with a large number of small districts has marked differences in local ability to finance schools. In such states the development of an equitable finance plan that will make possible adequate schools in all districts is difficult if not impossible. However, as districts are reorganized and larger districts evolve, the problem becomes simpler and a satisfactory solution is more practicable. In fact, in several states, district reorganization would probably contribute more to the equalization of financial support and of educational opportunity than has been accomplished thus far through improvements in the state provisions for financial support.

Financial Effect of Reorganization. If five districts with wide differences in ability were to combine into one larger district, the extremes in that particular area would be eliminated. If similar reorganizations were to be effected throughout the state, the range in local ability would be greatly reduced—probably to 10 or 15 to 1. The effect of reorganization on differences in local ability is illustrated in Chart III.

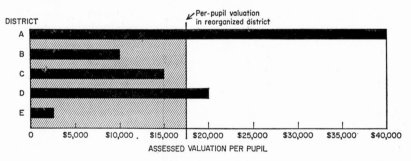

CHART III. *Effect of District Reorganization on Equalization of Local Ability to Finance Schools.*

Let us assume that District A, with 2,500 pupils, had $40,000 per pupil in actual valuation of property; District B, with 1,500 pupils, had $8,500; District C, with 3,500 pupils, had $15,000; District D, with 500 pupils, had $20,000; and District E, with 2,000 pupils, had $2,000. If a new district comprising these five original districts were organized, the range of 20 to 1 in ability would be eliminated and the valuation per pupil in the new district would be a little under $18,000.

Conclusions. A recent study of school district reorganization resulted in five significant conclusions, most of which have implications for school finance:

1. The program of state and local support for the schools has a close relation to school district reorganization. It is apparent, therefore, that the school finance program should be geared to the need for achieving the proper school district organizational structure.
2. State support systems, by certain features they contain, often help the poorly organized, inefficient school districts to the extent that an undesirable structure of local school district organization frequently is perpetuated.
3. The effects of a finance factor on redistricting depend almost entirely on the specific nature of the legislation pertaining to this factor and its relation to the total program of state and local support for the schools.
4. In many cases, the amount of money appropriated for a given feature of the school finance program is at least as important as the particular feature itself.
5. Although the findings are not entirely conclusive, there seems to be a relation between the per cent which state funds are of the total school cost and the progress made in school district reorganization, the progress tending to be greatest in the states in which the state aid is the highest.[4]

Small Schools

Few, if any, small school districts can be justified under any conditions, but some small schools are necessary and will probably be necessary for some years to come, because they are isolated. Generally speaking, small schools tend to be both expensive and unsatisfactory. Relatively small high schools are even more expensive and probably less satisfactory than small elementary schools. The small number of pupils per teacher usually found in such schools is the greatest single factor contributing to high costs, but the limited range of offerings possible tends to limit the adequacy of educational opportunity. Where small isolated schools are necessary, higher costs can be justified, but not otherwise. The per capita costs of education tend to be higher and the quality of the educational program less satisfactory in elementary schools having fewer than 175 to 200 pupils and in high schools having fewer than 250 to 300 pupils, than in larger schools.[5]

[4] Leslie L. Chisholm, *School District Reorganization,* Studies in Educational Administration (Chicago: Midwest Administration Center, University of Chicago, 1957), p. 6.

[5] Leslie L. Chisholm and M. L. Cushman, Chapter III in *Problems and Issues in Public School Finance,* R. L. Johns and E. L. Morphet, eds. (New York: Bureau of Publications, Teachers College, Columbia University, 1952), p. 103.

Some states have attempted to penalize all small schools, regardless of isolation, by providing the same amount of funds per pupil for small schools as for larger schools. On the other hand, other states have provided additional funds for all small schools, regardless of isolation, thus making it relatively easy for them to operate at the expense of the taxpayers of the entire state. Neither practice can be defended. Most states that have improved their finance plans during recent years have provided necessary additional funds for all small isolated schools but have required the local taxpayers to care for the extra expense of maintaining small non-isolated schools.

Differences in Ability and Effort

Some of the variations in ability and effort to support schools among and within the states, together with certain implications for financial support, are discussed later in this chapter. The important point to note here is that marked differences in ability are found within states and that they are maximized by faulty district structure. In small-district states it is impossible to provide reasonable equity for taxpayers, and consequently to assure anything closely approaching equality of educational opportunity for the children. Small and expensive schools are often perpetuated by the district structure and as long as such schools exist in non-isolated areas, the problem of equitable and adequate financial support is not likely to be solved.

The inadequate district structure is likewise one of the important reasons for differences in effort. In districts with extremely limited wealth, adequate educational opportunities cannot be provided unless the taxpayers make an excessive effort, and probably not even then, unless the state develops an unusually generous plan of financial support. Even if substantial state support were provided, marked variations in effort would be necessary if anything approaching equality of educational opportunity were to be assured.

The fact must be recognized, however, that even if all districts were properly organized and a sound state plan of financial support developed, there would still be variations in effort due to differences in interest of the people in their schools and in their attitude about financial support needed for a satisfactory program of education.

Unsound Legal Provisions

Legal provisions, in addition to those relating to district organization, frequently result in inequalities in educational opportunity. The intent of the laws probably is not to create or perpetuate inequalities, but the net effect of certain types of laws is definitely to do so. Many illustrations could be given, but a few should suffice to bring out some of the implications. For example, when the laws of a state provide that all or practically all state funds for schools are to be apportioned on a flat-grant basis, there are certain to be inequalities in educational opportunity, even in states in which all districts have been reorganized and are reasonably adequate. Laws limiting local levies that may be made for school support also tend to result in marked inequities. If property on which school taxes may be levied is assessed at a low percentage of actual valuation, adequate financial support may be impossible, especially when local levies are limited by law. When assessment ratios vary in different parts of a state, the inequities are likely to be particularly serious because the assessing practice will result in much lower support in proportion to ability in some parts of the state than in others.

Even laws providing for the election of county superintendents or of the state superintendent by popular vote may indirectly have considerable bearing on both adequacy and quality of educational opportunity in the various states. In fact, any legal provisions that result directly or indirectly in handicapping or preventing the citizens of properly organized districts from establishing and operating the kind and quality of schools needed to permit and assist every child to develop to his maximum potential have some effect on both the quality and the adequacy of educational opportunity.

VARIATIONS IN ABILITY

As previously noted, the citizens of a nation or of a community must have ability above that required to provide the bare necessities of life before they can afford a program of education beyond that incidental to the learning required to survive. The United States is considered one of the richest, perhaps even the richest, large nation in the world today. This wealth is due to a great extent to the development of the nation's human resources and to the ability to utilize most advantageously the natural resources for the benefit of the people. However, there are many indications that wealth, both among and within states, varies considerably. These variations have definite implications for the educational opportunities that can be provided in the future and, to some extent, may reflect and perhaps even result partly from the attention devoted to the development of human resources in the past.

Variations Among States

Before there can be any conclusion as to the variations in ability which exist and the extent of those variations, there must be agreement on the measures to be used. The statement has sometimes been made that every state could provide reasonably adequate educational opportunities for its children if its citizens were willing to make the effort. If that statement is correct, attention should be directed to means of encouraging the people in certain states to make greater effort to support their schools. If it is not correct, there are many other implications.

Measures of State ability. During pioneer days there might have been some justification for the contention that the best measure of the ability of the people in each state was the per capita wealth represented by the value of property in the state. However, as pointed out in an earlier chapter, property as a source of income of the people in the various states has rapidly declined in relative importance.

The measure most commonly used during recent years to determine ability is income of the people. Reliable data are now provided periodically by government agencies regarding annual income payments of the citizens of each state.[6]

When the income of the people of each state is known, it is possible to determine the per capita income, the income per child of school age (the ages 5 to 17, inclusive, are usually used) or the income per pupil in average daily attendance. The number of school age children in the total population varies considerably from state to state. For example, in 1957 the number of children ages 5 to 17 ranged from 367 per 1,000 adults aged 21 to 64 in New York, to 656 in New Mexico and 869 in Hawaii. Obviously, the per capita income would not be a good measure of ability of the various states to support schools, even though it might constitute a measure of ability to support certain other governmental services.

The income per child of school age (ages 5 to 17) is probably a better measure than the income per pupil in average daily attendance in the public schools, because all children in these age groups should be educated in some kind of school. If average daily attendance in the public schools were used, the children not attending any school, as well as those in private schools, would be ignored.

Questions have also been raised about use of the income of the people as a measure of ability. Some contend that since people

---

[6] Consult publications of the U.S. Department of Commerce, Office of Business Economics, for information on personal income by states for the various fiscal years.

throughout the United States must pay Federal income tax, the amount paid by individuals should be deducted from the income of the people in each state to determine the ability to support schools. There seems to be considerable merit to this contention. However, still another point has been advanced for consideration. Before the people of a state can support other than incidental education they must have an income above that required to provide the bare necessities of living. A good case can be made for subtracting, also, some figure representing the actual cost of living. Perhaps a reasonable and conservative figure would be the $600 exemption taken into consideration in calculating the Federal income tax.

Variations in State Ability. If the income payments per child of school age are used as a measure, it is apparent that there is considerable difference in the ability of the states to support schools. The difference between states high in ability and those low in ability seems to have declined somewhat over a period of years, but, nevertheless, it is a real difference. The most wealthy state, on the basis of this measure, seems to have between three and four times the ability to support schools than the least wealthy state has. This would mean, then, that for school support, the state with least wealth would have to make between three and four times the tax effort of the state with greatest wealth, if its schools were to be supported on a comparable basis.

Some have contended that while there are differences among the states, these differences are declining quite rapidly, and that within a few years they will be insignificant. The Committee for the White House Conference on Education assembled some information relating to this point for the years 1940 to 1953. The 1940 income per child of school age was adjusted in terms of 1953 dollars, to make the figures comparable. The facts assembled show that the *percentage of increase* during this 15-year period was between two and three times as great in the least wealthy states as in the most wealthy. These percentages are given in Table 6–2 for the five most wealthy and the five least wealthy states. However, this table also gives the actual dollar increase in income per child during this period. It is important to note that the dollar increase in income per child of school age was significantly greater in each of the most wealthy states than in any of the least wealthy. Thus not only were there more dollars available per school age child in the most wealthy states at the beginning of this period than in the least wealthy, but there was also a greater increase in dollars per child in the more wealthy than in the least wealthy. Do these facts support the idea that differences in ability will disappear in a short time, or do they indicate that the differences in income were actually more significant in 1953 than in 1940?

TABLE 6–2

INCREASE IN INCOME PER CHILD 5 TO 17 YEARS OF AGE, FROM 1940 TO 1953,
ADJUSTED TO 1953 DOLLARS

Five states with highest income			Five states with lowest income		
	Increase in Per Cent	Increase in Dollars		Increase in Per Cent	Increase in Dollars
Connecticut	43	$3,334	Kentucky	110	$2,432
Nevada	30	2,546	Alabama	116	2,096
New Jersey	43	3,262	South Carolina ...	111	2,055
Delaware	34	2,857	Arkansas	101	1,776
New York	34	2,950	Mississippi	119	1,644

Sources: Data from Report to the President (Washington, D.C.: Committee for the White House Conference on Education, 1956), Table 7, p. 67. Highest and lowest states are from Rankings of the States (Washington, D.C.: National Education Association, Research Division, December, 1957), Table 2.

Before drawing final conclusions, it should be helpful to take a look at the personal income available per school age child after deduction of Federal personal income taxes paid and basic expenditures for food, clothing, and shelter. The pertinent information for the five most able and the five least able states in 1955 is given in Table 6–3. It shows that net personal income per school age child was above $7,000 that year in each of the five most able states, and below $2,000 in all but

TABLE 6–3

PERSONAL INCOME PER SCHOOL AGE CHILD AFTER PAYMENT OF
FEDERAL PERSONAL INCOME TAXES AND DEDUCTION OF
BASIC EXPENDITURES FOR FOOD, CLOTHING AND
SHELTER, 1955

States	Estimates of School Age Population 5–17 Years	Net Personal Income after Deductions	Net Personal Income per School Age Child
FIVE HIGHEST:			
Connecticut	455,000	$ 3,553,000,000	$7,809
Nevada	50,000	373,000,000	7,460
New Jersey	1,074,000	7,873,000,000	7,331
Delaware	82,000	596,000,000	7,268
New York	3,160,000	22,738,000,000	7,196
FIVE LOWEST:			
Kentucky	784,000	$ 1,657,000,000	$2,114
Alabama	852,000	1,559,000,000	1,830
South Carolina	653,000	1,046,000,000	1,602
Arkansas	490,000	729,000,000	1,488
Mississippi	607,000	652,000,000	1,074

Source: Adapted from R. L. Johns, Ability and Effort of the States to Support the Public Schools. (Washington, D.C.: National Education Association, Legislative Commission, 1958), Table I, pp. 4 and 5.

one of the least able states. Furthermore, the ability of the most able state seems to be more than seven times as great as the ability of the least able.

It is apparent that there are marked differences among the states in ability to support schools. Insofar as financial support relates to educational opportunity, the most able states seem to have a decided advantage over the least able. The most able states could finance a reasonably adequate quality of education with much lower tax effort than the least able. This seems to mean that, if schools are to be financed entirely from state and local funds, the people in the least able states will either have to make much greater tax effort to support their schools than the people in the most able, or the children in the states with lowest ability will inevitably have to attend schools that are poorly financed. The implications of this information need careful consideration by everyone who is interested in adequacy as well as equality of educational opportunity.

Variations within States

There are greater variations in ability to support schools among the districts in most states than among the states. This would be expected, because the statewide figures are, in reality, averages based on data for individual districts that may vary widely in ability. Thus the range in ability within each state is lost sight of when the statewide figures are considered.

Another conclusion, supported by many studies, is that the range in ability among the districts in states in which districts have been reorganized is much less than in those that have many small districts. This is inevitably the case because, as previously pointed out, when several small districts with wide differences in wealth per pupil are combined to form one district, differences within the area are eliminated.

Before more exact conclusions regarding variations in ability can be reached, however, it is necessary to consider the possibility of agreement on procedures to be used in determining or measuring local ability.

Measures of Local Ability

A much better case can be made for using property as a measure, or in connection with a measure, of local ability to support schools than as a measure of state ability. As pointed out elsewhere in this book, in most states practically all of the local revenue for school support is derived from property taxes.

Equalized Assessments. If all property were assessed at full value, or even at a uniform percentage of full value, in every state the problem of determining local ability would be much simpler than it is under present conditions. However, the assessment practices in most states are far from uniform.[7] Studies in assessment ratios within states show a range of from less than 2 to 1 up to 8 or more to 1. The Colorado Legislative Council estimated the range in ratio of assessed to full valuation in various counties of the state ten years ago to have been approximately from 10 per cent to 85 per cent. A 1958 study by the Council showed that the ratio then ranged from 14.1 per cent in one county to 40.6 per cent in another.[8] The state average was found to be approximately 28 per cent.

Such variations result in many complications, not only in attempts to determine local ability, but in devising an equitable and satisfactory plan for financing schools, as pointed out in Chapter 10.

One difficulty arises from the wide differences of opinion over defining the full value of property. It cannot be the cost because in many areas purchase price or original cost of construction represents only a small percentage of present value. It cannot be sales price in all instances, because there may be sales among relatives, or under enforced conditions, where price is far below that for which other similar properties are being sold. This is not the place to discuss the technicalities involved in determining the actual value of property or deciding on the most appropriate assessment procedures, as the details of these matters are appropriately covered in books on public administration and manuals dealing with the subject.[9] Suffice it to say here that a reasonable objective is to determine fair market value under conditions where both willing sellers and willing buyers are involved.

The objective of all states is undoubtedly to attain uniform assessment procedures, but few states have made satisfactory progress in that direction thus far. Existing assessed valuations in most states, therefore, do not provide a satisfactory basis either for determining local ability or for prescribing local uniform effort.

The Assessment Ratio Plan. During the past few years several states, acting on the assumption that equalized values will not be attained in the near future, have established an assessment or sales-ratio plan for

---

[7] National Education Association, Committee on Tax Education and School Finance, *Equalization of Property Assessments* (Washington, D.C.: The Association, 1959).

[8] *Sales Ratio Study*, Part One, Report to the Colorado General Assembly, Research Publication No. 27 (Denver: Colorado Legislative Council, 1958), pp. 16–17.

[9] See, for example, William J. Shultz and C. Lowell Harriss, *American Public Finance*, 6th ed. (Englewood Cliffs, N.J.: Prentice-Hall, Inc., 1954), pp. 404ff.

determining local ability and as a basis for prescribing uniform local effort.

A recent study by Shenkel analyzed the assessment ratio studies made thus far in most states.[10] He pointed out that several states have developed what seem to be reasonably valid ratios. However, of the approximately 16 states attempting to use this plan, only a few have used it as effectively as desirable. If ability is to be determined by using this procedure, there must be careful sales-ratio studies based on a representative and adequate sample from every county of the state. Sample appraisals are also needed to supplement or adjust the data. Even then there may be difficulties, because some states prescribe different assessment procedures and rates for different kinds of property, and these requirements may result in inequities. Assessment of personal property represents a particularly difficult problem because sales-ratio studies usually do not produce valid data on personal property.

When the sales-ratio studies are properly made, the following procedures can be used not only in determining local ability but also in prescribing uniform local effort to finance the schools:

1. The state agency responsible for making the study should certify to the state board of education, at a designated time each year, the ratio for each county.

2. The state board of education should use this ratio as a basis for determining the funds that would be available if a uniform tax levy were made in each county on property assessed at state average or at a designated percentage of full valuation.

3. The ratio can be applied to the school districts in the county by finding the percentage the assessed valuation of the district represents of the county total valuation and multiplying this by the amount of funds that would be available if equalized valuation and a uniform levy were used.

4. Each district would have the option of making whatever levy is necessary to provide the funds required from a uniform effort, either by levying a higher or lower millage than the rate based on uniform assessment practice, or by accepting an adjusted assessment.

The Index of Taxpaying Ability. Some states, either because assessed valuations have not been equalized or because a satisfactory plan for determining assessment ratios has not been established, have developed and are using an index of local taxpaying ability. This index is designed to measure the relative ability of local school systems to pay property

[10] William Monroe Shenkel, *An Evaluation of Assessment Ratio Studies in Selected States* (Unpublished doctoral dissertation, University of Washington, 1957).

taxes and to determine the amount of funds each district should provide toward the cost of a foundation program.[11] In developing this index, states have used data based on appropriate economic factors (such as sales tax receipts, amount of passenger automobile license tax paid, value of farm products, and number of gainfully employed workers) to predict the relative proportion of the true value of property in each county or to predict the local taxpaying ability, which, when applied to the yield from a prescribed levy on the total assessed valuation of property in the state, will give the proportion of the total that should be provided by each county. The proportion for each district can be determined, as explained earlier. This procedure should probably be used only when no other adequate measure is available.

Variations in Local Ability

Recent studies in a number of states have indicated a range in ability in county-unit and other large-district states of from about 9 to 1 up to about 20 or 25 to 1. Thus, even when all districts are reasonably adequate in size, it is apparent that there is a considerable difference among the districts in ability to finance an educational program. If no state aid were provided in these states, the least wealthy districts would have to make from 9 to 25 times the effort as the most wealthy to finance a program providing reasonable equality of educational opportunity. The situation in the small-district states is, of course, much more serious, with the range exceeding 1,000 to 1 in one or two states.[12] This information, inadequate as it is in a number of states, points definitely to the following conclusions:

1. In no state can the least wealthy districts finance a reasonably satisfactory program of education from local funds without an unreasonable tax effort, and in many districts the effort required would be prohibitive.

2. The differences in wealth in small-district states are so great that no program of state aid is likely to solve all the problems until further reorganization occurs.

---

[11] Herbert A. Meyer and R. L. Johns, A Method for Calculating an Economic Index of the Taxpaying Ability of Local School Units (Gainesville: University of Florida, 1954; Mimeographed). See also: R. L. Johns and Herbert A. Meyer, "Distributing State Funds: How to Estimate Taxpaying Ability of Local School Units," The Nation's Schools, Vol. 49 (February, 1952), pp. 49–50; and The Index of Local Economic Ability in State School Finance Programs (Washington, D.C.: National Education Association, 1953).

[12] R. L. Johns, "Local Ability to Support Schools," in Problems and Issues in Public School Finance, R. L. Johns and E. L. Morphet, editors (New York: Bureau of Publications, Teachers College, Columbia University, 1952), Chapter VII.

3. Until further progress is made in many states in improving district organization and provisions for financing schools, inequalities in educational opportunity are certain to continue. Substantial numbers of pupils in many states cannot expect to have even reasonably adequate educational opportunities under present conditions.

VARIATIONS IN EFFORT

There are several possible measures of effort. The expenditures may constitute a very rough indication of effort, but do not actually measure it, because a state or district with high ability may with very little effort be able to expend a larger amount of funds than a less wealthy state or district could expend with much higher effort. Expenditures therefore give some indication of the investment in education but not of the effort being made to support the schools. Variations in expenditures are discussed in Chapter IV.

Local tax levies are likewise often considered an indication of the effort made by a school district. However, a relatively high levy in a district having a low ratio between assessed and actual valuation may constitute less effort than a much lower levy in a district with a relatively high assessment ratio.

Measures of State Effort

One of the most commonly used measures of the effort made by a state to support its public schools is the percentage of the income of the people represented by gross expenditures for schools. However, total reported expenditures include money from sale of bonds to be retired over a period of years. For that reason, the current expense, which is not likely to fluctuate from year to year, except as actual costs increase or the purchasing power of the dollar declines, is much better than total expenditure. Even more defensible is the revenue received by all districts in the state for school purposes during the year.

As indicated in the discussion of ability, the desirability of using the total net income of the people has frequently been questioned. Because these questions have some validity, the best measure to use may be the percentage the revenue available for support of schools constitutes of the net personal income of the people, minus the Federal personal income tax payments and basic expenditures for food, clothing, and shelter represented by the $600 exemption per person recognized and allowed in Federal income tax returns.

The local effort to support schools may be measured by dividing the local tax revenue of a school district by its equalized assessed valuation. Its assessed valuation can be equalized by either the sales-ratio or economic index technique. The quotient can be expressed as the equalized tax levy.

Effort of the States

In some states a much larger percentage of pupils attending elementary and secondary schools is enrolled in public schools than in others. The range is from about 70 per cent in Rhode Island to more than 98 per cent in a few states. This factor may have some bearing on the percentage of the net income of the people, less deductions as explained above, that is represented by revenues available to the public schools. This percentage ranges from about 3 per cent in the states making the least effort to 9 to 10 per cent in the states making the greatest effort. When revenues available for all elementary and secondary schools, including both public and private schools, are considered, the range is about 3.8 per cent to a little more than 10 per cent.

Table 6–4, which follows, gives for each of the six states with highest effort and for each of the six states with lowest effort in 1955, the percentage of the total school enrollment attending public schools, the percentage state and local public school revenue is of the net personal income less deductions, and the percentage the revenue for both public and private schools constitutes of the net personal income less deductions. It will be noted that some of the least wealthy states were making the highest effort and some of the most wealthy states were making the lowest effort. However, there are a number of exceptions, resulting from the attitude of the people in the various states toward schools and their support, or toward taxes and other aspects of government. As would be expected, the least wealthy states generally make a greater effort toward support of their elementary and secondary schools than the most wealthy.

As will be explained in later chapters, the percentage of revenues for support of the public schools derived from property taxes varies considerably from state to state. This variation in dependence on property taxes for school support may explain in part the range from the equivalent of 2.5 mills on full valuation of property in North Carolina to 13.5 mills in Oregon, as reported by James.[13]

---

[13] Henry Thomas James, *Toward a Unified Concept of State School Finance Systems* (Unpublished Ph.D. dissertation, University of Chicago, 1958).

TABLE 6–4

EFFORT OF THE STATES TO SUPPORT EDUCATION, 1955

	Per Cent of Total School Enrollment Attending Public Schools	Per Cent State and Local Public School Revenue Is of Net Personal Income *	Per Cent Revenue for Public and Private Schools Is of Net Personal Income *
SIX HIGHEST STATES IN EFFORT TO SUPPORT PUBLIC AND PRIVATE SCHOOLS:			
Mississippi	97.01	10.0	10.3
Louisiana	83.66	8.6	10.3
New Mexico	88.29	8.5	9.5
Iowa	88.92	8.3	9.3
South Dakota	89.81	8.2	9.2
Wyoming	95.86	8.9	9.2
SIX LOWEST STATES IN EFFORT TO SUPPORT PUBLIC AND PRIVATE SCHOOLS:			
Maine	84.39	4.1	4.8
Virginia	95.39	4.6	4.8
Massachusetts	76.95	3.6	4.7
Missouri	85.71	3.9	4.5
Connecticut	82.01	3.1	3.8
Nevada	94.53	3.5	3.8

* After Federal personal income tax and a $600 allowance for basic expenditures for food, clothing and shelter are deducted.

Source: Adapted from R. L. Johns, *Ability and Effort of the States to Support the Public Schools*. Legislative Commission (Washington, D.C.: National Education Association, 1958), Table IV, pp. 8 and 9.

Local Effort

Relative levels of local effort are difficult if not impossible to determine in many states due to variations in assessment practices. A high millage levy in a district may or may not represent high effort, depending on the assessment ratio in the district as compared to that in other parts of the state.

The range in levies for support of schools is influenced in a number of states by requirements established in connection with the foundation program. In some states, laws limiting the levy for school purposes may mean that the people in a number of districts are levying far less than they would be willing to make available if the laws permitted.

In spite of these factors it is not uncommon to find some districts in a state that are levying from two to six or eight times as much as other districts. Undoubtedly in many cases this represents a major difference in effort. In addition, certain districts, in states where the laws permit, may be receiving funds from other local tax sources, such as payroll or sales taxes. In many cases, however, these other sources of revenue are used in lieu of levies that would otherwise be made on property, and consequently property levies are less in some of those districts than in other districts that are not permitted or do not choose to use non-property taxes as a source of revenue.

A recent study in Kentucky attempted to determine the comparative local effort to support education among Kentucky counties. The percentage ratio was found between the total local tax receipts for public school purposes, including capital outlay and debt service, and the net income of the people. This percentage was found to range from .87 in one county to 2.98 in another. In other words, the reported range in effort among Kentucky counties was more than 3 to 1.[14] This study also reported that the assessed valuation ranged from 13.4 per cent of full value in one county to 45 per cent in another county. The true tax rate, based on assessment at full value, was found to range from 20¢ on each $100 of valuation in one county to 72¢ in another.

The range in actual local effort, although greatly influenced by the attitude of the people toward their schools, is materially affected by two other factors: (1) the amount of state aid provided and the plan used for apportioning the state funds, and (2) the number of small districts in the state. Other things being equal, the greatest range in local effort is likely to be found in states that have a large proportion of small districts of widely varying wealth and that provide only limited funds from state sources to assist in financing the schools.

SOME PROBLEMS AND ISSUES

The discussion in this chapter has directed attention to the wide range in educational opportunity, ability, and effort among the states and within many of the states. If this situation is to be improved there are many problems and issues which need to be faced and resolved, in addition to those discussed in the chapter. Among the more important that need careful consideration are the following:

Is Equality of Educational Opportunity Practicable and Desirable?

Theoretically equality of educational opportunity throughout the nation could be attained by abolishing all state and local taxes for

---

[14] "Where Does Your Community Stand in Financing of Schools?" *School Service Report*, University of Kentucky, Bureau of School Service, Vol. 1, No. 2 (February, 1959), pp. 17–21.

schools and using only Federal funds for school support. Likewise, equality within states could be attained by abolishing all local school support and using only state funds. Would either procedure be desirable? Would it actually assure equality?

If local support is to be utilized, equality of opportunity could theoretically be attained in either one of two ways: (1) limiting the effort and perhaps taking away and distributing to other districts some of the state funds now received by districts that have sufficient revenue to provide a reasonably adequate program, or (2) providing sufficient funds from state sources to enable all districts to have available as large an amount per pupil as is presently available in the more favored districts.

The adoption of any of the above procedures would seem to imply that equivalent funds per pupil or per classroom would mean equivalent opportunity. Obviously that would not be the case except under ideal conditions. Differences in communities and in backgrounds of the pupils, as well as in organization and administration of schools, would undoubtedly mean there would still be some differences in educational opportunity. However, the extremes that are now found might be reduced and the situation improved if more nearly equivalent funds were available.

The possibility of limiting local effort or taking funds from some of the more wealthy districts might appeal to a number of people who are concerned about high taxes and who believe that too much money is now being devoted to education. However, even those who tend toward this point of view would undoubtedly do some further thinking if they lived in some of the more favored districts. People usually like to think about building toward what is desirable instead of limiting opportunities that are now available in the more favored districts and states. However, there may be some improperly organized districts that are receiving indefensible subsidies, and perhaps these should not be continued. Under what, if any, conditions should revenues now available to certain school systems be taken away from those systems? Should all proceeds from taxes (property or non-property) collected in or from a community ever be used exclusively to support schools of that community?

If greater equality of opportunity were to be sought by providing additional funds for states and districts that make a reasonable effort but still have inadequate resources, a considerable sum of money would be required to bring them up to the level of support available to more favored districts in more wealthy states. Perhaps a more realistic objective would be to attempt to provide sufficient revenues to bring all districts up to some level of expenditure that would, if properly administered, assure reasonably adequate educational opportunity. This would not mean that equality of educational opportunity would be attained, because there would always be districts in which the people would be willing and would want to make a higher effort than required to assure a reasonably attainable level of support. Generally the more wealthy districts, with reasonable additional local effort, could have far more local funds available per pupil or per classroom unit than the least wealthy. Thus, unless some limitation were imposed on these districts, there would continue to be some inequality in resources available, and consequently some inequality in educational opportunity. These considerations seem to imply that equality of educational opportunity will probably never be attained in all states and communities. Is this conclusion justified? What steps can and should be taken to improve the situation even though equality may never be fully attainable?

Does a Closer Approach to Equality Mean Greater Centralization?

Soon after Australia began to be settled the people became concerned about educational services for the children, and especially about those in sparsely settled areas. A decision had to be made concerning the importance of educational opportunity for children of all settlers and as to the means for providing the opportunities considered desirable. The people in each community might have been expected to provide the kind of schools they were able to support. However, some of the leaders determined that such a procedure would not be equitable or desirable. They decided that the resources of each state should be used to support the educational program in the state, regardless of where the children lived. Consequently, the schools in Australia (as in many other countries) have developed largely on the basis of state rather than local support. An attempt is made to use the funds of the state to guarantee as good opportunities in the outlying areas as are provided in more wealthy areas.[15] This has been found to have both advantages and disadvantages. To a considerable extent control as well as support has been centralized. Some of the leaders apparently believe that there has been too much centralization and that the time has come to provide for some decentralization both in control and support.

In most states in America (with the possible exception of Hawaii)

---

[15] See *Education in Australia*, Bulletin No. 20 (Sydney, Australia: Commonwealth Office of Education, 1958).

almost the opposite development has occurred. People in most communities have developed their own schools. Some of these have been good; others have been far from satisfactory, either because the resources were so limited or because the insight of the people has not been adequate for the task. In most states, more than half of the financial support for schools is still provided by the community. In one-fourth, however, the state has assumed the major responsibility.

In this country, local responsibility, control, and local financial support generally have been emphasized. Many Americans have been pleased with, and in fact even proud of, this development. However, children in many communities and in a number of states have been seriously handicapped. The more favored communities usually have been in a financial position to pay much higher salaries for teachers, and consequently to attract many of the better teachers from less favored communities. The situation is gradually being improved in most states, but there are still marked inequalities and inequities. Many citizens vigorously resist proposals not only for Federal support for schools but also for increased state support, because they insist that the receipt of additional funds from other than district sources will mean increased Federal or state control of the schools. Authorities in school finance, however, insist that additional state and Federal support is needed, that it does not necessarily mean increased control or centralization, and that local responsibility and initiative can be strengthened if the plan of financial support is properly developed.

Should the various states in the United States have provided for substantial state support for schools from the beginning? If this had occurred, would most of the problems resulting from inequality of educational opportunity have been solved? What are the advantages and disadvantages of the Australian plan for financial support? Of the plans that have developed in this country? What steps can be taken to benefit from the advantages and minimize the disadvantages in the plan used in this country?

Should Expenditures for All Aspects of Local Government Be Considered in Determining Local Ability to Support Schools?

Major attention thus far has been centered on the problem of devising objective and equitable measures of local ability to support schools, without reference to other local governmental needs or problems. The theory has been that if valid measures of ability can be devised it will be possible to assure reasonable equity for all taxpayers, as far as effort to support schools is concerned. Perhaps, however, the problem has been oversimplified. There may be other factors that should have consideration.

People who live in cities or suburban areas often claim that they have heavy expenses for development of streets, utilities, police protection, and other essentials that are not needed in rural communities. When people in rapidly growing communities are attempting to support their schools and at the same time provide sewers, paved streets, sidewalks, and make other improvements, their financial burden may be much higher than that found in other areas.

Those living in rural areas, however, contend that they, too, have heavy expense. Provision of conveniences accepted as commonplace in urban and suburban areas may be even more expensive in rural areas. They insist that their taxes are in many cases high in proportion to their income and that to give special consideration to metropolitan areas would result in inequities. They point out that if the people in a city want parks for their own convenience, port facilities to increase the commerce and income, a city hall for service to the citizens, or other facilities or services, they should be willing to pay for them, just as the people in rural communities would have to pay for a community building, if they had one, or for other services or conveniences.

Is there any merit to the contention that all expenses of local government should be considered in determining the ability of a community to support schools? What would be the advantages or disadvantages of an attempt to develop such a plan? What steps can and should be taken to resolve this issue?

What Is the Best Measure of Local Ability?

Four possible measures of local ability have been briefly discussed in this chapter. These include: equalized valuation, based on partial or actual value of property; assessed valuation determined largely by local policy; a sales-ratio plan supplemented by appraisals, and an index of taxpaying ability. Perhaps others, including some adequate measure of income of the people, could be used if all pertinent information were available.

Many believe that state-equalized values provide the only satisfactory solution to the problem. However, there is much local resistance in many states to the idea of state equalization of assessments. Where assessors are elected by vote of the people in the county in which they reside, they are likely to, and in many cases do, oppose any state effort to raise assessments, regardless of how low they may be.

Some contend that there should be no effort to establish any sort of foundation program plan for financing schools until assessments are equalized. Many who are seriously concerned about inequalities in educational opportunity insist that improvements in state support need not wait until some uncertain future date when assessments can perhaps be equalized. They point out that if this policy were to be followed, children in many parts of the state would be penalized and handicapped merely because their elders have not been able to work out a satisfactory political solution to a difficult problem. They insist that, as far as school support is concerned, the same purposes generally can be accomplished through a formula as might be attained through equalized assessment. That is the reason they insist that the state adopt and make use either of a sales-ratio plan or of an index of taxpaying ability.

The sales-ratio plan, of course, has some weaknesses. Unless considerable sums are invested in a continuing study of sales price with reference to assessed value of property and in appraisals, and unless there is an adequate sampling, the ratio may not be fair and equitable. Some hold that sales-ratio studies in certain states may be subject to political manipulation. There may be a tendency for the legislature to pass a law freezing ratios or assessments to be used to those for a certain year. In fact, such laws have been passed in a number of states. Thus they believe that a far safer plan is to devise an index of taxpaying ability which is not subject to political manipulation or control. States that have developed and used good index plans seem to be reasonably well satisfied. Many of them have produced evidence to show that greater equity has been attained than if assessment practices were used. Few people seem to question the validity of the plan used in states where it has been properly developed. However, the index plan also has some weaknesses, and many believe it should be used only when other measures cannot be used for one reason or another.

What steps should the people in each state take toward solving this problem? What factors should be considered in determining the plan that would be most satisfactory? Which of the various plans should be most seriously considered for use?

SELECTED REFERENCES

American Association of School Administrators, Commission on School District Reorganization, *School District Organization*. Washington, D.C.: The Association, 1958. Chapters I–VI.

Burke, Arvid, *Financing Public Schools in the United States*, rev. ed. New York: Harper and Brothers, 1957. Chapters VIII, XX, and XXII.

Cyr, Frank, Arvid Burke, and Paul R. Mort, *Paying for our Public Schools*. Scranton, Pa.: International Textbook Company, 1938.

Groves, Harold M., *Financing Government*, 4th ed. New York: Henry Holt and Company, 1954.

Johns, R. L., and E. L. Morphet, editors, *Problems and Issues in Public School Finance*. New York: Bureau of Publications, Teachers College, Columbia University, 1952. Chapters I–IV.

MacLean, Malcolm S., and Edwin A. Lee, *Change and Process in Education*. New York: The Dryden Press, 1956. Chapters 3–7.

Morphet, Edgar L., Roe L. Johns, and Theodore L. Reller, *Educational Administration: Concepts, Practices, and Issues*. Englewood Cliffs, N.J.: Prentice-Hall, Inc., 1959. Chapters 10 and 22.

Mort, Paul R., and Reusser, Walter C., *Public School Finance*, 2nd ed. New York: McGraw-Hill Book Company, Inc., 1951. Chapters 1 and 10–12.

National Education Association, Research Division, *Rankings of the States*. Washington, D.C.: The Association, 1959, and subsequent years.

CHAPTER SEVEN

Legal Basis

for School Finance

No local school system in any state has any inherent right or authority to levy taxes or expend funds for schools. Similarly, no state board of education or state official has any inherent right or authority to apportion funds or to take any other action pertaining to school finance. All rights, duties, and responsibilities of state or local officials in any state must be authorized or prescribed by law. Consequently, knowledge of the constitutional provisions, laws, and regulations relating to the financing of schools is of basic importance for all who are concerned with school finance.

SIGNIFICANT LEGAL DEVELOPMENTS

Just as a new system of education designed to meet the needs and aspirations of the people had to be developed in this country, so provisions for financing the schools had to be devised. These provisions, of course, had to be evolved in keeping with the basic concepts and changing ideals of the people of the nation.

Early finance provisions were simple, crude, and inequitable according to modern concepts. This should not be surprising. One of the first concerns of the people, as their small communities were established, was to provide for schools. They soon began to be concerned about improving these schools, however, and removing some of the inequities

168

and injustices that became apparent. While voluntary cooperation was important and worked reasonably well for a time in most small communities, the need for local ordinances, state laws, constitutional provisions, and even court decisions became increasingly evident.

Some of the significant legal steps in providing for the financing of schools in the rapidly growing nation are summarized briefly below:

1. Although fees and rate bills continued for many years to be accepted methods of providing for the support of schools in communities in many parts of the nation, the greater equity of local tax support began to be apparent to the people in some communities, especially in the New England states, even before the new nation was formed. Local ordinances providing for the support of common schools through district tax funds began to be adopted.

2. When the nation was organized there had to be a decision, directly or indirectly, concerning the responsibilities of the Federal government for schools. Since, at that time, education was still considered largely a local responsibility, the subject was not directly discussed but, by implication, as explained later, the responsibility was left to the states and communities. This did not mean or imply that the Federal government should have no financial responsibility or concern for education. In fact, this responsibility and concern were clearly recognized at an early date.

3. The Ordinance of 1785 provided that Lot No. 16 (the sixteenth section) of every township should be preserved for the maintenance of a public school in the township. This provision was repeated and supplemented in the Ordinance of 1787.

4. The states, led by Connecticut in 1795, soon began to establish permanent funds for the support of the public schools. The Connecticut Act passed at that time provided that the principal sum received from the sale of lands belonging to the state, lying west of Pennsylvania, would remain a perpetual fund and the interest should be appropriated for support of schools in the state.[1]

5. States began one by one to provide that the schools should be supported by public tax funds. Following the example of Massachusetts, Pennsylvania adopted a law providing for tax support for public schools in 1833. Two years later a strong attempt was made to repeal the law, but vigorous support by Thaddeus Stevens and others prevented the repeal. In 1846 Horace Mann attempted to convince the people of New York that public schools should be tax supported. He stated: "Strange as it may seem, the subject of free schools and the right of a state to maintain them is never agitated in Massachusetts. . . .

---

[1] Connecticut Acts and Laws, 1795.

It is a thing universally taken for granted. . . ." [2] In 1849 New York provided for free schools throughout the state. Gradually this point of view was adopted by all states, and eventually fees and rate bills were prohibited by law.

6. After many bitter battles, one state after another, during the nineteenth century, adopted a constitutional provision or laws that prohibited the use of public tax funds for the support of denominational schools. This constituted a radical change in policy, since most schools in the beginning were religious institutions. The necessity for this policy became apparent partly because of controversies among various denominational groups and partly because it seemed the logical way to develop schools in this country. The wisdom of the policy has again and again been shown by subsequent developments and events.

7. Gradually communities in various states began to levy taxes for support of high schools. However, in many situations there was doubt as to whether such taxes were legal. In the famous Kalamazoo Decision in 1874 the Supreme Court of Michigan established the legality of taxes for secondary schools in that state. After summarizing developments and citing pertinent facts, the court stated:

> . . . Neither in our state policy, in our constitution, or in our laws do we find the primary school districts restricted in the branches of knowledge which their officers may cause to be taught, or the grade of instruction that may be given, if their voters consent in regular form to bear the expense and raise the taxes for the purpose. [3]

This decision also established the right of the people to levy taxes to support state universities; a right which had been authorized by law in certain states prior to that time.

8. The Federal government, from time to time, has demonstrated its interest in education by providing further land grants and financial support as explained in Chapter 13.

9. During the nineteenth century many states also began to recognize that schools could not be satisfactorily supported by local taxes and the income from state permanent school funds. Laws were passed providing for limited state funds to assist in the support of public schools throughout the state.

10. During the present century, and especially within the past 35 years, more and more states have begun to recognize the importance of assuring adequate educational opportunities throughout the state

[2] Thomas E. Finegan, editor, *Free Schools: A Documentary History of the Free School Movement in New York State* (Albany: The University of the State of New York, 1921), p. 102.
[3] Stuart v. School District No. 1 of Kalamazoo (1874), 30 Mich.: 69, 75.

and of establishing by law what is now called a foundation program plan, to assure that, through an equitable combination of state and local funds, adequate financial support will be available to assure these opportunities in every school system.

FEDERAL PROVISIONS AND RELATIONS

Since the Constitution of the United States makes no direct reference to education, under the provisions of the Tenth Amendment the basic responsibility for education has been allocated to the states. However, this does not mean that the Federal government lacks authority to finance, control, or regulate education. In fact, as will be pointed out under the discussion of the United States Supreme Court decisions, the Federal government has in many respects influenced and regulated certain aspects of educational development in the various states. This authority, which has not yet been fully defined or clarified, is found in the implied powers delegated to the Federal government in one or more clauses of the Constitution. Since most of these clauses state general principles, the powers, in some cases, have been more clearly defined by decisions of the Supreme Court than by the Constitutional provisions themselves.

Clause 1 of Section 8, Article I of the Constitution is generally referred to as the General Welfare Clause. Under the provisions of this clause and subsequent related court interpretations, there seems to be no doubt that Congress has the necessary authority to make any reasonable appropriations for the support of education. This authority has been exercised on a number of occasions. As pointed out by Edwards:

> . . . . It seems clear that the national government may tax and spend in the support of education, it may enter into voluntary agreements with the states for the mutual support of education, it may not spend funds for the primary purpose of regulating the educational policies of the states, and it may enforce whatever control measures are incidental but essential in the accomplishment of the purposes for which Federal funds are appropriated and spent.[4]

There are definite constitutional limits on the powers of the states relating to certain aspects of finance which may involve the schools. For example, Section 10 of Article 1 of the Constitution provides that no state may pass legislation impairing the obligations of contracts. Any

---

[4] Newton Edwards, *The Courts and the Public Schools*, rev. ed. (Chicago: University of Chicago Press), p. 5. Copyright 1955 by the University of Chicago.

session of the legislature may, of course, modify an expression of public policy adopted by a preceding session, unless that policy is expressed in the state or Federal Constitution. Thus, provisions which in effect become contracts between the state or its subdivisions and individuals or corporations in the state may not be cancelled.

According to a clause in the Fourteenth Amendment, no state may "deprive any person of life, liberty, or property without due process of law." Generally, since every state has police power, the legislature should be in a position to determine how and for what purposes it should be exercised. However, any person who feels that he has been unreasonably denied the use of his liberty or his property may appeal to the state courts and, if he is not satisfied, may appeal to the United States Supreme Court, which becomes the final arbitrator.

There are other provisions of the Constitution that have some implications for finance, as explained in Chapter 13, but those discussed above seem to have the most direct implications.

STATE CONSTITUTIONAL PROVISIONS

Since education in this country is a function of the respective states, in reality it becomes a responsibility of the people of each state. The people hold certain beliefs and attitudes about public education. These beliefs and attitudes are, in general terms, usually incorporated in the constitution and laws of the state. If the people believe in a liberal system of public free schools, they will provide for such a system. If they conceive of public schools as institutions which should be provided and financed within strict limitations, they will provide such limitations. The people of the state may make any provision for the establishment and support of the public schools they consider desirable, subject, of course, to limitations imposed or implied by the Federal Constitution.

Most state constitutions provide for the establishment and support of "public free schools." Practically all state constitutions provide for a permanent school fund, the principal of which is to be kept sacred and inviolate, and prescribe that the income is to be used for public school purposes. They also, either directly or by implication, authorize the legislature to provide additional funds for the support of the public schools. Constitutional provisions may, however, (1) prescribe the exact method of apportioning all funds, (2) prescribe the method of apportioning the income from the permanent fund but leave to the legislature the plan for apportioning other funds, or (3) provide that the legislature is to apportion all funds on the basis of some declared principle.

The constitutions usually also incorporate a provision that public tax funds may be used only for the support of public schools and public educational institutions. Other provisions having implications for finance may relate to taxation, sometimes including limitations on taxes for various purposes; the issuance of bonds; limitations on indebtedness; contractual obligations; and the expenditure and use of funds.

If constitutional provisions are restrictive, they are likely to handicap the educational program. Such restrictions cannot be removed by the legislature or in any other manner except by amendment of the constitution itself. Illustrations of undesirable restrictions are found in the Indiana and Kentucky constitutions, limiting school indebtedness to two per cent of the assessed valuation; in the Alabama constitution, limiting the local taxes which may be voted for school support in most districts to seven mills for all purposes; and in several other constitutions.

LEGISLATIVE PROVISIONS

While the United States Congress cannot determine the educational policies of a state, it can and often does influence policies. Federal laws cannot be concerned with the details of organization, administration, and operation of schools in a state, because that is a state responsibility. Therefore, they are concerned primarily with provisions relating to finance. The details of some of the more important of these laws are explained in Chapter 13. The primary concern here is with the influence on and implications for state policy.

Federal Laws

Every state is free to accept or refuse to accept funds provided by the Federal government for education. If the funds are accepted, however, as they have been in most cases, the state is bound to observe any conditions Congress may have attached with reference to the use and expenditure of those funds. Among the acts relating to the public schools which significantly influence developments in many states are the appropriations for vocational education, the Federal school lunch act, the funds provided under Public Laws 815 and 874 for school districts significantly affected by Federal activities, and the National Defense Education Act of 1958.

Local boards of education and school officials are generally more immediately and continuously concerned with the provisions and implications of state laws than of Federal laws. The state laws, within the limits prescribed by the constitution, determine the possibilities or limitations relating to organization, administration, financing and operation of the schools.

State Laws

The legislature of each state has what is commonly called plenary powers; that is, it may pass any laws it considers desirable and these laws will have to be observed unless they are later found to be inconsistent with provisions of the state constitution or to be in conflict with Federal Constitutional provisions. This finding, however, must be made by the courts on the basis of a controversy involving some issue which is presented for a legal decision.

Thus, the legislature of a state may pass laws relating to school finance which are wise and forward-looking or may enact laws which handicap the schools and prevent them from providing a satisfactory program of education. The adoption of sound laws does not mean that there will be a good program of education in every community, because laws cannot substitute for local leadership and responsibility. However, laws may determine, through financial and other provisions, whether local leadership has an opportunity to function effectively.

Laws may be changed at any time in the discretion of the legislature, except for aspects of certain laws relating to contracts or features restricted by constitutional provisions, as previously indicated. For example, the Indiana Supreme Court some time ago held:

> As the power over schools is a legislative one, it is not exhausted by exercise. The Legislature having tried one plan is not precluded from trying another. It has a complete choice of methods and may change its plans as often as it deems necessary or expedient.[5]

Laws Express Policies. Laws constitute an expression of state policy. If, in any state, a serious attempt has been made to agree upon policies that are wise from a long-range point of view, and if the policies relating to finance or to other aspects of the educational program have been thought through carefully, the laws are likely to be much sounder than in a state in which that has not been done. Ideas for laws come from many sources. If they come from special interest groups that are primarily concerned with legislation designed to promote their own objectives, they are not as likely to fit into a sound over-all conceptual

---

[5] State v. Haworth, 122 Indiana 462, 23 N.E. 946, 7 L.R.A. 240.

design as when they have been developed on the basis of careful study and through the cooperative effort of groups concerned with all aspects of education and state policy. Some of the difficulties in many states arise from the fact that much legislation relating to finance is of a patchwork nature and is sponsored by groups that have not had an opportunity to consider proposals in relationship to bona fide state-wide needs.

One of the major concerns in every state should be to see that policy is expressed in law without including details that discourage local responsibility and stifle local initiative. This problem is particularly serious in the field of finance because, as is commonly recognized, provisions relating to finance may either control or have serious implications for other aspects of the educational program. Furthermore, there has often been a tendency for the legislature to include more detail and greater limitations in legislation relating to finance than in other aspects of legislation. The legislature is properly concerned with problems of assuring prudential management and expenditure of funds and is constantly seeking ways of assuring that this objective can be implemented.

Criteria for Finance Legislation. The following criteria are suggested for guidance in planning new legislation relating to finance or in evaluating and revising existing legislation:

1. In the interest of equity and justice, the legislature should set forth the bases and procedures which must be used in determining amounts to be apportioned and in apportioning funds to local school districts.

2. The legislature should prescribe procedures to be used by local school systems in certifying tax levies and in obtaining, managing, and safeguarding funds and other assets of the district so local boards will not be handicapped by legal uncertainties or subject to suspicion because the public has no assurance that proper safeguards are provided.

3. The legislature should not deny local responsibility by limiting the opportunity of the citizens of a district to provide funds for financing schools, by attempting to place narrow restrictions on the purpose for which funds may be expended or on the procedures to be used in attaining those purposes.

STATE AND LOCAL REGULATIONS

While the basic financial policy should be prescribed by law in every state, there will probably always be a need for the state board of education or some other state agency to prescribe the sub-policies and rules and regulations for implementing the policies. These may be adopted by any agency of the state authorized by the legislature to assume the responsibility and may not be established unless that authorization is granted. The assignment of responsibility for finance regulations to some state agency primarily concerned with financial administration rather than with education, as has happened in several states, is likely to have unfortunate consequences for local school systems. An agency which is concerned primarily with economy and with keeping expenditures within certain limits is more likely to adopt restrictive and handicapping regulations than a state board of education which is or should be concerned with all aspects of the educational program.

The manner in which state board policies and regulations are developed is also important. If they are developed by some state official without consulting local school officials, they are likely to be less desirable than if they are developed through the efforts of a representative committee concerned with the implications of any policy for local initiative and responsibility. At least three important criteria should be used in developing and administering any necessary state regulations.[6]

1. The state should establish only those minimum standards that are universally applicable, are designed primarily to assure adequate opportunities for all children, and that in no way limit the freedom of the local school unit to go beyond the state's standards in education.

2. Compliance features should be avoided whenever there is reasonable possibility that local school systems with increased funds will exercise wise judgment in the development of their educational program. Special controls necessary to protect the educational rights of children under circumstances of educational expediency should be accompanied by provisions for automatically terminating them as soon as possible.

3. In making decisions regarding control, preference should be given to retaining control locally, particularly for those elements concerning which there is no certainty that the central authority will produce the best long-time results.

Local school finance policies and procedures must, of course, be consistent with and meet the requirements set forth in state laws and regulations. However, within these limits, local school boards have authority to, and should, establish such policies and regulations relating to finance and other aspects of the educational program in the local school system as they consider desirable. These likewise should be cooperatively developed, should conform to sound principles and should serve a constructive purpose.

------

[6] Adapted from National Education Association, Committee on Tax Education and School Finance, *Guides to the Development of State School Finance Programs* (Washington, D.C.: The Association, 1949), pp. 6–10.

DECISIONS OF THE UNITED STATES
SUPREME COURT

In spite of the fact that the responsibility for education has been reserved to the states, the Supreme Court of the United States has rendered several decisions that have rather direct implications for school finance. These decisions, of course, have come only on the basis of questions that have been brought before the Court. In this country the courts do not on their own initiative or volition rule on the constitutionality of law. Laws and administrative regulations are always assumed to be constitutional but may, of course, at any time be tested in an appropriate court.

> In deference to the fact that public education remains a state and local function, the Court has repeatedly expressed its reluctance to take the responsibility for interfering with state educational policy or practice, even when the rise of constitutional questions compelled it.
> Only in cases where local authorities have argued state function against federal supremacy has the Court consistently held against the state contention. . . .[7]

Four cases rather directly involving finance will be discussed briefly. A few others that obviously have important implications for finance will also be treated briefly.

Cases Directly Relating to Finance

Since questions involving education do not come directly before the Supreme Court, the involvement of education and of school finance is necessarily incidental, but in some cases it is quite significant.

Apportionment of Funds. One of the important early decisions of the Court had to do with the collection and apportionment of school funds. In this decision the Court upheld the State of Indiana in refusing to apportion state funds to schools that received township income from a Federal grant of land, until other state schools had attained a parity with the schools benefiting from the grant. Indiana was among the states early admitted to the Union, to which Congress had made a grant of the sixteenth section of land in each township "to the inhabitants thereof" for schools. Later admissions included provision for the

---

[7] Clark Spurlock, *Education and the Supreme Court* (Urbana: University of Illinois Press, 1955), p. 235. The authors are also indebted to Spurlock for helpful information on Supreme Court cases discussed on subsequent pages.

grants to be made to the state for its schools. Indiana was attempting to remedy inequities resulting from grants to townships, through what might be called a rough equalization plan. Justice Catron wrote, in giving the opinion of the Court:

> The law is a perfectly just one; but if it were otherwise and the school funds were distributed partially, nevertheless those receiving the bounty from the Congress have no right to call on this court to interfere with the power exercised by the state legislature in laying and collecting taxes and in appropriating them for educational purposes, at its discretion.[8]

This decision is interesting not only because of the principle upheld but because it dealt with an early effort of one of the states to achieve purposes now commonly recognized to be highly desirable in most states.

Use of Indian Funds. In another case, the Supreme Court upheld a contract made at the request of the Sioux Indians, providing that money due them under a treaty be paid by the Commissioner of Indian Affairs for the support of Indian Catholic schools. The Act of Congress involved declared it to be the settled policy of the government to "hereafter make no appropriation whatever for education in any sectarian school." The Commissioner of Indian Affairs pointed out that Congress had regularly authorized contracts with sectarian agencies for Indian education and had made payments for that purpose from public money. The Commissioner also directed attention to the point that Congressional limitation had been intended to be applied to the appropriation of public money and not to the funds belonging to the Indians as a matter of right and administered for them by the government. The Court held:

> These appropriations rested on different grounds from the gratuitous appropriations of public moneys under the heading, "Support of Schools." . . . They are moneys belonging really to the Indians. . . .
> . . . It seems unconceivable that Congress shall have intended to prohibit them from receiving religious education at their own cost if they desire it; such an intent would be one to prohibit the free exercise of religion amongst the Indians and such would be the effect of the construction for which the complainants contend. . . .[9]

In this case the question of public tax money, either state or Federal, was not involved. The question was one as to whether the Indians might use their own money for the purpose specified. However, the

---

[8] Springfield Township v. Quick, 22 How. 56 (U.S. 1859).
[9] Quick Bear v. Leupp, 210 U.S. 50, 28 Sup. Ct. 690 (1908).

"child benefit theory" which was later developed begins to be evident. *Free Textbooks.* The following case deals with free textbooks for pupils in private schools. A Louisiana statute had been passed authorizing free textbooks, purchased from public funds, to be provided for children in private schools. The child benefit theory was further developed in this case because the Court held that a state's obligation to all the school children in the state transcended a strictly literal observance of the principle of the separation of church and state. The Court stated:

> . . . we cannot doubt that the taxing power of the state is exerted for a public purpose. The legislation does not segregate private schools, or their pupils, as its beneficiaries or attempt to interfere with any matters of exclusively private concern. Its interest is education broadly; its method, comprehensive. Individual interests are aided only as the common interest is safeguarded.[10]

Transportation of Pupils. The next case summarized is perhaps one of the most interesting and controversial that has come before the Supreme Court. It involved the provision of free bus transportation for children attending parochial schools. The Court sustained the right of local school authorities, under a New Jersey statute, to provide free transportation for children attending parochial schools. It declared that the action of the authorities did not violate any provision of the Federal Constitution.

In this case the opinion of the Court was sharply divided. But in both opinions the "wall of separation" doctrine was advanced. Justice Black, speaking for the majority, stated:

> The state contributes no money to the [parochial] schools. It does not support them. Its legislation as applied does no more than provide a general program to help parents get their children, regardless of their religion, safely and expeditiously to and from accredited schools.
>
> The First Amendment has erected a wall between church and state. That wall must be kept high and impregnable. We could not approve the slightest breach. New Jersey has not breached it here.[11]

In a dissenting opinion, Justice Jackson stated:

> The funds used here were raised by taxation. The Court does not dispute, nor could it, that their use does in fact give aid and encouragement to religious instruction. . . . Here parents pay money to send their children to parochial schools and funds raised by taxation are used to reimburse them. This not only helps the children to get to school and

---

[10] Cochran v. Louisiana State Board of Education, 281 U.S. 370, 50 Sup. Ct. 335 (1930).

[11] Everson v. Board of Education, 330 U.S. 1, 67 Sup. Ct. 504 (1947).

the parents to send them. It aids them in a substantial way to get the very thing which they are being sent to the particular school to secure, namely, religious training and teaching.[12]

It should be noted that this case did not hold that states must provide transportation or funds for transportation for parochial school children but only that in the New Jersey situation, where transportation was authorized by state law, the use of funds for that purpose was permissible.

Cases Having Implications for Finance

In another Indiana case, involving teacher tenure, the Court held that the Indiana Legislature could not impair under Article I, Section 10, of the Federal Constitution a valid contract held by a dismissed teacher.[13] The Indiana Legislature had repealed a tenure law which, according to the Court, constituted a valid contract with the teacher. This, as pointed out in other cases, does not mean that a tenure law regulating contracts cannot be altered. In fact, the Court pointed out that while laws made by legislatures are ordinarily subject to amendment and repeal, the conditions provided by the laws are important. They may "contain provisions which, when accepted as a basis for action by individuals, become contracts between them and the state."

Several cases have involved the question of segregation. In a Missouri case the Court held that equal opportunity for a legal education must be provided within a state's own borders.[14] This indirectly involved finance. In a famous decision involving five cases in 1954, the Court held that: "In the field of public education the doctrine of 'separate but equal' has no place. Separate educational facilities are inherently unequal."[15] The decision has many important implications for finance as well as for other aspects of education in states which maintained separate schools for the two races.

STATE COURT DECISIONS

Only a few of the many thousands of laws relating to schools adopted over a period of years in any state are challenged in the courts. However, in some cases, the court decisions are very significant because they may hold a law or a portion of a law unconstitutional or may give

---

[12] *Ibid.*
[13] Indiana *ex rel.* Anderson v. Brand, 303 U.S. 95, 58 Sup. Ct. 43 (1938).
[14] Missouri *ex rel.* Gaines v. Canada, 305 U.S. 337, 159 Sup. Ct. 232 (1938).
[15] Brown v. Board of Education, 347 U.S. 483, 74 Sup. Ct. 686 (1954).

a different interpretation than seems implied when the law is read by lay citizens or school officials. In any case, when a law relating to school finance, or to other aspects of the educational program, has come before a court for decision, the opinion of the court should be carefully studied and considered in connection with the law itself. If it is not appealed, it becomes the accepted interpretation in the state. If it is appealed, it may either be reversed or upheld in a higher court.

When a question of law is being considered, the court always attempts to interpret the statute according to the intent of the legislature. Sometimes the intent is difficult to discover, but the court endeavors to make that determination if at all possible. The statute, therefore, must be read as a whole, because the language of one section may affect the interpretation of another. Furthermore, one law may have implications for another law dealing with related subject matter. When there are both general and specific provisions, the specific provisions control those which are more general. These points are important to keep in mind in drafting legislation as well as in attempting to understand the meaning of a particular law or section of the law.

Some Trends

The courts have held again and again that the maintenance of public schools is a matter of state concern and responsibility and that state interests take precedence over local provisions. Thus, if the state constitution or state law provides that boards of education are to have the power within limits prescribed by law to determine what is needed for the satisfactory operation of schools, no local agency of government can prevent the board from exercising that responsibility as authorized by law. In a Kentucky case involving the board of education and the city council of Louisville, the court required the council to levy the tax for school purposes certified by the board which the council had previously refused to levy. The court stated:

> If the maintenance of a public school is a purely municipal purpose, then the section would seem to be conclusive in the matter. . . . But . . . public education in this country . . . has never been looked upon as being at all a matter of local concern only. On the contrary, it is regarded as essential to the preservation of liberty—as forming one of the first duties of a democratic government. The place assigned to it in the deliberate judgment of the American people is scarcely second to any.[16]

The question as to what constitutes a uniform system of free schools, as commonly required in state constitutions, has frequently arisen.

---

[16] City of Louisville v. Commonwealth, 134 Kentucky 488, 121 S.W. 411.

Courts have generally held that "Uniformity does not mean identity, a dead level of sameness, a complete lack of distinction or discrimination. Uniformity does not preclude classification." [17]

Since school districts are agencies of the state, created for the purpose of providing educational opportunities for the children of the state, they do not have broad powers. Their powers are definitely limited to those expressly granted or conferred on them by necessary implication. It is thus uniformly held that there is no inherent power of school districts to levy taxes. If the power exists, it must be especially conferred by the legislature. It is not implied by the power to establish and maintain schools.[18]

A California case that reversed a previous decision on a similar issue has implications not only for school building planning and construction but obviously for finance. The issue was whether a municipal corporation's building regulations are applicable to construction of a public school building by a school district in the municipality. The court held that:

> The public schools of this state are a matter of state-wide rather than local or municipal concern; their establishment, regulation, and operation are covered by the Constitution and the State Legislature is given comprehensive powers in relation thereto. . . .
> Either the local regulation is ineffective or the state must bow to the requirement of its governmental subsidiary. Upon fundamental principles that conflict must be resolved in favor of the State.[19]

SIGNIFICANT LEGAL PROVISIONS
RELATING TO STATE AGENCIES AND OFFICIALS

It is well recognized that the legislature may not delegate its legislative powers to any agency or official. It may, however, delegate strictly limited legislative responsibility and broad administrative powers. In financial affairs, the legislature must necessarily prescribe the procedures for apportioning school funds and the principles upon which the apportionment is to be based. The responsibility for making the apportionment, however, is customarily delegated to the state board of education or to the chief state school officer. In making the apportionments, the board, or the state superintendent, simply applies the principles prescribed by the legislature.

---

[17] Edwards, *The Courts and the Public Schools*, p. 32.
[18] See Robert R. Hamilton and Paul R. Mort, *The Law and Public Education,* with cases. 2nd ed. (Brooklyn: The Foundation Press, Inc., 1959) pp. 117, 590.
[19] Guy Hall v. The City of Taft et al., 47 A.C. 179 (1956).

In an important decision, the Supreme Court of Maine held:

> The legislature has the right under the Constitution to impose an equal rate of taxation upon all properties in the state, including the property in unorganized townships, for the purpose of distributing the proceeds thereof among the cities, towns, and plantations for common school purposes. . . .
>
> The method of distributing the proceeds of such a tax rests in the wise discretion and sound judgment of the legislature. If this discretion is unwisely exercised, the remedy is with the people and not with the court. . . .[20]

In some states, broad authority is given to state officials to approve applications for funds or to withhold certain types of funds. In New York, for example, the Commissioner has been given the authority to withhold certain school funds as a means of enforcing requirements. In most cases, however, when such authority is granted the funds must be apportioned in full when the district meets the requirements.

To avoid the exercise of broad discretionary powers which might be abused, the intent in most states has been to prescribe objective measures to be used in apportioning funds and to state as objectively as possible the standards which must be observed. Under such conditions the district as well as the state officials can become familiar with the intent of the requirements, and the probability of misunderstanding is reduced to a minimum.

SIGNIFICANT LEGAL PROVISIONS RELATING TO LOCAL SCHOOL BOARDS AND OFFICIALS

School officials and students of finance in each state should not only become familiar with the laws and pertinent court decisions, but need to understand the general legal principles, some of which are discussed in the following paragraphs.

Custodianship Responsibilities

All school funds or monies credited to a district, or for which the district is responsible, are held in trust for the benefit of the public through education. They do not belong to the local board, to school officials, or, in a strictly legal sense, to the district. They should be managed and expended in such a manner as to provide for the most beneficial and economical use of the funds and to assure the best pos-

[20] Sawyer v. Gilmore, 83 A. 673, 109 Maine 169 (1912).

sible educational opportunities and facilities for those entitled to benefit from such a program.[21]

Fiscal Dependence or Independence

In some states, by law, all local school systems are fiscally independent; that is, the board of education has been made responsible by the legislature for determining and certifying the funds needed within the limits established by law for the operation of the schools, and for administering and managing those funds. In other states, the law provides that all local school systems are fiscally dependent; that is, some agency other than the board has the final authority to determine the amount of funds to be provided for the support of schools. In still other states, certain classes of systems are fiscally independent and others are fiscally dependent. However, even in states where fiscal dependence has been established by law the reviewing agency has only those powers assigned to it. Generally these agencies may not add or take out specific items in a budget, but in some instances they have the power to increase or decrease the budget total.

Fiscal independence established by law has been upheld by the courts in numerous cases. For example, a Kentucky court held:

> It [the legislature] meant to make the board of education entirely independent. . . . Where proper demand is made within the limits prescribed by law, the council will not be permitted to refuse to comply with the board's demands, unless it can show that the members of the board acted corruptly or in bad faith or that they embraced in their expenditures items not authorized by law. That in their opinion the demands of the board are excessive or extortionate is not sufficient.[22]

Taxation

There is no power inherent in the board of a district to levy a property tax or any other tax for school purposes. Taxation is a plenary power of the state which may be explicitly delegated, within limits, to local school districts or other agencies of government. The Supreme Court of Kansas held that:

> The authority to levy taxes is an extraordinary one. It is never left to implication. Its warrant must be clearly found in the act of the legislature. Any other rule might lead to great wrong and oppression and,

---

[21] Madeline Kinter Remmlein, *The Law of Local Public School Administration* (New York: McGraw-Hill Book Company, Inc., 1953), p. 39.

[22] Board of Education v. Townsend, 130 S.W. 1105, 140 Kentucky 248 (1910).

when there is reasonable doubt as to its existence, the right must be denied. Therefore to say that the right is in doubt is to deny its existence.[23]

Since a tax levied by a school district is, in effect, a state tax, it should be apparent that school districts may be required to levy taxes for school purposes regardless of whether the board or the people wish to levy the tax.[24] This principle becomes of great importance for states interested in establishing partnership foundation programs. A common requirement in connection with such programs is that all districts make a uniform local effort to support the program.

Management of School Funds

Local boards have only those powers for management and expenditure of school funds conferred on them by the legislature. When the legislature prescribes that certain grants-in-aid, or that the proceeds of certain local tax levies, must be used for specified purposes, they cannot be used for any other purpose. When general-purpose funds are provided the board has much more discretion in using those funds.

The law not only assumes that the board and school officials of each district will take every step possible to protect the public and the state from loss of funds or other assets through negligence or dishonesty but usually prescribes some of the safeguards considered essential. For example, cash transactions are seldom permitted, except in very small amounts, where purchases can most easily be cared for through petty cash funds. Even then, a complete accounting is customarily required or, if not required by law, should be prescribed by the board.

Even non-tax funds available to the schools are regulated by law in a number of states. These include cafeteria, student body, athletic, and other funds for which the board, either by law or by implication, is responsible. In every case the board should recognize its implied responsibility and establish proper safeguards for these funds.

The School Budget

The laws in most states require the preparation of an annual budget for most types of districts. While considerable discretion is left to the board and school officials, the budget must usually be prepared on the basis of certain standards and criteria prescribed either by law or by

---

[23] Marion and McPherson Railway Company v. Alexander, 64 Pac. 978, 63 Kansas 72 (1901).

[24] State v. Freeman, 61 Kansas 90, 58 Pac. 959, 47 L.R.A. 67.

regulations of the state board. A date is usually established by which the budget must be prepared and adopted by the board. In many states public hearings are required and, if required, must be held in accordance with the procedures prescribed by law.

As explained in Chapter 14, observance of all legal procedures does not mean that the budget will be satisfactory. A good budget, which can serve for guidance in conducting the financial affairs of the district during the year, can be prepared only on the basis of sound policies adopted by the board and through wise leadership on the part of the superintendent and other members of his staff.

Contractual Authority

There are certain principles of law pertaining to contracts and contractual procedures of the board of education which must be observed as carefully as principles relating to other aspects of finance. As pointed out by Edwards, the basic principles are as follows:

1. A contract, to be binding, must be entered into by parties who have the legal capacity to make it. Moreover, a board must have the legal authority to make a contract and the contract must be prepared in accordance with the provisions of law. For example, a board cannot make a contract with a teacher who does not possess a valid certificate, when such a certificate is required by law.

2. There must be a meeting of minds of the parties to the contract. That is, there must be complete agreement on the terms of the contract, including a definite offer and an unqualified acceptance. The action of a school board accepting an offer becomes official only when communicated to the party making the offer.

3. A contract must be in terms that are sufficiently definite to be enforceable.

4. An agreement does not constitute a contract unless it is based on some valid consideration.

5. An agreement that violates provisions of law or of a court decision relating to public policy is not a legal contract.

6. Contracts are made in relationship to the laws governing them. Thus, if the law requires local school systems to adopt a salary schedule to be used as a basis for paying teachers in the district, the schedule will become a part of the contract by implication.[25]

---

[25] Adapted from Newton Edwards, "Contractual Authority of School Boards," Chapter 2 of *Law and the School Business Manager*, Lee O. Garber (ed.) (Danville, Illinois: Interstate Printers and Publishers, Inc., 1957), p. 24.

School Indebtedness

The courts usually have held that the power to issue school bonds or other evidence of indebtedness exists only to the extent that it is granted in clear and unmistakable terms and is strictly limited to the authority granted by law.

In most states, bonds can be issued only when authorized and in the amounts authorized by vote of the people, and in many cases restrictions are placed on those who may vote. In a few states, a limited amount of bonds may be issued without a special election. In certain other states the issuance must be authorized directly by the legislature.

The procedures prescribed for authorizing, voting, issuing, and selling bonds or warrants must be followed in detail. Otherwise the entire issue may be invalidated.

In most states, school districts are authorized to make temporary loans to obtain funds needed for operation of schools during the current year. These funds may usually be borrowed in anticipation of tax receipts that have been included in the budget but have not yet become available. In most cases they must be paid back within the year in which they are borrowed. Other states have provisions for issuing registered or tax anticipation warrants under certain conditions.

The power to borrow is a definitely limited power and must not be abused by the district.

Insurance

There are many kinds and types of insurance, as explained in Chapter 18. Some of these are required of all districts in certain states, others are optional, and some may even be prohibited because the laws do not provide for expenditure of public tax funds for that purpose.

Where there is no statute covering a subject, common law is presumed to apply. Most states do not have statutes covering the liability of school districts. The common law principle which holds in those states is that school districts are not liable to pupils for injuries resulting from the negligence of their officers or employees. The state legislature may, however, enact legislation to replace the common law, as three or four states have done, and, in those cases, liability is recognized. In a West Virginia case where there was no statutory recognition of liability, the court held that:

> The general rule in this country is that a school district, municipal corporation, or school board is not, in the absence of a statute imposing

it, subject to liabilities for injuries to pupils in the public schools...
since such district ... acts as an agent for the state. ...." [26]

During the past few years several states have begun to consider
seriously the possibility of abrogating the common law principle, and
California, Washington, and New York have taken definite steps in
that direction.

In a Kentucky case the court stated:

> The legislature may make school boards liable for their torts or the
> torts of their agents and employees and we know of no reason why it
> may not take a middle course and empower them to protect, by liability
> insurance, persons injured by the negligence of their bus drivers, and to
> provide that liability to the insurer shall be determined by the final
> judgment obtained by the insured person.[27]

Officials in school districts in all states should understand that
even though the common law principle may be applicable to districts,
it does not protect employees who may be negligent and therefore
may be subject to suit.

SOME PROBLEMS AND ISSUES

Some of the problems and issues pertaining to legal aspects of school
finance will be considered on the following pages.

Does Support Under the "Child Benefit" Theory Aid
Children or Does It Aid Non-public Schools?

From decisions of the United States Supreme Court it is evident that
there can be no direct aid from public tax funds for the support of
sectarian schools.

Since the beginning of the present century the courts in Kentucky,
Iowa, Nebraska, New Mexico, and Missouri have held unconstitutional
arrangements made in certain communities in those states to teach
children at public expense in buildings owned by the church with
teachers belonging to religious denominations and in many cases wearing religious garb.

Probably the most serious situation was found in New Mexico
where in several counties in the northern part of the state it was
customary for religious orders to provide the buildings, select the
staff, and conduct the schools. These schools were supported by public

---

[26] Krutili v. Board of Education, 99 West Virginia 466, 129 S.E. 486.

[27] Taylor v. Knox County Board of Education, 292 Kentucky 167, 145 A.L.R.,
1333, 167 S.W. 700 (1942).

tax funds. Finally, controversy arose and the New Mexico Supreme Court in 1951 held the arrangement unconstitutional, stating: "In short, New Mexico had a Roman Catholic school system supported by public funds within its public school system." [28] The court prohibited the wearing of religious garb in the public schools and enjoined religious education at public expense.

The child benefit theory apparently began to be developed by the United States Supreme Court in the decision relating to the use of Indian tribal funds for education of children at parochial schools, but since tribal funds were involved, the issue was not clearly presented. It was definitely applied in the Louisiana case, when the Court held a Louisiana law, providing free textbooks for the school children of the state, constitutional.

The Federal government has also provided school lunch funds and surplus commodities for children in all schools that are willing to or can qualify. This constitutes another aspect of the application of the child benefit theory. The idea back of the legislation is that the lunches are for the benefit of the children, not for the aid of schools.

The question of providing transportation for children who attend sectarian schools has occasioned considerable controversy over a period of time. Such provisions have been held unconstitutional in Delaware, Missouri, Oklahoma, South Dakota, Washington, and Wisconsin. The courts have approved transportation for sectarian school pupils only in California, Maryland, and New Jersey.[29] New York and New Jersey have changed their constitutions to make transportation of parochial school pupils possible. Most states, however, still do not provide for or permit such transportation.

Many people hold that using funds for transporting pupils to sectarian schools is really a form of aid for those schools. In fact, some of the Justices, in the dissenting opinion, on the case Everson v. Board of Education advanced this point of view.[30]

The case for transportation seems to many people to be relatively clear-cut and simple. If the children are picked up along the road traveled by a bus which is transporting pupils to a public school, there would not seem to be any extra expense involved. However, if enough pupils attend the non-public schools the district might have to put on another bus or provide for an extra trip; additional cost would therefore be directly involved. If the children have to be transported beyond the regular public school route and directly to a parochial

[28] Zellers v. Huff, 236 P.2d, 949 N.Mex. 1951.
[29] National Education Association, *The State and Sectarian Education*, Research Bulletin, Vol. 36, No. 4 (December, 1956), pp. 187–188.
[30] Everson v. Board of Education 330 U.S. 1, 67 Sup. Ct. 504 (1947).

school, as is the case in New York, there is unquestionably considerable extra expense involved. This seems to many people to be a clear-cut case of aiding not only the children but the schools, because the non-public schools would have to provide the transportation if it were not provided at public expense.

Several of the Southern states have recently attempted to devise a plan which would permit public schools to be discontinued, as a means of avoiding integration. The idea is that public tax funds would be paid to parents to meet the expense of sending their children to non-public schools. Under this plan the "child benefit" theory would be carried to its logical conclusion. The tax money would be used for the benefit of the children, but clearly it would benefit the non-public schools.

What services should be provided at public expense for children who attend non-public schools? When does transportation become an aid to the school as well as to children? Could not the child benefit theory be carried so far that the aid provided would clearly be for the benefit of non-public schools?

What Procedures Should Be Used in Changing Laws Relating to Finance?

At practically every session of the legislature in most states several bills proposing to change certain aspects of the finance program are introduced, and some are passed. Usually what happens is that certain bills are sponsored by groups concerned with economy and many of these seek to impose new requirements or controls designed to assure greater efficiency. Other bills are sponsored by various groups in education. Some are sponsored by one or more groups concerned with certain aspects of the educational program. These various bills are likely to have widely different purposes. Some of the bills passed by the legislature may have an intent almost opposite that of other bills passed at the same session. The net result is that the state does not have a well-coordinated and integrated program or plan for financing schools, but rather a series of laws some of which may be beneficial and others, from a long-range point of view, harmful.

How can haphazard development of state laws relating to school finance be avoided? To what extent are educators responsible for the rather chaotic situations found in some of the states? How can the efforts of educators and of lay groups be better coordinated?

In several states, during the past few years, study groups have attempted to assess the strengths and weaknesses in existing plans and to develop a well-rounded program which, if enacted into law, would mean that the state would have a well-coordinated finance plan. On the basis of these studies several states have been quite successful in materially improving the legal provisions relating to school finance. In a few cases, however, certain phases of the carefully prepared bills introduced into the legislature have been amended to change some of the purposes or to impose controls not considered desirable by the study groups.

What would be the best procedure for a state to use in developing a sound program of finance? Would greater effort to get agreement on the characteristics of a sound program of finance and of sound financial laws be desirable? Would the organization of some state-wide group, such as the New York Education Conference Board, composed of prominent laymen and educators, facilitate the development of sound legislation?

How Much Detail Should Be Included in School Finance Laws?

In one state the laws relating to the major state appropriation for schools are relatively simple. They state the purpose, the amount of the appropriation, and a few general criteria to be used by the state board of education in making the apportionments. For example, they state that special adjustments are to be made for isolated schools but leave to the state board of education the matter of establishing standards for isolation and determining the amount of additional funds to be provided for schools found to be isolated. Procedures for determining uniform local effort are given in greater detail than most others. No requirements are established for participating in the fund except that the prescribed local effort must be made by each district.

Are these laws too general? What, if any, specifics should be added?

In another state, the opposite extreme is found. The legislature has prescribed a salary schedule including both training and experience. Districts are required to pay all teachers in accordance with the minimum salary schedule but may pay higher salaries if they desire. The procedure for determining classroom units is also set up in great detail but no adjustments are authorized for any small school. Provisions are made for units for principals and supervisors under conditions prescribed in detail in the law. The amount for transportation is based on approved costs and the procedures to be used in determining costs included are fully and carefully prescribed. The effort required for this aspect of the program is based on a uniform levy on assessed valuation even though assessment practices vary considerably.

There is a separate fund for current expense, other than teachers' salaries and transportation, based on a designated amount per classroom unit. A separate levy is required for participation in this fund. Districts must use the salary money only for teachers' salaries, the transportation money only for transportation, and the other current expense money only for other current expense. They must pay their teachers monthly over a ten month period and operate their schools for nine months. They can employ clerical assistance only when a school reaches a certain size. They cannot use any of the money for education of youth beyond the age of 21. The state board of education is not authorized to prescribe any regulations because the law is supposed to cover all points considered essential.

In the same state, a bill introduced at a recent session of the legislature included the following provisions:

> Beginning one year after this act becomes effective, any district operating a high school shall receive credit for classroom units operated in the grade levels of nine through twelve only if the following conditions shall prevail:
> 1. The total high school attendance shall exceed three hundred students in average daily attendance for a three year high school program or four hundred students in average daily attendance for a four year high school program.
> 2. Each such high school shall offer for those students preparing for higher education no less than one full year of required instruction in each of these fields: English grammar and composition, English literature, American history, world history, general science, biology, other specialized science such as chemistry or physics; and two years of mathematics, including general mathematics, or algebra, or geometry, and of foreign languages.
> 3. Each high school must have its school day organized into seven periods of no less than fifty minutes each including passing periods.

Do these laws or proposals include more details than are necessary? What criteria can be used in deciding how much detail should be included in state laws relating to finance?

Should Districts Be Authorized To Spend Public Funds for Publicity?

The laws in a number of states seem to express two concerns with reference to the relationship of school districts to the public: (1) that the districts should prepare and in many cases should publish at least an annual report; (2) that the districts should not spend public funds in an attempt to persuade the citizens of the community to support bond issues, tax levies, or other financial proposals.

Since the board serves as custodian for school funds held in trust for the education of children in a district, it is to be expected that an accounting to the public be rendered periodically. This accounting has a number of different aspects. Books and records are public property and are available for inspection by representatives of the public at any time. Periodic reports are prepared and the form for these reports is sometimes prescribed to assure that all pertinent information will be made available. Provisions in most states are made for auditing the accounts periodically so that the public will be assured that all funds are properly handled and expended in accordance with the provisions of law. There should be no question about the desirability of procedures designed to help the public keep informed regarding the financial stewardship of the district.

When tax levies need to be increased or a building program becomes essential in a district, groups may be, and often are, organized to oppose whatever proposal may be made. These groups may not bother to obtain all of the facts and may circulate information that contains only part of the truth or is misleading in other ways. If the board is not in a position to expend public funds to set forth the facts in the case, it may be at a decided disadvantage. The people may react unfavorably and the schools may be handicapped because most citizens have not had an opportunity to have access to pertinent facts on which their decision should be based.

Voluntary groups are sometimes organized to collect funds to be used in assembling and presenting pertinent information. In many cases these groups have rendered significant and helpful service. In others they have not had proper leadership or have not been able to get sufficient funds to make the facts available.

Probably most citizens believe that neither a school board nor any other agency of government should be permitted to use public funds for "propaganda" purposes. However, many would contend that there is a difference between propaganda and presenting factual information. Some of them at least would hold that the law should authorize expenditure of public funds for the purpose of explaining proposals and presenting facts. It is recognized, however, that in some cases it may be difficult to prepare a law that would cover the situation. What proponents of the proposal would consider factual information, opponents might consider to be propaganda.

How far should a board be permitted to go in using public funds to help to interpret the problems and needs of the schools? Can any safeguards be devised to assure that boards, under the guise of publicity, would not begin to propagandize?

Should States Abandon the Common Law Principle Relating to Non-liability?

Again and again, courts have recognized that damages have been suffered by individuals as the result of the carelessness of officials or employees of a district. Yet, under the common law which applies in most states, there can be no compensation by the district for these damages. For example, a North Dakota court held that "While the plaintiff's loss is a real one and the damages suffered by her are no doubt substantial, the law affords her no remedy." [31]

In a Kentucky case, the court held that:

> We followed the almost universal rule that a school district or a school board, in the absence of a statute opposing it, is not subject to liability for injuries to pupils of public schools received in connection with their attendance thereat.[32]

One of the problems in the few states that have legally recognized liability and therefore abrogated the common law principle arises from the fact that in some cases jury awards have provided what to many seem to be excessive amounts. One of the most interesting illustrations arose in the Dunsmuir (California) Joint Union High School District.[33] As a result of an injury suffered by a football player, a jury made an award of $325,000. The school carried liability insurance of $200,000. Eventually the Supreme Court of California had a hearing on the matter but the case was dismissed on stipulation of counsel, an agreement having been reached and the case settled in an amount reported as $137,500.

There has been consideration in a number of other states of the possibility of abrogating the common law principle. However, one of the reasons states have been slow to make the change, in the opinion of a number of people, has been concern over the possibility that high awards might involve some districts in financial difficulty.

If districts are permitted and authorized to carry liability insurance, a step would have been taken toward at least a partial solution of the problem. However, premiums on liability insurance have been increasing and, as noted above, the award might conceivably be greater than the insurance carried. Several of the states have recognized the desirability of this form of insurance and have attempted to provide adequate legislation.

---

[31] Anderson v. Board of Education, 49 North Dakota 181, 190 N.W. 807 (1922).
[32] Wallace v. Laurel County Board of Education et al. (1941) 287 Kentucky 454 (1941), 153 S.W. (2d) 1915.
[33] Welch v. Dunsmuir Jt. Union H.S. Dist. 326 P. 2d, 633 (1958).

The problem of extending workmen's compensation insurance to cover pupils is being considered by some. Campbell states:

Society needs such protection as much as the individual, because ultimately society must bear the burden, financial and otherwise, of the heavy losses which accidents entail.[34]

Since children of compulsory attendance age are required to attend school and have no option, a great many people feel that there should be some financial protection for these children and their parents against costs resulting from school accidents. If workmen's compensation insurance could be extended to cover pupils, it would be reasonably economical, because awards would be based on a well defined scale established by law for various types of disability. Furthermore, the simplified procedure for obtaining redress in workmen's compensation cases has to a great extent eliminated the expense and delay of costly court trials. It has been advantageous to workmen because they have not had to pay high level fees in connection with awards.

Is the common law doctrine of non-liability justified in modern American society? If the common law principle were abrogated, what would be the best procedure for assuring justice and equity both for the district and for the pupils and their parents?

SELECTED REFERENCES

Edwards, Newton, *The Courts and the Public Schools*, rev. ed. Chicago: University of Chicago Press, 1955. Chapters IX–XV.

Garber, Lee O., editor, *Law and the School Business Manager*. Danville, Ill.: Interstate Printers and Publishers, 1957. Chapters II, IV, VI, VIII, and IX.

Hamilton, Robert R., and Paul F. Mort, *The Law and Public Education*, with cases. 2nd ed. Brooklyn: The Foundation Press, Inc., 1959. Chapters 2, 3–8.

Hamilton, Robert R., and E. Edmund Reutter, Jr., *Legal Aspects of School Board Operation*. New York: Bureau of Publications, Teachers College, Columbia University, 1958. Chapters VI, VII, and X.

Morphet, Edgar L., "Fiscal Affairs," Chapter 7 in *Law and the School Superintendent*, Vol. 1 of the Legal Problems in Education Series, National Organization on Legal Problems in Education. Cincinnati: W. H. Anderson Company, 1958.

Morphet, Edgar L., Roe L. Johns, and Theodore L. Reller, *Educational Administration: Concepts, Practices, and Issues*. Englewood Cliffs, N.J.: Prentice-Hall, Inc., 1959. Chapter 2.

Remmlein, Madeline Kinter, *The Law of Local Public School Administration*. New York: McGraw-Hill Book Company, Inc., 1953. Chapters 2 and 9.

Spurlock, Clark, *Education and the Supreme Court*. Urbana, Ill.: University of Illinois Press, 1955. Chapters 1, 4, and 7.

[34] Douglas Argyle Campbell, *Workmen's Compensation Insurance: Principles and Practices* (Los Angeles: Parker, Stone, and Bayer Company, 1953), p. 14.

CHAPTER EIGHT

Local Financing
of the Public Schools

All three of the major levels of government—Federal, state, and local—have an interest in the public schools and all are involved in their financing, but the responsibility for the direct administration and supervision of the public schools is vested in one type of local government—the school district. This arrangement alone makes public school financing far more complicated in the United States than in those countries which provide for the financing, administration, and control of the public schools by central governments.

Students from foreign countries may well wonder why local tax revenues are provided for schools in the United States as well as state and Federal revenues. This arrangement certainly complicates school financing and it seems to divide responsibility. Would it not be better to finance the public schools entirely from state funds or a combination of state and Federal funds? This would make it possible to provide schools of approximately equal quality throughout the nation regardless of variations in local wealth or the aspirations of different communities.

The Federal government can levy and collect practically any important type of tax (with the possible exception of the property tax) more economically and efficiently than the state or local governments. Furthermore, the states can levy and collect practically any important type of tax more economically and efficiently than local governments.

Also, it is easier to develop equitable taxing systems at national and state levels than at local government levels.

Education is generally considered a state function. So why do not the states assume complete fiscal responsibility for the schools with such financial assistance as they may receive from the Federal government? If the public schools were completely financed by central governments in accordance with a "logical" fiscal plan, it would seem that the problems of school financing would be solved for local school administrators. It would follow then that, since local school administrators would have no financing problems, they could direct their energies entirely to developing and implementing the educational program.

REASONS FOR LOCAL FINANCIAL SUPPORT
FOR SCHOOLS

It is undoubtedly true that the Federal government could provide by a system of Federal taxes all the revenue now available to the public schools or any amount that is likely to be provided in the future. The Federal taxes could also be made more equitable in their effects on individuals and on individually owned or corporate private enterprises than existing state and local systems of taxation. Nevertheless, almost no one in the United States advocates complete Federal financial support of the public schools.

Our Federal System

The primary reason for this is that the government of the United States is a Federal government and not a national government. It has been so since its beginning. The name of our country, "The United States" and the fifty stars in the flag are symbols of this fact. Our Constitution allocates powers and responsibilities between the Federal government and the states. Laws are enacted by the Congress and by state legislatures. Public education developed by constitutional and legislative authorization of the states. It was provided in accordance with our plan of government. Therefore complete Federal financing of education would be inconsistent with our system of government. That fact alone is sufficient to explain why the public schools are not financed exclusively by the Federal government despite the fact that a completely logical taxing system might require it.

The Role of the States

It is also true that state governments could provide by systems of state taxation all the revenue now available or likely to be available to the public schools. State taxes could also be made more equitable in their effect on individuals and on individually owned or corporate enterprises. Despite this fact only a few persons in the United States advocate complete state financing of the public schools. This is difficult to explain unless the role of local governments in American life is fully understood. The words "home rule" in America mean the power and authority given to local governments as contrasted with the state government. The words "states' rights" mean the power and authority given to state governments as contrasted with the Federal government. One of the most interesting phenomena on the American scene is the continuing controversy over power and authority between the states and the Federal government and between the states and local governments. Times and conditions have changed and are still changing rapidly in the United States. Government services which at one time in our history could be rendered efficiently by one level of government can no longer be provided by that level. Changing conditions have forced the transfer of all or part of the responsibility for many government functions from lower levels of government to higher levels. This tendency toward "centralization" has been strongly resisted by many people who believe that important freedoms are lost through centralization of government.

The Trend toward Centralization. It is interesting to note that our economy has followed this same trend toward centralization. The small business man, the small farmer and the small manufacturer are finding it difficult to compete successfully with large enterprises. Therefore, we have seen the growth of big business, big industry, big farms, and big banking and financing enterprises to the point that, it is alleged by some, they dominate our economy. Resistance to centralization in the public economy may be due in part to resistance to centralization in the private economy. But on the other hand government control has frequently been used to retard centralization in the private economy. This of course has resulted in an extension of the sphere of control of central governments.

These national controversies are referred to in this book because they have important influences on attitudes toward school financing. There is a national trend toward centralization in both the public economy and the private economy. But the people almost instinctively resist further centralization because it is associated in their thinking with a loss of their freedom. The problem is how to obtain the benefits of centralization and at the same time suffer no loss in freedom. Specifically applied to public education, the problem is how to obtain the benefits of central taxation and at the same time retain freedom in decision making at state and local levels. This problem is dealt with extensively in the five following chapters.

The Role of Local School Districts

Let us now consider some specific advantages of local school financing. There are a number of reasons why there should be some local school financial support. There are many who believe that local financing increases local interest in the schools. It is also asserted that if the local people pay directly a substantial part of school costs, they will insist on more economical and efficient administration than if all funds were provided by the state and Federal governments.

Perhaps the best justification for some local school taxes is that this policy gives the local people the opportunity to provide better schools for their children than the foundation program of education provided by central governments. The foundation program provided represents the state wide political consensus. Thus, it has somewhat the characteristics of a minimum program in most states. Every district should have the freedom to exceed the minimum if it so desires. This freedom to exceed the minimum is not possible unless local taxes in addition to those required for the foundation program can be levied. This local freedom encourages local initiative to find new and better solutions to educational problems. Progress is hardly possible unless there is freedom to experiment and adapt to changing needs and conditions.

There is considerable evidence available to support this conclusion. Mort and Cornell found a positive relationship between the adaptability of local school systems and their freedom to tax and spend.[1] Woollatt found that new and promising educational practices were used most often in high level expenditure systems.[2] Those systems have sometimes been called "lighthouse" systems. The issue of some local school support versus complete support from the tax revenues of central governments has been summarized as follows:

> One's final conclusions concerning the value of local tax effort for schools will probably be decided in terms of his relative faith in conflicting values. If one believes that defensible theories of taxation and a

[1] Paul R. Mort and Francis G. Cornell, *Adaptability of Public School Systems* (New York: Bureau of Publications, Teachers College, Columbia University, 1938).
[2] Lorne Hedley Woollatt, *The Cost-Quality Relationship on the Growing Edge* (New York: Bureau of Publications, Teachers College, Columbia University, 1939).

uniform system of education are of paramount importance in determining this matter, he will accord but little value to local tax effort for schools. On the other hand, if one believes that local initiative, experimentation, and a large measure of home rule in education are of greater importance than tax theory and educational uniformity, he will place great value upon the desirability of local freedom to tax for school support.[3]

THE PROPERTY TAX

The property tax is the most difficult of all the important taxes to administer. As was pointed out in Chapter 5, the property tax finds less justification in accepted principles and theories of taxation than any other important tax. Despite these objections, the property tax is an important source of revenue for local governments (especially schools) and it will no doubt continue to be important. Probably the property tax will continue to decline in per cent of total school revenues but the total amount of school revenue derived from the property tax will continue to increase. The property tax must be retained for local school support if the policy of providing for local participation in public school financing is continued.

Variations Among the States in Assessing Policies

Evidence presented in a study made by the Bureau of the Census showed that the states varied widely in the per cent of true value at which property was assessed in 1956.[4] The range was from approximately six per cent of true value for most classes of property in South Carolina to approximately 60 per cent in Rhode Island. The ratio of assessments to true value was determined by comparing voluntary sales prices with assessed values. The median state assessed property at approximately 27 per cent of true value for most classes of property.

There are wide variations in most states in the per cent of true value at which different classes of property are assessed. For example, in Massachusetts, nonfarm residential properties were assessed at 42.2 per cent of true value, single family nonfarm houses at 39.5 per cent, acreage and farm properties at 25.4 per cent, vacant lots at 27.1 per

---

[3] R. L. Johns, Chapter VII in *Problems and Issues in Public School Finance* eds. R. L. Johns and E. L. Morphet (New York: Bureau of Publications, Teachers College, Columbia University, 1952), p. 236.

[4] U. S. Department of Commerce, Bureau of the Census, *Assessed Values and Sales Prices of Transferred Real Property*, Series G-CGA, No. 7 (Washington, D.C.: The Bureau, 1958).

cent, commercial properties at 55.9 per cent and industrial properties at 50.7 per cent.[5]

The total assessed value of property in the United States in 1956 was 272.4 billion dollars. Of this amount, 91.8 per cent was assessed by local assessors and 8.2 per cent by state authorities. The only properties assessed by most state agencies are railroads and other public utilities. However even these properties are not assessed by state agencies in some states.

It should not be assumed that the percentages of true value at which states assess property represent state policy as set forth in the laws of the respective states. For example, the laws of Alabama require that property be assessed at 60 per cent of true value, but property is actually assessed at about 20 per cent of true value for the state as a whole and individual counties assess property at from 14 to 28 per cent of true value. Similar conditions prevail in most states although variations may be greater or less. Therefore, it appears that in most states the policy is to give the major control of assessments to local authorities.

Administration of the Property Tax

Improvements in the administration of the property tax will affect both its equitableness and its palatability. There are a number of ways to achieve this, some of which are suggested in the following paragraphs.[6]

The assessment of property is probably the biggest single problem of property tax administration. In most states property is assessed by elected officials. It is only accidental if an assessor is trained in property appraisal. He is subjected to the usual political pressures on elected officials. Therefore, property assessments are far from equitable in many states. Different parcels of property within the same jurisdiction are assessed at widely varying percentages of true value. Large property holdings of individuals are often assessed at a lower per cent of true value than small holdings.

Property is frequently assessed at much different percentages of true value in different political subdivisions of the state. This causes great difficulty in school financing in those states having constitutional or statutory limits on the rates of local taxes or limits on the amount of bonds that can be issued as determined by a fixed per cent of the assessed valuation. Tax assessors actually exercise a large measure of

---

[5] *Ibid.*

[6] Property tax exemptions are discussed in Chapter 5.

control over educational expenditures in states that have limitations on tax rates.

State Services. How can this problem be solved? States which have the best property assessing practices have given some state agency considerable power to supervise and review local assessments. Some states give this agency power to make studies and to determine the ratio at which property is assessed in the major political subdivisions of the state. Some states have even given this agency the power to require all political subdivisions to assess property at least at a prescribed minimum per cent of true value.

Other states have provided a state agency primarily for offering leadership to local assessing officials. Such agencies provide in-service training programs for local tax assessors. These programs include training in the scientific appraisal of property. This approach offers much promise but when used alone, it may not be adequate.

Local Assessing Authorities. The state can be of great assistance in improving the administration of the property tax but there must be much improvement in the local arrangements for assessing property if much improvement is made. First, the position of tax assessor should be placed on an appointive rather than an elective basis. The position should have civil service status and appointment should be based on appropriate qualifications. This official should be a county official serving all subdivisions of the county as well as the county. Second, the trained assessor should be provided with an adequate number of qualified assistants to do a good job. All real estate should be discovered, recorded, and accurately appraised. Third, a non-elective appeal board should be provided to review protested assessments. Fourth, a single tax assessor and a single tax collector should be provided for all governments within the county.

In some states, counties are divided into different areas with a different assessor for each area. Assessments then must be "equalized" by a county equalization board in order to allocate county taxes when the county is used as a unit of administration.

In still other states, overlapping local governments sometimes have different assessors who assess the same property. Also some overlapping governments have different tax collectors. These duplicating and uncorrelated administrative arrangements add to the cost of the administration of the property tax and are irritating to the taxpayer.

Different points might be established within the county for the payment of taxes but it should be possible for a taxpayer to pay all his property taxes for different local governments at one office. If these measures are taken, the property tax will be made more equitable, tax avoidance will be decreased, the cost of administration of the tax will be reduced and the tax will be more convenient to pay. This will result in better public acceptance of the property tax.

In the states that do not use the county as an operating unit of local government, the largest unit of government available should be used for the administration of the property tax. It is not necessary for each unit of government receiving a property tax actually to administer the tax.

Classification of Property

The theory justifying the general property tax is that all property is sufficiently homogeneous that it can be lumped together and taxed uniformly. This theory has been increasingly challenged in recent years. Classification of property for taxing purposes gives consideration to differences in the characteristics of property other than true value as determined by the selling price of the property when a willing seller meets a willing buyer.

When property is classified for taxing purposes, different classes of property are assessed at different percentages of true value or different tax levies are made on different classes of property. Some of the purposes claimed for classification are as follows: (1) to promote more equity by adjusting the property tax to the yield of the property and to the ability to pay of property owners, (2) to increase the revenue yield (especially from intangibles) by reducing evasion, (3) to promote desirable economic effects by giving special tax treatment to improvements, residential property, and special types of industry.

The results of classification have not been too encouraging. When property classification policies are under consideration, a power struggle between different classes of property owners is the inevitable result. Property owners of each class naturally seek lower rates or lower assessments on the property they own. The net result of these struggles may have but little relationship to yield of property and ability to pay. There seems to be some agreement that intangibles should be assessed or taxed at a lower rate than tangibles. However, this policy has not generally resulted in securing a greater yield of tax revenue from intangibles. Whether it has resulted in more equity is a moot question.

A few states have classified forest and mineral lands for tax purposes. Such lands are taxed at low rates on the theory that no income is available until the products are harvested or mined. Then the products are taxed by severance taxes. This policy may be justified for it schedules the taxpayer's major tax liability at a time when he is receiving income from the property.

As was pointed out in Chapter 5, the wisdom of the use of the taxing system to give preferential treatment to certain segments of the economy is open to serious questioning. Classification of property for preferential treatment has the same effect as tax exemptions. Tax neutrality might be a more defensible policy than either classified property taxes or tax exemptions. Furthermore it is much easier to apply the ability to pay principle through more extensive use of state income taxes than to attempt to satisfy it by modifying the general property tax. In any event, the extensive classification of all types of property both tangible and intangible would add many complications to the administration of the property tax. There are many who believe that the administration of the property tax is already too difficult. Therefore, it seems that property classification is not likely to make the general property tax much more equitable or much more acceptable than it is now.

NON-PROPERTY LOCAL SCHOOL TAXES

The favorable influence on local initiative of local tax revenue for schools has already been emphasized. The property tax is the great local revenue producer for schools but it has a number of limitations, which have already been pointed out. Therefore, it is not surprising that many attempts are being made to secure local non-property taxes for schools. Boards of education in America generally have no machinery for the administration of taxes of any kind.[7] Boards of education do have the power to order the levy of a tax when authorized by law to do so or when authorized by vote of the electorate if such vote is permitted by law. That is, boards of education generally do not have employees with authority to collect taxes and the power to invoke the law on tax evaders. To that extent, most boards of education are dependent on other governments.

Boards of education sometimes do have treasurers under their direct control but those treasurers are only the receivers of revenue collected by other levels of government for schools, grants-in-aid, and other school revenues. Sometimes even the treasurers of school funds are employees of other local governments. It would be very inefficient tax administration if each unit of local government, including the school districts, had its own tax collectors.[8] Therefore, it is appropriate that some other unit of government perform the service of tax collector for school districts.

---

[7] There are a few exceptions—for example, Texas and New York.

[8] A school district legally is a state agency performing a state function and therefore is not strictly speaking a local government. But from the standpoint of tax administration a school district can be called a local government.

Estimated Local Non-property Tax Revenue for Schools

It is extremely difficult to ascertain accurately from financial reports the amount of local non-property tax revenue received by school districts. Some school districts receive local non-property tax revenue from taxes levied specifically for local districts, from non-property taxes levied by other local governments but shared with school districts, and from grants-in-aid from other local governments. The only non-property taxes completely under the control of school districts are those taxes which they have the power to levy.

The Bureau of the Census reported that school districts received $64,000,000 from non-property taxes in 1957.[9] Presumably the amount of such revenue was received by school districts from non-property taxes which they had the specific power to levy. School districts also received $193,000,000 of revenue from the local governments in 1957 according to the Bureau of the Census. It is assumed that this revenue was received by school districts from other local governments in the form of grants-in-aid or shared taxes. How much of this amount was derived from non-property taxes? Local governments excluding schools received 18.7 per cent of their local tax revenue from non-property taxes in 1957. Assuming that this percentage applies to the $193,000,000 received in local intergovernmental transfers, the schools received $36,000,000 in local non-property taxes from this source.

Therefore, it appears that school districts received a total of $100,000,000 from local non-property taxes in 1957. This is probably an underestimate because a considerable amount of local intergovernmental transfer is derived from shared non-property taxes. If it is assumed that all of the revenue received by school districts from local intergovernmental transfers was from non-property taxes, school districts received a total of $257,000,000 in local non-property tax revenue in 1957. The amount actually received was probably considerably in excess of $100,000,000 and considerably less than $257,000,000. In any event the total amount of local non-property tax revenue received by school districts in 1957 made up only a negligible percentage of total school revenues.

Efforts to Increase Local Non-property Tax Revenue

Local governments in recent years have increased their activity to obtain revenue from non-property tax sources. This is especially true

[9] U. S. Department of Commerce, Bureau of the Census, *Summary of Governmental Finances in 1957* (Washington, D.C.: The Bureau, 1958), p. 22.

of city and county governments. The property tax has been found not flexible enough in revenue to provide the government services demanded. County and city governments have sought and obtained some state shared tax revenue and some state grants-in-aid. County governments have usually been more successful than city governments in obtaining state assistance but most of the county aids have been for constructing and maintaining highways and bridges. Both county and city governments compete with school districts for "state aid" either in the form of shared taxes or grants-in-aid. In general, school districts have been more successful than other local governments in obtaining grants-in-aid. State governments have also aided local governments by using the state tax collection machinery to collect certain locally levied non-property taxes for local governments. This is sound policy, especially when applied to the types of non-property taxes that are levied by both the state and local governments, because it reduces the cost of tax collection and also the annoyance to the taxpayer.

We are particularly interested at this point in the trend of local governments, including schools, in obtaining a higher percentage of their tax revenue from non-property taxes. In 1942 all local governments including school districts obtained 92.4 per cent of their local tax revenue from the property tax. This had declined to 86.9 per cent in 1957. It is not a spectacular trend but it seems significant. Most of the increased local non-property taxes have gone to county and city governments. These governments have levied and are still levying many types of non-property taxes but the productive taxes in terms of revenue yield are sales taxes, gross receipts taxes, and payroll or flat rate income taxes. These taxes might all be considered regressive in their ultimate effect but they are probably less regressive than the property tax.

**Effect of Local Non-property Taxes on
School Financing**

Unfortunately the school districts most in need of non-property taxes can collect but little from that source. Only large urban districts containing concentrations of business and industry can obtain substantial amounts of money from non-property taxes. These districts are also usually the wealthiest districts as measured by the true value of property per pupil. The school districts with a low value of property per pupil frequently have high property taxes but usually they cannot obtain much revenue from non-property taxes because of lack of economic activities to tax.

The Effect on Equalization of Educational Opportunity. Numerous studies have shown that most measures of economic activity are highly correlated with the true value of property. Therefore, an increase in the use of local non-property taxes for schools will merely increase still further the wide differences in educational opportunity among school districts that already exist.

It can well be argued that more extensive use of property taxes by local school districts will also widen the existing differences in educational opportunity. That is true but states are already making wide use of techniques of apportionment of state school funds that partially equalize differences in ability to pay property taxes.[10]

The Effect on Tax Shifting. Furthermore, the geographical incidence of sales and gross receipts taxes can probably be shifted more readily than property taxes. People from school districts of little wealth frequently trade in wealthy urban districts. If local sales taxes are used for school support, then the people of wealthy districts actually tax the people living in nearby less wealthy districts in order to educate the children in wealthy districts. This is exactly the opposite of the equalization principle. It may be an expedient way for wealthy districts to obtain additional tax revenue but it is a difficult practice to justify on ethical grounds.

The local payroll or income tax is more difficult to shift to less wealthy districts than a sales tax. It can be shifted as far as people commute to work. The payroll tax is an interesting example of tax competition between cities and surrounding suburban areas. The tax was originally devised by city governments in part to tax people who live outside city limits but work in the city. Suburban areas then found it convenient to levy taxes on people who live in the city but work at industrial and business areas outside the large central city. It is true that payroll taxes apply to all workers in a jurisdiction whether resident or nonresident. But the possibility of shifting part of a tax to nonresidents is an attractive feature of any tax being considered by the tax levying authority or the people of a taxing jurisdiction. While taxation without representation was considered sufficient justification by Americans to revolt from the mother country, it is considered smart politics for communities or states to practice it on each other.

The Effect on State Finances. It may be that there is some virtue in the use of local non-property taxes for financing a part of school costs. But authorizing local non-property taxes will not enable the state to discharge its responsibility for assuring an adequate foundation program of education for every child in the state no matter where he may

[10] See Chapter 10.

live. The states have largely given up the levy of property taxes. Authorities on public finance generally recommend that the states leave the property tax entirely to local governments. The states received only a little over three per cent of their tax revenue from property taxes in 1957. Therefore, the states must finance their direct expenditures, extensive grants-in-aid to local governments, and extensive shared taxes with local governments almost exclusively from non-property taxes. This would seem to give the states a claim prior to the claim of local governments on non-property taxes. Furthermore the states can administer almost all types of non-property taxes more efficiently and economically than local governments.

The Effect on the Foundation Program. But more important than all other considerations, the states must assume a major responsibility for school financing if reasonably adequate educational opportunities are made available for all children. There has always been some difficulty in obtaining the support of some state legislators from wealthy areas for state appropriations for the public schools. For the educational leadership to advocate local non-property taxes for schools to the extent that they are considered by some as a substitute for general state aid is only giving support to those who have always opposed adequate foundation programs of education for all children no matter where they may live.

The evidence indicates that there should be extensive exploration of the possibilities of non-property taxes as a source of local school revenue *only after a reasonably adequate state foundation program has been established.* To authorize local school districts to levy a variety of special non-property taxes before an adequate state foundation program is established would not only delay the establishment of such a program but it would also result in increasing existing inequities in many areas.

Local governments other than school districts are more suited to the levy of non-property taxes than most school districts. If other local governments are able to obtain substantial amounts of revenues from non-property taxes, they should be able to operate without making such a heavy use of the property tax. In that event, more of the property tax would be available for schools.

TAX LIMITATIONS ON SCHOOL DISTRICTS

As has been previously pointed out, local governments in America have traditionally been supported primarily from the property tax. These units of local government have been given statutory and constitutional authority to levy property taxes either by a board for the local government or by a vote of the people or by both methods. Some states have had constitutional or statutory limits on local school property taxes since the time those taxes were constitutionally authorized. Other states have never limited the amount of local property taxes which may be levied.

Types of Limitations

There was a great increase in property tax limitations during the early 1930's because of the financial inability of many people to pay their taxes during the depression. These property tax limitations took the following principal forms: (1) an over-all limit on the property taxes that could be levied by all local governments, (2) a limit on the amount of taxes that could be levied by a board of education without a vote of the people, (3) a limit on the amount of school taxes that could be voted by the people, (4) limits on the purposes for which certain tax levies can be used.

There are also various combinations of these plans but probably the worst type of limitation from the standpoint of local school financing is the over-all limitation on the taxes which local governments may levy. This type of limitation puts local governments in undesirable competition with each other for the property tax.

Trends in Tax Limitations

There has been no trend in recent years to increase the severity of property tax limitations. A few states have relaxed their limitations somewhat, but not enough have done so to constitute a distinct trend. At this writing, tax limitations range all the way from a maximum levy in most school districts in Alabama [11] of seven mills on an assessed valuation that is approximately twenty per cent of true value to no limit in California, Connecticut, Maryland, Massachusetts, New Hampshire, New Jersey, Tennessee, and Vermont. If the purpose of these property tax limitations was to reduce school expenditures, it has failed because the total expenditures for schools have increased at about the same rate in states having property tax limitations as those having no limitations. Where property taxes were limited, school officials had no alternative but to press for more state financial support. They were successful in obtaining additional funds from state sources because the

---

[11] A few districts in Alabama have been given authority by special amendments to the constitution to levy a limited amount of additional millage for schools.

people demanded that the schools be financed from some source. The shift of part of the burden of school support from property taxes to state administered non-property taxes was a desirable end but it could have been accomplished without destroying the flexibility of the property tax.

Relationship of Tax Limitations to Assessing Policies

One of the most undesirable features of tax limitation provisions is that they are usually expressed in mills per dollar or cents per hundred dollars of assessed valuation. The ratio of assessed value to true value varies widely among the various political subdivisions in most states. A tax limit of twenty mills in a state which assesses property on the average at forty per cent of true value would be equal to: ten mills in a district where property is assessed at twenty per cent of true value; twenty mills in a district assessing property at forty per cent of true value; and forty mills in a district assessing property at eighty per cent of true value. This situation actually existed in Florida in 1959 as revealed by a statewide study. Therefore if tax limitations have any meaning whatsoever, they should be based on true value, not assessed value.

Setting Tax Limits

It may be advisable to set a limit on the tax rate which can be levied by a board of education without a vote of the people but there should be no limit on the rate which the people may vote. However there seems to be no reason why there should be a tax limit on boards of education if similar types of limits are not also placed on other units of local government. If a limit is placed on the tax rate which can be set by a board of education it should be placed high enough that the board can have reasonable flexibility in property tax revenue. If the limit is so low that the board always must submit for the approval of the electorate a tax rate much in excess of the amount it is permitted to levy without a vote of the people, then the limit is too low.

When is the tax limit which can be set by the board of education without a vote of the people too high? That is difficult to determine. Presumably the reason for having a limit is to prohibit a board from setting a tax rate that is so excessive it would put people in financial distress and otherwise injure the economy. It is doubtful if school property taxes in any district have ever actually put people in financial distress. Their financial distress was caused by general economic depression or other factors. Being financially distressed, they found it difficult to pay their tax bills as well as other bills.

What should be the tax limit, if any? Certainly a tax limit of ten mills on each dollar of the *true* valuation of property (or one dollar per hundred dollars of *true* value) to be levied without a vote of the people, will not be the primary cause of financial distress to people nor would it have any serious effect on the economy. Many school systems have had more liberal limits than that and there is no evidence in the literature that this authority has been abused to any appreciable extent. On the other hand there are many systems that are operating under much more severe limits than the one indicated above.

Actually the limit that it is feasible to set is determined more by the cultural history of the people in a particular area than by economic factors. If the people have been accustomed to paying relatively high property taxes for schools, they will accept a high limit. If they have been accustomed to paying low property tax rates for schools they are not likely to accept very high limits.

Earmarking Local Taxes

In some states, school districts earmark certain local tax levies for teacher's salaries, transportation, vocational education, school libraries, community services, and other special services. This policy places unnecessary restrictions on the board when it prepares and administers its budget. The needs of a service are seldom determined with accuracy by the yield of a tax levy. Almost always some services will be undersupported and others oversupported if the budget for each service is determined by the yield of a tax. About the only tax that should be earmarked is the debt service levy for bond retirement. All other local school taxes should be levied for general school purposes.

SCHOOL DISTRICT ORGANIZATION AND LOCAL SCHOOL FINANCING

In Chapter 6, it was pointed out that an efficient school district should have an absolute minimum of 1200 to 1500 pupils (6,000 to 7,500 total population), and that it could not approach maximum efficiency until it had 10,000 pupils (50,000 total population). The size and economic characteristics of school districts have considerable influence on local school financing. The greater the number of school districts within a given geographical area, the greater the difference in per capita wealth among the districts. The existence of large numbers of school districts is invariably accompanied by islands of poverty and islands of wealth.

In fact some wealthy small districts were deliberately organized to build a wall around some concentrated form of wealth in order to keep the taxes low on some favored enterprises. This is really an organizational device to provide partial tax exemption for the favored enterprises. The larger in area and population the school district, the less chance of giving favored tax treatment to concentrations of wealth.

Large districts with a diversified economy have other advantages. Such districts do not experience as much tax delinquency in distressed times as single industry districts. All the eggs are not in one basket. Wide fluctuations in property tax collections make fiscal operations difficult. Furthermore, a large school district with a diversified economy has better credit than a small district with a limited economy and it can sell bonds at a more favorable rate of interest.

A district can become too large for operational efficiency but it cannot become too large for local tax purposes. There are some who believe that some fiscal efficiency should be sacrificed in order to keep the schools close to the people. There is some merit to this point of view provided the educational program is not seriously affected by fiscal limitations.

Some states have attempted to preserve the educational efficiency of small districts of little wealth by providing for county-wide or intermediate unit-wide taxes that are shared with districts within the county or intermediate unit. This reduces somewhat the existing wide variations among the districts in financial ability. This is sometimes called "the second level of equalization" because it is a county or intermediate level of equalization above the state equalization program. If the intent of the second level of equalization is to provide a higher level foundation program for the constituent districts than the state foundation program, it is a justifiable policy. However, if the intent is to substitute county or intermediate unit equalization for state equalization, it is not good policy. County and intermediate units vary greatly in taxpaying ability. Only the state can equalize those differences by the use of equalized grants-in-aid. A poor county or intermediate unit can only equalize poverty.

FISCAL DEPENDENCE

A board of education is said to be fiscally dependent if it is dependent wholly or in part upon some other local government for its revenues or for budget approval. It is fiscally independent when no local government controls its revenues or its budget. There are various degrees and forms of fiscal dependence. All the local tax revenue of a board may be subject to the approval of another government but the local government may not have the power to approve or modify the board's budget. In other situations, the local government approves both the tax rates and budget items. In still other instances the board of education is completely independent of the local government but depends on it for a supplementary appropriation which it may or may not grant.

The worst form of fiscal dependence is granting to a non-school local government the authority to approve or disapprove individual budget items. Boards of education were established for the purpose of fixing responsibility for the educational program. When another local authority is given the power to determine the budget, and particularly individual budget items, the board of education is denied the authority necessary to carry out the responsibilities assigned to it.

Arguments for and against Fiscal Independence

Following are the principal arguments that have been advanced for fiscal independence:

1. Schools should be kept independent of partisan politics.
2. Education is a state function. An intermediary authority standing between the state and the local school board makes it impossible for the board to be in fact responsible to the state and the people.
3. Fiscal control of school boards by noneducational governmental agencies leads to *de facto* control of educational policies.
4. Control of school affairs by municipal or other noneducational local governmental agencies often leads to coercion in professional and technical matters and in the management of expenditures.
5. Fiscal independence leads to greater stability and continuity in educational planning.
6. Fiscal dependence leads to competition for the local tax dollar, thereby intensifying controversies between local governmental agencies and school authorities.
7. Fiscal dependence complicates school administration.
8. Fiscal independence is the only sure way to protect school funds from diversion to non-school purposes.
9. There is no evidence that fiscal dependence results in greater economy and efficiency.
10. The people should be able to express themselves on the important problem of education without having issues confused by a mixture with other governmental problems.
11. Separation of fiscal control from responsibility for educational results violates the basic administrative principle that authority and responsibility should go together.
12. It is desirable to keep educational control close to the people to preserve the elements of democratic government and to provide for the freedom essential for adaptability, adjustment, and invention.[12]

[12] E. L. Morphet, R. L. Johns, and T. L. Reller, *Educational Administration* (Englewood Cliffs, N.J.: Prentice-Hall, Inc., 1959), p. 456.

Following are the principal arguments usually advanced in favor of fiscal dependence:

1. There is a place for a unified and coordinated local financial structure. Intergovernmental relations are more complex and there is much duplication of effort and overlapping of functions when schools are independent of local government.
2. Determination of expenditures for all purposes should permit the weighing of the relative merits of each service. This recommends a single legislative authority.
3. Coordination of services in which the schools and local government are mutually interested is facilitated.
4. School services when delegated to local control and responsibility are in reality legitimate aspects of local government, the same way as police protection, public health, and similar services of general social significance.[13]

Unfortunately educational research has not shown the definite superiority of either fiscal independence or fiscal dependence. Well financed and poorly financed schools are provided under both plans.

Actually, which is the better plan depends perhaps more on social values than on the relative amounts of money received by the schools under the respective plans. There are those who believe that it is extremely important for the people to have the direct opportunity to determine the educational policies affecting their children and that those policies can be effectively determined only if they are separated from other issues of local government. Those holding this point of view believe that this can be accomplished only by giving boards of education fiscal independence.

There are others who believe that the only practicable way to determine how much of each local government service to provide is to place all of these services in competition with each other and then have the judgment rendered by a budget body that has the authority to control the budgets of all local governments including school districts. It is claimed by the supporters of this doctrine that the public economy would receive the same benefits from competition as the private economy. It is also claimed that an over-all budget approving body is needed to coordinate local spending. Thus, if it is believed that the direct determination of educational policy by the people is more important than the results to be achieved by fiscal coordination and intergovernmental competition, fiscal independence should be supported. If the reverse is believed, then fiscal dependence should be supported.

---

[13] *Ibid.*, pp. 456–457.

LONG TERM LOANS

Long term loans are of three main types: bonds, revenue certificates, and lease rental arrangements. A long term loan is defined as one that does not mature within the fiscal year in which the loan was obtained. Except under emergency circumstances, long term loans should be used only for the purpose of financing capital outlay expenditures.

School Bonds [14]

Boards of education are authorized to issue bonds (subject in most cases to approval by the voters) in 42 states and in seven states bonds for school construction are issued exclusively by non-school agencies. Bonds for school construction can be issued both by boards of education and by non-school agencies in a few states. Boards of education are not fully fiscally independent unless they have the authority to issue school bonds. Each state should provide a standard bond code for issuing school bonds and they should be made a legal investment for trusts. Some of the more important matters that should be included in the code are discussed in the following paragraphs.

Purpose of School Bonds. School bonds are almost always issued for the purpose of paying for capital outlay expenditures. Bonds have been issued in some instances to fund the floating indebtedness of boards of education incurred for current expenses. This is unsound fiscal policy and is now prohibited in practically all states. It was largely an emergency measure used during the Great Depression.

Boards of education commonly make some expenditures for capital outlay from current funds but when major capital outlays are necessary, boards usually issue bonds in order to spread payments for capital outlay over a period of years. This is a necessary policy. Most boards could not possibly make major capital outlay expenditures from current funds without seriously depleting their operating funds.

The borrowing of money for investment purposes is a common practice in the private economy. Private individuals, firms, and corporations commonly borrow money to invest in homes, furniture, land, business and industrial buildings, and producers' goods. Borrowing money is necessary for the functioning of the free enterprise, private economy. Investment is necessary for the production and consumption of eco-

---

[14] Most of the statistical information for this section was derived from Clayton D. Hutchins and Albert R. Munse, *Public School Finance Programs of the United States* (Washington, D.C.: U. S. Office of Education, U. S. Government Printing Office, 1955). The statistical information was adjusted in instances where evidence was available showing that changes had occurred since 1953–54.

nomic goods. Arrangements for borrowing money are necessary for investment. If borrowing for investment is sound fiscal policy in the private economy, it is equally sound in the public economy.

Term of School Bonds. A capital good should always be paid for by the time it is consumed. School buildings usually have a life of approximately fifty years. However, it is not recommended that school bonds be issued to mature over a fifty-year or even a forty-year period because interest charges would be excessive. For example, the interest would total approximately $1,000,000 on $1,000,000 of bonds issued at 4% maturing serially over even a forty-year period. Furthermore, the interest rate is higher on long term bonds than on short term bonds. The difference in the average interest rate of very long term bonds as compared with short term bonds may be as much as one per cent. This is especially true during periods when the dollar is gradually losing its purchasing power. Investors understandably do not wish to invest in securities that are likely to be paid in dollars worth considerably less than the dollars invested. The longer the term of the bond, the greater the risk. Therefore, investors demand a higher interest rate on long term bonds in order to compensate them for the additional risk incurred.

The number of years for which bonds may be issued ranges from 15 years in some school districts in New Jersey to 50 years in Maine. The average term permitted is approximately 26 years. However the typical bond issue actually sold probably matures over a twenty-year period.

Bond Limits. All states have some provisions of law restricting the incurring of indebtedness by boards of education. Usually bond limits are fixed at a prescribed per cent of the assessed valuation. The limits range from 2 per cent of the assessed valuation in Kentucky and Indiana to 50 per cent for some districts in Minnesota. Maryland prescribes no limit but all school bond issues must be approved by the state legislature. Alabama limits the amount of school bonds (warrants) which can be issued by requiring that the annual debt service may not exceed 80 per cent of the tax pledged.

The bond limits vary for different districts in some states. In Illinois the limit is 5 per cent for elementary schools and 5 per cent for high schools making a total of 10 per cent. In Texas there is no absolute limit but the state cannot purchase bonds when they exceed seven per cent of the assessed valuation and the total of debt service levies may not exceed 5 mills. Iowa, in addition to limiting school bonds to 5 per cent of the assessed valuation, limits the amount of school bonds that can be issued to the total that can be serviced by 7 mills. There are some other variations but in general ten states limit school bonds to less than 6 per cent of the assessed valuation, 13 states to from 6 to 9 per cent of the assessed valuation, 14 states to from 10 to 12 per cent of the assessed valuation, and ten states to 13 or more per cent of the assessed valuations.

It must not be assumed that these listed bond limits give an accurate picture of relative severity of the bond limits in the respective states. As has been pointed out previously in this chapter, states range from 6 to 60 per cent in the per cent of true value at which property is assessed. Furthermore the two states that have the lowest bond limits (2 per cent of true value) are reported as assessing property at only 22 to 29 per cent of true value. Therefore, the actual variations in the severity of bond limits are probably greater than those indicated above.

Unnecessarily restrictive bond limits have greatly hindered boards of education in constructing school buildings that were badly needed and for which the people were able and willing to pay. It is conceded that some type of bond limit is probably needed in order to enable the board to obtain more favorable interest rates. But bond limits in many states are inequitable and unrealistic. Since bond limits are usually based on a fixed percentage of the assessed valuation, the real limits actually vary as the ratio of assessed valuation to true valuation varies. For example, let us assume that a state has set a uniform bond limit applying to all districts of 10 per cent of the assessed valuation. But let us also assume that property is assessed in some districts at 20 per cent of true value and in other districts at 80 per cent but the state average practice is to assess property at 40 per cent of true valuation. These variations are not unusual. The effective bond limits based on average assessment practice in that state vary from 5 per cent in districts that assess property at 20 per cent of true value to 20 per cent in districts that assess property at 80 per cent of true value.

Assuming that bond limits are necessary, limits should be fixed at a given per cent of the true value of property (as is done in the State of New York) instead of a per cent of the assessed value. Unfortunately this is rarely done in the United States. Such a provision is practicable. A state agency could be given the authority to determine the true value of property in the district. This could be certified to the board and used to determine the maximum amount of bonds that may be issued.

What should be the limit on the amount of bonds that may be issued? It is difficult to suggest a rational basis by which to determine bond limits. The bond limits placed on boards do not correspond with their borrowing needs for capital outlay purposes. Wealthy districts may have more margin than needed and districts of little wealth never seem to have enough margin. No limit could be set high enough to give the least wealthy districts the margin needed because if a district of little wealth attempted to sell a bond issue disproportionate to its wealth, it would find no buyer. Only the state or the Federal government can remedy that kind of a situation. State participation in capital outlay financing is discussed in Chapter 11.

Despite the fact that bond limits cannot practicably be set high enough to meet the capital outlay needs of all districts, the limits should be set high enough to permit all districts to make a reasonable local effort to finance their building needs. For example, subject to appropriate supervision, boards of education might be given the authority to issue bonds for capital outlay purposes up to 4 per cent of the true valuation of property without a vote of the people and up to 10 per cent by vote of the people.

Approval of Bond Issues. Most states require that bond issues be approved at an election, 21 states require that issues be approved by a state agency, and 10 require that bonds be approved by a non-school agency.

It is common practice in the United States to require that school bonds be approved by a vote of the people. The argument usually advanced to support this practice is that property is usually pledged to pay local school bonds.[15] A bond issue, therefore, is actually a mortgage on the property of the community and it is argued that no person's property should be mortgaged without his consent. This argument is not so convincing when consideration is given to the fact that long term bond issues are paid in part by persons not old enough to vote at the time of the bond election. Furthermore, whether a bond election fails or passes is not a sure indication of whether the proposed building program is sound. Bond issues have failed when there was an urgent need for the projects proposed. On the other hand, bond issues have been approved by the people for many buildings that should not have been constructed.

The existence of thousands of expensive, inefficient, unnecessary small high schools in the United States is mute evidence that people will vote for unneeded buildings. In contrast, boards of education have failed to secure the approval of the electorate in districts where thousands of pupils were on double sessions at the time of the bond election.

One of the reasons why some boards of education construct facilities that are not really needed is that they sometimes consider it necessary to "give everybody something" in order to pass a bond issue. That is, the board believes it has to do something at practically every school center in order to get votes. This practice has undoubtedly raised the total of many bond issues beyond the amount necessary at a given time.

---

[15] A school bond is not actually a mortgage against the real and personal property of individuals in a district. It is merely a lien or evidence of a legal debt.

Is it not time to reconsider prevailing practices by which bond issues are approved? Ours is a representative democracy rather than a pure democracy. A board of education that has studied carefully its building needs with the advice and counsel of a professionally trained superintendent of schools, assisted by trained school plant consultants and a citizens' committee, is surely in a better position to appraise school building needs than is a popular electorate. School bond elections are expensive in money and in the time spent by school officials in attempting to secure the approval of bond issues.

It would seem to be sound fiscal policy to give boards of education authority to issue bonds without a vote of the people up to a prescribed per cent of the true valuation of property, and that additional bonds issued above that limit up to another prescribed limit be approved by a vote of the people. That practice is already followed in most states with respect to the levy of operating taxes for schools except that many states do not have an upper limit on the operating taxes that people may vote for schools.

If it is required that school bond issues be approved by a state agency, that agency should be the state education agency. No other agency is in as good a position to render service to a board of education in the process of approving the issue. The purpose of state approval of a local school bond issue should not be to "hold a lid" on bond issues but to furnish boards of education with the consulting service needed in planning their school plant programs. Some states have staffed the department of education with trained school plant specialists whose services are available to local boards in making school plant surveys. The services of state department personnel are also frequently supplemented by trained personnel employed by institutions of higher learning. Boards are also able to obtain valuable services from competent private school plant planning specialists.

No school bond issue should be proposed until an adequate school plant survey has been made. Therefore, a reasonable requirement for state approval of a bond issue would be that a competent survey be made. State approval could then be given, contingent upon the board using the proceeds of the bond issue only for the purpose of constructing buildings at centers approved by a competent survey. This type of approval might be considered by some as giving too much control to the state. But if boards of education were given authority with state approval to issue bonds without a vote of the people up to a prescribed limit, there would be less state control than actually exists when the state constitution requires that every bond issue be approved by a vote of the people. Furthermore, the plan suggested would surely result in better planned building programs than now prevail.

There seems to be no valid purpose whatsoever for requiring that school bond issues be approved by a local non-school agency. Such an agency is not usually so staffed that it can render the board of education any services in school plant planning. Approval of school bonds by a local non-school agency simply results in dividing the responsibility for the public schools without providing any compensating benefit.

Some states have imposed additional restrictions on the voting of bond issues. Examples of these restrictions are as follows: (1) permitting only freeholders (owners of real estate) to vote in bond elections, (2) requiring that bonds be approved by a majority of 60 per cent or more of those voting, (3) requiring that one more than 50 per cent of the electors who are freeholders participate in the election, (4) requiring that a majority of the assessed valuation of property owned by individuals be voted for a bond issue as well as a majority of the freeholders. These restrictions serve no useful purpose and are inconsistent with the principles of American democracy. A person who rents his home pays taxes in the form of rents. To deny him the right to vote on a bond issue on the assumption that he does not pay taxes is inconsistent with the facts. The provision that a majority of the property assessments must be cast for a bond issue actually determines the weight of a citizen's vote by the amount of property he owns. This is inconsistent with the American tradition of the equality of all citizens before the law.

Type of Bond. Thirty-four states permit only serial bonds to be issued. Some type of serial bond should be required in all states. Serial bonds mature annually over the life of the issue usually in smaller amounts during the first years of maturity and in larger amounts during the last years. The purpose of scheduling the maturing installments of principal in this manner is to provide for approximately equal total annual payments of principal and interest combined.

Serial bonds possess a number of advantages. The total interest cost to boards is reduced because interest ceases on bonds that are retired. It is unnecessary to build up large sinking funds to retire serial bonds because the sinking fund is used annually to pay both interest and principal. Also investors prefer serial bonds to straight bonds.

The serial-redemption sinking-fund bond is a variation of the serial bond. This type of bond issue is callable and obligations are paid off in serial order as rapidly as the accumulations of a continuing levy permit. Theoretically, this is a flexible instrument permitting the acceleration of debt retirement in good times and the deceleration when revenue declines. But since property taxes are usually pledged to retire bonds and the yield of such taxes is relatively inflexible, there may not be much advantage in issuing this type of bond.

A straight bond is the type which provides that the principal is payable in a lump sum at the expiration of the term of the bond. A twenty-year straight bond does not require any payment on principal until twenty years after the date of issue and then all the principal would be due. Such bonds require the building up of a sinking fund of sufficient size over the twenty year period to pay the entire principal at one time. The experience of boards of education and other public bodies with sinking funds has been unfortunate in many instances. There was always the temptation to divert funds from the sinking fund. This was frequently done and when bond issues were due they had to be refunded. Under the best of management boards were scarcely ever able to obtain as much interest on their sinking funds as the interest on their bonds. Fortunately straight bonds have been relegated to history and we should let them remain there.

School bonds are tax exempt and normally bear interest coupons that mature semi-annually. Installments on principal mature annually. These features are attractive to investors.

Many boards of education are issuing callable bonds. This is good practice because it gives boards the opportunity to refund their bonds and reissue them at a lower interest rate if the bonds were sold at a time when interest rates subsequently fell. It also gives the board the privilege of calling bonds for payment before maturity if it has the funds to do so. However, callable bonds are not as attractive to investors as non-callable bonds unless some special provisions are included. Such provisions may include such features as "bonds are callable on any interest date at a premium equal to one year's interest" or "no bonds are callable until ten years after date of issue" or similar features. Bonds should not be re-funded to extend the term of payment except in emergency circumstances. Re-funding for the purpose of extending the term of payment increases the total amount of interest paid because it increases the term of the bond issue.

Arrangements for the Issuance and Sale of Bonds. Bonds are technical instruments that must be issued strictly in accordance with the law. Superintendents of schools and members of boards of education normally do not possess the competencies necessary for issuing and selling bonds. Many bond issues and bond elections have been invalidated by the courts. Therefore, it is usually advisable for boards to obtain the services of a trained fiscal agent to supervise the details of the issuance and sale of bonds. Competent legal services are also necessary for calling bond elections. It is advisable also to secure an approving opinion on the bond issue from a nationally recognized firm of bond attorneys. Some states also require court validation procedures.

Laws usually require and should require that bonds be sold at public sale after due advertisement. The details of these procedures are too lengthy to include in a book of this type. This is an area of specialization in which it is usually a good investment to secure the services of trained specialists. However, fiscal agents and attorneys have been known to charge excessive fees for their services. Boards of education should be able to secure consulting help from the state department of education concerning the types of specialists that should be employed and the compensation they should expect to pay for those services.

Some authorities have advocated that the state issue and sell all school bonds. Under this plan, the state places its full faith and credit back of all local school bonds issued in behalf of local school districts. The district would initiate the issue. If it meets the requirements of the law, the state would sell the bonds and the local district would reimburse the state through annual debt service payments.

This plan would enable most boards of education to obtain better interest rates, it would reduce the cost of issuing and selling bonds and it would greatly simplify procedures for issuing bonds. It seems to the authors that this plan holds great possibilities.

Securing the Payment of Bonds. It is imperative that adequate security be given for the payment of bonds in order that boards receive the most favorable interest rates possible. When there is a doubt that a bond issue will be paid, it is not acceptable to the market, or if purchased, its interest rate will be high in order to compensate the buyer for the risk involved. It is poor fiscal policy as well as unethical for a board to default on the payment of the interest and principal on its bonded debt. A default not only injures the credit of the defaulting board but it also injures the credit of all other boards. Therefore, the state is fully justified in taking the measures necessary to prevent any board from defaulting on the payment of its bonds.

The bonds that are most attractive to the market are general obligation bonds that have a prior claim on the general revenues of the issuing body or that are secured by an unlimited tax. It is this latter type of bond that is usually issued by boards of education. After the bond issue is sold, the tax rate necessary to service the bond issue is fixed annually. If the assessed valuation falls, the debt service tax rate is automatically increased and if the assessed valuation increases, the debt service levy is automatically reduced.

The board should always build up its fund for debt service sufficiently to pay all interest and principal installments promptly when due. While serial bonds do not require large sinking funds, the fund should at least equal the annual debt service on a bond issue some months or even a year before the payments for any year are due.

Usually school bonds are made payable at some central bank for the region or the nation rather than at the board's depository. This is an attractive feature to potential purchasers especially if the depository of the board issuing the bonds is located in a small city. The bank paying the bonds is the board's paying agent. Banks charge a small fee for this service but this fee should never be deducted from the payments transmitted to the purchaser of the bonds. Any service fees charged for handling should be paid by the board. If the principal and interest is not paid on bonds at par with no deductions for handling charges, the interest rate is affected unfavorably.

One state (West Virginia) has made the state treasurer the paying agent for all bonds issued by local governments. If a local government fails to deposit with the state treasurer at any time sufficient funds to pay the debt service on its bonds, the state pays it immediately but reimburses itself from future grants-in-aid or state shared taxes payable to the defaulting government. This policy absolutely prevents a local government from defaulting or being negligent in meeting its debt service obligations. This is a sound policy because it improves the market value of all of the bonds issued by local governments.

Revenue Certificates

Boards of education make only a limited use of this type of debt instrument. A revenue certificate is payable exclusively from the proceeds of a particular tax or source of income that has been earmarked for the issuing body. City governing bodies make wide use of this type of security, but boards of education do not because they usually have no income except tax income. However, in a few states boards can issue revenue certificates against a special source of tax revenue available other than property taxes. In order for such certificates to be marketable, the tax must be irrepealable during the life of the issue and the annual debt service installments on the certificates must be appreciably less than the proceeds of the revenue pledged. This type of security is not as generally acceptable to the market as a well secured bond, in part because it is not as well known. Therefore, the interest rates on revenue certificates are usually higher than the interest rates on bonds with the same maturities. Because of this fact boards of education should issue bonds whenever practicable rather than revenue certificates. Legislation authorizing revenue certificates should include the provisions ordinarily included in a standard bond code in so far as they are applicable. In order to be marketable at a reasonable interest rate, the annual debt service on revenue bonds or certificates should not exceed 80 per cent of the revenue pledged.

Local School Building Authorities

School building construction was at a very low rate during the depression 'thirties and almost non-existent during World War II years. Bond and tax limitations had been tightened during the depression years. The school population increased rapidly in the post World War II years and major shifts in the population created additional building needs. School building costs rose rapidly after World War II. This combination of circumstances created a school building crisis after World War II that had not been solved in many states by 1959. The financial arrangements in many states were woefully inadequate to meet school building needs. Different steps were taken by the states to solve this problem, principally as follows: (1) loosening of bond limits and increasing assessments, (2) state assistance for capital outlay, (3) state school building authorities, and (4) local building authorities. All of these measures except local building authorities are discussed elsewhere in this book.

The local school building authority is a type of public corporation authorized by law to construct school buildings, to rent them to a board of education under a lease rental arrangement by which the board eventually obtains ownership, and to issue and sell securities and pledge for the payment thereof the rentals received from the board. This plan makes it possible to build school buildings in districts where bond limits prevent a board from constructing needed buildings. Actually local school building authorities were primarily established to enable boards of education to evade unrealistic bond limits. The existence of local building authorities is evidence of the fact that bond limits were unrealistic or that the state had not discharged its responsibility in assisting school districts to construct necessary school buildings. There is nothing more futile than unrealistic bond limits.

It would appear that a better solution to the building problem would be for the states to change their bond limits realistically and provide state assistance for capital outlay. But these sound, long range measures are sometimes difficult to accomplish and action cannot always be delayed. The local school building authority has provided at least one solution to the problem. It is not a perfect solution but thousands of school buildings have been constructed by local school building authorities and rented to boards of education. This is a more expensive method than issuing bonds to finance buildings. Interest rates are somewhat higher on the securities issued by local school building authorities than on school bonds. Furthermore, the rents have to be sufficient not only to pay the debt service on the securities issued by the authority but they must also pay the overhead of the authority.

The local school building authority has not solved the problem of the district with limited wealth. The rents must be paid from the resources of the board and if the rents are excessive there will not be sufficient funds left for operating the schools. Only state or Federal financial assistance can solve that problem.

One of the attractive features of local school building authorities is that they enable a board to obtain school buildings quickly without going through the expensive, lengthy, and controversial campaign usually involved in holding a bond election. Consequently boards of education, where building authorities are permitted, frequently obtain buildings through the authority rather than by calling a bond election even though bond limits permit the issuance of bonds. This is additional evidence that boards should be given the authority to issue bonds up to a prescribed limit without calling a bond election.

SHORT TERM LOANS

Short term loans are frequently used by boards of education to anticipate local taxes or state appropriations. Such loans should be retired in the fiscal year in which they are incurred. This type of loan is normally obtained to pay for current expenses. If loans for current expenses or current capital outlays are not paid during the year in which incurred, deficits accumulate that will eventually create a financial crisis. Deficits destroy a board's credit and eventually its ability to operate schools.

Floating debts, that is deficits that are carried over from one year to another, should never be accumulated. Some boards of education accumulated deficits of that kind during the depression years. Some even paid their bills in "script" which constituted mere promises of the board to pay when it had funds available. Some of the script or certificates of indebtedness bore interest and some did not. Many teachers and other employees were forced during the depression to accept their pay in certificates of indebtedness. These certificates naturally were not worth their face value and teachers were forced in some instances to discount their certificates as much as fifty per cent in order to pay their bills. These certificates were purchased in many instances by speculators who later received one hundred cents on the dollar for these certificates when the boards funded their floating debts. This was one of the most disgraceful episodes in the history of public school financing in the United States. Most states now prohibit boards of education from issuing certificates of indebtedness.

A board of education should pay the salaries of employees and other accounts on time. If its bank balance is not sufficient to pay accounts that are due and payable, it should have the authority to anticipate taxes and state appropriations by short term loans.

The board should not budget a longer school term than it can operate on the funds available. Any other policy merely "puts off" the evil day and adds to a board's difficulties. All reasonable economies should of course be exercised before reducing the school term. But the board's employees and its other creditors should not be expected to finance the schools. Some school districts during the depression actually requested teachers to work for a month or more without pay in order to keep the schools open. Measures of this type did not help to solve the financial problems of the schools. The people of America are able to afford schools and if they want public schools, sound fiscal arrangements should be made.

The need for tax anticipation loans can be minimized by a number of provisions. The July 1 to June 30 fiscal year is the best fiscal year for boards of education because it also corresponds with the board's scholastic year. The heaviest expenditure months do not begin until September and a fiscal year beginning July 1 permits a board to accumulate a balance prior to the opening of school. This is particularly true in states that provide a considerable amount of state appropriations for the public schools which is apportioned on the basis of one-twelfth of the total appropriations each month. The need for tax anticipation loans can also be reduced by setting the date on which property taxes are due early in the school year rather than late.

Some states have partially solved this problem by the state's obtaining a short term loan to anticipate state taxes. The state then apportions the proceeds of the loan to local districts and thereby eliminates or reduces the need for local borrowing. This plan usually saves interest. The possibilities of this plan should be fully explored in states where the flow of revenue requires considerable short term borrowing by local boards.

Boards also should carry a reasonable operating balance. The board should not end the fiscal year with a zero balance. It is good business to keep a reasonable working balance on hand at all times.

Short time construction loans are also used sometimes by boards. This type of loan is needed when a board has issued bonds but has not yet received the proceeds of the bond sale. Buildings may be urgently needed and the board may have started construction on a building before the proceeds of the bond sale have been received. This type of loan is payable from the proceeds of the bond issue. When properly regulated and administered, short term construction loans are desirable.

SOME PROBLEMS AND ISSUES

The problems and issues of local school financing are many indeed, as indicated by the content of this chapter. The following paragraphs deal with some special problems that may seem of less significance than those already presented but in specific situations they may become major problems.

Should Fees for the Support of the Public Schools Be Charged the Parents of Pupils?

This may seem to be a dead issue because progressive states many years ago made it illegal to charge fees for school support. But that practice is still permitted in some states. It is not unusual to hear suggestions that public school pupils, especially high school and junior college pupils, should pay a part of the cost of their education. How they can do so and attend school regularly is not explained. What is actually meant is that the parents who have more children in school should pay more of the cost of the public schools than parents with fewer children or families with no children in school.

A tuition fee of the same amount per pupil is one of the worst types of regressive taxes. Every person in the nation benefits from the public schools regardless of whether he has pupils in school. When men and even women are needed for national defense, it is the parents who reared the children that have supplied the needed man power. Parents not only have to send their children to school but they must provide for their subsistence. These facts are so well known that it seems unnecessary to refer to them. Our public schools should be free to all. Probably no tax worse than a tuition fee could be devised unless it would be a special tax levied on widows and orphans.

It is interesting to note that the issue of those attending public institutions paying a part of the cost of their education has been revived recently in connection with higher education. Tuition fees have been increased recently in public institutions of higher learning. There are demands that they be further increased. Also the National Defense Education Act of 1958 provided for student loans rather than scholarships for superior students. The original proposal was for scholarships. Almost half of the highest third in academic ability of high school graduates do not enter college. One principal reason for this is lack of money. Policies that make higher education more expensive than it now is will make this problem worse to the detriment of the nation as well as individuals. Should fees be charged for materials consumed in industrial arts shops and home making departments? Should fees be charged pupils attending public kindergartens and junior colleges?

Should Different Tax Sources Be Allocated to Different Levels of Government?

The use of the same type of tax by different governments has been a matter of considerable controversy. It has been urged by some that the different types of taxes be allocated to the different governments and that multiple use of the same tax be eliminated. For example, it has been suggested that only the Federal government should have the authority to levy personal and corporation income taxes, the states the exclusive authority to levy sales taxes and the local governments the exclusive authority to levy property taxes. Actually, in 1957 the Federal government levied 95 per cent of all personal and corporation income taxes and 54 per cent of all sales and gross receipts taxes. The states did not levy more than half of any major tax and local governments levied a little more than 96 per cent of the property taxes.

It would seem to be good policy for the Federal government to release some of its sales and gross receipts taxes to the state governments. Many fiscal authorities also recommend that state governments release the property tax entirely to local governments. It would also deem desirable for local governments other than schools to rely more heavily on non-property taxes and to release part of the property taxes they are now levying to school districts. But does it seem practicable to allocate completely different types of taxes to different governments? Each level of government needs some breadth to its tax base, and it needs stability and flexibility in its revenue sources. Furthermore, intergovernmental transfers through grants-in-aid and shared taxes complicate the allocation of tax sources.

Would the allocation of tax sources to different levels of government be of any substantial benefit to public school financing?

Should Capital Outlay Be Financed from Current Funds or from Borrowed Money?

Decisions on this problem must be made annually by thousands of boards of education. The total cost of a school building is much less when financed from current funds because interest charges are avoided. For example, the interest on a $1,000,000 serial bond issue maturing over a 25 year period will total $516,750 at an interest rate of 3½ per cent. This is almost fifty-two per cent of the cost of the buildings for which the bonds were issued. It is also argued by some that it is not ethical to burden the next generation with debts incurred by the present generation to construct buildings. These seem to be rather compelling reasons for constructing buildings entirely from current funds.

But as has already been pointed out in this chapter, most boards of education do not have sufficient current funds available to construct needed buildings. Furthermore, if a school building is completely paid for within twenty-five years of its construction, it has twenty-five years of "debt free" life, because a school building has a normal life of fifty years. Therefore, it might be argued that one-half of the cost of a building constructed from the proceeds of a twenty-five year serial bond issue is paid for from borrowed funds and half from current funds over a twenty-five year period. The next generation will benefit by buildings constructed by the current generation. Therefore, there seems to be no great injustice for the succeeding generation to pay part of the cost of the facilities from which it is benefiting.

Some large, relatively wealthy city school districts have been able to finance school buildings from current funds. Property taxes are levied annually to construct school buildings. These taxes are in addition to the taxes necessary for current operations. The yield of the taxes is sufficient in such systems usually to construct a number of school buildings annually. The construction program is as continuous as the current expense program. This is an ideal method by which to finance capital outlays. School systems of sufficient resources should use this method.

While most school systems must borrow money to finance capital outlay expenditures, no system should finance all such expenditures exclusively from the proceeds of bond issues. All boards of education should have some current funds available annually for school construction. Boards of education do not find it practicable to issue bonds each year. In the average system ten years or more frequently elapse between bond issues. A board may begin a ten-year period following a bond issue with relatively adequate facilities. If it is a steadily growing system, the buildings gradually become crowded. Eventually a school housing crisis develops and another issue of bonds is sold. This is not sound financing because housing conditions are not adequately provided for between bond issues. If some current funds could be made available each year for capital outlay, unmet building needs will not accumulate so rapidly. Buildings should be constructed and available when the pupils report to school. The capital outlay financing plan is not sound unless the plan makes it possible to construct buildings when needed. There are thousands of school systems in the United

States that are chronically two or three years behind in their construction programs. No plan is adequate which results in that condition.

For most school systems, it appears that a combination plan of financing school buildings partly from borrowed funds and partly from current funds is the best plan. Obviously the school systems of least wealth are not able to provide much revenue locally for current construction. Only the state or the Federal government can solve that problem. State provisions for capital outlay are discussed in Chapter 11. If the cash of the people of the community can be invested in United States government bonds bearing a higher rate of interest than school bonds, is it cheaper for the community to finance buildings by issuing bonds than by current tax levies?

Should School Bonds Be Tax Exempt?

Income from school bonds as well as the bonds of all state and local governments are tax exempt. However, Federal bonds are not tax exempt. Consequently the interest rate on well secured school bonds is less than the interest rate on United States government bonds of the same maturity. Investors in bonds are usually corporations, institutions, and individuals subject to relatively high income tax rates. Therefore, exemption of the interest on bonds from Federal income taxes adds to the attractiveness of the bonds.

It is asserted by some that the issuance of tax exempt bonds is not good public policy because it provides a means by which the wealthy purchasers of bonds can escape their just share of the tax burden. However, the purchaser of tax exempt bonds must sacrifice a part of his potential income by accepting a lower interest rate. The competition of tax exempt and non-tax exempt securities theoretically establishes the appropriate differential in income.

It is also argued that exemption of income from bonds issued by state and local governments is a Federal subsidy for those governments. However, it has not been established that it is unsound policy for the Federal government to provide financial assistance to state and local governments. Actually the Federal government is already doing this through a number of grants-in-aid. There are many experts in public finance who contend that the Federal government should further extend this policy. If exemption of the bonds of state and local governments from Federal income taxes is in reality a grant-in-aid it might well be a very equitable grant. It might be assumed that the governments most in need of aid are the borrowers. The borrowers of course receive greater benefits than the nonborrowers. Is it possible that the exemption of the bonds of state and local governments from Fed-

eral income taxes encourages those governments to borrow more funds
than would otherwise be borrowed? Is this good or bad in its ultimate
effect on the economy? Are investments sound policy only if they can
be made without borrowing money?

SELECTED REFERENCES

Anderson, William H., *Taxation and the American Economy.* Englewood
Cliffs, N.J.: Prentice-Hall, Inc., 1951. Chapters 6, 7, and 8.

Burke, Arvid J., *Financing Public Schools in the United States,* rev. ed. New
York: Harper and Brothers, 1957. Chapters 10 and 11.

Castetter, William B., *Public School Debt Administration.* Philadelphia: University of Pennsylvania Press, 1958.

Johns, R. L., and E. L. Morphet, editors, *Problems and Issues in Public
School Finance.* New York: Bureau of Publications, Teachers College,
Columbia University, 1952. Chapters 4, 7, and 12.

Linn, Henry H., ed. *School Business Administration.* New York: Ronald Press
Co., 1956. Chapter 12.

Morphet, Edgar L., Roe L. Johns, and Theodore L. Reller, *Educational Administration.* Englewood Cliffs, N.J.: Prentice-Hall, Inc., 1959. Chapters
10 and 20.

Mort, Paul R., and Walter C. Reusser, *Public School Finance,* 2nd ed. New
York: McGraw-Hill Book Company, Inc., 1951. Chapter 22.

National Education Association, *Tax Limitation Laws.* Washington, D.C.:
The Association, 1956.

———, *Valuation of Property, Assessments, and Sales Prices Compared.*
Washington, D.C.: The Association, 1959.

Poole, Kenyon E., *Public Finance and Economic Welfare.* New York: Rinehart & Company, Inc., 1956. Chapters 14 and 15.

Rosenstengel, William E., and Jefferson N. Eastmond, *School Finance.* New
York: The Ronald Press Co., 1957. Chapter 7.

Shultz, William J., and C. Lowell Harriss, *American Public Finance.* Englewood Cliffs, N.J.: Prentice-Hall, Inc., 1954. Chapters 8, 18, and 19.

CHAPTER NINE

State Provisions
for School Support

One way of assessing a state's policy towards education is to study its provisions for financing schools. Finance is a powerful instrument which may be used to facilitate or to retard the development of education. The amount of money provided, the purposes for which it may be used, and the conditions that must be observed in spending the funds greatly influence the kind and quality of education found in the public schools. Of course, a good basic plan for the organization and administration of education and for providing and encouraging local leadership and responsibility will facilitate prudential use of the funds and result in a better program of education than a poor plan. Thus, provisions for leadership, organization, administration, and finance, as evolved on the basis of the attitude of the people and their representatives, are significant determiners of the potential. It should be interesting and revealing, therefore, to examine the policy of the people toward education and its support and to ascertain some of the implications of the tangible expressions of that policy.

STATE POLICIES TOWARD EDUCATION

One of the primary purposes of the citizens of each state is to accomplish cooperatively through their public school system certain objectives relating to education. These objectives should attempt to assure

232

an adequate program of educational opportunities for all. The financial provisions are for the purpose of facilitating the attainment of individual, as well as state, educational objectives.

Possible or actual state policies toward public education and its financial support may be roughly described as follows:

1. Most citizens in the state want the best possible program of education for all children and youth regardless of wealth or poverty, progressiveness or conservativeness, attitude toward religion or politics, or other factors in the community in which they live. They consider schools to be a powerful means of improving life in the community, state, and nation. The adequacy and equity of the provisions for schools, including financial support, are studied and appraised continuously or periodically as a basis for determining weaknesses and planning improvements. Every effort is made to assure that financial support will be adequate for the needs in all communities and that organization, administration, and leadership are constantly improved to facilitate optimum use of all resources.

2. While there are many indications that most citizens are interested in and concerned about public education, they do not seem to give it top priority. They improve provisions for supporting schools from time to time when needs become obvious and urgent, but seldom make systematic studies to determine the status of the program except when serious problems arise. They seem to believe that the people in the various communities, regardless of their wealth or poverty, can provide good schools with a little state assistance if they want to do so.

3. The people in many parts of the state seem to have a laissez-faire or a complacent attitude toward public education. There is little professional leadership at the state level and practically no demand for such leadership. Excellent schools are found in some of the more wealthy and progressive communities but the situation in many of the less wealthy areas is far from satisfactory. However, during the past few years some lay and educational leaders, state and local, have begun to challenge the wisdom of existing policies and insist that greater attention must be given to the improvement of education and to the provision of more adequate financial support.

4. Many of the leaders in the state have apparently become suspicious and skeptical about the value of public education. On the one hand, they claim they want good schools and value local leadership; on the other, they criticize schools and educators and sponsor measures which make it impossible for good schools to be provided in many parts of the state. The people are interested in education, but there are many indications that they are even more concerned about high taxes

and increasing expenditures. Almost every step taken seems designed to give tangible expression to that concern.

Of course, no state can be classified under any one of the four categories listed above. Nearly every state has some desirable and some undesirable policies and provisions relating to education. It is encouraging that expenditures for schools have been increased greatly and that many improvements in the program for financial support as well as in provisions for organization, administration, and leadership have been made in most states since World War II. It seems apparent that most American citizens, regardless of the state in which they live, are generally seeking, in one way or another, to attain an adequate program of education. They seem to have a general idea that this objective cannot be reached unless schools are properly organized and adequate financial support is provided on a sound basis.

A statement in the foreword of a recent study of the costs of education in England may well characterize the situation in this country, too:

> In the changed position of industrial Britain in the modern world, it is conceivable that we shall henceforth have to accustom ourselves to living in a more or less permanent state of excitement about the education of all of our children from the primary school to the university. ... The public education system now carries greater responsibilities than ever before in determining both our technological future and the extent to which aspirations for self-advancement among all classes are satisfied or frustrated.[1]

NEED FOR STATE SUPPORT

Over three decades ago Cubberley wrote:

> The first important step in the provision of educational advantages for the children of a State has been taken when the people of that State come to recognize a broad and general responsibility for the education of all the children of the State, rather than for portions of them here and there. This recognition of responsibility is evidenced by the establishment of large-area taxing units and a wide pooling of maintenance costs. These mark attempts to equalize, in some important degree, the burdens of support for what is conceived to be for the common good of all.[2]

It is evident that the citizens of many states have not yet clearly recognized this responsibility or, at any rate, have not taken steps to

---

[1] Richard M. Titmuss, foreword to John Vaizey, *The Costs of Education* (London: Ruskin House, George Allen & Unwin, Ltd., 1958), p. 8.

[2] Elwood P. Cubberley, *State School Administration* (Boston: Houghton Mifflin Company, 1927), p. 450.

implement it fully. In only a small portion of the nation have large-area taxing units been established; in only a few states has the implementation of an *adequate* state-local program of financial support been attempted or even been given serious consideration by the people.

Most people in this country subscribe, in theory, to the idea that the schools cannot be financed satisfactorily on the basis of local funds alone. However, the situation with reference to state funds in certain states is somewhat like the status of local taxation for school support a hundred years ago. The idea had been accepted and implemented only in Massachusetts and a few other states when Horace Mann, in one of his famous addresses in New York (1846), affirmed:

> In this state [New York], however, and in most other states of our Union, and countries of the world, free schools are unknown. A fund may exist, a small tax may be levied upon property; but the residue of the cost of the school must be paid by those who send their children to it, and in proportion to the time of their attendance.[3]

Mann also had decided views on the distribution of school funds:

> I conclude, therefore, that every philanthropic and Christian view which we can take of the question,—how shall our educational resources be distributed?—points to a distribution of them which shall afford, as nearly as possible, an equality of advantages for all the districts in the town. If districts differ greatly in point of wealth, why should the tax money received from each, be handed back to it as soon as collected?[4]

Important Factors

The need of state support for schools should be much more obvious and is even more urgent at the present time than some years ago. There are two factors which make adequate state support for schools essential in every state: (1) variations in the ability of local school systems, and (2) trends in sources of income of the people.

Variations in Local Ability. Evidence concerning variations in local ability is presented in Chapter 6. This evidence shows that the differences have increased sharply with the growth of industrialization and other related trends in this country. The facts relating to differences in ability among districts within each state point not only to the need for state financial support for schools but also to a system of support which takes into consideration the differences in local ability. However, state

---

[3] Thomas E. Finegan, editor, *Free Schools: A Documentary History of the Free School Movement in New York State* (Albany: The University of the State of New York, 1921), p. 102.

[4] Horace Mann, *Eighth Annual Report of the Secretary of the Board of Education* (Boston: The Board, 1844), pp. 99–100.

support should not be expected to solve all of the problems resulting from small-district structure found in many states.

In a recent study of school finance in Canada the school trustees association made this interesting and pertinent observation:

> There are several reasons why local school districts should not be left mainly responsible for the support of education, among them are these:
>
> (a) The education a child receives must not be made dependent upon where he happens to be born or live.
>
> (b) Schools no longer provide merely a local service. With today's easy transportation, rapid communication and mobility of population, society demands a high standard of education for its own welfare.
>
> (c) With expanding industries and a growing shift of population from rural to urban centres, the level of education necessary, in both general and specialized fields, is higher than can be provided in small district schools.[5]

Changes in Sources of Income. As pointed out in Chapter 5, the sources of income of the people in the various states have changed considerably over a period of years. At one time a large percentage of the income of the people was derived from property. That no longer prevails. The rapid industrialization has resulted in marked and continuing changes.[6]

In all states, local taxes for schools are derived largely from property. If the sources of income for school support within a state are to bear any relationship to the sources of income of the people, there must either be substantial provision for state financial support or other local non-property sources of income for schools must be made available in the various states. The former is much more likely to occur than the latter and is much more defensible in light of the needs. As already pointed out, adding sources of income other than property for local support of schools would undoubtedly help with the financing but would tend to increase local inequities. Therefore, unless substantial state support from non-property tax sources is provided in every state, the sources of income for schools will bear little relation to the sources of income of the people. There are likely to be inequities both for pupils and taxpayers.

While the idea of state support is accepted in theory and to some extent has been incorporated in practice in all states, many people are still concerned about problems that may result from increased state support. This is a proper concern.

---

[5] Canadian School Trustees Association, School Finance Research Committee, *School Finance in Canada* (Saskatoon, Saskatchewan: M. P. Toombs, Secretary, College of Education, University of Saskatchewan, 1955), p. 90.

[6] R. L. Johns, *The Property Tax and Public School Finance*, N.E.A. Legislative Commission (Washington, D.C.: National Education Association, 1958), p. 4.

STATE SUPPORT IN RELATION TO STATE CONTROL

The statement is frequently made that "control follows the dollar." If this statement were inevitably true, it would mean that any amount of state funds provided for schools would result in some state control of the educational program and presumably that the larger the proportion of state funds, the greater the amount of state control.

There are a number of people and organizations in nearly every state that oppose any increase in state support for schools on the assumption that the increase would mean greater state control. The following quotation is typical of statements based on this assumption:

> Locally the desire appears to be for "more aid with less strings." In view of developments since 1930 and the current outlook, this pious hope is the equivalent of local surrender. A brief survey should convince most proponents of home-rule in school affairs that the opposite is more likely . . . each state's [school] system should be developed by the decision, and not through the default, of local units.[7]

Origin of State Controls

While various aspects of control are discussed in other appropriate places in this book, it seems desirable to review developments briefly here as a background for further consideration of the problem of state support. In the first place it should be recognized that state controls or requirements for schools did not originate with state aid. In fact the general assumption for many years was that local school systems could assume full responsibility for financing their schools. As Burke points out:

> After decentralized school systems were once established, states found that there were wide differences in school attendance, length of term, qualifications of teachers, and physical facilities. . . . States generally attempted to attain minimum standards at first through local support which resulted in very unequal tax burdens.[8]

The fact is that most states were not much concerned about the inequalities in local tax burdens until after the beginning of the present century. They were, however, increasingly concerned about assuring a minimum amount of education (primarily elementary education at

---

[7] The Tax Foundation, Inc., *Public School Financing, 1930–54: The Need for Local Solution to Rising Costs* (New York: The Foundation, 1954), p. 27.

[8] Arvid J. Burke, *Financing Public Schools in the United States,* rev. ed. (New York: Harper and Brothers, 1957), p. 395.

first) for all children, to be financed through public tax funds rather than through discriminatory rate bills, fees, and tuition charges.

States eventually learned that minimum standards could not be established and enforced in all districts unless sufficient funds were provided by the state to enable the districts to meet the expense involved in attaining the standards. The attempt to enforce standards for one aspect of the program in various communities often resulted indirectly in lowering other standards. Some districts simply could not make the tax effort necessary to meet state prescribed minimum standards and at the same time maintain satisfactory standards for all levels and aspects of the program. The burden on a number of districts finally became so obviously intolerable that state after state found it necessary to provide some state support.

Controls and Financial Support

While no conclusive studies have been made of state controls in relation to state support, there is considerable evidence to indicate that *the amount of state control is not determined as much by the amount of state support as by the procedures and policies followed by the state in providing the support.*

If a state assumes that only limited funds can be provided to assist the districts in financing their schools, it is likely to be greatly concerned with assuring maximum "economy" in the use of those funds. Moreover, if the legislature or officials of a state assume that local school systems are not to be trusted to plan sound procedures for meeting minimum standards and expending state and local funds, they will insist on a maximum of control.

Fowlkes and Watson studied state financial support of schools in relationship to local educational planning in a number of Midwestern states a few years ago. Some of these states provided very little support for schools while others made a substantial contribution through state funds. The authors decided that "No conclusion is justified that increases in state support result in an increased number of controls." [9]

The following observations seem to be justified: (1) There would be some state controls and requirements if there were no state aid; (2) Controls may be advantageous and desirable or may be limiting and undesirable; (3) Increased state support does not necessarily result in increased state controls; (4) Undesirable controls are likely to develop when the problem is ignored or when maximum emphasis is placed on

---

[9] John Guy Fowlkes and George E. Watson, *A Report on State Financial Support and Local Educational Planning* (Madison: University of Wisconsin, 1956, mimeographed), p. 80.

economy and efficiency in a narrow and restricted sense; (5) No control should ever be established at the state level that can more appropriately be provided by the local school system; (6) The objective in every state should be to devise a system of support that is adequate to meet the needs throughout the state and to restrict controls and requirements to those which are necessary to assure adequate and equitable educational opportunities.

KINDS OF STATE SUPPORT

Every person interested in current school finance problems should periodically review some of the early struggles, trends, and developments in this area. Since these are presented in detail in a number of histories of education and in some of the current books on school finance, only a brief summary will be presented here.[10]

Review of Early Developments

Connecticut, one of the first states to provide aid and the first to attempt complete state support, soon began to encounter difficulties:

> There was a time when the Common Schools of Connecticut were esteemed as the best in the world. . . . But within the last 20 years a change in all these respects had taken place.
> . . . It is cheaper as well as more grateful to pay a tax for the support of schools than it is to pay the same for jails and poorhouses. In Connecticut this right is denied and disputed. A tax may be levied on a district for the construction and repair of schoolhouses, but when a sum is to be raised additional to that which is to be received from public funds, it is left to those who have children to send to school. . . .
> This situation is unequal, anti-republican, and wrong, and it ought to be made odious. It should be held up in all its unfairness. The right of a town to tax itself should be embraced by all parties.[11]

It was natural that the states should have made many mistakes in attempting to provide financial aid for schools because most of the people did not see the problem clearly and none of them seemed to know what steps should be taken to bring about a satisfactory solution. Some assumed that the income from land grants would suffice to meet

---

[10] See, for example: Elwood P. Cubberley, *Public Education in the United States,* rev. ed. (Boston: Houghton Mifflin Company, 1934); Arvid J. Burke, *Financing Public Schools in the United States,* rev. ed., Chapters XV, XVII, XVIII, and XIX; and Paul R. Mort and Walter C. Reusser, *Public School Finance,* 2nd ed. (New York: McGraw-Hill Book Co., 1951), Chapters 19 to 23.

[11] Noah Porter, *American Journal of Education,* Vol. XIV (1850), pp. 244–75.

the need; others decided a state property tax for schools would solve the problem; still others thought limited state appropriations would suffice.

A major problem arose in developing plans and provisions for apportioning state funds. Funds have been distributed on almost every conceivable basis in one state or another at some time. Some states for a while apportioned funds to districts in proportion to the taxes paid. Others made per capita apportionments using the total population, the school census, some measure of attendance, or teachers employed. Even the number of houses, the number of able-bodied males over 21, and the number of families were used on occasion. A few established special funds for the particular purpose of helping poor districts.

One of the chief difficulties arose because states had not defined the purposes of state support. In fact, various purposes seem to have been accepted, by implication at least, at different times. One purpose was to aid districts in meeting standards established by the states. Another was to provide some assistance to all districts. Still another was to provide an incentive to districts to make greater local effort, and so on. Later, some states apparently came to accept equalization as one of their purposes. *However, equalization is not a purpose. It is merely a means to the end of assuring sufficient financial support to provide reasonably adequate educational opportunities for children throughout the state with reasonable equity for all taxpayers.*

In fact, purposes within a particular state have often been conflicting. The undesirable effects of one have sometimes offset the desirable effects of another. For example, funds provided as a reward for effort may make it impossible to assure reasonably equitable or adequate educational opportunities for children in many parts of the state.

As pointed out in the next chapter, it was not until the end of the first quarter of the present century that major purposes began to be clearly defined and procedures for attaining these purposes were available. Even after that time, however, the heavy hand of tradition continued to influence strongly policies followed in the various states. Many traditional practices have been continued and are still being followed in a number of states in spite of the fact that much more satisfactory ways of solving the problem have been available for some years and have been used in neighboring states.

The trend toward increased state support for public elementary and secondary schools has been noted. However, this trend has not been uniform among the states. For example in 1958–59, six states provided less than 20 per cent of the total funds for schools from state sources, whereas four other states provided more than 70 per cent of the total.

Classification of Funds

There are so many different kinds of state funds apportioned on such a large number of different bases that classification becomes difficult. Any system of classification has some advantages and some disadvantages. The plan adopted for use in studies and publications of the United States Office of Education seems to be as satisfactory as any developed thus far and consequently will be used here. According to this plan, funds and appropriations are classified on the basis of (1) use permitted and (2) basis for distribution and local tax effort required for participation.

Some funds may be used for general purposes and others only for specific purposes. Those which may be used for general school purposes without any restriction, or for any item of current expense, are called *general-purpose* funds. Those which may be used only for specific designated purposes, such as transportation or vocational education, are referred to as *special-purpose* funds. On the basis of the general plan for distribution and the local effort required for participation, funds may be listed as *flat-grants* and as *equalizing* or *foundation program* funds.

These two bases for classification may be combined as follows: (1) general-purpose flat-grant funds, (2) special-purpose flat-grant funds, (3) general-purpose foundation program or equalizing funds, and (4) special-purpose foundation program or equalizing funds.

It is interesting that all but eight states have one or more general-purpose flat-grants and all but one state have at least one special-purpose flat-grant. Several have as many as three or four general-purpose flat-grants and a few have as many as eight or ten special-purpose flat-grants.

The number of general-purpose equalizing grants in the various states tends to be somewhat smaller than the number of general-purpose flat-grants. All but eight states have one or two general-purpose equalizing grants.

More significant even than the number of funds or grants, from one point of view, is the percentage of funds distributed on various bases. Twenty-one states distribute more than 50 per cent of all of their funds as general-purpose flat-grants and six distribute more than 50 per cent as special-purpose flat-grants. In only 18 states are more than 50 per cent of the funds distributed as general-purpose equalizing grants and in only one state, Indiana, are more than 50 per cent distributed as special-purpose equalizing funds.

It is interesting to note there are several states that still have a rather large number of different funds or grants. Four or five different grants are quite common and as many as 12 or 15 are found in a few states. With so many different funds and grants it is to be expected that purposes are sometimes conflicting. As pointed out in various studies, local school systems are handicapped when the purposes for which the funds may be used are narrowly restricted.

The statement quoted below from the study by the Canadian School Trustees Association is pertinent for consideration not only in Canada, but also in this country.

> There are many kinds of grants serving many purposes. A pertinent question appears to be: "Would the elimination of all present grants and the substitution of one equalization grant in support of a minimum foundation programme adversely affect any phase of the school's work?" The simplification would save much time and money in departmental offices and ensure a known minimum programme in every classroom and give local trustees a little more responsibility and authority in determining the schools' offerings and equipment.[12]

Table 9–1 shows the number of different grants under each classification for 1949–50, 1953–54, and 1957–58 in the present 50 states.

TABLE 9–1

NUMBER OF STATE FUNDS OR GRANTS TO SCHOOLS

	Flat-Grants		Equalizing Grants		
Year	General Purpose	Special Purpose	General Purpose	Special Purpose	Total
1949–50 . . .	69	225	54	23	371
1953–54 . . .	90	217	60	28	395
1957–58 . . .	56	239	50	46	391

Source: U. S. Office of Education, *Public School Finance Programs of the United States,* U. S. Government Printing Office, 1950, 1954, and 1959 editions.

The purposes for which special-purpose funds are provided are many and varied. In addition to those which may be used for rather broad purposes such as for elementary schools, for secondary schools, or for instructional salaries, several states provide special funds or appropriations for administration and supervision, for school housing, for textbooks, for driver education, for pupil transportation, for school lunches, for health services, for libraries, for relief of emergency situations, for tax relief, for vocational education, for adult education, and so on.

---

[12] Canadian Trustees Association, *School Finance in Canada,* p. 89.

Bases for Apportionment

Fully as significant as the kind of grants or appropriations for schools may be the bases used for apportioning funds. Fortunately most funds are now apportioned on relatively objective bases. However, over two-thirds of the states continue to use some subjective basis, such as the approved budget or application, for apportioning certain funds. The percentage of funds distributed on these subjective bases is quite limited in all but three or four states.

The school census continues to be used as a basis for apportioning at least part of the funds in nearly half of the states. In most cases the percentage of the funds distributed on a school census basis is relatively limited but a few use the school census for apportioning more than 50 per cent of all funds. Other bases used for apportioning one or more funds include school enrollment, aggregate days of attendance, average daily attendance, average daily membership, number of teachers, number of districts, among others.

It should be obvious that some of these bases are much more satisfactory and equitable than others. The school census, for example, has long been recognized as quite unsatisfactory because the need for funds in a district is not directly related to the school census. As will be pointed out in the next chapter, the number of weighted pupils or the number of adjusted classroom units provides the only sound and defensible basis for determining need and for use in apportioning funds except for transportation. The question should continue to be raised as to why so many states, year after year, use bases for apportioning funds which have one or more unsatisfactory features. Until more states can get away from some of these unsatisfactory procedures, the situation will be far from desirable.

SOURCES OF STATE SUPPORT

State funds for support of schools are derived from income from permanent endowments established chiefly on the basis of the revenues from the early land grants, from earmarked state taxes, and from state appropriations from the general fund. The revenues from endowments constitute a little more than one per cent of the state revenues provided for schools. Only in Colorado, Idaho, Montana, Nebraska, North Dakota, South Dakota, and Wyoming do they constitute more than 10 per cent of all state funds.

A majority of the states, for reasons pointed out earlier, have abandoned the idea of obtaining revenues from earmarked taxes, that is from taxes levied specifically to provide revenue for school purposes. Less than 20 per cent of all funds came from this source in 1955–56. The states deriving more than 50 per cent of their state revenues for school purposes from earmarked taxes were Alabama, Kansas, Louisiana, Massachusetts, Minnesota, New Mexico, North Dakota, Texas, Utah, and Wyoming. Taxes earmarked for schools range from income, sales, and property taxes through license, poll, severance, and miscellaneous tax sources.

The only states that derive more than two per cent of their revenues for school purposes from state property taxes are Alabama, Indiana, Louisiana, Nebraska, Nevada, Texas, Utah, and Wyoming. In fact, only in two states, Nevada (14.0%) and Wyoming (27.4%), does more than 8 per cent come from state property taxes.

The general trend has been to eliminate state property taxes for schools, to reduce reliance on other earmarked tax sources, except in a few states, and to depend on appropriations from the general fund for the state funds used for school support. In other words there has been a distinct tendency for state revenues for schools to be derived from non-property tax sources and, consequently, the provision of state funds in most states results in broadening the tax base.

IMPROVING STATE SUPPORT PROGRAMS

It should be obvious that the fiscal policy relating to school support in every state and in the nation needs continuous analysis and review. Unless this is done, any existing inadequacies and handicaps are almost certain to be continued. Some of the major considerations and problems involved in improving state support programs are as follows:

1. Major improvements in state support programs require in each state some plan for assuring leadership and sponsorship for needed studies and analyses, as pointed out in Chapter 2. The leadership should come from both educators and laymen. The sponsoring committee or organization should be composed of leaders in whom the people of the state will have confidence.

2. Before there can be any satisfactory evaluation of the existing program or before sound long-range plans can be developed with any assurance that they will be acceptable, substantial agreement must be reached on the principles and characteristics of a satisfactory plan for financing schools. These principles and characteristics can then be used as guides for conducting studies and planning improvements.

3. The studies, which should be cooperatively planned and conducted, should involve a careful and systematic analysis of all aspects

of the program. All pertinent facts should be sought, analyzed, and evaluated in light of the principles and criteria agreed upon.

4. An excessive number of special funds is a serious problem in a number of states. The effects of these special funds should be carefully examined.

5. An especially acute problem frequently arises in connection with the question as to what should be done about existing flat-grants and special-purpose funds. If they are arbitrarily discontinued, there may be injustices. There is almost certain to be considerable dissatisfaction. The best opportunity to consolidate miscellaneous special funds is when additional state support can be provided.

6. In every state in which there are small districts there are special problems resulting from inadequate district organization which cannot be solved easily. These problems must be faced if a satisfactory financial plan is developed.

7. The determination of funds which should be provided through local uniform effort also creates serious problems in many states. Some contend that the program for financing schools should either not be improved until all property is assessed equitably or that the state should provide all funds needed and that local effort should be ignored. There is no justification for penalizing children because the adults of this generation have not worked out a satisfactory solution for the problem of assessments. A formula can be devised in every state for assuring equitable local effort by using either an assessment ratio plan or an index of taxpaying ability, as pointed out in Chapter 6.

8. A special problem is encountered in states in which, because of inadequate support or for other reasons, expenditures have been particularly low in certain districts. There are people who will take the position that increasing the funds to an adequate amount would result in unwise expenditures or extravagance in those districts. For example, a few years ago the Tax Foundation warned: "A further possibility is that the established minimum program may reach an expenditure level that results in an uneconomic use of state funds, particularly among the smallest units." [13] That is possible, but experience in the various states does not seem to justify the conclusion that a marked increase in needed funds for the least wealthy districts should be a matter of particular concern. It may take some of the less progressive districts a few years to make satisfactory adjustments. Some states have provided that, when expenditures in any district have been considerably below the amount provided by a new program, the allotment will be

---

[13] Tax Foundation, *Public School Financing, 1930–54*, p. 30.

increased over present expenditures by, for example, 25 per cent a year for four years before the maximum is included.

9. Some of the existing state funds are likely to have provisions involving matching, rewards for effort, or penalties for children rather than taxpayers. Similar proposals may be made with reference to new funds or even in connection with the foundation program. The fallacies in laws or proposals of this type should be carefully studied so provision can be made to assure that they are not perpetuated.

10. There are some who seek to impose special sanctions or controls on districts of any type. There are much better ways of promoting and assuring prudential use of the funds than through controls that are not necessary or desirable in a great many districts of the state and which, if imposed, would result in some handicaps or restrictions on all districts.

11. One of the problems that arises in a number of states, even after a sound plan for financing schools has been agreed upon, involves the appropriation of funds. The practice for many years, in a number of states, has been to appropriate a designated sum for the biennium. In a rapidly growing state an amount which is adequate the first year of the biennium is often inadequate during the second year.

PROCEDURES FOR APPRAISING PROVISIONS
FOR FINANCING SCHOOLS

As pointed out in a recent report:

> An ultimate test of financial policy is the wholesomeness of the educational conditions in each administrative unit. If the policies are sound, conditions will be *good* in the great cities, in the small cities, in the villages, and in the rural areas; they will be *good* in rich communities, in average communities, and in poor communities.[14]

How can the wholesomeness of the financial policies in a state be tested? Obviously, there should be systematic studies of all aspects of the educational program periodically as one basis for appraising the policies. It is equally important to determine the extent to which the entire plan of financial support is adequate and equitable. This cannot be done satisfactorily by studying any one phase of the plan in isolation, but will require a careful study of all aspects of state, local, and Federal provisions for financing schools. Some procedures which should be used in appraising the state provisions for financing schools are discussed briefly on the following pages.

---

[14] National Education Association, Committee on Tax Education and School Finance, *Guides to the Improvement of State School Finance Programs* (Washington, D.C.: The Association, 1958), p. 7.

The Use of Criteria

The criteria proposed in Chapter 10 which were developed specifically for appraising foundation program plans, or similar acceptable criteria, should be used as one basis for studying the program. An attempt shoud be made to determine whether each criterion is satisfactorily observed, and, after each has been studied, to ascertain the over-all implications.

Special Items to Be Studied

The discussion below directs attention to some items which are particularly important and should have special consideration.[15]

Are there any rewards for inefficiency or lack of economy? [16] In some cases the state provisions for financing schools tend to perpetuate inefficiently organized districts or schools, stimulate emphasis on certain aspects of the educational program through special appropriations, encourage uneconomical expenditures or promote inefficiency by various unsound but often unintentional features. All such rewards should be identified and eliminated.

Has provision been made for all essential elements of school costs? Some states provide funds only for certain special purposes and not for others. A number of states have provided more generously for certain aspects of the program (such as high schools or vocational education) than for others. A thorough examination should show whether the state plan helps to assure, or to retard the development of, a comprehensive and properly balanced educational program.

Are there any undesirable state controls? Most state requirements undoubtedly were not designed to restrict local initiative or responsibility. However, studies show that a number of states have enough limitations on taxes, on authority to vote bonds, or on ability of districts to use funds for the kind of program they desire, to discourage local initiative and responsibility.

Are the sources of revenue for school support reasonably related to the sources of income of the people of the state? This question involves the issue of the appropriate proportion of the funds derived from prop-

15 Adapted from Edgar L. Morphet, "The Foundation Program and Public School Finance," *State Government,* special education issue, Vol. XXV, No. 9 (September, 1952), pp. 192–196.

16 Illustrations may be found in "Some Effects of Finance Policies and Practices on the Public School Program," Phi Delta Kappa Commission on Support of Public Education, Edgar L. Morphet, Chairman, *The Phi Delta Kappan,* Vol. XXXIII, No. 1 (September, 1951), pp. 5–44.

erty taxes or from other tax sources in the various districts or on a state-wide basis.

Are the measures of need sound and realistic? Rough measures of need that represent only approximations or that include subjective provisions are no longer considered desirable.

Is local financial ability properly and equitably determined? When assessment practices vary, as they do in most states, the requirement for a uniform millage levy is not equitable. Either an assessment ratio or an index plan becomes necessary. In determining local ability, major sources of revenue other than property taxes should also be taken into consideration.

Is provision made for adequate financial support? Many states for one reason or another have made a gesture toward financing schools but have not gone far enough to assure that schools in all districts can be properly supported. If the state provides only a small appropriation, only a certain percentage of the cost (for example, 60 per cent), or omits entirely certain aspects such as transportation or capital outlay, provisions are almost certain to be inadequate.

Equity of the Program

A comprehensive study of expenditure programs was made by the Office of Education in 1950.[17] This study showed the range in current expense (except for transportation) per classroom unit in districts throughout each state. Expenditures were used because it was found impracticable to obtain information based on receipts from uniform local effort. The expenditures in the United States ranged from less than $1,000 in a few classroom units to over $12,000 in others. The range in some of the states was nearly as great as that found when all districts in the nation were considered. However, for one reason or another, the range in several states was relatively small. For example, in Utah the range was only from about $3,500 per classroom unit to about $6,500. This range, of course, reflected in part the impact of the relatively large districts found in the state, but it may have also reflected undesirable state limitations on tax levies and expenditure for the various districts.

Is the Plan Equitable? A much better procedure for determining the equity of the plan is illustrated by a study recently completed in Cali-

---

[17] Clayton D. Hutchins and Albert R. Munse, *Expenditures for Education at the Midcentury*, U. S. Office of Education (Washington, D.C.: U. S. Government Printing Office, 1953).

fornia.[18] In this study an attempt was made to ascertain for each of the districts (ranging from wealthy to poor) selected for study: (1) the amount of revenue available from state funds except those for capital outlay and transportation (funds for purposes such as capital outlay and transportation should not be included because they are not always directly related to the ongoing expenditure per classroom unit and would distort the picture for a number of districts); (2) the amount available from the uniform local effort required to participate in the foundation program, assuming that every district should at least make that local effort; (3) the number of classroom units in the district (using a formula similar to the one used in *Expenditures for Education at the Midcentury*). From this information it was possible to determine the amount available per classroom unit in each district by dividing the revenue from local and from state sources, and from local and state sources combined, by the number of classroom units.

When this procedure is used it is possible to hold local effort constant and thus study the probable impact of the financial program on educational opportunity and on equity. When expenditures are used rather than revenue, local effort is not held constant. In the California study, on the basis of uniform local effort, it was found that the elementary district having greatest ability per classroom unit (which received flat-grant funds but did not need equalization funds) had available over thirteen times the amount per classroom unit provided in the equalization districts. Even though high school districts were generally much larger and more wealthy than most elementary districts, the study showed that the amount available per classroom unit on this basis was approximately four times as much in the most wealthy high school district as in those benefiting from the equalization program.

Studies Show Problems. Studies made in a number of states show that when local effort is uniform, the revenues available per classroom unit in the most wealthy district within a state are often from two to several times those available in the least wealthy. Thus, it should be evident there are some serious problems to be faced in such states. The problems arise partly from the district structure. When there are many small districts there are bound to be extremes in wealth, and no state-local finance program can be developed that will even out such inequities. The studies also point to possible inadequacies in the equalization program. It may be that, as in the case of California, so much

[18] Edgar L. Morphet, with the assistance of Benjamin M. Harris and C. Earl Miller, Jr., *Financial Equalization in the Public Schools of California*, 1959 Legislative Problems No. 1 (Berkeley: Bureau of Public Administration, University of California, 1958).

emphasis has been placed on flat-grants that insufficient funds are made available for equalizing purposes.

Chart IV illustrates the situation found in one state, with flat-grants and a "weak district" equalization program, on the basis of the study suggested here. Selected districts are arranged according to wealth or ability. The amount available per classroom unit in each district from the local uniform effort and state funds, except for transportation and

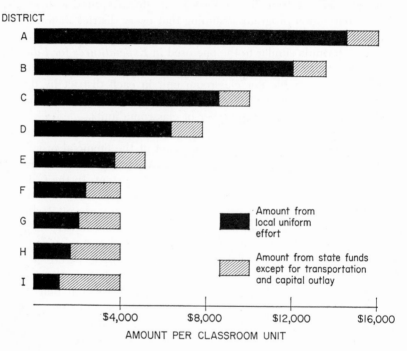

CHART IV. *Amount Available per Classroom Unit in Selected Districts from Local Uniform Effort and from State Funds.*

capital outlay, is shown by the length of the bar for the district. It will be noted that the most able district (A) has available approximately four times as much per classroom unit as any of the districts receiving equalization funds (F, G, H, and I).

The important conclusion that can be drawn from such studies is that either the taxpayers or the pupils (or both) in the more wealthy districts in a number of states have a decided advantage over those residing in less wealthy districts. If more favored districts choose to do so, they can virtually obtain a monopoly of the good teachers in the state. The less wealthy districts in such situations will constantly be confronted with the probability of losing their best personnel and, consequently, will always be handicapped.

The people in all states, therefore, should make studies of this type from time to time, and when serious inequities are found they should take steps to improve their financing plan or to improve their district organization, or probably both. Numerous studies conducted in many states show that the foundation program plan of school financing provides the best available solution for the problems discussed in this chapter. It is described in detail in the following chapter.

SOME PROBLEMS AND ISSUES

A few of the important problems and issues relating to state support of public schools are discussed briefly on the following pages.

Should Public Tax Funds Ever Be Used to Support Non-Public Schools?

In Chapter 7 the question, "To what extent can public tax funds be used to support non-public schools?" was discussed in terms of legal provisions and court decisions. The issue discussed here is not one of law but of principle. Laws and even constitutional provisions can be changed and are changed from time to time to conform to the prevailing philosophy held by the people. These changes can be good or bad, desirable or undesirable, from a long-range point of view. The issue discussed here then is: Should the American people consider or support any changes in law that would make it possible to use public tax funds for the benefit or support of non-public schools?

Issue Not Settled. Most people would hold that this issue was settled when the Constitution and the first ten Amendments thereto were adopted. However, as pointed out by histories of education, the issue was not resolved for the various states at that time. Church and private schools continued to receive aid for many years. In fact, in some states public schools in reality were not established and supported as such until about, or even after, the middle of the last century. One of the most bitter battles of that century involved the question of aid from public tax funds for non-public schools. According to Cubberley one of the most violent controversies over the division of public school funds among religious denominations for aid to their schools took place in New York City.[19] This controversy was eventually resolved in 1842

[19] Elwood P. Cubberley, *Public Education in the United States,* rev. ed. (Boston: Houghton Mifflin Company, 1934), Chapter VII.

when the legislature provided that no public aid should be given to any school in which "any religious, sectarian, doctrine, or tenet is taught, inculcated, or practiced."

However, while the issue was apparently legally resolved in practically all states during the 19th century by constitutional provisions that prevented the use of public tax funds for the support of non-public schools, the problem was not solved satisfactorily as far as many people were concerned. The issue has continued to be agitated from time to time in one place or another. During the past few years the controversy has been renewed in a number of quarters. Certain officials of the Roman Catholic Church have taken the position that there should be no Federal aid for schools unless funds are provided at least for services to parochial schools.[20] Some of them have insisted that the time has come to change, if necessary, both Federal and state constitutional provisions to make it possible for the people in any state who choose to do so, to make available funds for parochial schools or for services to those schools.

Points of View. The advocates of this point of view contend that:

1. In many European countries and in several provinces of Canada public tax funds are provided for the support of all schools, and that the people have benefited from such provision.

2. Unless tax funds are made available for the support of non-public schools, the state or the Federal government is in effect discriminating against such schools and their patrons.

3. The policy of requiring people to pay taxes to support public schools and of prohibiting the use of any of these tax funds for non-public schools in reality constitutes "double taxation"; those who choose to send their children to non-public schools not only have to pay taxes to support the public schools from which they do not benefit, but have to pay fees and tuition, representing another form of taxation, for support of schools their children attend.

Those who believe that public tax funds should be used only for the support of public schools and public institutions of higher learning contend that:

1. Policies and practices that have developed in other countries should not be used as a guide or as a precedent for policies in this country. Those who framed and approved the Federal and state constitutional provisions were aware of the problems which existed in other countries and wanted to establish a system of education which would not involve the people of this nation or of the various states in the

20 Paul Blanshard, *American Freedom and Catholic Power,* 2nd ed. (Boston: Beacon Press, 1958), Chapter 5.

nation in similar problems. They believed a system of public education was essential for the proper development of the citizens and that such a system could not flourish or make its maximum contribution in a climate which tended to encourage sectarian controversy in the field of education at the expense of all taxpayers.

2. There is no inherent discrimination against non-public schools in the system that has been established. The Supreme Court has held that states cannot eliminate non-public schools or prohibit parents from sending their children to those schools. Each citizen may choose to send his children either to public schools or to non-public schools of his choice.

3. There is no system of double taxation actual or implied. Every citizen has an obligation to support public schools and educational institutions established for the benefit of the individuals who attend as well as of the society in which they live. However, parents may, if they choose, send their children to a denominational or private school and pay the costs involved. They are not required to do this nor are they prevented from doing it.

Experience of Other Countries. The question of whether tax support should be provided for all schools is not as simple as it may seem to many people. In the first place, providing tax support would not resolve all controversies. Instead, it might set the stage for some that are even more serious than those encountered under present conditions. A study of what has happened in other countries should provide some insight into what might happen in the United States if the policy were to be changed.

Holland, for example, had what was recognized as a reasonably good system of public schools until shortly after the beginning of the present century. However, when the policy was changed to provide aid for denominational schools, competition for funds and prestige began to develop. The stronger denominations had a decided advantage and established vigorous schools in many areas. The weaker denominations had a struggle to establish and support even small schools. The fact that some of these schools were weak further complicated the problem. The public schools in many parts of Holland generally have declined in importance and prestige, with the result that the majority of the citizens are now being educated in various types of sectarian schools.

Studies made in some of the Eastern provinces of Canada, where tax funds are used to support denominational schools, indicate that small competing schools established by the various denominations are found in many areas. Schools in some of the communities tend to be more expensive and yet less adequately financed than necessary to provide satisfactory educational opportunities. Moreover, competing schools may have some advantages from the point of view of certain denominations but also have some serious disadvantages from a broader point of view.

What would be likely to happen in this country if the laws were changed to provide that public tax funds could be used to support non-public as well as public schools? Would the cost of education be likely to increase or decrease over present costs? What would happen in a community in which denominations decided to establish schools to accommodate all children of their faith and 70 per cent of the parents were Methodists or Catholics or Episcopalians or Jews?

Some Factors to Consider. Many people are even more concerned about what might happen to the United States as a nation than about the increases in costs which might result from a system of tax support for all schools. They believe, as many writers have pointed out, that the public schools have made a major contribution toward the development of this nation. Nearly 90 per cent of the present adult citizens have been educated in public schools. Except for some communities in which racially segregated schools have been maintained, these people, regardless of their religious faith, have had an opportunity to attend the public schools that served the area in which they live. They have played and worked with children of many denominations; have had an opportunity to develop common understandings and points of view; have learned to respect instead of suspect people with different religious faiths; have developed together as citizens of their respective communities, states, and of the nation.

Suppose, on the other hand, 60 or 70 or even a larger per cent of these adults had been educated in sectarian schools selected by their parents. What would have been the effect? Would they have developed as much common understanding as is found at present?

The question might well be raised whether this issue regarding aid to all schools, which seems theoretical to some, should even be discussed in this country. The point should be emphasized that it is not theoretical nor is it a religious issue. The fact that more and more parochial schools are being built and must be financed in many parts of the country means that many more parents will be concerned about the question of fees and taxation for schools. Consequently, the issue will have to be faced whether most people want to face it or not. It can either be compromised on the basis of expediency or resolved in the light of principles which should be carefully considered by all citizens concerned about the ultimate destiny of the nation.

Even more immediate as a problem is the question of aid for parents of children who attend non-public schools or of services for children who attend such schools. The question of direct payments to parents has been brought into prominence by the action of certain Southern states in providing for the possible abolition of public schools in the hope that they can thereby avoid integration. If payments were made to parents or some form of scholarships provided, as is done in a number of European countries, what would be the ultimate effect on public schools as now operated in various states? Would this plan ultimately and in reality be any different than a form of direct aid for all schools from public tax funds?

Should State Taxes Be Earmarked for Schools?

A tax is called "earmarked" when the proceeds are dedicated to a particular function and usually the yield of the tax determines the amount of the appropriation for that function. While the proceeds of non-earmarked taxes are deposited in a state's general fund subject to appropriation by the legislature, there is but little room for legislative discretion over an earmarked tax once it has been earmarked.

Although the practice of earmarking certain state revenues for schools has declined during the past few years, there are people in every state who believe it is desirable. Such points of view as the following are advanced in favor of earmarking:

1. There are so many demands on the general fund for supporting a multitude of state services and providing grants-in-aid for local agencies of government that the schools are likely to be short changed unless specific sources of revenue are earmarked. When there are so many demands on the general fund, the legislature is likely either to hold appropriations for schools below the minimum needs in order to balance the budget or to make appropriations in an effort to satisfy demands even though revenues may be short and appropriations cannot be paid in full.

2. If specific sources of revenue are earmarked for schools, local school authorities will always know what they can count on and can plan with assurance. Moreover, the people are likely to support additional taxes or increases in taxes and the legislature is more likely to make the levies if everyone knows that the proceeds are to be used for support of the public schools.

The arguments against state earmarking are usually about as follows:

1. The citizens of a state, including members of the legislature, who are opposed to a specific tax proposal are likely to resist increases in appropriations for schools when they know such increases would result in additional taxes of the type they oppose.

2. Earmarking of tax sources will not necessarily solve the problem of school support. If the sources earmarked are not adequate to meet

the needs or if revenues from these sources decline sharply, the schools may be worse off than if there had been no attempt at earmarking. Furthermore if more funds than are needed are available from earmarked taxes, the people and various agencies of government are likely to react adversely to the school program. They may feel that they have been cheated because, if the school people had not been over-ambitious in their demands, additional revenues would have been available for other purposes without increasing taxes.

Should Appropriations for the Public Schools Have the Same Status as Other Appropriations?

Many states have budget acts requiring that appropriations be reduced to the amount of revenue available in the event of a shortage in state revenue. When appropriations for a given fiscal year exceed the amount of revenue collected during that year plus the cash balance brought forward, the payments must be reduced to avoid a deficit. But how should they be reduced? Should all be reduced proportionately or should some be reduced more than others? If a state has bonds maturing, its credit would be seriously injured if it defaulted on its debts. Therefore, it would not be sound fiscal policy to scale appropriations for debt service payments, even in the event of a shortage in state funds. Appropriations for capital outlay might be made conditional on receipt of sufficient revenue to pay all state appropriations for operation and maintenance. This policy would restrict prorations to capital outlay appropriations. However, there are some good arguments against this policy. For example, some capital outlay appropriations may be so greatly needed that they can no more be deferred than appropriations for maintenance and operation. The only proper solution to this problem of course is for the legislature to raise sufficient revenue to pay in full the appropriations it has made. But if this is not done, is the only defensible policy for the state to reduce proportionately all appropriations to the funds available?

Some years ago the Supreme Court of Alabama, in interpreting the state budget act, ruled in effect that the appropriations for the "essential" functions of government from the state general fund must be paid in full and that "nonessential" appropriations only could be prorated. The court classified appropriations for education and public health as the principal "nonessential" appropriations. Consequently, education and health absorbed approximately 90 per cent of the state's deficit. This policy forced educational officials in Alabama to seek earmarked taxes for public education because the same ruling protected appropriations from earmarked taxes.

By constitutional provision in California, $180 per pupil in attendance during the previous year is required to be set aside as a first claim on the revenues of the state and made available for support of the public schools. However, from time to time, the amount provided by constitutional amendment has been found inadequate and has had to be increased.

Would priority for educational appropriations as provided in California have any decided advantages over what might be called "parity"? What are some of the possible advantages and disadvantages of each kind of provision?

How Much Emphasis Should Be Placed on Flat-Grants?

In a certain state most of the funds for schools are provided through flat-grants. A small "equalization" program was established about 15 years ago. This was designed only to aid the least wealthy districts. Since that time there have been several increases in state appropriations but most of the increases have been in the nature of flat-grants. Approximately 80 per cent of all state funds are apportioned on this basis and only a little over 20 per cent are distributed as equalization funds.

The superintendents and board members from many of the poor districts receiving equalization funds contend that they can never provide satisfactory schools under present conditions. They point out that their local tax levies are higher than the average levy in other districts in the state, that the salaries they can pay teachers are much lower than the average and that they are having many other difficulties.

The officials from some of the larger cities and more wealthy rural districts, some of the larger newspapers in the state, and representatives from some of the prominent lay organizations contend that most of the increases should go as flat-grants. They insist that:

1. There is considerable equalization in flat-grants because "the more wealthy districts pay more to the state in taxes than the districts receive back through a flat-grant," whereas in the less wealthy districts just the opposite is true.

2. The flat-grant plan of apportionment is sufficiently simple that everyone can understand it and therefore there will be no confusion. The funds have customarily been apportioned on the basis of the school census; the number of school census children can readily be determined and state officials can make an objective apportionment on the basis of the facts which everyone will accept. On the other hand, the

basis for distributing equalization funds is much more difficult to understand and has some subjective features.

3. The problems of the more wealthy districts are just as acute as those of the equalization districts. Because of the increasing costs of operating schools many of the more wealthy districts have higher levies now than they did a few years ago and the burden on property taxes in their communities is becoming serious. The people in these districts are just as much entitled to relief as those in the equalization districts. Since the wealthy districts educate a larger proportion of the children, flat-grants will do more good to a greater number than equalization grants.

4. The equalization grants are not fair or equitable. While districts participating in equalization must make a certain tax levy as a basis for providing local funds for the support of the program, the ratio between assessed and actual values varies considerably. Districts that are doing a poor job of assessing thus seem to need extra state funds chiefly because of their poor assessment practices.

Some of the leaders from equalization districts point out that:

1. While flat-grant funds do equalize to a limited extent, the equalization is more or less incidental and does not meet the need.

2. When flat-grant funds are increased, all districts are helped to some extent but differences in the ability of the districts to go beyond what the limited state appropriations will finance are just as great as they were before the flat-grants were provided.

3. While tax levies in some of the more wealthy districts have increased, the levies in the least wealthy have increased even more and consequently the situation is most serious in the poor districts.

4. The more wealthy districts have paid much higher salaries than the least wealthy districts for a number of years and consequently have been able to attract a large proportion of the better qualified and more promising teachers from these underprivileged areas.

5. Since assessment ratios are known for each of the counties, these can and should be applied as a basis for determining the amounts which should be made available through local effort.

What studies should be made and what facts provided as a basis for attempting to resolve this problem? Is this an issue which can and should be decided on the basis of facts or must it be decided in terms of attitudes and political power? How can a problem such as this best be solved?

Are "Incentive" Funds Ever Desirable?

Several years ago quite a bit of attention was given to incentive funds of one type or another. Many people had the idea that districts would do a better job of planning and financing a desirable educational program for their children if the state provided some incentive. Some proposals along this line continue to be made practically every year in some of the states and a number of them have been enacted into law. Some of these proposals come from educational groups, others from lay groups.

Ideas such as the following are seriously suggested from time to time: (1) that an additional $5.00 per pupil be made available to any district which levies a tax of at least one mill beyond a designated rate; (2) that an appropriation be made to provide for the extra costs of educating handicapped children but that these funds be made available only to districts that match them on a 50–50 basis; (3) that a special fund be made available to districts to provide for smaller pupil-teacher ratios in science classes, provided any district participating in the funds be required to make a one mill levy over and above that made for the regular program; (4) that a fund be established for use in reimbursing districts for 25 per cent of the cost of providing driver education including behind-the-wheel training. Should any of these be supported? Why?

Incentive funds are usually proposed or established for some particular aspect of the educational program. Such incentive funds, in effect, become special-purpose funds to be used for particular aspects of the educational program and for no other purpose. The argument used for each fund is that the purpose is desirable and that the districts should be given some stimulation and help in carrying out the purpose. What are the chief advantages and disadvantages of such funds?

What Should Be Done about Rewards for Preserving "Status Quo"?

Many kinds of rewards for effort have been identified in the past quarter of a century. Such rewards were relatively common in earlier programs of finance but are no longer recognized as desirable. However, they have been continued in some form in a number of state programs. Even more serious, in some respects, are certain other types of *rewards for preserving status quo*. Many such rewards have been inadvertently incorporated in one way or another in a number of state programs. Others have been provided because of pressures from vested interest groups which want to preserve or improve their own position regardless of the merit of their case.

One reward of this type is represented by an appropriation of state funds for tuition payments for out-of-district pupils. Because the district receiving the pupils has extra expense on account of the extra number of pupils involved, the state undertakes to pay part or all of this expense. A number of states at one time or another have established such aid. The problem was particularly serious in small district states such as Michigan, Ohio, and Oregon at some period during their development.

If districts had been properly organized, this problem would never have occurred. However, in cases where the high school district did not include the area from which a number of children attended, something had to be done to help with the expense. It was natural for people confronted with this situation to expect the state to help solve the problem. However, studies of the situation showed that in many cases the people living in elementary districts outside the boundaries of the high school district were being relieved of taxes and expense they should and would have paid had they been in the high school district. In effect, the state was providing a reward for preserving status quo. What should have been done to solve this problem? How can states with many small districts work out an equitable solution without providing a reward for continuing status quo?

Another reward of this type was developed by a number of states that attempted to provide funds to help meet the extra expense of operating all small schools and districts. When average practice was used in arriving at the need for extra funds, the basis was established for undesirable rewards for status quo. States which provided extra funds for all small schools soon found themselves in the position of subsidizing unnecessary schools and therefore providing them with a reward for continuing. These extra funds were provided by the taxpayers of the entire state. Thus, all taxpayers were penalized to some extent. How can the state help meet the extra expense of operating necessary small schools without providing incentives for all small schools to continue to operate? Would it be just as serious to penalize all small schools as it would be to reward all of them financially?

Other types of rewards for continuing status quo which have been used at one time or another in certain states include the following: (1) providing a weighting for high school pupils based on the costs of operation at the time when high school teachers had smaller classes because of accreditation requirements or were paid higher salaries than elementary teachers with the same training and experience; (2) developing a plan for encouraging district reorganization without providing funds to enable districts which should reorganize to construct needed facilities or provide for transportation; (3) providing sufficient flat-grants for all districts to enable wealthy small districts to operate at a very low levy instead of reorganizing to include some of the nearby less wealthy areas and having to make much higher levies to finance a satisfactory program; (4) providing extra funds for small districts to operate reasonably satisfactorily, but in such a way that if they reorganize they will lose state funds and have to make higher local tax levies to operate satisfactorily.

What other rewards for continuing status quo can be identified in various state programs? How can such rewards be avoided? Once they have been established, how can they be discontinued without involving open conflict with vested interest groups concerned? How serious are rewards for continuing status quo?

SELECTED REFERENCES

Burke, Arvid J., *Financing Public Schools in the United States*, rev. ed. New York: Harper and Brothers, 1957. Chapters XII, XV, XVIII, and XIX.

Chase, Francis S., and Edgar L. Morphet, res. dir., *The Forty-Eight State School Systems*. Chicago: Council of State Governments, 1949. Chapters VII, VIII, and IX.

Hutchins, Clayton D., and Albert R. Munse, *Expenditures for Education at the Mid-Century*. Department of Health, Education, and Welfare, U. S. Office of Education, Miscellaneous No. 18. Washington, D.C.: U. S. Government Printing Office, 1953.

——— and others, *Trends in Significant Facts on School Finance, 1929–30 –1953–54*. Department of Health, Education, and Welfare, U. S. Office of Education, Circular No. 498. Washington D.C.: U. S. Government Printing Office, 1957.

La Zerte, M. E., *School Finance in Canada, 1955*. Canadian School Trustees Association, School Finance Research Committee. Saskatoon, Saskatchewan: M. P. Toombs, Secretary, College of Education, University of Saskatchewan, 1955.

Morphet, Edgar L., Roe L. Johns, and Theodore L. Reller, *Educational Administration*. Englewood Cliffs, N.J.: Prentice-Hall, Inc., 1959. Chapter 22.

Munse, Albert R., and Eugene P. McLoone, *Public School Finance Programs of the United States, 1957–58*. U. S. Office of Education. Washington, D.C.: U.S. Government Printing Office, 1959.

Thurston, Lee M., and William H. Roe, *State School Administration*. New York: Harper and Brothers, Publishers, 1957. Chapter VII.

CHAPTER TEN

The Foundation Program

The discussion in the preceding chapter directed attention to some of the changes that have been made in provisions for financing various aspects of the educational program, and noted especially the wide variety of provisions and practices found among the states. It should be evident that not all of these practices are likely to be equally good. In fact, what has happened in a number of states is that a number of provisions incorporated in the law some years ago, and to which people have become accustomed, have been continued, either because their weaknesses have not been recognized by enough people or because substantial numbers would rather continue with these practices than face up to the difficult problem of making improvements.

Attention was also directed in the previous chapter to the fact that what is commonly called the foundation program concept has been adopted during recent years, at least to a limited extent, by most states, and that authorities generally have recognized this as a much better approach to the problem of financing schools than earlier plans, some of which are still being used.

EVOLUTION OF FOUNDATION PROGRAM CONCEPT

The foundation program concept is embodied in the idea that all students throughout each state, regardless of where they live or of the homes from which they come, should be entitled to participate in and receive maximum benefits from a program of education designed to meet their needs. In reality this is a statement of an objective to which most citizens throughout the nation have subscribed from the beginning.

"Equality of opportunity" has been accepted in theory as one of the major goals of a democracy. However, the idea has not been fully implemented, for many reasons, as pointed out in Chapter 6.

In practical terms, the foundation program concept implies and involves a plan for financing schools that requires equity for taxpayers as well as equity and adequacy of opportunity for students. It means that the resources of each state—and, by implication, of the nation—must be used to provide the financial support required to meet basic educational needs. Thus, the most wealthy citizens and the people in the most wealthy communities should be expected to make as much financial effort to support the foundation program of education as the least wealthy. To attain this objective would mean a change in the customary way of doing things for people in a number of states and communities.

Unsatisfactory Early Ideas

Although the term "foundation program" has not been used until recent years, it seems reasonable to assume that most citizens must have thought adequate educational opportunities, as envisioned at that time, could be provided through fees and rate bills commonly used to finance schools during pioneer days. When this plan was recognized as inequitable, people began to seek other means of financing the schools. The idea of a local tax on property to support schools must at first have seemed good to many. At least it was more equitable than the fees or rates. But again difficulties began to be evident, because some communities had much greater wealth and ability than others.

The early Federal land grants were undoubtedly provided partly in an effort to assure reasonably adequate and equitable educational opportunities for the children throughout each state. Even the proceeds from these grants did not suffice to meet the needs, and states began to make appropriations to help with school support. From a modern point of view most of these funds were apportioned on very crude bases. Providing the same amount per census child or per pupil did not meet the needs in the more sparsely populated and less wealthy districts. Apportioning part of the funds on a per teacher basis, as was done in some states, provided further help but still did not solve the problem.

Thus, the people in the various states and in the communities within each of those states continued to struggle with the problem of developing a satisfactory plan for financing their schools. Provisions were changed from time to time because they were found to be unsatisfactory, but new ideas usually did not prove to be much better. In fact, inequality seems to have been accepted by large numbers of people as inevitable. Citizens in the more wealthy areas were generally not too much distressed by the fact that children in the least wealthy communities had the poorest teachers, the shortest length of term, and generally the least satisfactory educational opportunities of any children in the state.

Although proposals for improving the situation were made from time to time by those who were concerned about the problem, there was insufficient knowledge available to make it possible for the people in any state to develop and implement a foundation program in the modern sense. In fact, not until after the beginning of the present century was much real progress made. Up to that time most of the concern in providing state aid seems to have been with (1) stimulation of the establishment of local schools and services not provided in many districts but deemed to be needed in all parts of the state; (2) stimulation and encouragement of local effort in the support of schools; and (3) provision of financial assistance for all districts to help them with their troublesome problem of obtaining sufficient revenue to organize and keep their schools in operation.

It seems to have been generally assumed that all districts could provide reasonably satisfactory schools if they wanted to do so, were willing to make the effort, and were given some encouragement and financial assistance. Nevertheless, the problem of "equalization" received some attention in a number of states even before the turn of the century, because it was becoming increasingly evident that some districts had much greater ability than others and that the least wealthy districts were having serious difficulties, even when some state aid was provided.

Early in the present century Cubberley made the first extensive study of the fiscal policies adopted by the various states, and of their experiences with those policies.[1] Cubberley noted the extensive use of special aid for encouraging or helping with the financing of designated aspects of the program and recognized the idea of rewarding communities for their effort as what he considered to be a principle. However, the practice now is generally recognized as an effort on the part of the state or some influential group to determine the specific purposes

---

[1] Elwood P. Cubberley, *School Funds and Their Apportionment* (New York: Bureau of Publications, Teachers College, Columbia University, 1905).

or phases of the educational program which should be encouraged and to promote those purposes through the use of special funds. Cubberley also recognized the need for greater assistance to the poorer communities than to the most wealthy, and thus directed attention to what is often called the "equalization principle." His studies and "principles" served a very useful and much needed purpose at that early date but did not provide a satisfactory basis for solving the most urgent problems. In 1922 Updegraff, on the basis of studies in New York and Pennsylvania, again directed attention to the need for greater emphasis on equalization but continued to stress the importance of stimulation.[2]

Origin of the Concept

The concept of the foundation program was first introduced and interpreted in the Strayer-Haig Educational Finance Inquiry in New York in 1923. This study showed the inconsistency between reward for effort and the principle of equalization. Attention was directed from equalization of school support to the idea of equalization of educational opportunity.

Strayer and Haig pointed out that:

> To carry into effect the principle of "equalization of educational opportunity" and "equalization of school support," as commonly understood, it would be necessary (1) to establish schools or make other arrangements sufficient to furnish the children in every locality within the state with equal educational opportunities up to some prescribed minimum; (2) to raise the funds necessary for this purpose by local or state taxation adjusted in such manner as to bear upon the people in all localities at the same rate in relation to their taxpaying ability; and (3) to provide adequately either for the supervision and control of all the schools, or for their direct administration, by a state department of education.[3]

They pointed out that the simplest method of financing schools to achieve the aim of the principle would be through uniform state-wide taxes on ability to pay. After commenting on the difficulty of centralizing the administration of funds without deadening local interest and initiative and on the problem of developing a suitable revenue system, they concluded that it would be desirable to inquire what measure of

[2] Harlan Updegraff, *Financial Support*, Rural School Survey of New York State (Ithaca, N.Y.: Joint Committee on Rural Schools, 1922).
[3] George D. Strayer and Robert M. Haig, *The Financing of Education in the State of New York*, Report of the Educational Finance Inquiry Commission (New York: The Macmillan Company, 1923), p. 173.

responsibility for financial support should be left to the localities, if the aims of the principle were to be attained. They then stated:

. . . The achievement of uniformity would involve the following:

1. A local school tax in support of the satisfactory minimum offering would be levied in each district at a rate which would provide the necessary funds for that purpose in the richest district.

2. This richest district then might raise all of its school money by means of the local tax, assuming that a satisfactory tax, capable of being locally administered, could be devised.

3. Every other district could be permitted to levy a local tax at the same rate and apply the proceeds toward the costs of schools, but—

4. Since the rate is uniform, this tax would be sufficient to meet the costs only in the richest districts, and the deficiencies would be made up by state subventions.[4]

This statement, in reality, presented a new theory in educational finance. It constituted the background for studies and developments that have resulted in revolutionizing provisions for financing schools in a number of states.

Paul R. Mort, both directly and through subsequent studies made by his students, has undoubtedly contributed more to the development of the foundation program concept than any other person. Starting with his study on *The Measurement of Educational Need*,[5] he has made and sponsored several other studies that have contributed greatly to the understanding of the needs, problems, and possibilities. Over the years he has developed a series of proposals which have made it possible for states to begin to implement the foundation program concept. As will be pointed out later, some of the original ideas, as should be expected, needed to be modified. The basic concepts, however, have proven to be sound, and later studies and developments have pointed the way to improvements essential for the development of satisfactory provisions.

Significance and Interpretation

One important contribution of the foundation program concept has been that it has helped to clarify fiscal relationships in the field of education between the state and the school districts. The financing of education in the various states might easily have become highly centralized and have been accompanied by so many restrictions and controls that local initiative and responsibility in education might largely have

---

[4] *Ibid.*, pp. 174–175.

[5] Paul R. Mort, *The Measurement of Educational Need* (New York: Bureau of Publications, Teachers College, Columbia University, 1925).

disappeared. The foundation program plan has provided a partnership basis for supporting the aspects of the educational program included in the plan. Both the state and districts provide on an equitable basis the funds needed to support the foundation program level of educational opportunity financed throughout the state. Beyond this program each district may provide funds to finance additional or higher quality services in accordance with the desires of the board and the citizens of the district, but within the limits of state laws or constitutional provisions.

The following statements regarding the foundation program concept should be of interest:

> The concept of the foundation program has proved highly useful as a device for differentiating the responsibility of the state as a whole from the additional responsibilities assumed by local communities on their own initiative.[6]

> The foundation program is more than a device for apportioning state aid for schools. In effect, it determines the level of education available to children in local units which have so little taxpaying ability that they can supplement it very little from local resources, no matter how great a tax effort they make.[7]

> Early systems of raising state revenues and apportioning them to schools lacked a rationale. Modern systems of state school finance are those which are based on research and planning. This provides a rationale which in its simplest form consists of sensibly determining: (1) What is to be financed. (2) How much it will cost. (3) What sources of revenue are available. (4) How the revenues may be tapped to meet the costs. (5) How to apportion state school revenue.[8]

> The concept of the foundation program is that of establishing an equitable fiscal partnership between the state as a whole and the individual school systems charged with the responsibility and privilege of operating the public schools.[9]

---

[6] Paul R. Mort and Walter C. Reusser, *Public School Finance,* 2nd ed. (New York: McGraw-Hill Book Company, Inc., 1951), pp. 400–401.

[7] Arvid J. Burke, *Financing Public Schools in the United States,* rev. ed. (New York: Harper and Brothers, 1957), pp. 445–446.

[8] Francis G. Cornell and William P. McLure, "The Foundation Program and the Measurement of Educational Need," Chapter VI in R. L. Johns and E. L. Morphet, editors, *Problems and Issues in Public School Finance* (New York: Bureau of Publications, Teachers College, Columbia University, 1952), p. 195.

[9] National Education Association, Committee on Tax Education and School Finance, *Guides to the Development of State School Finance Programs* (Washington, D.C.: The Association, 1949), p. 11.

CHARACTERISTICS OF
A SATISFACTORY FOUNDATION PROGRAM PLAN

It is generally recognized that any plan for financing public schools should make it possible to provide essential educational opportunities for all who should be educated, at a reasonable and equitable cost to the taxpayers. The ten characteristics of a satisfactory foundation program plan presented and discussed briefly below have been stated in various ways by different authorities but are generally accepted as basic guidelines for the satisfactory implementation or evaluation of any such plan.[10]

The plan of financial support for schools in each state should be designed to assure a foundation program providing essential, reasonably adequate, and well-rounded educational opportunities for all who should benefit from public education. This criterion evolves from the recognition of the basic responsibility of the state for the education of its people. It is generally believed this responsibility is such that the plan of financial support should provide for all necessary services and facilities required for a sound educational program in all communities. This financial program is often called "the foundation program."

Provision should be made for a bona fide state-local partnership plan for financing this foundation program of educational opportunity. The foundation program should be supported by an equitable combination of funds from local, state, and, insofar as applicable, Federal sources.

Each school district (or county) should be expected and required to make the same minimum local effort toward financing the foundation program. It would not be fair or equitable to expect the citizens of any efficiently organized district to make a greater tax effort toward financing the foundation program of essential educational opportunities than the citizens of any other such district. The same minimum effort, therefore, should be expected and required of all. Some states may prefer to use a uniform county effort, or some combination of county and district effort, rather than district effort alone, to provide local funds for the foundation program.

The state should provide for each district on an objective basis, the difference between the funds available from the required uniform mini-

---

[10] Adapted from Edgar L. Morphet, with the assistance of Ben M. Harris and C. Earl Miller, Jr., *Financial Equalization for the Public Schools of California—1959*, Legislative Problems No. 1 (Berkeley: Bureau of Public Administration, University of California, 1959), pp. 6–9.

mum tax effort and the cost of the foundation program. Objective procedures should be established for determining both the cost of the foundation program in each district and the funds which should be available from the required local tax effort. The state should guarantee that, when the required uniform tax effort has been made, sufficient additional funds will be provided from state sources to enable each district to finance and maintain its foundation program.

The plan for financing the foundation program should assure reasonable equity for all taxpayers. If public education is to serve all the people and is regarded as essential to the welfare and prosperity of the community, state, and nation, it follows that each citizen should share equitably in financing the foundation program. This means that (1) assessments should be uniform or some valid means of measuring local taxpaying ability should be devised and used; (2) each district (or county) should make the same minimum tax effort to support the foundation program; and (3) funds to support the program should be derived from property and other sources in equitable relationship to the sources of income of the citizens of the state.

The educational and financial provisions for the foundation program should encourage sound and efficient organization, administration, and operation of local school districts and schools. State funds should *not* be used to (1) subsidize or perpetuate inefficient or unnecessary small districts or schools; (2) relieve the taxpayers of any district of the necessity of levying the taxes considered essential in less wealthy districts for local support of the foundation program; or (3) encourage any uneconomical or inefficient practices. However, the state should not attempt, in the name of economy or for other reasons, to limit local initiative or responsibility or to restrict the program of education. Any district that chooses to maintain unnecessary small schools, or is inefficiently organized, should be expected to provide any additional costs of operating the foundation program from local tax levies above the uniform effort required for participation.

The foundation program plan should provide maximum opportunity and encouragement for the development and exercise of local leadership and responsibility in education. The exercise of local leadership and responsibility is considered of the utmost importance in every state. State plans and provisions, by establishing *maximum* standards and detailed requirements, can easily discourage such responsibility. Only those *minimum* standards and requirements that are necessary to assure adequate educational opportunities throughout the state should be considered desirable and acceptable.

The citizens of each local school system should be authorized to provide and finance such educational opportunities beyond the founda-

tion program as they desire. There should be provision for the citizens of each local school system, without handicapping restrictions, to vote or levy on themselves any taxes they consider desirable and necessary to provide additional or better educational services and facilities than those provided through the foundation program.

The foundation program plan should be cooperatively developed by representative citizens who have a genuine interest in and concern about public education. People who have an opportunity to help develop or improve any program or plan tend to believe in it and support it. The foundation program plan is likely to be best appreciated and supported when representative educators and lay citizens have had an opportunity to consider and agree upon the services and facilities deemed essential for a reasonably adequate program of education, and to determine the cost and method of financing such a program. The proposals should be developed through careful studies which have taken into consideration all pertinent evidence and concepts.

The program and procedures should emphasize continuous evaluation and sound long-range planning. The program should encourage and facilitate long-range state and local planning as contrasted with expedient action or shortsighted practices. It should be as simple as possible, avoiding complexities that do not contribute substantially to the main goals of education and of public school finance.

DEFINITION AND INTERPRETATION OF TERMS

Some of the more important terms and concepts commonly used in discussing the foundation program are explained briefly in the paragraphs which follow. Other somewhat more technical terms are explained in connection with the discussion of pertinent aspects of the subject presented later in the chapter.

Foundation Program. The terms "foundation program," "minimum program," "minimum-foundation program," and "equalization program" are often used interchangeably. Generally, the term "foundation program" has been preferred during recent years. In reality, it means the essential educational opportunities which should be provided through the public schools for all students regardless of the wealth of the district in which they live or attend school. It is the program which should be supported throughout the state on a partnership basis by an equitable combination of state and local funds. The use of this term is designed to center attention on the program of essential educational opportunities, but it necessarily has important implications for the provisions for financing schools. On the other hand, the term "equalization program" tends to center attention on the financial provisions rather than on the educational program itself.

Foundation Program Plan. This means the plan adopted for assuring essential educational opportunities through appropriate and equitable financial procedures. It is designed to assure that each district that makes the required minimum uniform local tax effort will have sufficient funds from state, local, and other sources to finance its foundation program. Under this plan, the state undertakes to provide the difference, if any, between the objectively determined yield from a uniformly required minimum local tax effort and the cost of the foundation program.

Foundation Program Funds. These are the funds required and used to support the foundation program. All state, local, and Federal funds involved in the support of the program are included. The term does not include state or Federal funds that may be provided for other educational purposes or the additional local funds which a district may provide in an effort to assure better educational opportunities than those provided from foundation program funds alone.

State Foundation Program Funds. These are the funds provided by the state to meet its responsibility for the cost of the foundation program for each district. These funds constitute the state's share of the cost of the foundation program for the district. They represent the difference between the funds provided toward the cost of the foundation program through the local uniform required effort, and the total cost of the foundation program for the district.

Local Foundation Program Funds. These funds constitute the local share of the total cost of the foundation program for the district— that is, the funds which must be provided through the required uniform local effort.

Financial Equalization. This term refers to the effect of any plan for financing schools, determined by whether (and the extent to which) the plan tends to provide funds for schools in such a way that those districts least able to finance a program of essential educational opportunities (a foundation program) with local funds receive proportionately more money from state sources than the more able districts.

Local Required Effort. This is the effort which every district (or county) must make to provide its share of the cost of the foundation program for the district. Proceeds from the local required effort constitute the local foundation program funds for the district.

Weighted Pupil. The weighted pupil is a unit of measurement used for determining the educational need of a school district. As more fully explained later, it involves a plan for assigning a weighting to pupils in various kinds and sizes of schools so that a pupil unit of need can be assigned a cost value and used as a unit for determining the cost of the foundation program.

Adjusted Classroom Unit. This is a unit of measurement based on class size weighted for various types and sizes of schools. It is usually based on the number of pupils in average daily attendance, or average daily membership, and therefore is related to or may actually be derived from the weighted pupil unit. The adjusted classroom unit can be used as a unit for measuring educational need and for determining the cost of the foundation program in any district.

Educational Need. The term "educational need" means and includes the essential educational opportunities which should be provided through the foundation program plan. Since an objective plan for measuring educational need is essential for the development of a satisfactory foundation program plan, usually either the weighted pupil or the adjusted classroom unit is used in measuring educational need, except perhaps for transportation service as explained later.

SCOPE AND ADEQUACY OF THE FOUNDATION PROGRAM

As previously indicated, the foundation program should constitute an expression of, and a plan for implementing, the state's responsibility for the essential educational opportunities to be provided through its public elementary and secondary schools. In reality, no aspect of the educational program which is considered essential should be omitted in any state. In practice, however, only a few states thus far have developed a comprehensive foundation program plan.

A comprehensive foundation program plan has decided advantages, if properly developed, over a partial or special-purpose foundation program. As pointed out by Mort and Reusser, the foundation program should include "(1) all the activities the state wishes to assure the communities of least ability to support schools, and (2) the whole range of expenditure involved." [11]

There is a difference between excluding important elements that are found only in part of the districts of a state and excluding features that are distinctly experimental or pioneering in nature. For example, let us assume that generally only the more wealthy districts in a state have provided services for exceptional children or have established kindergartens. If such services are considered essential, they should be included in the foundation program, even though they are not pro-

[11] Mort and Reusser, *Public School Finance*, p. 397.

vided in all districts. To exclude them would mean that they could not be provided in many of the least wealthy districts. It would be unrealistic in the light of the needs and demands of a modern program of education.

If most foundation programs are unsatisfactory as far as scope is concerned, even more are unsatisfactory in terms of adequacy of financial support. Several still have the characteristics of the obsolete "weak district" plan for state support. They seem to be predicated on the false assumption that if a state provides some "equalization aid" for the less wealthy districts, it has established a foundation program and therefore has met its major responsibility. No gesture in the direction of a foundation program can be considered adequate or realistic. For example, if the cost of providing essential educational opportunities is $400 per pupil, the establishment of a foundation program which guarantees $150 per pupil through a combination of state and local funds will not meet the need. A foundation program plan, to be satisfactory, must meet all criteria fully. It cannot be considered a good program if it conforms to seven or eight of the basic criteria and fails seriously to conform to two or three others.

PROCEDURES USED IN
DEVELOPING THE FOUNDATION PROGRAM

If a foundation program plan is to be sound and is to work the way it is intended, it must be carefully and scientifically devised to conform to sound principles and criteria. Failure to do so is almost certain to create problems and inequities. Two basically sound ideas as to how a foundation program should be developed are discussed briefly in the paragraphs which follow.

The Dollars-per-Unit-of-Need Approach

The idea back of the "dollars-per-unit" approach to the development of a foundation program is that, if a defensible cost per unit of need can be established and if valid procedures are used in determining need, in arriving at the amount required, and in apportioning funds, each local school system will be in a position to provide and finance the essential educational opportunities encompassed in the foundation program. This idea is sound. However, there are several problems which should be faced realistically, such as (1) determining the unit of cost to be used, and (2) convincing lay citizens, including legislators who must make the appropriation, that the cost per unit decided upon is needed to purchase the essential educational opportunities included in the foundation program. If people are not agreed on the opportunities which should be financed, they may have difficulty in agreeing upon the unit cost to be included.

The original plan for determining the unit cost of the foundation program provided for ascertaining the amount expended in typical or average districts in the state—that is, those districts presumably neither especially handicapped or especially favored because of their local ability. While this plan provides an objective basis for determining costs, it has some limitations which have been recognized for several years. Two of the most serious are (1) average practice is affected by existing customs and legal limitations and thus may not be desirable practice, (2) those who believe there are inefficiencies in the organization and administration of education may not consider average practice acceptable. Many may believe it is far beyond what should be provided in less wealthy districts whose expenditures have been considerably below the average. Furthermore, if revisions were made periodically on the basis of average practice, the unit cost figure would eventually become highly artificial since the standard for each revision would automatically be forced upward by the last previous revision.

More recently, much greater attention has been given to other means of determining unit costs. Attempts have been made to take into account trends in prices and wages, financial handicaps imposed on the districts, and other similar factors.

Perhaps the most promising approach has grown out of the cost-quality studies briefly discussed in Chapter 1. These studies show that (1) low expenditure districts cannot finance a satisfactory program of education, and (2) there are expenditure levels below which essential educational opportunity cannot be provided. Thus, an objective basis is provided for determining a unit cost figure not directly affected by or related to average practice.

The advantage of studies of this type is that they begin to direct attention to what it takes to provide adequate educational opportunities and away from practices which may be affected by limitations involving insight, understanding, or ability. One of the difficulties is that many people may not be willing to subscribe fully to the theory that greater expenditures for education tend to result in better education. The center of attention is necessarily still on the amount of dollars required per unit of educational need. This figure can be derived readily by experts but may not be easily understood by laymen who must support the program if it is to be adopted. To the extent that the amount proposed per unit is accepted and understood generally, the idea is both sound and practical. If, however, too many people question the findings and opinions of the experts, the unit appropriation may be limited or reduced and the program thus handicapped.

As taxes become higher and competition for the taxpayer's dollar becomes keener, more people may be inclined to raise questions concerning the amount of dollars per unit required to provide the essential services. The deductive definition of the kind and quality of education which can be purchased by a given number of dollars per unit may need more substantiation than has sometimes been provided.

The Services-and-Facilities-Needed Approach

The authors, in working with lay commissions and legislators in a number of states, have sometimes encountered considerable difficulty in convincing laymen and even some educators that a certain amount of money per weighted pupil or per weighted teacher is necessary to finance the foundation program. They have been concerned also about the problems and implications in using average practice. Gradually another procedure has been evolved for arriving at a defensible cost of the foundation program.

This procedure may be illustrated as follows: A committee of educators and laymen concerned with the development of a foundation program, and with a plan for financing that program, begins to work on the problem of determining what is needed for a satisfactory program of education in any school or school system in the state. One of the first questions raised usually is: How many children can be taught satisfactorily by an elementary or high school teacher? The committee is likely to be interested in the findings of research studies and in reactions of teachers, pupils, and parents in their own community and state.

Eventually, after much study and discussion, members of the committee may reach a conclusion which may be stated about as follows: "Some teachers can teach more children than others and do a superior job. However, other things being equal, the average teacher in a large school should not be expected to have more than 27 to 30 pupils in her class if she is to do a good job of teaching and to work effectively with individual pupils. The average class load should therefore generally not exceed this number of pupils. If it is much larger than this, both teachers and pupils will be handicapped. In the smaller schools the number of pupils per teacher should be somewhat fewer than in large schools, if the teachers are to do an equally good job. Of course, in a one-teacher school a teacher is needed even though there may be only ten or twelve children. However, small schools are expensive to operate and the foundation program should recognize the smaller pupil-teacher ratio only for necessary small schools."

From consideration of the teacher-pupil ratios the study usually moves on to such questions as: What quality of teachers and teaching is needed, and what preparation should be expected for good quality teachers? What other services are needed for a good program of instruction, such as principals, counseling services, librarians, and so on? In these discussions, most attention is usually centered on the instructional program, as it should be. Eventually, however, people begin to recognize, as a result of their studies, that many other services, as well as adequate facilities, are needed for a good program of education. They begin to develop the understanding necessary to reach agreement on services and facilities needed. When the essential services are agreed upon, these can be translated into costs and the cost per unit can be determined on a reasonably objective basis.

Advantages and Disadvantages

In the latter approach, the attention is centered on services and facilities needed and out of this study grow conclusions as to cost; in the former, attention is centered on cost, and on the basis of the figures arrived at, assumptions are made as to the services and facilities which can be provided.

The procedures used in developing such foundation programs as those found in Florida, Kentucky, and Ohio illustrate the "services-and-facilities-needed" approach. In Kentucky, for example, under the guidance of a state committee, local lay-professional committees were organized in practically every district to discuss the characteristics of a satisfactory foundation program of educational opportunity. These studies and discussions were continued in many cases for several months. The reports were then transmitted to the state committee, which summarized the returns. One interesting development was that in many cases more than 90 per cent of the people involved were agreed on some of the basic features of an essential program of educational opportunity. On the basis of these agreements the foundation program was approved by the Legislature.[12]

This procedure, too, involves some problems and difficulties: (1) Considerable time is required for large numbers of people to become

[12] See *Kentucky's Educational Puzzle—5,000 Citizens Report on Their Schools,* Information Bulletin No. 8 (Frankfort: Kentucky Legislative Research Commission, 1953).

informed and to establish bases for agreement; (2) some people may react on the basis of preconceived notions or prejudices and may not be willing to think through the problem; (3) there is a possibility that insufficient attention may be given to the findings and conclusions of studies that have been made in various parts of the country; (4) there is some danger that legislators may try to compartmentalize the program.

A foundation program developed in this manner has sometimes been called a "budget-based program." However, the procedure is designed to be used in *developing* the program, *not in attaching restrictions and limitations* to various aspects of the program. In fact, there is no greater need or justification for placing requirements and limitations on various aspects of a program based on a study of services and facilities than on a program developed on the basis of a "dollars-per-unit" approach. A unit cost figure can be derived in either case. A sound foundation program of educational opportunity can be established through either procedure.

Since the legislature must finally authorize the program and the financial support necessary to implement the program, it would seem that even greater attention must be given in the future to procedures which will result in widespread understanding of the problems and needs than has been necessary in the past. The question that must be resolved in each state is, What procedures will most likely result in the insights and understandings necessary to assure the adoption and financing of an adequate and satisfactory foundation program of essential educational opportunity?

MEASURES OF EDUCATIONAL NEED

One basic step in developing a satisfactory foundation program plan is to establish objective, equitable, and valid measures of educational need. If the measures of need are subjective, the determination of need is likely to be influenced by the judgment of state officials, and this, of course, might introduce inequities. If the measures of need are invalid, they would also be inequitable and would have adverse effects on the educational program.

While there is agreement that sound measures of need must be developed, there are differences of opinion as to whether a single measure should be used for determining all aspects of educational need, and as to the extent to which average practice should be used in deriving measures of need.

The Single Measure

Theoretically, a single measure for determining all aspects of need is desirable. Mort originally proposed the derivation and use of a single, all-encompassing unit. Studies have been made to determine the feasibility of developing such a unit, and on the basis of these studies a single unit of measurement has been proposed.[13] If a community is sparsely populated it will either have to operate small schools or provide extensive transportation, or perhaps operate some small schools and still provide some transportation. The cost per pupil in such communities would necessarily be greater than the cost in more densely populated communities.

The development of a single unit for measuring educational need would have advantages in analyzing the expenditures in different types of districts and among different states and in developing foundation program laws. Unless carefully developed, however, the single unit could serve either to retard consolidation because insufficient allowances were made to cover the cost of transportation and construction or, under different circumstances, it might unduly stimulate consolidation. When properly drawn, based on sound study, the law would neither reward nor penalize consolidation.

Most states have found it desirable to use two measures—one for current expense and capital outlay, and a separate measure for transportation. Several states use entirely different measures for current expense and for capital outlay, although this does not seem to be necessary. In fact, studies have shown that there is a long-range continuing relationship between expenditures for capital outlay and those for current expense.[14]

Units of Measurement

The pupil-teacher ratio is necessarily much smaller and the cost per pupil in attendance or in membership is much greater in small schools, in certain types of classes, and for certain grade levels than for regular classes in larger schools. It is therefore necessary to develop either a weighted pupil unit or an adjusted classroom unit for use in measur-

---

[13] See, for example, William P. McLure, *Effect of Population Sparsity on School Costs*, Contributions to Education No. 929 (New York: Bureau of Publications, Teachers College, Columbia University, 1947).

[14] F. E. Grossnickle, *Capital Outlays in Relation to a State's Minimum Educational Program* (New York: Teachers College, Columbia University, 1931).

ing educational need and in arriving at the foundation program cost. These units should be derived on the basis of careful studies if they are to serve satisfactorily as measures of need. Arbitrary compromises based on expediency are almost certain to result in inequities.

The chief problem with the weighted pupil unit is that it is difficult to interpret to legislators and other laymen. The adjusted classroom unit, although it is directly related in its derivation to the weighted pupil unit, is much easier for laymen and even teachers to understand. They can readily see the relationship between the number of teachers needed and program of services or facilities to be provided. This relationship is not so obvious in the case of the weighted pupil unit. More important than the question of which unit is to be used (a matter which can be appropriately decided by the leaders and the legislature of each state) is the method used in deriving the unit.

Either unit may be derived on the basis of average practice. However, as pointed out by Mort and Reusser,

> This has two very serious faults. First, practice on which the weightings are based varies from decade to decade. Second, it varies from state to state. The most serious variations are in the weightings given to secondary pupils as compared with elementary pupils. Sparsity corrections appear to be more uniform from state to state and more stable from decade to decade.[15]

Average practice provides definite criteria which may be used in developing units for measuring need. However, existing practice may tend to perpetuate undesirable and uneconomical practices and may indirectly even retard improvements.

Because of these difficulties, which have vigorously been pointed out from time to time by the authors of this book, increasing attention has been given during recent years to the derivation of units on the basis of service needs. The adjusted classroom unit seems to be well adapted to this approach.

The weighted pupil unit is usually used as a unit of cost for the foundation program as well as a unit of need. Thus, attention is centered on cost from the beginning, and people who are particularly tax-conscious may tend to resist improvements because the unit is directly associated with cost. This has usually not been the procedure in developing the adjusted classroom unit. Experience indicates that many people tend to be less concerned about the cost after they understand and have agreed upon the need than is the case when cost is an obvious consideration from the beginning.

---

[15] Mort and Reusser, *Public School Finance*, p. 493.

Deriving and Implementing the Adjusted
Classroom Unit

There are two points of view relating to the derivation of the adjusted classroom unit. One holds that the units should be derived in "pure" form from the studies and discussions and should cover needs for all employees and services. The other holds that the classroom unit should be "built up" in terms of services needed, starting with classroom teachers, then taking into consideration other pertinent factors and finally arriving at the same single-unit formula as would probably be derived if the first procedure were followed. The latter procedure will be used to illustrate how the unit is developed and what it means for measurement of educational need.

As previously explained, the committee responsible for a state-wide study, with the help of consultants, usually obtains evidence from studies of present and desirable practice in various types of communities, considers proposals regarding desirable programs made by local committees of educators and laymen which have been studying the problem, and eventually proceeds to develop a statement describing essential instructional and related services. This statement then becomes a guide for the development of classroom units to be used for measuring need. The statement tends to be both idealistic and practical. It usually envisions better services than are provided in the most backward districts but may not include the quality of services desired by the most progressive school systems. At any rate, it is not unduly restricted by considerations of average practice, although the committee will undoubtedly study data regarding these practices.

Units for Regular Teachers. Attention is usually centered first on the number of full-time teachers needed for regular classes in the larger schools (usually schools having more than 300 pupils). In most states the conclusion has been reached that there should be one teacher for about every 30 pupils in average daily membership, or for about 27 or 28 pupils in average daily attendance. Surprisingly enough, the number of pupils per teacher which has been accepted as desirable has usually been about the same for high schools as for elementary schools. The number in junior or community colleges has usually been somewhat less.

Attention is next usually directed to the small schools—that is, those having fewer than 100 to 150 pupils in attendance. In most cases the committee and consultants have agreed that where small schools are necessary because of sparsity of population and isolation (but not because of existing district boundary lines) sufficient units should be provided to enable such schools to conduct a satisfactory program, and that this will mean fewer pupils per teacher than in the larger schools. It is obvious that for any necessary one-teacher school there should be one unit. For other necessary small schools the formula developed usually provides for from 15 to 25 pupils per teacher, depending on the size of the school. For non-isolated small schools the same formula is used as for larger schools. (Provisions for determining isolation of small schools will be discussed later.)

Thus, suppose a district with 3,000 pupils in membership in several large schools (more than 300 to 400 pupils each) had one non-isolated school with ten pupils, an isolated one-teacher school with eight pupils, a non-isolated school with 30 pupils, and an isolated school with 100 pupils. If the conclusions from the illustration above are used, the district would have 100 classroom units for the 3,000 pupils in larger schools, one unit for the isolated one-teacher school, five units for the isolated 100-pupil school, one for the non-isolated 30-pupil school, and one-third of a unit for the non-isolated one-teacher school; or a total of 107⅓ units. These would be classroom units based on need for regular full-time teachers.

Units for Other Teaching Personnel. Unfortunately, many state programs have stopped at that stage and have not provided units for other needed instructional services. This has meant that the only way those instructional services could be provided would be to increase class size and, therefore, presumably lower the quality of the instructional program. For a realistic and comprehensive foundation program, it is necessary to provide units at least for kindergarten pupils, for exceptional children instructed in the schools, for vocational education and for adult education. Suppose, in this district there are 300 kindergarten pupils, and kindergartens are operated on a half-day basis. There would thus be five additional units for kindergarten teachers. There might be four additional units for teachers working with exceptional children, four units for the equivalent of four full-time vocational teachers, and 2⅔ units for full-time teaching equivalents for adult education. The district would thus have 123 classroom units for teachers.

Units for Other Instructional and Administrative Personnel. This still would not meet the need, because no provision would have been made for librarians, counselors, principals, supervisors, or others primarily concerned with instructional services. Studies in a number of states have shown that one additional classroom unit for other instructional services should be provided for each eight to ten classroom units for direct teaching services. In the district considered above there would be from 12 to 15 units which should be added if it is to have a realistic program. Thus, instead of 123 classroom units the district would have approximately 135 units.

Studies have shown that classroom units derived in this manner can also be used readily to measure the need for other current expense (except for transportation) and for capital outlay. However, the classroom units should include in all cases units for regular teachers, units for other teaching personnel, and units for other instructional and administrative personnel.

Measuring Educational Need for Small Schools

If the same plan is used for measuring educational need in all small schools, one of two things will happen:

1. When the formula used for determining units of need in large schools is used, every small school will be handicapped in that it will have to provide more teachers and other instructional services than included in the formula if it is to operate satisfactorily. Thus, the necessary small schools will be penalized along with those that are not necessary. Some states have used this plan.

2. When a small-school formula is used for all small schools, each school will have sufficient units to operate reasonably satisfactorily and thus, the unnecessary or non-isolated schools will be encouraged to continue. There would thus be incorporated in the formula a reward or incentive which would tend to perpetuate these schools. A number of states have used this plan, with the result that the people of the entire state are confronted with the necessity of having to help pay the extra cost of operating these schools.

The tendency during recent years has been to attempt to devise an objective plan for determining which small schools (that is, those having fewer than 100 to 150 pupils) are isolated and should be continued. This has no bearing on the question as to whether the non-isolated schools will continue to operate, because that is a matter which probably should be left for local determination. However, the people living in a district which chooses to continue the operation of such a school should pay the extra expense of operating the school.

Several states, such as Florida, Kentucky—and to a more limited extent, California—have devised and are using formulas of isolation as a basis for determining which small schools are to be allotted units on the small-school formula for the foundation program. For a one-teacher elementary school to be isolated, for example, one or more of the following conditions should apply: (1) It should be 18 or more miles from another isolated or large school; (2) pupils would have to be transported over roads that are impassable or extremely hazardous during part of the school year; (3) more than 10 per cent of the pupils would have to be on the bus more than three quarters of an hour, morning or evening. The distance may be decreased slightly for somewhat larger schools. In the case of small high schools, both the distance requirement and the time on the bus are usually increased somewhat.

Other Factors to Consider

Attendance During Current Year. In developing foundation programs or other state support formulas, the traditional practice has been to use the attendance of pupils during the previous year for determining need. This practice is not realistic, because rapidly growing districts may be seriously handicapped. For example, suppose a foundation program is developed on the basis of attendance of the previous year in a district which is entitled to 500 classroom units. If the attendance increased by 10 per cent during the year and no provision was made for recognizing this change, the district would have to provide an additional 50 teachers out of its own resources, or overload classes and teachers, as a means of carrying on its program. Most state aid formulas revised during recent years have included provisions for additional units based on increased attendance during the current year. This can readily be done by basing the first apportionment on the attendance of the previous year, then making adjustments for increases in attendance when later apportionments are made during the year. Provisions for this adjustment should be incorporated in all state foundation program plans.

Attendance or Membership? Another difficulty arises in states that base their units for the foundation program on average daily attendance. The attendance (and consequently the units) in certain districts may have decreased during a particular year solely as a consequence of epidemics or inclement weather. Several states have made adjustments to take care of this situation by (1) basing units on attendance during the first two or the best two months, (2) maintaining for each district, for the three preceding years, the ratio between average daily attendance and average daily membership and automatically correcting to the average for the district during any year when the ratio drops below its own average, or (3) changing from average daily attendance to average daily membership.

Services Beyond Regular School Year. A third factor, which has been overlooked in developing many foundation programs, is the educational services which may be needed beyond the regular school term. The units for the foundation program are customarily computed on a nine-month basis, or in a few cases on the basis of a nine-and-a-half or even a ten-months period. However, more and more districts are operating summer schools or continuing certain educational services during the summer months. Provision can and should be made for adding fractional units sufficient to meet the needs during these months. Thus, if there is a six-week summer school and the attendance would justify 90 classroom units on the basis of the six weeks, this would be the equivalent of 15 additional units based on a nine-month program. Units can be added for principals on the basis of one month for each additional month of service and for other instructional services on a somewhat similar basis. Unless these units are added to the foundation program, the less wealthy districts will generally not be able to provide the services and the program will be handicapped. The basic question is: Are these services needed to provide the essential educational opportunities which should be included in the foundation program? If they are, provision should be made to include them.

TRANSLATING NEEDS INTO COSTS

Traditionally, in developing a foundation program plan, the cost elements have been built into the unit. Thus, when the number of units is determined, all that is needed is to multiply this number by the foundation program cost allotment per unit to determine the cost of the foundation program. However, as indicated above, there are some inherent disadvantages in having the cost unit built into the unit for measuring need.

When the unit of need is based on a study of services and facilities necessary for an adequate foundation program of education, the cost must be determined separately. The units merely represent the educational needs for a foundation program. When it is found that a district has a certain number of units of need, there is no way, until further steps are taken, to determine how many dollars this need would represent. Translating units of need into units of cost, then, constitutes a separate step.

One way of determining the value which should be assigned to each unit of need would be to use the average cost per unit based on the current expenditure for education in the state. This would merely mean that the foundation program is to be set at the level of the average expenditure in the state. This procedure has sometimes been used.

A more common procedure has been to develop the cost unit allowances very much as the units themselves are developed. This is not done or should not be done as a means of controlling the program or expenditures but merely as a realistic means of developing understanding of financial needs and of making adequate provision for costs to be included in the foundation program. It would be a serious mistake in any state for those who are developing the foundation program to assume, or for the legislature to accept the idea, that steps taken to develop cost units should be used as devices for controlling or restricting foundation program expenditures in the districts.

Instructional Salaries

A question with which discussion of salary needs usually starts is: What should be the beginning salary of a properly certificated teacher who is a college graduate and has had no previous teaching experience? The next logical question is: How much, on the average, should properly certificated college graduates be paid, considering the fact that some of them have had no experience and some have had many years of experience? Other pertinent questions are: Do many districts employ teachers who are not college graduates? What would be a reasonably adequate salary for such teachers? Should most teachers have had training beyond college graduation? What would be a reasonable salary for such teachers? What about salaries for instructional personnel beyond the customary nine- or ten-month term? (That is, the amount for additional service provided through extra units for summer programs or service, as previously explained.)

Several state committees have agreed upon a fixed amount per unit which should be included for instructional salaries. Other state committees have taken the position that if a fixed amount is included for all districts, those which are now employing poorly prepared teachers probably would use the money in developing salary schedules for their presently employed teachers. Once that is done, they would not be in a position to attract better qualified teachers, because the only way they could raise their salary schedule would be to increase local effort. Some state committees, therefore, have decided to assign a somewhat lower value to a unit which is used for teachers who are poorly prepared and a somewhat higher value to units used for teachers who are particularly well prepared. Districts with poorly prepared teachers could thus increase the amount of their foundation program allotment by employing better qualified teachers.

Two arguments used against using this differential in most states are: (1) Districts should be assured of an adequate amount of money per unit, then should be free to determine how the money is to be used, and (2) the more alert districts will employ a higher proportion of well qualified teachers and consequently receive a somewhat larger share of the funds than the others. People in some states, in which a substantial proportion of the teachers are poorly qualified, may conclude that a differential is necessary for the present but should be discontinued at a later date. The evidence seems to indicate that reasonable differentials have stimulated improvement in the preparation of teachers in many areas where standards previously had been quite unsatisfactory.

Current Expense Other Than Salaries and Transportation

In many foundation programs, the amount included for current expense other than instructional salaries and transportation has been far too limited to meet the needs. Studies made in a number of states show that about 25 per cent of the amount needed per classroom unit for instructional salaries should be included in the program to meet the necessary expenses of administration, operation, maintenance, and other related current expense. The entire program may be handicapped if the amount included for such expense is too limited.

Transportation Expense

Since procedures for determining needs and costs for transportation are discussed in Chapter 12, there is no need to consider the problem in detail here. In a number of states, the cost of transportation is not included in the foundation program plan. In a few, a separate foundation program has been established for transportation. It would seem that the only defensible procedure would be to develop a sound plan for determining the cost of transportation, then to include the allowable cost in the foundation program for each district in the state.

Capital Outlay

As previously indicated, only a few states have included capital outlay in the foundation program thus far. There is still some difference of opinion as to whether it should be included in a general program or as to whether there should be a separate foundation program for capital outlay. This problem is further discussed in Chapter 11. If capital outlay is to be included, the amount needed per unit can be determined as explained later and that amount added to the other unit figures to arrive at the total value of the classroom unit, except for transportation.

Cost of the Foundation Program

The value of the classroom unit thus becomes the total of the amount included for instructional salaries, the amount for current expense other than salaries and transportation, and the amount for capital outlay if that is to be included in the foundation program. The cost of the foundation program for any district, then, will be determined by multiplying the total value of the classroom unit by the number of units in the district and adding the allowable cost of transportation. The cost for the program in the state can similarly be determined.

Some authorities have advocated cost-of-living adjustments in the value of the unit for school systems where such variations are found. The problem unquestionably needs further study. However, no state has provided a direct adjustment thus far in the current expense portion of the program. Most people point out that, when all factors are considered, variations within a state are usually relatively minor. Communities in which the higher costs are found usually have somewhat higher ability and hence greater local leeway, can more easily attract competent teachers, and have a number of advantages over the less favored areas. In fact, some contend that an adjustment should be made, as has already been done in some countries, to provide for higher salaries for teachers in the more isolated schools.

Proposals have also been made to provide in the law for the value of the classroom unit to be increased or decreased each year as the value of the dollar changes. The use of such an index would probably receive more serious consideration in a number of states if (1) the foundation program were financed at an adequate level, and (2) some way could be found to make the index applicable to both local and state funds involved in the support of the program.

STATE AND LOCAL SUPPORT

There are two major problems in determining the proportion and amount of the total cost of the foundation program to be provided by local effort and by the state. The first pertains to the percentage of the total cost of the program to be provided from state and from local funds; the second pertains to development of procedures for assuring uniform and equitable local effort.

Per Cent from Local and State Funds

In most states, practically all state funds are derived from sources other than property taxes, whereas most local funds for schools are provided through local property tax levies. Theoretically, therefore, except in those states which have state property taxes or substantial sources of local revenue derived from other than property taxes, the percentage of local funds to be used toward the cost of the foundation program on a state-wide basis should be somewhat related to the sources of income of the people of the state. If most of the income of the residents is derived from sources other than property, the largest percentage of funds for support of the foundation program should come from state sources. However, there is another factor to be considered. All or most districts levy some taxes for the current program in addition to those required for the foundation program, and many also have tax levies for bond retirement. Most of these revenues are derived from levies on property. It would seem, therefore, that the largest percentage of funds for support of the foundation program in all states should come from state sources. This percentage will vary from state to state but probably in most states from 60 to 80 per cent of the cost of the foundation program should come from state sources.

The procedures used in developing and implementing the foundation program have considerable bearing on the proportion of state and local funds used for support. Chart V illustrates this point.

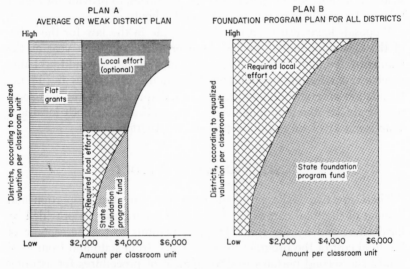

CHART V. *Two Kinds of Foundation Program Plans.*

Wealthiest District Plan. The original proposal relating to the foundation program presented the idea of determining the levy that would be required in the most wealthy district in the state to support the foundation program in that district on the basis of the number of units multiplied by the value of each unit. The plan has merit, in that all districts except the most wealthy would participate in and benefit from the foundation program; whereas the most wealthy district would have sufficient resources of its own to meet the costs. This plan would work reasonably well only in a large-district state, such as Utah, where it has been used in principle for a number of years. The range in wealth among districts in large-district states is sufficiently limited that the tax levy required for state support of the program in the most wealthy district would result in a reasonably substantial local contribution in each of the other districts. However, in the small-district states the plan would not work because the most wealthy district (often a small district) would have so much wealth that only a very low levy would be required to meet the complete cost of the program. If such a levy were applied in each of the other districts, the yield would be so small as to make the local contribution insignificant. The idea of keying the foundation program to the most wealthy district has, therefore, practically been abandoned, even in theory, in all except some of the large-district states.

The Key District Plan. Another plan frequently recommended during more recent years is to key the program to the largest wealthy district in the state. This plan would provide for determining the cost of the foundation program in the largest wealthy district and finding the levy required to provide complete support of the program in that district. This would be the required levy for each of the other districts and would result in reasonably substantial local contributions. In large-district states, the wealthiest district becomes the key district, and in those instances this plan would be identical with the plan previously discussed.

Foundation Program for All Districts. In the large-district states it becomes possible to establish a foundation program in which all districts, even the most wealthy, would participate. The proportion of funds which should be provided from local and state sources can be determined somewhat in relationship to the sources of income of the people of the state. The local levy can be set at a figure which would yield somewhat less than the cost of the program even for the most wealthy district, and this levy, of course, would apply to all other districts. Thus, all districts would participate and the extent to which the foundation program cost exceeds the yield of the required levy in the most wealthy district would represent tax broadening possibilities for all districts. This plan has been used in Florida for some years. (See Plan B in Chart V.)

Taxpayer Equity Plan. It is, of course, possible, after determining the cost of the foundation program in a state, to decide on the portion which, in terms of taxpayer equity, as previously explained, should be borne by the state and the portion by local school systems. Adjustments can be made to allow for local funds provided for enrichment of the program or for bond retirement. The local required levy or effort can then be set to provide the proportion of the cost of the program which should come from local funds. The remainder would come from the state. Thus, most of the districts in the state might participate or a substantial number might not, depending on the level at which the levy is set, and other factors.

Average or Weak District Plan. Several states have attempted to set a levy which would enable all districts with below-average ability to participate. Other states have had what is often called a "weak district" plan. The local levy in such states is set sufficiently high that only the least wealthy districts would lack sufficient funds to meet the costs of the foundation program. (See Plan A in Chart V.) Both of these provisions would have some serious disadvantages, especially in view of the fact that many of the districts in the state would have far more funds available from the local required effort, if made, than the cost of the foundation program. They therefore would have a decided advantage over the foundation program districts. Moreover, such districts, even though they might be considerably above average in wealth, might demand some share of state funds. The stage would thus be set for unwholesome competition between the wealthy and the least wealthy districts. Such a conflict would probably handicap the proper development of the foundation program, as it has in a number of states.

Completely State-Supported Programs

A few states, notably Hawaii, North Carolina, South Carolina, and Delaware, have attempted to establish completely state-supported foundation programs. In such cases the state undertakes to provide all of the funds needed for the foundation program and no required local effort is necessary. Such states avoid the complication of attempting to determine what constitutes equitable local effort but have involved themselves in some other difficulties. In the first place, there is serious question as to whether the state, over a period of years, will be as vigorous or as realistic in supporting the foundation program entirely from state funds as might be expected if there were a combination of state and local funds. In the second place, the impact of a completely state-supported program on local initiative and responsibility needs careful consideration. If the local school systems are not providing local funds toward the cost of the program, they may tend to feel that, since they are spending state money only, they can be less careful or prudent than would be the case if their own local funds were involved. Such an attitude tends to create suspicion and distrust on the part of the legislature and state officials and may result in creeping state controls which tend gradually to weaken local responsibility.

While there is apparently not enough evidence to justify the statement that completely state-supported programs are undesirable or indefensible, there is enough information available to point to the need for careful consideration of the problem.

Uniformity in Local Effort

Most of the foundation programs originally established provided for a uniform tax levy in all participating districts as a means of assuring that each district would make its proper local contribution to the cost of the foundation program. However, as previously noted, studies have shown that assessment practices vary greatly in many of the states and vary to some extent in practically every state. A uniform levy in such cases would result in serious inequities as far as taxpayers are concerned. Local levies combined with state funds would provide the full cost of the foundation program for each district, but the taxpayers in the various districts would not be making uniform effort. Therefore, the program would not be provided in relationship to ability and need.

To illustrate the problem, suppose there are two districts with the same number of classroom units and that each has an assessed valuation of $500,000 per classroom unit. In one district the property is assessed at 50 per cent of full cash value and in the other district it is assessed at only 25 per cent. On the basis of a 10-mill levy on assessed valuation, each district would provide $500 per classroom unit toward the cost of the program. In reality, however, the district assessed at 50 per cent of full value (if that is accepted as a standard) is providing what it should, whereas the other district, which is under-assessed, should be providing $1,000 per classroom unit instead of $500. Thus, because of under-assessment it is obtaining a subsidy of $500 per classroom unit from the state, which cannot be justified. The taxpayers of the entire state are helping to reward the district for its low assessment practices.

The remedy for this situation is to provide for uniform local effort instead of for a uniform local levy. Equity can be achieved, as explained in Chapter 6, by: (1) achieving uniformity in assessment practices (not likely to be attained in the near future in most states), (2) making adjustments on the basis of an assessment-ratio plan, or (3) making adjustments on the basis of an index of taxpaying ability. No foundation program can be considered satisfactory unless provision is made for uniform local effort based on taxpaying ability.

One other problem remains to be considered in connection with local funds. In most states, certain districts receive funds from Public Law 874, from Federal Forest Reserve funds, or from other Federal and miscellaneous sources. If the local required effort is based on property taxes, some adjustment should be made for these funds; otherwise districts will not be supporting the foundation program in accordance with their ability.[16] Thus, not only the yield from the required local taxes on property but also an equitable proportion of other revenues available to the local school system should be considered in determining ability to support the foundation program.

IMPLEMENTING THE FOUNDATION PROGRAM

If measures of need, cost units, and procedures for determining uniform local effort are objective, it should be possible for representatives from each local school system as well as from the state to determine and agree upon the cost of the foundation program for the district and the amount of local and state funds to be provided. Theoretically, there should be no serious problems in implementing and administering the program. However, in practice many problems arise in nearly every state. Some of the most important of these are discussed briefly on the following pages.

State Requirements and Controls

The foundation program plan should be considered basically as a sound and equitable procedure for assuring that each district will have sufficient funds from state and local sources to finance the essential program of educational opportunity. It should not be used as a basis for restricting or denying local control of education. In fact, it should serve to strengthen and improve the opportunity for more vigorous and meaningful local initiative and control. It should not be used as a means of forcing districts to conform to purposes conceived by the state legislature or by state officials unless those purposes clearly and definitely contribute to the improvement of education.

In an effort to assure reasonably adequate educational opportunities for pupils and prudent expenditure of funds, every state has estab-

---

[16] In states that use an economic index of taxpaying ability to determine the funds that should be provided by the local required effort, no special adjustment is needed for the Federal funds received under present laws.

lished some minimum requirements which must be met by all schools. Compulsory attendance, minimum length of term, certification of teachers, and other similar provisions are probably necessary to safeguard the interests and welfare of students and of society but, insofar as considered necessary, should be established for all districts, not just for districts which participate in foundation program funds. An ultimate test of a control should be whether it improves or injures the educational opportunities for the pupils.

Many states have gone much further than necessary in establishing detailed requirements which handicap and restrict districts. There is always a danger in such requirements, but the danger is particularly great when these requirements are imposed only on the least wealthy districts, because the precedent may thus be set for a control that could later be applied to other districts. The foundation program should neither be used as a means of establishing questionable controls, or of subsidizing or perpetuating indefensible practices to the extent that progress or improvement is discouraged.

One basic requirement is essential for the satisfactory implementation of the foundation program in any state. Every district must make the local tax effort found necessary to provide its share of the costs of the foundation program. Unless that requirement is established, the foundation program cannot be fully implemented. This requirement should apply to all districts. Even those districts which do not participate in foundation program funds, if there are any, should be required to make the levy necessary to provide the funds needed for full financing of the foundation program in the district.

If some districts choose to maintain unnecessary schools, they should be required to make the effort to finance those schools at the foundation program level of cost. If that is not required, the children may be deprived of essential educational opportunities. A good case can also be made for requiring areas maintaining separate elementary and high school districts to make an additional levy sufficient to meet the extra costs of operating those districts. Illinois has had such a requirement for several years.

Apportionment of Funds

When a foundation program plan is adopted in any state that has been apportioning a part of its funds on a flat-grant basis, the question arises as to what should happen to flat-grant apportionments to wealthy districts that do not participate in the foundation program. This is a difficult problem to solve. If the flat-grants are continued for all districts, the foundation program districts are involved in unnecessary accounting procedures and the stage is set for potential conflicts between districts that benefit most from flat-grants and those that benefit most from the foundation program. In such cases it is usually considered desirable to provide a minimum guarantee for districts which have been receiving flat-grant funds. Thus, after the cost of the foundation program has been agreed upon and the procedures for participation established, a provision can be incorporated in the law to the effect that no properly organized district shall be entitled to less funds per classroom unit than previously received from state sources. The Ohio law illustrates how this provision can be applied.

The legislature should, of course, be expected to appropriate for each year sufficient funds to meet the state's share of the cost of the foundation program. In some instances the law has provided for the local required effort to be increased sufficiently during any year to make up any deficit. However, if there is a major shortage such a provision would be impractical. A few states have provided that, if there is such a deficit, a uniform reduction would be made in the proportion of funds each district receives from the state. This would be inequitable because the least wealthy districts would be most handicapped. A better provision would be that the cost of the foundation program is to be reduced proportionately for all districts. Every effort should, of course, be made to assure that the program will be financed in full each year so that none of the districts will be at a disadvantage.

The foundation program funds provided by the state should never be made available on a reimbursement basis. The least wealthy districts will not have the resources to meet expenses with the expectation that they will be reimbursed by the state at a later date. The funds should therefore be apportioned periodically each year. The best plan would be to provide for an apportionment to be made monthly, beginning the first month of the fiscal year. The first apportionments can be tentative, if necessary, and adjustments can then be made in later apportionments.

When standards are established for determining which small schools are isolated, corrections for such schools can be made at the time the apportionment is computed. Once the status of a small school has been determined, there should be no need for reclassifying the school for several years unless new highways are constructed or other factors that might affect the isolation are changed. Similarly, when the formula provides for a differential for salaries of instructional personnel on the basis of training of teachers for the current year (not for the past year, because this would tend to discourage districts from employing better trained teachers) any necessary adjustments can be made at the time the foundation program costs for each district are finally computed.

It should be clearly understood by state as well as local school officials that procedures established for determining foundation program costs are to be used only for that purpose and are not to be used to restrict or regulate local expenditures. For example, it would be a serious mistake to require any district to use only for transportation any funds included in the foundation program on the basis of transportation need, because such a requirement would restrict the decision making prerogative of the board and might encourage extravagance. It would be equally unfortunate to have a similar provision involving funds for current expense other than instructional salaries and transportation.

Some state teachers' associations have favored safeguards to assure that a proper proportion of the money will be used for instructional salaries. In some cases, salary schedules have been tied in with the foundation program plan. This, however, has involved some difficulties and seems to be unwise. A few states have insisted that a certain percentage of all state funds be used for salaries. Such a provision would be meaningless and unworkable. The only provision that would have any meaning would be to require that the amount included in the foundation program for instructional salaries be used for salaries. Even such a general provision might, on theoretical grounds, be objectionable to some.

If capital outlay is included in the foundation program, a reasonably good case can be made for requiring that the capital outlay portion of the funds be set aside and used only for that purpose or for debt service. This point is discussed further in a later chapter.

SOME PROBLEMS AND ISSUES

There are many important problems and issues relating to the development and implementation of foundation programs. Only a few can be discussed on the following pages.

Who Should Provide the Leadership in Developing or Improving the Foundation Program?

In a number of states there has been no serious study during recent years of the impact on educational opportunities and on taxpayers, of the program for financing schools. In these states, no individual or group has attempted to obtain the evidence on a state-wide basis which may be used in determining the extent to which the program conforms to acceptable criteria or in ascertaining inequities which may exist in the finance plan as it applies to the various districts. In some states that have relied heavily on flat-grants for financing their schools, the legislature apparently has found it easier to increase these grants than to make major revisions in the program. Districts benefiting from flat-grants may tend to resist changes, and other districts may not have sufficient information to support their claims for additional funds apportioned on a different basis.

Who should take the leadership in making studies and getting thinking started, in states which have no foundation program plan or are having difficulties with their foundation program?

National groups, of course, make studies from time to time, and some of these studies point to potential problems. For example, the study to which reference has already been made, *Expenditures for Education at the Mid-Century,* presents charts which indicate serious problems in a number of the states. However, no national group is likely to be in a position to take the leadership in getting studies started in any state.

Sometimes university professors, with the help of their graduate students, can make a series of studies that will have considerable impact. However, there is a tendency in some states to consider these merely as "studies" and not be concerned about the practical implications. It takes more than such studies, in many states, to get thinking started, but not much progress can be made unless such studies are made.

In a number of states the teachers' association has taken the responsibility for proposing to the legislature improvements in provisions for financing schools. In some cases these suggestions have largely constituted proposals for providing more money for schools. In too few cases have they been based on studies which provided the background for sound suggestions. In other states, the department of education has taken the leadership and sometimes has prepared suggestions on the basis of studies. However, the department may also be under some handicap, particularly if the teachers' association leadership feels that its opportunity for leadership is thereby decreased.

An analysis of developments indicates that the most significant progress has usually come as a result of studies sponsored by the governor, by the legislature, or by some cooperative group. For example, in Ohio the legislature adopted a resolution requesting a comprehensive study of education, and out of this study came proposals that resulted in material improvements in the entire finance plan. This study was carried out with the cooperation of prominent lay citizens and educators throughout the state. There seems to be general agreement among leaders in Ohio that most of these improvements could not have been made, at least at that time, without such a study.

In Wyoming, a legislative interim committee became interested in the study of education and developed the idea of appointing a citizens' committee to assume the responsibility for the study. As in the case of

Ohio, while the general plans were developed by the sponsoring committee, the studies were carried out cooperatively by educators and laymen, including not only educators from the public school system but from the university. Conferences were held in various parts of the state from time to time, to discuss problems and attempt to get agreement on objectives. A state-wide conference sponsored by the governor resulted in substantial agreement on proposals, and a plan materially revising and improving the finance program was adopted by unanimous vote of the legislature.

Many other illustrations could be given. In Kentucky, for example, the Legislative Research Commission sponsored some of the original studies but soon found it desirable to stimulate the organization of a state-wide committee, which sponsored further studies resulting in revision of the program. In New York the Education Conference Board has, for years, carried out various studies concerning all aspects of the finance plan and its implications for the educational program. As a result of these studies, numerous improvements have been proposed and many have been adopted.

These comments should not be interpreted to minimize the importance of the state department of education, the state education association, the state school boards association, or the parent-teacher association, in providing statewide leadership. Such groups should cooperate and participate in making state studies but the legislature must make the final decision on educational appropriations and changes in the laws. The support of the governor for these proposed changes is also extremely important. If educational agencies and organizations only are involved in initiating changes, especially changes which involve increasing educational expenditures, the proposals are usually suspect as being self-interest proposals. In order to avoid the charge of bias, it would seem desirable for the legislature, which represents all people and all groups, to initiate the study.

What handicaps would the state board or the state teachers association encounter in planning finance studies? In view of all pertinent factors, what seems to be the best plan for providing leadership and assuring that appropriate studies are made at the time they are needed?

What Consideration Should Be Given to the Most Wealthy Districts?

In many states the most wealthy districts are politically among the most powerful. At least, they have sufficient influence that they can usually block proposals they may not approve.

The people living in the most wealthy districts generally pay a larger proportion per capita of the taxes which go into the state general fund than those in the least wealthy districts. Many feel that the money paid in the way of taxes should, at least in part, be "their" money, and object to the idea of paying sales, income, or other taxes into the state treasury unless they can receive back "their share."

Even the educational leaders in a number of the more wealthy districts are likely to overlook the fact that their wealth is derived from the resources which happen to be located in the district (or because they have been able to extend their boundaries to include some particularly rich resources), or that the taxpaying ability is as high as it is because people from outlying areas largely support the businesses and industries located in the district. In most cases, if a foundation program were developed and no other state funds made available to the public schools, some of the more wealthy districts would not participate—at least until a larger percentage of the districts were reorganized. Generally there would be opposition to the adoption of such a program which would not directly benefit some of the more wealthy areas.

What should be the policy in such states? Should the wealthy areas receive special flat-grant funds even though in terms of equity they might not be entitled to such funds? Should tax sharing be considered as important as equalization?

How Should the Foundation Program Affect Small Schools or Districts?

In one state the foundation program provides an adjustment for all small schools. Every school, because it is small, is credited through the foundation program with more money per pupil than a larger school. The people in many of the larger school systems have pointed out that it is unfair to subsidize all small schools—that in so doing, the state is helping to perpetuate the unnecessary and expensive small schools. They have insisted that if people in a community want to continue a small school they should have the privilege of doing so but that the taxpayers of the entire state should not help to take care of the extra cost of continuing the school. Those who live in small districts contend that they should have a right to continue their schools and should be entitled to full state support.

A state committee recommended that only isolated small schools should be entitled to a smaller pupil-teacher ratio in the foundation program than the large schools. They recommended that a plan be developed for determining which small schools were isolated and which were not. They further insisted that the non-isolated schools receive from the foundation program only the number of units in relation to pupils that they would have received if the pupils had been in large schools. This committee further recommended that school districts having fewer than 100 pupils in average daily attendance be required to make an extra levy of a couple of mills to be eligible to participate in the foundation program unless the school operated by the district was an isolated school.

Who was right in this controversy? What safeguards can and should be established to assure that unnecessary, expensive schools are not perpetuated through the foundation program?

How Should Local Uniform Effort Be Determined?

In a certain state the law prescribes that each district participating in the foundation program must make a prescribed levy on the assessed valuation of the property in the district. This plan has been in operation for 15 years. Studies show that the foundation program has improved the financial condition of many districts and therefore has enabled them to provide better educational opportunities. Most districts are satisfied with the program. Some districts insist that it is not equitable. Some of the larger districts which do not participate, state that unless the program is made more equitable they will resist any further increases in the level of support. There is some talk that the state should abandon the foundation program entirely and distribute funds on a flat-grant basis. Others insist that the requirement for local effort be discontinued. They advocate that the foundation program be supported entirely by state funds and bring out the idea that this would be much more equitable and would be much simpler to administer. Some insist that the local required effort is, in reality, a state tax and should either be recognized as such or discontinued.[17]

A committee has recently been studying the problem and has obtained information on the developments in a number of other states. The study shows that there are marked variations in assessment ratios within the state in which the problem exists. The range, in fact, exceeds 3 to 1. This information has strengthened the opinions of those who hold that the foundation program should be discontinued and flat grants substituted, as well as of those who believe the foundation program should be supported entirely by state funds. However, the study shows that while a large proportion of the states still use a fixed levy based on

---

[17] Henry Thomas James, *Toward a Unified Concept of State School Finance Systems* (Unpublished Ph.D. dissertation, University of Chicago, 1958).

assessed valuation, many others seem to be achieving reasonable equity without waiting until assessments are uniform.

Would it be better to discontinue the requirement for local effort and provide either a state-supported foundation program or state support through flat-grants? Which would be superior? Should attempts be made to improve a foundation program plan until assessments are fully equalized?

What Level of Financial Support Should Be Provided Through the Foundation Program?

In several states the foundation program actually constitutes a "gesture" toward financing schools. The level of support has been so low that it helps only the poorest districts. In Indiana, for a number of years, it was realistically called the "School Relief Fund."

One of the major issues in several states involves the level at which the foundation program should be supported. Many believe it should be relatively low to avoid providing poor districts with more funds than they can use wisely.

One proposal is that the level of support should be set with reference to the point at which the marginal dollar expended for public schools returns the same values as the marginal dollar expended for other purposes.[18] Is this a defensible basis for determining the level at which the foundation program should be supported? If so, how can it be applied?

Several writers have proposed that expenditures for education should include those necessary (1) for the renewal of the citizenry and (2) for the improvement of the citizenry. With this in mind, James suggested that the expenditures for renewal of the citizenry be roughly approximated by estimating the productive life of a member of the labor force at 45 years, and accepting 1/45 or 2.2 per cent of the personal income payments as the amount to be expended for renewal.[19] He also estimated, on the basis of statements from economists, that about one per cent of the personal income payments would be necessary for improvement of the citizenry. Thus, on this basis, about 3 per cent of the personal income of the citizens of the state might be used in establishing the level of state and local support of the foundation program. To what extent is this defensible? What other bases should be used in arriving at a decision regarding the level of financial support for the foundation program?

---

[18] See Procter Thompson and Eugene S. Lawler, "Taxation and Educational Finance," Chapter IV in *Problems and Issues in Public School Finance*, eds. R. L. Johns and E. L. Morphet, p. 118.

[19] James, *op. cit.*, p. 91.

SELECTED REFERENCES

Burke, Arvid J., *Financing Public Schools in the United States*, rev. ed. New York: Harper and Brothers, 1957. Chapters XIV and XVI–XX.

Chase, Francis S., and Edgar L. Morphet, *The Forty-Eight State School Systems*. Chicago: Council of State Governments, 1949. Chapters VII to IX.

Committee for the White House Conference on Education, *A Report to the President*. Washington, D.C.: U. S. Government Printing Office, 1956. Pages 51–71.

Fowlkes, John G., and George E. Watson, *School Finance and Local Planning*. Chicago: University of Chicago Press, 1957.

Johns, R. L., and Edgar L. Morphet, editors, *Problems and Issues in Public School Finance*. New York: Bureau of Publications, Teachers College, Columbia University, 1952. Chapters I, V, and VI.

Morphet, Edgar L., Roe L. Johns, and Theodore L. Reller, *Educational Administration*. Englewood Cliffs, N.J.: Prentice-Hall, Inc., 1959. Chapter 22.

Morphet, Edgar L., and Erick L. Lindman, res. dir., *Public School Finance Programs of the Forty-Eight States*, Office of Education Circular No. 274. Washington, D.C.: U. S. Government Printing Office, 1950. Chapters V and VI.

Mort, Paul R., and Walter C. Reusser, *Public School Finance*, 2nd ed. New York: McGraw-Hill Book Company, Inc., 1951. Chapters 20–26.

Munse, Albert R., and Eugene P. McLoone, *Public School Finance Programs of the United States, 1957–58*. U. S. Office of Education, Washington, D.C.: U. S. Government Printing Office, 1959.

Rosenstengel, William Everett, and Jefferson N. Eastmond, *School Finance*. New York: The Ronald Press Company, 1957. Chapters 4 and 5.

CHAPTER ELEVEN

State Provisions
for Financing Capital Outlay

The present day problem of providing satisfactory school plant facilities is much more complicated and far more expensive than at any previous time in the history of the nation. The rapid growth in most states and the increasing urbanization of many communities have made small schools obsolete in many areas. The demands of a modern program of education, the improvement in roads and transportation, the increasing density of population, and other similar developments indicate that in a few years there will be practically no elementary schools enrolling fewer than 300 to 600 pupils and only a limited number of high schools with fewer than 500 to 1000 pupils, except in sparsely populated areas.

While school sites in some rural areas may still be purchased for only a few dollars, the minimum cost in many urban and metropolitan areas has increased to several thousand dollars an acre and satisfactory sites are increasingly difficult to obtain at any reasonable cost. Both standards for construction and construction costs have increased rapidly. In late 1959 the index of construction costs for school buildings, using 1939 as 100, had risen to approximately 236.

The construction of a single large elementary school in many communities now involves not only difficult and complicated planning, but also an investment of a half million or more dollars. A single comprehensive high school requires even more complicated planning and is likely to cost from a million and a half to five million dollars.

THE TRADITION OF LOCAL SUPPORT

The provision of school sites, buildings, and equipment has been considered a local responsibility until comparatively recent years. In fact, the tradition of local responsibility for financing capital outlay is still strongly entrenched in many states. Many people believe that if the state assists in financing the current cost of operating schools, districts should be expected to provide their own buildings. However, studies in many parts of the country show that there are serious building shortages and inadequacies and that many school systems cannot provide suitable facilities from local resources.

There have been great variations in local effort to provide school facilities. However, if every district made a reasonable and continuing financial effort to provide satisfactory school buildings on the basis of a carefully developed plan, there would still be problems. The most serious would be found in small-district states because of the range in wealth or ability. Some of the more wealthy districts could meet their housing needs with very limited effort while some of the least wealthy or rapidly growing districts could not possibly make the local effort required to finance either schools or buildings.

Even in the large-district states there will be problems in providing satisfactory buildings in all communities if the construction has to be financed entirely out of local funds. In county-unit states, as indicated previously, the range in ability is, of course, much less than in small-district states, but is still ten or more to one in most of these states. Thus, the least wealthy counties in a county-unit state would have to make at least ten times the effort required of the most wealthy to provide satisfactory school buildings.

If there is only limited state support for the current operating program, the problem of financing school buildings will be more acute both in small- and large-district states than would be the case if a satisfactory and adequate foundation program had been developed and fully financed in those states. In other words, a good state plan of financial support for the current operating program will help, but will not solve the problem of financing the school plant program.

Many who believe that the tradition of local responsibility for financing school plant construction should be continued contend that the chief problem arises from the fact that limitations on indebtedness for school plant purposes are too low. There is considerable evidence to indicate that indebtedness limitations are not only unrealistically low in several states, but that they may be lower in practice than actually seems to be the case because assessed values may represent only a small percentage of actual values. In such situations, raising the limits on indebtedness would help many districts. Relating the limits to actual valuation rather than assessed valuation would remove some of the existing inequities resulting from variations in assessment practices. However, if the limits were removed entirely, the problem would not be solved for the less wealthy districts because they could not finance the needed construction.

When school buildings are financed with local funds, the costs must be paid in most communities entirely from the proceeds of property taxes. However, in many communities, and particularly in suburban communities, many of the parents who have children attending school may not own any property. Many who have considerable taxpaying ability are likely to derive much of their income from sources other than property. If buildings are to be financed from the proceeds of property taxes, those who are not property owners may escape much of their responsibility for helping finance the buildings needed to house the pupils of the community.

Thus, the tradition of exclusive local responsibility for financing school plant construction is not sound or realistic in any state. The wealthy communities may have ample resources to provide excellent buildings to house all of the children. The communities of average wealth may be able to provide reasonably satisfactory buildings if they are willing to make a high tax effort. However, the least wealthy communities will not be able to afford satisfactory buildings unless state or Federal funds are provided to assist in meeting the costs.

TRENDS IN STATE SUPPORT

Although no state had developed a continuing plan for assisting local districts with capital outlay expenses before 1900, shortly after that time, a few began to recognize the problem and to provide some assistance. The establishment of state standards for buildings and sites undoubtedly contributed to this development. Some communities, for one reason or another, had constructed schools on sites that were obviously undesirable, or had built structures that were hazardous to both children and teachers. As a result, states began to recognize the need for establishing minimum standards for school construction. However, it soon became apparent that there were districts that could not finance the construction of buildings in accordance with those standards. It also became obvious that small districts in certain rural areas could not consolidate their schools because they could not finance the construction of a centrally located school.

Alabama took the first step toward continuing state aid for school plant construction in 1901, by providing aid for rural school buildings. In 1903, Delaware provided aid for the erection of school buildings in Negro districts. In 1904, Louisiana, by constitutional amendment, authorized the legislature to issue bonds to construct buildings in areas not able to finance such construction. In 1909, South Carolina provided aid on a matching basis for rural school buildings. North Carolina and Virginia, in the meantime, had provided funds that could be used for loans to districts. During the next 25 years, several states provided funds, usually on a matching basis and chiefly for aid in consolidations.

In 1927, Delaware took the first major step toward support of school construction by providing state funds to meet most of the costs and requiring only a small local contribution. A few states that were developing foundation programs began to permit limited state funds to be used for capital outlay or debt service but no state seems to have developed a continuing partnership plan based on recognition of capital outlay costs as an essential part of the foundation program before 1935. In that year, Alabama developed a minimum program plan including funds for capital outlay and debt service. However, since the amount included in the foundation program was inadequate to meet all needs of the program, the legislature and the state board began to allocate for teachers' salaries some of the funds seriously needed for plant construction. The amounts remaining for capital outlay and debt service proved to be totally inadequate.

In the report of his 1941 study, Weller noted that the states still had "crude and inequitable distribution systems in which the principles of equalization are neither recognized nor applied ... or else simple devices for loaning money to districts by the State on easy terms." [1]

He reported that of the twelve states making some limited provisions for financing capital outlay, three were "groping toward some recognition of principles or procedures required by equalization." These were Delaware, New York, and Ohio. However, Alabama should have been added to that list.

During the five-year period from 1945 to 1950, many states began to be seriously concerned about the problem and several provided more realistic state assistance for financing capital outlay than had even been considered prior to the war. The building situation had become acute in many communities due chiefly to inability to construct buildings during the depression years, to restrictions on civilian construction of

---

[1] Gerald D. Weller, *State Equalization of Capital Outlays for Public School Buildings* (Los Angeles: University of Southern California Press, 1941), p. 5.

all kinds during World War II, and to rapid growth in population. Studies showed that many of these communities could not begin to meet their needs from local resources and that states would have to provide assistance if pupils were to be housed satisfactorily.

In 1947 Florida developed the first plan based on studies and designed to determine the amount each district would need annually if every building were to be replaced at the end of its normal life expectancy. Thus, Florida took a major step toward providing for the financing of school plant construction on a continuing pay-as-you-go basis with a state-local partnership plan.

Other states began about the same time to develop other kinds of plans. A few attempted to incorporate the financing of capital outlay in the foundation program. Even more, however, established special funds for capital outlay purposes, some of which were apportioned partly on an equalizing basis. For example, Washington developed an equalized matching plan in which the state first provided between 25 per cent and 75 per cent of the cost in needy districts but later modified this so the actual range extended to approximately 90 per cent of the cost. However, emphasis was placed on meeting emergency needs rather than on a continuing program. New York and California developed what may be considered loan-grant plans, including provisions for loaning money to certain types of districts which the districts were to repay in whole or in part in accordance with their ability. New York was the first state to incorporate a cost-of-construction index in its formula and thus provide for increases in state funds for buildings as construction costs were increased.

By 1950, some 20 states had provided assistance of some sort to aid at least certain types of districts with school plant construction. Since that time, a few other states have developed plans of one type or another and at the present time approximately three-fifths are providing some assistance. This number does not include a few states that provide loans for districts at a designated rate of interest.

CHARACTERISTICS OF A SATISFACTORY PROGRAM

In 1950, representatives from the U. S. Office of Education and the University of California at Berkeley cooperated in a study of state provisions for financing public school capital outlay programs. After presenting in considerable detail and analyzing the provisions made by each of the states, the authors of the study concluded:

> Notable developments have occurred in recent years. . . . Much of the thinking continues to deal with emergencies rather than with the

long-range program. . . . Some plans show little recognition of commonly accepted principles of State financing of education. There is, however, in the plans now in operation a significant recognition of the State's responsibility for participation in financing capital outlay costs, and there are in practice procedures which should point the way toward the development of long-range programs that will meet the capital outlay needs and avoid the present practice of meeting emergencies. It may be expected that a long-range program, developed in light of sound principles of educational finance, should emerge in many States in the next decade.[2]

On the basis of their experience in conducting the study and in attempting to evaluate existing programs, the authors concluded that every satisfactory program for financing school plant construction should have certain characteristics, which were presented in Chapter 6 of the report. In a follow-up study, Morphet and Reller re-analyzed the proposed criteria or characteristics, grouped them under certain headings, and added a few not included in the previous report. These are given below:

General Guidelines:

1. Each state should make provision for state participation in the financing of capital outlay programs.
2. The state program for financing capital outlay should be developed through sound, comprehensive studies.
3. An acceptable program should provide adequately and equitably for all essential school plant needs.
4. The state plan should provide for both emergency and long-range needs.
5. All districts should be eligible to participate in accordance with needs.

Guidelines Pertaining to Finance:

1. The state plan for financing capital outlay should be developed as an integral part of the foundation program of education.
2. Provision should be made in the program for state grants or grants and loans rather than for loans alone.
3. The program should be financed through an equitable combination of state and local revenue.
4. Funds for the program should be derived chiefly from current state revenues and insofar as practicable from current local revenues.
5. An objective formula for apportioning funds should be included in the law.
6. The program should provide for equitable local tax effort.
7. Each local school system should have a reasonable margin of local tax leeway and bonding ability.

---

[2] Erick L. Lindman, Clayton D. Hutchins, Edgar L. Morphet, and Theodore L. Reller, *State Provisions for Financing Public School Capital Outlay Programs*, U. S. Office of Education Bulletin 1951, No. 6 (Washington, D.C.: U. S. Government Printing Office, 1951), p. 148.

Guidelines to Administration:

1. The program should be administered by the state department of education.
2. The program should place maximum emphasis on local responsibility and state leadership.
3. Comprehensive local school plant studies should be required.
4. Each local school system should develop and adopt a long-range program.
5. The state program should assure that all necessary facilities can be provided at permanent school centers.
6. Building plans and specifications should be submitted to the state department of education for checking as to conformity to a few broad minimum standards.
7. Except for funds provided strictly for emergency programs, districts should be permitted to use capital outlay funds provided through the program either during the current year or to place such funds on deposit so they can be accumulated over a reasonable period of years and used as needed.
8. The basic state and local capital outlay funds should be required to be used for bona fide capital outlay purposes or for debt service under certain conditions.[3]

ANALYSIS OF STATE SUPPORT PROVISIONS

It should be apparent from the previous discussion that emergency or temporary provisions made by a state will not meet the needs during coming years, unless the emergency provisions are extended at each session of the legislature. However, such provisions tend to encourage expedient action. They may even discourage or make impossible sound long-range planning. Moreover, numerous requirements tend to be established in connection with emergency programs in an attempt to assure that the money will be used to provide housing for as large a proportion of the improperly housed children as possible. Such controls may be regarded by the sponsors as necessary for the emergency but might not be acceptable for any long-range program. However, when emergency provisions are continued from year to year, people tend to become accustomed to some of the controls. Thus, there is danger that such controls may become a permanent although undesirable part of the program.

In failing to recognize the financing of capital outlay as a long-range problem, several states have resorted to bond issues and have encouraged the participating districts to incur heavy indebtedness in order to

---

[3] Edgar L. Morphet and Theodore L. Reller, *State Provisions for Financing Public School Capital Outlay Costs,* Field Service Leaflet No. 1 (Berkeley: University of California, Department of Education, 1952).

provide funds to meet urgent construction costs. The continued issuance of bonds may eventually involve both the state and some of the districts in financial difficulty. Unnecessary costs are added for interest and, because of the heavy indebtedness, interest rates may be higher than would otherwise be the case.

The procedures used in the various states that are attempting to help with the financing of school plant construction cannot easily and neatly be classified. Some states have authorized several distinct funds designed to provide aid for certain types of districts or to help with certain problems. These funds may have somewhat different purposes. Some states also have elements of two or three kinds of programs incorporated in a plan that seems to defy classification. In the following paragraphs, some of the most interesting provisions found in one or more states are briefly discussed and analyzed.

State Loans

Several states, through their permanent school fund or some other fund or combination of funds, have authorized loans to school districts for capital outlay at a prescribed rate of interest. Such a procedure not only helps to assure a sound investment and source of income for the state fund but makes it possible for all districts to sell their bonds at a reasonable rate of interest.

The larger and more wealthy districts usually have no difficulty in marketing their bonds and consequently may obtain a more favorable rate of interest through public sale than through a state loan. However, the smaller and less wealthy districts may benefit from state purchase of their bonds or by obtaining money as a loan from the state through some other procedure. While this plan may help certain districts to obtain loans when they would otherwise not be available or to obtain a reasonable interest rate, it does not help many of them with their basic problem—obtaining sufficient funds to finance needed construction. Even the state has to be assured that the loan will be repaid and cannot afford to loan money to a district beyond its reasonable borrowing capacity.

During the past few years, however, several states have related the idea of a state loan or bonding authority to the idea of a continuing program of state assistance in financing capital outlay. Thus, once a continuing plan is established, districts may, if authorized to do so, borrow money from a state bonding authority in anticipation of their continuing annual state allotment and the yield from the local required levy for capital outlay, as explained later. Thus, the bonding or borrowing capacity of a district may, in effect, be removed from local valuation and related to its actual housing needs. Some such provision seems to be essential and has become an important factor in a few states in assuring the satisfactory operation of the continuing program.

A committee in New York State studied various aspects of this problem in 1957.[4] This Committee proposed the establishment of a State School Financing Authority for New York as "the most effective and most efficient instrument yet proposed to accomplish the general objectives for which our Committee was constituted." It was proposed that the authority should have two main functions:

1. At the request of the local school district, to advise and assist in the preparation of a bond issue for sale, and
2. At the request of the local school district, to buy bonds of the district from the district.

It seems obvious that these functions would have maximum value if related to a continuing state-aid plan for financing capital outlay as indicated above.

Flat-Grants

Since several states use flat-grants as a means of providing state assistance for financing the current school program, it would be expected that some would resort to flat-grants in an effort to assist in the financing of school plant construction. Such grants provide some assistance to all districts but are not equitable and do not meet the need. When a grant constitutes only a small amount, it is designed more as an encouragement or a stimulation than as realistic assistance. When it constitutes a substantial amount per school or per district regardless of wealth, it is obviously inequitable.

Incentive Funds

Incentive funds for school building construction were first used to encourage consolidation of schools. In some cases, the fund was tied in with dollar-for-dollar matching requirements. This often nullified the purpose for which the grant was provided because some of the districts were not able to make available the local matching funds required. In other cases, it constituted more of a gesture than anything else because the amount provided was too small to be realistic and districts could

---

[4] *Schools for New York,* A Report of the Governors' Committee on the Marketing of School Bonds (Albany: The Governor of the State of New York, 1957), pp. 12 and 20.

not afford the additional funds from local effort that would be necessary to construct satisfactory buildings. In other situations, where the amount has been relatively realistic, it has made some consolidations possible.

In a few states, the building fund has been designed as a means of stimulating not only consolidation of schools but district reorganization. For example, one state provided $25,000 toward school plant construction in reorganized districts. In some instances, however, where five or six districts should have been combined into one, two districts were established apparently because each had an opportunity to get $25,000 toward financing its building.

Studies show that there are better ways of financing school buildings than through incentive funds.

Grants-in-Aid to Needy Districts

Practically all emergency programs that have been developed have been based on the assumption that assistance should be given only to the districts that have most urgent needs. Districts which expect to participate in such funds usually have to make detailed applications that are reviewed by one or more state agencies as a basis for determining need. An effort has been made by several state agencies to establish objective criteria as a basis for determining priority and need. However, the fact remains that considerable state discretion is involved and specific state requirements and controls are usually deemed necessary to assure that districts do not take advantage of the situation. Under a program of this sort, districts may find themselves in a position of attempting to do what is required by the state in order to qualify for urgently needed funds, instead of working out a program designed to meet their own needs.

For many years, authorities have pointed to the danger of incorporating subjective factors and state discretion in provisions for apportioning funds to school districts for current operation. The dangers are just as great in the capital outlay field and should be zealously avoided.

Another form of aid to needy districts used in a few states is closely akin to the old idea of "aid to weak districts" for the current school program. If this type of aid is developed on a realistic basis and the funds are apportioned on an equitable formula, it may not be as dangerous as a system based on approved applications. However, the state is more likely to impose undesirable controls on "weak" districts than on all districts. Moreover, the amount included in the program is not likely to be adequate if only the poorest districts are eligible

Loan-Grants

A few states, such as California and New York, have pioneered in what is sometimes called "loan-grant" plans. Such plans constitute a step forward in that the ability of a district over a period of years is considered in scheduling repayments. Districts which cannot make full repayment with a reasonable and uniformly required local effort over a period of 25 to 30 years may have the unpaid portion of the loan cancelled. The unpaid portion then actually becomes a grant.

One of the chief difficulties with the loan-grant plan is that maximum emphasis is placed on borrowing as a major means of financing school plant construction. Districts may be required to issue bonds to their full capacity before they are eligible to participate in the program. Thus, a rapidly growing district might have to keep itself bonded to capacity over a period of many years and constantly have heavy debt service and other costs. Another difficulty arises from the fact that some states have tended to specify in great detail just what can be constructed as a means of safeguarding the state's interest and reducing the unpaid portion of the loan to a minimum. If the state itself issues bonds to finance its grant obligations, the emphasis on financing buildings through loans is maximized.

Building Authority Plans

Pennsylvania has been generally recognized as the state that pioneered the "Building Authority" plan, although some elements of the plan were developed in a number of local school systems in certain states (notably Kentucky) before the Pennsylvania plan was adopted. Several other states during recent years have incorporated at least certain elements of the plan in their state programs, notably Georgia, Indiana, Maine, and Wisconsin. Some of the bills presented to Congress for Federal assistance for school plant construction have apparently been designed partly to stimulate states to establish building authorities.

The chief difficulty with the Authority plan is that it tends to be used as a way of avoiding the basic issues and difficulties found in a state. For that reason, there have been legal problems in establishing the state Authority and putting it on a practical operating basis in a number of states. After the difficulties have been overcome, however, the Authority plan has made it possible for many districts to obtain a building when otherwise they would not have been able to finance the needed construction.

From one point of view, the Authority plan results in increasing debt limitations without changing the constitutional limitation. However, experience has shown that this does not solve the basic problem for local districts even though a state Authority may finance the construction of buildings designed to meet their needs. The Authority must rent buildings to these districts in order to recover its investment. However, experience has shown that the least wealthy districts cannot afford to pay the rent required without handicapping their operating program. Therefore, the state has to provide money for these districts so they may pay their rent. This constitutes a further subterfuge. The question might well be raised as to whether the state is gaining any-thing by establishing indirect procedures for doing something that can be done as well or perhaps even better by setting about to solve the problem directly.

Long-Range Continuing Plans

Only a few states thus far have deliberately undertaken to establish continuing long-range provisions for financing capital outlay programs. Some of the emergency provisions seem to be gradually evolving into continuing plans but most of them lack some of the desirable qualities of a sound plan, as pointed out earlier.

A long-range plan, such as developed in Florida, Kentucky, and New York, provides for a certain amount to be made available each year, from state and local effort combined, to each properly organized district for capital outlay purposes.

As indicated earlier, the Alabama plan provides no safeguards as to the proportion of the total included in the minimum program to be used for capital outlay. When the Florida foundation program was established, the $400 per classroom unit provided in the program for capital outlay purposes was added to the amount authorized for each district for the current operating program. The yield from the equivalent of a six mill levy based on state-wide equalized assessments was considered the local contribution. Each school system was required to set aside and use for capital outlay or debt service purposes, either currently or on an accumulative basis, the entire $400 per unit. However, no provision was incorporated in the law for changing the amount allocated per unit as the cost of construction changed and consequently it soon became inadequate. A later session of the Legislature provided that $200 per additional pupil would be made available to each district annually to help meet the building problems resulting from growth. Provision had been made prior to that time for the $400 to be paid entirely from state earmarked funds in order to facilitate loans to districts and thus make it possible for all districts to meet emergency needs.

When the Kentucky foundation program was established, provision was also made for including $400 per classroom unit for capital outlay. However, the levy required for local participation was separate from that required for participation in the current program. This procedure was designed to assure that at least the $400 per classroom unit would continue to be available in each district and that there would be no encroachment on this portion of the fund because of needs in other areas. Thus, it was established as a special-purpose equalizing or foundation program fund.

The New York plan constitutes a combination of loans and grants-in-aid. In this respect it is similar to the California plan but fortunately does not incorporate many of the controls and requirements found in the latter plan. The New York plan provides an amount per elementary pupil and per secondary pupil based on costs in 1951. However, a cost-of-construction index is incorporated, assuring that the amount per pupil is increased as the cost of construction increases. In order to qualify, school districts must have an indebtedness equivalent to 7.5 per cent of the total valuation of property in the district. The State provides the debt service payments in excess of the yield of a 3 mill levy on full valuation. The district begins to repay the advances without interest when the debt service tax rate drops below three mills. If the loan is not repaid at the end of 30 years, the remaining portion becomes a grant.

The chief feature of the continuing long-range plans discussed above, as well as of those that seem to be evolving in certain other states, is that an attempt has been made to assure that they are developed in accordance with sound principles of school finance. They are not merely expedient devices—nor are they ideal plans, since all of them seem to have incorporated some compromises and adjustments to existing conditions. At any rate, they constitute important steps in a direction that seems to be desirable and most of them have fewer undesirable characteristics than most of the emergency or other plans.

DEVELOPING A SOUND PROGRAM

The problem of developing a sound plan for financing capital outlay cannot be solved without giving careful consideration not only to the principles of finance but to some special problems that relate to the capital outlay field. Among those are the following:

1. *What should be considered as capital outlay costs?* While the accounting manuals give bases for classifying expenditures, the line cannot be drawn in some instances as readily as the manuals would indicate. For example, capital outlay includes expenditures for buses as well as for library books. Yet the chief concern here is with sites, buildings, and equipment, and the financial problems relating thereto. If a state can develop an adequate foundation program for current operating costs and services such as transportation, it seems that it should be possible for it to develop a sound plan for financing the school plant program.

2. *How can fluctuating annual costs be met?* The need for operating services, and in fact for most aspects of the educational program, continues year after year with some increases or decreases in costs due to changes in school population, value of the dollar, and other factors. However, the need for capital outlay does not involve the same amount per year except perhaps in some of the larger districts where the construction of one or more new buildings a year may be necessary to replace obsolescent structures or provide for growth. The question then becomes: How can a plan for financing school plant construction be devised that will meet all needs under these conditions?

3. *How can rapid growth needs be met?* The school plant problem is much more acute in rapidly growing districts than in other districts. Where there is a rapid growth, the growth frequently outstrips the resources. It is not unusual in such districts to find the valuation per pupil declining year after year, at least until new industries begin to develop in the area.

4. *How can a state plan be devised to take into consideration all variations in local methods of financing school building construction during prior years?* Variations in practices within most states are striking. Some districts continually make a high effort and bond themselves practically to the limit to provide buildings; others make no effort until the situation becomes acute; still others make a small levy each year, meet all buildings needs and still have an operating program financed far above the level found in most other districts.

5. *How can districts best be encouraged to establish or maintain adequate standards for school plant facilities?* It is a well known fact that many people in some districts are satisfied with the structures that house their children, no matter how ancient or hazardous these structures may be, unless some incident occurs that focuses attention on the problem. In other communities the people have been accustomed to buildings that meet adequate standards. These buildings may cost two or three times as much per classroom or per square foot as buildings constructed in other communities in the same state.

Studies of the Problem

Considerable attention has been given to the problem of state provisions for financing school buildings over a period of years. For example, Updegraff was concerned with the problem in his New York study in 1922 and proposed that a varying percentage of actual costs should be allowed according to the valuation per teacher.[5]

Mort first proposed that capital outlay could and should be financed by adding a percentage to the foundation program cost allowance for current operation.[6] The first attempt to measure the need for capital outlay in a state foundation program was made by Grossnickle, who found that over a period of years on a state-wide basis there was a fairly constant relationship between capital outlay and operating expenses (approximating 14 per cent at that time). He proposed that a fixed percentage of the current expense program should be added for capital outlay.[7] In the State of Washington, Lindman became interested in combining matching and equalization and proposed what he called "an equalized matching formula" for the apportionment of building aid.[8]

Average practice was commonly used, as previously indicated, in early studies and thinking about foundation programs. Weller, using average practice, worked out a proposal including a standard unit for housing, measurement of need for the unit on the basis of attendance, and cost allowances.[9] Strevell, in studying problems in New York, found that the measurement of capital outlay need in sparsely settled areas could be based on the same measures used for determining need and apportioning funds for current expense.[10]

Other studies have been concerned with the operation of state programs and attempts to evaluate those programs. For example, Wardle, attempting to determine the equity in the financial aspects of the California program, discovered that there were not only marked inequities but also undesirable controls that were tending either to perpetuate

---

[5] Harlan Updegraff, *Financial Support*, Rural School Survey of New York State (Ithaca: Joint Committee on Rural Schools, 1922).

[6] Paul R. Mort, *State Support for Public Schools* (New York: Teachers College, Columbia University).

[7] F. E. Grossnickle, *Capital Outlay in Relation to a States Minimum Education Program* (New York: Teachers College, Columbia University, 1931).

[8] Erick L. Lindman, *Development of an Equalized Matching Formula for the Apportionment of State School Building Aid* (Seattle: University of Washington Press, 1948).

[9] Weller, *State Equalization of Capital Outlays for Public School Buildings.*

[10] W. H. Strevell, *State Aid for Central School Building* (New York: Bureau of Publications, Teachers College, Columbia University, 1949).

unwholesome practices or to handicap school districts in planning their programs.[11]

Angel, in a study of the control provisions in various state programs, noted that while every program includes some requirements, the emergency programs seem to include considerably more undesirable controls than most other types of programs.[12] He noted that the assumptions made regarding a program seem to affect the amount of control. For example, the assumption in Florida seems to be that the state has an obligation to develop an adequate and realistic partnership plan for financing capital outlay needs. Only limited controls have been incorporated in the Florida program plan and few of these seem to handicap local school districts. On the other hand, in California the assumption seems to be that the state can invest only limited funds in capital outlay, that the problem is temporary and that, during the emergency, these funds must be used with maximum economy to meet most urgent needs. The California program was found to include many detailed controls that limit and handicap participating districts.

On the basis of these studies and the experience of various states, it is now possible for the people in every state to proceed to establish a sound program involving state assistance for financing school plant construction. Because of variations in ability in the various states, the adequacy of the programs established is almost certain to vary unless assistance is provided through Federal funds. However, there seem to be two basic problems of concern to many states: [13]

1. What steps politically and otherwise can be taken to avoid or remove limitations, obstacles, and inequities that prevent the people in many districts from doing what they should and, in many cases, would like to do to help themselves?

2. How can legislatures be persuaded that sound long-range programs should be developed and established instead of relying on emergency provisions that may not be basically sound or defensible?

Among the specific problems which must be faced and resolved satisfactorily in every state are the following:

The Measurement of Need

The development of some sound and equitable plan for measuring need is essential as a basis for determining school plant requirements

---

[11] Orrin D. Wardle, *Equity in the Financial Aspects of the California State School Building Aid Program* (Unpublished Doctoral Dissertation, University of California, 1957).

[12] Frank Angel, Jr., *Controls in State Programs for Financing Public School Plant Facilities* (Unpublished Doctoral dissertation, University of California, 1959).

[13] Edgar L. Morphet, "State Responsibility for New School Construction," *American School Board Journal* (May, 1957), pp. 30–32 and 70, Vol. 134.

in each district. As previously indicated, this problem is complicated by the existence of a number of related issues.

The fact should be recognized that no perfect measure of need has been developed thus far. However, when attention is centered on attempts to develop a measure for needs that exist at a particular time, the problem is much more complicated than if the interest is in developing a measure for continuing needs. Since states should be concerned with the development of long-range programs, attention here will be centered on this problem.

Studies and experience thus far seem to indicate that either the weighted pupil or the adjusted classroom unit constitute the best and most defensible means available thus far for measuring continuing need for school plant facilities. They are undoubtedly far more satisfactory than a designated number of square feet per pupil, the requirement of maximum bonding or taxing effort, the submission of applications for approval, or similar provisions which tend, both by implication and application, to result in undesirable and unwholesome state controls over local school programs.

In Chapter 10 attention was called to the fact that most states seem to find the adjusted classroom unit more satisfactory for measuring and explaining units of need for the current program to the legislature and to lay groups than the weighted pupil. This also seems to be true with reference to building needs. If the classroom unit is based on a desirable number of pupils per teacher, with adjustments for necessary small isolated schools, it is obvious that each classroom unit should not only provide for classroom space but for related corridor, office, and other essential space. Studies have shown that the amount of space needed tends to be proportionate to the adjusted classroom unit. This unit has an added advantage if it is used in a state for the current program. The problem, then, is not complicated by the necessity of devising new plans for measuring needs for capital outlay.

The only information required, therefore, to determine units of capital outlay need for a district, if this plan is used, is the number of pupils in membership or in average daily attendance in the regular program, in various special programs, and in different grade levels, if differences in space requirements in elementary and high school are found to be significant. The number of units for school plant needs for a district, therefore, become the number of units of educational need for the current operating program, with one possible exception. Studies have shown, as will be explained later, that there are special needs in rapidly growing districts that cannot be financed without special provisions for growth. The number of adjusted classroom units based on the growth over the preceding year, therefore, needs to be determined as a separate figure.

Translating Needs into Costs

The costs of construction per adjusted classroom unit including related service areas can readily be determined in a state for any given year by appropriate cost studies. These studies should include elementary and high schools, large and small schools, and should be so planned that costs per square foot as well as per classroom unit can be determined. To the actual school construction costs, of course, must be added a reasonable allowance for purchase and improvement of sites, an adequate amount for equipment, and the necessary interest costs if funds are to be borrowed. The funds included in the program should be sufficient to provide for all aspects of school plant capital outlay needs for all essential educational facilities.

Before establishing the cost figure to be used it is necessary to get agreement on the kind and quality of construction to be financed. The state would not be in a defensible economic position if it were to finance only the lowest cost construction because repairs and other maintenance costs would tend to become excessive. On the other hand, the state could not afford to assure for each district sufficient funds to enable it to construct the more elaborate buildings that may be desired in some districts. What is needed is a good school plant that can be operated and maintained economically and will serve satisfactorily to house the educational program.

Once the allowable costs per classroom unit (or per elementary and secondary classroom unit) have been ascertained, it is possible to determine the amount needed annually. For example, if it is assumed that the average building should last approximately 50 years without replacement or major alterations, the costs per classroom unit should be divided by 50 to ascertain the amount that must be included in the foundation program each year. Suppose the cost per classroom unit including related service areas, sites, and site improvement, is $40,000 in a given state at the present time. Forty thousand dollars divided by 50 gives the annual amount to be included in the foundation program, or $800 per classroom unit. Unless this amount is available each year from state and local funds for each unit in the state, sooner or later the plan will be found to be defective and adjustments will have to be made.

It should be obvious that merely providing for the cost as it is at a given time will not suffice. As the costs of construction change, the amount per classroom unit should be changed. Provision should be made in the program for adjustments on the basis of changes in the construction cost index as has been done in New York State for some years.

This plan for computing costs may have some advantages beyond the foundation program for capital outlay. Everyone who has studied expenditures for capital outlay recognizes the fact that they fluctuate considerably over a period of years in most districts, depending on how much construction is needed. If costs could be allocated and reported annually for the life of a building, the expenditure figure would be much more stable and meaningful than under present conditions.

Determining Local Ability and Effort

If school construction costs are to be financed on a partnership foundation program basis the state should use procedures for determining local ability and effort similar to those used for the current program. Suppose, for example, the amount to be included in the program each year is $800 per classroom unit (about $30 per weighted pupil). If the state should undertake to provide approximately half of the annual amount required for capital outlay in the foundation program on a state-wide basis, the local required effort could be ascertained by determining the levy necessary to provide $400 per classroom unit for all units in the state on the basis of the total valuation. The computation would thus give the approximate amount to be provided by the state from non-property tax sources and, at the same time, the approximate amount to be provided by the districts through the local required effort, or generally, from property taxes. Thus, each district would have to make the same minimum tax effort as each other district and the state would provide the difference between the amount provided through district effort and the $800 per classroom unit multiplied by the number of units in the district. The local uniform effort, of course, should be based on actual value of property in the district, or on some uniform measure of taxpaying ability, as in the case of the current operating program. If this is not done, there will be serious inequities in a number of states.

Problems Resulting from Growth

As previously pointed out, the number of classroom units should be computed for each district on the basis of the growth over the previous year as well as for the total membership or attendance. Thus, if 30 pupils in membership are used for determining classroom units and there is a growth of 300 pupils in the district, there would be ten additional classroom units, plus one unit for special services, for growth.

The reason for this can be shown by a simple calculation. If it is assumed that buildings should last approximately 50 years, the $800 per unit would finance the cost of buildings needed to provide for growth if money could be borrowed over a period of 50 years. However, if the maximum time within which a loan must be repaid is 25 years, there would have to be $1600 available per unit, or an extra $800 per year over a period of 25 years, to enable a district to finance expansion in its building program due to growth.

Emergency Aspects of the Program

The continuing long-range program for financing capital outlay would work out satisfactorily without further adjustments if districts had no accumulated needs or rapid growth problems and if classrooms or buildings could gradually be replaced over a 50-year period. However, many districts, particularly those in metropolitan and other rapidly growing areas, have accumulated a backlog of needs and, in addition, have growth problems. The continuing long-range plan, sound as it is in principle, will not meet the needs of such districts unless provision is made for what may be termed the "emergency" or immediately urgent aspects of the program. The basis for meeting these emergency needs, however, should be an inherent part of the long-range plan.

The chief difficulty is that, while the continuing program provides the amount required for replacing all plant facilities over a period of 50 years, it does not provide directly for meeting the substantial costs that must be met in the immediate future if accumulated needs and growth are to be cared for.

If all districts had adequate borrowing capacity to bond in sufficient amount to meet their accumulated needs and growth problems, there would be no serious difficulty except for the extra interest costs involved. However, many districts do not have such capacity. To provide for the emergency or immediately urgent aspects of the program, therefore, the state should establish a bonding or loan Authority. Provision should be made for any district that needs to do so to apply for a loan, the principal of which should not exceed 75 to 80 per cent of the value of the unit times the number of classroom units, multiplied by the number of years for which the loan may be made. Thus, if a district has 1,000 classroom units, for each of which $800 is allotted, it would have available each year $800,000 through the continuing foundation program that could be used in financing construction. If it could borrow three-fourths of that amount or $600,000 per year over even a 20-year period, it would have a borrowing capacity of $12,000,-000. The principal and interest due on the loan annually could then be repaid out of the foundation program allotment which would be sufficient to pay the principal, the interest, and leave some margin for other current capital outlay needs. Additional needs beyond that could be met by an extra local levy for capital outlay if the district desires to make that effort.

The question might well be raised as to what districts would do when they already have a substantial outstanding indebtedness. Generally speaking, such districts have made considerable progress with their building and will not have as large unmet needs as districts of equal wealth which do not have such loans. However, as will be explained later, districts should be permitted to use their capital outlay funds to help retire existing indebtedness unless they have unusual accumulated needs. If there are any districts in the state in which indebtedness is excessive, the state might need to meet the costs of retiring such indebtedness that required more than a designated levy established somewhat in accordance with the plan now used in New York State.

The idea of a state bonding Authority is not simply a theory, since it has been applied in one way or another in practice in several states. Florida was one of the early states to develop the plan. To be sure that the bonds could be marketed advantageously, as much as needed of the proceeds from a designated tax source was pledged by constitutional provision for a period of years to be used in retiring bonds issued by the Authority.

In principle, there is considerable difference between a state bonding authority and a building authority. Assuming that requirements for participation have been met, a bonding authority would be concerned only with the matter of marketing bonds and making funds available to various districts in accordance with the amount authorized. It would not need to make policy decisions which might affect the educational program. On the other hand, a building authority would have difficulty avoiding such policy decisions because it would be concerned with building plans and construction.

IMPLEMENTING THE PROGRAM

Any program that seems good in theory can become an undesirable program if it incorporates undesirable controls and restrictions or if it is not properly implemented. Thus, some states have encountered difficulty with their program for financing the costs of current operation because some undesirable features have been tied on to the plan in one way or another or because it was not fully financed.

Some of the important matters to be considered in implementing the program for financing capital outlay are briefly discussed below.

State Supervision and Administration

For some reason a number of states have established a special agency to develop regulations and to administer and supervise provisions for financing school plant construction. This agency is usually presumed to be primarily concerned with finance but tends sooner or later to become involved in policies that affect the educational program.

As indicated in the statement of characteristics, authorities are generally agreed that all state responsibilities relating to the school plant program should be vested in the state board of education rather than in some agency that is not directly concerned with the educational program. There is no more reason for establishing a separate board for administering the financial aspects of the school plant program than for establishing such a board to administer the financing of the current foundation program. The establishment of separate boards tends to result in delays and confusion for local school officials and to involve them in requirements and restrictions that are considered undesirable.

Requirements for Participation and Other Controls

Some problems of controls relating to the foundation program for current operation were discussed in Chapter 10. Similar problems are involved in provisions for capital outlay. However, for some reason many states have been more successful in avoiding undesirable restrictive controls in the current program than in the capital outlay program. The danger from such controls apparently has not yet been fully understood in some of the states in which the controls have developed.

On the basis of studies of the problem and of the experience in various states, it seems that the following requirements are desirable and that few or no other requirements should be established:

1. Every district should be required to make the local uniform effort essential for the proper operation of the program. If this were not done some might go along without any effort for a few years, then suddenly find that they were in difficulty and needed state funds. Such districts, however, would not have accumulated the local funds necessary for proper operation of the program.

2. A county-wide or large area study or survey should be required as a basis for determining the location of permanent elementary and secondary school centers. (Junior college centers should also be determined if they are included in the program.) This survey should include an area much larger than the typical district because if the study is restricted to the boundaries of smaller districts it may not be possible to locate permanent centers satisfactorily. Studies or surveys should be made in accordance with standards and regulations established by the state board. Unless permanent centers are identified, districts may not have a satisfactory basis for developing a sound capital outlay program.

3. Each local school board should adopt a long-range program providing for construction at recognized permanent centers and should establish priority plans for such construction. This program should be modified from time to time as necessary on the basis of re-studies made when population trends show that additional centers are needed or that some centers should be reclassified.

4. Each district should be authorized to use funds available each year for needed construction or to accumulate these funds for a few years before using them. The funds should be available for use only for bona fide capital outlay purposes relating to school plant development or for debt service.

5. A district should be authorized to negotiate loans to obtain funds and to finance needed construction based on growth or on accumulated needs. Loans that would obligate capital outlay funds for a period of perhaps ten to fifteen years definitely should be authorized on application of the local board. Some states may prefer to require the authorization for loans for a longer period to be approved by a majority of the qualified electors in the district.

6. Districts should probably be required to show that there are no pupils on double sessions or in obsolete buildings before using foundation program funds for retirement of indebtedness incurred before the program was adopted or for construction not directly related to urgent instructional needs. Funds should be permitted to be used only at permanent centers or for necessary minor alterations at temporary centers.

7. Plans for proposed construction should be submitted to the State Department of Education by all districts to assure that safety and other minimum essential requirements established by the state are observed.

8. Districts should be permitted to make additional levies or use any funds from local sources to provide higher quality buildings or facilities than included in the state program. There should be no state limitation on the number of square feet per pupil or other maximum standards for construction.

The Problem of Small Districts

Small and inadequately organized districts constitute one of the most serious stumbling blocks in the way of the development of a satisfactory state program for financing capital outlay. If funds are made available to all districts regardless of size, some of the small districts are almost certain to use these funds to construct buildings at places where they cannot be justified and thus to perpetuate an inefficient plan of organization.

The Missouri Citizens Commission for the Study of Education, after a thorough study of the problem, recommended that state capital outlay funds for all districts below a specified size (for example, 500 pupils) should be held in escrow in the state treasury to the credit of the district.[14] These funds could be used for short term loans to other districts with urgent building problems. When any such district joins a district of adequate size, or several small districts organize into a more adequate district, the accumulated funds for the districts involved would be released to be used for construction of needed facilities.

Some such plan seems to be highly desirable, in fact necessary, in states having small districts. The fact that accumulated funds would be available when districts reorganize would mean that reorganization would be facilitated because needed buildings could probably be constructed without undue handicaps or delays.

The Financial Plan

The foundation program plan for financing capital outlay provides that a large proportion of the on-going construction costs will be financed from current funds, as they should be. The state portion should be financed from revenue receipts, as the current operating program is financed at the present time. This is far more defensible than for the state to issue bonds to finance a program which in reality is a continuing program. The year-to-year needs for capital outlay should be considered a part of the current operating expense.

The districts would also finance their current construction in part from current funds. However, these funds would not be adequate to meet all needs in many districts. Therefore, especially in small districts and in rapidly growing districts of limited wealth, loans would be necessary. However, the loans could be provided through a state bond-

---

[14] Missouri Citizens Commission for the Study of Education, *Better Public Schools for Missouri Children* (Jefferson City: The Commission, 1952), Chapter XI.

ing agency or could be obtained in the customary manner through local bond issues. The proceeds from the capital outlay portion of the foundation program for any district could be used in part to retire its loan, or extra taxes could be levied for debt service if the district considers such effort desirable. The state might need a provision to guarantee sufficient funds to assure that outstanding loans authorized under the program would be repaid as due each year regardless of fluctuations in the construction index.

There would be a number of problems involving equity in inaugurating programs of this sort. Most of these would not be serious if the plan is properly developed. However, districts that have made little or no effort for a number of years but have urgent needs should probably have special attention. Such districts may have to borrow heavily and therefore need to make extra levies for a few years to bring their program up to date. A good case could be made, however, for requiring districts that, over a period of years, have made less than the effort specified for participation in the capital outlay portion of the foundation program, to make an extra levy for that purpose for a few years. Thus, if the required levy on equalized valuation is four mills and a certain district has made no levy for capital outlay or debt service for the past ten years, it might be required to make an extra levy of at least one mill for each two mills deficiency for the ensuing ten years.

FEDERAL FUNDS FOR SCHOOL CONSTRUCTION

Some Federal funds have been available for school construction in various types of districts over a period of years (see Chapter 13). During the depression period, the districts in best position to take advantage of these funds were the more wealthy districts. In the war years, only districts with urgent needs resulting from war connected activities were eligible for Federal funds for school construction. Since the war, districts materially affected by Federal activities have been eligible for such funds through Public Law 815.

Three observations are pertinent:

1. Because of variations in ability of the states, some states will not be able, at least for many years in the future, to provide adequate school plant facilities unless Federal funds are available.

2. Federal funds will not solve the construction problem in states that have numerous small and inadequate districts or that have not developed a sound state plan for assisting with the financing of school construction.

3. If Federal funds should become available for school plant construction they should be used to supplement and strengthen the state plan. Those that are now available or may become available to particular districts in the future should be recognized in developing state plans for financial support in those districts. Unless some adjustment is made, such as eliminating from the capital outlay portion of the foundation program of the district the number of classroom units housed in buildings constructed with Federal funds, those districts may obtain an advantage to which they are not entitled.

SOME IMPORTANT PROBLEMS AND ISSUES

Many problems relating to control, adequacy, equity, and other matters pertinent to the financing of capital outlay should have further study. A few of the important issues in this area are discussed briefly on the following pages.

What Plan for State Support of Capital Outlay Is Best?

As pointed out in this chapter, almost every conceivable type of provision for financing capital outlay can be found in some state at present. One or two states seem to be moving toward complete or practically complete state financing of school buildings. Others are depending on the building authority plan and seem to be reasonably well satisfied with developments. A few provide limited grants with the expectation that such grants will enable the districts to solve their own problems. Others emphasize loan-grant plans. Only a handful of states have made a serious effort to develop a continuing long-range plan based on sound principles of finance.

In this chapter considerable attention has been devoted to the application of the foundation program concept to the financing of capital outlay for school facilities. Since the foundation program, when properly developed, is considered the best plan for financing the costs of current operation, it seems logical to assume that this plan in principle should also be the most logical for financing capital outlay. Is that assumption justified? What are the weaknesses in the foundation program plan discussed in this chapter? Can these be overcome or would some other plan be more advantageous?

As noted previously, the state could, in theory, assure adequate school plant facilities in all districts if it would agree to take care of all costs after a district had made a maximum bond effort. For example, the state might provide that, when a district had issued bonds amounting to 5 per cent of the actual valuation of property in the district, the state would make available any funds beyond that amount needed for buildings. What would be some of the difficulties encountered in trying to apply this plan?

There must be some reason to explain the fact that nearly two-fifths of the states have not provided any funds to assist with the financing of school building programs. It may be that buildings are being properly financed in those states on a local basis. What does the evidence show? Perhaps the people in such states feel that the problem is only temporary and will straighten itself out in a few years. Is this point of view justified? On the other hand the people may believe the state simply cannot afford to get into the financing of school plant construction. Can this point of view be supported?

Will State Support Increase the Cost of Providing School Buildings?

Some people who oppose state aid for school plant construction have contended that state funds would add to the already high costs. They point out that most districts seem to be getting along reasonably well with the buildings they have. They insist that just as salaries, and consequently school costs, were increased in many districts when state aid was provided for current operation of schools, so school plant costs will increase. If state funds become available for buildings, many districts will want to use those funds to construct buildings that are more expensive than they would otherwise provide.

Those who favor state support point out that if buildings are not provided when and as needed, the educational program for the pupils will certainly be handicapped. They point to instances where teachers cannot do as effective work as they are capable of doing because they and their classses are handicapped by outmoded and improperly planned buildings. They insist that state money is being spent uneconomically to pay the salaries of teachers who have to work under unsatisfactory conditions and consequently cannot do their best work because of those conditions.

They hold that it will not cost any more to construct good buildings with state assistance than if they were financed locally. In fact, it might not cost as much in the long run if all districts were in a position to provide adequate buildings at permanent centers. They call attention to districts that have constructed buildings where they were not needed and that this has sometimes been done in an effort to avoid district reorganization. They contend that adequate buildings will cost a certain amount regardless of the plan of financing. The difference would be that if buildings were financed locally the entire cost would be borne by property taxes, whereas if state aid is provided, the state portion would come from non-property tax sources in most states and the tax base would thereby be broadened.

Is there any likelihood that school plant program costs would be increased if every state developed a plan for helping to finance construction? Should the tax base for financing capital outlay be broadened?

Should State School Building Authorities Be Established to Provide School Plant Facilities?

In a certain state there has been considerable discussion for several years concerning the need for state support for school plant construction. The leaders seem now to be agreed that some plan for state assistance is necessary. However, they are sharply divided concerning the plan they consider desirable.

One group, following the leadership of a prominent state senator, is advocating the establishment of a state school building Authority. He and his supporters insist that the present 5 per cent constitutional limitation on school indebtedness is reasonable and should not be changed. They point out that if this limit were increased some districts would become extravagant in planning their buildings and would unnecessarily burden the citizens with heavy indebtedness. The senator and his substantial group of followers insist, in fact, that a lot of money is being wasted now through local planning and construction of school buildings; that there is no need or justification for individual plans for buildings in many parts of the state; that the development of plans by local architects results in many inadequacies and unnecessarily expensive features; and that local contracting and supervision of construction is expensive and inefficient. They want the state building Authority to be authorized not only to borrow the money necessary to finance construction but to be responsible for the planning and construction of buildings. They contend that much money could be saved by central planning and by the use of standard plans in many parts of the state. They point out that all districts will need to do is to provide information concerning their enrollment trends and housing needs, then when the buildings are provided, pay an annual rental to the housing authority.

The chairman of the Senate Committee on Education, who has served in that capacity for a number of years, seems to be emerging as the leader of another group of people who insist that a state building

Authority plan is unwise. They point out that the present 5 per cent limitation on bonds for school purposes is not only unrealistically low but is inequitable because it is based on assessments that vary considerably from county to county. They hold that the building Authority plan would in reality be a subterfuge, an indirect method of meeting the basic problem. They insist that local initiative and responsibility are just as necessary in planning school buildings for a community as in providing for the educational program. "Centralization," they insist, "may be advantageous in some cases and disadvantageous in others. It is likely to involve considerable red tape and delay and result in just as much inefficiency and high costs as decentralization with all of its problems." They point out that many districts would not be satisfied with buildings planned and constructed chiefly by people in a state building Authority who are not very familiar with local educational problems. They insist that interest rates would be high and that the least wealthy districts would not be able to pay rent for buildings unless the state provided assistance.

Which group has the more defensible position? What are the conditions under which a building Authority would be superior to other plans? Is state construction of school buildings a possibility that should be given serious consideration? What would be its advantages and disadvantages?

Assuming that these two groups are sincere in wanting to find a satisfactory solution to the school building problems of the state, what procedure should they use in attempting to determine which point of view is more defensible? Is there a compromise solution that might be desirable in such a case?

How Can Undesirable State Controls Be Avoided?

Almost everyone knows that school officials in some local districts, if left to their own devices, will do very unsatisfactory jobs of planning to meet educational needs. There are a few situations in which a board has constructed a gymnasium with a large public seating capacity, an elaborate auditorium, or even a stadium, while pupils continued in obsolete buildings or even on double sessions. In city districts, school buildings have sometimes been constructed or additions made to buildings in centers where such facilities were not as urgently needed as in other parts of the district. In such cases the board has usually blamed "public pressure" or has justified its action on the basis that such steps had to be taken in order to get public approval of a bond issue. When state aid for school buildings is contemplated, many people become concerned that such extravagances and inefficiencies will be commonplace. They are concerned that districts will build costly "palaces" instead of buildings designed to meet the needs.

Those who are especially concerned about this problem insist that the state establish detailed requirements and controls if it is to provide funds to assist in financing school buildings. They are not willing to leave to districts, with state guidance and leadership, the matter of determining the size of classrooms, the amount of corridor space, or the kind of construction most appropriate for the community. They insist that districts participating in state aid must use state money only for classrooms and directly related service areas; that the space provided not exceed a certain number of square feet per pupil; that any special service rooms be multi-purpose rooms; and that districts have no local leeway whatever to go beyond state standards.

The philosophy of those who advocate detailed state requirements and controls seems to be that local school officials are not to be trusted, and that decisions made at the state level affecting costs and finance are likely to be much wiser than decisions made at the local level.

Do any states seem to have unnecessary and unwise controls? What are some of these controls? Is there serious danger that too few requirements may be established and that inefficiency and extravagance may result? To what extent can state leadership and advisory services substitute for and eliminate the necessity of requirements and controls?

In some states, those who insist on rigorous controls have advocated the establishment of an agency other than the state department of education to be responsible for supervising the financial aspects of the program. In some cases, when such an agency has been established, the responsibility for decisions regarding requirements, needs, and compliance has rested largely with the special agency. Even though the theory, in some cases, has been that the state department of education should determine and certify educational needs, the finance agency seems in most cases to have controlled or greatly influenced policy.

Should the state board of education assume all responsibility for administering, through the state department of education, provisions for state aid for school buildings, or is another agency necessary to handle financial matters? If two agencies have been established with overlapping responsibilities, what, if any, steps can and should be taken to straighten out the situation?

Should State Funds for Capital Outlay Be Provided for All Districts?

The recommendation of the Missouri Citizens Commission that state capital outlay funds for small districts be held in escrow by the state was discussed briefly in this chapter. Some would insist that every district, regardless of its size, should be entitled to receive state funds annually since it is required to make the same local effort as other districts. This point of view does not seem defensible because it should be evident to everyone who looks into the problem that two- and three-teacher districts would either not use the funds advantageously for buildings or, if the laws permitted, would seek to use such funds to reduce their levy for operating expenses or to pay higher salaries for teachers.

If the state portion of the funds, at least, is held in the state treasury to the credit of the district, it can be released at any time for urgent building needs at a permanent center in the district or when the district is reorganized. However, some have doubts about the idea of providing that such funds be held in the state treasury. They believe that there might be a temptation for the legislature to use the funds for other purposes so they would eventually not be available to the reorganized district.

Is the idea of holding state funds in escrow to the credit of small districts desirable? If so, to what size districts should this provision apply? Should both state and local funds for capital outlay be held by the state or should this provision apply only to the state portion of the funds?

There are some exceedingly wealthy districts in nearly every state that could easily finance all the buildings they need with a limited bond issue or with a continuing low tax levy. Many would insist that these districts are not entitled to any state funds because, when the formula is applied, they would have available more local revenues from the required tax effort than the program would provide for the district. However, officials from such districts, and perhaps many of the citizens, are likely to insist that they should be entitled to some state funds. Is this point of view defensible? If so, how can the provision of funds be defended in terms of principles of equity for pupils and taxpayers? Are there other principles that would be applicable in attempting to resolve a problem such as this?

There are differences in points of view as to whether the capital outlay funds included in the foundation program should be permitted to be used for any educational purposes at the discretion of the district or should be required to be set aside and used for capital outlay or debt service. Good theory seems to indicate that there should be no earmarking of funds within the foundation program. However, as some states have learned, funds supposed to be used for capital outlay purposes tend to be used for other purposes under certain conditions. For example, when a board has a large balance or reserve in the capital outlay portion of its budget and the salaries of teachers have lagged behind the cost of living, teachers are likely to insist that part of the reserve money be used to increase salaries. Once it is used for that purpose, however, it is no longer available for capital outlay and, after the precedent has been set, increasing amounts may be used for other purposes during future years.

Many believe that funds for capital outlay purposes should either be provided through a separate special-purpose foundation program, or if incorporated in the foundation program, should be required to be set aside to be used only for the authorized purposes. Studies indicate that over a period of years every district will need a certain percentage of its current expense budget for capital outlay purposes and unless that percentage is set aside to be used for capital outlay, the district will in effect be incurring a deficit which must be made up during future years.

Can special funds for capital outlay purposes be justified or should full discretion in the use of all funds be left entirely to local boards of education? What are the disadvantages of setting aside funds for capital outlay? What are the advantages?

SELECTED REFERENCES

Burke, Arvid J., *Financing Public Schools in the United States,* rev. ed. New York: Harper and Brothers, 1957. Chapter XXI.

Hutchins, Clayton D., et al., *Financing Public School Facilities,* Office of Education Bulletin 1959, No. 32. Washington, D.C.: U. S. Government Printing Office, 1959.

Johns, R. L., and Edgar L. Morphet, editors, *Problems and Issues in Public School Finance.* New York: Bureau of Publications, Teachers College, Columbia University, 1952. Chapter XII.

Lindman, Erick L., et al., *State Provisions for Financing Public School Outlay Programs,* Office of Education Bulletin 1951, No. 6. Washington, D.C.: U.S. Government Printing Office, 1951.

Morphet, Edgar L., Roe L. Johns, and Theodore L. Reller, *Educational Administration: Concepts, Practices, and Issues.* Englewood Cliffs, N.J.: Prentice-Hall, Inc., 1959. Chapters 19 and 22.

Mort, Paul R., and Walter C. Reusser, *Public School Finance,* 2nd ed. New York: McGraw-Hill Book Company, Inc., 1951. Chapters 18 and 21.

Rosenstengel, William Everett, and Jefferson N. Eastmond, *School Finance,* New York: The Ronald Press Company, 1957. Chapter 5.

CHAPTER TWELVE

Financing
Special Services

Boards of education in most school districts are often confronted with conflicting demands: (1) to add services not traditionally included in the educational program which, if added, would increase the costs of education; (2) to eliminate services or to reduce the cost of services already provided.

In nearly every community there are some citizens who contend that the schools have already taken over services that properly belong to and should be provided by the homes or by other community agencies or institutions. Other citizens, however, insist that there are still unmet needs so closely related to education that they can better be provided through the schools than through any other agency. Conflicting demands such as these pose problems that cannot easily be resolved in many communities.

State legislators are likewise faced with demands to add to or to eliminate services provided by the schools, and to increase or decrease appropriations for various aspects of education. The dilemma presented by such demands is not likely to be resolved in the near future. Basically the problem is not one of finance but of conflicting points of view and values relating to the schools and the educational program.

As a matter of historical fact, the common schools were organized in this country to teach a limited number of subjects, generally referred to as the three R's. As schools of higher grade were organized, the offerings and services at first were also rather narrowly restricted. However,

334

a majority of the people in many communities gradually became convinced that such a restricted educational program would not meet the needs of a rapidly developing nation. They insisted that broader curricula and additional services would facilitate the educational process. Consequently, both the elementary and the high school curricula were gradually expanded and many new services were added. Provision began to be made for the services of professional administrators and supervisors, for kindergartens, for special programs for handicapped children, for health and attendance services, for transportation, and for a variety of other services, some of which have been added only recently.

As such changes were contemplated or approved, problems of finance arose. It became apparent that generally the larger and more wealthy communities were among the first to establish such services, because resources were available to provide necessary financial support. Many of the less wealthy communities learned that, because of limited financial ability, the cost of certain services would be prohibitive and consequently did not attempt to provide them.

Demands soon began to be made on the state for assistance in financing some of the newer services. The logical way for legislators to satisfy these demands seemed to be to make a special grant or appropriation for each new service added or for each special aspect of the educational program that seemed to involve financial problems for the districts. This was done in many states. However, studies began to show that these attempts to solve the problem had resulted in some unanticipated difficulties. The establishment or continuation of a variety of special aids or special purpose funds began to be seriously questioned.

Since many states have continued certain special aids and since demands arise periodically in most states for the establishment of new funds to help with the financing of some limited aspect of the educational program, it seems desirable to consider in this chapter some of the problems, developments and possibilities in financing special services.

PROBLEMS IN FINANCING SPECIAL SERVICES

The first extensive study of state aid for special educational projects in the public schools was made in 1928.[1] This study pointed out that practically every state had provided some kind of special aid for one aspect or another of the educational program. For example, in 1913 aid was provided in many states for agriculture, home economics, libraries,

---

[1] Lester N. Neulen, *State Aid for Educational Projects in the Public Schools* (New York: Teachers College, Columbia University, 1928).

manual training, industrial training, teacher training, evening schools, the employment of a superintendent, and, in some, for capital outlay, district reorganization, and various other purposes.

By 1923 every state was providing one or more special aids, the number having been considerably increased during World War I. The states making greatest use of such aids were Minnesota, South Carolina, Connecticut, Rhode Island, New York, Pennsylvania, and about twelve others which used special aids extensively but not quite as generally as those listed. A few states, such as Illinois, Colorado, and Utah, had made little use of special aids.

The use of special aids began to decline, however, soon after the studies relating to the development of a sound equalization program had been carried out by Strayer and Haig, and by Mort in New York, and especially after the completion of several studies that cast doubts on the desirability or efficacy of such aid. For example, Neulen found that mandatory state legislation, state leadership, and certain other devices seemed to be as effective in many cases in providing stimulation for local districts as special aids.[2] Wrightstone studied the effects of substituting an equalization program in New York State for a series of special aids.[3] He found that, under the equalization program, many communities that had not previously received a special subsidy for or provided services such as kindergartens, were tending to establish or expand those services. He found, further, that many of the previously subsidized services were continuing to expand, and concluded that the equalization program was as effective as special aids in stimulating improvement in these services.

Burke made a comprehensive study of the financing of special aids in connection with the reorganization of school districts in New York State.[4] He concluded that the central problem was one of providing sufficient state support and apportioning the funds in such a way that school districts could reorganize without increasing taxation merely because of reorganization. He pointed out that high tax rates in reorganized districts could not be avoided unless the program of equalization support was developed on a realistic basis, and unless proper corrections were made for sparsity, sufficient subsidies were provided for transportation, and adequate provision was made for financing school buildings.

---

[2] *Ibid.*, p. 78.

[3] J. W. Wrightstone, *Stimulating of Educational Undertakings* (New York: Teachers College, Columbia University, 1933), Chapter VIII.

[4] Arvid J. Burke, *Proposed Changes in Financial Support for Rural Schools of New York State* (New York: Teachers College, Columbia University, 1936), p. 225.

Chase and Morphet classified the special aids being provided as (1) special-purpose flat-grants and (2) special-purpose equalizing grants.[5] They concluded that "The provision of a number of special-purpose funds often tends to result in undesirable forms of state control which might be avoided through a properly developed system of aid, chiefly involving general-purpose funds."

Special Aids and Control

Numerous studies have directed attention to the relationship between special aids and control. Special aids are presumably provided to enable districts to carry out some purpose considered important for the educational program by the state. However, the fact that a fund is made available to the district for a special purpose tends to mean that districts which participate must (1) meet all requirements established in connection with the use of the fund, (2) set aside and use some district funds for that purpose, (3) maintain a special account, sometimes a special bank account, for the fund and (4) continue to meet the requirements and provide necessary funds for that aspect of the program, even though other aspects may be neglected.

It seems evident that the provision of special-purpose funds may help to stimulate the development of certain aspects of the educational program, although the stimulation may be no greater than that provided through a properly developed and adequately financed foundation program. The provision of special aids tends to stimulate the districts to give major attention to the purposes for which funds may be provided, even though other equally important purposes may be neglected. It tends to freeze certain funds for designated aspects of the program, and thus to limit local initiative and responsibility in determining how the educational program in the district can best be developed.

The amount of funds provided by the state for special purposes has sometimes been determined not by the needs but by the effectiveness of the efforts of certain pressure groups. For example, those who are especially interested in services for handicapped children or for vocational education might persuade the legislature to provide more generously for the financing of these services from state funds than could be justified in terms of the needs when all aspects of the educational program are considered. Furthermore, when special aids are provided, support for the educational program may be divided. Those who are

---

[5] Francis S. Chase and Edgar L. Morphet, *The Forty Eight State School Systems* (Chicago: The Council of State Governments, 1949), p. 127.

interested in one aspect or another of the educational program may give so much attention to the matter of obtaining funds to finance services in which they are interested that they devote comparatively little time or effort to the support of the general school program.

Apportionment and Use of Funds

The provision of Federal funds for special purposes has had a decided impact on practice in many of the states. For example, the fact that the Federal government has made available funds which can be used by the states for certain aspects of vocational education and for school lunches, when certain conditions and requirements are met, has meant that a number of states and communities have been stimulated to provide special funds or appropriations for those purposes. The possibility of obtaining funds from state or Federal sources when certain requirements are met has proved to be a powerful but unbalancing stimulant to many districts.

Most special-purpose funds have been apportioned to districts either as flat-grants or on a matching basis. The flat-grant apportionment does not meet the needs in less wealthy districts. The matching grant is even more inequitable for the less wealthy districts because such districts, in order to meet matching requirements, must either make an excessive effort or provide funds which should be used for other aspects of the program.

During more recent years provision has been made in a number of states for reimbursement of local costs for designated services over and above a certain amount or up to a prescribed maximum. These provisions also tend to be inequitable because the more wealthy districts are usually in a better position to provide and finance adequate services than the less wealthy and consequently may receive greater reimbursement from the state.

One other problem in connection with special-purpose funds should have careful consideration. In most states the funds provided for any special-purpose are usually inadequate to meet the need in the various districts. If the cost of the program were met fully by state funds the question would be largely one of the extent to which the local program is distorted or unbalanced as a result of the provision of these funds. When state funds are inadequate to meet the needs, however, districts that attempt to provide the services must use substantial local revenue if satisfactory services are to be provided. This means that the least wealthy districts are most likely to be handicapped and to have their local program distorted by the provision of special aids.

The fact that many school systems in a large proportion of the states still lack essential educational services of one kind or another is likely to continue to result in demands for establishing new kinds of special aids or for increasing the funds provided for other specialized services. To a local citizen, a teacher, a legislator, or anyone who has not carefully studied the implications of special aids, the logical solution may seem to be to provide funds for special purposes. However, one serious difficulty in most instances arises from the fact that funds for support of the entire educational program are inadequate. If adequate funds were made available through a properly developed foundation program plan, and if districts had ample leeway beyond the financial requirements for participation in the program to provide funds needed for emerging service requirements, there would be little demand and less need for special-purpose appropriations. The solution to the problem, therefore, seems to be to provide in all states a realistic and adequate plan of support for a reasonably comprehensive foundation program of services.

TRENDS IN SPECIAL AIDS

Three types of developments have occurred as foundation programs have been approved. Some states, when they adopted a new program, discontinued most of the special-purpose appropriations. Others discontinued some of the special aids but continued others without any material change. Most states seem to have adopted the foundation program to provide for what has sometimes been considered the "regular" school services but did not materially change any of the special aid provisions.

The Office of Education made an analysis in 1953–54 of the service factors recognized in allocating state funds to the public schools.[6] No attempt was made in this analysis to distinguish between the service factors recognized through separate appropriations or special aids and those for which special provision was made in the equalization program or in connection with some other kind of general-purpose aid. The extent to which some of these factors are recognized by special aids will be pointed out later. This analysis showed that 20 states recognized kindergartens; 8 included junior colleges; 15 aided adult education or evening schools; 6 in the Midwest provided for teacher training; 39, the education of exceptional children; 41, vocational education; and 18, tuition payments. Other factors recognized included administration

---

[6] Clayton D. Hutchins and Albert R. Munse, *Public School Finance Programs of the United States,* U. S. Office of Education (Washington, D.C.: U. S. Government Printing Office, 1954), pp. 35 and 36.

and supervision, for which 25 states made special provision; textbooks and libraries, recognized by 16; pupil transportation, by 40; school lunches, by 9; health services, by 5; and libraries, by 5.

As previously noted, the establishment of special state aids for one aspect or another of the educational program represented an early and pronounced trend. After studies had paved the way for the establishment of a sound foundation program and had directed attention to some of the handicaps arising from the system of special aids, there was a definite trend in some states to reduce materially the number of separate funds. However, the demand for financial subsidies for some of the newer services has tended to offset many of the gains in a number of states during recent years. The result is that the number of special aids or special provisions in general-purpose programs has not appreciably declined during this period. Among the states that have made the most notable progress in reducing the number of special aids are Florida, Idaho, Montana, and New York.

Perhaps it has been fortunate that there has not been as much tendency to earmark local levies or funds for special aspects of the educational program as to make special state appropriations. Most states, of course, require that special levies be made and the proceeds set aside to retire bonded indebtedness. Several, as previously noted, provide for special levies for capital outlay, some for library purposes, a few for vocational education, several for retirement of teachers or other school employees, and one authorizes a special levy for community services by schools.

PROVISIONS FOR EXTENDING THE EDUCATIONAL PROGRAM

From time to time, local school systems and states have been concerned with one aspect or another of the problem of extending the educational program. One of the first concerns was with the problem of lengthening the school term, since schools in many pioneer communities operated less than three months during the year. In fact, it was not until well after the beginning of the present century that even a six-month term was provided for all schools. However, the establishment of a state standard requiring a certain minimum length of term did not solve the problem in many communities because they were not in a position to finance an extended term from local resources. The state, therefore, found it necessary to provide additional funds for schools. This was done in most cases by increasing the appropriations, but in some states special funds or appropriations were provided for rural schools or for certain types of less favored communities. By the middle of the present century the average length of term had been increased to nine months in most states but there were still districts in a few states that provided a term of only seven or eight months.

During the past few years considerable attention has again been centered on the problem of increasing the length of the school year. A number of the larger cities have, for some time, operated schools for nine and a half or ten months and other school systems are considering a similar extension. Several states have provided by law for small increases in the number of days taught and have increased state appropriations accordingly.

Summer Programs

Leaders in a number of communities and in several states, however, have raised questions as to whether the needs can be met merely by extending the length of term for the traditional program. Some have advocated the development of all-year schools, not so much to increase the length of term for individual pupils but more as a means of utilizing buildings and teachers effectively and thereby reducing the cost per pupil. Studies have brought to light sufficient problems, however, that few communities have attempted to establish the four-quarter, twelve-month plan, providing for three-fourths of the children to be in school at all times and one-fourth on vacation at all times.[7]

Many communities and several states have established or are considering the establishment of summer schools of various types. Some are concerned only with extending the academic program, but many others are interested in providing a variety of educational activities and including, of course, additional work in academic subjects. These schools are conceived by many as providing special opportunities for the academically talented as well as affording needed remedial work and related enriching experiences for many others.

The provision of summer programs, however, creates special financial problems. Unless there is state assistance, the least wealthy districts are not able to operate summer schools except on a fee or tuition basis that discriminates against children whose parents have limited incomes. State financial assistance, therefore, is necessary if a satisfactory program of summer educational activities is to be operated in all communities. Theoretically, all a state would need to do would be to provide additional funds on a classroom unit or pupil basis—that is, increase proportionately the amount provided for the regular term. However,

---

[7] See, for example, *The All Year School* (Tallahassee, Florida: State Department of Education, April, 1957).

for the present at least, only a small proportion of the children in many communities will be enrolled in summer educational activities, and some school systems—particularly smaller ones—may not be willing to undertake a summer program because of the high costs involved.

A few states have attempted to solve the problem by providing a special fund or appropriation for summer schools. This, however, has not worked satisfactorily in most cases because measures of need have been defective. A few states have provided in their foundation programs for adding units for summer schools on a proportionate basis. Thus, if the regular term is nine months and provision is made for a nine-week summer school program, 25 per cent would be added to the value of the classroom units for the regular program. This adjustment is made only for the units actually used in the district for summer school purposes. Through a plan developed along these lines it should be possible for every state to provide for summer educational activities without the necessity of establishing a separate fund or appropriation specifically for that purpose.

Different Age Groups

Another problem that has concerned many school systems and states has been to provide for age groups not generally included in the regular school program. For example, the common schools as originally established in this country included work only for children in what is now called the elementary grades—in fact, often only in the lower grades. However, districts soon began to attempt to provide work in higher grades. The issue as to whether provision could be made for financing this extended program was largely settled in the famous *Kalamazoo* decision, to which reference is made in Chapter 7. In that case the Supreme Court of Michigan held that the levy of taxes for high school purposes made in 1872 in Kalamazoo was legal. The court held that the facts cited clearly and conclusively demonstrated a general state policy ". . . in the direction of free schools and in which education, and at their option the elements of classical education, might be brought within the reach of all children of the state. . . ." [8]

States soon began to include high school attendance in determining the number of children for which funds were apportioned. In most cases there was no special fund or apportionment established for high school purposes but in some states, particularly those where there are a large number of separate elementary and high school districts, the apportionment continues to be made separately for elementary and for high schools.

---

[8] Stuart v. School District No. 1 of Kalamazoo (1874), 30 Mich. 69, 75.

Kindergartens. Other issues in this area, however, still remained to be settled. Communities began to press for the establishment of kindergartens, and in some cases, during more recent years, of nursery schools. In some states the laws or even constitutional provisions had to be changed to make this possible. State after state began to include kindergartens along with elementary and high schools in making financial provisions for schools. Some states have provided a separate special-purpose appropriation to assist in financing kindergartens or nursery schools. However, classroom units for kindergarten attendance (for example, one unit for each 25 pupils taught by the same teacher [9]) have usually been added to the "regular" units as a basis for determining foundation program costs. In a few states a limited increase in local effort, in addition to that required for the foundation program, has been prescribed for districts providing kindergartens.

Adult Education. The demand for adult education created another problem. Most apportionments at first did not include provisions for adults. Some state law prevented local school systems from collecting taxes and providing funds for adults beyond the age of 21, and of course these laws had to be changed before realistic provisions could be made. State funds gradually began to be provided for adults as well as for regular elementary and secondary school education. By the middle of the present century some 15 states, as previously noted, had made some rather direct provision for state aid for adult education. About half of these provided separate or special appropriations for adult and evening schools; the remainder included provision for adult education in the foundation program. The latter seems to be the most sensible and satisfactory plan, as it eliminates the necessity for a separate special-purpose fund and the cost can be included in the foundation program merely by adding to the units for elementary and secondary schools the number of units in each district for adult education, determined on the basis of standards and requirements established by the state (for example, one-fifth of a unit for every 180 clock hours of instruction in classes having 15 or more students). However, adult education still occasions considerable controversy in a number of states.

Junior Colleges. The idea of providing junior or community colleges to include work in grades 13 and 14 began to be vigorously advocated only during the present century. By the middle of the century a few states were financing some junior colleges in connection with their universities; eight had provided for junior colleges through their public school finance program, and communities in a number of other states

---

[9] Some states assume that kindergartens should be taught on a half-day basis and allocate one unit for each 50 pupils.

were attempting to provide these facilities and services at district expense. In most states (California and Florida have been notable exceptions) junior colleges have been developed only in certain communities, are frequently supported partly by fees, and a state-wide junior college system has not even been closely approached. Several states, however, have begun to use a foundation program plan for financing junior colleges. While the classroom unit has commonly been used for measuring need it is usually based on a class load of from 15 to 20 students (for example, one unit may be allotted for every 450 student semester hours registered). Some reasonable local effort, in addition to that necessary for the elementary and high school program, is usually required. Flat-grant apportionments are no more satisfactory for financing junior colleges than for other aspects of the educational plan.

PROVISIONS FOR EDUCATIONAL SERVICES
TO SPECIAL GROUPS

In addition to extending the educational program by increasing the length of the school year and by providing for new age groups, the people in many school systems have found it necessary to provide services for special groups whose needs were not satisfactorily being met through the traditional program. Some of the provisions that have been made, and the procedures used in financing these services, will be discussed briefly in the following paragraphs.

Vocational Education

Before World War I the people in a number of school systems and in a few states had become dissatisfied with the typical academic program provided in most public schools and were seeking to meet other needs. However, in most secondary schools the courses offered were largely of a college preparatory nature. There was only limited provision for the large percentages of high school students who would not attend college. As a result of the increasing dissatisfaction, accentuated by deficiencies made evident by preparations for participation in World War I, the Smith-Hughes Act was passed in 1917. It has been amended and supplemented by a number of acts since that time, as explained in Chapter 13. The various acts relating to vocational education have provided for the apportionment of funds to states to assist in financing programs of vocational education that meet Federal requirements. All states have accepted these funds and most of them have provided special appropriations to be used along with Federal funds in helping to finance vocational education in high schools in the various districts. Apparently only eight or nine of the 50 states do not directly provide state funds to assist in financing vocational education but expect districts to expend sufficient local funds to meet the Federal matching requirements.

The influence of Federal policy is evident in the policies followed by the various states in providing funds for vocational education. Although the Federal government does not require the establishment of a separate fund, most states have either followed Federal precedent or have apparently assumed that a separate fund would be necessary to provide adequately for vocational education. Approximately three-fourths of the states still have a separate appropriation that can be used only for vocational education in accordance with the purposes prescribed by the state and the Federal government. Furthermore, most states have followed Federal precedent in apportioning funds for this purpose. Usually the Federal and state funds are made available to districts for reimbursement of certain expenses incurred for vocational education, including salaries of teachers. However, several difficulties are involved, among the most important of which are the following:

(1) The provision of separate funds tends to divide the interests of people, with the result that many in vocational education seem to have been more concerned with the appropriations for vocational education than for the regular programs; similarly, other educators have been primarily concerned with appropriations for the regular program.

(2) The reimbursement plan assumes that districts will have money to spend and that later reimbursement will be adequate; in reality, the less wealthy districts are most likely to be handicapped by this plan.

(3) Provision of state and Federal funds on some matching ratio, whether the local matching is at a dollar-for-dollar rate or, as is frequently true, on the basis of three or four dollars of local funds to one dollar of state and Federal funds, not only handicaps the least wealthy districts but tends to distort the local program. In some cases, in order to meet these matching requirements, local funds have been used for vocational education which, in reality, should have been used for other aspects of the program. This does not mean that vocational education has been overfinanced but, in some of these communities, other aspects of education have been relatively underfinanced.

Florida was one of the first states to integrate vocational education into the foundation program, although New York and a few other states had earlier taken some steps in this direction. The Florida plan provides for including units for vocational education along with other classroom units as a basis for determining the costs of a foundation program. The units for vocational education are computed in accordance with standards prescribed by the State Board of Education, allotting, in general, one unit for the equivalent of each full-time teacher authorized. The same value is assigned to each of these units as to each other classroom unit for the regular term. Where vocational teachers are employed on an eleven- or twelve-month basis instead of on a nine- or ten-month basis, a proportionate increase is made in the value of these units on the same basis as for other units used for an extended program of education. One advantage of this plan is that it provides for the development of vocational education in accordance with needs and eliminates some of the handicaps formerly faced by districts with limited ability.

Education of Exceptional Children

Many years ago educators began to recognize that there were some children who required special services, and in some cases special classes, if they were to be educated satisfactorily. These included children with defective speech, hearing, or vision; children with physical handicaps; home-bound or hospitalized children; those who were mentally subnormal; and the unusually talented. The smaller or more backward school systems either ignored the problem or attempted to meet the needs without special provisions. The larger school systems began to recognize the necessity of special provisions and to find that extra costs were involved.

The people in the various states gradually began to take an interest in the problem, and some states made special financial provisions of one kind or another to assist the districts. By the middle of this century most states had recognized the education of exceptional children as a service factor to be considered in allocating state funds for schools. The tendency, as in the case of most new services, has been for states to establish special funds for one aspect or another or for several aspects of the program.

At present, approximately half the states have one or more special-purpose appropriations designed to assist districts in meeting their needs in this area. Some of these appropriations are for narrowly restricted purposes. For example, a certain appropriation in one state may be used only for the technically defined "severely mentally retarded" children, another may be used only for cerebral palsied children, and so on. Other appropriations found in a few states are for the education of orphan children, the education of veterans' orphans, the education of island children, and for a few other specialized groups.

Some of the state appropriations provide a designated number of dollars per student included in the program; others directly or indirectly require some local matching; but most provide for the reimbursement of costs up to a designated amount or for reimbursement of "excess costs" beyond those required for education of children in the regular program. In addition to the problems inherent in restricted special-purpose appropriations, many of these provisions indirectly handicap the less wealthy districts. For example, when provision is made for reimbursement of expenditures within designated limits, the less wealthy districts are likely to be handicapped because of the difficulty of advancing funds. Moreover, if the reimbursement provided is below the actual cost of a satisfactory program, the less wealthy districts will not be in as favorable a position as the more wealthy to care for any extra costs involved.

During more recent years a few states have included this service in the foundation program. Usually the attendance of children in special classes is excluded from the computation used in determining units for the regular program. Units for special education may then be allotted to districts on the basis of one unit for each special class organized for ten or more children, or perhaps even for five or more home-bound or hospitalized children, or for each full-time teacher utilized in this program. Since this unit provides for fewer pupils per teacher, it automatically includes extra funds per pupil for other expenses of operating the program. This plan seems to be much more satisfactory and equitable when properly developed than any kind of special-purpose aid provided thus far.

Driver Education

Driver education is a relatively new service for many school systems. In a few states it has been required by law. These states have usually provided a special-purpose appropriation designed to help meet the expenses of conducting this program. Since this is a new service that involves considerable additional expense for students in certain age groups, many are inclined to think the only way to meet the financial need is through a special appropriation. However, since every child attending certain high school grades should participate in and benefit from a properly developed program of driver education, the financial need probably can be determined readily and can be met most satisfactorily merely by increasing the amount per unit included in the foundation program. This should be more equitable than another special-purpose appropriation.

PROVISIONS FOR TRANSPORTATION AND
FOOD SERVICES

Most school systems now provide both transportation and food services. These, of course, involve extra costs. Most states have directly recognized the need for assistance in meeting the expense of transportation. Several, along with the Federal government, have made special provision for assisting with costs of the school lunch program.

Transportation Service

In densely populated districts where children live within walking distance of the schools there is no extra cost involved for transportation of pupils to school. In most districts, however, there is considerable extra expense because of the need for purchasing buses and for operating and maintaining an adequate transportation service. Whether the district owns the buses or contracts for bus service, the cost must be met at public expense, unless it is provided by parents—a practice that denies equality of educational opportunity or equity for taxpayers.

All but seven or eight states provide some form of financial assistance to districts for transporting pupils. About one-half the states have established a separate fund which may be used only for transportation expense. A few have two or three special funds—one of which may be used, for example, only for purchasing buses, another for regular transportation, and the third for the transportation of the physically handicapped.

In the states in which there is no financial assistance for transportation expense, consolidation of schools tends to be retarded and the least wealthy and most sparsely populated areas are seriously penalized. If these districts finance transportation from local funds they must make extra effort over and above that required of other districts that have little or no transportation costs. When small schools are consolidated in these states, local taxpayers must meet any extra expense involved in the consolidation, because of the necessity of transporting pupils.

Several states provide a flat amount per pupil toward meeting the cost of transportation. This is not equitable, because the cost per pupil, other things being equal, is considerably greater in the sparsely populated areas than in areas having sufficient pupils to justify larger buses with shorter trips. Another common procedure is for states to reimburse districts for a certain percentage of the expenditure for transportation. Such a procedure may reward uneconomical practices in some districts, but its most serious defect arises from the fact that the less wealthy districts are in least favorable position to meet the unreimbursed portion of the costs. Thus, if a state provides for 60 per cent reimbursement, every district would have to meet the other 40 per cent of its costs, and many could not do so without excessive local effort. There is some evidence to indicate that the plan for reimbursement for expenditures, or a percentage of the expenditures, may tend to lead to undesirable state regulations and controls.

The present situation might be summarized by the statement that there are some unsatisfactory features and inequities in most plans for state support of transportation that have been developed thus far. Many of the present provisions are little more than makeshift devices for giving some assistance for financing the cost of transportation.

There are two theories regarding the most defensible procedure for state participation in the financing of transportation costs. One holds that transportation costs should be determined on a different basis from that used in determining weighted pupil or classroom units; the other, that a single measure of need should be used for all aspects of the program.

Obviously transportation need on a state-wide basis is not directly related to the number of classroom units or weighted pupils in the districts. The necessary costs of transportation are affected by such factors as: (1) the number of pupils transported who live more than a prescribed distance from the school they attend; (2) the area served by transportation—that is, the distance the pupils have to be transported; and (3) perhaps road conditions or topography. Obviously it would cost more to transport children over poor roads or mountainous roads than over modern highways that are free from sharp curves and steep grades. However, studies have shown that in many areas poor roads and sparsity, and perhaps even sparsity and topography, tend to be related.

Studies made in a number of states also show that when appropriate information is available a formula can be devised for determining the density of transported population in each district and assigning the cost per transported pupil in districts with a given density in such a way that there is reasonable equity for all districts.[10]

In simple terms, the procedure used in developing a formula involves: (1) ascertaining the bona fide expenditures for the current expense of operating transportation in each district on a uniform basis and adding for district-owned buses, a percentage of the cost of the buses to care for depreciation (for example, 10 per cent each year,

[10] Roe L. Johns, "Determining Pupil Transportation Costs," *The Nation's Schools*, Vol. 43, No. 2 (February, 1949), pp. 48–49.

assuming a ten-year period of service); (2) determining the number of pupils transported who live beyond reasonable walking distance to a school; (3) finding the cost per transported pupil in each district; (4) calculating the density of transported population per square mile of area served; (5) arranging districts in 12 to 14 groups, according to density, ranging from those with the least density of transported pupils to those with the highest density; (6) plotting a curve of best fit, as a basis for determining the allowable cost per pupil in each density grouping. This plan, of course, can be more easily and perhaps even more equitably developed and utilized in large-district states than in small-district states, but it can be adapted for use in the latter.

Another theory, as pointed out in Chapter 10, holds that there should be one encompassing measure for all aspects of foundation program needs, including transportation. In accordance with this theory of a unitary measure of need, population sparsity is used as a basis for correcting pupil units or teacher units, to allow for both the school size factor and for the transportation factor, or for the latter where small schools have been eliminated.[11] This procedure was used in West Virginia for a while but has since been modified.

Another problem involves the question as to whether state funds for transportation should be included in the foundation program or should be kept as a separate special-purpose fund. There are many advantages in including transportation expense as a part of the foundation program. In the first place, the total cost of the foundation program is financed from state and local funds, whereas, if transportation is financed separately, the funds obviously must come from state sources. In the latter case there seems to be some danger that undesirable state controls may be imposed in an effort to hold down costs. In the second place, when transportation funds are separate they must be used entirely for transportation, whereas, if they are included in the foundation program any portion not used for transportation can be used by the local school system for other aspects of the educational program.

Food Service

The question as to whether school lunches should be provided for pupils entirely or partly at public expense is still controversial in many communities and in the minds of many citizens. However, the program has developed rapidly, particularly since the National School Lunch Act was passed in 1946. Funds are provided for assistance to schools

---

[11] William P. McLure, *Effect of Population Sparsity on School Costs*, Contributions to Education, No. 929 (New York: Bureau of Publications, Teachers College, Columbia University, 1947).

for the lunch program and for the purchase of milk, and in addition substantial amounts of surplus commodities are provided. Approximately one-eighth of the states have followed the pattern of the Federal government by providing state aid for school lunches or for the food service program. Thus, another special-purpose fund has been established in these states.

Policies in the various school districts still vary considerably. In some districts the entire cost of the service and part of the cost of food is financed from a combination of Federal, state, and local funds. In many other districts only limited local funds are provided, with the result that the cost to pupils for lunches includes not only the cost of food but of other services, and in some cases even part of the cost of facilities.

The question might well be raised as to whether additional states should provide special-purpose funds to assist with the food service program. If a food service program is to be established for all schools there would seem to be no need or justification for a separate special-purpose fund. The cost of providing these services—and, if desirable, even a reasonable proportion of the cost of providing the food—could be determined through studies in various types of districts and this amount added to the classroom or weighted pupil allotment for the foundation program. This would be much simpler and more defensible than attempting to handle the problem by means of a special appropriation.

OTHER PROVISIONS

There are, of course, several other kinds of special-purpose funds found among the states, and theoretically many others could be added in the future. A major problem in most states is: How can adequate and equitable provision be made through the foundation program so a number of existing funds can be eliminated? Another problem is: How can the state best anticipate and make satisfactory provision for meeting developing needs so there will be no bona fide demand or justification for new special-purpose appropriations?

Three additional special provisions made by a number of the states are discussed briefly below.

Compensation of Employees

Although there would seem to be no need or justification for a separate appropriation for salaries of teachers or for compensation of other kinds of employees, several state legislatures have seen fit to establish one or more special funds for this purpose. The intent presumably has been to assure that adequate funds will be provided and used in all districts for salaries of teachers and other designated personnel. However, when only a few hundred dollars per teacher are set aside in a special salary fund, as is done in some states, the action seems to constitute little more than a gesture, and the gesture itself seems to be indefensible. As late as ten years ago about one-fourth of the states had one or more appropriations for the specific purpose of aiding with the payment of salaries of teachers. Since that time a few states have eliminated special appropriations for this purpose at the time a comprehensive foundation program was established. However, approximately one-eighth of the states have continued the practice in one form or another. Several states have established special funds to be used for salaries of superintendents or of supervisors. A number provide for partial or complete payment of the salaries of county superintendents. Since foundation program provisions relating to salaries have been discussed in Chapter 10 and further attention is given to state salary policies in Chapter 15, no further consideration of the problem seems necessary at this point except to emphasize the fact that there seems to be no need or justification for continuation of separate appropriations for salary purposes. It might seem that an exception should be made for salaries of county superintendents, but if the state is to assist in financing county school services, as should be appropriate, it appears that provision should be made in the foundation program for these services.

A few states have established special funds for sick leave or for salaries of substitute teachers. This need, of course, should be recognized but there should be no reason for a special fund. Studies have been made in a number of states and can be made in others to determine the percentage allowance that should be made for payment of substitute teachers. Provision can readily be made to include this amount in the foundation program allowance per classroom unit or per weighted pupil.

Provisions for retirement and Social Security seem to need further attention. In some states the practice has been to expect each local school system to finance the costs other than those paid by the employee. Obviously this is not equitable, because the least wealthy districts are in less satisfactory position to meet these costs than the more wealthy. The most equitable plan is to include in the foundation program for each district the amount required to finance these aspects of the program rather than to charge each district with its share of the cost.

Text and Library Books

State policies relating to the provision of textbooks vary considerably. In some states the parents of pupils in all grades are expected to buy textbooks needed. Other states provide the cost of textbooks for elementary grades but not for high school grades. Still others provide textbooks or funds intended to meet the cost of textbooks in all grades.

Library books, of course, are generally expected to be provided at public expense, but the funds available have been so limited in a number of districts that the unsatisfactory policy of soliciting book donations to meet part of the library need has been followed. Several states, recognizing that the cost of providing an adequate supply of library books from local funds would require greater effort on the part of poor than of wealthy districts, have established a special fund for that purpose.

If the cost of text and library books is to be met from public tax funds, it obviously should be included in the foundation program. Again in this instance there seems to be no need for a special fund or appropriation. The cost of text and library books per pupil or per classroom unit can readily be determined and this amount added to the foundation program allowance.

There might seem to be a special problem in states where the textbooks are actually purchased and provided by the state. However, analysis indicates there is no adequate justification for a separate fund even in these states. The amount can be included in the foundation program allowance and districts charged with the cost of books in accordance with their allotment.

School District Reorganization

Over a period of years a number of states have sought to stimulate district reorganization through special grants of one kind or another. Most of these grants have had relatively little effect, either because (1) there were hidden subsidies in existing laws which tended to reward small districts for continuing as separate districts or (2) the grants provided were so limited that they did not meet the extra costs of reorganization.

Studies made in a number of states have shown that desirable reorganization in many situations is not likely to occur if, as a result, the local tax effort would have to be increased to support the program.

In a study in California, Freudenthal found that if all districts were reorganized and only unified districts existed in the state, three per cent of the cost of the foundation program would be shifted from state funds or from non-property taxes to the district or to property taxes.[12] He concluded that many districts that should reorganize would not do so under existing conditions because local property taxes would have to be increased to an extent that would seem unreasonable and, in many cases, would be inequitable. This was true in spite of the fact that the state plan provided a special state subsidy for unified districts for the first five years of their existence.

If district reorganization is to be encouraged rather than handicapped by financial provisions, the following conditions seem essential:

1. The cost of the foundation program should be determined on an adequate and realistic basis and the local effort required should be equitable and reasonable.

2. Provision should be made in the foundation program for including all reasonable and defensible costs of the educational program, including capital outlay, so that the local tax effort does not have to be increased beyond the uniform minimum requirement when districts are reorganized. If the people in any area choose to maintain an inadequate district they should be expected to make a higher levy to meet the extra cost of maintaining such a district.

Approximately one-third of the states have some form of state subsidy for inter-district tuition payments. Fortunately, the number has been declining, largely because studies have shown that such subsidies tend to encourage the perpetuation of unnecessary small districts. In a number of instances the state subsidy has been sufficient to enable the existing districts, particularly those that do not provide a high school program, to operate on a lower levy than would be necessary if they were to join a high school district. Under such conditions reorganization is retarded because it would mean the loss of state subsidies and consequently an increase in the local tax levy. A more defensible plan than state subsidies would be to require all elementary school districts to make the same effort required of unified districts for participation in the foundation program, except where a higher levy to meet the extra costs resulting from the continuance of indefensible small districts would be in order. For any extra costs over and above the foundation program, the elementary district should, of course, be expected to make any additional levies necessary to pay the difference on a per pupil basis to the district the pupils are attending.

---

[12] Daniel K. Freudenthal, *Relationships between Local School District Unification in California and the Financial Support of Public Education* (Unpublished doctoral dissertation, University of California, 1959).

SOME PROBLEMS AND ISSUES

Many of the issues relating to the establishment of special-purpose funds for different aspects of the educational program have been brought out or implied in the discussion in this chapter and in some of the other chapters of this book. Among the issues which should have further special consideration by both layman and educators are the following:

What Services Should Be Financed from School Funds?

In reality there are two major issues implied by this question: (1) What services should school districts be authorized to provide and finance from public funds? and (2) What services should the state assist in financing?

As indicated by the discussion in this chapter, educational services have been expanded considerably over a period of years. Some of them had not even been thought of by people who lived a few generations ago. In the days when children brought their lunches to rural schools, or walked to school in villages, the idea of a school lunchroom would have seemed absurd. However, conditions and ways of looking at problems have changed considerably. The cold lunch is no longer considered desirable as a daily diet. Furthermore, it is recognized that children from many homes have inadequate lunches and, unless some provision is made, their educational progress would be handicapped.

In the horse-and-buggy days the idea of driver education provided by schools would have seemed ridiculous. However, when present-day accident records are considered and other related developments analyzed, it seems apparent to many that driver education should be a required phase of the program of every high school. Some, however, hold that driver education should be conducted by an agency other than the schools and consequently do not believe that school funds should be used for that purpose. Even though this difference of opinion exists, most people seem to consider some form of driver education provided by some agency, to be highly desirable.

The fact that these and many other services have become an accepted part of the educational program in many communities does not mean that the educational situation has been stabilized. There continue to be many new demands. Physical and dental examinations at public expense are accepted as a recognized aspect of the educational program in many communities but not in others. Even some medical services are provided by a few communities. There is now a demand for special classes for the exceptionally talented children in many schools, and even for special schools for such children. Many would like to see special funds provided to stimulate the organization of such classes and to meet the extra costs involved in developing a program for such children.

Educational television is a comparatively recent development. Perhaps few would attempt to predict the future except in very general terms. There are indications that the development of satisfactory television programs may add to rather than decrease the costs. A few states have provided special funds for television or audio-visual services, or are operating television stations and programs. Many are wondering how the costs of these services can best be met. Some financial assistance is being provided at the present time by philanthropic organizations such as the Ford Foundation. But this is not a long-term solution to the problem.

Many are concerned about the problem of juvenile delinquency. Studies indicate that many problem children can be identified before they become delinquent. Some advocate that special educational facilities, including 24-hour youth schools in a different environment, should be provided for such children. Some think these schools should be operated as a definite part of the educational program; others think they should be operated by juvenile authorities. The establishment and operation of such schools would involve considerable extra expense, but many contend that the net result would be not only to save many youngsters from becoming delinquents but would constitute an actual economy for society.

In some states, many of the larger school systems either have or are attempting to provide kindergartens, but others for one reason or another have not begun to consider the problem seriously. In many states junior colleges are found only in a few centers but have not even been seriously discussed in other centers where need is no less evident. In fact, except for grades 1–12 that are presumably available for all children in every state, there are no educational services that are universally provided or required. The question, then, naturally arises as to whether the foundation program should provide only for financing the services generally provided for pupils in grades 1–12 or whether it should also include some services provided only in the more progressive communities.

Some of the leaders in one state have proposed that: (1) the foundation program be defined to include all essential educational services; (2) units be included in the program for any such service in any district as soon as it is provided in accordance with state minimum standards; (3) the local uniform effort to be the only effort required for any or all services for grades 1–12; (4) a reasonable extra local effort be required and considered as local funds available toward the cost of the foundation program for (a) any district that provides kindergartens and (b) any district or group of districts providing a junior college at a recognized center. What are the strengths and weaknesses of this proposal? What should be included in the foundation program and what should be omitted? For what services, if any, should additional local effort be required?

Are Separate Appropriations and Provisions for Financing Vocational Education Desirable?

As pointed out in this chapter, the typical procedure has been for the states to provide separate funds and appropriations for programs of vocational education that meet accepted standards. These seem to have worked reasonably well, but studies have called attention to a number of difficulties and inequities. Many are concerned about the tendency toward separateness and isolation.

In a certain state, separate appropriations have been provided for the various aspects of vocational education for a period of years. Those in vocational education seem to be reasonably well satisfied with the plan and want to continue. However, several leaders have proposed that provisions for vocational education on a broader basis be included in the foundation program and that the separate appropriations be discontinued.

There has been much vigorous discussion of this problem. Many in vocational education claim that eliminating the separate appropriation would affect the program adversely. They insist that more money can be provided for vocational education through special appropriations than would be feasible through the foundation program. They point out that vocational education has many supporters who are always in a position to help persuade the legislature to provide generous appropriations.

On the other hand, some of the leaders, including a few people from vocational education who advocate the foundation program plan, point out that the situation in the state is not particularly wholesome or desirable. They insist that failure on the part of many vocational people to support the general appropriation provides a handicap. They state that more adequate provision for vocational education could be made in the foundation program than through separate appropriations, and that the entire plan would become more equitable than it is at present.

Many of the vocational people respond by calling attention to the fact that there are separate funds provided by the Federal government and that a change in state policy might affect adversely the position of the state in the Federal program. They indicate that discontinuance of state appropriations might tend to set a precedent for abolition of the Federal appropriation.

What are the merits to these respective points of view? If vocational education were included in the foundation program, what are some of the special problems and factors that would need to be considered? Would there be any justification for separate state, or even Federal, appropriations for vocational education if the plan were changed as recommended by some of the state leaders?

What Provision Should Be Made for Financing Purchases of School Buses?

In several states provision is made in the state plan of financial support to assist districts in the current costs of transportation but not in financing the cost of purchasing school buses. Several provide for reimbursement of a certain percentage of expenditures for transportation other than for buses. Many who have studied the situation call attention to two problems: (1) Districts that contract for transportation services are favored in the reimbursement program because the contract price includes a portion of the cost of purchasing the bus, whereas this is not included, either directly or indirectly, for districts owning their own buses. (2) Districts that provide their own transportation have to find funds from some other source to purchase buses, and when neither bond funds nor state funds are available for this purpose they either have to make an extra levy to meet the cost or use funds that should be available for other aspects of the program. There are further difficulties in some of the states: (1) There is no provision in the law for short-term loans, other than those than can be repaid during the year, and (2) If bonds are issued for the purchase of buses as well as for constructing buildings, some of these bonds may not be retired for 20 or 25 years, while the life of the average bus may not be expected to exceed 10 or 12 years.

A committee that studied the problem in one of these states has recommended the following steps:

1. A study should be made to determine the cost and life expectancy of buses and the annual cost that should be allowed per transported pupil for depreciation on buses.

2. This annual cost should be added to the per pupil allowance for the current expense of transportation determined on the basis of density

of transported pupils. This adjustment, of course, would be made only for districts that own and operate their own buses.

3. Provision should be made for all districts that need to do so, without a vote of the people but with state approval, to issue warrants for a period not to exceed seven years, to be used in financing the purchase of buses.

4. These warrants, when approved by the State Department of Education as to necessity and reasonableness, should be purchased as an investment by the State Teachers Retirement Fund.

5. Districts should be encouraged to work out a plan for staggering purchase of buses so they replace several buses periodically rather than one or two buses a year, thus enabling them to receive the benefit of better prices than would be available if single buses were purchased.

6. The state should explore the possibility of obtaining bids for bus bodies and chassis, the lowest of which would be accepted and could be used by districts in purchasing their own buses.

What are the advantages and disadvantages to this proposal? What refinements should be made if it is to work satisfactorily? Is there a better and more defensible plan for providing state assistance in the purchase of school buses? If so, what plan should be proposed?

How Should Adult Education Be Financed?

Many contend that there are so many different possibilities in the field of adult education that no satisfactory policy can be developed for state assistance. Some insist that only the cost of Americanization or illiteracy classes should be provided through public funds. Others would include various types of vocational classes but not courses devoted to general cultural improvement. Many would contend that recreational classes, including those designed to develop hobby interests, should not be financed either from state or local funds.

Should there be a distinction in methods of financing various kinds of adult education? If so, what kinds of courses should be financed fully at district and state expense? Are there some that should be financed partly from public tax funds and partly on a tuition basis? Should others be supported entirely from fees and tuition? If so, what courses should come in each category?

Many contend that the cost of adult education per student should be less than the cost per pupil of providing elementary and secondary education. They point out that adult classes are usually conducted in public school buildings and that the only extra housing cost is in providing limited special facilities. The costs of operation and maintenance, theoretically, should be less per student than the cost for public schools. What do the facts show about the costs of adult education? Do these vary as much on the basis of the kind of courses provided as public school costs? What implications do these variations have for the plan for financing adult education?

In many states, financing adult education is recognized only as a local responsibility. The assumption is made that communities that desire to provide adult education can do so if they want to and that the state should not enter into the situation. However, in several states the legislature has recognized that the state has a responsibility and has provided funds either through the foundation program or through a special appropriation to assist school districts in financing adult education.

What is the effect on adult education opportunities in a state when the responsibility for financing the program is left entirely to local school systems? If provision is made by the state to assist in the financing, should extra local effort be required as a basis for participation? Should the state participate in financing certain aspects of adult education and not in others? If so, what criteria can be used as a basis for making the distinction?

SELECTED REFERENCES

American Association of School Administrators, Commission on School District Organization, *School District Organization*. Washington, D.C.: The Association, 1958. Chapter IX.

Burke, Arvid J., *Financing Public Schools in the United States*, rev. ed. New York: Harper and Brothers, 1957. Chapters XVIII, XIX, and XXI.

Johns, R. L., and E. L. Morphet, editors, *Problems and Issues in Public School Finance*. New York: Bureau of Publications, Teachers College, Columbia University, 1952. Chapters V, VI, and IX.

Morphet, Edgar L., Roe L. Johns, and Theodore L. Reller, *Educational Administration: Concepts, Practices, and Issues*. Englewood Cliffs, N.J.: Prentice-Hall, Inc., 1959. Chapter 22.

Mort, Paul R., and Walter C. Reusser, *Public School Finance*, 2nd ed. New York: McGraw-Hill Book Company, Inc., 1951. Chapter 24.

Munse, Albert R., and Eugene P. McLoone, *Public School Finance Programs of the United States, 1957–58*, U. S. Office of Education. Washington, D.C.: Superintendent of Documents, 1959.

Rosenstengel, William Everett, and Jefferson N. Eastmond, *School Finance: Its Theory and Practice*. New York: The Ronald Press Company, 1957. Chapters 2, 5, and 21.

Thurston, Lee M., and William H. Roe, *State School Administration*. New York: Harper and Brothers, 1957. Chapters VII and XI.

CHAPTER THIRTEEN

Responsibility
of the Federal Government
for Financing Education

The participation of the Federal government in the financing of public education is the most important controversial issue concerning school financing in the United States. It is an issue as old as the nation itself because the Federal government has participated in the financing of education from its beginning. It is the one educational issue considered of sufficient importance to be included in the platforms of the two major political parties.

This must seem strange to foreign observers for the following reasons: (1) no country (with the possible exception of Communist Russia) has demonstrated a greater faith in mass education than the United States, (2) the central governments of most modern foreign countries play major roles in the financing of education, (3) the Federal government of the United States already participates directly or indirectly in the financing of several hundred educational activities.

After reading reports [1] of the educational activities of the Federal government, the foreign student might well conclude that this issue had been resolved because of the extensive Federal participation in the financing of education. But as will be shown in this chapter, the Fed-

---

[1] For example: Charles A. Quattlebaum, *Federal Educational Activities and Educational Issues Before Congress*, Volumes I & II (Washington, D.C.: U. S. Government Printing Office, 1951); and Clayton D. Hutchins, Albert R. Munse, and Edna D. Booker, *Federal Funds for Education, 1956–57 and 1957–58* (Washington, D.C.: U. S. Government Printing Office, 1959).

eral government has no well defined national educational policy, and the role played by it in the financing of education is relatively minor as compared with the roles played by state and local governments.

Why is it that we have not developed a national educational policy? [2] Why is it that the Federal government provides only a small part of the funds spent for public education? There are many reasons for this. As was pointed out in Chapter 4 education is one of the most important functions of government both in terms of the amount of money involved and the number of people affected. It affects everyone in the nation directly or indirectly and it vitally affects the total economy. The failure to resolve this issue, therefore, is not due to any lack of recognition of the importance of education. Neither can it be assumed that the failure to resolve this issue has been due primarily to the strength of the opponents of public education. It is true that a small minority of persons in the United States are opposed to tax supported public schools. But 87 to 90 per cent of the people of the United States have attended public schools. Also, many if not most of the persons patronizing private schools are also firm supporters of tax supported public schools. Therefore, one must search deeper in order to identify the real causes of the controversy over Federal aid to public education.

The real reason for the bitterness of this controversy is that it has become involved with a number of other important national issues. Education has become the battleground for testing many important principles of law, theories of government, theories of economics, and philosophical values.[3] The great number of studies made on the Federal aid issue is evidence of its importance. In 1951 Quattlebaum listed 42 governmental commissions, advisory groups, and private voluntary organizations as having made studies of this problem during the previous 20 years.[4] A great many additional studies have been made during the past ten years. It appears that interest in the issue of Federal aid will continue.

It is impossible in a book of this length to give a comprehensive treatment of the subject of Federal aid to education.[5] Only some of the more important phases of the problem can be presented. This chapter will deal with some of the important national issues involved in Federal aid, a brief review of the history of Federal aid to education, and some

---

[2] Some insist that we do have a national educational policy, but that it is a negative one.

[3] Edgar L. Morphet, Roe L. Johns, and Theodore L. Reller, *Educational Administration* (Englewood Cliffs, N.J.: Prentice-Hall, Inc., 1959), p. 167.

[4] Quattlebaum, *Federal Educational Activities,* pp. 69–128.

[5] Some authorities on school finance object to the use of the term "Federal aid" and prefer the term "Federal support." The authors use both terms considering them as being synonymous in meaning.

important problems and issues involved in providing for Federal aid to public education.

NATIONAL ISSUES AFFECTING FEDERAL AID TO EDUCATION

If the issue of Federal aid to education could have been isolated from other important national issues, it would probably have been resolved many years ago. Some of the more important of those issues are discussed below.

Division of Powers Among Governments

The Tenth Amendment to the Federal Constitution provides: "The powers not delegated to the United States by the Constitution, nor prohibited by it to the States, are reserved to the states respectively or to the people." Since the Federal Constitution makes no specific reference to education, it has been assumed that education is the legal responsibility of the states. The governmental powers of the states are plenary except for the powers that have been delegated to the Federal government or withheld from the states by some provision of the Constitution. On the other hand, the Federal government is a limited government with no powers except those specifically conferred on it by the Constitution or those powers which can reasonably be implied as necessary to exercise the powers and responsibilities specifically granted.[6]

The Constitution in addition to being a broad statement of principles also provides broad specific grants of power to the Federal government. Since the Federal government has no specific grant of power to finance, regulate, control, or operate schools, colleges, institutions or educational programs, its authority to do so must be found in its implied powers. It is in the area of implied powers that the controversy centers.

As will be shown later in this chapter, it is a historical fact that the Federal government has assisted in the financing of many types of public educational institutions including the public schools; it has regulated and controlled public education to some extent and it has operated practically every type of educational institution and numerous special programs. In fact it is still doing so. It is interesting that this exercise of implied powers has never been successfully challenged in

---

[6] Newton Edwards, *The Courts and the Public Schools*, rev. ed. (Chicago: University of Chicago Press, 1955), p. 1.

the courts. The issue is not whether the Federal government has any implied powers with respect to education but to what extent those powers should be exercised. It is not possible to define neatly by constitution or statute the limits of the exercise of the implied or discretionary powers of government or the times when they should be exercised or the objects for which they should be exercised.

The implied powers of the Federal government have caused bitter controversy between the states and the Federal government. It was one of the fundamental issues of the War Between the States. It is a basic issue in the current controversy over desegregation in the public schools and institutions of higher learning. It is an old issue and also a burning issue of the present.

One of the earliest issues causing the formation of political parties arose over differences in opinion concerning the relative roles of the Federal and state governments. The present-day term "states' rights" (also an old term) means many things to many people. But in general it emphasizes the powers of the states and de-emphasizes the powers of the Federal government. It was inevitable that the issue of Federal aid to education would become associated in the minds of many people with these old issues. Therefore, the position that many people take with respect to Federal aid to education is not determined by the virtue of the proposals, or the reality of the need for Federal aid but by their thinking concerning these old issues.

Controversy over the Effect of Government Expenditures on the Economy

The tremendous increase in the expenditures and activities of the Federal government during the past 30 years has been accompanied by bitter controversy. As has been pointed out in Chapter 3, expenditures have increased at all levels of government but the increase has been far greater at the Federal level than at any other. The point of view of many modern thinkers is that this is a necessary and desirable trend because: (1) Only government (especially central governments) can provide many of the essential services needed by a modern civilization, (2) The expenditures of government are necessary for maximizing production and consumption of goods and services and minimizing unemployment.

The classical view is that government taxing and spending should be limited to providing the minimum of necessary government services because: (1) Continued increases in government spending will eventually result in socialism and the welfare state, (2) Socialism will destroy the free enterprise system and eventually result in the loss of other liberties. These two sharply contrasting views are the heart of much of present-day political controversy.

The modernists do not fear an increase in the public economy; the classicists fear it greatly. The modernists among other things have been called liberals, radicals, and socialists; the classicists among other things have been called conservatives, reactionaries, and economic royalists. The hurling of epithets by each side has not contributed to the resolution of this issue.

Those not fearing the effects of government spending generally support increased revenue for education at all levels of government and especially at the state and Federal levels. Those fearing the effects of government spending generally oppose increased spending for education at all levels, especially by the Federal government. The classicist or conservative generally opposes increased spending for public education, not because he is opposed to public education, but rather because of his opposition to increases in governmental spending in general.

The General Welfare Clause of the Constitution

Section 8 of Article I of the Constitution deals with the powers granted to Congress. Clause 1 of Section 8 of Article I reads as follows: "The Congress shall have Power To lay and collect Taxes, Duties, Imposts and Excises, to pay the Debts and provide for the common Defense and general Welfare of the United States; but all Duties, Imposts and Excises shall be uniform throughout the United States." Although this clause deals with such important matters as levying and collecting taxes, the payment of debts and providing for the common defense, it is commonly called the "general welfare clause" because of the great controversies over the meaning of the words "and general welfare of the United States." At the time the Constitution was adopted, probably only a few people realized the significance of those words.

The eighteenth and last clause of Section 8 of Article I grants Congress the final power: "To make all Laws which shall be necessary and proper for carrying into Execution the foregoing Powers, and all other Powers vested by this Constitution in the Government of the United States, or in any Department or Officer thereof." This eighteenth clause gives a broad grant of implied powers to Congress. The meaning of Clauses 1 and 18 became a matter of bitter controversy very early in our history.[7] James Madison and Alexander Hamilton took the lead in presenting the opposing points of view. Madison argued that the words

---

[7] Morphet, Johns, and Reller, *Educational Administration*, p. 69.

"and general Welfare of the United States" confer no additional powers on the Congress to tax and spend and, therefore, the power of Congress to tax and spend is limited to those purposes specifically enumerated by the Constitution. Hamilton held that these words did confer additional power on Congress to tax and spend for purposes other than those specifically enumerated in the Constitution and that Congress had the power to tax and spend for any purpose that it deemed to be for the general welfare.

Hamilton and Madison did not resolve their differences. In fact controversy over this issue still continues but the details have changed somewhat. The Supreme Court in some relatively recent decisions has supported some of Hamilton's contentions. The Court in a ruling on the Agricultural Adjustment Act held that "the power of Congress to authorize expenditures of public moneys for public purposes is not limited by the direct grants of legislative power found in the Constitution." [8] The Supreme Court in ruling on the Social Security Act held that the decision as to whether an expenditure was for the general welfare must be made by Congress provided that it is not a display of arbitrary power. The Court also held in this decision: "Nor is the concept of general welfare static. Needs that were narrow or parochial a century ago may be interwoven in our day with the well being of the nation. What is critical or urgent changes with the times." [9]

The authority of Congress to tax and spend for public education has been clearly established by these and other opinions by the Court. Actually the legal power of Congress to appropriate and spend money for public education has never been challenged in the Supreme Court. But the rulings of the Court have not settled the controversy between the "liberal constructionists" and the "strict constructionists" of the Constitution. The battle still continues but the major issue has changed from the legal power of Congress to tax and spend for the general welfare to the wisdom of the policy of doing so. What laws are "necessary and proper" (Clause 18) "to provide for the general Welfare of the United States" (Clause 1)? That issue will never be finally resolved because what is necessary and proper for the general welfare "changes with the times."

The general welfare clause has been used extensively during the past 30 years to justify the expansion of old Federal activities and the addition of new activities of the Federal government. The advocates of extension of services of the Federal government now contend that Congress not only has the power to promote the general welfare but

---

[8] United States v. Butler, 297 U.S. 1, 56 Supt. Ct. 312 (1936).
[9] Helvering v. Davis, 301 Cr. S 619, 57 Sup. Ct. 904 (1937).

also the duty to do so. This point of view is vigorously opposed by the classicists who bitterly fight practically any extension of Federal spending except for the national defense. Therefore, the Federal aid to education issue is actually a part of the old Hamilton-Madison controversy.

Limitations on Congress

Section 9 of Article I of the Constitution sets forth the powers denied to Congress. Two of the subsections of this section have some relationship to the financing of education. Subsection 4 reads as follows: "No Capitation or other direct Tax shall be laid, unless in Proportion to the Census or Enumeration herein before directed to be taken." This provision of the Constitution has effectively prevented Congress from levying a property tax. It is obviously impracticable to levy a property tax in proportion to the census. The last time Congress attempted to levy a property tax was during the Civil War. Had it not been for this provision of the Constitution, Congress probably would have levied property taxes very early in our history.

This subsection also prevented Congress from levying income taxes. This limitation was removed by the Sixteenth Amendment to the Constitution ratified in 1913. It reads: "The Congress shall have power to lay and collect taxes on incomes, from whatever sources derived, without apportionment among the several States, and without regard to any census or enumeration." This amendment greatly increased the taxing powers of Congress. As pointed out in Chapter 5, the Federal government now obtains more than 81 per cent of its revenue from income taxes. This broadening of the taxing powers of Congress has made it possible for the Federal government to extend greatly the Federal services provided. It also greatly improved the equity of our taxing system.

Subsection 5 prohibits Congress from laying taxes or duties on articles exported from any state. This provision and the provisions of Subsection 4 as amended by the Sixteenth Amendment are the only specific limitations on the taxing powers of Congress except a provision of Clause 1 of Section 8 of Article I requiring that "all Duties, Imposts and Excises shall be uniform throughout the United States." Therefore, it is apparent that Congress has very broad taxing powers. The enormous amount of revenue collected annually by the Federal government is evidence of that fact.

The Federal government has another important advantage in obtaining revenues. When taxes are levied nation-wide, the difficulties of competition among state and local governments are avoided. The income tax both personal and corporation is levied nation-wide. A person or corporation cannot escape the income tax by moving to another political jurisdiction within the nation. But the income taxes of state and local governments can be avoided by moving into a jurisdiction not levying the tax. The same thing is true of any tax levied by state and local governments. Therefore, "tax competition" limits the potential tax revenues of state and local governments.

The Federal government does not suffer from this limitation. It might be argued that the Federal government faces international tax competition. That is probably true to some extent but international tax competition does not have nearly as great a restraining influence on taxation as the tax competition among state and local governments.

Limitations on the States

Section 10 of Article I of the Constitution sets forth the powers denied the States. There are only a few provisions of this Section that are related to the financing of education. Subsection 1 includes the provision that no state shall pass any law impairing the obligation of contracts. Subsection 2 provides: "No State shall, without the Consent of the Congress, lay any Imposts or Duties on Imports or Exports, except what may be absolutely necessary for executing its inspection Laws; and the net Produce of all Duties and Imposts, laid by any State on Imports or Exports, shall be for the Use of the Treasury of the United States; and all such Laws shall be subject to the Revision and Control of the Congress. [Subsection 3] No State shall, without the Consent of Congress, lay any Duty of Tonnage. . . ." These are the only limitations placed on the taxing powers of the states by the Federal Constitution. They are relatively minor and, therefore, place no serious restrictions on the states with respect to the levy and collection of taxes.

But it should not be assumed that Section 10 of Article I of the Constitution contains the only Federal limitations on the states in the operation of systems of public education. The Constitution as interpreted by the Supreme Court is the supreme law of the land. Any law of any state on any matter including education that is in conflict with any provision of the Federal Constitution is null and void if so declared by the United States Supreme Court. People who argue that the Federal government should have no control whatsoever over public education seem to have overlooked this fact. It would be impossible to have a Federal government of the United States if the states could nullify its Constitution. Therefore, some measure of Federal control of public education is inescapable. The issue of Federal control of public education is so important that some specific instances are presented in the following paragraphs.

Equal Protection of the Law. Section 1 of the Fourteenth Amendment provides in part ".... No State shall make or enforce any law which shall abridge the privileges or immunities of citizens of the United States; nor shall any State deprive any person of life, liberty, or property, without due process of law; nor deny to any person within its jurisdiction the equal protection of the laws." It was this amendment plus subsequent rulings of the Supreme Court that firmly established the supremacy of the Federal Constitution and all of its provisions.

One of the most dramatic rulings by the Court was made on May 17, 1954. The Court had before it five cases dealing with segregation in the public schools. Segregation by race was declared unconstitutional in the public schools. "We conclude that in the field of public education the doctrine of 'separate but equal' has no place. Separate educational facilities are inherently unequal. Therefore, we hold that the plaintiffs and others similarly situated for whom the actions are brought are, by reason of the segregation complained of, deprived of the equal protection of the laws guaranteed by the Fourteenth Amendment." [10]

It is interesting to note that the 1954 ruling of the Court reversed a ruling it had made in 1896 dealing with the question of racial segregation on public transportation facilities. The Court ruled in that case that separate but equal facilities were constitutional.[11] The 1954 *Brown* ruling not only controls the policies of the states but the policies of boards of education wherever situated. This decision overthrew the "states' rights" theory in so far as certain aspects of public education are concerned.

Decisions of the Court dealing with highly controversial matters are not always accepted by the losers as being the "supreme law of the land." Segments of the public continue to resist the implementation of the Court's decisions on controversial matters. This is particularly true of the 1954 ruling on segregation. Controversy over the segregation issue does not produce a climate favorable to the financing of education. This observation is not for the purpose of questioning the correctness of the ruling of the Court but rather to point out its fiscal effect.

Separation of Church and State. The relationship of the schools to religion is regulated by the Federal government under authority of the First and Fourteenth Amendments to the Constitution. The First Amendment provides "Congress shall make no law respecting an establishment of religion, or prohibiting the free exercise thereof; ...." The

---

[10] Brown v. Board of Education, 347 U.S. 483, 74 Sup. Ct. 686 (1954).
[11] Plessey v. Ferguson, 163 U.S. 537, 16 Sup. Ct. 1138 (1896).

Supreme Court of the United States has held that the provisions of the First Amendment also apply to the states because of the following provision in the Fourteenth Amendment: "No State shall make or enforce any law which shall abridge the privileges or immunities of citizens of the United States; . . . ." Therefore any privilege or immunity granted a citizen of the United States by the Federal Constitution cannot be denied by the states.

The Court in the case of *Illinois* ex rel. *McCollum v. Board of Education* [12] and in *Everson v. Board of Education* [13] held that the intent of the First Amendment was to erect a "wall of separation between church and state." In these two opinions and in other opinions the Court has declared that the Federal government and state governments may not levy any tax large or small to support religious activities. Neither can they use property provided from tax funds for religious instruction nor can they provide for an established church.[14]

These opinions, however, have not fully settled the matter of the use of tax funds for religious activities. The Court has held in certain opinions on the use of tax funds for transportation and textbooks for pupils attending parochial schools that the use of tax funds for such purposes is an aid to the child and not to the school and therefore not unconstitutional. This is another opinion of the Court concerning education that is highly controversial. While the Court did not rule that a state *must* use its tax funds to provide textbooks and transportation to children attending parochial schools, it ruled that it *could* do so. This has resulted in pressure being brought on public school officials in many communities to spend tax funds indirectly to aid parochial schools even though they do not wish to do so. This is an indirect type of Federal control.

Impairment of Contracts. As has been pointed out, Section 10 of Article I of the Constitution contains a provision prohibiting a state from passing a law impairing the obligation of contracts. School financing involves many different types of contracts. School boards, for instance, issue bonds that are important financial contracts. The Federal prohibition against the impairment of contracts has undoubtedly improved the credit of boards of education as well as the credit of all state and local governments. This type of Federal control seems to be applauded by almost everyone. In fact it is not generally recognized as a control but the fact that it is a control makes it a valuable asset to school financing.

One ruling of the Supreme Court previously referred to has signifi-

[12] 333 U.S. 203 (1948).
[13] 330 U.S. 1 (1947).
[14] Morphet, Johns, and Reller, *Educational Administration*, p. 170.

cance in relation to teacher retirement. The Court has held that "A legislative enactment may contain provisions which, when accepted as a basis of action by individuals, become contracts between them and the state or its subdivision . . ." [15] Teacher retirement laws should be so drafted as to make it clear that provisions for retirement constitute a contract between the teacher and the state.

HISTORICAL DEVELOPMENT OF FEDERAL AID

Practically every department of the Federal government at one time or another has expended some of its appropriations for education either directly or indirectly. There is no accurate historical record available of all of the Federal funds that have been expended for education. Actually no office or agency of the Federal government can give an accurate statement of Federal funds being expended directly or indirectly for education. Even objective investigators working independently cannot arrive at the same total of Federal funds expended for education during any given fiscal year. Therefore, it would not be possible to present an accurate history of Federal aid even if space permitted. However, it is possible to present certain examples of Federal aid that throw some light on its development.

Early Land Grants

The national interest in education was revealed even before the adoption of the Constitution. The Ordinance of 1785 included the provision "there shall be reserved the lot number 16 of every township for the maintenance of public schools in each township."

The policies enunciated in the Ordinance of 1785 were put into effect in 1787 by a Federal contract for the sale of lands to the Ohio Company. The Ordinance of 1787 contained these often quoted words expressing Federal educational policy at that time: "Religion, morality and knowledge being necessary to good government and the happiness of mankind, schools and the means of education shall be forever encouraged." The Ordinance, providing for the contract of sale in 1787, also first reserved certain townships to endow a university.

Most of the states admitted to the Union since 1789 were first administered and organized as territories. The Federal government administered the territories and consequently actually founded the public school systems of many states. This direct responsibility of the Federal government for education in the territories probably contrib-

---

[15] Indiana *ex rel.* Anderson v. Brand, 303 U.S. 95, 58 S. Ct. 443 (1938).

uted to Federal interest in education when the territories became states.

The Congress in 1802 adopted the same general policy of giving support to public education that was adopted by the Congress of the Confederation 17 years earlier. When Ohio was admitted to the Union in 1802, Congress initiated its policy of setting aside public lands for public education at the time of the admission of a state to the Union.

The policy of setting aside the sixteenth section of each township for the public schools was followed for states admitted between 1802 and 1848. When the Oregon territory was established in 1848, Congress set aside two sections of each township for the public schools. This policy was continued until 1896 when Utah was granted four sections in every township. Similar grants were made other western states admitted after that year.

The Federal government made a number of other kinds of early grants for the public schools. The most important of these grants were as follows:

(1) grants of funds in lieu of land grants in Indian territory; (2) additional land grants under the Internal Improvement Act of 1841; (3) grants of saline lands; (4) grants of 5 per cent of the funds received by the Federal government from sale of public lands in the states; (5) payment to the states of 25 per cent of the income from national forests and 37.5 per cent of the income received from the extraction of non-metallic minerals for the benefit of roads and public schools; and (6) the allocation of surplus Federal revenues to the states in 1836.[16]

Swift made a comprehensive study of land grants for schools.[17] He reported that the domain granted specifically for schools by the Federal government to the thirty public-land states totalled 121,110 square miles, an area larger than Italy, and ten times as large as Maryland. This does not include 120,004 square miles of additional domain granted to the states by the Federal government which was used in part for the public schools, 19,953 square miles of school land in Alaska or 78,428 square miles of land given by the states to the public schools.

Unfortunately this rich heritage of land grants for the public schools was badly mismanaged by many states. Swift reported that eleven of the thirty land-grant states had badly mismanaged school lands.[18] In a number of states most of the domain was sold for a small part of its present worth. The money derived from the sale of the school lands was deposited in a permanent school endowment fund. But in a number of

---

[16] Morphet, Johns, and Reller, *Educational Administration*, p. 173.
[17] Fletcher Harper Swift, *Federal and State Policies in Public School Finance in the United States* (Boston: Ginn & Company, 1931), p. 59.
[18] *Ibid.*, p. 62.

states, the fund was squandered and it exists only in the form of a debt of the state. However, a few states managed their lands wisely and the income from those lands is substantial.

It was the hope of some in the early days that the income from school lands would be sufficient to pay for most of the cost of the public schools. However, this was a vain hope even if the public lands had been well managed in all cases. But the early land grants and early grants of funds had great significance for the public schools. These Federal grants stimulated the interest of the states in public schools. When the states found that the income from Federal grants was insufficient to support their schools they began to provide state grants-in-aid. Therefore, the early Federal grants in effect established the precedent for state aid for the public schools.

Two characteristics of these early land grants were of great significance. First, they were for general public school purposes. Second, the Federal government exercised no control whatsoever over education as a condition for receiving the grants. Authorities on school finance almost unanimously recommend general Federal aid for the public schools in preference to aid for specific educational purposes. Despite this fact, as will be pointed out later in this chapter, practically all Federal grants-in-aid to the public schools after 1862 have been special-purpose grants.

The early Federal grants demonstrated the fact that the Federal government can give Federal aid without Federal control. But the history of the management of those grants is not proof that absolutely no Federal control is a wise policy. Perhaps the states would have benefited from some Federal requirements concerning sound fiscal management of the grants. Such controls would not have interfered with the prerogative of the states to determine educational policy.

The Morrill Acts

The first Morrill Act was passed by Congress in 1862. This act provided for a grant of 30,000 acres to each state for each representative and senator then in Congress. This same grant of land was made available to states thereafter admitted to the Union. The act provided for the giving of script to those states in which the public lands were insufficient to make up the allotment. It was provided that the land be sold and the proceeds used for the "endowment, maintenance and support of at least one college where the leading object shall be, without excluding other scientific and classical studies and including military tactics, to teach such branches of learning as are related to agriculture and the mechanic arts in such manner as the legislatures of the states may respectively prescribe." Another stated purpose of the act was "to promote the liberal and practical education of the industrial classes in the several pursuits and professions of life."

This original Morrill Act is the first instance of the Federal government's providing a grant for specific educational purposes. It will be noted that Federal control was limited to specifying that agriculture, mechanic arts, and military tactics must be taught in those institutions. No limitation was placed on the other types of subjects that might be taught. Also, the act specifically placed the determination of the educational policies of the land-grant institutions in the hands of the respective legislatures.

This act is of great significance because it again demonstrated the national interest in education. It also showed that, when existing educational institutions did not provide adequately for the "general welfare," the Federal government could and would take action. At the time the Morrill Act was passed, the institutions of higher learning were largely classical and academic in character. They catered primarily to the select few. The land grant colleges have been called "people's colleges." The curricula of these colleges included subjects that were not "academically respectable" in 1862. But educational programs of the land-grant colleges grew in popularity. The influence of these colleges has been so great that they have contributed substantially to liberalizing the educational programs of many non-land-grant colleges. In 30 states, a land-grant college is also the principal state university.

The land grants were supplemented by regular grants-in-aid when it was found that those grants were insufficient to accomplish the purposes of the act. The second Morrill Act in 1890 further strengthened the original act. It also placed upon the Secretary of the Interior certain responsibilities for administering the act. He delegated those responsibilities to the Bureau of Education. The Bureau was succeeded by the Office of Education which is administering the provisions of the act at present.

The Congress has increased the range of activities of the land-grant colleges by a number of acts. For example, the Hatch Act of 1887, the Adams Act of 1906, the Purnell Act of 1925, the Bankhead-Jones Act of 1935, the Research and Marketing Act of 1946 and other acts greatly increased the funds available for agricultural experimentation. The research conducted by the land-grant institutions has been a major factor in making American farmers the most productive and American people the best fed of any in the world.

The Smith-Lever Act

The Smith-Lever Act was approved by Congress in 1914. It provided for extension services by county agricultural and home demonstration agents, 4-H leaders, and specialists in agriculture and homemaking, and for the professional training of teachers in these areas. This act was far more specific in detailing the purposes for which the grant could be spent than the grants provided by the Morrill Act. Actually, the services provided under the Smith-Lever Act were practically non-existent prior to its passage. This act is additional evidence that the Congress, when it deems it desirable to do so, will provide for or stimulate the provision for educational services not being furnished by the educational organization.

The extension services provided under this act are not an integral part of the system of public education. The service at the local level is usually allocated to the control of the county governing body. Boards of education, especially county boards, have sometimes subsidized the extension service but they have no authority over it. The state director of the extension service is usually associated with a land-grant college but this is about the only direct relationship to the system of public education.

The extension services have made a major contribution to the dissemination of the results of the research conducted on agricultural experiment farms. The home demonstrators have also made major contributions to home and family living. The extension services have brought the "people's colleges" to the people. It should be remembered that the extension services were inaugurated before the days of radio and television. Therefore, these workers were the major communicators of new and improved practices in agriculture and homemaking.

The success of the Federally subsidized extension services undoubtedly influenced the states and institutions of higher learning to establish additional extension services and adult education programs.

The Smith-Hughes Act

Between 1862 and 1917 the Federal government seemed to be concerned primarily with inadequacies in the programs of institutions of higher learning. No new Federal act of any major significance to the public schools was passed by Congress during this period. In 1917, Congress passed the Smith-Hughes Act which provided funds for vocational education below college level. A continuing appropriation was provided for vocational education in agriculture, trades and industry, and homemaking. Provision was also made for teacher training in these fields. The original Smith-Hughes Act required dollar-for-dollar matching by the states and local units. Some states provided all of the matching funds required from state revenues. Other states required local units to match the state funds dollar for dollar and thereby provide half of the matching funds required by the Federal government. This retarded the development of vocational education in some of the least wealthy districts because of their inability to provide the required matching funds.

Some other acts which supplemented and broadened the Smith-Hughes Act were: the George-Reed Act of 1929, the George-Ellzey Act of 1935, the George-Deen Act of 1937 and the George-Barden Act of 1946.

The Smith-Hughes Act provided the first special-purpose grants made available to the public schools by Congress. Vocational education was not a new educational idea. A number of school systems had established some types of vocational education programs prior to 1917. For example, some 500 agricultural high schools had been established by 1909. Some schools in forty-four of the forty-seven states in 1911 offered training in homemaking. A number of city systems had developed trade schools or trades courses in regular high schools. However, most high school pupils did not have access to suitable kinds of vocational programs.

At the beginning of the twentieth century most lay people—and also most educators—believed that the high school program should be largely academic in character. The prevailing belief was that if a high school student was not interested in college preparatory work, he should not go to high school. High schools did not become mass education institutions until after World War I. Following that war, however, there was a remarkable increase in the demand for secondary education. The development of vocational education, which was stimulated by the Smith-Hughes Act, contributed to providing for the needs of large numbers of pupils whose needs could not have been served by the high school programs generally available prior to 1917.

Although the matching of Federal vocational funds was a significant problem in the early years, it is no longer of much consequence. All states far more than match vocational funds. The typical state provides from state and local sources five times as much financial support for vocational education as the Federal vocational grants. In a few states Federal vocational funds represent less than 10 per cent of the total money spent on vocational education.

Grants-in-aid for vocational education have been criticized on the grounds that such grants tend to turn the educational programs in the direction of the subsidized purpose. This was no doubt true in the years immediately following 1917. But that was probably one of the purposes of the Smith-Hughes Act. Any special-purpose grant influences the direction of the educational program. Therefore, a special-purpose grant of any kind, state or Federal, contains an element of control.

Some Federal Relief Measures Affecting Education

In the decade between 1930 and 1940 the nation suffered the worst financial depression in its history. The depression actually became world-wide in its effects. The major attention of the nation in those years was directed toward finding a solution for our economic difficulties. One school of thought was that if we did nothing, the economy in time would adjust itself. Another theory was that the Federal government could break the depression by "priming" the economy with Federal spending.

Franklin D. Roosevelt was inaugurated president in 1933, and he promptly initiated his New Deal program for economic recovery. One of the principal elements of the New Deal was an accelerated program of Federal spending for the primary purpose of stimulating the economy. Almost twenty per cent of the labor force was unemployed and millions of people were destitute. Therefore, the immediate purpose of many of the New Deal measures was to provide employment and to give relief to destitute persons.

Little planning had been done on Federal projects by which this could be accomplished. It was recognized that government spending would be most effective if the projects selected for Federal spending were intrinsically worth while. Therefore, it is not surprising that considerable Federal relief money was made available to the public schools.

The Federal relief appropriations did not represent a change in Federal policy toward education. In fact, only one of the present Federal appropriations had its origin in a relief measure. Therefore, a description of the various types of Federal relief measures affecting education will not be presented. Most of these emergency relief appropriations were administered by newly-created agencies.

Following is a list of some of the more important relief agencies that gave financial aid to public education either directly or indirectly. Only the principal educational activities of these agencies are indicated. It must be remembered that all these agencies were created primarily for relief purposes so their non-educational activities were far more extensive than their educational activities.

1. The Civilian Conservation Corps was established in 1933 and abolished in 1943. This agency carried on organized educational activities for men in CCC camps. Over 2.7 million men participated in these activities.

2. The National Youth Administration was established by the executive order of the President in 1935 and was liquidated in 1944. This organization provided work relief for thousands of secondary and college students and enabled them to continue their education. The NYA also established special schools in some states.

3. The Federal Emergency Relief Administration was established in 1933, superseded by the Works Progress Administration in 1939, and abolished in the early 1940's. These organizations carried on extensive programs of school building construction, maintenance, and repair; paid the salaries of many teachers on a relief basis in a number of states; supported educational projects for adult education, nursery schools, vocational rehabilitation, part-time employment of college students, and literacy and naturalization classes; and provided labor for school lunch rooms.

4. The Public Works Administration was established in 1933 and abolished in the early 1940's. It made grants for school buildings (first on the basis of 30 per cent Federal funds and 70 per cent state and local funds and later on a 45 to 55 basis) and made loans for school building construction. This matching requirement limited the benefits of the PWA largely to the school districts of greatest wealth.

5. The Federal Surplus Commodities Corporation was established in 1935. It purchased and distributed surplus commodities to school lunch rooms operated on a non-profit basis. Some cash assistance to lunch rooms was also provided primarily for the purchase of surplus foods locally. This organization was administered by the Department of Agriculture. These lunch room aids were made available for lunch rooms operated by private schools as well as public schools. This was justified on the basis that lunchroom assistance is an aid to the child and not the school.

The policies developed by the Surplus Commodities Corporation culminated in the National School Lunch Act of 1946. This was later supplemented by an act providing special aid for the school milk program. Those acts apparently have made school lunch assistance a continuing policy of the Federal government. This program has stimulated the construction and operation of thousands of school lunch rooms throughout the United States. The extensiveness of this program is indicated by the fact that in 1956–57 the Federal government expended $83,915,000 for the School Lunch Program and $61,032,000 for the Special Milk Program. The schools and other eligible institutions also received $146,-

632,000 in the form of surplus commodities from the Direct Distribution Program.

Defense and War Federal Educational Activities

The past and present educational activities of the Federal government related to defense and war are far too extensive to treat in detail in a volume of this length. They were justified on the grounds that they were necessary to provide for the common defense and to promote the general welfare. These activities in terms of money expended have been far more extensive than all other educational activities of the Federal government combined. Appropriations for most of the war and defense educational activities of the Federal government have been passed by Congress with little opposition from any quarter. For example, Federal expenditures for veterans education exceeded 15 billion dollars in the twelve-year period 1944–1955. Federal expenditures for the vocational education of high school youth totalled approximately 300 million dollars during this same period. But there was far more opposition to the small appropriations for vocational education than to the huge appropriations for veterans education.

Numerous proposals were made for general Federal aid to the public schools during this period and in the years preceding and following this period. All of these proposals have been defeated in Congress. Apparently there is stronger public approval for providing for the common defense than for promoting the general welfare. But as pointed out elsewhere in this book, general expenditures for public education help to provide for the common defense as well as to promote the general welfare.

Following are some of the educational activities of the Federal government for defense and war.

Educational Institutions Operated by the Armed Services. The Military Academy was established in 1802, the Naval Academy in 1845, the Air Force Academy in 1954, the Army Medical School in 1893, the Army War College in 1902, superseded by the National War College in 1946, and the Air University in 1947. In addition, the armed services operate elementary and high schools at some service posts both at home and abroad. This is an incomplete list but it gives some indication of the scope of the institutions operated by the armed services.

Educational Programs Administered by the Armed Services. An act of Congress in 1866 provided that "Whenever troops are serving at any post, garrison, or permanent camp, there shall be established a school where all men may be provided with instruction in the common English branches of education and especially in the history of the United

States." Many thousands of men were trained under this program and it probably was the forerunner of the Armed Forces Institute which was established in 1945. This program is very extensive in nature. It provides educational training in many areas of knowledge. It is a voluntary off-duty program which in 1955 served about one-half million persons. In addition to these programs, the Army, the Navy, the Air Force, the Marines and the Coast Guard all conduct or sponsor other types of educational programs that are useful to service personnel when they return to civilian life.

The War Production Training Programs. The war production program was initiated in the years immediately preceding World War II. It was a crash program for the training of workers needed in industries producing goods required for national defense and war. The Office of Education administered this program. The Office worked through state education agencies in carrying out the purposes of the act. Some 7.8 million workers were trained under this program.

The Office also worked with degree-granting institutions in organizing short courses for the training of physicists, engineers, chemists, and production supervisors. Other important programs administered by the Office of Education during the war included the training programs for rural war production workers and the student war loans program.

Wartime and Peacetime Use of Higher Institutions. During World War II, the Federal government made wide use of the facilities of institutions. The Army specialized training program had been established on more than 300 campuses by 1943. The V-12 program of the Navy provided similar college opportunities for Navy personnel. These programs were not established for the purpose of giving military training to service personnel but to train persons in civilian professions necessary for national defense. These programs enabled many colleges to continue operating during the war. If these programs or similar programs had not been made available many colleges would have been compelled to cease operations during this period because of the extensive mobilization of manpower. Many thousands of students benefited from these programs.

Since World War II, the Federal government has contracted with the institutions for a great deal of research on projects of interest to it. These should not be thought of as grants-in-aid to the higher institutions but rather as purchases by the Federal government of certain services furnished by higher institutions. This seems to be a wise policy because it is certainly less expensive than it would have been had the Federal government established its own agencies to do the needed research. These research programs have also been of value in training graduate students.

Federal Impact Area Aid. Congress passed the Lanham Act in 1941 for the construction, maintenance, and operation of community facilities in the areas where the defense and war activities created unusual burdens for local governments. Schools received considerable Federal aid for building construction and for current expenses under the provisions of this act.

The Lanham Act was superseded by Public Laws 815 and 874 in 1950 which continued approximately the same types of benefits provided by the Lanham Act.

Veterans Training Programs. Public Law 178 of 1918 provided for the vocational training of the disabled veterans of World War I and Public Law 16 of 1943 provided for the training of the disabled veterans of World War II.

The most important of the acts providing training for veterans was Public Law 346 of 1944, which has been commonly called the "GI Bill of Rights." This bill contained extremely liberal provisions for the education of veterans. It provided reasonable allowances for the payment of the cost of books, tuition, and subsistence. The educational training allowed included practically everything from dancing to advanced graduate study in the United States or abroad. The educational training of the veterans of the Korean War was provided for by Public Law 550 of 1952, the "Korean GI Bill."

It is estimated that by 1959 some 10,000,000 veterans had received benefits under these bills at a total cost of almost 20 billion dollars.

The immediate effect of these two bills was to double college enrollments after World War II. The long-range effect was to popularize college education for the masses and bring it within the aspirations of millions of young men and women who prior to World War II would not have seriously considered going to college. Another long-range effect was to raise the production and cultural level of individuals and of the nation. It has been estimated that the increased income taxes collected from veterans because of their higher earning power will more than reimburse the Federal government for their education before most of them are forty years of age.

The National Defense Education Act of 1958. This act authorized the expenditure of 887 million dollars over a period of four years for: providing loans to students in institutions of higher learning; providing equipment for and remodeling of facilities for science, mathematics, and foreign language teaching; providing graduate fellowships for those interested in teaching in institutions of higher learning; providing assistance for guidance, counseling, and testing services and identification and encouragement of able students; providing centers for teaching modern foreign languages; providing assistance for research and experimentation in the more effective use of television and other related audio-visual media; and providing assistance for certain area vocational programs. State legislatures were required to pass special legislation before they could take advantage of some of the provisions of the act.

The National Defense Education Act contains the provision, "Nothing contained in this act shall be construed to authorize any department, agency, officer, or employee of the United States to exercise any direction, supervision, or control over the curriculum, program of instruction or school system." This provision makes it clear that Congress does not want any Federal department, agency, or officer to exercise control over education, but that Congress itself wants to control education. Congress controls education by appropriating funds for special educational purposes and requiring that those funds be spent for those purposes.

The primary impetus for this act came from the scientific advances of military significance made by Russia. These advances were dramatized by the launching of Sputnik I. That was the reason, perhaps, the act was named the National Defense Education Act.

Some Other Federal Programs

In 1920, the Federal government provided an appropriation to be matched by the states for the rehabilitation, including the training, of disabled civilians. This act was superseded by Public Law 113 of 1943 which provided Federal assistance to the states for the vocational rehabilitation of injured persons.

Public Law 507 of 1950 established the National Science Foundation, "to promote the progress of science; to advance the national health, prosperity, and welfare; to secure the national defense; and for other purposes." The Foundation is particularly directed to advance education in the sciences. The Foundation provides grants for basic research and fellowships for graduate students of the sciences. It also sponsors conferences and institutes for students of science, including high school science teachers, and promotes the development of science libraries.

Congress has authorized a number of educational exchange programs by six separate acts, the most important of which is the Fulbright Act (Public Law 584, 79th Congress). These programs have done much to promote international understanding.

The International Cooperation Administration was created in 1955 as a semi-autonomous unit within the Department of State. One of its major functions is to administer programs of technical education in the undeveloped areas of the world. The International Cooperation Administration uses Federal funds to secure the cooperation of American universities and colleges with foreign universities in improving teaching, curriculum, research, and extension.

Summary of Federal Educational Activities

The Federal educational activities described in this chapter should not be considered a complete inventory. Only those activities of particular significance to public education have been mentioned. Table 13–1 presents a summary of Federal expenditures for 137 educational programs in 1956–57. The total expended for these programs was $1,997,825,000. These programs do not include all the Federal educational activities during that year.

Of the $656,632,000 expended for programs for elementary and secondary schools, $291,579,000 in cash and commodities were allotted to the school lunch and school milk programs and $172,835,000 for aid to Federally affected areas. Expenditures for these two programs comprised 71 per cent of all Federal expenditures for elementary and secondary schools in 1956–57.

Federal expenditures for the programs included in Table 13–1 totalled $3,501,406,000 in 1948–49, but $3,039,062,000 of this amount was expended for the education, training, and vocational rehabilitation of veterans. Excluding the veterans' programs, Federal expenditures for education increased from $462,344,000 in 1948–49 to $1,186,221,000 in 1956–57.

A major educational program was added by the National Defense Education Act of 1958, which is not included in programs reported in this table.

TABLE 13–1

SUMMARY OF FEDERAL FINANCIAL SUPPORT
FOR 137 EDUCATIONAL PROGRAMS IN 1956–57

Type of Program	Amount (thousands)
Elementary and Secondary Education	$ 656,632
Higher Education	220,920
Research in Educational Institutions	133,328
Veterans' Education, Training and Vocational Rehabilitation	811,604
Adult Education	87,220
In-Service Training of Civilian Personnel	3,485
Education of Military and Merchant Marine Personnel for Defense	34,497
International Education	50,139
TOTAL:	$ 1,997,825

Source: Clayton D. Hutchins, Albert R. Munse, and Edna D. Booker, *Federal Funds for Education 1956–57 and 1957–58*, U. S. Department of Health, Education and Welfare, Office of Education (Washington, D.C.: U. S. Government Printing Office, 1959), pp. 17–19.

METHODS OF DISTRIBUTING FEDERAL AID

Many different methods have been used in distributing Federal aid. Following are the principal methods by which funds have been distributed:

(1) Allotted on the basis of *land areas,* (2) distributed in proportion to *population* figures, (3) awarded to the States as *flat-grants,* (4) given on condition that *matching funds* are provided from State and local revenues, (5) provided as the *cost of an educational program* or of operating a school, (6) apportioned to meet a Federal obligation such as *payments in* lieu of taxes on Federally owned property, (7) allocated as *equalization aid* to provide greater assistance to the financially weaker areas, (8) paid to cover the *cost of tuition* and of other educational expenses of individuals, and (9) granted in accordance with *contracts for services* on research programs in various colleges, universities and industries.[19]

The only Federal fund for the public schools distributed at least partly on an equalization basis is the school lunch appropriation. The most commonly used method is the matching basis which takes no account of differences in the taxpaying ability of the states. This is the most inequitable method used in distributing Federal aid. The most equitable basis is the equalization method, and probably the next most equitable method would be to distribute Federal funds on the basis of the census of children 5–17 years of age. An appropriate combination of these two methods might be the most desirable plan.

SOME PROBLEMS AND ISSUES

Numerous bills proposing substantial general Federal aid for the public schools have been before Congress during the past twenty-five years. Congress has passed no bill of this type during that period although it has approved a number of special aids. Some of the issues involved in this problem are discussed in the following paragraphs.

What Is the Evidence for and against Federal Aid?

Many arguments have been presented for and against Federal aid. A listing of these arguments is of little value because the arguments usually presented seldom contain the assumptions or evidence by which they can be tested. In order to evaluate the evidence available on this

[19] Hutchins, Munse, and Booker, *Federal Funds for Education,* 1959, pp. 5–6.

issue, certain key questions are presented below. If the weight of available evidence indicates that the answers to these questions should be in the affirmative, then Federal aid to education is a sound national policy. If the evidence indicates that these questions should be answered in the negative, then Federal aid is not a sound national policy.

Are There Critical Differences Among the States in the Educational Opportunities Available to Children? The evidence presented in Chapter 6 of this book shows that there are critical differences among the states in the educational opportunities available to children.

Is It Impossible for All States to Provide Adequate Educational Opportunities for Their Children Without Making a Relatively Excessive State and Local Tax Effort? The Committee for the White House Conference on Education studied this question. It was found that seven states in 1953–54 would have to levy state and local taxes for schools equal to five per cent or more of the total personal income of the people in order to maintain the national average expenditure per classroom unit at that time.[20] On the other hand, seven states could have spent less than two per cent of the personal income of the people and maintained the average expenditure per classroom unit. Actually the national average expenditure per classroom unit in 1953–54 was far less than the amount necessary to provide an adequate educational program. The evidence is conclusive that it is impossible for all states to provide an adequate educational program for all children without a relatively excessive state and local tax effort.

Is an Adequate Educational Program in All States Necessary for the National Defense and the General Welfare? The necessity of education for the national defense is self evident, so it seems unnecessary to review it. One of the important acts passed by Congress in 1958 was named "The National Defense Education Act." The educational activities of the Federal Goverment during World War II indicate the necessity of mobilizing the educational resources of the nation in order to win a war.

In 14 states, 20 per cent or more of the selectees registered for the armed forces failed the Armed Forces Qualification Test during the period July 1950 to June 1951.[21] The level of education available in these 14 states during the previous 20 years was much below the national average. In 14 states less than seven per cent of the selectees failed these tests and in most of these states the level of education during the preceding 20 years exceeded the national average. Modern

---

[20] The Committee for the White House Conference on Education, *A Report to the President* (Washington, D.C.: U. S. Government Printing Office, 1956), p. 64.

[21] National Education Association, *Educational Differences Among the States* (Washington, D,C,; The Association, 1954), p. 11.

wars are won in the classrooms as well as in the factories, on the farms and on the battlefields. With the continued advance of science and technology this will be even more evident in the future than in the past.

It is also equally evident that education is necessary for the common welfare. The effect of education on the production and consumption of goods and services was described in Chapter 3. The necessity of education for useful citizenship in a democracy was shown in Chapter 4. Education or lack of education is not local in its effects. We are a mobile people. The 1950 census shows that one American out of four had left the state of his birth. Therefore, adequate educational opportunities in each state are necessary to promote the general welfare in all states.

Is It Possible to Provide Federal Aid to Public Education Without Undesirable Federal Controls? The answer is in the affirmative because Congress has provided certain grants for education without Federal control. Prior to 1862 all Federal grants of land and money to the states for the public schools and higher institutions were general purpose grants. They contained no Federal controls whatsoever.

Even a special-purpose grant can be made by Congress with no Federal controls by Federal officials. The National Defense Education Act of 1958 is an example. But, as has been pointed out in this chapter, a special-purpose grant is itself an undesirable type of control. In Chapter 9 it is pointed out that even state special-purpose grants contain an undesirable element of state control. It is not to be inferred that special-purpose grants are always harmful to education. But maximum benefits are provided by general-purpose grants. Therefore, the Federal government can maximize the benefits received from the funds appropriated and eliminate undesirable Federal controls entirely by providing substantial general-purpose grants.

Will Federal Aid Improve the Equity of Our Taxing System for the Public Schools? In Chapter 5 it is shown that the property tax constitutes the largest single source of tax revenue for the public schools and that the property tax is the most inequitable of all of the major sources of the tax revenue of government. It is also shown that, due to the interlocking nature of our economic system, the wealthier states can shift a considerable portion of the incidence of their taxes to the least wealthy states. The income tax is the most equitable of all major types of taxes. The Federal government collects 95 per cent of all of the income taxes collected by all governments in the United States. The Federal government derives more than 81 per cent of its total tax revenue from income taxes. Furthermore, the Federal government can administer income taxes more efficiently and with fewer undesirable effects on the economy than the states. Therefore, substantial Federal educational appropriations will considerably improve the equity of the taxing system for the public schools.

The authors have encountered many arguments against Federal aid for education but have found no evidence showing that Federal aid is an unsound national policy. Is there any valid evidence that Federal aid is an unsound national policy?

What Is the National Educational Policy?

It has been said that we have a national educational policy that is negative. That is not quite true because numerous acts of Congress providing for grants of land and money for public education have contained clauses showing the national interest in education. The necessity of education for a democratic form of government has been recognized by national leaders from the beginning of our history as a nation. But an analysis of the acts of Congress providing Federal aid for education does not reveal any well defined educational policy. If it can be assumed that the national policy can be inferred from the acts passed by Congress providing Federal aid for education, then the Federal policy can be described as to repair or "shore up" education. The Federal government, despite its professed interest in education, has done but little to aid public education until some national crisis developed and it was suddenly discovered that the educational system was not adequate to meet national needs. At least that has been the national policy since 1862. The Morrill Act was passed during the Civil War, the Smith-Hughes Act was passed during World War I, numerous acts providing for emergency relief were passed during the 1930's, numerous acts shoring up educational programs were passed during World War II, and the National Defense Education Act of 1958 was passed during a period of national alarm over Russia's educational and scientific progress. To let things go and do nothing until there is a breakdown is a repair program. To take care of things in advance, according to plan prevents a breakdown and is a maintenance program. The Federal educational policy since 1862 has been a repair program rather than a maintenance program.

The Federal government could provide for the common defense and promote the general welfare more effectively by establishing an educational policy which would substitute a maintenance program for its present repair program. The Federal government will have a maintenance program for education when Congress appropriates sufficient general-purpose funds for public education, in addition to the amount of funds each state can raise by a reasonable state and local tax effort, to provide an adequate foundation program of education in every state.

What factors account for the failure of the Federal government to develop a sound educational policy?

How Should Federal Funds for Education Be Distributed?

The equalization basis involves the calculation of the cost of a defined program, the calculation of the amount of funds that can be raised by a prescribed uniform local effort [22] and the payment by the central government of the part of the cost of the program that can not be met from the prescribed local effort. The flat-grant method is the distribution of funds on a uniform basis with no allowance for differences in taxpaying ability. Bills have been before Congress proposing that Federal aid be distributed on the equalization basis, the flat-grant basis, and a combination of these bases.

The equalization basis is a sound method of distributing state funds as pointed out in Chapter 10. It is an equally sound method of distributing Federal funds for education. But the equalization method has one limitation as an exclusive method of distributing Federal funds. If all Federal funds were distributed on the equalization basis, a number of the more wealthy states would receive no funds unless the Federal appropriation were exceedingly large.

The advantages of central governments administering many non-property taxes and sharing the proceeds with local governments were emphasized in Chapter 5. This policy makes it possible to develop more equitable taxing systems. It is applicable to the Federal government as well as to state governments. Therefore, it would seem that methods of distributing Federal funds should incorporate both the principle of equalization and the principle of tax sharing of non-property taxes. For example, a Federal act providing general-purpose funds for the public schools should appropriate sufficient funds on an equalization basis to assure an adequate foundation program of education in every state and in addition should appropriate a substantial amount to be distributed to all states on the basis of the census of children 5–17 years of age. The per capita flat-grant should be included as a part of the guaranteed foundation program in the states receiving equalization aid.

---

[22] See Chapter 10 for a full explanation of the equalization or foundation program method of distributing school funds.

What techniques should be used in determining the cost of the foundation program of education supported by the Federal government?

Should Federal Funds Distributed To The States Be Administered By One Agency?

Experience with the administration of the Federal educational appropriations described in this chapter has shown that the best plan is to administer educational funds at the Federal level through the United States Office of Education and that the Office of Education should deal directly with the respective state education agencies and not with local school districts in distributing Federal funds. It is extremely confusing to the states to be compelled to deal with a number of different agencies at the Federal level concerning educational matters. The Office of Education is staffed with educational experts and they understand educational administration far better than the staff of any other Federal agency. The coordination and centralization of the administration of Federal educational funds distributed to the states will greatly improve the efficiency of the administration of those funds.

Federal agencies should not deal directly with local school districts. That procedure is likely to open the way to undesirable Federal controls. During the 1930's a number of independent Federal agencies dealt directly with local school districts. This sometimes created conflicts between state policy and Federal policy. The state education agency knows the needs and conditions of local school districts within that state much better than a Federal agency.

What educational funds now administered by non-educational Federal agencies should be administered by the United States Office of Education? Would there be any danger in providing that all educational funds distributed to the states be administered by one agency?

SELECTED REFERENCES

Allen, Hollis P., *The Federal Government and Education*. New York: McGraw-Hill Book Company, Inc., 1950.
Anderson, William, *The Nation and the States: Rivals or Partners?* Minneapolis: University of Minnesota Press, 1955.
Commission on Intergovernmental Relations, *A Report to the President for Transmittal to the Congress*. Washington, D.C.; U. S. Government Printing Office, 1955.

Educational Policies Commission and Problems and Policies Committee, *Source Book on Federal-State Relations in Education.* Washington, D.C.: National Education Association and American Council on Education, 1945.

————, *Federal-State Relations in Education.* Washington, D.C.: National Education Association and American Council on Education, 1947.

————, *Education and National Security.* Washington, D.C.: National Education Association and American Council on Education, 1951.

————, *Public Education and the Future of America.* Washington, D.C.: National Education Association and American Council on Education, 1955.

Edwards, Newton, *The Courts and the Public Schools,* rev. ed. Chicago: University of Chicago Press, 1955. Chapter I.

Hales, Dawson, *Federal Control of Public Education.* New York: Bureau of Publications, Teachers College, Columbia University, 1954.

Hutchins, Clayton D., Albert R. Munse, and Edna D. Booker, *Federal Funds for Education 1956–57 and 1957–58,* U. S. Department of Health, Education and Welfare, Office of Education. Washington, D.C.: U. S. Government Printing Office, 1959.

Morphet, Edgar L., Roe L. Johns, and Theodore L. Reller, *Educational Administration.* Englewood Cliffs, N.J.: Prentice-Hall, Inc., 1959. Chapter 8.

Quattlebaum, Charles A., *Federal Educational Activities and Educational Issues Before Congress,* Volumes I & II. Washington, D.C.: U. S. Government Printing Office, 1951.

Spurlock, Clark, *Education and the Supreme Court.* Urbana: University of Illinois Press, 1955.

CHAPTER FOURTEEN

The Development
and Administration
of the School Budget

The right of the people or their representatives to determine the purposes of government, the governmental services provided, the amounts expended for those services, and the taxes levied is closely associated with the development of popular government. That right is associated with many other rights, freedoms, and privileges enjoyed by people living under a democratic form of government. Therefore, the superintendent of schools and the board of education should not take budgetary procedures lightly.

BRIEF HISTORY OF BUDGET DEVELOPMENT

The modern term "the budget" has an interesting history because it also is associated with the development of popular government. The budgetary practices of governments in the United States had their origin in England. Whether the Parliament or the King had the right to levy taxes and to determine the purposes for which the tax proceeds were expended were major issues in the development of popular government in England.

As early as 1314, Parliament insisted that the King spend money for the purposes for which taxes had been levied. But it was not until the end of the seventeenth century that the Parliament wrested the power to levy taxes from the King.

The authority to make the budget was originally in the hands of the King and ministers appointed by him. After the Revolution of 1688 this authority was transferred to a cabinet theoretically responsible to Parliament but that policy did not become fully effective until after 1742. At that time it became the cabinet's responsibility to prepare the budget and present it to the House of Commons. Thus, it became the constitutional right of the people to control their finances through a popularly elected legislature.

The basic budgetary procedures developed by England are now followed in principle by all modern democratic countries. The budget is developed by the executive branch of government and presented to the legislative branch. The legislative branch of government approves the budget with such amendments as it deems wise and levies taxes to pay for the expenditures approved. The executive branch then administers the budget. This may seem like a very simple and natural arrangement. But it took hundreds of years for the people to wrest from ruling monarchs the authority to levy taxes and to determine governmental expenditures. The extent to which this right is recognized is considered to be one of the surest indications of the degree to which popular government has been developed in a county.[1] Therefore, the budget is not just a document containing a list of receipts and expenditures but it is a process by which the people in a democracy exercise their constitutional right to govern themselves.

Developments in the United States

The word budget is not mentioned in the Constitution of the United States. But it is clear that the framers of the Constitution intended that the basic principles of the English budgetary system be followed. Section 9 of Article I provided that "no Money shall be drawn from the Treasury, but in Consequence of Appropriations made by Law;" Section 8 of Article I gave Congress the exclusive power to levy taxes, and; Section 3 of Article II requires that the President "from time to time give to the Congress Information of the State of the Union, and recommend to their Consideration such Measures as he shall judge necessary and expedient; . . ." This provision with respect to the President was the constitutional origin of the President's budget message but its history is much older than our Constitution.

While the basic principles under democratic government for the proper allocation of authority with respect to the budget were recog-

---

[1] Henry C. Adams, *The Science of Finance* (New York: Henry Holt and Company, 1899), p. 109.

nized early in our history, it must not be assumed that modern budgetary procedures were practiced during those times. Actually, primary attention was given to the allocation of authority rather than to the improvement of government by budgetary procedures. Hamilton, as the first Secretary of the Treasury, tried to perform the services of a real finance minister by presenting a budget of all Federal services to Congress. But Congress was jealous of the executive branch and would not tolerate it. Gallatin also attempted to formulate plans for developing a budget which were broad in scope and purpose, but he was unsuccessful.[2]

It was not until 1920 that Congress passed the first bill providing for a national budget but it was vetoed by President Wilson. Almost the same bill passed Congress the following year. It was approved by President Harding and became law in 1921. That act laid the foundation for the present budgetary system of the Federal government.

Some states adopted budget systems before the Federal government but a number of states did not establish comprehensive budget systems until the 1930's.

Municipal Budgeting. Municipal governments and not the Federal or state governments took the lead in developing budgetary practices in the United States. In 1899 the National Municipal League drafted a model municipal corporation act that included proposals for a budget system under the direct supervision of the mayor. In 1906 the New York Bureau of Municipal Research was established. One of its first reports bore the title "Making a Municipal Budget." New York City soon adopted a municipal budget and became a laboratory in financial administration. The Bureau published the experiences of the city and aided greatly in spreading budgetary practices nation-wide.[3]

School Budgeting. Accurate historical information concerning the development of school budgeting is not available. However, it appears that the development of school budgeting paralleled the development of municipal budgeting. Municipal budgeting practices undoubtedly had a strong influence on the initiation of school budgeting. Twente made the first comprehensive study of budgetary practices in city school systems.[4] His study of 363 city school systems in 1921 showed a wide divergence in budgetary practices but that budgets of one type or another had become widespread by that time.

---

[2] W. F. Willoughby, *The National Budget System* (Baltimore: The Johns Hopkins Press, 1927), p. 5.
[3] Arthur E. Buck, *Public Budgeting* (New York: Harper and Brothers, 1929), p. 13.
[4] John W. Twente, *Budgetary Procedure for a Local School System* (Montpelier, Vt.: Capital City Press, 1922).

The following major aspects of school budgeting are presented in this chapter: (1) the purpose of the school budget, (2) principles or criteria for school budgeting, and (3) the budgetary process.

PURPOSE OF THE BUDGET

The purposes of the budget have evolved somewhat in accordance with changes in our concepts concerning the structure and role of government. When government was by unlimited monarchy, the budget was not an issue. There was only one branch of government, the administrative branch, and it was not accountable to the people or to any other branch of government.

Allocation of Authority

As democratic forms of government developed, monarchs were either overthrown or their powers limited. This involved the establishment of a legislative branch of government as well as an administrative branch. As soon as two branches of government were created, a struggle developed over their respective powers. The judicial branch of government probably was established originally to limit the powers of the executive branch primarily but as constitutional government developed, the judicial branch has also assumed limited powers over the legislative branch.

As pointed out above, the legislative branch was not satisfied with depriving the executive branch of the power to tax. It also won the power to determine the amount of money to be appropriated and the purposes for which it could be spent. This left the executive branch only the power to spend appropriated money for the purposes specified by the legislature. Thus, the first purpose of budgetary procedure was to provide for an appropriate allocation of authority between the executive and legislative branches of government.

Comprehensive View of Services

It must not be assumed that full agreement has been reached by the executive and legislative branches on the proper allocation of authority in fiscal matters. Jealousy of the executive branch has caused some legislative bodies to deprive themselves of the executive services necessary to develop a comprehensive fiscal plan. Such bodies have attempted to develop financing plans without counseling with the executive branch. The inevitable result was unbalanced fiscal plans resulting in over-appropriation for some governmental services and under-appropriation for others. The need for executive coordination became so apparent that most legislative bodies now require the executive branch to present to them a coordinated budget for their consideration. The purpose is to provide a comprehensive view of all services in order to make equitable provision for each service.

Estimates of Receipts and Expenditures

Another fiscal problem was the difficulty of obtaining accurate estimates of receipts and anticipated expenditures. When the appropriations exceeded the receipts during a given fiscal year, the result was a deficit. The evil effects of deficit financing have long been recognized. Therefore, it became an accepted purpose of budgeting procedures to provide an accurate forecast of anticipated receipts and expenditures over a definite period of time. For the Federal government this period is one year, for most states, two years, and for boards of education, one year.

Balancing Receipts and Expenditures

Problems of balancing expenditures with receipts developed two opposing points of view. When a budget is out of balance (that is, when proposed expenditures exceed anticipated receipts) it can be brought into balance by reducing expenditures, by increasing taxes, or by doing both. For some, the budget should be used to hold down governmental costs by reducing expenditures. According to this school of thought, the proper budgetary procedure is to ascertain what present taxes will yield and then hold the total of appropriations to the total of anticipated tax receipts. There are others who believe that when a budget is out of balance, the proper budgetary procedure is to increase taxes sufficiently to make the total tax receipts equal to the total of the projected expenditures. Neither of these two extreme points of view usually prevails, because in practice budgets in the United States are usually balanced both by increasing taxes and reducing proposed expenditures. Therefore, a purpose of budgetary procedures is to provide a basis for keeping revenues and expenditures in reasonable balance.

Basis for Accounting

Orderly fiscal administration is not feasible without an adequate system of financial accounting. Sound budgetary procedures cannot be developed without the aid of financial accounting. On the other hand, financial accounting without the aid of a budget is not of much benefit to management. As shown in Chapter 16, accounting is not merely a listing of receipts and expenditures in ledgers. Accounting makes it possible to ascertain whether funds have been expended in accordance with a plan for attaining the purposes for which the funds were provided. Therefore, an important purpose of the budget is to provide a basis for accounting.

Determining Quality and Quantity of Services Needed

During recent years an important purpose of budgetary procedures has been to provide a systematic plan for studying the quantity and quality of governmental services needed not only to survive but to maximize the rate of progress in improving the quality of living. As pointed out in Chapter 3, government is essential for survival. It is a necessary and important part of our economy. Conceptions as to what governmental services should be provided in the public sector of our economy and the quantity and quality of those services change with the times. Therefore, governmental services must be continuously appraised in terms of the needs of the people. The annual and biennial development of budgets provides a vehicle for facilitating this process. Efficient and necessary governmental services cannot be provided from appropriations based on haphazard guesses of costs.

The newer view is that the budget should start with a study of the services needed. Of course, the ability to finance needed services must also be given due consideration. But the ability to finance needed services is not fixed, nor does it have absolute control over the budget. No one has yet determined what proportion of our total national income should be spent for governmental services in order to maximize the quality of living. The evidence presented in Chapter 3 shows that we have much greater ability to finance governmental services than was formerly believed. Governmental services such as education increase the productivity of the private economy more than the cost of the original investment. Therefore, when this matter is considered from a national viewpoint, the educational budget should be determined by the educational services needed, not by abstract concepts of financial ability. If some school districts and some states must give greater emphasis to fiscal capacity than educational needs in determining their school budgets, it means that we have not yet developed adequate state and Federal plans to finance needed educational services.

A Plan for Attaining Purposes

The last purpose of budgetary procedures to evolve, and perhaps one of the most important, is to provide a plan for attaining the purposes of an institution or service. Burke defines a school budget as "a plan for attaining the purposes of the institution."[5] As shown above, budgetary procedures have many purposes. These purposes are all valid but if an institution or service does not attain the purposes for which it was designed, government is ineffective. Therefore, the institution or service should define its purposes before the budget is developed, and the budget should provide the fiscal plan necessary to attain those purposes.

PRINCIPLES OF SCHOOL BUDGETARY PROCEDURES

There have been a number of studies of school budgetary procedures during the past thirty-five years. Vosecky in 1957 made a comprehensive study of the recommendations contained in those studies. The recommendations on which there was consensus he summarized in the form of principles for appraising school budgetary practices. Following are the principles proposed by Vosecky:

1. The superintendent of schools should be responsible for the preparation of the budget document.
2. The budget document should be the result of the cooperative efforts of all who are concerned with the educational needs of the children and youth.
3. Budget preparation should be a continuous process, with the annual budget being a part of a long-range program.
4. The initial step in the preparation of the school budget should be the formulation of a definite educational plan.
5. The second step in budget construction should be the preparation of the spending plan, which is a translation of the educational plan into estimated costs.
6. The final step in the construction of the budget document should be the preparation of the financing or revenue plan.
7. It should be the responsibility of the superintendent of schools to present and interpret the school budget.
8. The budget should be adopted before the beginning of the fiscal year for which it is to serve, but only after the legislative body having power to adopt it has had ample time for analysis and review.
9. After its adoption, the budget should be accurately and carefully recorded in the official minutes of the body adopting it.
10. The administration of the budget should be the responsibility of the superintendent of schools.
11. There should be provisions for continuous appraisal of the budget document and the budgetary procedure.[6]

---

[5] Arvid J. Burke, *Financing Public Schools in the United States,* rev. ed. (New York: Harper & Brothers, 1957), p. 3.

[6] Eugene William Vosecky, *A Study of Budgetary Procedures in Selected East Tennessee County School Systems* (Unpublished doctors dissertation, University of Tennessee, 1957), pp. 60–119.

It might be argued that these are not principles but rather useful criteria to use in appraising school budgetary procedures. But whether principles or criteria, authorities on school finance and business administration are generally agreed that they constitute some valid guides for developing sound budgetary policies and procedures. These guides are discussed in connection with the description of school budgetary processes presented in the next part of this chapter.

SCHOOL BUDGETARY PROCESSES

School budgeting in well-managed school systems consists of a number of important processes. The most important school budgetary processes are:

(1) The determination of the purposes of the educational program
(2) The development of an educational plan to achieve the purposes agreed upon
(3) The preparation of a budget document to forecast the expenditures and revenue necessary to implement the educational plan during a stated period of time
(4) The presentation, consideration, and adoption of the budget
(5) The administration of the budget
(6) The appraisal of the budget

These processes are discussed in the following sections of this chapter.

Determination of the Purposes of the Educational Program

The importance of reaching agreement on the purposes of the educational program was emphasized in Chapters 1 and 2. There is no real basis for determining what educational services, facilities, and funds to provide unless at least some measure of agreement has been reached on the purposes of the educational program. A parallel issue is "who should be educated" because the range in the ability, age, and interests of the children, youth, and adults served determines to a large extent the breadth of the purposes of the educational program.

Much emphasis is given in modern educational literature to the desirability of providing opportunities for wide participation in the determination of policy. This is particularly important in determining educational policy. The educational policy of a school district directly and critically affects all parents having children in school. Educational policy has a profound influence on the economy and on the national welfare. Therefore, all citizens regardless of whether they have children in school have a vital interest in educational policy.

It is true that we have a representative democracy rather than a pure democracy. We are willing to delegate to our elected representatives in Congress and in state legislatures the authority to determine many governmental policies. But we have insisted on keeping the schools very close to the people. We do not want the Congress to determine the educational policies of a school district. We give our state legislatures the authority to determine some matters of educational policy but we also insist on a large measure of "home rule" in educational matters.

The Role of the Board of Education. Our local school government structure typically consists of an executive branch headed by a superintendent of schools and a legislative branch consisting in most cases of a board of education elected by the people. It might seem to foreign observers that since our government is a representative democracy, surely the people would trust the local board of education to determine educational policy. They do so in a great many matters, but as pointed out elsewhere in this book, some matters of educational policy are determined by referendum. Therefore, the trust given to the board is not unlimited.

Boards of education in the United States typically consist of from three to nine members. Individual citizens are not willing to detach themselves completely from the determination of educational policies and leave these matters exclusively to boards of education. Boards of education do not act for themselves but for the people. Therefore, we insist that meetings of the board be open to the public, that reports be made regularly to the people and that the records of the board be open to public inspection.

Most individual schools in the United States have parent-teacher associations. Thousands of special citizens' committees are engaged in the study of educational policies. Therefore, the superintendent and board of education who believe that it is their job to determine purposes, to develop the educational plan, or to make the school budget without consulting with the general public seem to be unaware of the cultural history of the people of the United States and the many battles that have been fought by the people to gain the right to govern themselves.

Providing Opportunities for Participation. The problem is, how can the people be given the opportunity to participate in developing the school budget? Obviously thousands of people cannot gather around one table and make entries of receipts and expenditures in a budget document. But the budget document reflects the educational policies that have been adopted either intelligently or unintelligently and either democratically or undemocratically. It is in the areas of determining who shall be educated, what shall be the purposes of the educational program, and what educational plans are necessary to attain the purposes agreed upon that opportunities can be provided for broad participation in developing the budget. Parent-teacher associations should be primarily concerned with these vital policy matters rather than with such trivialities as how to raise money to buy a curtain for the auditorium. During recent years thousands of special citizens committees have come into existence primarily to provide citizens with broader opportunities to participate in the determination of educational policies many of which directly affect the school budget.

The Climate for Participation. Probably the most difficult task of educational leadership is to create the climate and to provide the means and arrangements by which the people of a community can reach consensus on educational policy. Experience has shown that democratic government cannot succeed if consensus is attained blindly and unintelligently. We also know from the researches of social psychologists that consensus is not likely to be attained democratically unless people have the opportunity to interact in a climate of freedom. People who have not had much opportunity to participate in decision making and who have not had the advantage of good educational opportunities are likely to have only a limited concept of the possibilities of education. Their aspiration level is likely to be low because of lack of understanding and information. Even people who have had good educational opportunities are frequently confused concerning the purposes of education primarily because they have been largely isolated from the determination of educational policy.

There are many ways by which boards of education and superintendents can give citizens opportunities to participate in the development of the budget. A prerequisite for the success of any program involving wide participation in policy development is a favorable attitude on the part of the board, the superintendent, and principals. If it is apparent to the people that the board, the superintendent, and the principals welcome their participation, then the way to participation is opened. But if these officials are so jealous of their legal prerogatives or so insecure in their roles that they are fearful of the consequences of democratic procedures, then the way to participation is closed.

The Responsibility of the Superintendent and the Board. The superintendent and the board should take the initiative in opening the way for wide involvement of the people. Instead of resenting citizens committees that "pry into the board's affairs," the board should initiate citizens committees either by appointment or by developing plans for their appointment. Citizens committees, parent-teacher associations, civic groups or any group interested in school affairs should be encouraged to study educational policies and services. These groups should be supplied with all available information and if some needed information is not available, the administration should cooperate in obtaining it.

When the board is considering educational policy with respect to who should be educated, what should be the purposes of the educational program, and what educational plans are required to attain different purposes, or other policy matters of general interest, all interested groups and individuals should be invited to study these issues. The press, radio, television, published reports, and other means can be used to keep the public informed concerning school problems, conditions, and needs. Of course, any group should have the privilege of studying any educational issue at any time it desires to do so. But it is particularly desirable that citizens groups in cooperation with the school staff, have the opportunity to study a policy before the board takes final action.

Channels of communication should be provided so that study groups can present their findings to the board. It is recognized that the board has the legal responsibility of making the final decision on many matters and that all informal groups must act in an advisory capacity to the board. But the decisions reached by the board after the public has been furnished full information and after the public has had an adequate opportunity to discuss the issues under consideration are likely to be more acceptable to the public and better educationally. In other matters such as tax and bond elections and elections to select school board members, the people make the final decision.

How Lay Citizens and Teachers Can Participate. We are concerned at this point primarily with how the people can participate in the development of the budget. A superintendent of a school system with a total population of approximately 50,000 desired to give the public more opportunity to participate in the development of the budget. The superintendent and the board decided to hold public hearings on the budget at each school in the district in order to give the patrons of each school center an opportunity to study the school budget document. The first meeting at a school was well advertised by press and radio. Three lay persons other than the board appeared at the meeting. There was no greater success in getting people to attend the hearing at the next meeting. The plan was abandoned. Few people are interested in studying a statistical budget document.

Another board in another school system of about the same size announced that it was considering the advisability of establishing kindergartens. The board also invited parents to meet with the board at one of the schools in order to explore the problem. When the board arrived at the meeting, the auditorium was filled to capacity. Following an evening of general discussion, the board appointed a citizens committee to work with the professional staff in making an extensive study of the desirability and feasibility of establishing kindergartens. The committee, after considerable study and after meeting with parents at all elementary school centers, recommended that kindergartens be established. The board approved the recommendation. It required an increase in the tax rate that had to be submitted to the people. The increase in the tax rate was voted by an overwhelming majority.

These two cases are cited in order to illustrate the types of issues in which to involve people in the development of the school budget. The people are interested in educational services, the purposes of those services and how the purposes of the educational services can be attained rather than in the budget document. Therefore, people should be given the opportunity to participate in the processes of budget development in which they want to participate and can participate.

Determining the Educational Plan

It has already been pointed out that the budget should be based on an educational plan and that the educational plan should be developed to attain the educational purposes agreed upon. Therefore, the educational plan should be comprehensive in nature. It should include a statement of the purposes of the educational program. It should include both short-range and long-range plans for attaining the purposes of the program. It should present the quantity and quality of the educational services proposed. It should include alternatives and show the advantages and disadvantages of each alternative. The short-range plan for a fiscal year is more limited than the long-range plan. An alternative might be acceptable or at least expedient for one year but not acceptable for the long-range plan.

If the educational plan is to be useful in preparing the budget it must be specific enough in essential details that budget estimates can be prepared that reflect the educational plan adopted. Therefore, the plan should include specific information on such questions as the following:

1. Who should be educated? That is, will educational opportunities be limited to grades 1 to 12, or should the program include kindergartens, a junior college, and adult education opportunities?
2. What will be the probable enrollment in each age group or school program during the next five to ten years?

3. What additional sites, buildings, equipment and personnel will be needed during the next five to ten years?
4. For how many days during the year should the schools be kept open?
5. Should sufficient staff be employed to operate the schools during the summer months for enrichment and recreational purposes?
6. Should the school plants be planned to serve community purposes as well as the regularly organized school program?
7. What should be the pupil load per teacher?
8. What level of qualifications should be possessed by teachers?
9. What provisions should be made for exceptional children?
10. What provisions should be made for clinical and guidance services?
11. What provisions should be made for pupil transportation?
12. Should senior high schools be comprehensive high schools, or should special vocational schools be provided?
13. Should special teachers of art, music, and physical education be provided for elementary schools, or should elementary rooms be self-contained?
14. What variety of educational programs should be provided in junior and senior high schools?
15. Should a school lunch program be provided, and what should be its characteristics?
16. What health services should be provided by the school system? [7]

Other important items could be added to this list. Before a budget can be constructed which reflects the educational plan, decisions must be reached on matters of this kind. Each aspect of the educational plan should be developed as a policy. It should not be assumed, however, that the statement of the educational plan is simply a list of items. The statement should be broad enough in scope to present a picture of the total educational program and the purposes of that program but at the same time provide the specific information necessary for accurate budgeting.

After policies are adopted, many need not be reconsidered each year but there should be opportunity to do so.

The Preparation of the Budget Document

The budget document consists basically of the educational plan, the spending plan, and the financing plan. After the educational plan has been agreed upon, the superintendent and his staff should have the responsibility of preparing the budget document, because this step involves the translation of the educational plan into costs. If the plan is a part of the budget, the educational budget is a professional document rather than a financial balance sheet.

---

[7] Edgar L. Morphet, Roe L. Johns, and Theodore L. Reller, *Educational Administration* (Englewood Cliffs, N.J.: Prentice-Hall, Inc., 1959), pp. 440–441.

Reference has already been made in this chapter to an appropriate allocation of authority and responsibility between the executive and legislative branches of government. Experience with popular government generally has shown that when the legislative branch prepares the budget document, the result is usually an uncoordinated document that fails to present a comprehensive, balanced picture of governmental services needed. Therefore, the budget document should not be prepared by the board of education or by a finance committee of the board.

The Tentative Budget. The superintendent and his professional staff should not assume that the responsibility of preparing the budget document gives them the authority to determine the budget. That authority belongs to the board of education. Therefore, the superintendent should prepare the budget in tentative form. The tentative form of the budget should reflect the educational policies adopted by the board and, when no clear-cut policy has been established, should include various alternatives showing the estimated costs and the relative educational values of each alternative. Descriptions of these alternatives should identify the types of educational services proposed and the facilities necessary to provide the services. Different levels of quality of services and goods should also be presented. Unless the board and the public have the opportunity to consider different alternatives, they have no real basis on which they can give an intelligent approval of the budget.

Budget development is a continuous process. Preparation of the budget for the succeeding fiscal year should start at least at the beginning of the current fiscal year. Superintendents who do long-range budget planning actually start planning more than a year before the budget is adopted. Appropriate lay and professional committees should begin functioning when budget planning begins. The board and the public should be considering and reaching agreement on different alternatives throughout the year. Therefore, when the budget document is finally presented to the board, it should consist largely of agreements which have been reached previously.

Form of the Budget. The form of that part of the budget dealing with the spending plan and the financing plan will vary somewhat in different states and different districts depending upon the requirements of state law and the accounting system used by the districts. Following, however, are some generalizations concerning the content of the spending plan and the financing plan that are applicable to practically any school budget.

1. The estimates of receipts and expenditures should be listed in accordance with the revenue sources and expenditure account classifi-

cation of the accounting system used by the state and the district. This is necessary for proper budget administration.

2. The budget should present a comprehensive picture of anticipated receipts and expenditures from all funds. When the purposes of a particular fund are restricted, a separate budget must be made for that fund. For instance, a board may have a general fund which can be spent for any school purpose, a bond fund consisting of the proceeds of a bond sale, and a debt service fund consisting of the proceeds of a tax levied specifically to pay the debt service on bonds which have been issued. Separate budgets must be made for the bond fund and the debt service fund, but the consolidated budget should present a total picture of anticipated receipts and expenditures from all funds. Some special funds, of course, are necessary, but unnecessary earmarking of funds should be avoided. The difficulty of budgeting and accounting is greatly increased by a multiplicity of funds.

3. The budget should provide for a small contingent fund to provide for emergencies and inaccuracies in estimates. Most authorities suggest that the contingent fund need not exceed 2 per cent of the budget if estimates are made carefully.

4. The budget should provide for a reserve cash balance sufficient to care for operating expenses at the beginning of a fiscal year before receipts are available. This balance should not be considered as a surplus but as the operating balance necessary for the board to pay all bills on time without having to resort to short-term borrowing.

5. The data on receipts and expenditures should include at least the receipts and expenditures for the previous fiscal year, the budget for the current fiscal year, and the estimates for the succeeding fiscal year.

6. Some other types of information which should be included in the budget are: the assessed valuation; tax rates required; schedule of maturing indebtedness; salary schedules for different classes of personnel; trends in average daily attendance, enrollment, and educational load; trends in receipts and expenditures adjusted for differences in the purchasing power of the dollar; various types of unit cost analyses; appropriate data on comparable school systems; anticipated costs of additional educational services included in the proposed budget; estimated costs of needed educational services not included in the proposed budget; and any other type of information needed by the board and the public to make intelligent decisions concerning the budget.

The Performance Budget. If the budget consists exclusively of a formal statement of receipts and expenditures, the emphasis is on what is to be expended, not on what is to be achieved. Some authorities on school budgeting recommend a performance budget which includes a brief description of what is to be achieved after each item of expenditure.[8] This considerably increases the length of the budget but it provides some information by which individual items in the budget can be appraised. It should not be assumed that the performance budget is a substitute method of including the educational plan in the budget. The performance budget presents a somewhat atomized statement of the educational plan. Therefore, a definite, comprehensive statement of the educational plan is needed even if the performance budget is used.

It is not absolutely necessary to use a performance budget to show what is to be achieved. The supplementary material included in the budget should be presented in such form that emphasis is given to showing what is to be achieved. The various alternatives presented in the educational plan, for example, should indicate what can be achieved by each alternative.

The Budget Calendar. The processes recommended in preparing the budget require the making of many studies, the collection and interpretation of many types of statistical data, the projection of estimates, and the consideration by the board and the public of many alternatives. These things will not happen without planning. Therefore, the superintendent and his staff should develop a budget calendar at the beginning of the year. This calendar should include at least a schedule showing the responsibilities assigned to different persons and groups, the time when each type of information is due, the time for assembly of the budget document, the time for presenting the tentative budget and the time for final adoption.

Balancing the Budget

There has been much emphasis given in the press and in popular periodicals to "balancing the budget." The popular concept of balancing the budget is to juggle receipts and expenditures by addition and subtraction so that expenditures will not exceed receipts. If this is all that is involved in budgeting, any clerk who is competent to add and subtract should be able to balance the budget. This concept of the budget could be described as a balance with two pans, one for receipts and one for expenditures. The only problem is to balance two pans by shifting weights. What is to be accomplished is not in the picture or is a very small part of it. Those holding this concept of budgeting frequently do not even move a weight from one pan to the other. They start with the weights in the receipts pan as a fixed quantity and simply remove enough weights from the expenditures pan to balance the scales. The favorite motto of those following this procedure is "cut the suit to

[8] Henry H. Linn, editor, *School Business Administration* (New York: The Ronald Press Company, 1956), pp. 169–170.

fit the cloth." Their minds are closed to what is needed on the expenditures side.

The modern concept of a balanced school budget can be described as an equilateral triangle, the base of which is the educational plan, one side the spending plan and the other side the financing plan.[9] According to this concept, the educational plan must be balanced along with receipts and expenditures. If the educational plan is not balanced with educational needs, the school budget is not balanced even though expenditures may be made mathematically equal to or less than receipts. The authors accept this modern concept of school budgeting because educational needs never have been nor ever will be provided for adequately under the old concept of money balancing without regard to educational needs. When the authors use the term "the school budget" in this book, that term includes the educational plan as well as the spending and financing plans.

Presentation, Consideration, and Adoption of the Budget

As pointed out previously, the board should have the opportunity to consider various alternatives in the educational plan at different times throughout the year. Many decisions affecting the budget for the ensuing year will have been reached by the board long before the budget document is finally presented to the board. Therefore, the proposed budget is not "news" to board members when it is presented because they have been appropriately participating in the preparation of the budget throughout the year. Neither will it be news to the public if proper procedures have been followed in giving the public an opportunity to participate in the development of the budget. Publicity through newspapers, radio, television, reports, and other means should be given to various aspects of the school budget throughout the year. The publicity should emphasize what is achieved by the educational program as well as what it costs.

The superintendent should present the budget document to the board several weeks before the board finally adopts it. No board should be asked to adopt a budget the day it is presented. The superintendent should also present an oral interpretation of the proposed budget to the board and the public. Copies of the proposed budget should be made available to the mass media of communication and other interested groups and individuals.

Public Hearings. Opportunities for public hearings should be provided. These hearings usually mean little if there has not been broad

---

[9] Henry H. Linn, editor, *School Business Administration* (New York: The Ronald Press Company, 1956), p. 138.

participation in the development of the budget. Boards of education and superintendents who work in isolation in determining school policies usually have only a few persons present at a budget hearing. Those persons usually consist of representatives of a taxpayer's league, if one has been organized, and a few reporters for the mass media of communication. The majority of the people interested in the educational program do not attend budget hearings because they cannot participate effectively. Legal requirements for hearings do not assure effective hearings. The public hearings which are significant are the opportunities provided throughout the year for many lay and professional groups to study different elements of the educational program. It is only through this process that significant numbers of people can gain an understanding of the school budget and make their wishes known.

Approval of the Budget. The budget should be approved before the beginning of the fiscal year. This is impossible in some states because state appropriations in legislative years are not made until after the beginning of the school fiscal year. This is unfortunate because it prevents desirable advance planning.

As was pointed out in Chapter 8, the board of education should be given final authority to approve the budget. If another local governmental agency is given that authority, responsibility for the educational program is unnecessarily divided. The board of education is held responsible by the people for the educational program, therefore, the board should be given the final authority to approve its budget.

In some states, boards of education are required to submit their budgets to the state department of education for approval. This approval, if required, should become primarily a consulting service. It should be limited to checking the budget to see that it complies with the law and that estimates of state, Federal, and local revenues and anticipated expenditures are realistic. Neither the state department of education nor any other state agency should be given the authority to make decisions concerning the budget which should be made locally. However, the state department of education should provide local boards of education with appropriate consulting services in connection with budget development regardless of whether approval is required.

Administration of the Budget

The superintendent and his assistants are responsible for administering the budget. The administration of the budget involves: (1) the controlling of expenditures so that the educational plan is accomplished, (2) the development of work plans for each undertaking in the budget,

(3) the implementation of work plans. There must be centralized administration and coordination of the budget if the program envisioned in the budget becomes a reality. If various persons are given the authority to make expenditures without central control, the result is chaos. The budget is not intended to put a strait-jacket on educational expenditures, but if unrestricted spending is permitted for one item, sufficient funds will not be available for other items of expenditure. Therefore, expenditures must be controlled in order to keep the educational program in balance as well as to keep total receipts and expenditures in balance.

Budget Control. The budget should not be filed away and referred to only at infrequent intervals. If budget estimates are to serve as a guide they must be used constantly. Most authorities recommend that budget estimates be transferred immediately to the top of the appropriate columns in the account books. This makes it possible to observe the amount budgeted for each account without having to refer to a copy of the budget. It also serves as a reminder of the amount budgeted for each account as entries are made.

It must not be assumed, however, that proper budget controls are being exercised unless accrual accounting is used. If entries are made in an expenditure ledger only when payments are actually made, the balance available in the budget for a particular account cannot be ascertained by subtracting the total of payments to date from the amount budgeted. Under accrual accounting, as soon as contracts are let or purchase orders signed, the obligations so incurred are charged immediately to the affected account as encumbrances. When the corresponding bill is paid, the procedure is to credit the account with the original encumbrance and charge the final payment to it.

If accrual accounting is not used, it is necessary to keep a separate record of unpaid obligations against each account, add them to payments to date, and subtract the total from the amount budgeted in order to ascertain the unobligated balance in the budget for that item.

The superintendent should make a monthly financial report to the board which shows clearly the board's financial condition in relation to its budget. It is important for the board to be aware at all times of its operating condition. The board has no basis on which to approve budget amendments or even expenditures unless it knows its status with respect to its budget.

Work Plans. Work plans must be developed and put into operation for each undertaking in the budget. Buildings must be constructed, repaired, and operated; supplies, books, and equipment must be purchased and distributed; programs must be organized; persons must be employed; many other things must be done to carry on the educational program. Therefore, the superintendent should initiate procedures early in the year which result in the accomplishment of all planned undertakings. It is inefficient and destructive of morale when goods and services are not received at the time needed. Work plans should also take into consideration the flow of revenue available to the board. That is, payments should be scheduled so as to minimize short-term borrowing.

Work plans for administering the budget also involve the allocation of some budgeted accounts to individual schools and services. For example, a total sum may be budgeted for instructional supplies. If no plan is provided for budgeting by individual schools such items as instructional supplies, library books, and certain types of equipment, an over-aggressive principal may requisition a disproportionate share for his school. Many boards of education have provided budgets for individual schools that give the principal and his faculty considerable authority to determine within a given budget what items are most needed at that school. The funds are actually retained by the board, but the budget serves as a control on the requisitions submitted by a particular school.

Budgets for individual schools are usually determined by some type of objective formula such as a fixed amount per pupil in average daily attendance. Care should be exercised, however, in using objective formulas of this type. It is quite possible that the needs for different types of programs are different. The replacement needs for an old school plant are much greater than for a new plant. But the first-year outlay for library books and special equipment is much greater for a new school than an old school. If properly developed, individual school budgets aid in the administration of the budget.

When the budget is approved, the budget appropriation for each item constitutes authorization for making expenditures for that item up to the amount budgeted. In practice, however, boards usually require superintendents to refer major items of expenditure to them for approval before incurring the obligation.

Budget Amendments. Despite careful estimating, receipts may be more or less than estimated and needed expenditures for different budget accounts may also vary. Therefore, it is usually necessary to amend the budget from time to time during the year. If too much has been budgeted for one account and not enough for another, the board should have the authority to reduce the budget for the one account and increase it for the other provided the transfer is not made from a trust or special purpose fund to an unauthorized purpose. The board should also have the authority to use the contingent fund and unanticipated receipts to provide for account shortages. However, the board should not amend its budget so as to incur a deficit. A deficit should never be incurred except perhaps in a time of disaster. Continued deficits inevitably result in a financial breakdown of the school system.

The board should also be concerned if its balance at the close of a fiscal year is considerably less than at the close of the previous fiscal year. That means that the board spent more during the fiscal year than its revenue receipts. In the succeeding fiscal year, either revenue receipts must be increased or expenditures reduced if a deficit is to be avoided.

Appraisal of the Budget Document and Budgetary Procedures

The budget document should be appraised in terms of its purposes. Therefore, the budget document should be evaluated on the basis of the following criteria:

1. Does it provide for an appropriate allocation of responsibility and authority between the board of education and the superintendent?

2. Does it provide for relatively accurate, systematic estimates of receipts and expenditures?

3. Does it provide a comprehensive view of all services and make equitable provision for each service?

4. Does it provide a basis for keeping revenue and expenditures in reasonable balance?

5. Does it provide a basis for financial accounting?

6. Does it contain a statement of the educational plan and the purposes of the educational program?

7. Does it contain sufficient appropriate supplementary information to enable the board and the public to understand the budget?

Check lists such as the one developed by DeYoung [10] are also useful in checking the form and format of the budget document.

Appraisal of the budgetary processes is as important as appraisal of the budget document. A good budget document cannot be produced without the use of sound processes in its preparation and if the budget is not properly administered, the document is of little value. Some questions concerning budgetary processes which should be studied and used as a kind of check list are:

1. Has there been wide public participation in the study of the purposes of the educational program and the development of the educational plan?

---

[10] Chris A. DeYoung, *Budgeting in Public Schools* (Garden City, New York: Doubleday, Doran and Co., 1936), p. 474.

2. Is there wide agreement in the community concerning what the purposes of the educational program should be?

3. Is there wide agreement in the community concerning what the educational plan should be?

4. Have the superintendent and the board cooperated fully with all lay and professional groups making bona fide studies of the schools?

5. Have the superintendent and the board initiated lay participation in the development of the budget?

6. Has adequate publicity been given to the school budget during its development?

7. Has development of the school budget been a continuous process?

8. Has there been long-range planning as well as year-to-year planning?

9. Was a budget calendar prepared and has it been adequate?

10. Was the preliminary budget prepared in time for the board to receive it several weeks before it had to be adopted?

11. Did the board and the public have the opportunity to study alternate educational plans for different types of educational services and different levels of quality?

12. Did the board adopt the budget prior to the beginning of the fiscal year?

13. Were the budget items entered in the account books?

14. Was accrual accounting used for budget control?

15. Were work plans developed to implement the budget and were those plans adequate?

16. Were instructional supplies on hand when needed by the teachers?

17. Were requisitions handled without unnecessary delay at the central office?

18. Did the superintendent provide the board with monthly financial reports showing clearly the financial position of the board with respect to its budget?

19. Were needed amendments made to the budget and were those amendments made in accordance with the law and the policies of the board?

20. Was the budget administered with sufficient flexibility to make reasonable provision for changes in the requirements of educational activities?

21. Did the board avoid an operating deficit during the fiscal year?

22. Were the budget document and the budgetary processes evaluated during the year?

SOME PROBLEMS AND ISSUES

Some special problems and issues associated with budget development and administration are presented in this section.

Should Budget Appropriations Be Made in Great Detail?

If budget appropriations are made in lump sums for broad categories of expenditure, great flexibility is provided for administering the budget, and budget amendments are minimized. The flexibility may be so great, however, that the budget appropriations may not be very useful for accounting purposes. Furthermore, if too many items are covered under a lump-sum appropriation for a broad category, there may be over-spending for one item at the expense of another. This can be prevented only by providing a budget appropriation for each important item and regulating expenditures on all items in accordance with budget appropriations or as those appropriations may be amended.

If budget appropriations are made in great detail, there is usually less flexibility in budget administration, but expenditures may be more equitably distributed among all items of need. Therefore, the choice seems to be between maximum flexibility and minimum budget control and minimum flexibility and maximum budget control. In practice, a reasonable compromise must be made between these two alternatives.

Budget accounting is made easier if budget appropriations correspond with the accounting ledgers. If the budget appropriations are made in less detail than shown in the accounting ledgers, special provisions must be made for general budget accounting.

It is recognized that some special budget forms will be required, regardless of the detail of the general budget, if budgets for certain items are provided for individual schools. These special individual school budgets may be considered as synonymous with work plans for allocating certain items, such as instructional supplies, to individual schools. They need not complicate the monthly financial report which reconciles payments made and obligations incurred with budget appropriations.

A strict line item budget, administered under laws or regulations that make it difficult or impossible to transfer a surplus in a budget appropriation for one item to another item in which there is a deficit, is not good fiscal administration. The purpose of such a budget is to hold expenditures down rather than to make the budget an instrument for implementing the educational program. Strict line item budgeting is one of the worst types of earmarking. This type of budget is seldom found in the public schools but some states require strict line item budgets for state institutions.

Some boards of education give the superintendent the authority to transfer budget appropriations from one item to another within a broad budget category without securing a budget amendment. However, all transfers among major budget categories should be made by budget amendment approved by the board. This provision makes it possible to make budget appropriations in as much detail as the accounting system without unnecessarily restricting budget flexibility and it does give budget control over all important items of expenditure. What other criteria should be used to determine the detail of budget appropriations?

What Factors Have Retarded the Use of Good Budgetary Procedures?

Numerous surveys made by the authors and others show that only relatively few school systems in the United States use all or practically all of the practices and processes recommended in this chapter. All school systems of any size have some kind of a budget. But the budget document may range all the way from one page containing lump-sum estimates of receipts and expenditures to a comprehensive presentation of more than a hundred pages which details the educational plan, the spending plan, the financing plan, and a wealth of supplementary information useful in interpreting the budget. Very few budgets make any reference to the educational plan. Only a few budgets contain adequate supplementary information. A considerable number of school systems involve educational personnel other than the central office personnel in budget development. But only a few school systems involve a significant number of lay persons other than members of the board in budget development.

Good budgetary procedures have been known to the profession for a long time. Moehlman [11] in 1923 and Engelhardt and Engelhardt [12] in 1927 presented many of the elements of modern school budgeting. DeYoung in 1936 recommended budgetary practices far in advance of those generally followed almost a quarter of a century later. [13] Some

---

[11] A. B. Moehlman, "A Scientific Budget for City School Districts," *Twelfth Annual Proceedings*, National Association of School Business Officials (Kalamazoo: The Association, 1923), p. 139.

[12] N. L. Engelhardt and Fred Engelhardt, *Public School Business Administration* (New York: Bureau of Publications, Teachers College, Columbia University, 1927), Chapter 22.

[13] Chris A. DeYoung, *Budgeting in Public Schools* (New York: Doubleday, Doran and Company, Inc., 1936).

authorities have stated that it takes about fifty years from the time a good educational practice has been validated for it to come into general use. This seems unnecessarily long in a critical area such as school finance. No doubt constitutional and statutory limits on taxes have retarded budget development in some states. Unnecessary earmarking of state funds in some states has probably been a hindrance to good budgeting. The dependent fiscal status of some boards has certainly denied those boards the freedom necessary for good budgetary procedures. Many superintendents do not have an adequate number of assistants.

But the impression persists that the lack of a broad concept of budgetary processes on the part of superintendents and boards of education is the greatest single factor retarding the progress of budget development. Much emphasis is being given today to the improvement of educational leadership. The improvement of educational leadership in school budgeting procedures will quickly result in improved educational programs in many school districts. What are some other factors that are retarding school budget development? What budgetary processes are most likely to be neglected? Why?

How Should Increases in the School Budget Be Explained?

School budgets will increase annually in most school districts for many years in the future. The reasons for this were analyzed in Chapter 4. But there is constant public opposition to increases in the school budget although increases are inevitable. Therefore, the superintendent and the board should provide a full explanation of all budget increases. If school officials provide wide opportunities for lay citizens to participate in budget development, many persons will discover for themselves the reasons for increases in the budget. This is perhaps the best possible method for convincing lay persons of the necessity for budget increases. But many lay citizens have difficulty in locating the information necessary for evaluating budget increases and others do not know how to process and interpret data once they have found it.

The superintendent has ready access to all school records. He is a professionally trained person. He has or should have the competence necessary to locate, process and interpret data relating to school costs. Therefore, the superintendent and his staff should prepare for inclusion in the budget a complete and objective analysis of all proposed budget increases. The analysis of increases in costs should take into consideration at least the following factors:

1. Increases due to increases in school enrollment
2. Increases due to a decline in the purchasing power of the dollar
3. Increases due to adding new educational services

4. Increases for expanding existing special services
5. Increases for the purpose of improving quality
6. Increases in salary necessary for the board to compete with other employers for the quality of personnel required
7. Increases due to unusual capital outlays

Let us assume that a superintendent presents a $5,500,000 budget to his board which is $500,000 in excess of the budget for the previous year. This ten per cent increase in the budget should be fully explained in terms of the reasons listed above and other appropriate reasons. It is not sufficient to explain, for example, that salaries are being increased by 6 per cent.

Let us assume that the cost of living is increasing at the rate of 2 per cent per year as it did during the decade ending with 1959. Let us assume that the general economic productivity or standard of living is rising at the rate of 2 per cent per year as it did during the decade ending with 1959. Salaries need to be increased 2 per cent to provide for the declining purchasing power of the dollar and another 2 per cent for the salaries of school employees to keep pace with the general rise in the standard of living. Therefore, only a 2 per cent increase is actually available for increasing the quality of personnel. What other factors should be considered when budget increases are being analyzed? How can these best be interpreted?

SELECTED REFERENCES

Burke, Arvid J., *Financing Public Schools in the United States*, rev. ed. New York: Harper and Brothers, 1957. Chapters 1 and 2.

Burkhead, Jesse, *Government Budgeting*. New York: John Wiley and Sons, Inc., 1956.

DeYoung, Chris A., *Budgeting in Public Schools*. Garden City, N.Y.: Doubleday, Doran and Company, Inc., 1936.

Hagman, Harlan L., *The Administration of American Public Schools*. New York: McGraw-Hill Book Company, Inc., 1951. Chapter 15.

Hunt, Herold C., and Paul R. Pierce, *The Practice of School Administration*. Boston: Houghton Mifflin Company, 1958. Chapter 20.

Johns, R. L., and E. L. Morphet, editors, *Problems and Issues in Public School Finance*. New York: Bureau of Publications, Teachers College, Columbia University, 1952. Chapter 10.

Linn, Henry H., editor, *School Business Administration*. New York: The Ronald Press Company, 1956. Chapter 5.

Miller, Van, and Willard B. Spalding, *The Public Administration of American Schools*. 2nd ed., Yonkers-on-Hudson, N.Y.: World Book Company, 1958. Chapter 17.

Morphet, Edgar L., Roe L. Johns, and Theodore L. Reller, *Educational Administration*. Englewood Cliffs, N.J.: Prentice-Hall, Inc., 1959. Chapter 20.

Mort, Paul R., and Walter C. Reusser, *Public School Finance*. 2nd ed. New York: McGraw-Hill Book Company, Inc., 1951. Chapter 9.

Ovsiew, Leon, and William B. Castetter, *Budgeting for Better Schools*. Englewood Cliffs, N.J.: Prentice-Hall, Inc., 1960.

Shultz, William J., and C. Lowell Harriss, *American Public Finance*, 6th ed. Englewood Cliffs, N.J.: Prentice-Hall, Inc., 1954. Chapter 6.

Smithies, Arthur, *The Budgetary Process in the United States*. New York: McGraw-Hill Book Company, Inc., 1955.

CHAPTER FIFTEEN

Finance

and Personnel

Problems of finance in relationship to personnel probably challenge more of the attention and occupy more of the time, directly or indirectly, of local citizens, boards of education, and school officials than any other problem relating to schools. This is appropriate. The success of the educational program in any school system is largely determined by the competency and contributions of the personnel employed. But personnel who can develop and operate good schools do not materialize or operate on the basis of wishful thinking. There must, first of all, be sufficient funds to assure that adequate salaries can be paid. However, adequate financial support is only one essential element in the picture. The attitude toward schools and school personnel on the part of the community, the board, and the administration; policies established by state law and regulations of the board; the quality of leadership provided by the superintendent and his staff; the ways of working on school problems; and many other factors must be favorable if there is to be an adequate and effective program of education.

Expenditures for personnel (certificated and non-certificated) in most school systems constitute from 80 to 85 per cent of the funds expended for the current operation of the schools. Policies relating to the provision and expenditure of these funds largely determine the quality of education in the community. It is important, therefore, that not only boards of education and school officials but all citizens in each community recognize the significance of this fact and make every effort to assure that all conditions are favorable and conducive to a good program of education.

From time to time various school systems have found themselves confronted with an interesting and troublesome problem. If financial support has been so limited or personnel policies have been so unsatisfactory that the schools are not doing a good job, many people become dissatisfied and critical. This tends to make it difficult or impossible to obtain additional support. When inadequate funds are responsible for the difficulty, only exceptionally competent leadership on the part of the board, the citizens of the community, and the administrative staff, or the provision of additional funds from state sources, can establish a basis for resolving the dilemma. If, however, the difficulty has arisen largely because of unsatisfactory or inadequate personnel policies, it seems apparent that prompt, vigorous, and effective attention to the improvement of those policies should provide a satisfactory basis for improving the school program.

POLICIES RELATING TO PERSONNEL

Since this book is concerned primarily with finance it would be inappropriate to attempt to discuss personnel policies in detail. However, personnel policies have so many implications for finance, as well as for the educational program, that brief consideration of some of the essentials is important.

Policies relating to personnel may be stated in law, in local board regulations, and in administrative directives, or they may be unwritten and consequently somewhat intangible. Both the written and unwritten policies are important in every community. Written policies serve for guidance and must, of course, be observed until they are repealed or revised. The unwritten policies are often the most difficult with which to deal. They are expressed through the attitude of the people of the community, of the board, and of the administrative staff toward teachers and other employees. This attitude determines the climate or conditions under which school personnel have to work. It may indirectly affect, and in some cases determine, what is included and what is not included in written policy. If the attitude is favorable to schools and to school personnel, working conditions are likely to be better and morale much higher than if the attitude is one of distrust, suspicion, and criticism. In fact, the attitude of the people of the community may determine whether the funds provided for salaries, and the salaries paid, are adequate or inadequate, and even have a decided effect on whether these funds are used wisely or unwisely in terms of the personnel services provided.

Characteristics of Satisfactory Policies

Policies constitute an expression of the values the people of a state or community, the members of a board of education, and the superintendent attach to school personnel and their services. They are to some extent an expression of the philosophy or point of view and therefore are significant in determining the potential and the limitations. Good personnel policies should:

1. Make clear that the dignity and worth of individual members of the staff are to be recognized and respected in the operation of the educational program;

2. Provide for and encourage creativeness and originality on the part of all members of the staff;

3. Emphasize the importance of competency and quality in staff selection;

4. Encourage and provide opportunities for continuous improvement on the part of all members of the staff;

5. Assure adequate compensation, insofar as practicable, under a plan that will be recognized as fair and equitable by all concerned;

6. Recognize that the best possible working conditions for all staff members are necessary to facilitate development of a good program of education;

7. Be stated in written form sufficiently definite to be meaningful, but not so detailed or expressed in such a way as to restrict desirable initiative, and, of course, should be readily available for the guidance of all staff members;

8. Be developed with the cooperation and participation of appropriate staff members who are concerned with or will be affected by their implementation.

Development of Policy Statements

The procedure used in developing policies relating to personnel may be as significant as the policies themselves. If the board and superintendent do not respect the staff enough to seek their cooperation in preparing statements that are vital to morale and to the satisfactory functioning of the program, the staff sooner or later will become aware of that philosophy and this awareness is almost certain to affect their attitude and their work.

The procedure to be used in developing or in revising statements of policy relating to personnel should be very carefully thought through in every school system. Even these procedures should be worked out with the cooperation of the staff and, if that is done, the members of the staff will undoubtedly have an opportunity to participate in developing the policy statements. The citizens of the community should also be vitally interested in these policies. Many boards, therefore, have involved lay citizens, along with staff members, in the process of developing or revising policies to be proposed for adoption. Of course, in the final analysis, the board must adopt policies before they can become official, but the proposals should originate, or at least be worked through, with the staff members and perhaps with leading citizens, and should have their concurrence. This is essential if policies are to be satisfactorily implemented.

NEEDS, STANDARDS, AND ASSIGNMENTS

The number of persons to be employed and the standards or qualifications established for each of the various kinds of services and positions will largely determine the amount a school system must include in its budget for salaries. The policies established for the system will have a direct bearing on its ability to attract and retain people who have the desired qualifications. The policies and working conditions will be closely related to the issue as to whether the funds used for salaries will be utilized effectively—that is, whether a high quality and level of services will be provided by the persons serving in various positions.

Determining Need

The number of pupils or size of a school system is obviously related to the number of employees needed by the system. However, policies relating to the educational program and services also have a decided bearing. For example, a school system that, as a matter of policy or expediency, maintains classes averaging between 30 and 35 pupils will need considerably fewer teachers than a school system of the same size that has classes averaging between 25 and 30 pupils. If equal qualifications were maintained in the two systems, the cost of teachers' salaries would be considerably greater in the latter than in the former.

Whether systems provide or do not provide kindergartens, classes for exceptional children, vocational education, driver education, and other services, will be other factors that must be considered in determining the number of instructional employees needed.

The number of non-instructional personnel needed will also depend on policies relating to a number of matters. For example, if secretarial service is provided at each school, the number of secretarial employees in the schools will obviously be greater than if the need for this service is not recognized. A district that contracts for most of its repairs will need fewer district employees than one that has its own maintenance staff.

Thus each school system needs to study carefully the problem of staffing policy. Any system can find itself in a position of employing more or fewer people than are needed to provide effective services. The objective should be to study carefully all aspects of the program, determine the kind and quality of services needed for an effective program of education, establish policies that will assure adequate staffing, and use these policies for guidance in determining personnel needs.

Standards or Qualifications

Most school systems recognize, in theory, that all employees should be well qualified. Unfortunately, every year some districts employ a less well qualified superintendent than needed to provide educational leadership for the community and its schools, contract with teachers who are less competent than others who might have been obtained, or employ custodians and other non-certificated personnel who lack essential qualifications and consequently will not provide efficient service.

The absence of clearly stated policies regarding standards or qualifications for employees often leads to inefficient practices. A careful study to determine each kind of service needed, and to ascertain the competencies required if that service is to be provided satisfactorily, should be made periodically in every school system. On the basis of such studies, school systems can proceed to develop standards and qualifications for all positions ranging from that of assistant custodian to the position of superintendent of schools. Qualifications for positions will include factors such as age, kind and quality of preparation, nature of previous experience, character, and other important considerations. The qualifications established for each kind of position should be designed to assure that only persons who have the competencies deemed necessary will be considered for appointment. The objective, of course, should be to employ for each position the most competent person who can be located after diligent search and who seems to be best qualified to render the service required. The establishment of adequate minimum standards or qualifications will not in itself assure that the most competent person available will be selected for a position, but will provide a safeguard against the employment of people who are likely to render unsatisfactory service.

Administrative Policy

When sound personnel policies have been adopted, defensible procedures have been used in determining personnel needs, and adequate qualifications and standards have been established, the foundation has been laid for a good personnel program. However, the assumptions made and policies followed in administering the program may, in the final analysis, determine whether it is satisfactory or unsatisfactory—that is, whether or not it results in good schools. For example, if the administrator believes that new teachers should be assigned to schools or classrooms in the low socio-economic areas in which some of the more experienced prefer not to serve, or that teachers or principals who display originality or creativity are potentially disturbing elements in the school system, or if he periodically ignores the basic principles of human relations, he is almost certain to create personnel problems. This means, then, that the superintendent should be an excellent personnel administrator. His objective in assigning teachers, principals, and other staff members should be to place them in positions where they can serve most effectively and satisfactorily. His purpose in working with employees should be to stimulate and challenge them to make their maximum contribution. A major objective of the program should be to build a team of competent people who cooperate effectively in developing the best possible schools.

DETERMINATION OF SALARY POLICY

Salary policies constitute one important aspect of general personnel policies. There has been a decided tendency during the past quarter of a century for districts to develop written statements relating to salary policy. These are usually developed with the cooperation of the staff or through the joint efforts of representatives from the staff and citizens of the community. These groups, however, can only *recommend* salary policy, and the board may or may not approve the recommendation. However, when committees have done a good job of developing sound policies, the recommendations usually have been approved by the board without material alteration.

The purpose of salary policies is to give assurance to the community that sound procedures will be observed in compensating employees, to give assurance to the staff that recognized policies rather than haphazard procedures will be followed, and to provide guidance to the administrator and his staff in developing satisfactory procedures for obtaining and retaining the services of competent personnel.

There are, of course, a number of factors that need be considered in developing salary policies in any community. Among the most important are the following:

1. If minimum standards are established by the state, they, of course, must be observed. These standards may be reasonably adequate or may

424 FINANCE AND PERSONNEL

be entirely too low to be realistic. The state plan for apportioning funds to school districts may determine the extent to which, or whether, many districts can exceed those standards.

2. The local attitude toward education and toward salaries may limit the action the board can take. The prospects of developing adequate salary policies are much more encouraging in communities where people want good schools and recognize that adequate salaries are necessary than in communities where indifference or sharply divided opinion is the rule.

3. The supply of and demand for teachers tend to affect possibilities. During periods when teachers are in short supply many communities are more willing to establish adequate policies than at other times.

4. Economic trends have a bearing on possibilities. When prices are rising there may be more concern about adequate salaries and policies than when they are falling. Rising prices may also create concern because of increasing tax loads.

Suggested Policies

Suggestions for salary policies or schedules have been made in connection with a number of studies. The following are adapted from those proposed for teachers by the Winnetka Citizens Advisory Committee.[1]

The salary plan should: (1) meet reasonable competition for good beginning teachers without attempting to offer the highest starting salary, (2) assure dignified living standards for maturing personnel, (3) assure relief from hardship for heads of households, (4) contribute an uplifting influence to the dignity and prestige of teaching in the United States, (5) attract and hold teachers and principals of the highest quality, (6) stimulate increased graduate study through the Master's degree, (7) encourage study, research, and travel beyond the Master's degree, (8) provide adequate and dignified maximum salaries for those teachers for whom teaching is only a part of their career, (9) provide markedly distinguished salaries for those teachers who, in the tradition of the community, make substantial and measurable contributions to education in the district and in the United States, (10) provide a relatively long period for salary improvement before reaching maxima, but with safeguards against automatic advancement if a teacher's work is unsatisfactory, (11) provide annual increments of sufficient amount to be "felt," (12) contrary to long-established tradition, provide an

---

[1] *Report of the Winnetka Citizens Advisory Committee on Teacher Salaries* (Winnetka, Illinois: The Committee, 1958), pp. 12 and 13.

opportunity for teachers to achieve professional distinction and corresponding salary recognition without leaving teaching for administrative or supervisory office, (13) recognize any special economic factors in the community, (14) serve the long-term needs of the district, the board of education, and the faculty, and not be merely a temporizing, stopgap measure.

The Citizens Advisory Committee of San Diego included the following in its recommendations to the board concerning salary policies for the district: [2]

1. To determine the salary of an employee by reference to one of four pay schedules: (1) Teachers' Schedule, (2) Principals' Schedule, (3) Classified Employees' Schedule, and (4) Special Services Schedule;

2. To pay certificated personnel who are employed on an annual contract basis in ten, eleven, or twelve equal monthly payments, depending on the duration of the contract;

3. To place no employee on the schedule at a reduced rate in salary when the schedule for any category has been materially revised or a new schedule has been adopted, unless the entire schedule has been revised downward or his classification has been changed;

4. To allow employees leaves of absence on account of their own illness or a death within their immediate family, as prescribed by the Education Code or rules and regulations of the board;

5. To publish in written form the policies, rules, and procedures covering the payment of all employees in order to provide understanding of these provisions;

6. To provide for the periodic evaluation of salary policies and practices through the appointment of appropriate committees;

7. To adopt salary schedules that will assure that salaries paid teachers in the district compare favorably with averages in minimum-maximum salaries paid in other comparable school districts.

STATE PROVISIONS RELATING TO SALARIES

As previously pointed out, state laws and regulations may affect rather directly the salary provisions and possibilities in the various school districts in the state. If only limited funds for schools are provided from state sources, the salary possibilities in each school system will be determined chiefly by the willingness and the ability of the citizens in the district to provide funds for schools. In such states, sal-

[2] *Report of the Citizens Advisory Committee on Salary Policy to the Board of Education,* San Diego Unified School District (San Diego, California: The Committee, April, 1954; Mimeographed), pp. 3–5.

aries in the least wealthy districts may generally be expected to be much lower than those in the most wealthy. However, when an adequate and realistic foundation program has been established, all districts in the state, regardless of their wealth, should be in reasonably satisfactory position, unless restricted by other state laws, to develop fairly adequate salary schedules.

Many states, because of concern about this problem, have taken one step or another relating directly to salaries. Several have established state minimum salary schedules. West Virginia is supposed to have established the first state minimum salary law in 1882. By 1905, Indiana, Rhode Island, Pennsylvania, and North Dakota had enacted similar laws. By 1937, twenty had some kind of minimum salary legislation; by 1951 there were 31 (or 33 including Alaska and Hawaii).[3] Since that time the trend seems to have changed to some extent. A few states that previously had minimum salary schedules have taken steps either to discontinue the state schedule or to modify and simplify the schedule.

In general there are three types of state minimum salary laws relating to teachers: (1) those that provide a state minimum salary schedule recognizing both training and experience (some 17 states); (2) those that fix minimum salaries on the basis of two or more flat rates but with no recognition of experience (about 9 states); and (3) those that fix the minimum salary as a single flat amount (about 7 states).

Interest of states in minimum salary schedules first developed largely because salaries paid in some districts were obviously totally inadequate. Those who were concerned with the problem apparently assumed that if a state minimum salary schedule could be established by law the problem would be solved. However, it was soon discovered that many poor districts could not maintain a desirable pupil-teacher ratio or a satisfactory length of term and pay the minimum salaries required for all teachers. Since state laws in many cases require a certain minimum length of term, the only alternatives for these districts were to maintain only the minimum term, increase the number of pupils per teacher, employ only teachers with minimum training, and levy excessive taxes.

An illustration of the problem is provided in the analysis made by the Indiana School Study Commission in 1948,[4] noting that: (1) The number of units allotted for instructional personnel was considerably less than the number needed; consequently, all districts that were able to do so employed teachers in addition to those included in the state program. (2) The state was providing approximately 80 per cent of the

---

[3] National Education Association, Research Division, *State Minimum Salary Laws for Teachers, 1950–51* (Washington, D.C.: The Association, 1950).

[4] Indiana School Study Commission, *An Evaluation of the Indiana Public Schools* (Indianapolis: The Commission, 1949), pp. 387–403.

amount required in the salary schedule for an eight month term, and the less wealthy districts in many cases, which through necessity had undesirably large classes, were restricting their schools to an eight month term and were tending to avoid the employment of better trained teachers because they could not provide the additional local revenues to pay the salaries required.

The tendency in most states during recent years seems to be in the direction of attempting to develop an adequate and realistic plan for financing schools from state and local revenues. Progress in this direction facilitates the development of adequate salaries rather than minimum salaries as the basic salary policy.

LOCAL SALARIES AND SALARY SCHEDULES

The salaries teachers should receive, and the plan for paying these salaries, have involved much discussion in practically every community and state since schools were first established. Both still involve considerable controversy in many areas.

Salary Levels

Education and other governmental services, of course, are in a much different position from business and industry. If salaries of public employees are increased, the cost must be met through the proceeds of taxes levied on and paid by the citizens. Almost everyone watches taxes carefully. Many assume that the more money they pay for taxes the less they have for private use. However, as pointed out in an earlier chapter, certain governmental services, and particularly education, may contribute to the productivity and to the taxpaying ability of the people —a fact not commonly recognized. On the other hand, if salaries paid by business and industry are raised, the increases must come either from increased production per man hour or from profits, or be passed on to the consumer in price increases. There is very little the consumer can do directly about price increases for products he wants. Yet these increases may almost be equivalent to hidden taxes, from one point of view. The consumer has to pay them if he purchases the goods, whereas he, along with others, may have the means rather directly at hand to keep down or limit tax levies and price increases for public services.

For some reason many citizens fail to realize that, in a capitalistic society, the values people hold are reflected in part by the prices they are willing to pay for products and services. Thus, the salaries paid teachers in the various states and communities are always partly a reflection of economic conditions and partly an indication of the importance attached to education and teaching by the citizens.

The problem the American people are trying to resolve in this regard is: *How much should teachers and other school employees be paid to attract to the profession sufficient people with adequate competence and qualifications to provide the kind of schools and education needed in this country?* It is apparent that this problem has not been satisfactorily resolved. Salaries of teachers in particular have tended to lag behind those of equally well prepared people in business and industry. As a result, an insufficient proportion of highly competent people have been attracted to education, the schools have not accomplished as much as the people seem to expect, and many have been critical. These criticisms will be beneficial if they result in a re-orientation of the thinking of the people and the development of better perspectives regarding the significance and role of public education. They will be harmful if they result in decreased support and lowered morale.

Salary levels for teachers and other school employees have varied considerably, both among and within states. For example, an NEA study showed that approximately two per cent of the teachers employed in 1957 were paid under $2,000 and approximately two per cent received salaries of over $7,000. Slightly more than 16 per cent were paid less than $3,000, and approximately eight per cent had salaries greater than $6,000.[5]

The average salary of teachers in states such as California and New York, during recent years, has been nearly twice as high as the average in states such as Arkansas, Kentucky, and Mississippi.[6] This marked difference has made it possible for many of the states paying among the highest salaries (usually among the most wealthy states) to attract large numbers of teachers from those paying lowest salaries (usually among the least wealthy states). Similar conditions, of course, prevail within states in which there are wide ranges in average salaries paid teachers in the various districts.

The widest range in salaries tends to be found in those states with little state support and a large number of small districts. A somewhat smaller range is found in states with properly organized districts and a reasonably well developed foundation program plan of financial support.

Provisions for salaries also differ considerably among districts. For many years, salaries in most districts were negotiated with individual

---

[5] National Education Association, "Status of the American Public School Teacher," *Research Bulletin,* Vol. XXXV, No. 1 (February, 1957), p. 23.

[6] National Education Association, *Rankings of the States,* Research Division (Washington, D.C.: The Association, 1959), Table 23, p. 18.

employees. Districts commonly paid men more than women, high school teachers more than elementary teachers, and some individuals in each group more than others. Such hit-and-miss provisions led to dissatisfactions. As districts increased in size, the need for some better plan was recognized by all concerned. Within the last half century most school districts have developed salary plans or schedules for teachers based chiefly on training and experience, but many small districts have not. Many of the larger districts have also developed schedules for compensation of noncertificated employees, but smaller districts have lagged in this respect, also. Some districts have schedules for all members of the administrative and supervisory staff, but many do not. In most districts, the salary of the superintendent is still negotiated with the board, except districts generally try to keep somewhat in line with salaries paid in other districts comparable in size and wealth.

Some Trends in Developing Schedules

A salary schedule is simply a plan for compensating individual members of any group of employees, such as principals, teachers, secretaries, or custodians. This plan may be good or bad, satisfactory or unsatisfactory in whole or in part. According to Givens:

> Salary schedules for teachers are social inventions that have been developed by insight and ingenuity to meet the problems of personnel administration in the schools.[7]

A brief consideration of some of the trends in developing salary schedules should be helpful.

1. As previously indicated, there has been a distinct trend toward the development of salary schedules for all groups of school employees. It seems apparent that in the near future every school system in the nation should have some definite salary plan.

2. There has been a marked trend toward the establishment of single salary schedules for teachers. In the single salary schedule, the plan for paying salaries is based on the training and experience of the persons employed. There are no distinctions based on grade placement, sex or other similar factors. The single salary schedule in some cases applies also to junior college districts.[8]

3. For certain types of employees there has been considerable consideration of job evaluation as one basis for salary schedules and

---

[7] Willard E. Givens, "Analysis of Single Salary Schedules," National Education Association *Research Bulletin,* Vol. XXV, No. 3 (October, 1947), Foreword, p. 76.
[8] *Ibid.,* p. 77.

placement on schedules. This has been particularly evident in the development of schedules for non-certificated employees and to some extent has been considered in connection with schedules for administrative, supervisory, and certain other types of positions. In industry there have been many studies involving job evaluation, and according to Davis,

> Job evaluation is an accepted management practice which sets each job value into proper relation with each other, primarily for wage purposes. It provides what is usually called an *internal alignment* of jobs. This alignment is established by a scientific procedure which is sometimes considered to be so "objective" that most human relations conflicts over wages are removed.[9]

4. Cost and standard of living factors have been increasingly emphasized during the past few years. It is generally accepted that school employees must be able to maintain an adequate standard of living if they are to work effectively. It is evident, however, that the objective of salaries that will enable all employees to maintain an adequate standard of living has not been attained. For some years the Heller Committee has been making periodic studies of the budgets of salaried junior professional and executive workers and of wage earners in the San Francisco Bay area. The budget, in each case, was of a family comprising husband and wife, a boy of 13, and a girl of 8. The budgets reported for the year 1958 were $9,202 for the salaried junior professional and executive worker and his family, and $6,435 for the wage earner buying a home.[10]

5. For a number of years, minimum salaries provided in schedules gained more than maximum salaries. However, there is some indication that during the last few years maximum salaries are tending to increase as much as or at a somewhat higher rate than minimum salaries, thus tending to restore the balance that was upset by special cost-of-living and other adjustments resulting from post-war and other economic developments.

6. For a time the average number of increments included in schedules tended to increase slightly. However, during the past few years there has been a tendency, perhaps partly as a result of the trend toward more adequate minimum salaries noted above, to reduce slightly the number of increments. In a number of school systems there

---

[9] Keith Davis, *Human Relations in Business* (New York: McGraw-Hill Book Co., Inc., 1957), p. 309.

[10] The Heller Committee for Research in Social Economics, of the University of California, *Quantity and Cost Budgets for Two Income Levels: Prices for the San Francisco Bay Area, September, 1958* (Berkeley, California: The Committee, University of California, 1959).

has been an effort to provide maximum salaries in each category that are approximately twice those established as a minimum. Few systems, however, have been able to attain this objective.

7. The fact that proper preparation is essential for satisfactory teaching in modern society has become increasingly recognized. As a means of encouraging people to complete their college training before beginning to teach, as well as of providing an incentive for teachers who have not completed their college degrees to do so, the differential in salaries for the two groups has gradually been increased in a number of school systems. Many systems also recognize that there is a place and need for teachers who have experience and have completed preparation beyond the Master's degree; consequently there has been a tendency to add another column to the schedule. There has also been some tendency for the increments between the steps based on experience to be increased.

8. There has been a slight trend toward the consideration of factors other than training and experience, for teachers as well as for other groups of employees. For example, some systems have adopted or experimented with a plan for attempting to evaluate and recognize merit and provide special increments for merit. Others have made some provision for dependency allowances, and so on.

9. The length of service during the year for various school employees has been increased in many systems. Sometimes this has been accomplished by increasing the length of the term, and many times by providing for needed educational and other services during the summer months. Schedules in many systems thus provide for adjustments for length of service beyond the regular school year.

PROCEDURES IN DEVELOPING SCHEDULES

Since the success of a salary schedule plan depends largely on the satisfaction of those who are involved and concerned, the procedures used in preparing the plan are of considerable importance. When any changes are proposed, decisions must be made as to who initiates the process, who carries out the study, and who prepares the report. The initiative in bringing up the issue may rest with the teachers, with the board members, with the superintendent, or even, perhaps, with representative citizens of the community.

Kinds of Patterns

Three general kinds of patterns are recognized in developing proposals for salary schedule improvement. These are (1) the administration-sponsored plan, (2) the teacher-sponsored plan, and (3) the cooperatively-sponsored plan.[11] According to the National Education Association, most plans were administration-sponsored until comparatively recent years.[12]

In administration-sponsored plans, several procedures have been followed. In many districts, during earlier years, the board authorized work on the schedule, the superintendent and perhaps members of his staff did the work, and then he submitted the plan for approval by the board. In more recent years, many boards of education have appointed a citizens advisory committee or a teachers' committee to conduct the study and propose changes. Sometimes the board has engaged the services of a consultant or a group of consultants to conduct the study and propose improvements.

All the evidence indicates that there has been greater teacher participation in initiating improvements and drafting salary schedules during the past few years. In teacher-sponsored plans, the local association usually organizes a salary committee and this committee gathers the data, makes a study, and eventually develops a proposal for revising the schedule. After the proposal has been approved by the teachers' group it is presented to the board for action.

In cooperatively-sponsored plans, teachers and representatives from the administration usually meet together to consider the problem, plan and carry on the study. The committee that actually makes the study usually comprises representatives from the teachers' groups, the administration, and perhaps the board, and in many cases includes representative lay citizens.

As pointed out by Reller,

> This trend of wider participation is also supported by the view that in a democratic society the various parties involved in a matter should participate in working out basic policy decisions. This point of view requires that teachers, secretaries, and other personnel groups, as well as administrators and citizens, be represented in the development of schedules.[13]

There are many indications that the question of procedures to be used in developing salary schedules, whether for teachers or for other

[11] *A Study of Policies and Practices Related to Developing Salary Schedules for Teachers* (Berkeley: University of California, Department of Education, Field Service Center, and California Association of School Administrators, Area VI, October, 1958; Mimeographed), p. 6.

[12] National Education Association, Research Division, "The Preparation of Teachers' Salary Schedules," Part I, Administrative and Fact-Finding Procedures *Research Bulletin*, Vol. XIV (January, 1936), pp. 11–46.

[13] Theodore L. Reller, "Finance and Personnel," Chapter XI in *Problems and Issues in Public School Finance*, R. L. Johns and E. L. Morphet, editors (New York: Bureau of Publications, Teachers College, Columbia University, 1952), pp. 364–65.

school groups, is one of the most troublesome and controversial being faced in many school districts. It is certainly no longer satisfactory to most teachers for the board and the superintendent to make all decisions regarding policy without consulting them. This procedure is no more satisfactory to non-certificated personnel than to those who are certificated. However, it may be equally unsatisfactory, as far as the board members and perhaps the administration and citizens of the community are concerned, for teachers or non-certificated employees to develop their own salary proposals. If the salary proposals have been developed by any group of employees, the employees are likely to support their proposals regardless of whether they are realistic in terms of the economic situation of the community or of the position in which the board and the administration may be placed at that particular time.

Characteristics of Satisfactory Procedures

On the basis of commonly recognized principles of human relations and of operational procedures in a democracy, it would seem that the following are characteristics of satisfactory procedures:

1. Any group or individual may initiate a suggestion for a study or revision of a salary schedule. Obviously the board and the administration should not stand back and wait for employees to initiate the suggestion, nor should employees wait for the suggestion to come from the board or the administration.

2. In times of economic change all parties concerned should recognize the desirability of a periodic restudy of the situation. Perhaps such a restudy should be made annually as a matter of policy. The fact that a review of the situation has been undertaken does not mean that salary schedules should be revised annually. Another possibility would be to institute a restudy any time there has been a significant change in the cost of living or any time such a review is suggested by representatives from any of the groups concerned.

3. When a restudy is considered desirable (and it should be recognized as desirable any time such a study is seriously suggested by representatives of one or more of the groups most concerned) provision should be made promptly for the establishment of a committee to make the study. The policies for selecting this committee should be agreed upon in advance. Some members of the committee should be selected by the group whose salaries would be affected (for example, teachers or non-certificated employees), some by the administration, and perhaps some by the board. One or more board members might serve on the committee; however, there are some who believe that board mem-

bers should not actually serve on the committee but should feel free to attend all meetings.

4. Periodically, at least, representative lay citizens should be involved in the study of salary policy and salary schedules. They will generally be more concerned with basic policies than with details and therefore may not need to be involved in those aspects requiring consideration of some of the more technical problems.

5. Consultants should be brought in to help in planning, carrying out the study, or arriving at recommendations, when, after careful consideration, the committee decides that such consultants could be helpful. It would be a mistake to ignore or to refuse to consider the possibility of using consultants when there are serious difficulties within the committee or the community that might not otherwise be resolved. On the other hand, it would be an equally serious mistake to rely entirely on the consultants for the study and recommendations.

6. The objective of all who are involved in the salary committee should be (1) to review and reconsider policies to determine whether they are satisfactory or should be revised, (2) to proceed to gather all pertinent evidence which might have a bearing on the situation, and (3) to attempt to reach agreement on what would be most desirable.

7. When the study has been completed and a report prepared, the presentation should be made to the board by the committee. In the meantime, however, periodic progress reports should have been made so the board will be informed of all the major developments.

8. The objective of both the board and the committee should be to reach concurrence on what should and can be done in the way of improving the schedule for the ensuing year or years. It is always unfortunate when a committee takes the position that its proposal, which necessarily involves value judgments, must be accepted without change. It would be equally unfortunate if the board were to take the position that it is abdicating some of its responsibility unless it finds an opportunity to whittle down or to change some of the major proposals.

PROBLEMS RELATING TO SALARY SCHEDULES

Some of the more important problems that may arise in connection with the development of salary schedules are considered briefly below.

1. *In the schedule for teachers, and perhaps for administrators, what recognition should be given and what allowance made for training and experience?* Most schedules provide from four to six columns for training differentials and from six to 15 steps in the various columns for

experience differentials. In schedules for many districts there still needs to be a column for persons who have not completed their college work. The first regular column is generally devoted to those who hold an A.B. degree and are properly certificated. Most systems have a column for teachers who have completed from 16 to 18 hours above the A.B. degree; but some do not. Practically all have a separate column for those who have completed the Master's degree and are properly certificated. Many have another column for those who have completed from 16 to 18 hours above the Master's, and some have a column for persons who hold the Doctor's degree.

The experience steps are usually smaller in number for the less well-prepared teachers than for the others. Questions as to the differences in beginning salary to be established for each column, as well as to the differential for each year of experience, need to be carefully considered. Some school systems hold that greater increments or increases should be provided for experience during the first few years than after several years of service.

2. *Under what conditions should credit be given for additional college work, in-service training, travel, and other factors?* Some school systems have permitted teachers to receive credit toward salary increments for a wide variety of activities. Unquestionably these provisions have been abused in some cases. Every system, therefore, needs to have carefully developed policies regarding these matters.

3. *Should provisions be made in the salary plan for annual cost-of-living adjustments when necessary?* The question is quite controversial and needs to be resolved by every system. Perhaps one of the biggest obstacles arises from the dissatisfaction with the Consumer Price Index as a measure of cost-of-living changes for school personnel. Theoretically, if a satisfactory measure could be devised and if an adequate salary plan could be agreed upon and implemented, changes could be made periodically on the basis of adjustments in a cost-of-living index.

4. *How should the question of extra assignments be handled?* In practically every school system there are some people who have extra assignments either regularly or periodically. For example, custodians are frequently expected to serve for night or Saturday meetings; dramatics teachers have various productions at other than school hours for which they are responsible; and coaches have special duties on Saturdays, at nights, and at other times. The problem is complicated by the fact that many teachers—for example, English teachers—must spend extra time at nights and on weekends reading themes and grading papers, and this factor is not always recognized. Several systems provide at least nominal extra pay for extra duties. Other systems have attempted to work out adjustments in the program so the teacher who

has night or Saturday responsibility will be relieved insofar as possible for an equal time during the regular school day. Provisions are made by most school systems for extra compensation for necessary night and week end responsibilities when no relief in time or load can be provided during the day. All school systems attempt to provide proportionate extra compensation for persons employed for more than the regular school year.

5. *Should dependency allowances be established?* Studies show that in many school systems married men and other employees who have a heavy dependency responsibility have to supplement their pay by obtaining part-time jobs elsewhere. This is not satisfactory either for the person or for the school system. If the principle of equal pay for equal service is recognized, dependency allowances seem to be ruled out. If all salaries are adjusted upward in an effort to take care of those with a large number of dependents, the compensation for many may be greater than can be justified or provided on the basis of the economic condition of the community. A few school systems, following the pattern established by some of the Federal services, have provided dependency allowances. Some countries, such as France, have for some time had a plan providing for dependency allowances for all school employees.

6. *Should extra compensation be provided for persons who render superior service?* This question, frequently raised with reference to salaries of teachers, is one of the most controversial that has come up. For many years professional organizations tended to oppose any system of merit pay. Lay citizens generally, however, have insisted on some further consideration of the problem. During the past few years various plans of merit pay for teachers have been proposed and some have been adopted for use in a number of systems. The question obviously needs to be considered but cannot easily be resolved, as pointed out later in an issue dealing with this problem.

7. *Should salaries of administrators be related in any way to those for teachers?* Studies have shown that salaries of teachers have increased proportionately more rapidly than those for administrators. This may be an indication that teachers' salaries were relatively too low or merely that, as the cost of living increased, greater adjustments had to be made in salaries of teachers than in those of administrators, in order to make it possible for teachers to continue to serve in the profession. A number of school systems have tried during the past few years to establish some ratio plan for determining the amount of salaries that should be paid to administrators and supervisors. Others have developed rather arbitrary and sometimes expedient plans for determining what these salaries should be.

8. *When a new plan is adopted, how can the transition best be made from the old to the new schedule?* If the new schedule provides increments for all and makes no other change in columns and steps, there should be no problem of adjustment. Often, however, reclassifications result from the adoption of a new schedule. The plan generally followed is to provide that persons whose salaries would be decreased when the new schedule is developed are retained at their existing salaries. If any would have unusually great increases, provision might be made for the full adjustment to cover a two or three year period.

9. *How much credit should be given for experience in other school systems?* Practices in this regard vary considerably. The tendency during recent years has been for most districts to provide for recognition of some experience elsewhere. Many systems credit only half of the experience; others limit the credit to a designated number of years. Each system needs a guiding policy to assist in resolving problems in this area.

OTHER ECONOMIC BENEFITS

While salaries are important in establishing the basic economic position of each group of employees, the fact has been increasingly recognized that other benefits should have as careful consideration as salary policy. A policy that attempts to provide reasonably adequate salaries without considering other economic benefits or working conditions is not as satisfactory as a similar policy that places considerable emphasis on the other benefits.

For this reason most groups devote considerable attention to this problem. For example, the Winnetka Citizens Advisory Committee carefully considered what it called "supplemental employee benefits," and recommended a supplementary retirement plan, provisions for group life insurance, a comprehensive medical expense insurance program, and disability insurance. The report stated:

> With the establishment of these new employee benefit plans, the Winnetka school system will have policies comparable to modern industrial practice and well in advance of current educational practice. They should be of material aid in attracting and holding the quality personnel we need in Winnetka.[14]

While all the states now have retirement plans, either for teachers or including teachers and other employees, many of these plans are not realistic or adequate in the light of recent developments. Some of them limit the salaries that may be used in computing retirement benefits;

---

[14] *Report of the Winnetka Citizens Advisory Committee*, p. 51.

others fail to provide for survivors, and some are not on a very sound actuarial basis. Development of sound and adequate retirement provisions, perhaps supplemented by state provisions comparable to those for Social Security (see Chapter 18), seem to be essential in every state.

The provisions of workmen's compensation laws are applicable to teachers and other school employees in most states, as they should be. Although these seem to have been working out reasonably satisfactorily, improvements are needed in many states, and existing provisions should probably be supplemented by plans for group life, accident, and even liability insurance.

Practically all of the larger school systems have reasonably adequate provisions for certain kinds of leaves of absence. In some cases these provisions are state-wide. Usually sick leave may be taken without loss of compensation, up to a designated number of days per year, cumulative up to several months over a period of years. Many small school systems, however, have no provisions along this line, or have inadequate provisions. For example, in some cases teachers who have to be absent must pay the salaries of substitutes. Provisions for sabbatical leave are found in some of the larger but in practically none of the smaller systems. Perhaps some statewide sabbatical plan could help with this problem.

Assurance of reasonable security in employment has significant economic implications. Some states have gone so far in providing tenure for teachers that discharge of incompetent teachers seems unduly difficult and expensive. Others have no provisions for tenure or continuity of service, especially for smaller districts. It would seem that reasonable assurance that employees who are rendering effective service are not subject to loss of position at the mere whim of a board or superintendent should be expected in all states.

SOME PROBLEMS AND ISSUES

Although researchers have tried to establish objective criteria for salary schedules for more than half a century, it is generally conceded that these standards have not yet been determined. The size of our country and the social and cultural backgrounds represented make these criteria a complex task.[15]

As implied by this statement, indicated by the discussion in this chapter, and dramatized by many developments in the field, there are

[15] Margaret Stevenson, "What Is the Need? Not Merit Rating but Sound Personnel Policies," *NEA Journal,* Vol. 46, No. 6 (September, 1957), p. 13.

a great many unresolved problems and issues relating to personnel and finance. A few of the most controversial are discussed on the following pages.

Should "Collective Bargaining" Procedures Be Used in Determining Salaries for Teachers?

Some teachers take the position that they are, in reality, "workers" and that the board, and perhaps the superintendent, represent "management." These teachers apparently believe the only way they can get good salaries is to establish their own committee, make their own studies, and reach their own conclusions. They seem to feel that, in the meantime, the board and community should be kept in the dark as to what they are doing. When the study has been completed and the teachers have agreed upon what they think would be desirable, they insist on an opportunity to present their demands at a meeting of the board. If the board approves the proposal, the group is satisfied until the next year, when the same procedure may be followed again, except that the demands may be considerably increased. However, if the board should refuse to accept the proposal, the teachers are likely to take their case to the public and try to show that the board is unreasonable. They may even attempt to develop an organization to assure that some of the board members whose votes have been unfavorable will be defeated in the next election.

Procedures similar to these have sometimes resulted in unfortunate developments involving the schools. As a result of teacher-board controversies many people may get the impression that there is something wrong with the school system. Some may consider the teachers unreasonable; others may blame the board. Thus the community tends to be divided. However, some apparently believe this procedure has its advantages. They insist it tends to stimulate people to become better informed about their schools and, thus, may ultimately result in more adequate salaries than would otherwise be obtained.

In some cases this procedure seems to have been carried to an extreme. When the board has indicated that some increases might be made but that the resources will not permit all increases proposed, the teachers' committee has insisted that there be no compromises. If the administrator has seemed to side with the board in his analysis, the committee has, in some cases, attempted to hold him up before the community as a person who is unfavorable to teachers and thus to discredit him. A few teachers in some communities have insisted that they did not want common ground with either the superintendent or the board and that the only way they can make progress is to keep the superintendent and board on the defensive.

There are other communities in which the superintendent, board, and teachers seem to be making a sincere attempt to work together. Teachers recognize that the board has serious problems in attempting to assure adequate support for the schools without excessive tax levies, while the board grants that teachers' salaries have not been adequate. The board, the teachers, and the superintendent discuss periodically their common problems and attempt to develop procedures that will make it possible to arrive at a satisfactory solution. The procedures in studying salary schedules in these communities seem to have most of the characteristics suggested earlier in the chapter.

Many of those concerned would not question the desirability of "collective bargaining" procedures in other areas but doubt whether they should generally be used in determining teachers' salaries.

Are teachers justified in taking a "collective bargaining" attitude with reference to salaries? What about other employees? Should teachers and other employees take the position that there is common ground and that they should seek to discover it, or should they take the opposite position?

How Should Salaries of Administrative and Supervisory Staff Members Be Determined?

In some school systems the position is taken that administrators and supervisors are paid for their administrative competence and leadership qualities, and that these have no relationship to their preparation and experience as teachers. However, authorities point out that principals and others are leaders of teachers as well as administrators. Many hold that there should be some defensible relationship between salaries of teachers and those of administrators and supervisors. If the relationship that exists is accidental, it may be out of line. Administrators may be paid too much or too little in proportion to the salaries of teachers.

On the assumption that some relationship should exist, attempts have been made to devise a formula that can be used in developing a schedule for salaries of administrators and supervisors. Such a schedule probably would have the following characteristics:

1. It should use a ratio based on teachers' salaries, so that adjustments in one are automatically reflected in the other.

2. Allowance should be made both for additional time served and for additional responsibility.

3. There should be experience increments equal in number to about one half the number of steps in the teachers' schedule.

4. The level of training should be recognized as in teachers' schedules.[16]

The formula proposed and approved in principle by the Anchorage, Alaska, board is substantially as follows:

$$S = T [M + E (M \times R)],$$

where S = the *administrator's salary*

T = the *time ratio* between the regular school year for teachers and the length of the year for which administrators are employed.

M = the *maximum teachers' salary* in the column where the administrator would be placed on the basis of his professional preparation

E = the *experience ratio* for administrators and supervisors

R = the *responsibility ratio* for administrators and supervisors

Thus, if the length of term for which most teachers are employed is taken as 1.00, an extra percentage (for example, .025), based on careful calculations, should be added to the ratio for each week the administrator or supervisor serves beyond the regular term. This would be the *time ratio*.

In terms of the *experience ratio*, the administrative schedule might have six steps, the first represented by the ratio .50, the next, .60, and so on. More or fewer steps could, of course, be used if desirable.

The *responsibility ratios* would range from .01 to perhaps 1.00. Thus principals might be assigned a ratio on the basis of number of teachers in the school, responsibility, or a combination thereof, ranging from .10 to .50. The superintendent's responsibility might be 1.00, or in large school systems would probably be higher.

It might be desirable to spread over a period of time the salary advantage an administrator would gain at first, in moving from his place as a teacher on the schedule to that for a principal. Thus the above formula might be modified by subtracting from the formula as given the factor D, which would be the difference between the salary for the administrator's place on the teacher's schedule according to his training and experience, and M, or the maximum for that salary classification if he were a teacher. In still other communities, $\frac{D}{2}$ might be used

[16] Robert B. Howsam, Edgar L. Morphet, John G. Ross, *Proposed Salary Schedule for the Professional Staff of the Anchorage Independent School District* (Anchorage, Alaska: Board of Education, 1959; Mimeographed), p. 39.

instead of D. Other formulae have of course been proposed by other persons concerned with the problem.[17]

Should salaries of principals, supervisors, and other professional employees bear some agreed-upon ratio to salaries that would be paid those persons if they were serving as teachers? If so, what formula should be used?

A few years ago Haisley proposed a special formula for determining salaries of superintendents of schools. This formula was made up of six factors, including: (1) a base index number to be credited to superintendent, indicating a minimum status equal to that of a teacher at maximum salary, (2) a measure of the size of the school system in terms of the pupil membership, (3) size and responsibility of the job, represented by the number of teachers employed, (4) wealth of the community, (5) the amount of state and Federal money received by the local district, and (6) the personal qualifications of the superintendent.[18]

Should a formula be used in determining the salary of the superintendent of schools? If so, what would be a satisfactory formula?

What, if Any, Provision Should Be Made for "Merit" in Salary Schedules?

As pointed out in this chapter, many lay citizens insist that salaries of teachers should in some way be related to competence. When salary increases are proposed they frequently state they would be willing to see much higher salaries paid for the most competent teachers but that increasing salaries for all teachers would be equivalent to wasting a lot of money. They insist that industry has had and used successfully merit pay plans for a number of years and that these plans could readily be adapted for use by the schools.

Many teachers and administrators have tended to oppose merit pay. They call attention to the fact that merit pay plans are used only for certain types of positions in industry and that seniority is the major factor in determining salary for many other types of positions. They point out that most salary schedules in education are based on training and experience and that the training factor supplemented by experience is superior to the seniority factor alone. They moreover call attention to the difficulty of establishing any effective plan for determin-

---

[17] See for example Willard S. Ellsbree and John E. Phay, *Salary Study of the Sacramento City Unified School District* (Sacramento, California: City Teachers' Association, February, 1959, Mimeographed), pp. 31–35.

[18] Otto W. Haisley, "The Superintendent's Salary," *American School Board Journal*, Vol. 118, No. 2 (February, 1949), p. 35.

ing merit in teaching and point to the danger that subjective factors will enter into any merit rating plan. Davis states,

A merit wage system is primarily a procedure for one person to make subjective judgments about another, which means that it is fraught with human relations problems and is one of the most difficult of all personnel practices to administer. Its human problems cluster around the merit-increase philosophy, the rating process, and the use of rating data for merit increases.[19]

A recent University of California study led to the following conclusions:

(1) Industry, business and government do not pay employees on a merit program base to the extent which is sometimes assumed or to the extent claimed by some proponents of merit pay programs for teachers.

(2) The purposes and nature of the work situation in business and teaching have little in common.

(3) Large gaps in thinking must be bridged before common ground is found for those who are in one way or another interested in or involved in the merit-pay question.

(4) If the purpose of merit-pay is to raise the level of teaching performance, serious questions can be raised as to whether it alone holds much promise; if the purpose of merit-pay programs is to reward outstanding teachers, then consideration should be given to various possible ways of offering rewards.[20]

The report made several suggestions for school districts considering the merit-pay question, including: (1) establish the purposes of the proposed program and secure the acceptance of these purposes by the parties affected; (2) establish a committee representative of the various interested parties to study the question and then to develop proposals for the district in question; (3) provide essential resources for the committee, to make the necessary studies; (4) consider the relationships of any proposal to the basic teacher salary question in the district; (5) provide for a widespread review of various aspects of the proposal as they are developed; (6) regard any program adopted as highly tentative and provide for its review in the light of results; (7) consider and develop any program as but one element in an expanded program of improving conditions within the school system, recognizing that many factors affect teaching performance.

---

[19] Davis, *Human Relations in Business*, p. 317.
[20] Theodore L. Reller, Robert B. Howsam, and Richard B. Jones, *Merit Pay?— What Are the Issues?* (Berkeley: Field Service Center, Department of Education, University of California, 1957, Mimeographed), pp. 20–21.

The recent Utah School Merit Study concluded:

> The Committee is not ready to recommend any one merit salary program any more than it is ready to recommend any one evaluation procedure. However, as in the matter of evaluation, the Committee believes that experience and research both in and out of Utah suggest some guidelines for a sound approach.[21]

The Committee then proposed a "professional merit" salary program, based on training and experience, that provides for additional increments for "good performance growth," beginning at the end of five years, and another special increment, beginning at the end of seven years, for the "Master Professional" teacher showing excellent performance growth. At the end of any two years of decrease in performance on the part of any teacher, the salary increment would be decreased to its "good" or "regular" status.

In the light of all the discussions and developments connected with merit rating, should school systems attempt to incorporate the idea in their salary schedule? If the attempt is made, what are some of the difficulties? What steps can be taken toward resolving the problem of merit rating?

Should Adjustments in Salaries Be Made on the Basis of a Cost-of-Living Index?

Several school systems, such as Milwaukee, Duluth, and Stamford, have related salaries to the Consumer's Price Index. The idea has been proposed in a number of school systems and even has been considered by several states as a basis for determining the amount of the apportionment for salaries, or even for the foundation program.

Some of the arguments in favor of using a cost-of-living index to adjust salary amounts in a schedule are as follows:

1. Many discussions and controversies regarding salary adjustments could be avoided.

2. The use of an index would provide for an automatic plan for adjustments and would eliminate subjective factors.

3. Salaries would automatically increase or decrease as the cost of living increases or decreases.

Some of the points brought out in opposition to the use of the Consumer's Price Index, and perhaps by implication to the use of any index, are as follows:

---

[21] Utah School Merit Study Committee, *Utah School Merit Study* (Salt Lake City: The Committee, State Capitol, November, 1958), Report and Recommendations, p. 25.

1. The Consumer's Price Index does not necessarily mean that the cost of living is higher in one community than in another but merely shows the extent to which the cost of living has increased in each city for which an index is given.

2. The Consumer's Price Index does not reflect adequately the cost of living for a professional person because it is based largely on the needs of industrial workers.

3. Salaries for teachers and many other school employees in most school systems have not caught up with increases in salaries paid many other kinds of workers; and, consequently, if any cost-of-living index were tied to present salaries it would simply result in adjustment upward or downward of salaries that are already inadequate and would not provide for desirable improvements.

It has been suggested that before there is any attempt to use a cost-of-living index to adjust salaries, there should be more realistic and comprehensive studies of standards of living and of budget requirements for various standards of living. Perhaps studies such as those made by the Heller Committee might be extended to other groups and to other parts of the country as a basis for determining desirable salaries for teachers and other school employees. Perhaps another step should be to devise a cost-of-living index for professional people and to use this index instead of the Consumer's Price Index for determining adjustments in salaries of teachers.

In considering this issue, the fact should not be overlooked that the standard or level of living for all people in this country is increasing at the rate of about 2 per cent per year. This increase is largely a result of the increased productivity of the economy as pointed out in Chapter 3. Thus, the application of a cost-of-living index would not provide directly for teachers or other school employees to share in this increase in the productivity of the nation. It would appear, therefore, that even if salaries of teachers in any state and community were adequate and equitable, there would be a fundamental defect in using a cost-of-living index that corrects only for the changes in the purchasing power of the dollar.

How could a satisfactory cost-of-living index for teachers be determined? Would this be suitable for other school employees? How could corrections be made for increases in productivity? What, if any, procedures can be suggested for moving away from the necessity of the annual or periodic salary negotiations now found in many communities?

Are State Minimum Salary Schedules for Teachers Desirable?

As pointed out in this chapter, a number of states have adopted minimum salary schedules for teachers. Most teachers in those states would hesitate to see such schedules discontinued because of the fear that local boards would use for other purposes some of the funds that should be used for salaries, or would pay certain teachers disproportionately higher salaries at the expense of other teachers.

The points usually advanced in favor of state teachers' salary schedules include the following:

1. The state schedule establishes a general plan that should be followed by districts in providing salaries for teachers; that is, it assures higher salaries for teachers with better training and longer experience than for those with more limited training and experience.

2. It does not limit what boards can do in developing schedules, but sets a floor beyond which districts may go if they desire to do so.

3. The encouragement for salaries higher than the minimum will come from more wealthy districts that are in a position to pay higher salaries, and, in order to be competitive, the less wealthy districts will also have to pay higher salaries.

Those who oppose state schedules point out that:

1. No one yet knows the best answer to the problem of devising salary schedules. The fact that the state legislature or the state board of education approves a certain plan for minimum salaries based on training and experience tends to indicate that this is a good plan and that districts should follow the general pattern.

2. A state minimum salary schedule is meaningless for the more wealthy and more progressive districts and tends to become the maximum in many of the less wealthy districts.

3. Many districts that could do more than provided in the state minimum do not do so because they tend to accept the state minimum as a desirable schedule.

4. There are much better ways of assuring adequate salaries for teachers than through the establishment of a state minimum salary schedule, and these ways will not be explored as long as the state schedule is in effect.

Many states that have not adopted detailed schedules have established a minimum salary that must be paid any person employed as a teacher. In some states, certain groups of teachers have periodically sponsored proposals that would raise the minimum to approximately the maximum paid in the average district, on the assumption that this would result in improving all salaries. However, those who oppose such a step have pointed out that merely raising the minimum salary by law would not solve the problem of providing adequate financial support for salaries. Thus, if the minimum were too high, many local school systems would not be in a position to maintain present increments or to pay a desirable maximum for the most experienced teachers. The net result might be to cause those systems to raise the minimum to nearly the maximum and thus indirectly to penalize the more experienced teachers.

A few states have laws providing that a certain percentage of the amount included in the foundation program for each district must be used for salaries of instructional personnel. This obviously would not be realistic or equitable, if only because of variations in transportation costs. As a result, several states have excluded transportation and capital outlay provisions. Would this be a reasonable procedure for assuring that all districts would pay reasonably adequate salaries? Is any such guarantee necessary?

Suppose each state were to develop an adequate foundation program and give some assurance that necessary funds would be annually provided to finance the program in full. Would there be any need for the state to guarantee salaries? Would there be any danger that some districts would use too much money for other purposes? What safeguards, if any, are needed to assure that adequate salaries will be paid in all districts?

How Can Adequate Salaries for Noncertificated Personnel Be Assured?

Most of the attention in the laws and in the literature seems to have been given to the problem of assuring adequate salary schedules and salaries for teachers and other members of the instructional staff. Aside from the minimum wage laws that apply to all workers and in most cases have little significance for school personnel, there seems to be no provisions in most states requiring that certain funds be set aside or used for salaries of non-certificated personnel. In many cases there is no legal requirement that salary schedules be established for these personnel. Many believe that the relation between salaries of teachers and those of other school employees should be governed by the laws of supply and demand. Thus, if secretaries are in short supply, a school system should expect to pay as much for a competent secretary as for a competent teacher, or more. Others oppose this point of view and insist that the nature of the work and the preparation required by various kinds of employees should be the major factors in determining salary policy.

As a practical matter, most school systems will have to pay secretaries, custodians, and other personnel roughly the "going" wage in the community for such personnel. If the salaries authorized are too low, the schools cannot employ or retain competent people. Moreover, some of the employees in many communities belong to unions and there would be difficulties with the unions if salaries were too low.

Since principals, teachers, and non-certificated employees must work in close co-operation on a number of aspects of the school program, many believe that special steps should be taken in every school system to assure that each group understands the basis for and supports the general idea behind the salary schedules for other groups. For that reason, provisions are made in many salary studies for representatives from non-certificated employees to serve on teachers' salary schedule committees and for teachers to serve on committees to study schedules for other groups.

What procedures should be used by a school system in developing a satisfactory salary schedule for non-certificated employees? What are some of the factors to be considered? Should the same policies and principles be used in adjusting these schedules as in adjusting schedules for teachers?

SELECTED REFERENCES

American Association of School Administrators, *Staff Relations in Public Schools.* Thirty-third Yearbook. Washington, D.C.: The Association, 1955. Chapters 7 and 8.

Chandler, B. J., and Paul Petty, *Personnel Management in School Administration.* Yonkers, N.Y.: World Book Company, 1955. Chapters 8, 9, 12–14, and 17.

Davis, Keith, *Human Relations in Business.* New York: McGraw-Hill Book Company, Inc., 1957. Chapters 1–6, 17–18, and 24.

Elsbree, Willard S., and Edmund Reutter, *Staff Personnel in Public Schools.* Englewood Cliffs, N.J.: Prentice-Hall, Inc., 1954. Chapters 4–11, and 13.

Gauerke, Warren E., *Legal and Ethical Responsibilities of School Personnel.* Englewood Cliffs, N.J.: Prentice-Hall, Inc., 1959. Chapters 1–3.

Johns, R. L., and E. L. Morphet, editors, *Problems and Issues in Public School Finance.* New York: Bureau of Publications, Teachers College, Columbia University, 1952. Chapter XI.

Miller, Van, and Willard B. Spalding, *The Public Administration of American Schools,* 2nd ed. Yonkers-on-Hudson, N.Y.: World Book Company, 1958. Chapters 12, 13, and 17.

Moore, Harold E., and Newell B. Walters, *Personnel Administration in Education.* New York: Harper and Brothers, 1955. Chapters 3, 8, 10, and 12.

Morphet, Edgar L., Roe L. Johns, and Theodore L. Reller, *Educational Administration: Concepts, Practices, and Issues.* Englewood Cliffs, N.J.: Prentice-Hall, Inc., 1959. Chapter 16.

National Education Association, Research Division, *The Status of the American Public School Teacher.* Washington, D.C.: The Association. Research Bulletin, Vol. XXXV, No. 1, February, 1957.

Yeager, William A., *Administration of the Noninstructional Personnel and Services.* New York: Harper and Brothers, Publishers, 1959.

CHAPTER SIXTEEN

Financial
Accounting

No institution of any size, public or private, can operate effectively without adequate accounting services. The educational enterprise is one of the major activities of government. It is one of the major enterprises in every community, both in terms of the volume of financial transactions and in terms of the importance of the service.

School accounting can be classified in two broad categories: statistical and financial. Statistical accounting includes all quantitative information on the educational enterprise except financial data. Examples of statistical accounting are pupil accounting, personnel accounting, inventories—of textbooks, library books, supplies and equipment—and similar records. Statistical accounting is necessary for effective use of financial accounting as well as for other purposes.

We are concerned in this chapter only with financial accounting. While it is true that financial accounts record transactions involving only money, accounting procedures vitally affect the administration of the educational program and no program is better than its administration.

Most school administrators are not accountants, but they should know the function and general structure of an adequate school financial accounting system in order to be able to assure that it is properly organized and administered. Administrators must have this competency if they are able to provide proper leadership for the business administration of the schools.

450

Gregg [1] has described the administrative process in terms of the following seven components: (1) decision making, (2) planning, (3) organizing, (4) communicating, (5) influencing, (6) coordinating, (7) evaluating. Financial accounting directly or indirectly affects each of these components of the administrative process.

The financial accounting needs of school districts vary greatly due to size, state laws, and relationship to other units of local government. Some school systems keep accounts by hand, some by accounting machines, some by punched card machines, and some by combinations of these methods. No one system of accounting can be used by all school systems. Therefore emphasis is given in this chapter primarily to a description of the objectives and characteristics of financial accounting that are common to all systems rather than to the description of a system of accounting.

OBJECTIVES OF SCHOOL ACCOUNTING

Financial accounting is much more than bookkeeping. While budgeting, accounting, and reporting are different components of fiscal administration, they are so closely interrelated that each must be planned to be consistent with the other components. Financial accounting is not an end in itself. It is for the purpose of enabling business management to be of maximum service to the educational program. Following are some of the business management operations in which financial accounting plays a vital part:

1. Budgets must be prepared annually. The information furnished from accounting records is essential for budget development and administration.

2. Boards of education have financial dealings with other officials, institutions, and agencies. These include tax collectors, treasurers, depository banks, bonding companies, insurance companies, purchasers of securities issued by the board, retirement systems, state and Federal income tax collectors, county and municipal governing bodies, state agencies, and other boards of education. Financial records are essential for the orderly conduct of business with all these parties.

3. A method must be provided for authorizing expenditures. The approved budget itself is a general authorization for spending money. But budget controls are necessary and pre-audits of expenditures must be provided for. Pre-audits of expenditures cannot be made unless cash and accrual accounting records are available.

[1] Roald F. Campbell and Russell T. Gregg, *Administrative Behavior in Education* (New York: Harper and Brothers, 1957), p. 274.

4. In order for the schools to operate, purchases must be made and contracts must be let. Purchases include a wide variety of supplies, equipment, services, materials, real estate, and other items. Contracts are made for personnel services, building construction and repairs, insurance, loans, and for other transactions. Authorized procedures must be followed and forms developed for recording these transactions.

5. The board must pay for the obligations it has incurred. Therefore the board must develop procedures by which it can ascertain what it owes. Invoices must be checked to see that the board has received the goods it purchased and that it is paying the price agreed upon. The length of time worked by employees must be verified and the amount owed employees under contract determined. Buildings under construction must be inspected and the proportionate part of the contract due at a particular time determined.

6. The payments made by the board must be recorded systematically, and the records must show at least to whom or to what agency or organization the payment was made and for what purpose.

7. The board must have revenue if it is to pay its obligations, so revenue must be procured by local taxation, state and Federal appropriations, sale of property, insurance adjustments, loans, or other sources. These receipts must be systematically recorded by source and by the fund or purpose for which they can be used. Special fund accounts must also be kept in order to meet the requirements of law and to discharge trust obligations. Receipts may be for current purposes, for capital outlay, or for trust and agency purposes.

8. Many activities involving financial transactions are carried on at individual schools. These activities may be supported entirely from non-tax funds or only in part from tax funds. Some activities such as cafeteria operation are partly commercial in character. The board has responsibility for general supervision over all of these activities even though they may not be operated from the central office. The board and the superintendent cannot exercise supervision over these activities unless financial records are kept.

9. The board and its employees must be able to prove from the records that all funds have been faithfully accounted for and that no funds have been stolen, lost, or misused. Accounts will be audited; therefore the financial accounting system must provide the information essential for an adequate audit.

10. The board must make reports of its financial operations to the public. Therefore account classifications of the budget, the accounting system, and the financial reports should be consistent and appropriate.

11. Reports are made to the state, to the United States Office of Education and often to other agencies and organizations. Therefore the

accounting system must meet state requirements, and the information provided should be comparable with that provided by other school systems.

12. Business management policies need to be evaluated. Therefore the accounting system must provide the information necessary for appropriate research. Cost analyses are of particular importance in evaluating certain policies. For that reason the accounting system should lend itself to making the needed cost analyses. Financial economy and efficiency consistent with the implementation of the educational program are always desirable. The board cannot make decisions which result in real economy and efficiency unless it has the financial records and other types of records necessary to furnish essential information.[2]

The above list does not include all of the financial activities of the board but it gives some indication of the number and importance of the activities vitally dependent on financial accounting. It also indicates some objectives of school accounting.

THE DEVELOPMENT OF
SCHOOL FINANCIAL ACCOUNTING

School financial accounting has evolved from the fiscal operations of boards of education. Each accounting record should serve some useful purpose or it should be discarded. If some purpose related to business management is not being served by existing records, the accounting system should be expanded to include the needed additional records.

The financial accounting system should provide a complete history of all of the financial transactions of the board and should provide the information necessary to carry on the business management operations described in the preceding section of this chapter. An analysis of those operations shows that at least the following types of records are needed.

1. *A financial plan integrated with the educational plan.* This is the budget described in Chapter 14.

2. *Control accounts.* These are necessary for recording the board's financial transactions with other officials, institutions, and agencies and persons.

3. *Receipt accounts.* The board has many types of receipts from many different sources. The purposes for which different types of receipts may be used are frequently restricted. These accounts are neces-

---

[2] Adapted from Edgar L. Morphet, Roe L. Johns, and Theodore L. Reller, *Educational Administration* (Englewood Cliffs, N.J.: Prentice-Hall, Inc., 1959), pp. 448–449.

sary for budget administration and planni: 3 and for compliance with legal provisions concerning the use of different types of receipts.

4. *Expenditure accounts.* The board spends funds for many functions, objects, program areas, units, and activities. These accounts are necessary for budget administration and planning, analysis of expenditures and costs, and for compliance with legal provisions concerning the purposes for which school funds may be expended.

5. *Subsidiary accounts.* These accounts are necessary to record the financial transactions of special activities not recorded in the general receipt and expenditure accounts.

6. *Original documents.* Original documents are necessary for the substantiation of all ledger entries. The accounts of the board cannot be audited if original documents are not available.

7. *Financial reports.* The information contained in the accounts must be summarized periodically in an orderly manner in order to facilitate business administration and to provide reports to the board, to other agencies, and to the public.

Developing Uniformity in School Accounting

As public education developed, all school systems were compelled by necessity to establish some type of a financial accounting system. As school systems grew in size, it became necessary for all school systems with any considerable volume of financial transactions to establish all the types of financial records listed in the preceding paragraph. Sometimes the records were adequate and sometimes not. But a persistent problem was the lack of uniformity of the information provided by different school systems. Different definitions were frequently used for the same terms and widely different classifications were used for receipts and expenditures. Consequently it was impossible to obtain comparable information from different school systems within the same state or to compare the school financial statistics of one state with those of other states.

Almost one hundred years back in educational literature, references can be found to the need for comparable statistics but it was not until 1899 that a Committee of the National Education Association made some broad, general recommendations for uniformity in financial accounting.[3] That committee recommended that expenditures be classified as current, capital and other.

The National Committee on Uniform Records and Reports was organized in 1909. This was the first national committee to make an inten-

---

[3] Henry H. Linn, editor, *School Business Administration* (New York: Ronald Press Company, 1956), p. 178.

sive study of this problem. As a result of the work of the Committee, the U. S. Office of Education in 1913 published the first edition of Circular 204, "Financial Accounting for the Public Schools." It is interesting to note that in that same year the Comptroller of New York City in cooperation with the Bureau of Municipal Research published a "Handbook of Municipal Accounting." [4] Municipal accounting practices have undoubtedly had some influence on school financial accounting. But school operations are dissimilar to municipal operations in many respects. Therefore, it was inevitable that the two systems would differ as they were developed.

The work of one individual, Hiram C. Case, Chief, Statistics Division, New York State Department of Education, gave a tremendous impetus to developing uniformity in school accounting. He developed a handbook in 1916 for recording school expenditures which became known throughout the nation as the "Case Handbook." [5] It presented the first systematic and well organized method of recording school expenditures. Case worked in cooperation with representatives of the U. S. Office of Education, the National Association of School Accounting Officers,[6] and Teachers College, Columbia University to produce this handbook. The influence of the Case Handbook became nation-wide. Many states developed accounting handbooks using Case's work as a guide.

The United States Office of Education subsequently published many other circulars and bulletins promoting uniformity in statistical and accounting data. In 1957 the Office, in cooperation with the American Association of School Administrators, the Association of School Business Officials of the United States and Canada, the Council of Chief State School Officers, the Department of Rural Education of the National Education Association and the National School Boards Association developed and published a revised handbook on school accounting. The introduction to this handbook contains the following statement:

> Universal use of the standard accounts and terminology in this handbook will: (a) help to insure appropriate initial recording of financial data; (b) improve the accounting for school funds; (c) improve school budgeting; (d) establish a sound basis for cost accounting; (e) improve the accuracy of local, State, and national summaries; (f) facilitate comparisons of financial information among communities and among States; (g) enable local and State educational authorities to obtain more suit-

---

[4] *Ibid.*, p. 178.

[5] Hiram C. Case, *Handbook of Instructions for Recording Disbursements for School Purposes* (Albany, N.Y.: C. F. Williams and Sons, Inc., 1916).

[6] Now known as The Association of School Business Officials of the United States and Canada.

able needed information for policy determination; (h) improve the accuracy of educational research; and (i) facilitate and improve reliable reporting to the public on the condition and progress of education.[7]

Uniformity in financial accounting terminology and standard accounts has not been fully accomplished. But great progress has been made since the beginning of the century.

BASIC SCHOOL FINANCIAL ACCOUNTS AND RECORDS

Some of the basic school financial accounts are discussed in this section. School systems vary greatly in the accounts needed and the volume of transactions but all school accounting systems should be based on the same principles. The kind of forms used will depend upon whether accounts are kept by hand, by accounting machines, or by punched card machines; and upon the special needs of the school system. Therefore the functions of the basic accounts are emphasized in this chapter rather than the accounting forms.

Budget Accounting

Some aspects of budget accounting have been discussed in Chapter 14. The budget is probably the most important document of the accounting system. It provides a plan for coordinating all financial operations.

If the spending of the board is in accordance with the spending plan and the financing plan contained in the budget, the accounting system must provide at all times the information necessary to ascertain (1) the amount of revenue received to date and the amount receivable by the end of the fiscal year, (2) the payments made to date for each budget appropriation and the amount for which each budget appropriation is obligated or encumbered and, (3) the true balance in each budget account.

There are three principal bases of accounting: (1) cash, (2) accrual, and (3) modified accrual.

Under the cash basis of accounting, revenues are recorded only when actually received, and expenditures only when cash payments are actually made.

---

[7] Paul L. Reason and Alpheus L. White, *Financial Accounting for State and Local School Systems*, U. S. Department of Health, Education and Welfare, Office of Education (Washington, D.C.: U. S. Government Printing Office, 1957), p. XVI.

Accrual Accounting. Under the accrual basis, revenues are recorded when earned or when levies are made regardless of when revenue is actually received, and expenditures are recorded as soon as they result in a liability regardless of when the payment is actually made.

Under the modified accrual basis, revenues are usually recorded on a cash basis and expenditures on the accrual basis.

Accrual accounting requires more labor and more space on accounting forms than cash accounting but it provides much more information. For example, four columns are normally required for accrual accounting of an expenditure item for which there is a budget appropriation. One column is needed for each of the following: (1) budget appropriation, (2) encumbrances, (3) payments, (4) unencumbered balance.[8]

When the books are opened, the budget appropriation for the expenditure item is recorded. When a purchase order is signed or a contract approved, the amount is entered in the encumbrance column. When payment is made, the amount is charged to the payment column and the amount of the original encumbrance is credited to encumbrances. The unencumbered balance in the budget appropriation at any time is the difference between the budget appropriation and the sum of payments plus net encumbrances.

This type of accounting can be done by hand but much labor can be saved by the use of accounting or punched card machines. When the original documents for an expenditure are processed, a voucher jacket or cover sheet with appropriate coding can be used for posting by an accounting machine or for punching the cards necessary for posting by a tabulator printing machine.

If cash accounting only is used for expenditures, separate accounts must be kept of encumbrances if the real balance in a budget appropriation is ascertainable. If these records are kept accurately and up-to-date more labor is probably required than under accrual accounting because it is necessary to consult two separate records in order to ascertain the balance in the budget appropriation.

Fund Accounting

A fund is defined as a sum of money which must be spent for specific activities, objects or purposes. It is a separate entity and the receipts and expenditures and other financial transactions of a fund must be accounted for separately. Examples that are common to most school systems are the general fund, the bond fund, and the sinking fund for

---

[8] Some accounting machines utilize six columns: (1) budget appropriation, (2) encumbrances, (3) net encumbrances, (4) payments, (5) net encumbrances plus payments, (6) unencumbered balance.

debt service. But there may be special funds for such limited purposes as teachers' salaries, buildings, transportation, library books, guidance services, and similar items. The number of funds should be kept to the minimum, consistent with good business management practices. Numerous special funds complicate accounting, restrict the flexibility of budgeting, and sometimes get the educational program out of balance. As pointed out in Chapter 12, some states make school appropriations in the form of a number of special appropriations with restricted purposes. This creates unnecessary fund accounting.

Differences Between School Accounting and Commercial Accounting. The common practice is to keep a general ledger of receipts and disbursements and a depository ledger for each school fund. School accounting uses double entry bookkeeping in a limited sense because each entry in the receipt ledger is debited to the depository account and each entry in the expenditure ledger is credited to the depository account. But the full accrual, double entry bookkeeping which is so useful in industry and business is not fully adaptable to school financial accounting. The purpose of industrial and business bookkeeping is to produce a balance sheet of assets and liabilities in order to show profit and loss over a given period of time. The purposes of school financial accounting do not generally include the production of profit and loss statements. The exception is the commercial aspect of the operation of a school farm or a school cafeteria. Double entry commercial bookkeeping can be adapted to enterprises of that type.

Accountants not familiar with school operations sometimes recommend that schools use the full accrual double entry type of bookkeeping used by industry and business. If this is done the result is usually confusion and unnecessary labor without the production of additional information actually needed by the school administrator.

Control Accounts

Control accounts [9] are necessary (1) for reconciling the records of the board with the records of other officials, institutions, agencies, and persons with whom the board does business (2) for reconciliation with receipts and expenditures ledgers, and (3) for property control. The control accounts for funds include the treasurer's accounts, depository accounts, check registers for payrolls, check registers for vouchers, and periodical summaries of cash. Debt records should include accounts payable and records of long and short term obligations. Capital records

---

[9] Sometimes called general accounts or books of original entry.

should be kept of stores, furniture, and equipment, real estate, and plant structures.[10] Receipts records should provide detailed information concerning the status at all times of taxes levied and taxes collected and of all other types of revenue and non-revenue receipts.

The kinds of control accounts and records kept by board of education employees and by the employees of other local governments vary from state to state. But employees of the board of education should either keep or have easy access to all of the control accounts necessary for efficient business administration.

Receipt Accounting

Detailed information is needed for all types of receipts. That type of information cannot be obtained from depository ledgers, therefore a receipts ledger should be kept for this purpose. The receipts accounts should show for each receipt: (1) whether it is revenue or non-revenue, (2) the source, and (3) the fund to which it should be deposited.

Revenue receipts are "additions to assets which do not incur an obligation that must be met at some future date and do not represent exchanges of property for money." [11] Examples are income from taxes, state appropriations and interest on deposits.

Non-revenue receipts are "amounts received which either incur an obligation that must be met at some future date or change the form of an asset from property to cash and therefore decrease the amount and value of school property." [12] Examples are money received from sale of bonds, sale of property and insurance adjustments.

The United States Office of Education has proposed the following classification of basic receipt accounts:

Basic Receipt Accounts

REVENUE RECEIPTS

10–40 Series

10. REVENUE FROM LOCAL SOURCES
    11. TAXATION AND APPROPRIATIONS RECEIVED
        11-a. Taxes Received from School District Levies
            11-a-1. Property taxes
            11-a-2. Non-property taxes

---

[10] Linn, *School Business Administration*, p. 189.
[11] Paul L. Reason and Alpheus L. White, *Financial Accounting for State and Local School Systems*, U. S. Department of Health, Education and Welfare, Office of Education (Washington, D.C.: U. S. Government Printing Office, 1957), p. 230.
[12] *Ibid.*, p. 230.

Basic Receipt Accounts—Cont.

11-b.   Taxes Received from Local Governmental Units Other than School Districts

    11-b-1.   Property taxes

    11-b-2.   Non-property taxes

11-c.   Appropriations Received from Local Governmental Units Other than School Districts

12.   TUITION FROM PATRONS

    12-a.   Regular Day Schools

    12-b.   Adult Education

    12-c.   Other Tuition from Patrons

13.   TRANSPORTATION FEES FROM PATRONS

14.   OTHER REVENUE FROM LOCAL SOURCES

    14-a.   Earnings from Permanent Funds and Endowments

    14-b.   Earnings from Temporary Deposits and Investments

    14-c.   Net Receipts from Revolving Funds or Clearing Accounts

    14-d.   Rent from School Facilities

    14-e.   Rent from Property Other than School Facilities

    14-f.   Gifts and Bequests

    14-g.   Miscellaneous Revenue from Local Sources

20.   REVENUE FROM INTERMEDIATE SOURCES

30.   REVENUE FROM STATE SOURCES

    30-a.   State

    30-b.   Federal Money Received through the State

40.   REVENUE FROM FEDERAL SOURCES

NON-REVENUE RECEIPTS

50–70 Series

50.   SALE OF BONDS

60.   LOANS

    60-a.   Short-term *

    60-b.   Long-term

70.   SALE OF SCHOOL PROPERTY AND INSURANCE ADJUSTMENTS

    70-a.   Sale of Real Property

    70-b.   Sale of Equipment

    70-c.   Net Insurance Recovery

INCOMING TRANSFER ACCOUNTS

80–90 Series

80.   AMOUNTS RECEIVED FROM OTHER SCHOOL DISTRICTS IN THE STATE

    80-a.   Tuition

    80-b.   Transportation

    80-c.   Miscellaneous

90.   AMOUNTS RECEIVED FROM SCHOOL DISTRICTS IN ANOTHER STATE

    90-a.   Tuition

    90-b.   Transportation

    90-c.   Miscellaneous [13]

* Payable within five years but not payable before the end of the current fiscal year.

---

[13] *Ibid.*, pp. 6–7.

It will be noted that the receipt accounts are coded. Coding of accounts reduces the labor of accounting and aids in systematizing record keeping. Each state or local school district can develop its own coding system. But the code numbers used in the accounts should be the same as those used in the budget document.

The uniform classification of receipts throughout the nation will greatly facilitate the production of comparable information from all state and local school systems.

Expenditure Accounting

Expenditures can be classified in many ways. The broadest way to classify expenditures is by current transactions and capital transactions. Current transactions, commonly called current expense, is the total of all expenditures made during a given period of time except expenditures for capital outlay and debt service.

Capital outlay is defined as "An expenditure which results in the acquisition of fixed assets or additions to fixed assets. It is an expenditure for land or existing buildings, improvement of grounds, construction of buildings, additions to buildings, remodeling of buildings, or initial or additional equipment. It includes installment or lease payments on property (except interest) which have a terminal date and result in the acquisition of property." [14]

Debt service is defined as "Expenditures for the retirement of debt and expenditures for interest on debt, except principal and interest of current loans." [15] In well-managed school systems, debt service payments are made only to retire debt incurred for capital outlay purposes. Therefore expenditures for capital outlay and debt service can both be considered capital transactions. As pointed out previously, loans to pay for current expense should be retired in the fiscal year in which the debt is incurred. The financial transactions involved in retiring a loan within the fiscal year in which it is incurred are not recorded as debt service expenditures.

Classifying Expenditures. During the past forty years, the most commonly used method of classifying expenditures has been by function. This is sometimes called the function-character classification. The current expense transactions usually have included six categories as follows: (1) Administration or General Control, (2) Instruction, (3) Operation of Plant, (4) Maintenance of Plant, (5) Auxiliary Services, and (6) Fixed Charges. The capital transactions have usually included two categories: (1) Capital Outlay and (2) Debt Service.

[14] *Ibid.,* pp. 218–219.
[15] *Ibid.,* p. 222.

The expenditure accounts provide many sub-items for these eight broad categories. The sub-items may differ among the states and among school systems depending upon need. The difficulty in securing uniformity has been primarily to obtain general agreement on what sub-items to include under each broad category.

Many criticisms have been made of the functional classification of school expenditures. Purists in accounting have claimed that many sub-items are classified by object and not by function. There has been great difficulty in obtaining uniformity in classifying expenditures. The system does not provide all of the information needed for cost accounting. But despite its defects, the functional classification of school expenditures has proved to be a very useful and very flexible system. Using it as a base, school systems generally have been able to expand the system in accordance with their needs without destroying basic uniformity.

The United States Office of Education recently has recommended that nine broad categories be provided for current expense. Following is a condensed outline of the recommended expenditure accounts.

Condensed Outline of Basic Expenditure Accounts

ADMINISTRATION

100 Series

110. SALARIES
120. CONTRACTED SERVICES
130. OTHER EXPENSES

INSTRUCTION

200 Series

210. SALARIES
    211. Principals
    212. Consultants or Supervisors
    213. Teachers
    214. Other Instructional Staff
    215. Secretarial and Clerical Assistants
    216. Other Salaries for Instruction
220. TEXTBOOKS
230. SCHOOL LIBRARIES & AUDIOVISUAL
240. TEACHING SUPPLIES
250. OTHER EXPENSES

ATTENDANCE AND HEALTH SERVICES

300–400 Series

300. ATTENDANCE SERVICES
    310. Salaries
    320. Other Expenses
400. HEALTH SERVICES
    410. Salaries
    420. Other Expenses

*Condensed Outline of Basic Expenditure Accounts—*Cont.

1140. CUSTODIAL AND DETENTION CARE OF CHILDREN
1150. WELFARE ACTIVITIES
1160. NONPUBLIC SCHOOL PUPILS
    1161. Instructional Services
    1162. Attendance and Health Services
    1163. Transportation Services

CAPITAL OUTLAY

1200 Series

1210. SITES
1220. BUILDINGS
1230. EQUIPMENT

DEBT SERVICE FROM CURRENT FUNDS

1300 Series

1310. PRINCIPAL OF DEBT
1320. INTEREST ON DEBT
1330. PAID INTO SINKING FUNDS
1340. SCHOOLHOUSING AUTHORITY
1350. OTHER DEBT SERVICE

OUTGOING TRANSFER ACCOUNTS

1400 Series

1410. DISTRICTS IN THE STATE
1420. DISTRICTS IN ANOTHER STATE
1430. TUITION TO OTHER THAN PUBLIC SCHOOLS [16]

It will be observed that this recommended system provides an expansion of the old system by substituting three new categories—Attendance and Health Services, Pupil Transportation Services, Food Service and Student Body Activities—for the old category, Auxiliary Agencies. A new category—Community Services, is added. This more detailed functional classification of expenditures should improve uniformity in accounting because it provides a more logical classification of present day school expenditures.

It is also recommended that instructional expenditures at least be recorded by program area. This facilitates both budget administration and cost analysis.

No one method of classifying school expenditures will serve all purposes. All school systems need to classify expenditures at least by fund and function. Other recognized methods of classifying school expenditures are by (1) activity or program area, (2) object, and (3) educational unit such as a school. Large school systems frequently use all of

---

[16] Reason and White, *Financial Accounting for State and Local School Systems,* p. XIX.

these classifications. School systems will need to classify expenditures by activity or program area as educational planning becomes a part of the budgetary process.

Object classification is useful for cost comparisons. In practice the functional classification can be expanded sufficiently to include most of the object classifications needed. Thus what accounting purists claim to be a weakness of the system is actually a strength.

Classification of expenditures by school is necessary if costs by individual schools are desired. It requires considerable accounting labor to classify all expenditures by individual schools. Each school system should determine whether the additional information provided is worth the extra cost of individual school accounting.

Subsidiary Accounting

School systems generally keep a number of subsidiary accounts which are not carried in the general budget and the receipt and expenditure ledgers except to the extent that profits from subsidiary activities are transferable to general fund receipts or expenditures for subsidiary activities are made from the general fund. The most common subsidiary accounts are: (1) special trust funds, (2) stores, (3) school lunch funds, (4) student activity funds, (5) petty cash funds, (6) school plant maintenance shop records, (7) school bus and shop records.

Special trust funds usually originate from gifts. Such funds can be used only for the purposes specified by the donors. Special accounts are necessary to show that such funds have been expended in accordance with the conditions attached to the gifts.

When a storehouse is maintained, records should be kept which show both the physical inventory and financial transactions. Stores may be financed directly from the general fund or from a working capital fund.

School lunch funds may be administered either by the central office or by individual schools. When the school lunch fund is administered by an individual school, it is known as an internal account.

Student activity accounts are usually administered by individual schools. Boards of education have a responsibility for internal accounts although these do not include tax funds. Any funds administered under the auspices of the school are school funds. A board of education should require all schools under its jurisdiction to follow uniform accounting and budgeting procedures in administering all internal accounts. The minimum accounts which should be required are a depository ledger, a receipts ledger, and an expenditure ledger. These ledgers should be supported by the original documents usually required for keeping accounts. Principals should make financial reports monthly to the board.

All internal accounts should be audited at least annually. Because many student activity accounts are so small, it is common practice to consolidate all internal funds (except lunch funds) into one depository account, but ledgers are kept for each account.

Some boards of education provide centralized accounting for all internal accounts including both lunch room and student activity accounts. If machine accounting is used, much labor on the part of school principals and their assistants can be saved.

Petty cash funds are used sometimes when it is more expeditious to pay cash than to process invoices for payment by check. Such funds may be used either in internal accounting or in accounting by the central office. When a person administering a petty cash fund submits invoices, the amounts are charged to the proper expenditure account.

Special accounts are needed for school plant maintenance shops operated by the board. These accounts usually show the cost of various types of repairs by individual schools. This information is important for determining whether a job should be done by the school plant maintenance crew or by private contract. It is useful for both budgeting and cost accounting.

Special accounts are essential for the efficient management of a fleet of district owned buses serviced by a district operated bus repair shop.

Records should be kept for each bus unit and for the shop. Information from this type of accounting is essential for determining operating efficiency of individual bus units, whether a bus unit should be replaced and whether a particular type of repair should be made by the school bus shop or by private contract. These records facilitate budgeting and cost accounting.

Clearing Accounts

Clearing accounts are used for recording the gross amounts of money received and paid out without inflating the totals of the regular receipt and expenditure accounts.

The transactions which should be recorded through clearing accounts generally concern one of the following: (1) Activities financed wholly or in part by revenue produced by the activity, (2) prepayments or advancements, (3) abatements, (4) exchanges of one asset or liability for another asset or liability, (5) interfund transfers, (6) current loans, and (7) insurance adjustments.[17]

It is essential that the board exercise control over all school connected

---

[17] Reason and White, *Financial Accounting for State and Local School Systems,* p. 105.

activities and that records be kept and reports be made of all types of financial transactions. But the records should be so kept that the financial reports give a true picture of the financial status of the board. For example, school food service funds are in effect revolving funds including funds received and paid out continuously to provide lunches for pupils. School lunch funds cannot be used for regular school operations. A current loan obtained and retired during the year represents no increase in the fiscal capacity of the board. The use of clearing accounts for transactions of this type make it possible for the board to report all financial transactions without inflating regular receipt and expenditure accounts.

If the board subsidizes any activity in the clearing accounts, the amount of the subsidy must be reported in the regular expenditure account. If the board receives any net revenue from such an activity which can be used for general school purposes it must be recorded in the regular receipt account. All other financial transactions of clearing accounts should be excluded from regular receipt and expenditure accounts.

Original Documents

Financial accounting in reality begins with original documents. The budget and minutes of the board are the primary original documents because they provide evidence of the authorization of expenditures. Other original documents of importance are contracts, evidences of receipts, numbered checks or voucher checks, check stubs, bank deposit slips, numbered requisitions, numbered purchase orders, invoices, payrolls and evidence supporting payrolls, individual record cards for each employee, and similar documents. Records of this type are necessary to support ledger entries. Accounts cannot be audited unless adequate supporting evidence in the form of original documents is available. Original documents should be easily available and filed in a systematic manner.

The original evidence supporting receipts should show that all funds sent to the board were received and deposited to the credit of the board. The original documents supporting payments should show that the payment was authorized, that the services paid for were received, that the goods paid for were received in good condition in the quantity and quality ordered, and the amount paid was the correct amount. If the original documents are adequate, it should be possible to destroy the ledgers and reproduce them from the original documents.[18]

---

[18] Morphet, Johns, and Reller, *Educational Administration*, p. 452.

Cost Accounting

Cost accounting is frequently confused with expenditure accounting. In fact the words "costs" and "expenditures" are frequently used interchangeably in educational literature. Cost accounting is defined as: "That method of accounting which provides for the assembling and recording of all the elements of cost incurred to accomplish a purpose, to carry on an activity or operation, or to complete a unit of work or a specific job." [19]

The difference between costs and expenditures can be easily demonstrated by determining costs and expenditures for contracted and district owned transportation. Let us assume that District A contracted for its transportation and paid private contractors $180,000 during a fiscal year for transporting 3,000 pupils to school. The contractors furnished the equipment and paid all costs of operation including insurance. The expenditures totalled $60 per pupil and, ignoring the time of the superintendent and principals spent in supervising transportation, the cost of transportation was $60 per pupil. Technically, this supervisory time should be charged to the cost of transportation, but in practice supervisory time is not usually broken down into detailed categories of duties.

Let us assume that District B owned and operated its own buses and had its own repair shop. Let us assume that it expended $90,000 during the year for the salaries of bus drivers and all other expenses of operating and repairing buses and that it purchased no new buses. Expenditures were $30 per pupil but costs were considerably more. Let us assume that the board operated 40 buses which originally cost $5,000 per bus. Assuming that school buses have an average life of ten years, the depreciation cost was $500 annually for each bus. The total cost of bus depreciation was $20,000 during the year. Let us also assume that the board paid $4,000 annually for insurance, $4,000 for interest on a short term loan for the purchase of the buses and that the depreciation cost of the bus repair shop was $2,000 per year. The total cost of school transportation during that year, ignoring the cost of supervisory services provided by the superintendent and principals, was $120,000 or $40 per pupil.

It should not be assumed that District B is operating its transportation services more economically than District A unless conditions affecting transportation costs are approximately the same in the two districts. For example, District A may be serving 1200 square miles of territory and District B, 600 square miles. The roads over which buses operate

[19] Reason and White, *op. cit.*, p. 220.

may be much better in District B than in District A. This illustrates the difficulties of comparing the costs of one district with the costs of another district. *Unit Costs are comparable in evaluating the economy of management only when conditions beyond the control of the board that affect costs are comparable.* This generalization applies to all types of cost comparisons.

There are many kinds of unit costs and they have many uses. Unit costs are frequently used in developing and interpreting the budget and in interpreting the annual report. Large sums of money included in the budget or the annual report have little meaning to the public unless analyzed in terms of logical and understandable units. A $6,000,000 budget for current expense means little to the public except that it is a huge sum of money. When this huge sum is interpreted as a current expense budget of $295 per pupil per year or $1.64 per pupil day, it is more understandable. A parent can compare the cost of $1.64 per pupil per day in school with the cost of employing a baby sitter for a day.[20]

Some type of a per pupil measure is also commonly used as the cost unit for a program area, an activity, or a school. Average daily attendance, average daily membership, and enrollment have all been used. Average daily attendance has been used most frequently in comparing educational expenditures and costs of the states and school districts. Average daily membership is probably the best unit cost measure because it is more closely associated with need for expenditure than either average daily attendance or enrollment. Unfortunately all school systems do not keep records on average daily membership.

Average daily membership has another advantage as a cost unit. Let us assume that a district operates elementary schools, high schools, a junior college, and an adult education program, and that unit costs are being calculated for these program areas. The average daily membership of the elementary and high schools can be readily determined. The equivalent average daily membership of the junior college can be determined by dividing the total student semester hours for which students are registered by 30. A load for a full time student for an academic year is approximately 30 semester hours. The equivalent average daily membership of adult classes can be determined by dividing the total student clock hours of adult instruction by 900. A typical public school pupil has 900 clock hours of instruction in a nine-months school year.

The expenditure account should show instruction expenditures by program area. Other expenditures which cannot be recorded by program area can be allocated by appropriate formulas.[21] When the expenditures

[20] Morphet, Johns, and Reller, *op. cit.*, p. 458.
[21] Excellent suggestions for prorating expenditures are presented in Chapter 8. Reason and White, *Financial Accounting for Local and State School Systems.*

for each program area are determined, the amount per student in average daily membership for each program area can be readily calculated. Calculations of this type usually include only current expense items. Therefore it is not a true measure of total costs. A true measure of total costs would also include depreciation on buildings and equipment and interest paid on notes and bonds issued for capital outlay purposes.[22]

The expenditure and subsidiary accounts and the non-financial statistics regularly recorded should provide the information needed for essential cost accounting. Extensive cost accounting involves considerable expense. Therefore, all cost accounting should serve a good purpose.

MACHINE ACCOUNTING

The keeping of accounts and records requires much labor, and labor costs are increasing. Machine aids that reduce labor save money. Many types of machines minimize errors and make possible the recording of more complete information with but little extra cost.

The least expensive type of mechanical aid for record keeping is a duplicating board. This device can be used by very small school systems. Different forms with carbons can be locked in the board in perfect alignment. Entries are made by hand. Entries on two or three forms can be made simultaneously by this method. It is especially useful in processing payrolls and accounts payable.

Many school systems now use accounting and payroll machines. Several kinds of good machines are available. They vary in cost, capacity, and operations performed. The types of machines which should be purchased depend on the volume of financial transactions and on the purposes for which the machines are to be used. These machines are expensive and should be used for as many operations as practicable. Many improvements have been made in recent years in accounting and payroll machines. Some authorities believe that the volume of work is sufficient in school systems of four thousand or more pupils to justify the purchase of such machines.

The use of punched card machines is increasing. These are the most expensive of all accounting machines. But these machines can be used for processing and recording many types of school statistics. Punched card machines can be used for many business office functions, school census and child accounting, test scoring and recording of results, mail-

---

[22] A broader concept of school costs might even include the value of the labor of employable students.

ing lists, and performing the statistical computations necessary for many types of research.

Punched card equipment can be installed on a cumulative basis. Some equipment can be used by school systems with as few as 3,600 pupils. The equipment suitable to a school system of 3,600 pupils is not capable of being used for as many purposes as a complete installation. Spencer [23] has shown that a school system with as few as 15,000 pupils can efficiently use the following equipment:

3 key punches	1 large tab or 2 small tabs
1 verifier	1 or 2 sorters
1 collator	1 small computer
1 interpreter	1 test scorer
1 reproducer with mark sense	

This equipment can handle most of the financial and pupil accounting and some research for a school system of this size. Large school systems require a much more extensive and more expensive installation. The larger the system, the greater the possible saving by the use of punched card equipment.

Accounting machines automatically produce the unencumbered balance in a budget appropriation account when each item is posted. Therefore, the unencumbered balance is available at all times. When punched card machines are used for accounting, the cards must be run through the tabulator printing machine to ascertain the unencumbered balance.[24] Therefore, accounting machines are more useful than punched card machines if the unencumbered balance is needed continuously. But punched card machines can be used for a very wide variety of accounting and statistical purposes. Therefore, some large school systems use both accounting machines and punched card machines.

SOME PROBLEMS AND ISSUES

Financial accounting might seem to be the one area of educational administration that could be completely tied up in a neat bundle with no loose ends. The special problems and issues presented in the following paragraphs are indications that there still are a number of loose ends in school financial accounting.

[23] Richard E. Spencer, "Do Punched Card Methods Save Money?" *School Management* (August, 1958), Vol. 2, No. 8, pp. 35–38.
[24] The information on the cards may be transferred to tape or record disk machine units to speed up this process when a great volume of work is involved.

How Can the Revenue Receipts for a Fiscal Year Be
Reconciled with Expenditures for That Year?

Taxpayers frequently ask the following question: "Where does the money come from and where does it go?" This is a rational question and school officials should be able to answer it. But it is not easy to obtain a completely accurate answer to this question from the school account books now in general use for the following reasons: (1) the funds available for expenditure include revenue receipts, non-revenue receipts and balances brought forward; (2) expenditures include all 6 to 9 functions [25] of current expense plus debt service and capital outlay. Expenditures for capital outlay are made from both revenue and non-revenue receipts.

As pointed out in Chapter 4, if expenditures for all functions of current expense are added to expenditures for capital outlay and debt service for a fiscal year, the grand total is a gross expenditure total which cannot be reconciled with revenue receipts. This gross expenditure total is an inflated total because it not only includes expenditures for capital outlay but also expenditures for debt service to retire bonds issued for capital outlay.

Some method is needed to reflect current tax effort by expenditures as well as by revenue receipts. The following method is suggested for reconciling revenue receipts with expenditures: (1) keep a subsidiary account of capital outlay expenditures, (2) credit all non-revenue receipts to this capital outlay account,[26] (3) credit all expenditures for capital outlay made from revenue receipts as a receipt to this account.

Construct a pie chart of revenue receipts which includes the following: (1) each revenue receipt by source for the fiscal year, (2) the income received from incoming transfer accounts, (3) the balance brought forward not including the balance in the capital outlay account.

Construct a pie chart of expenditures from revenue receipts which includes the following: (1) expenditures for each function of current expense, (2) expenditures for capital outlay from revenue receipts, (3) expenditures for debt service, (4) expenditures for outgoing transfer accounts, (5) balance at the close of the fiscal year not including the balance in the capital outlay account.

Following is an application of this method of reconciling the revenue receipts of a school system with its expenditures from revenue receipts.

---

[25] Depending upon the number of major classifications given to current expense.
[26] Non-revenue receipts ordinarily should be expended exclusively for capital outlay because they are obtained either by borrowing money or depleting assets.

Where the Money Came From, July 1, 196– – June 30, 196–

Revenue Receipts Plus Opening Balance:

1. Balance at Beginning of Fiscal Year .... $ 446,564.67
2. Federal Funds 60,950.86
3. State Funds 2,106,734.77
4. Local Property Taxes 1,116,166.25
5. Other Local Revenue Receipts 87,046.67
6. Transfers from Other School Systems 3,000.00

TOTAL $3,820,463.22

Where the Money Went, July 1, 196– – June 30, 196–

Expenditures From Revenue Receipts Plus Closing Balance:

1. Administration .... $ 58,817.22
2. Instruction 2,313,794.54
3. Operation of Plant 146,392.32
4. Maintenance of Plant 81,850.67
5. Auxiliary Agencies 204,804.64
6. Fixed Charges 57,133.48
7. Adult Schools 43,521.00
8. Capital Outlay 115,474.81
9. Debt Service 351,580.33
10. Balance at Close of Fiscal Year 445,094.21
11. Transfers to Other School Systems 2,000.00

TOTAL $3,820,463.22

These data can be used to construct pie charts or other types of charts which are useful in helping the public to understand technical financial reports. In preparing financial reports for popular consumption it is important that such terms as auxiliary agencies, fixed charges, capital outlay, and debt service be defined in terms that can be generally understood.

What other method can be used to show from where the money comes and where it goes? What do increasing or decreasing balances mean?

What Financial Reports Should Be Made and to Whom?

In general superintendents make financial reports to the local board of education, to the state department of education, and upon request to the United States Office of Education.[27]

Reports to the Board of Education and the People. The superintendent should prepare monthly and annual statistical financial reports for his board of education. The reports are necessary for the board to dis-

---

[27] Some districts also make financial reports to intermediate educational units and to other units of local government.

charge its responsibility of exercising general control over the financial operations of the district. The data for the statistical financial reports should be taken from the financial accounts of the board. The monthly and annual statistical reports should not only present a picture of the receipts and expenditures for each fund but should also present a reconciliation with the budget. Therefore, the budget, the financial accounts, and the financial reports should all follow the same account classifications. When financial reports grow out of the financial accounts, statistical financial reporting becomes a routine, standardized procedure minimizing the expenditure of labor. Monthly financial reporting makes it possible to detect accounting errors early and it also stimulates prompt posting of ledgers.

Some states require that the annual statistical financial report of the board be published in a newspaper. This practice may have some justification but it should not be assumed that many lay people will read or can interpret the statistical financial report because it must of necessity be technical in nature.

Many superintendents periodically prepare reports on the total educational program. Reports of this type present descriptions of educational activities as well as financial activities. The purpose of these reports is to show what has been achieved and what is needed as well as what has been expended. The best type of report is presented in simple and interesting style which can be read and will be read by many people. Financial data are presented in a non-technical fashion. Liberal use is usually made of charts, illustrations, and pictures. Reports of this type should be widely distributed because they are reports to the people. The best reports present information in such manner that the people can make intelligent judgments on educational policy. This is essential if large numbers of people participate effectively in budget development. Therefore, the comprehensive school report should present a look at the future as well as a history of the past.

How should the annual report be developed and published?

Reports to the State Department of Education. Annual statistical financial reports should be made to the state department of education on forms prescribed by the state. The state should call only for the information provided by the minimum accounts required by the state. If the annual financial report required by the state meets the requirements of a local board of education, duplicate copies can be made of the report. This saves labor. If the financial report is not broad enough in scope to meet local requirements, the local report should be in greater detail.

The state should publish annually, or at least biennially, the essential financial statistics for all school systems. In some states, statistics for small, common school districts are frequently summarized and presented by intermediate districts. Comprehensive financial statistics for all school districts are needed by the legislature and the state education agency for planning state programs of school financing. Financial statistics for all districts are also required for many types of research studies.

Should the states publish popularized financial and statistical reports? If so, in what form?

Reports to the United States Office of Education. The regular biennial survey of the United States Office of Education provides financial statistics for all states and territories but not for all individual school systems. There is a considerable demand for comparable financial statistics for local school systems from all states. Therefore, the Office periodically requests selected school systems to file financial reports on its own forms. City school systems are classified by size and a considerable number of systems from each group are included.

Forms are furnished by the Office of Education because the account classifications vary somewhat among the states. If the statistics from different school systems are to be made comparable, the account classifications must be the same. It requires some extra labor to prepare this report for the Office which includes some statistics other than financial statistics. The Office has no authority to require that reports be made to it, but all systems requested to file reports should co-operate and file reports. If this is not done, there will be no authoritative nation-wide figures.

The respective departments of education of the states and territories are also requested to file annual statistical reports with the Office of Education. These reports include state or territory summaries only. The states are not required to file these reports with the Office but all states do so. Some states are not as prompt as they should be in filing reports with the Office; this delays the publication of national statistics. More time is usually required to collect statistics and prepare reports in the states with large numbers of small districts than in states with only relatively few local districts. The consolidation of unnecessary, small districts will facilitate reporting.

The accuracy and speed of reporting at all levels of government will be improved as more uniformity is achieved in school financial accounting practices.

Should the Federal government require all states and territories to furnish financial and statistical information to the United States Office of Education? What types of financial and statistical information should be available for all states?

Should Each State Require a Uniform Financial
Accounting System for Its School Systems?

There would seem to be a number of advantages if all school systems
in a state used the same financial accounting system. But as has already
been pointed out in this chapter, the financial accounting needs of
school systems vary. The accounting needs of a small school system
with 50 teachers or less differ considerably from the needs of a school
system with 5,000 teachers. Therefore, no one system of accounting
should be prescribed by the state for all school districts.

However, the state should prescribe the minimum accounts which
must be kept by all districts. It should also publish manuals for classifying receipts and expenditures and guides for recording receipts and
expenditures. Local school districts should have the authority to establish additional accounts as their needs require, but uniform procedures
should be followed in keeping required accounts.

States should exercise great care in establishing uniform minimum
standards for financial accounting. Each state may like to consider
itself unique, but there is little evidence that the basic, minimum
school financing accounting needs of each state are unique. There is
much more to be lost in unique accounting practices than there is to be
gained. On the other hand, there is much more to be gained by following standard, uniform accounting practices than there is to be lost.
The safest policy for a state to use in establishing state minimum
requirements for basic accounts is to follow the recommendations of the
United States Office of Education insofar as practicable. It is only by
this policy that substantial uniformity in school financial accounting
among the states can be achieved. When a state prescribes minimum
standards for basic accounts which vary from national practice, the
variations should not be so great as to make it impossible to reconcile
the financial statistics of that state with the statistics of other states.

What are the advantages, if any, of a state or a local school system
having its own unique system of classifying receipts and expenditures?

SELECTED REFERENCES

Davis, Clifford M., A Manual of Accounting Principles and Procedures For
    Student Activity Funds. Evanston, Ill.: Association of School Business
    Officials of the United States and Canada, 1957.
Johns, R. L., and E. L. Morphet, editors, Problems and Issues in Public
    School Finance. New York: Bureau of Publications, Teachers College,
    Columbia University, 1952. Chapter 14.

Linn, Henry H., editor, *School Business Administration*. New York: Ronald Press Company, 1956. Chapter 6.

Morphet, Edgar L., Roe L. Johns, and Theodore L. Reller, *Educational Administration*. Englewood Cliffs, N.J.: Prentice-Hall, Inc., 1959. Chapter 20.

Mort, Paul R., and Walter C. Reusser, *Public School Finance*, 2nd ed., New York: McGraw-Hill Book Company, Inc., 1951. Chapter 12.

Reason, Paul L., Emery M. Foster, and Robert F. Will, *The Common Core of State Educational Information*. U. S. Department of Health, Education and Welfare, Office of Education. Washington, D.C.: U. S. Government Printing Office, 1953.

Reason, Paul L., and Alpheus L. White, *Financial Accounting for State and Local School Systems*, U. S. Department of Health, Education and Welfare, Office of Education. Washington, D.C.: U. S. Government Printing Office, 1957.

Rosenstengel, William Everett, and Jefferson N. Eastwood, *School Finance*. New York: Ronald Press Company, 1957. Chapter 11.

CHAPTER SEVENTEEN

Spending and Safeguarding School Funds

The central purpose of business management is to maximize the educational returns per dollar invested in education. That is also one of the major purposes of all of the administrative, supervisory, and instructional services for the educational enterprise. Since the underlying purpose of business administration is basically congruent with the purposes of all other educational services, it is concerned with every facet of the educational enterprise. However, business administration has some special responsibilities for the judicious spending of money, the safeguarding of money, and the protection of persons and property.

The purpose of school business management is not to "save money" but to use it wisely. Economy in the spending of school funds is achieved only when school funds are wisely invested. It is not economy to refuse to spend available funds for meeting the needs of the educational program. An unnecessarily large cash balance at the end of any year is not an indication of economy in school financial administration but rather an indication of an inferior investment policy.

In order to make wise investments in the educational enterprise, school funds must be expended judiciously and they must be safeguarded against loss or misuse as a result of dishonesty, misfortune, or misappropriation. This chapter is concerned primarily with these two important aspects of financial administration—the judicious spending and the safeguarding of school funds.

478

CENTRAL CONTROL OF SPENDING

Central control of the spending of funds included in a budget must be provided if a budget is of any use. This is true of any type of budget in government or business. Central control must be provided for the general budget administered by the central office for the school district. This control is exercised by the superintendent and his assistants in accordance with law and the regulations of the board. The school principal and his assistants exercise central control over the internal accounts of an individual school. This control must be exercised in accordance with law and the regulations of the board and under the supervision of the superintendent.

As was pointed out in Chapter 14 the judicious spending of school funds begins with the development of spending and financing plans based on a soundly conceived educational plan. The first step in implementing the educational plan is to purchase the goods and services necessary to carry it out. From the standpoint of operational procedure, spending can be divided into two broad categories: (1) the employment and payment of regular personnel, (2) other purchases initiated by requisitions, orders and contracts, the payments for which are substantiated by invoices or claims.

PAYROLL ADMINISTRATION

Most school revenues are expended for paying the salaries and wages of employed school personnel. In 1958–59 the public schools employed more than 1,400,000 teachers, principals, superintendents, and other certificated instructional and administrative personnel. The non-certificated employed personnel including custodians, bus drivers, secretaries, clerks, bookkeepers, maintenance workers, and similar personnel (not including lunch room employees) totalled more than 300,000. Therefore payroll administration is a major operation in all except the smallest school systems. Payroll administration is concerned with the following operations: (1) establishing and maintaining payrolls, (2) obtaining evidence of service, (3) preparing the payroll document, (4) drawing and delivering checks, and (5) making entries into the account records. In a large school system, different operations may be allocated to several different divisions of the business administration office. In a small school system, one person may be responsible for all operations. But regardless of the size of the system, all of these tasks must be performed by someone if the payroll is properly administered.

Establishment and Maintenance of the Payroll

No person can be placed on the payroll unless he has been legally employed by the employing authority for the district. The method of making recommendations for employment varies among school districts in the United States and it also varies for different classes of employees within the same district. But the final employing authority is the board of education. Therefore, the names of all employees of a board should be included in its minutes.

Start and Stop Orders. Before the name of a person is entered on the payroll, a start order should be prepared which includes at least the following information: (1) the exact name of the person concerned, (2) the exact time when employment starts, (3) the type of service rendered, (4) the place where it is rendered, (5) the title or classification of the position, (6) the credit for prior service, and (7) the salary or wage rate.

Before a person's name is removed from the payroll, a stop order should be prepared giving at least the following information: (1) the exact name of the person concerned, (2) the exact time that employment ceases, (3) the reason for termination of employment (4) the vacation leave due, and (5) the salary due. Employment and termination of employment must be done with proper authority. Therefore, the minutes of the board should show approval of the employment and termination of employment of all regular employees.

Salary and Wage Schedules. The salary rate of teachers and other instructional employees of the board is usually determined by salary schedules approved by the board. When this is done, it is not necessary to include the salary of each instructional employee in the minutes of the board each year because it can be determined from the appropriate salary schedule.

It is good practice to establish salary or wage schedules for all non-instructional employees of the board. If the compensation of any instructional or non-instructional employee is not determined in accordance with a salary or wage schedule approved by the board, the salary or wage of the person must be recorded in the minutes of the board.

Types of Payrolls. Payrolls are usually divided into several sections depending on the size and needs of a district. A very small district may have only one payroll. Medium-sized districts may have two payrolls —one for instructional personnel and one for all other personnel. Large districts may have separate payrolls for instructional personnel, custodians, bus drivers, maintenance employees, clerical and secretarial personnel, and similar classes of employees. Payrolls for some classes of employees may be made monthly and for others every two weeks.

Pay Calendars. Pay calendars should be established for making payrolls. It is important for each employee to know at the time of his employment exactly the dates on which he will receive payments for his services. This is necessary for the employee to meet his personal financial obligations. These time schedules should be met promptly. It is destructive of morale when employees fail to receive salaries or wages on time.

Pay calendars should be so structured as to prevent the work load of the payroll office from becoming too heavy at any one time. That is one of the reasons why divisions of the payroll are advisable for large school systems. It is common practice to pay professional staff members on a monthly basis. This requires less work than payment on a semi-monthly basis. There is a growing tendency to pay teachers in twelve installments for twelve calendar months because it meets the spending needs of teachers better than payment in nine installments for nine months.

The wages of employees in industry are normally paid weekly. Non-professional employees of boards of education usually prefer payment more often than once per month. It requires considerable labor to prepare weekly payrolls. Therefore the two-week pay period for non-professional board employees seems to be an appropriate compromise between the customary weekly pay calendar in industry and the monthly pay calendar.

Maintaining the Payroll. Once a person's name has been entered on the payroll, it remains until a stop order removes it. This facilitates the preparation of payrolls for successive pay periods. However, if a person's status changes with respect to position or wage or salary rate, the start order must be amended accordingly. Maintenance of the payroll is a continuous process because it must be amended every time there is a change in personnel or a change in the status of individuals.

Regardless of whether the payroll is divided, names should be grouped on the payroll in accordance with budget appropriation and expenditure accounts. This greatly facilitates budget control, expenditure accounting and reporting. Entries on the payroll should be coded for expenditure classification. Coding is made much easier if the names are grouped on the payroll by account classification.

Evidence of Service

The payroll must be supported by evidence of service obtained by timekeeping. The word "timekeeping" may not seem appropriate for professional personnel because as a rule they are not timed by the hour. But the central office should not take it for granted that salaried personnel work for the number of days for which they are scheduled to work during a given pay period. Methods of timekeeping vary for teachers and non-certificated employees, but records should be kept of the time worked by all employees. To pay employees without verifying the time worked is as unsound as paying an invoice without verifying that the goods were received.

The school principal should, at a specified time prior to each pay period, make a certified report to the central office of the time worked by all employees at his school. Similar reports should be made to the central office by department heads for employees not assigned to individual schools. Regular time registers should be kept and time reports prepared from the register. The time report should show the reasons for absence and also the substitute assigned to the vacancy if a substitute was employed. This is necessary in order to give due credit for sick leave not in excess of the number of days of sick leave earned.

Preparation of the Payroll Document

The procedures outlined so far only provide for entering on the payroll the name, the salary or wage rate, and the amount earned. Before checks can actually be drawn, considerable other information must be on file and made a matter of record. Numerous deductions are now being made from salary checks, including: (1) teacher retirement, (2) income tax and social security, (3) group insurance, and (4) other types of deductions permitted by the board and authorized by the employee. It requires extra accounting labor for the board to make these deductions. Actually the board serves as the paying agent of its employees for many purposes without cost to the employee. This is a convenience in some instances and in others it is required by law. In all cases the person preparing the payroll must have on file the specific authority to make the deduction and the amount of the deduction or the method of determining the amount of the deduction.

With all the required information available, the payroll document can be prepared showing: (1) name, (2) salary or wage rate, (3) amount earned, (4) deductions or additions because of under or over payment on previous payrolls, (5) each deduction made and paid to others, (6) the amount of the check to the employee. The payroll should then be checked or pre-audited by an authorized person and approved in accordance with the regulations of the board.

Drawing and Delivering Checks

When the information necessary for preparing the payroll has been assembled and recorded and the payroll approved, the procedure can be standardized. The next operations are: (1) drawing the check to the employee, (2) making entries on the check stub or employee's remittance advice, (3) posting the individual earnings ledger or card, (4) posting the payroll journal. These operations are done manually in small school systems. Fortunately these operations are ideally suited for mechanization. All four operations can be done simultaneously by a number of standard accounting machines. This saves much labor and minimizes errors.

These four operations are also adapted to punched card payroll accounting. This type of payroll accounting is especially suitable for large school systems.

Employees should not be expected to go to the central office for their checks unless it is more convenient. If the employee goes to the central office for his check on the board's time, it is expensive for the board. If he goes to the office on his own time, it is unfair to the employee. Paying employees promptly and delivering their checks to them costs the board very little but it aids greatly in building morale and in improving human relations.

Entering into the Account Records

Payroll accounting should be closely coordinated with expenditure accounting and budgetary control. If the names on the payroll have been grouped and coded in accordance with expenditure account classifications, it is not necessary to enter the name and the amount paid to each individual for each payroll period in the expenditures ledger. Only the total for each account classification for each payroll period should be entered. This will save considerable labor. It is not necessary to repeat the details of the payroll in the expenditures ledger because the details are entered on the individual earnings ledger or cards and on the payroll journal.

It is customary to distribute payroll charges to the different expenditure accounts directly from the payroll journal. This speeds up the financial accounting, budgetary control and reporting processes.

Individual Employee Records

It is evident that efficient payroll administration is impossible without adequate information for each employee. This can be provided only by establishing a systematic individual record for each employee. Records of individual employees are needed for purposes other than financial accounting. Therefore, the individual record system should be planned to serve all functions of administration. The information most needed for payroll administration includes: (1) the individual earnings record, (2) the service record, (3) the sick leave record, (4) the certificate rank for certificated personnel, and (5) record of authorized deductions.

OTHER PURCHASES AND PAYMENTS

The expenditure of school funds for regularly employed personnel is originated by employment contracts as described in the preceding section of this chapter. The other purchases of the board are made by purchase order, contract, and other means permitted by law and regulations of the board. They are substantiated by invoices or claims. There should be some type of written evidence of the origin of every expenditure made by the board. If this evidence is not available, there is no basis for encumbrance accounting or for determining the validity of the accounts payable. The condensed outline of basic expenditure accounts presented in Chapter 16 gives an indication of the variety of expenditures made by the board.

Space does not permit a description of the technical procedures to follow in originating each type of expenditure and the methods to use in pre-auditing invoices, contracts, and claims for determining accounts payable. Procedures and methods vary among school systems. These generalizations, however, apply to all school systems that have good school business management policies: (1) all expenditures are made in accordance with the budget adopted by the board or as it may be amended, (2) all expenditures are originated by an authorized person in accordance with law and the regulations of the board, (3) written evidence of the origin of every expenditure is provided, (4) all expenditures are substantiated by invoices, contracts or claims, (5) payment is made by the board only when evidence shows that the board purchased the goods or services specified in the invoices or claims submitted for payment and that it received the goods and services it purchased.

The term "purchasing" could be applied in a broad sense to any expenditure made by the board. However, it is usually applied to the purchase of supplies and equipment by the board. This type of purchasing is discussed in the following paragraphs because it involves some special problems.

Specifications for Supplies and Equipment

Many kinds of supplies and equipment are purchased by boards of education. The quantity, quality, and kinds of supplies and equipment purchased directly affect the educational program. Supplies and equipment cost money and they create storage and distribution problems. Purchasing procedures involve the determination of: (1) what is needed, (2) what quality is needed, (3) what quantity is needed, (4) when it is needed, (5) where it is needed, and (6) what it will cost. Efficient purchasing results in having the right item in the right place at the right time at the right cost.[1]

Efficient purchasing of supplies and equipment is impossible without the use of properly developed specifications. *The teachers, custodians, maintenance workers, and others using supplies and equipment should work with the business office in developing specifications.* Before specifications can be drawn, quality standards must be determined.

Developing Quality Standards. Following are some important concepts concerning the development of standards.

1. Standardization is an economical means of defining quality. It enables the purchasing agent to secure the value and the quality needed without excessive cost and with a minimum of negotiation.

2. Standardization is the process of establishing agreement on the quality needed. The established agreement is the standard upon which the specification is based.

3. Value analysis is the process of objectively studying every item to be purchased and eliminating every cost factor which does not contribute to the value of the item.

4. Standardization promotes efficiency and saves money because:

(a) It makes possible larger purchases of fewer items at a lower cost.

(b) It reduces the time for specification writing and expands the list of known and proven items.

(c) It reduces repair and maintenance costs.

(d) It speeds up delivery schedules.

(e) It reduces inventories.

(f) It reduces volume of disposals.

(g) It reduces storage and warehousing costs.

(h) It is conducive to more definite planning.

---

[1] Henry H. Linn, editor, *School Business Administration* (New York: Ronald Press Company, 1956), p. 251.

(i) It simplifies office work.

(j) It improves interdepartmental coordination.[2]

Simplification is not the same as standardization but standardization usually results in simplification. When quality standards are developed those standards should be studied in relation to the needs of various schools, departments, and classes. For example, the paper needs of many departments, schools and classes may be satisfied by the same standard. It is uneconomical to buy more different types and sizes of paper or other items than are necessary to meet needs.

Linn has proposed the following questions for consideration when quality standards are being considered:

1. Does the product have a long or short term use?
2. Does it have a repetitive use, that is, when used up will it be replaced?
3. Will a better quality result in a saving of manpower?
4. Will educational results be commensurately better with a higher quality of material?
5. Is a prestige factor involved?
6. Does the product present any safety hazards to teachers, pupils, and employees?
7. Is an adequate supply of the product available for replacement when purchases must be made?
8. Is the material truly economical from a short range or long range point of view?[3]

Cooperative Development of Specifications. The development of good specifications is a laborious process. It is obvious that appropriate specifications cannot be developed by employees of the business office working in isolation. It is equally obvious that teachers and other school employees lack the technical knowledge to prepare many types of specifications. Therefore, arrangements should be made for broad participation in determining the supplies and equipment needed and the quality standards required. Even when appropriate arrangements are made for pooling the knowledge of all school employees, additional information may be required for developing proper specifications for some items.

Some needed information may be obtained from performance test-

---

[2] Adapted from William G. East in the *Proceedings,* Association of School Business Officials of the United States and Canada (Evanston, Ill.: The Association, 1957), pp. 269–270.

[3] Henry H. Linn in the *Proceedings,* p. 228.

ing.[4] Some performance tests may be made by school employees. Large school systems may find it desirable to establish their own testing laboratories. Other school systems may find it desirable to use state, regional or national testing laboratories for some purposes.

Standard specifications that are of some value can be obtained from a number of sources. Some of those sources are as follows:

1. Federal Bureau of Standards—ordinarily known as Federal Specifications (The General Services Administration, Washington 25, D.C.)
2. Specifications of American Standards Association (ASA) (70 East 45th Street, New York 17, N.Y.)
3. Specifications of American Society for Testing Materials (ASTM) (1916 Race Street, Philadelphia 3, Pa.)
4. Specifications of American Society of Mechanical Engineer (ASME) (29 West 29th Street, New York 18, N.Y.)
5. Specifications of New York State Division of Standards and Purchases (103 Washington Avenue, Albany, N.Y.)

Form of Specifications. Long-form specifications should be used for large quantity purchases. It usually requires considerable labor to prepare detailed specifications. However, when specifications are once prepared, they may be used until there is evidence that revision is needed.

Short-form specifications may be used for small quantity purchases. Brand-name buying is one type of short-form specification. Brand-name buying for some items has the following advantages:

1. It saves time in soliciting quotations and in ordering.
2. It eliminates the need for elaborate testing if a warranty is required.
3. It is accepted and even demanded by the users. Brand-name specifications however may reduce competitive bidding except where competition exists among suppliers of the same brand.

Some other suggestions for preparing specifications are:

1. Be sure that the specifications are clear, concise, and include all the information necessary for submitting bids.
2. Simplify procedures as much as the law permits, provided sound business policies are followed. Do not require special bid deposits or bonds except where large sums are involved. The requirement of bid deposits and bonds costs money and reduces competition.

---

[4] George Ronald Larke, "Inspection and Tests of Material Quality of Instructional and Other Supplies" (Unpublished doctor's dissertation, University of California, 1958).

Quantity Purchasing

Quantity purchasing has advantages and disadvantages. Following are some advantages of large quantity, infrequent purchases:

1. Better unit costs are usually obtained and freight costs are usually reduced.

2. Budget control is made easier.

3. Principals and department heads are required to plan well ahead.

Some disadvantages of large, infrequent purchases are:

1. Principals and department heads, knowing that purchases are to be made once a year, sometimes pad requests.

2. Large quantity purchases require more storage space. Storage space costs money. The original capital outlay cost of storage space usually ranges from $7 per square foot in a warehouse to more than twice that amount in a school building.

3. It is expensive to maintain a large inventory. The larger the inventory, the greater the cost for storage space, interest on money invested, obsolescence, deterioration, and insurance. The National Metal Trades Association has estimated that it takes approximately 24 per cent of the original cost of the inventory to carry it for a year.[5]

Economy in purchasing is not always achieved by purchasing the largest quantities possible. More frequent purchases in smaller quantity for some supplies may actually be more economical than large quantity infrequent purchases. The smaller quantity purchases are also more adaptable to changes in teacher preferences. A small quantity purchase does not mean a trivial purchase. It has been estimated that it costs approximately $3.50 to process a requisition, a purchase order, an invoice and a check. It is absurd to purchase a $2.00 item through this procedure. Trivial purchases should ordinarily be made through petty cash accounts. Purchases should be made in large enough quantity to obtain quantity prices but not in such quantity as to incur extra costs greater than the saving made by quantity purchasing.

Bidding Procedures

Purchases should be based on competitive bids for all important items. A number of states specify by law the maximum amount of the purchase which can be made without securing competitive bids. The amount has been set so low in some states, that the amount of money saved on many items does not justify the extra labor and additional time required for securing competitive bids. If the law permits, the board

---

[5] Adapted from Thomas Linton in the *Proceedings*, pp. 233–234.

should establish reasonable policies with respect to the amount of the purchase above which competitive bids must be secured. The amount above which competitive bids must be secured should not be set so low that competitive bidding, which results in no advantage to the board, is required on many items. The amount should not be so high as to eliminate competitive bidding on items that could be more advantageously purchased by competitive bidding.

Competition is the basis of all bidding, both public and private. The underlying purposes of purchasing by competitive bidding are:

1. To give all recognized and responsible vendors equal opportunity in furnishing supplies and equipment to the district.
2. To prevent the favoring of one vendor over another.
3. To keep district taxpayers informed on business matters pertaining to schools.
4. To prevent fraud on the part of the purchasing official.[6]

Obtaining Bids. Bids can be secured: (1) by advertising and obtaining sealed bids based on formal contract and proposal forms, (2) by informal sealed bids, (3) by letter quotations, and (4) by negotiation.

The formal advertised contract bid is commonly used for the most important purchases. Bid deposits or bonds are usually required. The formal contract forms usually include: (1) the general conditions of the contract, (2) the specifications, and (3) the proposal form.

Informal sealed bids are frequently used for purchases which are not so large as to require formal contract bids. Bids of this type follow the general pattern of formal bids. The bids are based on specifications and can be made as binding as formal contracts. But bid deposits are not required and the time of advertising can usually be reduced.

Letter quotations are sometimes used for obtaining prices on small items for which there is not much bidding competition. Quotations from several vendors, while not the same as competitive bids, do enable the board to make purchases at more favorable prices.

Negotiated bids are also sometimes obtained for items for which vendors' bids cannot be secured. Such items are usually of a highly specialized or unusual type.

Awarding Contracts

The bid invitation usually includes the phrase, "the award will be made to the lowest and most responsible bidder," or some equivalent statement. The easiest policy for the board to follow is to award the

---

[6] University of the State of New York, *Purchases and Stores* (Albany, N.Y.: State Department of Education, 1955), p. 37.

contract to the bidder submitting the low bid on the specifications. Other things being equal, this should always be done. But strict adherence to low bid gives no weight to the service provided by the bidder or to the extent to which he will stand back of his product. Therefore, it is to the advantage of the board to award the contract to the lowest and most responsible bidder rather than the low bidder even though it may at times involve the board in some controversies. Sometimes the product furnished by the low bidder technically meets specifications but the workmanship is poor. The board can protect itself from this contingency by including in the specifications for some items a statement somewhat as follows, "must be the best workmanship known to the industry."

The board and staff must maintain good relationships with bidders as well as protect their own interests. The board reduces its chances of securing good competitive bids in the future if bidders feel they have been dealt with unfairly. Sometimes the specifications are at fault. Bidders may have misunderstood the specifications. The board may not be satisfied with the product obtained on low bid because the specifications were inadequate. In circumstances of this kind the board should reject all bids and call for new bids on revised specifications. The bid invitation should always include the statement, "the board reserves the right to reject any and all bids." This protects the board against unsatisfactory bids as well as unsatisfactory specifications.

Requisitions and Purchase Orders

Purchases of supplies and equipment should start with requisitions. The schools, departments, and offices authorized to originate requisitions should be specified in the regulations of the board of education. Requisitioning is made much simpler if standard lists of supplies and equipment are made available to the persons authorized to file requisitions. These standard lists should be based on specifications which are also available to the persons originating requisitions. Each item should be numbered and coded so that the specification for the item can be identified. This eliminates the necessity of writing detailed descriptions of each item on the requisition. It also enables the purchasing officer to determine accurately what is wanted.

It is not always possible to requisition all supplies and equipment from standard lists. The requisition should be numbered and include at least the following information: the school or department, the name of the person originating the requisition, when required, where to ship, the description and/or code number of the item, the quantity, the unit price and the amount. If the person originating the requisition is not able to estimate the unit price and the amount, that information is furnished by the purchasing office.

The requisition is filed with the business office. If the amount requested is within the budget of the school or department and if the items requested are within the policies of the board, the requisition is approved. If the supplies or equipment are on hand, the requisition is sent to the warehouse and the amount is charged to the budget of the school or department. If the supplies or equipment are not on hand, a numbered purchase order is signed. As soon as the purchase order is signed it is entered as an encumbrance against the budget appropriation for the appropriate account. It is also charged against the budget for the department or school if the item is chargeable to that budget.

One copy of the purchase order is sent to the vendor, one to the originator of the requisition and at least one copy kept by the business office. When the goods are delivered, the originator of the requisition checks the delivery against the invoice and the purchase order. If the goods are received in good condition and they are in the quantity and of the quality ordered, the invoice is approved. Any exceptions should be noted and that information along with the invoice and purchase order should be sent to the business office.

The requisition, the purchase order, and the invoice serve as voucher collateral for determining the payment to be made. These original documents are assembled, pre-audited and processed for payment by check. Voucher jackets are frequently used for assembling and filing these documents. If the voucher jacket is coded for the proper accounts, accounting operations are facilitated.

When quantity purchasing is done, requisitions are consolidated. This greatly reduces the number of purchase orders and invoices which must be processed. In practice most school systems make both quantity purchases for all schools and departments and also purchases for individual schools and departments. The persons originating requisitions should do sufficient advance planning to keep the number of individual requisitions within reasonable bounds.

OTHER MEANS FOR EFFECTING ECONOMIES IN SCHOOL EXPENDITURES

The board of education should explore all possibilities for eliminating any excessive expenditure for a given amount of goods and services. Competitive bidding has already been emphasized. But there are other possibilities for conserving school funds. Some of those possibilities for many school systems are as follows: (1) district owned and operated school buses serviced by a publicly owned bus shop, (2) the operation of a school plant maintenance shop, (3) the operation of a warehouse, (4) the centralized financing of school lunch rooms.

The feasibility of utilizing these operations to save money depends largely on the size and needs of the school district and the managerial competencies of the administrators employed by the school district. A well administered system of district owned and operated school buses may provide school transportation at 25 per cent less than the cost of contracting for that service. An efficiently operated school plant maintenance shop may provide for school plant repairs at 40 per cent less than by private contract. The operation of a central warehouse or warehouses may be necessary in some districts to make maximum savings by quantity buying. The centralized financing of school lunch rooms may provide better food services at a lower cost in many districts These operations are described in Chapter 19.

SAFEGUARDING MONEY

The broad concept of safeguarding money involves practically every phase of educational administration and organization. If insufficient funds are invested in education, the money that is expended does not yield as high a return per dollar as a larger investment. If the system of taxation for school support is inequitable, the result will be an under-investment in education, an unfavorable incidence on the private economy, or both. If the organizational plan perpetuates unnecessary small, inefficient school districts or school centers, the result is lower educational returns per dollar invested than should be received. If planning does not result in an appropriate synchronization of the educational plan, the spending plan and the financing plan, the result is lower educational returns per dollar invested than should be received. If school funds are not expended judiciously, less education is purchased than should be expected from the money expended.

These broad aspects of the conservation and safeguarding of money have already been presented. But school funds can be lost or misused due to dishonesty, accident, carelessness, misfortune, or ignorance of the law. The special measures which should be taken by a board to protect itself and the people from loss of funds due to these causes are presented in this section.

Protection of School Funds in Depositories

When school funds are deposited in a commercial bank they should be fully protected at all times. The standard method for protecting school funds in depositories is to require the depository bank to escrow collateral in another bank equal to the amount of the deposit. The escrowed collateral is under the control of the board of education. When the collateral is escrowed, a receipt is sent to the board of education by the bank in which the collateral is escrowed and a copy is sent to the depository bank. The bank which owns the collateral continues to collect the interest earned on the collateral. If the depository bank fails, as much of the collateral is sold as is necessary for the board to recover the full amount of its deposit.

The escrowed collateral should be in the form of United States government securities and such municipal bonds as are approved by the board.

The bank in which the collateral is escrowed should be financially independent of the depository bank. It can be either a Federal Reserve Bank or a commercial bank. Usually the bank in which the collateral is escrowed is larger than the depository bank. It is also usually a correspondent bank for the depository bank. If the bank in which the collateral is escrowed is a correspondent bank for the board's depository bank, it normally does not charge the depository bank for this service. A board of education thus can have its bank deposits fully protected at all times at no cost either to the board or the depository bank. Therefore, a board should not select a bank as its depository unless that bank agrees to protect its funds fully at all times by escrowed collateral.

The laws of some states require that the procedures just described be followed for protecting all deposits of school funds. Every state should have such a law. The reasons for this are obvious. The Federal government and the state governments require that deposits of Federal and state funds be protected by collateral. A considerable part of the assets of a school depository bank may be in the form of collateral escrowed to protect deposits of Federal and state funds. If the depository bank fails, the Federal and the state government have a prior claim on the bank assets. This reduces the amount of the bank's assets which will be available for returning to the board the amount of school funds it deposited.

Insurance by the Federal Government. The Federal Deposit Insurance Corporation insures deposits up to $10,000 for each account in most banks. But $10,000 of insurance is entirely inadequate to protect the deposits of boards of education in all except very small school districts. The F.D.I.C. insurance does provide complete protection for the deposits made by most private persons. If the board of education does not protect its deposits with escrowed collateral, school funds on deposit are not safeguarded as well as the deposits of private persons. It is inexcusable negligence on the part of a board of education for it to fail to provide adequate protection for school funds on deposit.

The F.D.I.C. insurance can be used to protect deposits of internal funds for individual schools provided no one account exceeds $10,000. Some boards of education require that all internal funds be turned over to the board of education in order to provide centralized accounting services and more control over the administration of internal funds. If this is done, deposits of internal funds can be protected by escrowed collateral in the same manner as other school funds.

Surety Bonds

Bonding of school officials and employees not only protects the district against loss but it also stimulates officials and employees to keep better records and to follow more business-like procedures in handling school funds.

The principal types of surety bonds in which boards of education are interested are: (1) fidelity bonds to insure against the dishonesty of an individual, (2) public official bonds to insure against malperformance or nonperformance of duties by public officials, and (3) contract bonds to insure against nonperformance of contracts. Also of interest is the broad form money and securities policy which can protect an official or school employee from suit by a surety company to recover from an individual any funds which were lost due to no fault of that individual. These types of protection are discussed in order.

Fidelity Bonds. All persons handling or having access to school money or negotiable merchandise should be under a fidelity bond of some type. The principal types of fidelity bonds are: (1) *individual bonds,* (2) *name schedule bonds,* (3) *position schedule bonds,* and (4) *blanket bonds.*

The individual bond is written on an individual in the sum required by the board, and the cost of the bond is determined by the amount for which the individual is insured. It is usually the most expensive type of fidelity bond.

The name schedule bond covers a number of individuals listed in the same schedule. It furnishes the same protection as the individual bond. The premium is usually less than the total of the premiums of individual bonds carried on the same individuals.

The position schedule bond does not require the listing of the names of individuals occupying the position. The board is insured against the dishonesty of a person occupying the position. This type of bond is particularly useful in positions in which there is a rapid turnover of personnel. The bond has to be changed only when positions are added or abolished.

The blanket bond is now being used widely. It is probably the best type of fidelity bond for the average school system. A blanket bond can be used to cover all school employees. Additions and deductions of persons covered can be made without notifying the company and without premium change during the year. Losses can be recovered without identifying the individual causing the loss, provided it can be established that the loss came within the terms of the bond.

Public employee blanket bonds are of two principal types: (1) the honesty blanket position bond and (2) the honesty blanket bond. In writing an honesty blanket position bond, employees are divided into classes according to the insuring risks involved. Employees are usually classified as: (1) executives and those who actually handle money, securities, or negotiable merchandise, (2) those who do not handle money securities, and merchandise but have access to these valuables, (3) those who represent little or no risk. The higher the proportion of persons covered in the low risk groups, the lower the premium. This type of policy pays up to the bond limit for each person involved in the loss. The typical coverage provided is a minimum of $2,500 and a maximum of $25,000 for each person.

The honesty blanket bond insures the district against the dishonest acts of all employees except those covered by statutory public official bonds. It pays up to the bond limit for any one loss. This type of bond requires a minimum coverage but prescribes no maximum coverage.

Public Official Bonds. These bonds are usually called statutory public official bonds because all states require that certain classes of public officials be bonded. All officials who are responsible for the disbursement, collection, custody, or care of school funds should be covered with a public official bond. These usually include the superintendent of schools, the tax collector, the treasurer, and members of the board of education.

The public official bond is much broader in its coverage than the fidelity bond. It not only protects the board from the dishonesty of an individual but it also protects the board from loss due to his ignorance, negligence, or carelessness and from loss of funds in the custody of a public official due to burglary or fire. The public official bond is a written obligation guaranteeing that a public official will faithfully perform his duties and that he will honestly account for all funds and property that come into his possession. Public policy requires a very broad coverage in a public official bond.

Contract Bonds. A contract bond is a surety bond which guarantees the performance of some contract or agreement. Following are the different types of contract bonds with which boards of education are concerned:

1. A *bid bond* is furnished by a contractor when he submits his bid. It is a guarantee that if his bid is accepted he will sign the contract and furnish a performance bond acceptable to the district.

2. A *performance bond* guarantees faithful performance of the contract in accordance with its terms. A contract for school construction should contain a maintenance clause whereby the contractor provides a guarantee against defective workmanship and materials for a stated period after acceptance of the work.

3. A *payment bond* guarantees that the contractor will pay in full all the suppliers of labor and materials. This may be a separate bond or it may be included in the performance bond.

4. The *supply bond* guarantees that certain materials will be furnished or supplied.

It is customary and required by law in some states to award building contracts to the lowest responsible bidder. Contract bonds help to eliminate incompetent and dishonest contractors from bidding. If the contractor does not have a good reputation or if he is overcommitted financially, a surety company is not likely to issue him a bond. Therefore, contract bonds should be required for all construction contracts of any importance.

When bid bonds are required, if a contractor is awarded the contract and then refuses to furnish a performance bond, he must pay damages up to the amount of the bid bond. This usually amounts to about 5 per cent of the contract.

The New York State Department of Education in its handbook, *Insurance,* has pointed out the following advantages of contract bonds:

1. The school district knows that a contract will be completed either by the contractor or the surety company, at a stipulated price.
2. Incompetent or dishonest contractors have difficulty in obtaining contracts because they will not be able to qualify for a surety bond if their reputation is poor.
3. Construction progress is aided since payment of bills for labor and material is guaranteed in the Performance Bond or as a separate Payment Bond. Supply houses usually make prompt shipments to contractors whose credit has been established.
4. Deserving contractors are often aided by surety companies to finish a troublesome contract. Without this aid the contractor might be in serious trouble.[7]

---

[7] University of the State of New York, *Insurance* (Albany, N.Y.: State Department of Education, 1956), p. 56.

Broad Form Money and Securities Policy. This is not a surety bond but it offers a wide range of protection. Following are the coverages provided by this type of policy:

1. Combination of Safe Burglary, Robbery and Theft policies
2. Loss of money and securities within the premises caused by "destruction, disappearance, or wrongful abstraction" thereof
3. Loss of or damage to property other than money and securities (except by fire) caused by safe burglary or robbery
4. All damage (except by fire) to the premises caused by robbery or safe burglary
5. Loss of money and securities occurring outside the premises caused by "destruction, disappearance or wrongful abstraction" thereof when being conveyed by a messenger
6. All loss of or damage to property other than money and securities caused by robbery or an attempt thereat outside the premises while such property is being conveyed by a messenger
7. Loss of money and securities by fire
8. Loss of money and property from an unlocked safe
9. Loss of money stolen from the cash register in the cafeteria
10. Damage to a safe and other property if explosives are used to gain entry to the safe
11. Damage to a locked cash register from which money is stolen
12. Disappearance of money being conveyed by the school district treasurer to the bank for deposit
13. Loss of money from the school safe when the school principal or other employee is forced to open the safe for robbers [8]

This type of policy will even cover the loss of school funds stolen from the house of a public employee or from any location named in the policy where funds are temporarily kept. There is a premium charge for each location named in this policy.

The public official bond protects the district from losses of funds in the custody of the bonded official, but it is not an insurance policy for the school official. The public official is held liable for the disappearance of school funds regardless of circumstances. The surety company assumes his place to make good any loss to the school district. But the surety company can sue the bonded individual to collect from him the amount of the loss it has paid plus the expenses it has incurred in recovering its losses. This is true even though the funds disappeared through no fault of the person bonded. The broad form money and securities policy will protect the public employee up to the amount of coverage from personal losses not due to dishonesty on his part.

If a district carries broad form money and securities insurance or burglary and theft insurance it should be carried with the same com-

[8] *Ibid.*, pp. 47–48.

pany that provides it with fidelity and public official bonds. When this practice is followed there is no need to prove just who caused the loss. If two different companies are involved, the district must be able to prove that it was either a school employee who was responsible or that it was a non-school employee who was guilty. If the district cannot prove whether it was a school employee or a non-school employee who was responsible, neither company will pay. If the insurance and bonds are furnished by the same company, it must pay in either event.

Handling Cash

The handling of cash should be minimized in school operations. Taxes are collected by the tax collector and turned over to the treasurer. Payments are authorized by the board of education. This provides three independent points of control because the accounts of the board must be reconciled with the accounts of the treasurer and the accounts of the treasurer must be reconciled with the accounts of the tax collectors or other agencies sending money to him. The board makes its payments by check. It is true that some small invoices may be paid from petty cash accounts but the board sets up petty cash accounts by check and the expenditures from petty cash accounts can readily be audited.

But considerable cash comes into the hands of the board's employees from a number of sources. This cash is from non-tax sources, but it is school money regardless of its sources, and it should be handled with as much honesty and propriety as tax money. Some of the sources of cash handled by school employees are: instructional materials fees, school lunch funds, sales from store rooms and school stores, donations and gifts, tuition fees in some states, and a host of student activity funds. Some cash from student activity funds may be handled in part by students.

Accounting procedures for these types of funds have been described in Chapter 16. However, if cash is not properly handled, it may never get into the accounts. Procedures for handling cash should be established so as to minimize the chances for losing funds by theft or carelessness. Students sometimes sell tickets or merchandise for which they receive cash. If supervision is inadequate, there is unnecessary temptation for students to take funds that do not belong to them. If cash is carelessly left unguarded it provides an unnecessary temptation to custodians, maids, and any employee or student. School officials and administrators who permit cash to be handled in such a manner as to create unnecessary temptation are morally if not legally contributing to delinquency.

Following are some general suggestions for the handling of cash:

1. Cash should be deposited in a bank to the proper account as soon as practicable. Cash kept on school premises invites burglaries which result in property damage as well as loss of money.

2. Payments should not be made by cash when they can be made by check without undue inconvenience.

3. At least two and preferably three persons should be involved in the control of a particular sum of cash—for example: collector, treasurer and disburser. Records should be kept by each of these agents and these records should be compared. To illustrate: the ticket seller receives numbered tickets; he sells tickets and gives to the principal or his agent the cash he received, the unsold tickets, and a signed statement of the cash turned in; the principal or his agent gives the ticket seller a receipt; and the cash is deposited in the bank. The receipts, the numbered tickets and the bank deposits serve as independent original documents verifying that the cash was properly handled. An important point is that a bank deposit slip is no evidence that the person receiving funds deposited all the money that came into his possession. The person depositing cash should have written evidence from another person which will establish that he deposited all the money he received.

4. Cash kept on school premises should be carefully guarded at all times or placed in a secure safe or vault.

Investing School Funds

Boards of education frequently have funds on hand that will not be needed for some time. Considerable interest may be earned on these funds. For example, idle funds may be invested in United States Treasury Bills or other appropriate Federal securities. Funds may be placed on time deposit if permitted by law and they are properly protected by collateral. The principal of any investment should be fully protected. The amount of interest earned is of secondary importance to the security of the principal. Funds should be invested in securities that mature or can be liquidated at the time needed by the board without loss of principal.

Auditing School Accounts

Auditing of accounts is a standard procedure followed by business and industry as well as government. The principal purposes of the school audit program are as follows:

1. To protect employees and the board
2. To furnish assurance to the public that school funds and property are being properly administered

3. To furnish objective, complete, and accurate financial statistics on educational operations

4. To determine the adequacy of internal checks

5. To determine the adequacy of financial accounting procedures and records

6. To determine the adequacy of property records and inventory procedures

7. To determine the adequacy of internal accounting procedures

8. To assist in developing improved business administration and financial accounting procedures and policies

The two principal types of school auditing are internal auditing and external auditing.

Internal or Pre-Auditing. Internal auditing is ordinarily done by employees of the board. The primary purpose of internal auditing is to minimize mistakes and to avoid legal and financial trouble. School internal auditing consists principally of pre-auditing before action is taken.[9] Pre-auditing operations consist primarily of: (1) giving advance approval to requisitions, purchase orders, contracts, or other actions which result in a commitment of the board, (2) careful checking of all original documents prior to approval of payments. Pre-auditing operations should not result in undue delay in the processing of requisitions and purchase orders for supplies and equipment or in the processing of invoices, claims, and payrolls for payment. But adequate internal auditing gives maximum assurance to the board that its financial policies are being currently observed and that errors are minimized. It also reduces the chances of unfavorable criticisms of the board and the superintendent in the post-audit report.

External Auditing or Post-Auditing. External audits are usually post-audits. Following are some characteristics of post-audits:

1. They are made after the year's work has been completed.

2. External audits are made by independent auditors. That is, the auditor should not be an employee of the board or subject to its control.

3. An external audit is made of the operations for each fiscal year.

4. The audit is made soon after the close of the fiscal year.

5. The audit report is formally presented to the board and a copy given to the superintendent.

Post-audits of school accounts should be made by auditors trained and experienced in public accounting. Auditors employed by the board should be: (1) Certified Public Accountants, (2) Registered Accountants, or (3) accountants licensed specifically for the purpose of examining government accounts.

---

[9] An internal audit could be an audit made by an employee of the board in anticipation of an external audit.

Some states provide state auditors for school districts. These auditors should be trained to examine school accounts. If state auditors do not provide the board with competent auditing service, the board should have an additional audit of its accounts made by a qualified public accountant.

Auditors should perform only the services they are employed to render. It is not the function of the auditor to criticize educational policy or to recommend changes in the educational program. Auditors are not educational experts and they should not make recommendations in areas in which they have no competence or for which they have no responsibility.

Following is an outline of the more important records which the auditor should examine:

1. The minutes of the board of education
2. The school budget
3. Original documents relating to the authorization of expenditures
4. Original documents relating to the making of payments
5. Ledgers, registers, journals, and other account books
6. The internal accounts of individual schools if that is a part of his employment contract
7. Tax collections and delinquencies
8. All revenue and non-revenue receipt records
9. Bank accounts
10. Investments
11. Sinking funds, bond funds, capital accounts, trust funds, and all other special funds
12. Deeds to property and property inventories including stores inventory
13. Insurance policies
14. Cash not deposited in banks
15. Surety bonds carried

Audit reports should include at least the following:

1. A letter of transmittal
2. A statement describing the scope and limitations of the audit
3. A summary of findings
4. Recommendations for improving financial accounting and other appropriate business administration procedures
5. The necessary financial statements and schedules
6. Other statistical information within the scope of the audit

A good auditing program gives the public assurance that school affairs are being faithfully administered. It protects those who are responsible for funds and it protects the public. Therefore, the board should establish sound auditing policies and employ competent auditors for both internal and external accounting.

Many boards of education use qualified employees from the central office to audit the internal accounts of individual schools. Although auditors from the central office are board employees they are external to the school being audited. The board should employ competent personnel for auditing the accounts of individual schools. This same personnel can also be used to help with the internal auditing of central accounts. If the board does not have competent accountants in its employ, it should engage competent public accountants for auditing individual school accounts.

SOME PROBLEMS AND ISSUES

Some additional problems relating to spending and safeguarding school funds are presented in the following paragraphs.

Should Bid Awards Be Made Only at a Formal Meeting of the Board?

All meetings for opening bids should be open to bidders. But competitive bids have to be obtained for many purchases. If the board requires that the successful bidder for each bid invitation be determined at a board meeting, the result is: (1) an excessive number of board meetings, or (2) excessive delays in making bid awards. Furthermore, it requires a great deal of time to open and tabulate bids, to determine whether the products offered by bidders meet specifications and to determine the lowest and most responsible bidder. If these operations are all carried out in board meetings, entirely too much time is required of board members. On the other hand, no board of education wants to give to its superintendent or to its purchasing agent the full responsibility for making all bid awards. Neither does the superintendent nor the purchasing agent wish to accept full responsibility for making all bid awards.

The board of education should adopt policies for making bid awards that will substantially resolve these difficulties. Following are some policies that should be considered:

1. The superintendent, or his representative, is given the authority to make bid awards for purchases which cost less than a specified amount. The board makes the bid award for all purchases above this specified amount.

2. When the amount involved is sufficiently large to require that the

bid be awarded by the board and when considerable time is required for tabulating bids and determining whether products meet specifications, bids will be opened and processed by the superintendent or his representative prior to the board meeting in order that the board may make the bid award with a minimum expenditure of time.

What should be the maximum amount of the purchase for which the superintendent or his representative should be authorized to make the bid award?

Should the Board Approve Each Item Before an Expenditure Can Be Made?

Boards of education need to spend money continuously throughout the fiscal year. If every item of expenditure must be approved by the board before it is made, the board would have to be in session almost continuously or there would be undesirable delays in making many needed expenditures. For example, if the sewerage system became obstructed, it would be ridiculous to require the superintendent to call a board meeting to authorize him to employ a plumber to remove the obstruction.

One of the major purposes of a board in approving a budget is to provide advance approval of expenditure for the items included in each budget appropriation up to the amount of the budget appropriation. As pointed out in Chapter 16, monthly financial reports providing a budget reconciliation should be presented to the board. If expenditures are being made at a greater rate than they should be, as indicated by the budget status, the board can instruct the superintendent to reduce the spending rate. The board can also establish allotments of budget appropriations for each quarter or other specified period of time. If the superintendent makes an illegal expenditure, the board can recover on the bond of the superintendent. It is much more important for the board to exercise proper budgetary control than for it to spend the major part of its time in checking requisitions and invoices. It is good practice, however, for the superintendent to secure prior board approval for a major expenditure even though it is included in the budget.

The problem of securing prior approval before incurring an expense is also associated with the problem of obtaining prior approval by the board before making payment. It is standard procedure to present payrolls and accounts payable to the board for approval. But if no check can be drawn without prior approval by the board, the work of the business office cannot be spread evenly over the month. Furthermore, discounts may be lost on some purchases if payment is not made promptly. Therefore, many boards of education have made provision for the payment of certain accounts prior to formal approval by the board. If payment is improperly made for any item, recovery can be made by the board on the bond of the responsible official. The board should adopt policies that will enable it to pay its bills promptly and at the same time provide proper safeguards.

If payrolls are made every two weeks, should the board be called into session every two weeks to approve payrolls before checks can be given to employees? Under what conditions should a superintendent and his staff make purchases without specific approval by the board?

How Should Petty Cash Funds Be Administered?

Petty cash funds are issued to authorized persons in order to expedite the purchasing of certain low-cost items. It is impossible for a school principal or a department head to anticipate every possible item that is needed. Sometimes an emergency that could not have been anticipated creates the need for the item. The item needed may not be in stock at the warehouse. There may be but little need to stock the item because it is seldom needed. The item may cost only $1.00 and it is stocked by a local hardware store. The school may be located ten miles from the central office. Let us assume that the item is a small part for a machine in the industrial arts shop and that the machine cannot be operated until the part is replaced. The regular procedure is for the principal to file a requisition with the central office for the item.

If the regular purchasing procedure is followed, it may take a week to ten days for the principal to receive the item he needs and the cost of processing may be several times the cost of the item. It is in order to avoid absurd and inefficient operations of this type that petty cash funds are used.

The procedures for administering a petty cash fund are as follows:

1. The person authorized by the board to have a petty cash fund signs a check requisition for the amount of the fund authorized. Let us assume that the amount authorized is $50.00.

2. A check is issued to the person signing the check requisition.

3. The person having the petty cash fund periodically submits to the central office paid invoices substantiating purchases that have been made from the petty cash fund.

4. A check is issued by the central office to the person operating the petty cash fund in the amount of the paid invoices submitted and this check restores the fund to its original amount of $50.00.

5. The central office distributes the payments substantiated by the paid invoices to the appropriate expenditure accounts and charges them to the appropriate budget appropriations.

6. In auditing a petty cash fund, the cash on hand plus the paid invoices on hand that have not been turned in must always equal $50.00.

7. When closing out a petty cash fund, the operator of the fund must turn in to the central office paid invoices and cash that total $50.00.

It is obvious that unrestricted spending from petty cash accounts may remove part of the incentive for principals and department heads to do adequate advance planning. It can also lead to paying higher prices than can be obtained by central purchasing. Therefore, the total operations of each cash fund should be carefully defined in the regulations of the board.

What criteria should be used in defining the limits for the use of petty cash funds?

Should State School Auditors Be Employees of the State Department of Education?

Auditors are employed by the state department of education in some states to audit the accounts of local school districts. This practice has been defended for the following reasons:

1. Auditors employed by the state department of education are familiar with school financial accounting procedures.

2. Auditors employed by the state department of education can help enforce the policies and regulations of the state board of education.

3. Auditors employed by the state department of education are better informed on general educational policies and can be of greater assistance to local school districts than other auditors.

Some objections to the employment of auditors by the state department of education are as follows:

1. State department of education auditors are not truly independent auditors. Accounts of local school districts are interwoven with the accounts of the state department of education.

2. Auditors from the state department of education may be perceived by local school officials as a threat. There is a danger that state department officials may use auditors to exercise unwarranted control over local school affairs. In any event the employment of auditors by the state department of education puts it in a less favorable position for exercising true leadership.

3. There is a danger that state department of education auditors may interfere with local educational policy.

What are some other advantages and disadvantages of employment of school auditors by the state department of education? Does state auditing cost less than private auditing?

SELECTED REFERENCES

Burke, Arvid J., *Financing Public Schools in the United States*, rev. ed. New York: Harper and Brothers, 1957. Chapter 2.

Grieder, Calvin, and William E. Rosenstengel, *Public School Administration*. New York: The Ronald Press Company, 1954. Chapter 19.

Hunt, Herold C., and Paul R. Pierce, *The Practice of School Administration*. Boston: Houghton Mifflin Company, 1958. Chapter 20.

Johns, R. L., and E. L. Morphet, editors, *Problems and Issues in Public School Finance*. New York: Bureau of Publications, Teachers College, Columbia University, 1952. Chapter 13.

Linn, Henry H., editor, *School Business Administration*. New York: Ronald Press Company, 1956. Chapters 7, 8, 9, and 11.

Miller, Van, and Willard B. Spalding, *The Public Administration of American Schools*, 2nd ed. Yonkers-on-Hudson, N.Y.: World Book Company, 1958. Chapter 17.

Morphet, Edgar L., Roe L. Johns, and Theodore L. Reller, *Educational Administration*. Englewood Cliffs, N.J.: Prentice-Hall, Inc., 1959. Chapters 20 and 21.

Morrison, H. C., *The Management of School Money*. Chicago: University of Chicago Press, 1930.

Mort, Paul R., and Walter C. Reusser, *Public School Finance*, 2nd ed. New York: McGraw-Hill Book Company, Inc., 1951. Chapters 10 and 11.

Rosenstengel, William Everett, and Jefferson N. Eastmond, *School Finance*. New York: Ronald Press Company, 1957. Chapters 12, 13, and 14.

University of the State of New York, State Department of Education, *Accounting and Reporting*. Albany, N.Y.: State Department of Education, 1956. Chapter 11.

——, *Insurance*. Albany, N.Y.: State Department of Education, 1956.

——, *Purchases and Stores*. Albany, N.Y.: State Department of Education, 1955.

CHAPTER EIGHTEEN

Protecting

Property and Persons

The general purpose of insurance is to provide for the shifting to others or the sharing with others of risks that are greater than it is wise for an agency, institution, person, firm, or corporation to carry individually. Some special types of school insurance have the additional purpose of providing an arrangement whereby a board of education may discharge an obligation for which it is morally responsible but not legally responsible under existing laws.

The board of education has property, money and securities in its custody that are subject to loss or damage from many causes under many different circumstances. The board and its employees in the course of operating the school system may cause financial loss or bodily injury to others for which they are legally or morally responsible. The board has the legal responsibility in some states and the moral responsibility in all states to "save harmless" [1] its employees for injury done to others during the lawful performance of their duties. The board has the legal responsibility in some states and the moral responsibility in all states to provide financial protection for its employees who are injured during the course of the performance of their duties. There is a legal responsibility in some states and a moral responsibility in all states for the board to provide financial protection for students who are injured during the course of receiving instruction.

---

[1] That is, the board assumes the liability of the employee.

Thus the financial risks of a board are very complex and its moral obligations very numerous. The development of an adequate insurance program for a school district involves many considerations. The laws of the states vary widely in: (1) the types of insurance coverage and the amounts of the coverage for different types of risks that a school district must carry, (2) the types of insurance coverage that are permissible, and (3) the degree of liability of the board for loss or injury caused to others or suffered by others as a consequence of operating schools.

Boards of education differ greatly in: (1) the types of risks incurred, (2) the financial significance of risks, (3) the spread of property risks and (4) financial ability to bear risks. No one insurance program is suitable for all districts. In fact, no one insurance program is equally suitable for any two districts unless it occurs as a rare statistical coincidence. Therefore, the insurance program of each district should be tailored to its needs. This requires much study and intelligent planning. The purpose in planning the insurance program is to obtain the maximum of needed protection at the minimum cost. The principal types of protection needed by boards of education are presented in this chapter.

In terms of "who furnishes the protection," insurance can be classified as: (1) commercial, (2) state, (3) self-insurance. Commercial insurance is procured from private companies. Some types of insurance are provided by a few states and this is called state insurance. When a district builds up an insurance reserve fund in order to spread its losses from insurable risks over several years, it has self-insurance. Primary emphasis is given in this chapter to commercial insurance.

FIRE INSURANCE

School buildings and their contents represent major investments by the board. The loss of a major building and its contents would be a financial disaster to all except the largest school districts unless that building was adequately insured at the time of the loss. The cost of replacing a school plant may be several times the annual revenue receipts of a school district. The revenue receipts totalled only approximately $200 per child enrolled in some inadequately financed school districts in 1958–59. It required approximately $800 per pupil in 1958–59 to construct the cheapest type of low-cost permanent buildings.[2] Assuming that the cheapest type of buildings would be constructed in inadequately financed districts, the building replacement cost of all

---

[2] Actually, no district should construct buildings of this type.

buildings would be approximately four times the annual revenue receipts in such districts.

In some better financed districts in 1958–59, revenue receipts totalled approximately $400 per child enrolled. It cost approximately $1200 per pupil in 1958–59 to construct buildings of medium quality. Assuming that the better financed districts would construct buildings of medium quality or better, it would require at least three times the revenue receipts of the better financed districts to replace all buildings. Therefore, the loss of school buildings is a serious matter in all districts, but the less wealthy the district the greater the possibility of financial disaster.

Spread of Risks

If a district owns only one building, it has the maximum possible risk because it may have to replace its entire plant at one time. If a district owns many buildings located on widely separated sites, the chance of having to replace its total plant at one time is so remote as to be nonexistent for all practical purposes. For example, a large district may own 100 or more buildings located on separate sites. If a district owning 100 buildings loses one building which houses one per cent of its pupils, the loss would equal only approximately 3 per cent of its revenue receipts for one year. Therefore, the smaller the district and the fewer the number of buildings owned on separate sites, the greater the risk from the loss of a building.

It should not be inferred that because risks from building losses are proportionately greater in some districts than in others, building insurance is unimportant in low risk districts. It is important in all districts but building insurance is of critical importance in districts that risk financial disaster from building losses. The history of school building losses unfortunately reveals that frequently the districts that have the greatest need for insurance are the most inadequately insured.

Some of the most important points to consider when insuring school plants against loss by fire and other causes are presented in the following paragraphs.

Coverage Needed

The ordinary fire insurance policy insures against direct damage caused by fire and lightning. The extended coverage endorsement extends the coverage to insure against other perils. The extended coverage endorsement usually covers loss caused by windstorm, explosion, riot, civil commotion, aircraft, vehicles, and smoke. In some sections of the nation, insurance protection from loss caused by earthquake should be provided. The board should not gamble on what is likely to be the cause of building losses. All probable causes of building loss should be covered. If the probability of loss from a particular cause of loss is small, the cost of including it in the coverage is small.

Vandalism and malicious mischief insurance can be provided as a separate clause in a fire insurance policy. This protection usually is not available unless the extended coverage indorsement is also included in the policy.

Appraisal of Insurable Value

Fire insurance should be based on the sound insurable value of a building and its contents. The sound insurable value of a building is defined as the cost of replacing it at current prices less the cost of non-insurable items (excavations, fillings, certain parts of foundations, and underground sewerage, piping, and wiring), less depreciation.

Boards of education can employ a commercial appraisal company, an architect, or a qualified construction contractor to determine the sound insurable value of its buildings. Insurance companies will also give an estimate of the sound insurable value of a building. That estimate is usually based upon a square or cubic foot unit price.

It is highly important that accurate appraisals be made both of buildings and contents. Following are some reasons why accurate appraisals are necessary:

1. The district must provide proof of loss. The following quotation is taken from a typical fire insurance policy: "the insured shall give immediate written notice . . . of any loss . . . furnish a complete inventory of the destroyed, damaged, and undamaged property, showing in detail quantities, costs, actual cash value, and amount of loss claimed." Lump-sum estimates of the loss of building contents are not satisfactory. The actual cash value of each item must be shown in order to establish loss.

2. When coinsurance is carried, insurance equal to or above a fixed per cent of insurable value must be carried if a coinsurance penalty is to be avoided. Accurate appraisals are necessary for the board to determine the amount of insurance it must carry in order to avoid penalty.

3. Even if coinsurance is not carried, the board will likely overinsure or underinsure its buildings if accurate appraisals are not available. If a board overinsures its buildings, it wastes the taxpayers' money. If it underinsures, it exposes the district to possible financial disaster.

4. Building insurance rates are lower than the rates on contents. Accurate appraisals correctly differentiate between items that should be classified as a part of the building and those that should be classified under contents. If an item can be properly classified as a part of the

building, it should be so classified in order to take advantage of the lower rates available.

Duplicate copies of the inventory of the contents of a building should be made and one copy kept in the central office. If only one copy of the inventory is made and that copy kept in the insured building, it might be destroyed in the fire that destroyed the building. In that event, it would be difficult to establish proof of loss of contents. An inventory of contents should be made annually but that inventory should be revised during the year if there are any substantial additions to insured contents. Ideally, a perpetual inventory should be kept, but that requires an excessive amount of clerical labor.

Flat Insurance and Coinsurance

Flat insurance is a contract which includes no penalty for failure to insure property equal to or above a given per cent of its true value. In other words, it contains no requirement relative to coinsured value. The insured may place any amount of coverage he desires on his property. Property may be insured at a low per cent or high per cent of insurable value, but the insured may never collect more than the amount of the coverage nor more than the insurable value. The rates for this type of insurance are usually higher than for coinsurance.

Coinsurance contracts provide rates in proportion to the percentage of coverage. The higher the percentage of coverage of insurable value, the lower the rates that are charged. For example, different rates are established for 50, 60, 70, 80, 90 and 100 per cent of coverage of insured value. If a district carries coinsurance, it must insure its property at the per cent agreed upon to avoid a coinsurance penalty when a loss occurs.

In order to qualify for a reduced rate, the board agrees to carry insurance equal to the amount specified in the coinsurance clause. If the board does so, it will recover the entire amount of the loss up to the face amount of the policy. If the contract is for 80 per cent coinsurance and the board carries only 40 per cent of the amount required, it can recover only 50 per cent of the loss up to the face amount of the policy.

Many boards of education find it advisable to carry 80 per cent coinsurance on most buildings. The following schedule illustrates how 80 per cent coinsurance operates.

	Case 1	Case 2	Case 3	Case 4
Value of property at time of loss	$400,000	$400,000	$400,000	$400,000
Amount of insurance required by 80 per cent coinsurance	320,000	320,000	320,000	320,000
Amount of insurance carried	160,000	320,000	320,000	160,000
Loss due to fire	80,000	80,000	350,000	380,000
Amount recovered from insurance	40,000	80,000	320,000	160,000

Determination of Fire Insurance Rates

Insurance rate schedules are developed by rating bureaus. In some states the insurance commission approves or disapproves schedules suggested by the rating bureaus. But all rate schedules are based on the schedules developed by rating bureaus.

Schools are rated under the School and Institution Schedule. This schedule is divided into two parts, one for fire resistive buildings and the other for non-fire resistive buildings. Base rates are established for each schedule which reflect the type of construction, the quality of the fire protection in the community in which the school is located, and the experience record of losses for the class of risk. Each community is graded for its fire department equipment, its personnel, its water supply, and its alarm service. Various charges and credits are given for features of the building that cause or prevent school fire losses.

The rate make-up sheet shows these charges and credits. These charges and credits should be studied carefully. The rating organization upon request will send an engineer to check the conditions that produce charges. He will make recommendations for changing a charge into a credit or at least eliminating the charge. The cost of making the recommended changes should be compared with the savings to be made from receiving a credit. All conditions which result in a saving to the district should be corrected. If the condition constitutes a hazard to pupils, it should be corrected even if there is no saving. When conditions have been corrected, action should be taken to see that the insurance rate has been adjusted accordingly.

The easiest and the least costly way to earn credits is to incorporate credit features when a building is constructed. The rating bureau should be consulted when a new building is being planned. It is easier and less costly to change a plan than a building.

Term Insurance

Boards of education can save considerable money by purchasing term insurance. The three-year rate is normally 2½ times the one-year rate and the five-year rate 4 times the rate for one year. Therefore, five-year term insurance is the most economical insurance to buy.[3]

Boards of education can spread the cost of the premium over the term of the policy by the budget plan or the installment plan. Under the budget plan for a five-year term policy: (1) five policies each equal to 1/5 of the amount of the policy are written, (2) policies are written

---

[3] Except state or self-insurance.

for 1, 2, 3, 4, and 5 year terms and the premiums are paid when the policies are written, (3) as each policy expires it is replaced with a five-year term policy, (4) during the first year of the budget plan the premiums cost 60 per cent of a straight five-year term policy but after a few years they will be 20 per cent of the premium for the five-year term policy.

Under the installment plan, a single five-year term policy is written and the insured pays 25 per cent of the five-year premium during the first year and 78 per cent of the first year's premium for each of the remaining four years. The insured pays approximately a 3 per cent higher premium under the installment plan but the first year payment is less. Either of these plans is recommended depending upon the needs of the district.

Blanket Insurance

A fire insurance contract that covers several properties is called blanket insurance. Ninety per cent or more coinsurance must be carried on blanket insurance. An average rate for all buildings is calculated rather than a separate rate for each property. There is generally no saving in blanket insurance but it is becoming quite popular. Following are some of the advantages of blanket insurance:

1. The coinsurance penalty on an individual piece of property may be avoided as long as the total coverage satisfies the coinsurance requirements.

2. Record keeping is simplified and it is easier to keep check on maturing policies.

3. Property that is moved from one building to another is automatically insured without policy modification.

Builders' Risk Insurance

Builders' risk insurance is for the purpose of protecting the owner's interest in the building during the course of construction. Boards pay contractors in installments during the course of the construction of a building. Those payments are based on the per cent of completion of the building but payment does not correspond exactly with the per cent of completion. Payments to contractors should always be a certain per cent less than the per cent of building completion as determined by the contract agreement. Despite this withholding of payment, the board acquires an increasing interest in the building as the builder proceeds to construct it. There are three types of builders' risk insurance: (1) building-in-process, (2) automatic coverage, (3) completed value.

Under building-in-process insurance, the owner specifies at various stages in the construction the coverage desired but at all times the coverage must be 80 per cent of the value of the building. If the coverage drops below 80 per cent at any time and there is a loss, the owner will suffer a coinsurance penalty. The disadvantage of this type of insurance is that the owner is usually always underinsured or overinsured.

Under automatic coverage insurance, coverage begins as value begins and increases as construction progresses. Monthly reports of the progress of construction are made on a specific date each month. Premiums are based on the completed value of the building. One hundred per cent coinsurance is required and the recovery is limited to the estimated completed value of the building.

Under completed value insurance, one hundred per cent coinsurance is required but the coverage increases automatically as construction progresses. No reports are required unless the estimated completed value of the building changes. Losses are paid in full if 100 per cent coinsurance is carried. If the insurance carried is less than the completed value of the building, losses are paid on the basis of the ratio of insurance coverage to the actual completed value. The completed value is generally considered the best type of builder's risk insurance. Monthly reports are not required and as long as accurate estimates are made of the total cost of the project, adequate coverage is provided.

OTHER TYPES OF
BUILDING AND CONTENTS INSURANCE

Other types of building and contents insurance of interest to school districts are: boiler and machinery insurance, glass insurance, and inland marine insurance.

Boiler and Machinery Insurance

The following types of school property can be insured under boiler and machinery insurance: boilers, furnaces (excluding hot air furnaces), water pressure tanks, hot water storage tanks, refrigerator units, air compressor tanks, motors, compressors, and air conditioning units.

Each type of coverage provided in this type of policy is very specifically described. A boiler and machinery insurance policy names objects and defines "accident" for each type of equipment. Furthermore, the coverage for boilers may be limited coverage or broad coverage. Therefore, each policy must be examined carefully to determine the different kinds of protection provided.

The insurance company is not required to make inspections but it has the right to do so at any time. It makes periodic inspections for its own protection and may suspend insurance if a board, after receiving written notice from the company, fails to correct a dangerous condition. This inspection service is of great value to the board. The prevention of accidents in situations involving danger to persons is more important than the recovery of financial losses.

Glass Insurance

Glass insurance is not generally recommended for school districts The money value involved is not great. If the glass breakage rate is high, the insurance rate will be high. In fact it is difficult to obtain glass insurance where the breakage rate is excessively heavy. This is one risk the district can afford to bear. Adequate supervision and the development of pupil responsibility for the school plant will probably provide the best protection against excessive glass breakage.

Inland Marine Insurance

As the name implies, this type of insurance was originally designed to protect property being transported on the high seas. Inland marine insurance companies now write certain types of "floater" policies for the protection of certain types of property not only at fixed locations but also when it is being moved about. Expensive equipment which is moved about is used for such activities as audio-visual programs, music groups, and sports teams. Protection by this type of insurance is given against loss from transportation, fire, lightning, windstorm, and theft. Coverage against breakage can also be obtained. Whether it is advisable for a district to carry insurance of this type depends largely on the seriousness of the risk involved.

Burglary, Robbery, and Theft Insurance

Insurance companies distinguish between burglary of open stock, safe burglary, robbery, and theft. Therefore, the district should carefully examine its policies in order to be assured that it has the different types of coverage needed.

Open stock includes merchandise, fixtures, and equipment for which vault or safe equipment is not provided. It does not include money and securities. A mercantile open stock policy protects a school district against burglary of property other than money and securities. The coverage applies only during hours when the premises are closed. Also there must be visible evidence of forcible entry. A theft indorsement to the mercantile open stock policy is provided by some companies at a premium increase of 75 per cent.

The mercantile safe burglary policy insures against loss of money and securities and other property within a safe or vault. But there must be evidence of forcible entry into the safe or vault. It also covers damage to the property and premises resulting from burglary.

Messenger robbery insurance and interior robbery insurance can also be obtained.

It is recommended that a broad form money and securities policy be obtained to protect money and securities rather than several separate types of protection. The broad form money and securities policy is described in Chapter 17.

In order for a district to be adequately protected at all times against loss of money, securities and other types of merchantable property, the following types of insurance are needed: (1) broad form money and securities insurance, (2) mercantile open stock insurance, (3) public official dishonesty bonds, and (4) floater insurance. When any of these coverages overlap, they should be excluded from all except one policy.

LIABILITY INSURANCE

At the present time, only a few states hold school boards liable for the torts (negligent acts) of their agents or employees. In order for a school district to be held liable, generally a statute must make school districts liable for torts. Many writers have pointed out the injustice of this legal theory in a democracy. It is alleged that it was derived from the "divine right of kings" theory under which the king can do no wrong. Popular governments take the place of kings in the United States but under this theory they incongruously hold the rights of a king.

The trend of court rulings has been to increase gradually the liability of boards of education. If a private person suffers property damage or personal injury from the negligent operation of a district school bus, he has the moral right in a democracy to recovery of his losses even if he does not have the legal right. Boards of education, therefore, have the moral responsibility to provide protection to others from losses caused by the negligent acts of the board's agents and employees. This can be provided through liability insurance. However, it is not legal for boards of education to provide the important types of liability insurance in all states. It should be legal in all states. The principal types of liability insurance are general liability and automobile liability.

In states where school districts have immunity from liability, a liability insurance policy should include a waiver whereby the company agrees to waive the right to decline to pay for losses covered in the policy on the ground that the district is not legally liable.

General Liability Insurance

General liability insurance includes the following different types of insurance coverage:

1. Owners', Landlords', Tenants' Liability—Accidents arising out of the ownership, maintenance or use of premises and operations incidental thereto.
2. Owners' Protective Liability—Accidents arising out of operations performed for the insured by independent contractors.
3. Contractual Liability—Liability assumed by the insured under any contract or agreement.
4. Products Liability—Accidents occurring away from school premises arising out of the use of or the existence of any condition in goods or products manufactured, sold, handled or distributed by the insured.
5. Professional (malpractice) Liability—Accidents resulting from errors, mistakes, or malpractice on the part of doctors, dentists, nurses, dental hygienists and others.
6. Liability of School Employees—Accidents resulting from negligence on the part of school employees while such employees are acting within the scope of their employment.[4]

It is generally recommended that the board select the needed coverages and obtain comprehensive liability coverage. It can be written in one policy even including comprehensive automobile coverage, or the board can obtain two policies, one for comprehensive general liability and the other for comprehensive automobile liability.

General liability insurance does not protect the district against injury to its employees as a result of its negligence. That protection, as well as other types of protection, is afforded through workmen's compensation insurance.

Automobile Liability Insurance

Following are the types of automobile liability coverage which can be obtained by boards of education:

1. Owned Automobile Liability—Accidents arising out of the ownership, maintenance or use of the insured's automobiles.

---

[4] University of the State of New York, *Insurance* (Albany, N.Y.: State Department of Education, 1956), p. 30.

2. Employers' Non-Ownership Liability—Accidents arising out of the operation of automobiles used in connection with the business of the insured but not owned, hired or leased by the insured.
3. Hired Automobile Liability—Accidents arising out of the operation of automobiles hired by the insured for use in the business of the insured.
4. Liability of School Employees—Accidents resulting from negligence on the part of school employees while such employees are acting within the scope of their employment.[5]

It is recommended that boards obtain protection for automobile liability either by including it in a comprehensive general liability policy or by obtaining a comprehensive automobile liability policy.

A district is eligible for fleet rates when it operates five or more vehicles. The rate reduction increases as the number of vehicles increases.

WORKMEN'S COMPENSATION INSURANCE

Workmen's compensation insurance for public employees is compulsory in about half the states. It should be compulsory for all states. Workmen's compensation insurance is to protect the employee and the employer from loss caused by accidental injury of the employee or by disease of the employee arising in or because of his employment.

The following benefits accrue to the employee:

1. Compensation during the period of disability subject to defined limits of time and rates of compensation.
2. All reasonable medical and hospital expenses.
3. Compensation for permanent, partial, or total disability.
4. Burial expenses.
5. Death benefit for survivors.

The employee need not prove negligence on the part of the district in order to be eligible for benefits.

The district receives the following protection:

1. Protects against loss imposed by law for damages caused by injury or disease suffered by employees and arising in or because of employment.
2. Defends the insured in suits.
3. Pays all costs taxed against the district arising out of legal proceedings.

Most rates for workmen's compensation insurance are developed by the National Council on compensation insurance. In most states these rates must be approved by state compensation rating bureaus. Rates

[5] *Ibid.*, p. 30.

vary for different job classifications. For example, the rates per $100 of salary in New York State on July 1, 1955 for school employees were:

Teacher	$ .21
Clerk	.21
Janitor	2.60
Bus Driver	1.10

Rates may be increased or decreased by experience rating. Additional workmen's compensation insurance should be provided by a well administered accident and disease prevention program. Adequate mechanical safeguards should be provided. Safety education should be emphasized. An employee who has lost an arm or leg is never fully compensated for his loss by the few dollars he receives from workmen's compensation insurance. An accident and disease prevention program saves the board money and it provides additional protection for the employee.

RETIREMENT AND SURVIVORS' BENEFITS

Retirement is not usually thought of as a type of insurance. But retirement provides protection for both the employer and the employee. The employer is protected because he is not compelled by humanitarian reasons to keep aged employees on the payroll long after their usefulness has largely terminated, simply to keep them from starving. The employee is benefited because he is financially able to retire, when because of age or health he should retire. If an employee knows that when the time comes for him to retire he can do so without being destitute and dependent on others, his morale is greatly improved. Good morale contributes to better quality of work.

Survivor benefits are needed to protect an employee's survivors. This is especially important for young employees who have not worked long enough to build up a significant equity in a retirement system. One of the major purposes of Federal social security legislation is to provide survivors' benefits for the mass of workers.

Under the traditional theories of "rugged individualism" each individual should provide independently for his own financial security. Experience has shown that in an urbanized, technological, industrialized society, individual provision for financial security is not practical or feasible for most people. Therefore, more and more emphasis is being given to such "fringe benefits" as retirement, survivors' benefits, disability benefits, and workmen's compensation benefits. In some types of industry and business many additional fringe benefits are provided. Unless boards of education provide the major types of fringe benefits for their employees that are provided for the employees of business and industry, school boards will be in a very unfavorable position in the competitive labor market. The quality of employees obtained and retained depends on the fringe benefits provided as well as the salaries paid.

Fringe benefits should not be considered as an extra cost to the board but as part of the salary paid. Teacher retirement, for example, is almost always on a participating plan. The board or the state pays part of the cost and part is paid by the teacher. The part paid by the teacher is withheld from his salary and the part paid by the employer can be considered as money which would have been paid to the teacher. In any event the employer's contribution is in effect an addition to the salary. It is in the public's interest as well as the teacher's interest that his total real salary not be paid to him each month.

Practically all states have some kind of a system of teacher retirement but many states do not provide retirement for other school employees. This social distinction seems strange in a democracy. The principles of democracy and equity are not satisfied unless all full-time school employees are covered by retirement protection.

Adequate Retirement Systems. A complete retirement system should include at least the following: (1) a pension upon retirement, (2) a disability allowance, (3) survivors' benefits when an employee dies prior to being eligible for retirement, (4) survivors' benefits when an employee dies after being eligible for retirement.

A teacher retirement system may provide for all the types of coverage needed, but the provisions may be inadequate. An adequate teacher retirement system should provide at least the following levels of benefits:

1. An annual pension equal to 2 per cent times the number of years worked times the average annual salary for the highest ten years with normal retirement age 60 years and mandatory 70 years.

2. Survivors' benefits equal to those provided by Federal social security.

3. A reasonable disability allowance after 10 years of service.

4. Provision that retirement be paid at actuarial rates to the surviving spouse if the employee dies after being eligible for retirement.

Teacher's retirement and survivor's protection at the levels described can be provided by an employee's contribution of 6¼ per cent of his salary matched by his employer, making a total contribution of 12½ per cent. There should be no limit on the amount of the salary upon which the percentage of retirement contributions can be based.

It is not suggested that the above plan is an ideal teacher-retirement plan. It is presented merely to illustrate what is meant by a reasonably adequate retirement plan. Many states provide retirement plans which are very inadequate because the deduction from the teacher's salary and employer's matching constitute too low a percentage of the salary. Many states also limit the amount of the salary on which retirement may be based. The benefits which can be provided by existing rates must be computed by competent actuaries. The cost of providing additional benefits should be similarly determined. The adequacy of retirement protection is determined by the level of contributions.

Teacher retirement funds are trust funds. They should be fully protected by law from loss or diversion. The investment policies of retirement reserves should be sound. Safety of principal is more important than rate of interest received.

Federal Social Security. Some states have combined teacher retirement with Federal Social Security. There seems to be little or no advantage to this arrangement. In fact, there may be some disadvantages. Federal Social Security is provided entirely from contributions made by the employee and the employer. There is no subsidy for social security provided from the general revenues of the Federal government. The Federal government serves only as the banker and administrator of Federal Social Security funds. There is some evidence that the risks are less for some types of protection provided by Social Security for teachers than for employed persons generally. That is particularly true of survivors' benefits.

Ohio and Florida for some years have provided survivors' benefits for teachers as a supplement to their regular retirement systems. The experience of these states indicates that survivors' benefits and other benefits for teachers can be provided at lower rates within the states than the same benefits can be obtained through Federal Social Security. In any event there is no reason to believe that the Federal government can provide old age and survivors' benefits for teachers at lower cost than the states.

One benefit of Federal Social Security is that the insured can take his equity in the system with him if he moves from one state to another. This cannot be done under the retirement provisions of many states. However, a few states have provided that as many as ten years of service may be transferred to another state. This is good public policy. The number of years of service which can be transferred should probably be increased.

There seems to be no serious objection to making teachers eligible for Federal Social Security benefits in addition to the benefits provided by their own retirement system. Under this plan, Federal Social Security is kept completely separate from teacher retirement.

Local Retirement Systems. Local school systems started teacher retirement systems long before state retirement systems were inaugurated. Many of the large school systems developed sound systems. But
many of the smaller school systems set up inadequate systems and many
of these were not actuarially sound. Experience has shown that state retirement systems are usually better administered and more soundly
financed than local systems. It is far more efficient to have one state
teacher-retirement system than a multitude of local systems. A multitude of local systems creates problems when teachers transfer from one
system to another within the same state. The only justification for a
local retirement system or a separate system for college and university
professors is an inadequate state system. The remedy, of course, is to
establish an adequate state system. In many states, college and university professors and the professional personnel of public school systems
are members of the same retirement system.

STATE INSURANCE

The success of state retirement systems is the most striking example
of the benefits of state insurance. School employees and boards of education are able to buy far more protection for school employees through
state retirement systems than can be purchased through commercial
insurance companies at the same cost.

If it is agreed that it is a desirable objective of school business administration to purchase the maximum amount of needed protection at
the minimum cost, then the provision for state insurance is sound
public policy. A few states have established state systems for insuring
school buildings. A study by Viles showed that Alabama, North Dakota, and South Carolina have provided state insurance for school
buildings for many years at rates which have been 40 per cent less
than commercial rates and that state insurance fund reserves have
been increasing in those states.[6] North Carolina has provided state insurance at 46 per cent less than commercial rates and Wisconsin at 50
per cent less.

The Association of School Business Officials of the United States and
Canada made a study of the ratio of recoveries from school building
fire insurance to premiums paid for the period 1935 to 1945.[7] The As-

---

[6] N. E. Viles, Sr., *School Property Insurance,* U. S. Department of Health, Education and Welfare, Office of Education (Washington, D.C.: U. S. Government Printing Office, 1956).

[7] Insurance Committee Report, *Proceedings,* Association of School Business Officials of the United States and Canada, 1948. (Evanston: The Association, 1948).

sociation reported that only approximately 32 per cent of each premium dollar was returned to boards of education for fire losses.

Viles reported that during the five-year period 1948–52 the losses paid by stock and mutual companies insuring school buildings amounted to only 35.3 per cent of premiums received for school fire insurance.[8] There was an astonishing variation among the states in the loss ratios during this five-year period. The losses paid by insurance companies were less than 20 per cent of premiums paid in 8 states and more than 45 per cent in 11 states. This would seem to indicate that some states need to give far more emphasis to fire prevention than has been given. It would also indicate that there should be far more variation among the states in fire insurance rates than now prevails. Insurance companies have apparently been making up for their losses in some states by making high profits in other states. It would seem to be more equitable if the states that have low loss ratios would be given much lower rates than the states with high losses. Numerous other studies generally corroborate these findings. For some unknown reason, boards of education generally pay higher fire insurance rates in proportion to losses than private persons.

A few states provide state insurance for automobile liability. Some seventeen states have state compensation insurance funds. Experience with different types of state insurance has shown that when state insurance plans are soundly planned and properly administered, considerable money can be saved by state insurance for practically all important types of coverage.

SAFEGUARDING RECORDS

It is impossible to express the value of records in terms of money. Therefore, ordinary insurance coverage is of no value. The only protection for records that can be obtained is to prevent their destruction or loss. Insurance against loss or destruction of records must be self-insurance obtained by providing appropriate storage space and protective devices for irreplaceable items.

Records are of four principal types, as follows: (1) vital records which are irreplaceable and which if reproduced do not have the same value as originals, (2) important records which can be reproduced but at a considerable expense of time and labor, (3) useful records whose loss will cause some inconvenience but which can readily be replaced, and (4) nonessential records which should be destroyed after proper

---

[8] Viles, *op. cit.*, p. 21.

authorization in order to conserve storage space and eliminate a fire hazard.

There are three principal types of protective equipment: (1) vaults, (2) safes, and (3) insulated record containers. Each of these different types of equipment varies considerably in its fire resistance rating, depending on its quality.

The National Fire Protection Association has presented excellent suggestions for safeguarding records in its booklet "Protection of Records." The following degrees of protection are recommended:

1. *Vital records*—should have protection which will assure that the records will be preserved even if there is a complete burning-out of the section of the building in which they are located. This degree of protection may be achieved by housing the records in fire-resistive vaults or safes. Six-hour or four-hour vaults or four-hour safes are recommended for most buildings.

2. *Important records*—should be given the protection recommended for vital records to the greatest possible extent. If it is physically impossible to so protect them, and the building is fire-resistive, important records may be kept in the next best equipment available, but this storage should not be considered as protecting the records against an all-out fire.

3. *Useful records*—should, as a minimum, be housed in closed steel containers located where they will be least exposed to combustibles, but this should not be regarded as full protection against fire.

4. *Nonessential records*—require no special protection so far as their value is concerned. Records of this class should be segregated from more valuable records. Any unneeded records should be disposed of in order to eliminate a fire hazard and to save space.[9]

SOME PROBLEMS AND ISSUES

Some special problems and issues relating to school insurance are presented in this section.

When Is Self-Insurance Feasible?

The self-insurance of a school district is usually not as desirable as state insurance because the risks are spread wider under state insurance than under self-insurance. Some large school districts in the United

---

[9] Adapted from National Fire Protection Association, *Protection of Records—Consolidated Reports of the Committee on the Protection of Records* (Boston: The Association, 1947).

States are considerably larger in population than a number of states. Self-insurance for many types of coverage is feasible in these large districts.

The purpose of self-insurance is to provide the needed protection at less cost than the cost of obtaining the same protection from commercial insurance companies. Self-insurance does not mean no insurance protection. If real self-insurance is provided, an insurance reserve trust fund is provided for the particular type of insurance desired. This reserve fund should be sufficiently large to enable the board to pay the losses covered by the fund in the year in which the losses occur. The board is uninsured to the extent that the fund is insufficient for this purpose.

Following are some suggestions concerning the establishment of self-insurance plans by school districts:

1.   Only relatively large school districts should provide self-insurance and this should be done only when adequate state insurance is not available.

2.   The board should not attempt to insure itself against extremely hazardous risks which, if assumed by the board, could result in financial disaster for the district.

3.   The number of risks should be sufficiently large to permit the law of averages to operate smoothly.

4.   The risks should be geographically scattered. Risks should be independent of each other. For example, a district with 100 buildings located on widely separated sites has a much greater spread of risks than a district with only three buildings on three sites.

5.   No one risk should constitute a high per cent of the gross coverage. For example, the insured value of one building should not constitute a high per cent of the total building coverage.

6.   The self-insurance fund should be created gradually. That is, a fractional portion of the risk should be assumed by the fund when it is established. As the fund grows, the portion assumed by the fund can be increased.

7.   The self-insurance fund should be fully protected at all times and established as a trust fund. Investment of trust fund reserves should be in accordance with sound policies for the investment of public trust funds.

What is the minimum sized school district in which self-insurance should be considered? For what types of coverage would self-insurance be undesirable?

Should There Be Competitive Bids on Insurance Contracts?

It has been the practice in many districts to award the school insurance business to local agents regardless of cost. Some local businessmen insist that the board make all possible purchases from local vendors even if prices are higher. The argument advanced is that the board should give its business to local taxpayers. But the board has a responsibility to all of the citizens of the district. Furthermore, in most districts a substantial portion of school revenues is provided from state sources. The board has no obligation to subsidize local businessmen.

The belief is growing that insurance should be purchased by competitive bidding. Despite the popular belief to the contrary, all insurance companies do not charge the same rates for the same protection. A number of companies, both stock and mutual, have on file with the state insurance department what is known as "file deviation agreements." These agreements authorize the companies having such agreements on file to discount manual rates by a percentage approved by the department. Other companies offer dividends to policy holders based largely on loss experience.

It is probably better for a board to receive informal bids on insurance than legally advertised sealed bids which might obligate the board to award the insurance contract to the lowest responsible bidder. When informal bids are used, allowance can more readily be made for quality and extent of services offered. The rating of an insurance company can be obtained from *Best's Insurance Guide* and also from the state insurance department. Would widespread competitive bidding on school insurance gradually reduce the rates? Is competitive bidding desirable for all kinds of insurance?

Many boards of education divide their fire insurance business among all the insurance agents in the district. The authors, in making a survey of a large school system, noted that forty-eight companies shared in each policy. When a loss occurred, the board received forty-eight checks. One loss involving only a total of $70.00 was paid in that manner. It involved considerable accounting labor to record all transactions with so many companies.

Some boards have solved this problem by dealing with only one broker who represents all the fire insurance companies in the district. Under this plan, the board pays only one premium check and receives only one check for each loss.

Other boards have partially solved this problem by limiting the number of companies that may share in the insurance on a particular building.

If fire insurance contracts are awarded on the basis of competitive bids, only one company may be awarded all of the board's fire insurance business. Is that bad public policy? Would the board have as much protection from one company as from several companies? If the board awards all of its fire insurance to one company, should it require that company to reinsure with other companies?

SELECTED REFERENCES

Ackerman, S. B., *Insurance: A Practical Guide*. New York: Ronald Press Co., 1952.

American Association of School Administrators, *Managing the School District Insurance Program*. Washington, D.C.: The Association, 1953.

———, *School District Liability*. Washington, D.C.: The Association, 1953.

Linn, Henry H., *School Business Administration*. New York: Ronald Press Co., 1956. Chapter 11.

———, and S. C. Joyner, *Insurance Practices in School Administration*. New York: Ronald Press Co., 1952.

Lucas, G. G., and R. H. Wherry, *Insurance Principles and Coverages*. New York: Rinehart & Company, Inc., 1954.

National Board of Fire Underwriters, *Fire Safe School Buildings*. New York: The Board, 1954.

Salmon, Paul, *Fire Insurance Principles and Practices*. Evanston: Association of School Business Officials of the United States and Canada, 1958.

University of the State of New York, State Department of Education, *Insurance*. Albany: State Department of Education, 1956.

Viles, N. E., Sr., *School Property Insurance*, Department of Health, Education and Welfare, Office of Education, Washington, D.C.: U. S. Government Printing Office, 1956.

CHAPTER NINETEEN

Central Services
of Business Administration

Business administration of a school system is established in order to provide the services essential for attaining the educational plan. Budgetary procedures, financial accounting, the spending and safeguarding of money, and the protection of persons and property have already been described. Business administration is also concerned with the storage and distribution of supplies and equipment, school plant planning, custodial services, school plant maintenance, school transportation, and school lunch management. These services are described briefly in this chapter.

ORGANIZATION FOR
BUSINESS ADMINISTRATION SERVICES

Two important conclusions relating to school organizational structure can be drawn from the many studies that have been made of business administration services. First, business administration policies, procedures, and processes vitally affect the educational program. Second, each service of business administration is closely related to all other business administration services.

Coordination of Services

Since the business administration of a school system vitally affects its educational program, a rational plan of organization must provide

528

for the coordination of business administration and educational administration. Coordination of all services can be achieved most expeditiously by making the superintendent the chief executive of the board of education with the responsibility for coordinating all services. A number of school systems have experimented with the dual system of administration which provides for one chief executive for business affairs and one for educational affairs. Under this system each executive is coordinate with the other in authority and each reports directly to the board. The dual system has almost invariably resulted in conflict and inefficient administration. Successful business and industrial enterprises use a single executive to coordinate all activities. All activities of any enterprise, public or private, are interrelated. In educational administration, it is even difficult to classify many activities as primarily educational or primarily business. Therefore, efficient administration of the schools is not likely to be attained unless all the activities for which the board of education is responsible are coordinated by a single executive.

Since all business administration services are closely interrelated, a rational plan of organization requires that these services all be coordinated by a single executive. In very small school systems, this person should be the superintendent himself. In larger school systems, the coordinating executive should be an assistant to the superintendent with the title of assistant superintendent for business affairs, or a similar title indicating the area of responsibility.

Effect of Size of Districts on Business Management Services

Very small school systems in the United States can provide only limited central business administration services. From the standpoint of finance, a primary purpose of all organization and administration is to purchase the maximum amount of educational opportunity per dollar expended. If a school system is too small to provide the administrative and supervisory services necessary to obtain the educational returns that should be expected for the funds expended, the district should be reorganized into a district of sufficient size to be potentially efficient.

The arrangements described in this chapter for providing business management services are more suitable for school systems with 2,000 and more pupils than for very small school systems. A school system must be large enough to produce the volume of work necessary for providing central business administration services at a low unit cost if those services are established. The evidence obtained from numerous surveys of local school systems indicates that the potential savings from providing central business administration services are not maximized until school systems reach the size of from 10,000 to 20,000 pupils. This is not to suggest that the potential savings from business administration should determine the minimum size of local school districts. Many other factors such as density of population, natural barriers, and community interests should be considered.

It is possible for a district to be so large that lines of communication will be overextended for some types of central business administration services if only one service point is established. For example, it may overextend communication lines to distribute supplies and equipment from one central warehouse in a school district with 200,000 or more pupils. In districts of this size, two or more service points may need to be established for certain types of business administration services if maximum efficiency is attained. The arrangements for business administration services differ somewhat in school systems that vary in size. But the principles of sound business management are the same in all school systems.

Physical Facilities Needed

The location of the physical facilities provided for business administration services and all other central administrative and supervisory services influences the efficiency of those services. The office of the assistant superintendent for business affairs should be located in the central office facilities for the school district. The central office facilities for the district should include adequate and suitably arranged space for the superintendent of schools and all other administrative and supervisory personnel whose activities need to be closely coordinated. Communication and coordination are hindered if administrative and supervisory personnel who need to work with each other on many activities are housed in separate buildings.

There are some distinct advantages in housing the offices of a board of education and the central staff in a separate office building. The location of the central offices in a building separate from the city hall or the county court house usually provides a more suitable climate for conducting educational affairs. Psychologically this arrangement tends to remove the schools at least partially from partisan politics. Furthermore, if the board of education is dependent on the governing body of the city or the county for its office facilities, it sets a precedent for extending dependency to other matters. Any factor that tends to extend the dependency of boards of education on other local governments is considered undesirable by most authorities on educational administration.

The physical facilities for business administration also include warehouses, school plant maintenance shops, and school bus shops. Efficiency is promoted when all of these facilities are located on the same site, unless the district is so large as to require two or more service points for some of these services. These services are closely interrelated and communications are facilitated when the physical facilities are located on the same site. If the site is large enough to provide a suitable environment for the central offices and sufficient space for the shops and warehouses, there is some advantage in locating all of these facilities on one large site. This arrangement minimizes the time spent by personnel travelling to and from the central offices and the other facilities.

The central facilities should be readily accessible to the public and to the personnel located at school centers. Therefore, the central facilities should be located as near the population center of the district as is feasible and adequate parking space should be provided.

STORAGE AND DISTRIBUTION

The management of supplies and equipment involves the operations of receiving, storing,[1] distributing, and recording. The purpose of supply and equipment management is, without loss or damage and at a minimum cost, to get the goods required to the point of need at the right time in the quantity needed.[2] Therefore, these operations are all closely interrelated.

Receiving Supplies and Equipment

As pointed out in Chapter 16, some responsible person must receive the goods purchased by the board. This is absolutely necessary in order to establish the validity of some of the original documents upon which the board authorizes payments and bases its financial accounting. Some responsible person must check the goods delivered against the purchase order and the invoice or bill of lading. If the goods received are damaged or differ in quantity or quality from the specifications upon which the order was based, adjustments should be made or the board advised before payment is made. Obviously this type of checking should be done by a responsible person.

---

[1] Some pieces of large equipment may never be stored.
[2] For an excellent discussion of supply management, see Henry H. Linn, editor, *School Business Administration* (New York: Ronald Press Company, 1956), Chapter 10.

The problem of checking deliveries immediately raises a number of questions. Who should receive deliveries of goods purchased by the board? Should goods be received only while schools are in session or should some goods be received during the summer months?

Different arrangements may be provided for receiving supplies and equipment in large school systems than in small systems, but the problems are the same. If goods are received from vendors at individual schools, they are usually checked by the principal, his assistant, or the custodian. It is desirable for the board to order and accept delivery of many types of goods during the summer months in order that they be made available at the beginning of school. It is desirable of course that the principal and at least one custodian for each school be employed on a year-round basis. But this is usually not practicable except in large schools. Therefore, in many cases, no person is available at individual schools during the summer months to receive deliveries from vendors. The real question is whether it is better to receive goods at a central warehouse or at individual schools or at both places. This immediately raises the question of storage.

Storage of Supplies and Equipment

When goods are received they must be stored or put to use at the point of need. Some large pieces of equipment may be received at the point of need and put to use without the necessity of storage. But it is more economical to purchase practically all supplies and many small items of equipment in quantity and this involves storage. Thus the problem of whether storage space should be provided at a central warehouse or at individual schools or at both places must be faced. The solution to the problem of storage cannot be found without also solving the problem of receiving.

Centralized receiving and storing has some advantages and disadvantages. The principal advantages are:

1. Competent personnel are always available for checking deliveries.
2. Financial accounting and prompt payment of bills are facilitated.
3. Suitable storage space for quantity purchasing can be constructed more economically at one point than at all schools.
4. Inventories and other control records can be maintained more efficiently.
5. It facilitates quantity purchasing of a great number of items.
6. It provides a method for returning surplus stock from a school so it can be sent to a point of need.
7. It saves time and money in reducing the volume of spot purchases.[3]

[3] Edgar L. Morphet, Roe L. Johns, and Theodore L. Reller, *Educational Administration* (Englewood Cliffs, N.J.: Prentice-Hall, Inc., 1959), p. 463.

The principal disadvantages of centralized receiving and storing are:

1. Goods are originally stored at some distance from the point of need. This involves the extra cost of distribution to schools from the warehouse.

2. It is impracticable to store certain bulky items such as fuel and certain heavy pieces of equipment at a central warehouse.

Thus, it seems that there is no one best plan for receiving and storing all supply and equipment items. Some items should be centrally received and stored and others should be received and stored at the point of need. Furthermore, even when supplies are centrally stored, it is not practicable to deliver all items to the ultimate point of need from the warehouse. The ultimate point of need for many items is the classroom. Thus, storage space must be provided at each school. All supplies cannot be consumed immediately when they are delivered. The ultimate point of need for other items may be the school plant maintenance shop, the school bus shop, or the central offices.

At an individual school at least the following separate storage spaces are needed: (1) A central storage space for instructional supplies, (2) a central storage space for custodial supplies, (3) storage space in each classroom, special service room, and general service room.

A central warehouse is not practicable for a very small school system. In order for a central warehouse to be practicable, the volume of work should be sufficient to justify the employment of at least one person for service at the warehouse for twelve months in the year. If this is not done, goods cannot be received and distributed expeditiously. Some authorities recommend a central warehouse if a system has six or more school buildings of reasonable size located on separate sites. This would be the approximate equivalent of a school system with 2400 or more pupils.

Following are some criteria for determining whether an item should be received from the vendor at the central warehouse or at the point of need:

1. Bulky items such as fuel and heavy pieces of equipment should be delivered by the vendor to the point of need. Any item for which the cost of delivering from the warehouse to the point of need is substantially greater than the extra charge made by the vendor for delivering the item to the point of need instead of the central warehouse should be delivered by the vendor to the point of need.

2. All other items should be received from vendors at the central warehouse if one is provided.

The Warehouse. Deliveries from the warehouse to the schools are usually made by the school plant maintenance trucks. Sometimes school transportation service trucks may also be used for this purpose. Location of all of these facilities on the same site eliminates much travel time when trucks are being used for different purposes.

Functional planning of the warehouse and all other school facilities will pay rich dividends. Following are some factors that should be given consideration:

1. The warehouse should be of sufficient size to provide the central storage space needed. The size needed depends, of course, on the size of the school system, but it also depends on the purchasing policies of the board. As pointed out in Chapter 17, if the board purchases supplies and equipment in quantity only once each year, more storage space is needed than if the board makes quantity purchases several times annually. The evidence favors quantity purchasing several times each year.

2. Streets or roads should be adequate for access by trucks.

3. Loading and unloading platforms should be efficiently arranged.

4. The building should be so designed that modern labor-saving equipment can be used.

5. The storage space should be so designed that the stock can be classified and old stock moved first. If the stock is not properly classified, control records are difficult to administer.

6. The shelving and other storage facilities provided should be so designed as to minimize the labor required to store and distribute goods.

7. The building should be of fire-resistive construction. The building should be designed so as to minimize the cost of insurance and the losses due to fire, water, theft, fungus, vermin, and other causes. A non-fire-resistive abandoned school building usually makes a very poor warehouse.

8. Adequate office space should be provided for the personnel in charge of the warehouse.

The Distribution of Supplies and Equipment

Items stored in the central warehouse must eventually be distributed to the point of need. It is important that needed items be delivered promptly. It is also desirable that the number of trips necessary for delivering items from the warehouse to the points of need be minimized in order to eliminate unnecessary transportation costs. Therefore, it is important that school principals and others authorized to make requisitions on the warehouse do some advance planning in order to anticipate needs over a reasonable period of time.

When items are being drawn from the central warehouse, the usual procedure is as follows:

1. The principal, or other person authorized to make requisitions, files a requisition with the business office.

2. The approved requisition is sent to the warehouse.

3. The goods are packaged and delivered to the point specified in the requisition.

This seems to be a simple procedure, but it is not quite as simple as it seems. First, the person filing the requisition is usually required to state the amount of the item he has on hand as well as the amount he needs. He cannot do this unless he has a continuing stock record for his store room. Second, the requisition is not automatically approved by the business office. Since no school system has unlimited supplies and equipment available in its warehouse, some plan must be developed for making an equitable allocation of supplies and equipment among individual schools. As explained in Chapter 14, this is usually done by establishing budgets for individual schools or by developing some type of allocation formula for supplies. When the requisition is approved, it is charged to the budget or allocation for the school or other service operated by the board. This involves control record keeping. Third, when items are drawn from the warehouse, the transaction should be reflected in the warehouse records.

Control Record Keeping

Accounting responsibility does not cease when school funds are converted into supplies and equipment. Control record keeping for supplies and equipment serves some purposes that are similar to the purposes of financial records. Following are some of the major purposes of control records for goods purchased by the board:

1. To establish the faithfulness of the stewardship of those having custody of merchantable goods.

2. To prevent the theft, loss, wastage, or misuse of supplies and equipment.

3. To prevent over-purchasing or under-purchasing of individual items.

4. To facilitate budget control and administration.

5. To aid in budget development.

6. To provide the information necessary for certain types of cost accounting.

7. To provide for the orderly storage and distribution of supplies and equipment.

When goods are received at the warehouse, control record keeping starts. Many different types of control record systems are used. The kind of system used should be determined by local needs. But an adequate record system for any warehouse must provide at least the following information: (1) the items received—from whom, when, and in what quantity; (2) the items sent out—to whom, when, and in what quantity; and (3) the items on hand and in what quantity.

The following control record system is used for many central warehouses:

1. Entries are made on the appropriate stock record card when items are received.

2. Principals and other authorized persons send requisitions on the warehouse to the business office for approval.

3. Approved requisitions are sent to the warehouse and goods are packaged for delivery.

4. A delivery slip is made in duplicate and sent with the goods to the point of delivery.

5. An authorized person at the point of delivery signs for the goods, retains one copy of the signed delivery slip and returns the other copy to the warehouse.

6. An inventory is taken of the warehouse stock periodically, preferably each month.

This should be considered a minimum control record system for a warehouse. It is possible by this system to determine the items received and their disposition; but it is possible to determine the items on hand only at the time an inventory is taken.

A better system is to keep a perpetual inventory of the warehouse stock. The stock record card can be designed with three columns to show the quantity received, the quantity sent out, and the quantity on hand. Under this system an inventory should be taken at least annually to verify the stock record. Some authorities are of the opinion that the extra labor required for a perpetual inventory is not justified for a school warehouse.

When items are delivered to a school, entries should be made on the school records. The principal or his designated representative should keep these records. If the item is equipment, it should be entered on the equipment inventory. If it is a supply, it is usually delivered to a storeroom at the school. The principal should set up a control record system for each storeroom. It need not be as elaborate as the control record system for the central warehouse, but it should serve the same purposes.

The Stock Catalogue. A stock catalogue should be made of all items carried in the warehouse. All items should be numbered and coded to the specifications. A stock catalogue should be in the hands of each requisitioning authority. A well-organized stock catalogue facilitates the location of items in the warehouse. It greatly reduces the labor of preparing requisitions and keeping records. It also minimizes errors of those who file requisitions and those who make deliveries.

SCHOOL PLANT OPERATION AND MAINTENANCE

School plant operation and school plant maintenance are closely related but separate activities. Plant operation involves the cleaning, heating, cooling, lighting, ground maintenance, and other activities necessary for keeping the plant open and in use. Plant maintenance is concerned with the repair of buildings and the repair and replacement of equipment. It is beyond the scope of this book to present a detailed description of school plant operation and maintenance procedures. But school funds can be conserved and the physical environment of the educational program improved by efficient operation and maintenance. Therefore, certain general policies for school plant operation and maintenance are presented in the following sections of this chapter.

School Plant Operation

The typical modern school plant represents an investment of several hundred thousand dollars. Some school plants cost several million dollars. These modern plants contain many kinds of costly equipment. A building houses several hundred or even several thousand pupils. The health and safety of these pupils and their teachers are affected by the quality of the custodial service provided. No real savings have ever been obtained by providing low-quality, cheap custodial service. Good business management requires that custodial services be recognized as essential to the educational enterprise. Following are some policies for administering custodial services that should be considered:

1. A high quality of custodial service should be provided for all schools. No one school plant should be given preferred custodial treatment.

2. School custodians should be employees of the board of education. Contracted custodial service has generally been more costly and less satisfactory than service provided by school employees.

3. School custodians should be selected on the basis of appropriate qualifications. Such factors as education, age, health, character, experience, willingness to learn, and ability to work with others should be considered when selecting custodians.

4. The custodians as well as other personnel at a school should be under the direct administration and supervision of the school principal. It is not good administrative organization to make custodians administratively responsible to the superintendent of buildings and grounds. Such an arrangement usually breeds conflict.

5. If there are several custodians at a school, one should be named head custodian. Lines of authority and areas of responsibility should be well defined and clearly understood. Teachers should not be authorized to give direct orders to custodians except in emergencies.

6. Work schedules for custodians should be carefully planned. The principal is responsible for developing or assisting in developing work schedules. The purpose of work schedules is to equalize work loads and to plan for the orderly rendering of necessary custodial services without undue disturbance to educational activities.

7. School custodians should be provided with in-service training programs. Most school custodians have had little or no custodial experience prior to employment by the board. In some school systems, the superintendent of plants and grounds makes arrangements for the in-service training program. Sometimes competent, experienced, school custodians can be used to instruct inexperienced employees.

The dividing line between maintenance and custodial services is not very wide. Poor operational procedures will create maintenance problems. Custodians should be trained in preventive operational maintenance. Custodians may also be trained to make simple repairs and non-complicated adjustments in equipment. This will save many trips to the school by maintenance employees. However, custodians should never be permitted to endanger themselves and others by making dangerous or complicated repairs and adjustments.

8. A sufficient number of custodians should be employed for each building to do a satisfactory job. Various formulas have been proposed for determining the number of custodians needed. For example, it has been suggested that one custodian should be employed for each ten teachers or 18,000 square feet of floor area. These ratios might be fairly satisfactory under average conditions. But the type of floor surface, the labor-saving machinery provided, the amount of ground maintenance required, the type of heating system, and other factors affect the custodial load. It is good policy to provide labor-saving equipment but some buildings are more adapted to the use of such equipment than others. A careful study should be made of all of the important factors affecting custodial load before determining the number of custodians needed for a particular building.

9. School custodians should generally be employed for twelve months. Some custodians are needed at school buildings during the

summer months but usually the entire staff is not needed. Many school systems augment the maintenance crew with school custodians during the summer months. This plan has the advantages of providing extra help for the maintenance staff during its heavy work season and of giving summer employment to custodians. Much of the heavy turnover in school custodians is due to the failure of boards of education to provide them with twelve months of employment. It is not economical practice to train a competent custodian and then lose his services.

10. School custodians should be consulted when developing custodial policies and operational procedures for a school. Custodians will better understand the policies they help to develop and they will implement them more effectively.

11. Salary or pay schedules should be developed for custodians. These schedules should give due recognition to experience and quality of service.

12. Custodial employees should have the benefits of retirement and/or social security, survivors' benefits, sick leave, vacation leave and workmen's compensation insurance. Unless the board of education provides fringe benefits for custodial employees similar to those provided by business and industry, it will be able to employ only low-grade workers.[4]

School Plant Maintenance

An annual expenditure of from 1.5 to 2 per cent of the replacement cost of most buildings is usually required to keep them in proper repair. Poorly constructed buildings cost more than 2 per cent of their replacement cost for maintenance and well constructed buildings may require an annual expenditure of only one per cent. Since school buildings usually have a life of approximately fifty years, there is no real economy in original low-cost but flimsy construction. Buildings constructed of inferior materials are more expensive in the long run and they are not as satisfactory for housing the educational program as well constructed buildings. Therefore, school plant maintenance starts with school plant planning.

Sound construction will reduce but not eliminate the need for maintenance. All buildings and equipment need maintenance. When boards of education are short of funds, it is common practice to reduce the budget appropriation for plant maintenance. That is just as unsound a policy as incurring a current deficit. Deferred maintenance almost al-

---

[4] Adapted in part from Morphet, Johns, and Reller, *Educational Administration*, pp. 467–468.

ways costs more money eventually than if the repairs were made at the time needed. When a board permits its school plants to deteriorate more rapidly than normal due to lack of maintenance, it is suffering a loss of funds. A building deteriorating due to lack of maintenance is in effect a slowly burning school building for which no recovery from insurance is possible. The only insurance against this type of loss is a sound maintenance program. Buildings represent invested school funds. It is just as essential to safeguard buildings from loss as it is to safeguard money.

Organization for School Plant Maintenance. The school plant planning department of a school system should be closely coordinated with the school plant maintenance department. In many school systems, these departments are combined. Plans of organization differ for school systems that differ in size. But the principle of coordination should apply to all plans of organization. Titles also differ in accordance with responsibilities. For example, the supervisor for plants and grounds may be responsible for both school plant planning and school plant maintenance. If the system is large enough to have an assistant superintendent for business affairs, the supervisor of plant planning and maintenance is normally administratively responsible to him. If the school system does not have an assistant superintendent for business affairs, the supervisor should be administratively responsible directly to the superintendent.

If a school system is large enough for separate departments of plant planning and plant maintenance, the heads of these departments should both be administratively responsible to the assistant superintendent for business affairs. This is desirable in order to assure the coordination of these two services.

The Plan for Maintenance. The board of education must adopt a plan for maintaining school buildings. The three alternative plans are: (1) maintenance by contract, (2) maintenance by school employees, and (3) a combination of maintenance by private contractors and school employees.

Some of the principal advantages of board employment of its maintenance workers are as follows:

1. Maintenance costs less for many types of jobs because profits are not involved. A number of studies have shown that boards of education for school systems of medium size and above can save as much as 40 per cent of the cost of maintenance by employing their own maintenance workers and properly administering the maintenance program.

2. The time involved in getting a job done is reduced because no time is spent in advertising for bids and letting contracts.

3. The board can require a higher quality of work from its own employees than of private contractors.

4. Private mechanics are difficult to obtain for small jobs. This frequently causes delays in making needed repairs.

5. School plant maintenance can be planned and scheduled more efficiently if the board has its own employees.

Some of the disadvantages of the board providing all of its maintenance by school employees are as follows:

1. Some types of jobs require heavy expensive equipment that is rarely used.

2. Some types of jobs require highly specialized mechanics that are rarely needed. It would not be economical to employ these mechanics full time.

3. Some major school repairs cannot be made while school is in session without disrupting the educational program. This requires a heavier maintenance staff for the summer months than it is economical to employ for the full year.

It appears that a combination plan of maintenance by school employees and private contracting is the most practical plan for the average school system. Each major repair job should be carefully studied to determine whether it is better policy to have it done by private contract or board employees. The objective is to obtain the best service possible at the lowest cost.

The School Plant Maintenance Shop. The volume of work is not sufficient in very small school systems to justify the establishment of a school plant maintenance shop. Such systems may find it desirable to employ one or two general repairmen. But major repairs must be contracted.

School systems with a number of buildings should provide a school plant maintenance shop. The size of the shop and the number and types of employees required depend on the volume of work and the types of jobs done by the maintenance employees. The jobs done usually include the repair and maintenance of buildings and equipment, the upkeep of school grounds including grading and draining, the construction of shelves and simple equipment, minor building alterations, the delivery of supplies and equipment, the adjustment of machinery and equipment, and similar tasks.

Well staffed maintenance departments include a supervisor or supervisors, general repairmen, carpenters, plumbers, steam fitters, electricians, a heating engineer, painters, and laborers. The maintenance shop should be furnished with the equipment needed for the jobs undertaken. An adequate number of maintenance trucks should be provided.

Operational Procedures. A good school plant maintenance program requires careful planning. A good program saves money, aids the educational program, promotes health and safety, and improves public relations. Following are some recommended operational procedures and policies for the school plant maintenance program:

1. Preventive maintenance should be one of the basic maintenance policies. For example, it is less expensive to eliminate conditions causing roof leaks, dry rot, and termite damage than it is to make repairs.

2. When repairs or maintenance are needed, action should be taken at once. Deferment causes extra costs. For example, an unrepaired roof leak will cause plaster or ceiling board damage and rot or rust of roof supports. If exterior wood work is not repainted before the old paint cracks and peels, an expensive scraping job must be done before the building can be repainted.

3. Regular schedules for certain types of maintenance should be developed for each building. This is necessary to implement a preventive maintenance policy. Planned schedules of maintenance are also necessary to spread the work over the year and to schedule maintenance that is disruptive of the school program during summer months.

4. Buildings should be inspected regularly for needed repairs by the school plant maintenance supervisor in cooperation with the school principal. The principal should report immediately any urgent repairs needed. Urgent repairs should be made at once. Less urgent repair and maintenance jobs should be scheduled at times when the work load is not heavy.

5. General repairmen should be used as much as possible for a number of small jobs to be done on a building at one time. It is very uneconomical to send several men at different times or even at the same time when each does a job that requires only a few minutes of time. Labor union regulations in some communities prevent the full implementation of this policy.

6. Careful pre-planning should be done before a major repair job is undertaken. The job should be carefully studied to determine the number and types of workers needed, the material needed and the equipment needed. School funds are wasted when workmen arrive at the job and find that the materials and equipment needed have not been delivered.

7. Adequate supervision and inspection should be provided. A crew of maintenance workers needs leadership. The workers need to know what is expected of them and they need a plan for doing the job if it is a major undertaking. Inspection of the work is necessary to assure quality and safety.

8. The board of education should designate the persons authorized to file requisitions for repairs and work orders. These requisitions should be filed with and approved by the business office. In emergencies, the persons authorized to file labor requisitions should be given the authority to deal directly with the maintenance supervisor. But records should be made of all such transactions.

9. The maintenance department should keep records of all jobs done. The records should show the labor and materials used on each building by types of jobs. These records are essential for cost accounting and for budget development. They are also necessary for determining which jobs should be contracted and which should be done by the board's employees.

10. A stock record control system should be established for the storeroom. Bulky materials such as lumber should be delivered by vendors to the storeroom or to the job instead of to the central warehouse.

11. Broken or damaged school equipment either should be repaired at schools or removed to the maintenance shop for repairs. It should not be allowed to accumulate at individual schools. When equipment is taken from a school, it should be removed from the equipment inventory of that school.

12. Salary or pay schedules should be developed for maintenance employees. Pay should be adequate but the hourly rates need not be as high as are paid skilled workers in the construction trades by private industry. One of the reasons for the high hourly rates for construction workers in private employment is the seasonal nature of their employment. The school plant maintenance worker has steady employment.

13. Employees should be provided with the same fringe benefits as other school employees.

SCHOOL TRANSPORTATION

School transportation is becoming an important item in the school budget. The cost of transportation for the public elementary and secondary schools has increased from $35,600,000 in 1925–26 to more than $400,000,000 in 1958–59. The number of pupils transported has increased from 1,100,000 in 1925–26 to approximately 11,000,000 in 1958–59. Approximately 31 per cent of the public school pupils are transported to school.

It might have been anticipated that the number of pupils transported would decrease as the farm population decreased. But the improvement of roads and the consolidation of schools has much more than made up for the loss in the number of farm children. The migration of the population of the cities to the surrounding rural territory has caused a great increase in the non-farm rural children who must be transported. Special transportation services are now being provided for physically handicapped pupils in many districts. The factors which have caused increases in school transportation during the past one-third of a century are still operative. Therefore, increases in school transportation costs are likely to continue.

It is interesting to note that the increases in total school transportation costs have about kept pace with the increases in the total number of pupils transported without making allowance for the decrease in the purchasing power of the dollar since 1925–26. In terms of the purchasing power of 1947–49 dollars, the per pupil cost of transportation was $43 in 1925–26 and approximately $29 in 1958–59. This reduction in per pupil costs has been due largely to improvements in the efficiency of school transportation service.

Purposes of School Transportation

School transportation is essential for the operation of most modern school systems. Transportation is provided for normal pupils who live beyond a reasonable walking distance from school and for physically handicapped pupils living any distance from school if they need transportation. Transportation is frequently provided for normal pupils who live within a reasonable walking distance but who live on routes dangerous for walking.

The school bus has also become an extension of the classroom in many school systems. The bus can be used to extend the learning experiences of pupils much as a library or laboratory. Therefore, the purpose of school transportation is not only to transport pupils to and from school but to extend the educational horizon.

But school transportation can be expensive. It is not good business management to spend more on transportation than the amount necessary for providing safe, comfortable, and hygienic service for the pupils in need of transportation. Some suggestions are presented in the following section of this chapter for providing that type of service.

Transportation Service Policies

The board must define its transportation service policies before bus routes can be established and time schedules developed. This involves the determination of: (1) how far normal pupils must live from school in order to be entitled to transportation, (2) whether transportation will be furnished to pupils who live within the established walking distance but must walk to school on dangerous streets and roads with no sidewalks, (3) what types of physically handicapped pupils are entitled to transportation, (4) how far pupils are required to walk to the main bus line from side roads, (5) whether the bus will stop in front of each pupil's home on the main route or only at spaced stops limited in number by a required minimum distance between stops, (6) the maximum time that transported pupils arrive at school before it opens or wait for a bus after school is dismissed, and (7) the maximum speed at which buses will be permitted to operate.

All of these policies affect transportation costs, all affect quality of service and some affect the safety and health of pupils. The problem of the board is to determine what quality of transportation service is really needed to enable pupils to attend school and to protect their health and safety. For example, a board could establish the following transportation service policies: All pupils who want to ride a school bus are entitled to service, buses will give door-to-door service whether on main roads or side roads, no pupil will spend more than thirty minutes riding a bus to school, no transported pupil will arrive at school more than five minutes before it opens or wait for a bus more than five minutes after it is dismissed and buses will not operate at a speed of more than thirty miles per hour. This would be very high-quality service but it would be quite expensive. It would be difficult to justify the extra costs required for this level of service.

It is impossible to suggest transportation service policies that would be suitable for all districts. Variations in climate and traffic hazards and other conditions require variations among districts in service policies to provide equivalent levels of service. Following are some policies that may provide a reasonable quality of service in a district with average climatic and traffic conditions:

1. Physically normal pupils living more than 1½ miles from school are entitled to transportation.

2. Pupils with physical handicaps that make walking difficult or dangerous, living any distance from school are entitled to transportation.

3. Pupils living on roads or streets with heavy traffic and no pedestrian sidewalks or paths are entitled to transportation if they live one-half mile or more from school.

4. Buses will not travel side roads from the main bus routes unless pupils live more than a mile from a main route.

5. High school pupils will not spend more than one hour and elementary pupils more than forty-five minutes in riding a bus to or from school.

6. Transported pupils will not arrive at school more than fifteen

minutes before school opens or wait for a bus after school has dismissed more than fifteen minutes.

It is not suggested that these policies are ideal. They are presented only to illustrate the types of decisions with respect to service policies that boards of education must make.

The Establishment of Bus Routes

After the board has established its transportation service policies, it must then determine the bus routes and the number of buses needed. The preparation of a spot map of transported pupils is necessary to provide the other information needed. The spot map should include at least the following: (1) different symbols showing the residence of each elementary and high school pupil entitled to transportation, (2) the location of each elementary and each high school, (3) the type and condition of each road on which pupils live, (4) the principal hazards on each road on which buses must be operated.

In establishing routes and bus stops, consideration should be given to the following factors:

1. It is more economical to use one large bus than two small buses for the same route.

2. It reduces transportation costs to use the same bus for two routes.

3. It reduces transportation costs to establish a limited number of bus stops on a route. The stops should be made at non-hazardous locations.

4. It increases transportation costs to make unnecessary side trips.

5. The bus runs fewer miles when empty if the driver lives near the beginning of the route.

In making decisions on the number of routes and buses needed, the factors affecting transportation costs should be considered along with the quality of service provided.

District-Operated versus Contracted Transportation

Approximately two-thirds of the school buses in the nation are publicly owned. The national trend is toward public ownership. In 1936 boards owned only 37 per cent of the school buses in operation.

Following are the advantages usually found for public ownership:

1. It is more economical because fleet operation is more efficient than individual operation, and profits are eliminated.
2. Better service is provided, because school employees are more responsive to supervision than private contractors.
3. Better equipment is provided, because private contractors frequently cannot finance proper equipment.

4. Better drivers can be selected, because the board is not restricted to the man who can buy a bus.
5. Routing and scheduling are more efficient, because the board owns the equipment and can control it.
6. The educational program can be carried out more effectively, because the board can use its own equipment for educational trips more readily than it can use contracted equipment.[5]

The principal advantages of private contracting are that the board knows at the beginning of the year what its transportation costs will be and contracted transportation requires less management by board employees.

The advantages of district operated buses far outweigh the disadvantages in most districts. However, in some situations public utility facilities may provide good service at a low cost. The board should study each situation in the district and select the method of transportation that provides the best service at the lowest cost.

Standards for School Buses

The standardization of school bus equipment has made it possible for boards of education to obtain good equipment at a much lower cost than would have been possible without standardization. National school bus standards [6] were first developed in 1939. The state departments of education and the principal body and chassis manufacturers developed these recommended standards cooperatively. The standards have been revised from time to time. The minimum standards adopted by most states are based on the national standards. Different climatic and topographical conditions in the states make it desirable to provide variations in some specifications. However, the basic national standards are applicable in all states. For example, the national standards prescribe the same width and height for all bus bodies. This made it possible for manufacturers to use mass production methods in constructing bus bodies and to reduce prices. This was not possible so long as different states and even different districts within states had different specifications with respect to height and width of bus bodies.

The national standards have also emphasized safety in bus equipment. The standards have been tested for twenty years and modified as the need arose. Therefore, no district should purchase school buses which do not meet these minimum standards.

---

[5] Morphet, Johns, and Reller, *Educational Administration*, p. 474.
[6] *Minimum Standards for School Buses*, rev. ed. (Washington, D.C.: National Commission on Safety Education, The National Education Association, 1954).

The Selection and Training of Drivers

No school bus is any safer than its driver. The driver can also maximize or minimize operation costs. Therefore, the qualifications of the school bus driver are quite important.

Driving a school bus is not a full-time job. The typical bus driver may spend no more than fifteen or twenty hours per week in driving the school bus. It is not economical for a board to pay a full-time salary for a part-time job. It is difficult in many districts to employ competent, adult men at a part-time salary for a part-time job. Therefore, numerous attempts have been made to provide full employment for bus drivers by giving them other part-time jobs such as custodians, mechanics, plant maintenance workers, and lunchroom workers. Some drivers have been able to secure part-time private employment to supplement their salaries. These measures have not completely solved the problem in most districts.

Many districts have had successful experience with women drivers. The safety records of women drivers have generally been equal to or better than that of men drivers. Usually there are more competent women drivers available for part-time service than men drivers.

Other districts have used student drivers successfully. The state of North Carolina has had outstanding success with the use of large numbers of student drivers.

Driver Training. No driver should be permitted to drive a school bus without special training. The operation of a school bus is not the same as the operation of an automobile. Each driver should have a special driver's license for operating a school bus. Competent instructors should be obtained for training drivers and substitute drivers. After taking the driver-training program, each driver should be carefully tested for his competency to drive a bus. Each driver should drive his route with an empty bus at least once before carrying children.

Drivers should also be trained to observe symptoms that the bus needs adjustment or repair. Drivers should not be expected to diagnose symptoms. That is the responsibility of the mechanic. But properly trained and alert drivers report such symptoms as a slipping clutch, an overheating engine, the failure of the engine to idle properly, peculiar noises for which there is no apparent explanation, excessive play in the steering wheel and loose brakes.

Maintenance of School Buses

The proper maintenance of school buses saves money, improves service and promotes safety. If the board owns its buses, it must provide for its own maintenance program. If buses are contracted, they should be inspected periodically to assure that the buses are safe for pupils.

Boards owning only a few buses must contract for bus maintenance and repair. This is usually not as satisfactory as maintenance by board employees.

If a board owns fifteen or more buses, it is usually sound policy for it to provide its own bus shop. In well-equipped and well-administered shops serving a considerable number of buses, one mechanic is usually employed for every fifteen to eighteen buses. A bus shop serving 80 or 90 buses may have fewer mechanics in relation to the number of buses served than a shop servicing only 25 buses because of the possibility of greater specialization of work. Some helpers are also needed who are not trained mechanics.

The responsibilities of supervising and managing district-owned school buses are so great that a transportation supervisor is needed if twenty or more buses are operated. The supervisor should be administratively responsible to the assistant superintendent of business affairs, in systems having one, and directly responsible to the superintendent in other systems.

The Maintenance and Repair Program. Major emphasis should be given to preventive maintenance. There is a difference between a maintenance program and a repair program. The differences between a preventive maintenance program and a repair program have been well described by the New York State Department of Education as follows:

With Preventive Maintenance	*Without Preventive Maintenance*
1. Adjustments are made before wear results from maladjustment.	1. Adjustments neglected until wear has resulted.
2. Worn parts are replaced before failure damages other parts.	2. No worn parts are replaced until they break.
3. Small, or inexpensive parts suffice to restore to good order.	3. Costly parts, or whole units, are required.
4. Everything on bus works well or is promptly restored to good order.	4. Several things are not working "quite right" or do not work at all.
5. Work is done at a convenient time and place. Major repairs are accomplished during vacation periods.	5. Work is done when breakdown occurs. Work is done where breakdown occurs or towing is involved.
6. There is a fairly even flow of work for mechanics.	6. Mechanics are rushed at one time and idle the next.
7. Parts are on hand when replacements are scheduled.	7. Parts frequently have to be ordered after breakdowns occur.

With Preventive Maintenance	*Without Preventive Maintenance*
8. It is possible to predict repair costs with some degree of accuracy.	8. The need for repairs is relatively unpredictable. A snow storm may produce a number of failures.
9. There are no interruptions in the school schedule due to breakdowns.	9. Trips are delayed or missed while repairs are made.
10. The risk of accidents due to mechanical failures is reduced.	10. The risk of accidents due to mechanical failure is increased.
11. The public has confidence in the transportation service.	11. The public is skeptical of the safety and reliability of the transportation service.[7]

The bus shop should be equipped to do most of the repairs needed. Some types of jobs require expensive equipment which is not often needed. If the number of buses served does not justify the purchase of the equipment, the job should be contracted.

Buses should be inspected and serviced regularly. Some boards of education save money by fueling buses from their own pumps. This is usually practicable only where a fleet of considerable size is operated. Service trucks should be provided for mechanics. It is also good policy to provide a spare bus for about every thirty buses. This bus can be used to replace a bus which is brought to the shop for repairs. A spare bus makes it possible to space work more evenly.

Shop Records. Stock room control records of all items stored at the shop should be kept. Individual records should be kept of the cost of keeping each bus in repair. Records should also be kept of the gasoline and oil consumed by each bus. These records are necessary for cost accounting and budget development. When the cost of keeping a bus in good operating condition becomes excessive, it should be replaced.

SOME OTHER PROBLEMS AND ISSUES

A brief treatment has been given in this chapter of some of the major problems of supply and equipment management, school plant operation and maintenance, and school transportation. Major emphasis has been given to the financial and business management aspects of these services because that is the purpose of this book. It should not be assumed from the treatment presented in this book that policies with respect to

---

[7] The University of the State of New York, State Department of Education, *Transportation* (Albany, N.Y.: State Department of Education, 1955), pp. 64–65.

these and other central services should be determined largely by money considerations. The purpose of the service and the quality of service needed are more important than the amount of money which might be saved. Some other problems relating to the services of business management are presented in the following paragraphs.

How Should Business Management Save Money?

School business management can provide services at less cost by paying low wages; by eliminating such benefits as retirement, social security, sick leave, and vacation leave, and by otherwise exploiting labor. While these measures apparently reduce cost, they invariably lower the quality of service provided.

One of the outstanding features of the American economy is that business and industrial management has been able to pay labor high wages by means of continually increasing the productivity of labor. The productivity of labor has been increased by education and by the utilization of new and improved machines and processes. This system has produced the highest standard of living in the world.

The public school system is an important part of the American economy. Therefore, school business management should save money by improving the productivity per man hour of labor and not by exploiting labor. This is good public policy and it is sound economic policy. It provides better services at a reasonable cost, it improves public relations and it has a desirable effect on the economy.

Should the public schools pay wages comparable with those paid by business and industry? Is there any evidence that boards of education can employ skilled or unskilled labor at a lower cost than industry? Is there any evidence that boards of education can employ competent managerial talent at a lower cost than industry? Does a low-wage school system have the same effect on the private economy as a low-wage industry?

What Central Services Should Be Provided
for School Lunch Rooms?

The school food service program is now a major operation. The annual cost of the school lunch program in 1958–59 exceeded one billion dollars. More than three-fourths of this amount has been financed by collecting payments for lunches from pupils.

More than half of all public school pupils are served by the school food service program. The demands for this service are increasing. The

552   CENTRAL SERVICES OF BUSINESS ADMINISTRATION

increase in the size of schools and the consolidation of schools have made it impossible for most pupils to go home for lunch. Millions of mothers are now working and do not have the time to prepare lunches for their children. There is an increasing awareness of the importance of proper nutrition.

Despite these facts, most school lunch rooms in the United States are operated by local schools with but little help from the central office. Each principal is expected in most school systems to manage the financing of the school lunch program operated at his school. It is true that the board usually provides and equips the lunchroom and furnishes public utilities. The principal may also receive some Federal aid in the form of cash or commodities from the National School Lunch and Special Milk programs. But he must obtain most of his funds from payments made for lunches. Principals serving schools located in communities of low socio-economic levels face serious financial difficulties. The proportion of children needing free lunches is high in these communities but the financial ability is low.

Other school systems have developed very different school lunch policies. Some of the policies followed by school systems that provide the best school food service programs are as follows:

1. The board of education, the superintendent, and school principals accept responsibility for the school lunch program as an important part of the total program.
2. The financing of the school lunch program is centralized. All receipts of school lunchrooms are sent to the central office and pooled with any state and Federal funds available for the lunch program. This pooling of resources prevents the penalization of small schools and schools compelled to carry a heavy free lunch load because of the socio-economic level of the population. In practice, Federal funds and surplus commodities are largely used to remove inequalities.
3. All purchasing except for some authorized perishables is done on a wholesale basis by the central office. All payments are made, and all financial accounts are kept by the central office. Budgets are made for each lunchroom, and cost accounts are kept for each lunchroom, but all lunchrooms are financed as one program.
4. In systems of efficient size, a trained school food service supervisor is employed. The supervisor works closely with the principal and school lunchroom managers. She plans menus in cooperation with lunchroom managers; carries on an in-service training program for lunchroom workers; works closely with the business office in purchasing, storing, and distributing food, equipment, and lunchroom supplies; keeps the lunchroom accounts; and in general coordinates all phases of the lunch program. She is a part of the business management office.
5. Lunchroom managers and their assistants are appointed by the board on the nomination of the superintendent and the recommendation of the principal. They are administratively responsible to the principal.

6. Lunchroom facilities are functionally planned for food service operations. Those operations include receiving, storing, preparing, and serving food; cleaning utensils; disposing of garbage; and keeping control records. The capacity of storage facilities provided for lunchrooms is coordinated with the capacity of central storage facilities.[8]

What other central services should be provided for the school lunch program?

How Much Tax Support Should Be Provided for the School Lunch Program?

This is a highly controversial issue. In a free-enterprise economy, it is natural to assume that each parent is responsible for feeding his own children. To provide school lunches from public funds might seem socialistic. But parents are required by law to send children of school age to school. Compliance with this requirement prevents most parents from giving their children warm, nutritious lunches on school days.

Opposition to the establishment of public schools in the United States was originally based largely on the assumption that it was socialistic. As each new public school service has been added, the charge has been made by some that it was socialistic and that it was taking away a parental responsibility. Some school people have also felt that the school lunch program was not an appropriate educational function.

From a financial standpoint, it would be more economical to provide the entire cost of the school lunch program from tax funds than to require pupils to pay for their lunches. This would eliminate the labor of collecting payments for lunches from pupils. It would also make nutritious lunches available for all children. The increased volume would lower the real total cost per lunch.

Despite these facts there are many strong supporters of the public schools who believe that it is unsound public policy to extend the financing of the public schools to include complete tax support of the school lunch program. It is argued that there must be some stopping place beyond which tax support for the public schools might not be wisely extended. If there is no stopping place, tax support for the public schools might be extended to furnishing clothing and complete medical and dental care for all pupils.

Following are some important questions concerning school lunch financing policies:

1. Should Federal aid for the school lunch and school milk programs be abolished or increased?

---

[8] Adapted from Morphet, Johns, and Reller, *Educational Administration*, p. 482.

2. Should state aid for the school lunch program be provided?

3. Should tax support for the school lunch program be limited to the provision of buildings and equipment and the furnishing of utilities?

4. Should the cost of management and supervision of the lunch program be provided from tax funds?

5. Should sufficient tax support be provided for the school lunch program that the price of school lunches will represent only the wholesale food cost?

6. Should complete tax support be provided for the school lunch program?

SELECTED REFERENCES

Burke, Arvid J., *Financing Public Schools in the United States*, rev. ed. New York: Harper and Brothers, 1957. Chapter 6.

Featherstone, E. Glenn, *Pupil Transportation Responsibilities and Services of State Departments of Education*, Office of Education. Washington, D.C.: U. S. Government Printing Office, 1956.

Johns, R. L., and E. L. Morphet, editors, *Problems and Issues in Public School Finance*. New York: Bureau of Publications, Teachers College, Columbia University, 1952. Chapter 13.

Linn, Henry H., editor, *School Business Administration*. New York: Ronald Press Company, 1956. Chapters 10, 13, 15 and 16.

Morphet, Edgar L., Roe L. Johns, and Theodore L. Reller, *Educational Administration*. Englewood Cliffs, N.J.: Prentice-Hall, Inc., 1959. Chapter 21.

Southern States Work Conference, R. L. Johns, ed., *School Lunch Policies and Standards*. Tallahassee, Florida: State Department of Education, 1952.

University of the State of New York, State Department of Education, *Transportation*. Albany, N.Y.: State Department of Education, 1955.

———, *School Lunch*. Albany, N.Y.: State Department of Education, 1955.

———, *Purchases and Stores*. Albany, N.Y.: State Department of Education, 1955.

———, *Operation and Maintenance*. Albany, N.Y.: State Department of Education, 1955.

Index

Financial accounting (*Cont.*):
  expenditure accounting, 462
  expenditures, 461, 472
  fund accounting, 457
  machine accounting, 470
  original documents, 467
  receipt accounting, 459
  records, 456
  reports, 473
  revenue receipts, 459, 472
  subsidiary accounting, 465
  uniform, 476
Financial administration (*see* Business administration)
Financial effort:
  differences, 149
  inequalities, 138
  local, 160, 291, 299
  local required, 271
  measures of state, 158
  state, 159, 160
  variations in, 158
Financial equalization, 271
Financial support:
  characteristics of a satisfactory program, 306
  differences in points of view, 23
  effect, 18
  Federal, 197
  foundation program, 262
  level, 300
  local, 197, 303
  need for state, 234
  need for understanding, 23
  plan, 268
  property tax, 200
  reasons, 197
  role of local school districts, 199
  role of the states, 198
  state, 304
  state provisions, 232
  summary of Federal, 383
  trend toward centralization, 198
Financing schools:
  foundation program, 262
  local, 196
  provisions, 26, 246
Finegan, Thomas E., 170, 235
Fire insurance, 508 (*see also* Insurance)
  appraisal, 510
  blanket, 513
  coverage, 509
  insurable value, 510
  rates, 512
  risks, 509
  value, 510
Fiscal dependence, 184
Fiscal independence, 184
Fiscal relationships, 266
Fiscal year, 226
Flat-grants, 241, 310
  emphasis on, 257
Florida State Department of Education, 341
Food service, 348, 350, 551 (*see also* School lunch)
Ford Foundation, 356
Foster, Emery M., 477
Foundation program, 262, 270
  adequacy, 272
  apportionment of funds, 293
  capital outlay, 286, 316
  characteristics of a satisfactory plan, 268
  comprehensive plan, 272

Foundation program (*Cont.*):
  concept, 263, 265, 267
  costs, 284, 287
  current expense, 286
  definition, 29
  definition and interpretation of terms, 270
  development, 295
  dollars-per-unit-of-need approach, 273
  evolution of concept, 263
  funds, 271
  implementation, 292
  improvement, 295
  instructional salaries, 285
  interpretation of terms, 270
  kinds of plans, 288
  leadership, 295
  level of financial support, 300
  local effort, 291, 299
  local funds, 271
  local support, 287
  measures of educational need, 277
  needs, 284
  origin of concept, 265
  other factors, 283
  plan, 271
  procedures used in developing, 273
  scope and adequacy, 272
  services-and-facilities-needed approach, 275
  small schools, 298
  state controls, 292
  state funds, 271
  state and local support, 287
  state requirements and controls, 292
  state support, 290
  translating needs into costs, 284
  transportation expense, 286
  wealthy districts, 297
Fowlkes, John Guy, and George E. Watson, 238, 301
Freudenthal, Daniel K., 354
Funds:
  classification, 241
  equalizing, 241
  flat-grant, 241, 310
  foundation program, 241
  general purpose, 241
  incentive, 259
  special purpose, 241

Galbraith, John Kenneth, 80, 136
Garber, Lee O., 186, 195
George-Barden Act, 376
George-Deen Act, 376
George-Ellzey Act, 376
George-Reed Act, 376
General-purpose funds, 241
Givens, Willard E., 429
Government (*see also* Federal government; State)
  allocation of tax sources, 228
  amount of taxes collected, 109
  benefits received, 120
  grants-in-aid, 110
  state and local taxes, 136
  tax collections, 109
  tax collections by level of government, 114
  trends in types of taxes, 113
  types of taxes, 111
Governmental expenditures, 60, 63, 66, 104, 105